Business Analytics

Progress on Applications in Asia Pacific

Business Analytics

Progress on Applications in Asia Pacific

Editor

Jorge L. C. Sanz

World Scientific

NEW JERSEY • LONDON • SINGAPORE • BEIJING • SHANGHAI • HONG KONG • TAIPEI • CHENNAI • TOKYO

Published by

World Scientific Publishing Co. Pte. Ltd.
5 Toh Tuck Link, Singapore 596224
USA office: 27 Warren Street, Suite 401-402, Hackensack, NJ 07601
UK office: 57 Shelton Street, Covent Garden, London WC2H 9HE

National Library Board, Singapore Cataloguing in Publication Data
Names: Sanz , J. L. C. (Jorge L.C.), 1955– editor.
Title: Business analytics : progress on applications in Asia Pacific / editor, Jorge L. C. Sanz.
Description: Singapore : World Scientific Publishing Co. Pte. Ltd., [2017]
Identifiers: OCN 953841567 | ISBN 978-981-31-4930-4 (paperback) | 978-981-31-4929-8
Subjects: LCSH: Management--Asia--Data processing. | Management--Pacific Area--
Data processing. | Decision making--Asia--Data processing. |
Decision making--Pacific Area--Data processing.
Classification: DDC 658.4038--dc23

British Library Cataloguing-in-Publication Data
A catalogue record for this book is available from the British Library.

Printed in Singapore

Contents

Preface

The need for improving enterprise operations and finding new business models continues to attract the attention of practitioners and researchers. There have been different schools of thought and approaches followed for over a century, ranging from Taylor's ideas to more modern attempts to design and run organizations. The study of these broad enterprise and societal concerns has invariably been based on using ***data***. This data may be collected at different levels of the phenomena of interest, going from individuals to more aggregate levels in organizations or involving broader relationships that cut across industries or significant segments of the world's population. Considering the long-standing pursuits for supporting decision-making in enterprises and innovation in society based on data evidence, it would be inaccurate to state that *working with data* entails any **new science**. Indeed, many data-centric research activities and methodologies have been commonplace for decades and used in many disciplines and applications, ranging from biology to statistics, from engineering to business and from computing to social sciences.

An authentic subject of inquiry for researchers, practitioners and educators is to enlighten *what the actual news about data truly is*. This inquiry is important because there has been renewed interest in data-centric decision-making and innovation in the last five years. Admittedly, this impetus has been propelled by marketing statements and overloaded language, also generating confusion among different stakeholders. Shedding light, not adding to the overall chaos, remains as the primary role of academics and practitioners. To that end, the first trend to surface is that *digital capabilities* (sensors, computing devices, communication and storage technologies) have commoditized to the point of giving enormous power to *almost everybody*. The wide-spread and cost-effective availability of these devices has enabled significantly more end-users to access tools previously only provided to privileged users within enterprises.

This trend intensified in the 1990s when traditional glass-house software applications became intensively driven by individual departments outside the traditional Information Technology (IT) Line-of-Business (LoB). This distributed power was disseminated pervasively in enterprises as computing capabilities moved into workstations and laptops, thus enabling a new form of end-user in all organizations. Simultaneously, miniaturization enabled sensors to take a prominent role everywhere and mobile devices have finally dominated the telecommunications market to the point of making cellular phones replace conventional telephony services in many countries. In just a few decades, enterprises have gone from corporate-controlled provision of IT to individual-centric capabilities enabled by all these technological factors. These 'empowered individuals' have multiplied to the point of yielding the so-called 'bring your own device' (BYOD) strategy adopted by virtually all global enterprises to equip their own employees with internal enterprise applications.

The second trend is the continued pressure for cost-reduction in enterprises. The rationalization of resources has been supported by automation in virtually all LoBs. Automation and standardization have co-evolved, with positive and negative consequences. For example, they have jointly enabled the delivery of cost-effective services in some industries but simultaneously, have also limited the ability to co-create better services in the business-to-consumer segments of the economy. As a result, the need for organizations to reposition *individualization* in their consumer services is paramount. The drive to improve '*customer experience*' (sadly confused with a more limited form of *digital experience*) has revamped the prominent role of data, involving customers, providers and entire ecosystems. This renewed interest is the result of the challenge of achieving *service scalability* for millions of customers while preserving some quality, viable costs and a degree of individualization in said provisions.

The third trend is the availability of high-speed, high-density storage devices that allow for huge data sets to be better integrated and used simultaneously. This technological capability has significantly reduced trial-and-error cycles in the pursuit of discovering patterns potentially buried in these unexploited data sets. The latter is being accomplished by reducing the time taken to visualize and process massive quantities of information. In a relatively short period, massive amounts of data have been collected from almost all interactions across socio-technical systems, involving sensors, information produced by people, computer systems, enterprise processes and practices, with structured or unstructured representations including videos, images and sound. Cheaper and higher-density storage has been a key complement to computing power and high-speed networks, giving rise to producing and consuming data much more pervasively in all organizations and society in general.

A much shorter compute-visualize cycle and better integrated massive data sources have enabled new data-centric methods to build upon existing techniques already available from a wealth of other disciplines. As a consequence, old ideas have then taken front seats in research and practice due to their becoming viable through more widely accessible tools at minimal costs. Indeed, the fact that many ideas borrowed from classical disciplines can now be tried and tested without central IT intervention has become a propelling force for using and analyzing data. The subject of inquiry and techniques remain largely as an evolution of existing capabilities, enacted by the advent of technological innovation taking place in the information and communication (ICT) industries. Simultaneously, these technological advances have revealed new opportunities for improving life conditions and helping organizations perform better. The opportunity in all applied fields is thus paramount and exciting.

Depending on the specific discipline, field of science or institution where data is used, the above trends take on different brand names. In enterprises, for example, the opportunity to make better-informed decisions and innovate by using suitable data sources is called ***Business Analytics***. This brand name should be preserved distinctly from other siblings such as '*data analytics*' and '*big data*'. The importance of this difference is not rhetorical at all. First, not all data that matters to an enterprise has the size implied by the word *big*. In fact, 'big' is a relative adjective when applied to data and thus, a moving target with the advent of new ICT generations. All technical topics dealing with architecture and platforms to suitably host and process 'big' data sources are unquestionably important areas of education, research and practice. These subjects are usually addressed in computer science curricula and stay within the concern of the information technology division in enterprises. Likewise, the analysis of data, i.e., 'data analytics', requires a wealth of knowledge mostly borrowed from statistics and optimization disciplines, and calls for the ability to extract and process data by using selected tools and related information technology support. As computing capabilities for analysis have also moved outside the IT glass-house and reside now in the sphere of individual workers, the analysis of data is no longer the exclusive prerogative of skillful IT professionals. This means a huge departure from past practices in enterprises. Complex open-source packages for modeling, accessible clients for data residing in cloud infrastructures and visualization tools deployed in desktops and laptops equip virtually any end-user with the instruments needed to carry out significant analytical tasks. There is no longer a need to rely on heavily specialized IT to 'extract' and 'process' data.

These trends leading to 'democratization' and 'empowerment' of end-users enacted by data integration policies and ICT capabilities bring new expectations and significant pressures on anyone working in a modern enterprise. Not surprisingly, with many decades of evolution in statistics and optimization, and after a decade more of ICT capabilities, tools for data analysis have begun to lower the 'barrier of entry' for those professionals not having a deep background in mathematics and computing. Many such tools are also becoming progressively embedded into *actual work practices* by their being further specialized to competences mastered by those professionals working in the corresponding LoBs. For example, a marketing professional focused on campaign management will execute analytics as part of the customary processes emerging in the marketing department. These analytics capabilities encapsulate and insulate the business expert from previously complex details and data manipulation needed, although it does not free the user from understanding the meaning of the data analysis work needed.

The advent of actionable data[1] in enterprises has boosted higher expectations on the discovery of new productivity gains, the design of new ideas for growth and the provision of better services for customers and employees. These activities are the essence of what all professionals do for a living in almost every enterprise. This statement should then not be taken lightly as its implications are profound: the opportunity to impact all enterprise competences through digital capabilities has become so prominent that the interplay between business and IT is today more critical than ever. Automation continues to rise and vigorously moves into previously unimaginable competences, deeply impacting conventional professional roles in business. The demand for data availability across functions is pressing organizations to deconstruct conventional silos. It would not be an exaggeration to state that a virtually inseparable business-IT liaison is changing the way most business professions are being deployed nowadays. The trend is remarkable in almost any LoB, including finance and accounting, marketing, strategy management, sales, customer operations, product design, supply chain, personnel, manufacturing, distribution channels and the list goes on to include virtually all main competences in for-profit and non-profit organizations. Knowledge of conventional business practices has begun to commoditize at a very high pace while employers begin to expect '*appetite and ability to analyze data*' as a skill desired from existing employees and new hires.

However, no data analysis is fruitful or even meaningful in social sciences without a proper understanding of the behavior of the actors and organizational capabilities through which the involved data is generated. This means that data is not separable from the understanding of the phenomenon where it has been originated. Indeed, there is no '*raw data*',

1 For a lack of a better term, *actionable data* denotes here the availability of data accompanied with the distributed computing and storage capabilities to make effective use of it.

as masterfully explained by Lisa Gitelman,[2] a posture that builds upon the work of Geoffrey Bowker, in his *Memory Practices in the Sciences*,[3] and others. It is somehow unfortunate to see a certain analytics pretense to '*obtain insights from data*' by divorcing the method of inquiry from the actual principles that generate data and materialize its observation. In simple and practical terms, this means that the *analysis of footprints* cannot and should not be separated from those processes and practices in organizations or the behavior of customers and partners where the data may emanate from. This is the central thought that characterizes Business Analytics as a distinct discipline: the field of applied research that attempts to formally model the deep interplay across competences, process / practice / behavior and technical systems. The subject of study in Business Analytics is then deep and vast, and its epistemological connotations (including its relationship with *Business Informatics*) go well beyond the purpose of this book.[4]

The importance of bringing Business Analytics to a wider audience in organizations and professionals have given rise to a new Center and Masters of Science Program in the National University of Singapore (NUS). The focus of both Center and Program is on Business Analytics. This NUS Center also comes to foster opportunities and offer a platform to support a number of Undergraduate activities in several Schools on Campus, including the Business Analytics Undergraduate program from the NUS School of Computing. The Center counts today with over 40 different external partner organizations in Asia-Pacific with which all Masters students carry out individual projects as part of their curriculum requirement for graduation. This book is the first volume in a series reporting the progress made in applications of Business Analytics with many of these organizations. The book has been edited as a compilation of 32 chapters describing in a high-level style some of the work carried out with many of these enterprises.

---

2 This remark has been made much more drastic in *Raw Data is an Oxymoron*, edited by Lisa Gitelman and published by MIT Press in 2013. The author offers a deep analysis on the nonsensical intention to attribute intrinsic objectivity to data.

3 In the words of G. Bowker: '**Raw Data is both an oxymoron and a bad idea**', in *Memory Practices in the Sciences*, MIT Press, 2005.

4 Of course, in all cases the term *business*, as used in *Business Analytics*, should be understood in a wide sense and not as a synonym of *for-profit*.

The absence of excessive detail is due to the intention of making the material accessible to a wider audience of practitioners and business or information systems students interested in analytics. In part, some simplification has also been necessary to preserve confidentiality of certain sensitive information from the work done. In most of these papers, the specific names of these enterprises has consequently been reserved also for confidentiality reasons, a preference left open for each partner organization to decide.

The authors of all the papers in this collection were Masters students at the time of the editing of this book (late 2015) and the vast majority has completed the program since then. This means that these projects are all very recent and therefore, provide a useful picture of the maturity of Business Analytics in Asia Pacific. Most headquarters in the region are located in Singapore and thus, the content of the papers addresses problems and opportunities emerging in different countries and in some cases, also beyond Asia-Pacific. Furthermore, with the continuation of this series in the upcoming years, the velocity of change of the Business Analytics domain in enterprises will become more apparent. Some interesting signs of growing complexity in many organizations can already be observed. If this trend were to be summarized with a single statement, the characterization of the maturity would be: '*organizations are complementing classical business reporting with more advanced explanatory and predictive capabilities*'. But the state of this evolution varies in each enterprise, even by LoB, so any generalization would be inconvenient and probably, also wrong. This fact has been validated by work carried out in different competences of these organizations at the same time through these projects and others not reported in this book.

The organization of the book proceeds as follows. The first *seven chapters* address some business analytics applications related to different industries: consumer packaging, electronics, transportation maintenance and package manufacturing. The companies covered are all sizable multinationals with large operations in Asia Pacific. These papers cover a variety of competences, including operations, products, services, information technology and pricing.

The next eight chapters are focused on financial services, covering banking, insurance and reinsurance segments. These papers are of varying complexity and focus on different topics and capabilities in these industries, ranging from customer-oriented business analytics applications to risk assessments and from strategy to improving management reporting activities.

The following six chapters are oriented to consumer business analytics, covering a range of different capabilities such as travel planning, bicycle rentals, skin care, retail websites, price optimization, and the list goes on.

The next two chapters are concerned with an increasingly important and challenging problem of improving customer experience in the transportation industry. Different operations in two industry segments are addressed: airports and trains.

The next five papers address different finance problems relevant to finance and accounting, corporate finance and procurement operations. The industries involved include government, healthcare manufacturing and stock markets. In one of these papers, an extension of the conventional Buffett Indicator to specific industries is presented along with rich experimental work for the United States. This and the other chapters addressing improved business intelligence and more complex models of financial indicators show the 'mix bag' evolution of business analytics in different competences for related industry segments.

The final four chapters cover an interesting and wide mix of industry topics, going from pharmacy services in healthcare centers to an attempt to create a method for doing business analytics more systematically, and from consumer services to a deep-dive into knowledge extraction from unstructured data sources.

In closing, these 32 chapters with short and long papers compose an interesting and useful snapshot of some of the exciting progress made on applied business analytics in Asia-Pacific. Upcoming volumes in this series will provide an opportunity to gauge the *speed of evolution* of Business Analytics in the geography across different LoBs and industry segments.

Prof. Dr. Jorge L. C. Sanz
Director Business Analytics Center
School of Computing – Business School
National University of Singapore
Chief Innovation Officer – Retail Banking, IBM Corporation

Acknowledgments

The editor would like to thank all the authors for their hard work in writing the papers and preparing them for publication in this book. One or more academic advisors in the National University of Singapore have reviewed each of these papers. While the names of the advisors are not reserved or confidential, the list is too extensive. But it would not make full justice to name only a few of them. Thus, a word of sincere gratitude goes to all involved colleagues from the School of Computing and Business School of NUS for their support as Affiliated Professors to the Business Analytics Center and/or for advising in the individual projects: Khim Yong Goh, Ashok Charan, Stephane Bressan, Singfat Chu, Tuan Phan, Hock Hai Teo, Kian-lee Tan, Danny Poo, Keith Carter, Lucy Chen, Mabel Chou, Jussi Keppo, Yong Meng Teo, James Pang, Ke-Wei Huang, Richard Ma, Roland Yap, Marcelo Labre, Tong Wang, Chee Yong Chan, Jack Jiang, Rudy Setiono and Jin Song Dong.

In particular, very special thanks are due to Prof Jussi Keppo and Prof Siau Cheng Khoo for their co-directing the Masters Program in the Business Analytics Center and to Prof Kian-lee Tan, Prof Chung Piaw Teo, Prof Jungpil Hahn for their support to both practicum and curriculum as Head of Computer Science, Decision Sciences and Information Sciences, respectively. Also, the endless commitment from Dean of School of Computing, Prof David Rosenblum, and Dean of Business School, Prof Bernard Yeung is gratefully acknowledged.

These papers and overall work in NUS Business Analytics Center would not be possible without the enthusiastic endorsement and support from a significant network of enterprises working with the Business Analytics Center. Executives and senior managers from a wealth of companies and non-profit organizations are due a word of deep gratitude for their partnership: Allianz, ANZ, AXA, Axiata Group, Changi Airport Group, Bikes 99, Cognizant, Data Innovation Lab (AXA), DBS, Defense Science and Technology Agency, GfK, IBM, Institute for Infocomm Research, JLL, Johnson & Johnson, Lenovo, Levi's, Marina Bay Sands, Ministry of Home Affairs, MoH Holdings, National University Health System, Nielsen, OCBC, Optum, PayPal, Procter & Gamble, SAP, SAS, SIA Engineering Company, Singapore General Hospital, SMRT Corporation, Swiss Re, Tetra Pak, UBS, Unilever and Wing Tai.

A word of special recognition is also due to Janet Chow for her strongest commitment to support the Program and Business Analytics Center for several years and to Ness Burton for going through all the papers with great dedication and carrying out a huge editing job at very short notice.

Finally, the editor needs to gratefully acknowledge World Scientific Publishing business operations leaders for their patience and understanding of having gone through endless reviews and last-minute changes to improve the book.

Prof Jorge L. C. Sanz
National University of Singapore

CHAPTER 1

Leveraging of Big Data from Manufacturing Facilities to Create New Business Insights

Gemma Braganza

ABSTRACT

Standardizing the capture of manufacturing data can enable meaningful data visualization to occur. Once fully realised, the capability envisaged in this project the 'Data Vault' will link multiple manufacturing systems from global production facilities to enable performance comparisons, cost optimization, and performance models to enable meaningful business insights in a set of user-defined dashboards.

1. INTRODUCTION

Proctor and Gamble (P&G) owns multiple hair care plants around the world, each producing thousands of tonnes of conditioner per year. The conditioner is produced via a process that generates unique manufacturing data for each production lot. This manufacturing data is often assessed by lot, to confirm that the conditioner was made as intended, and complies to the requirements of the formula recipe. Currently, the millions of data points captured via the manufacturing systems are assessed on an individual production lot basis, with occasional manual compilation to compare across multiple production lots.

In funding the Data Vault project, P&G has committed to enabling a significant improvement in how this data which is captured, collated and compared. This will enable greater business insights into manufacturing processes, and enable performance and cost optimization from the interpretation of collated, structured, visualised and modelled data.

2. PROBLEM STATEMENT

The creation of the Data Vault will enable new business insights into the data related to the production of conditioner. Several aspects of the data project are being completed in parallel to ensure that the end user can visualise and interpret data. Key considerations include: the structure of captured data, the frequency of extraction, optimal local and global storage, and the creation of any calculated fields until the dashboards are executed.

3. STATE OF THE ART

The Data Vault project involves the collaboration of a multi-functional, multi company, global team to deliver an end-to-end data system. Ensuring a seamless communication between the needs of the end user to the design and construction of the database is key to the success and timely delivery of this project.

Specifically for the visualisation, Tableau has been utilised to build prototypes to enable effective communication of possibilities to the end user, and requirements to the external vendor.

To deliver the required visualisation and business insight, the structure and efficiency of the database has been considered and defined. Calculated fields, which either consist of logical or mathematical calculations, have been envisioned and defined.

4. SOLUTION: DESCRIPTION OF APPROACH

The Data Vault project is designed to bring the conditioner manufacturing data from global manufacturing facilities into one standardised structure, and enable a centralised database whereby users can visualise, analyse and optimise the conditioner-making process.

The current structure of the data flow from equipment to the end user reports is visualised below. Data is captured from the manufacturing equipment and visualised in real time via Factory Talk software. Data captured from multiple sensors on the equipment is passed through the FactoryTalk Server to the Historian Server where it is stored. The manufacturing plant can subsequently generate reports based on specific requirements, with data filtered to individual needs.

This structure allows for individual reporting at each manufacturing location, for an individual production lot process. The reporting is sufficiently granular to enable analysis of the process for a specific lot; it can hence provide confirmation that the lot was made according to the required process (Figure 1).

To develop any further analysis, such as performance of the processes across multiple production or plants, requires further data analysis and manipulation. Currently, such analysis would typically include basic charting of process parameters, with the interim step required of importing, collating and cleaning the data to make visual comparisons. Further statistical analysis and modelling of the process parameters to enable optimization or predictive capabilities requires significant time input and data manipulation, which is rarely undertaken. A previous attempt at this type of analysis compared in-process measures to final product properties to try and establish the driver behind product that did not conform to consumer requirements. To enable the work to be done with available resource and within a required time frame, a sample of production lots was taken (approximately 5 per cent of available data) at the extreme ends of the product property measure, and approximately 10 per cent of the process parameters were assessed to determine a relationship between the two. Clearly, if it were easier to access, collate, visualise and analyse data on a larger scale, then it would be more likely to determine any relationship that may exist between process parameter and product properties.

The Data Vault project aims to bridge this gap and enable cross plant or cross lot analysis to occur in a standardised way. The following shows the overall structure of data storage and flow (Figure 2):

4.1. Work flow

The Historian database, Data Vault Database and visualization design are all being developed in parallel. This is to enable feedback from the end

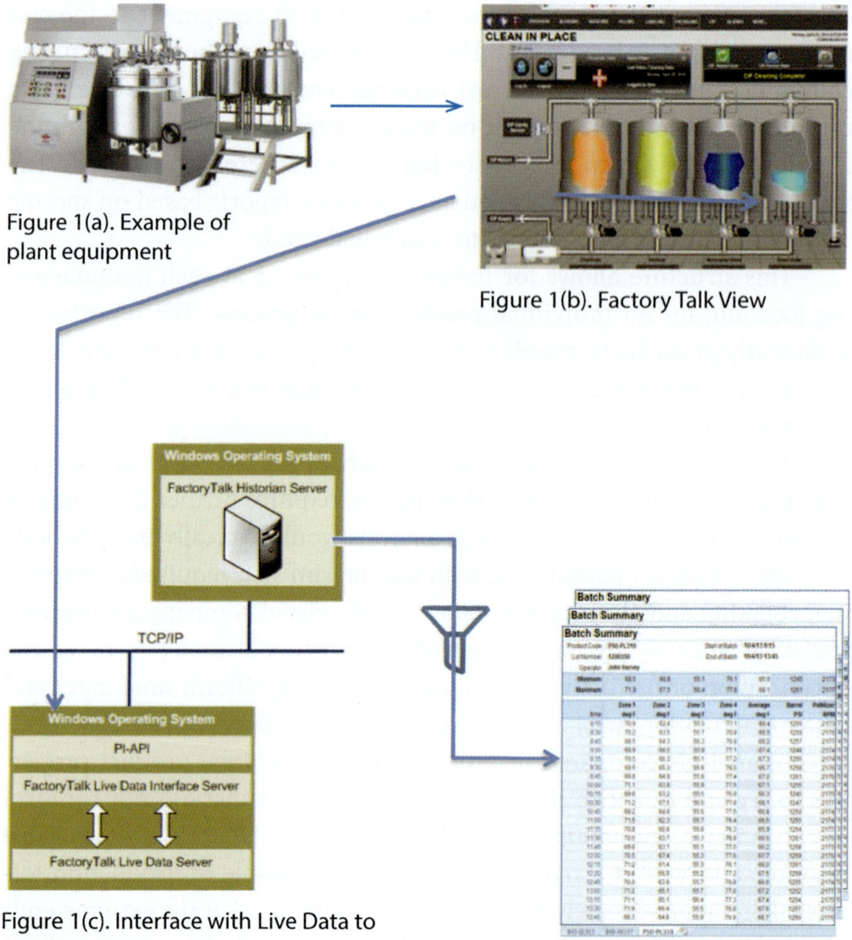

Figure 1(a). Example of plant equipment

Figure 1(b). Factory Talk View

Figure 1(c). Interface with Live Data to Historian Server

Figure 1(d). Report example from SyTech.

Figure 1: Production process data.

user to be right across the data flow to ensure that data needed by the end user to make business insights is captured in the Historian database.

4.2. Historian database standardisation

The Historian has several advantages that are being utlised across this project:

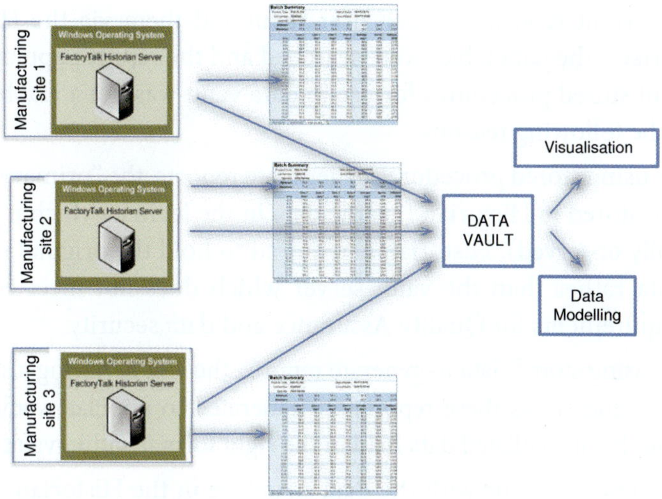

Figure 2: Data storage and flow.

- Define tags and displays that are standard across different manufacturing sites
- Share data and integrate seamlessly with other systems
- Configurable from anywhere on the network; access stored data remotely
- Scalable Architecture from single station HMI to multi-client/multi-server system [4]

By implementing a standardised data structure, data from all sites can be leveraged. There are several attributes that have been defined to ensure the needs of the end user have been met:

- All required tags are captured in the database
  - During the development of the project, several tags (e.g. status of equipment, measurements from sensors) were added to the tables of data held in the Historian.
  - The frequency of data captured has been defined. This depends on the level of granularity that is needed by the end user, and in how much detail comparisons need to be made.
  - The structure of the data within the Historian has been modified to meet the needs of Data Vault. The initial structure involved the use of stored procedures to generate end user reports. This meant that

for current reports, as each user requested them via the Historian interface, the data tables were searched and the report populated. The use of stored procedures for use in data vault was not a viable option for the following reasons:

- By using stored procedures to generate reports, the "primary data" is not stored in Historian (i.e. the data in the form at which it is originally observed). Historian is required to hold the original reported data rather than the vault server which does not meet company requirements for Quality Assurance and data security.
- By using stored data to generate reports, the risk of having a slow system emerges as these reports are generated to populate vault, rather than having collated data held in the right format within vault.
- As updates occur with the data structure in the Historian, updates would not automatically occur in any stored procedures if operated from the Vault; this could lead to poor data quality/ errors in the Vault. By keeping all data tables stored in the required format within the Historian, any updates and changes are made to the original data structure and are less likely to cause on-going upkeep needs for the Vault.

The work flow for the Historian database definition is finished in the early stages of the Data Vault project, since much of the structure already exists in the manufacturing facilities. The changes and requirements need to be defined early on in the project, and are then fed into the Data Vault database design implementation.

4.3. Data vault database

The Data Vault will store all required data for visualization in one place from each of the manufacturing sites and units in a structured form. During the work process, a full list of fields that must be pulled from the Historian is defined, as well as fields that must be calculated within the database. The definition of calculated fields will be discussed further below.

The work flow for the Data Vault database starts with this definition, which essentially lists data fields that should be captured, the database structure, and a clear definition of calculated fields. This should link directly to the location in the Historian database for the data field, and also to the fields that are used to create the visualisations. This definition is then used by the external vendor to create the Data Vault database.

4.4. Visualisation

The initial representation of the data is to be in dashboards that show key parameters important to the end user. Key steps include determining the needs of the end user, the business questions that the dashboards could help to answer, and defining specific functional requirements for each dashboard to enable their creation by the external vendors. By definition of the dashboard requirements at the initial stages of the project, the requirements have been fed back throughout the data flow.

Following the definition of these dashboards is collaboration with the external vendor. This is to ensure the requirements are met, the testing of dashboards to ensure that data is visualised correctly, and releasing dashboards to the organisation. Re-application of other existing business dashboards is also in the scope of the Data Vault project. The mapping of these for their new purpose will follow this work.

4.5. Work flow challenges

A parallel work flow brings several challenges:

- No database available to start visualisation designs. This makes it difficult for customers/ end users to envision final output when data cannot be seen, and it is difficult to create functioning dashboards. Without prototypes made with data, it is difficult for the vendor to understand the business question. This was overcomed for the most complex data by the creation of dummy databases.
- Multiple re-loops with vendors to ensure that the structure was as required in the Historian database. This had the potential to incur additional project costing due to additional work outside of the original scope

- Delays occurred where full definition of dashboards was not complete. Full scope of dashboards was needed to ensure that the overall project scope was within budget before engaging Data Vault external vendors.

As the implementation is ed by an external vendor, future needs have to be considered to ensure that minimal changes are required, as such alterations will be costly to implement and have significant time frames associated with them.

4.6. Dashboard definition

The following were key steps required in defining the end user experience.

Understand the needs of the customer

Initial scoping meetings to understand the needs of the customer were completed. This shared the scope of the data available within the database, and examples of how similar data has been utilised across different business units. These were completed with cross functional teams (engineering, upstream and downstream process communities). The teams were encouraged to share their current analysis methods employed on data provided from the manufacturing site to determine the most frequent way the data would be interpreted, and where time savings could occur. Brain storming sessions also generated ideas for new ways in which the data could make business decisions. Viable ideas and most frequently used data were rated to determine the dashboards of highest importance. This would enable choices to be made if there were any budget constraints limiting the number of dashboards that could be created.

The second stage of iteration involved creation and sharing of prototypes to show how the visualisations could look and function. These were then reviewed with the customer to help with further refinement and spark new ideas for dashboards. Refinement included suggestions to make the dashboards easier to filter, more intuitive, or different statistical analysis that would be helpful for users.

4.7. Develop actionable designs

To develop the prototypes into actionable designs, dummy databases were created for several dashboards. This involved manual download of individual reports from the manufacturing facilities, and merging the data into sufficient size to enable interpretable visualization and statistical analysis. This then enabled the creation of working prototypes.

A key consideration for this work was which software to develop and implement the visualisations in. There are many options available from commercial software; two approaches were compared.

Tableau software had been used prior projects to interpret and share manufacturing data. This software is easy for internal employees to develop new dashboards, enabling a flexible and adaptable set of dashboards to meet ever-changing business needs. The license strategy meant the software was available for multiple users to develop new dashboards and interpret the data.

The corporate strategy is to use Spotfire, which is less user friendly and has less flexibility than Tableau. The licenses are not as easily available and dashboards would be managed corporately, making small or quick changes or new dashboard implementation difficult.

This assessment is represented in Gartner Survey Analysis: Customers Rate Their BI Platform Functionality [5] (Figure 3).

Because of the ease of use of the Tableau software, prototypes were developed internally via Tableau, and converted to Spotfire via the external vendor who would be connecting to the corporate systems and connecting to the data stored in Data Vault database.

4.8. Determination of requirements for Historian/ Data Vault

Once the design work had begun, the requirements for Historian/ Data Vault were further refined. This included ensuring the list of data fields for Data Vault was completed as per the visualization needs, and that the structure was simple and in line with the Historian structure.

Follows an extract of the definition required. Over 100 fields (both calculated and directly sourced from Historian) have been defined to populate the Data Vault database along with the frequency of data and the refresh schedule required from the Historian Database.

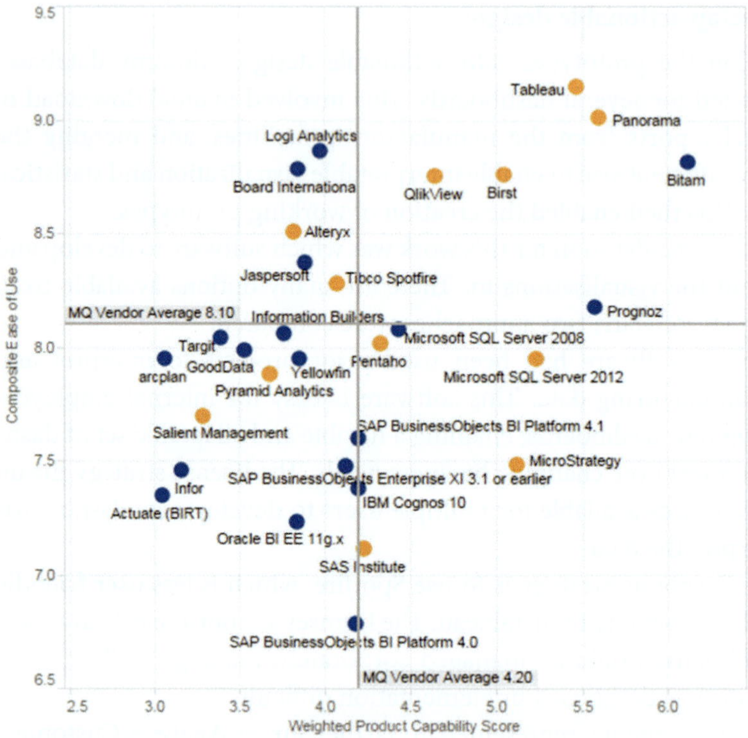

Note: The orange color dot indicates an above-average complexity of analysis score (see Note 3); the blue color dot indicates a below-average complexity of analysis score.
BI = business intelligence; MQ = Magic Quadrant
n = 1,551 (see Figures 1 and 2)
Chart represents customer perception and not Gartner's opinion, and may feature vendors that (in Gartner's opinion) do not deliver the functional capability described.

Source: Gartner (October 2014)

Refresh schedule	Vault Table	Vault Module	Field Names for Users	Historian Table	Vault Logic	Notes
Every 3 hours	Site	Additional site info for maps	Latitude		Google maps	
			Longitude		Google maps	
			Country		Plant Country	
			Description			
			Area		area column	
			Site		Plant Code	

During this process it was noted that the Historian structure was not sufficient for the needs of Data Vault. Refinement and additional work was required to modify the structure and available data tables within the Historian database.

4.9. Creation of calculated fields

With a dummy data set, it was possible to define the calculated fields that would be needed to create visualisations. These can be created within the visualization software (ideal for some of the statistical interpretations). However, this tends to lead to longer load times for each of the dashboards. Creating these within the database where possible should enable quicker loading of dashboards. Calculated fields are based on the data provided by the Historian database, but interpreted in a way that would enable superior level business insights into the data analysis. Some examples of calculated fields required to design the dashboards are.

- **Determining a relative time**

  When comparing multiple production lots, comparisons much occur at the same relative time point, rather than the actual time point e.g. time after the manufacture has begun. This relative time field becomes a calculated field.

- **Determining when a specific part of the making process is in progress**

  It is often of interest to the customer to understand when a critical part of the making process is occurring. Often, this can be implied from multiple attributes collected from the manufacturing data e.g. it can be implied that the product within the tank is being transferred to storage when the weight is decreasing. In the Historian database, only the weight decrease is captured. To be able to visualise this data, it must have a new column within the Data Vault database.

- **Determining the capacity of specific equipment**

  Understanding if equipment is running efficiently can help determine whether maintenance is needed e.g. the amount of energy used to run equipment may change over time, and may be indicative of the need for special cleaning or replacement. This may be more cost-effective to monitor rather than scheduled physical checks of the equipment. Calculated fields can be used to calculate the efficiency of certain equipment, given other parameters captured within the database. These have been defined and are ready to be implemented within the Data Vault database.

- **Standardisation of human-input data**

  Where operators in the manufacturing site have input data manually into the system, there may be differences in the formatting. Logic to enable the database to interpret these as the same factor is required for summary statistics in the end visualisation. An example might be in comparing different formulas. A name may be input as Conditioner1; conditioner-1; Conditioner-01. Therefore if trying to average a statistic, these would not be recognised as being within the same formula. The logic should be able to encompass not only lists of formulas that are currently available, but also cover potential new formulas to ensure that minimal upkeep is needed for the database.

Some further refinement of defined calculated fields will be required when the final database is ready. Currently, the calculated fields are validated with a limited data set collated from one manufacturing site. When the database becomes live and is populated by significantly larger amounts of data, it may be that the logic set is not sufficient e.g. where logic is provided to standardise human-input data, there may be a larger variation in the way they are being captured.

4.10. Develop success criteria of the design/ functionality/ timing for external vendor

Success criteria have been developed around the required functionality of each dashboard including details of the following:

Key business question
Report Layout/Screenshot/Mock-up
Selection Criteria/Filter Criteria
Main Heading
Sub Heading
Different dashboard views
Default Settings
Adding process limit comparisons
Totalling/Calculation/Statistical requirements
Sorting
Page Breaks
Interactive Capabilities

Expected performance was also defined, such as time to load, and also timings on when the implementation will be needed.

The design criteria document details cannot be shared for confidentiality reasons.

4.11. Collaborate within the team and vendor to execute the dashboard

Collaboration with the Dashboard vendor has begun, and initial prototypes executed where dummy-data sets are available. This work will be ongoing until the Data Vault database is ready to be connected and final dashboard executions can be developed. Vendor documentation principles, which determine the degree of work and their understanding of the design criteria, is also in progress. These assist with finalizing costing quotations and ensuring that the project is delivered within the agreed budget.

Collaboration with the Data Vault vendors will also begin soon; the database structure is defined with the fields list fixed.

5. DISCUSSION

The project has moved P&G closer to the implementation of the biggest advance in manufacturing data analytics in the beauty category. The full integration of the Research and Development group and Product Supply organization means that a seamless approach to manufacturing data analytics is being developed, ensuring that the needs of all users can be included in the work scope. Manipulating or collating data currently available ensures that the dashboards will be immediately utilised for business decisions.

This work is also important in the role it may play in future innovation. Enabling access to this data for modelling and simulation gives huge possibilities of manufacturing processes can be leveraged to develop new innovations.

6. CONCLUSION AND FURTHER WORK

A multifunctional team (across internal functions) together with external vendors is required to execute this data management project. By running several aspects in parallel, end user input into the early stages of database design has ensured that their requirements can be met. This will lead to quicker implementation of the dashboards, and rapid exploitation of the new capability.

6.1. Further work

The current work status comprises the first half of this project. The second half of this project will cover the following areas:

- Database creation to meet needs of dashboards
  - Consultation is required with the Data Vault external vendors to ensure the database is created as required. This includes the creation of calculated fields, and the validation that these fields are calculated correctly.
- Dashboard creation by external vendors
  - Once the database is ready to create the dashboards, there will be several iterations to ensure they have the functionality as required. Validation of any on-dashboard calculations, such as summary statistics, will be required.
  - Transfer of available dashboard design into this project is required (different business unit dashboards for reapplication). This requires communication of field mapping and validation of the dashboards.
- Training, onboarding and future planning
  - Development of training material and roll out plans for both research and development organization and the product supply organization will be required to ensure successful project completion.
  - Define areas of potential analysis
- Data Modelling (If project timing allows)
  - Utilisation of dashboards to make business recommendations comparing different attributes across sites- engineering opportunities, R&D opportunities, and opportunities for modelling the data will also be explored.

REFERENCES

1. Rockwell Software (2015) Human Machine Interface http://www.rockwellautomation.com/rockwellsoftware/hmi.page

2. Rockwell Software (2013) Factory Talk ® Historian SE Live interface User Guide http://literature.rockwellautomation.com/idc/groups/literature/documents/um/hseld-um024_-en-e.pdf

3. SyTech Incorporated (2015) Report from Historians http://www.sytech.com/product_xlreporter_history.asp

4. Rockwell Software (2015) Factory Talk ® View SE http://www.rockwellautomation.com/rockwellsoftware/products/factorytalk-view-se.page#features

5. Gartner, inc. (2014) Gartner Survey Analysis: Customers Rate Their BI Platform Functionality, ID:G00262302 Analyst(s): Rita L. Sallam, Josh Parenteau

CHAPTER 2

Price Erosion and Sales Volume Analysis of China Smart-Phone Market

LIN Fangbin

ABSTRACT

In the competitive smart-phone market in China, price is one of the most critical factors affecting customers' purchase decisions. The objectives of this study are:

- To depict price erosion patterns and sales volume trends across major smart-phone market players,
- To predict the smart-phone prices on multiple levels and dimensions, and
- To identify pricing strategies of Lenovo and its key competitors in China

The final output of this study is a fully automatic visualization dashboard that will be able to accommodate a big dataset of at least three years, from December 2013 to 2016. Besides, it will make the whole analysis more efficient and accurate in capturing the pattern of price erosion and sales volume and make it more user-friendly.

1. INTRODUCTION

One of the mainstream smart-phone brands in China, Lenovo gathered data for price, monthly sales volume, model features for own and competing brands in China from December 2013 to April 2015, and would like to turn it into winning strategies. This study helps Lenovo clean and structure this data, and create an Excel-based visualization dashboard to monitor how the price and sales volume of certain products evolve across dynamic dimensions (time, provinces, brands, etc.) and to predict how the price of a model will change in the next few months.

This study was proposed by the internal business units of Lenovo (marketing departments, procurement management teams, etc.) to help them monitor the sales of Lenovo's own or competing products, and to revise its pricing/marketing strategies.

2. PROBLEM STATEMENT

There are four important steps to be taken to achieve the above mentioned goals. These are:

1) **Product identification**

   Products of a particular model (e.g., iPhone 6 Plus) can come in batches and sold in different provinces, and can be bundled with the service contracts offered by different telecom service operators in a certain province. Attributes such as provinces and telecom service operators help to define a "product". This is different from elsewhere. iPhone 6 Plus should be deemed as one product, even if it is sold in different cities. However, in this study, items sold in different provinces are treated as different products. Similarly, items having contracts with different telecom service providers are treated as separate products. Thus, iPhone 6 Plus sold in Beijing and Shanghai are two different products, while the same phone having service contracts with CMCC and China Unicom are also two different products. In this study, multiple attributes are combined into composite keys in order to better define the "products". In other words, only items identical in every attribute of a key are deemed as the same "products". The attributes forming the composite keys are introduced in Sect. 4.

2) **Data cleaning**

The dataset for this project is extremely big; is cluttered and unstructured. It contains more than 700,000 smart-phone records, each of which represents the details of a batch of products sold in a transaction. Each record has more than 40 attributes including the launch time, model name, brand, unit price, provinces where the transaction happened, feature information, and so on, to describe the products sold in the transaction. There are empty values, "NA" values, wrong values, or duplicate records in the dataset. For example, for a selected "product", either there is no launch price, or there are two different launch prices. Such uncleaned dataset will have negative effect on modeling and data visualization. Therefore, a cleaned and structured dataset is critical for this study.

3) **Capturing price erosion trend**

Simply showing the change of the average price across time may not be a good solution to determine the trend of price erosion in extreme situations. For instance, there are three products of brand A sold at different unit prices because of quantity discount. A1 sold 8000 pieces for 1050 Yuan/piece, A2 sold 8500 pieces for 1000 Yuan/piece and A3 sold only 10 pieces for 4000 Yuan/piece. If average price is used to capture the price erosion trend for the whole brand, the nonimportant but highest price of A3 will interfere with the trend to a great extent.

4) **Analysis conduction**

It is necessary to conduct the analysis in an accurate and user-friendly way. The data is analyzed for different dynamic dimensions such as brands, provinces, etc. Every time the dimensions used for filtering changes, for example, when the brands are changed from Samsung to HTC, the data selected for the analysis will change accordingly. In addition, data validation, calculation, and graphing process will need to be reworked. It is not possible for the business units to do entire processes manually every time the dimensions change. What is also disadvantageous about the manual adjustment is that manual work may not be accurate – any typo, wrong data matching or wrong data selection may lead to incorrect results. From this perspective, a tool is required to make the analysis reproducible, accurate and convenient.

3. STATE OF THE ART

No such analysis was ever conducted for China's smart-phone market. However there was a similar study by Lenovo for Brazil PC market for the price erosion and sales volume patterns for all the mainstream PC products. These were the products from 12 domestic and international PC brands as shown in Figure 1, and their total annual sales volume accounted for more than 90 per cent of the total annual PC sales in Brazil from 2010 to 2014. This analysis analyzed the price erosion and sales volume trends of these 12 brands from their launch to 12 months later. Launch month did not necessarily refer to a fixed or identical calendar month e.g., product A was launched in December 2013 while product B was launched in March 2014. Even though they were launched in different calendar months, the price erosion and sales volume trends of product A from December 2013 to November 2014 and the similar trends of product B from March 2014 to February 2015 can be analyzed for the same timeline because the criteria for analysis was from the products launch to 12 months after the launch. This study of China's smart-phone price erosion and sales volume analysis is comparable in its ideologies with Brazil PC analysis.

3.1. Brazil PC analysis: composite keys for products identifications

In Brazil PC analysis, nine features of a PC are combined into composite keys to identify a product, which include keyboard, screen-size, screen resolution, CPU, brand, city where the PC is sold, WIFI, battery, and model name. As products of the same category (electronic products), most of the above features are also used to compose the keys to identify smart-phone products.

3.2. Brazil PC analysis: based on a clean dataset

Brazil PC analysis was based on a clean dataset, e.g., all the records with NA or missing values in sales volume or price column were deleted. All the records without adequate data about previous month's sales volume or price information were also deleted. In the current analysis, similar data cleaning process is applied. The data cleaning process will be illustrated in more detail in Sect. 4.

3.3. Brazil PC analysis: capture price erosion and sales volume pattern

In Brazil study, price erosion meant the price discount at *X* months from launch. The launch month can be any month during January 2011–December 2014. Sales volume was *(volume sold in X months from launch)/*

(total volume sold during January 2011–December 2014) as percentage. Price index and sales volume within 12 months from launch are plotted separately month on month. Price index and sales volume are combined as "price index >12 mths" and "sales volumes >12 mths" in the graph.

Figure 1 shows the price erosion and the sales volume pattern detected:

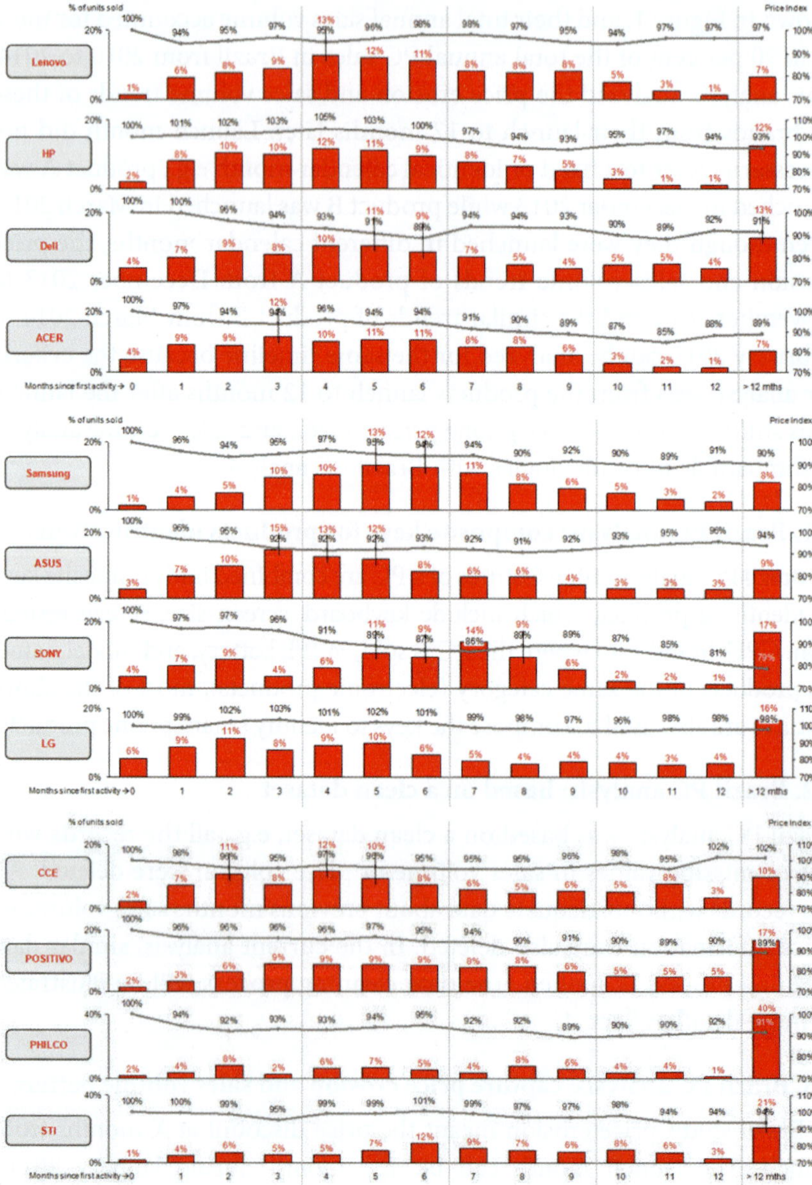

Figure 1: Pattern of price erosion and sales volume for 12 brands.

3.4. Brazil PC analysis: detecting competitors' marketing strategies

Brazil PC analysis also successfully detected the marketing strategies of Lenovo and its competitors. Figures 2–5 show how the marketing strategies are detected:

Figure 2 indicates that the prices of products from Lenovo's major competing brands, HP and LG, increased in the first three months post-launch. Unlike these, other two major competing brands, Asus and Acer, were engaged in aggressive price discounts within the first three months and achieved more than 30 per cent of their total annual sales volume ascribed to such discounts. At this stage, Asus and Acer lead the sales volume. Compared to them, Lenovo has less competitive price discount, and sees slower sales.

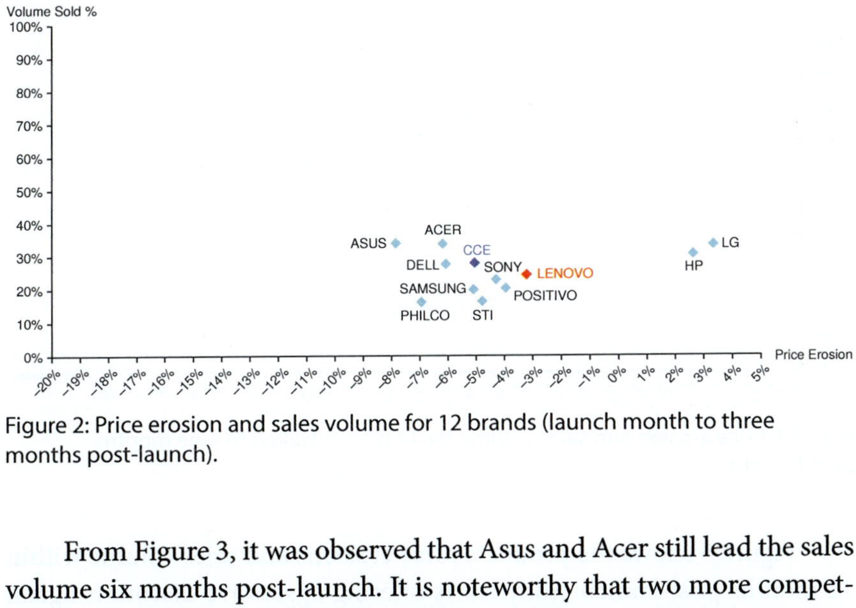

Figure 2: Price erosion and sales volume for 12 brands (launch month to three months post-launch).

From Figure 3, it was observed that Asus and Acer still lead the sales volume six months post-launch. It is noteworthy that two more competing brands Dell and Sony are even more aggressive in pricing discount. For Lenovo, the price discount is still not competitive.

Figure 4 illustrates the products' price erosion and sales volume nine months post-launch. A very important finding at this stage is that HP and Acer start offering more aggressive price discounts while Dell stops. Lenovo and CCE are still less aggressive than major international brands, but Lenovo is about to start offering higher discounts. Besides, Lenovo's sales volume inches up to second position, marginally behind Acer.

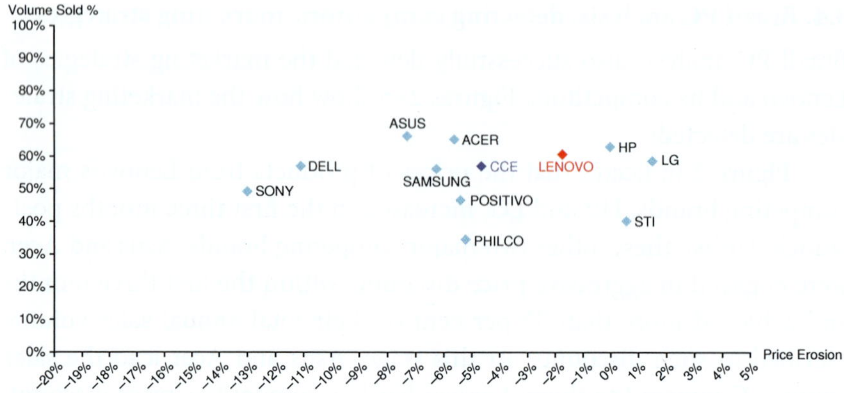

Figure 3: Price erosion and sales volume for 12 brands (four to six months post-launch).

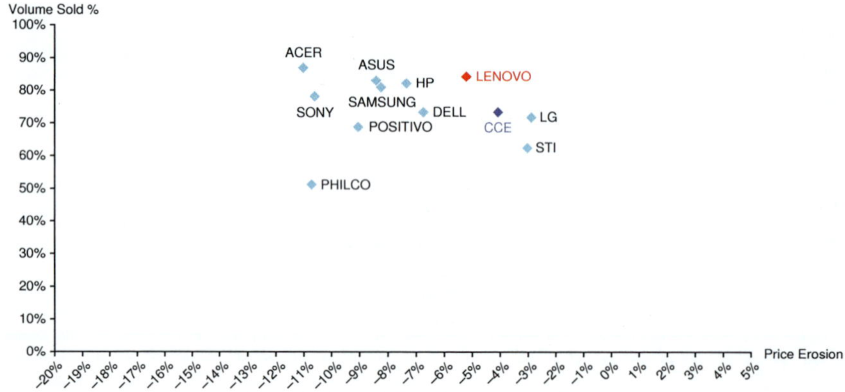

Figure 4: Price erosion and sales volume for 12 brands (seven to nine months post-launch).

Figure 5 shows the products price erosions and sales volume within 12 months post-launch. Sony starts offering aggressive discounts again, while Acer continues to be aggressive. Lenovo now inches up to the first place in sales volume.

Generally speaking, Acer tries to keep leading the sales volume by long-term price discounts and is getting more and more aggressive. Sony and Dell also keep discounts across the year, but the aggressive and non-aggressive types appear alternatively across the year. Lenovo is slower than these brands in its sale or, in other words, in its inventory clearing process and does not offer deep discounts compared to others.

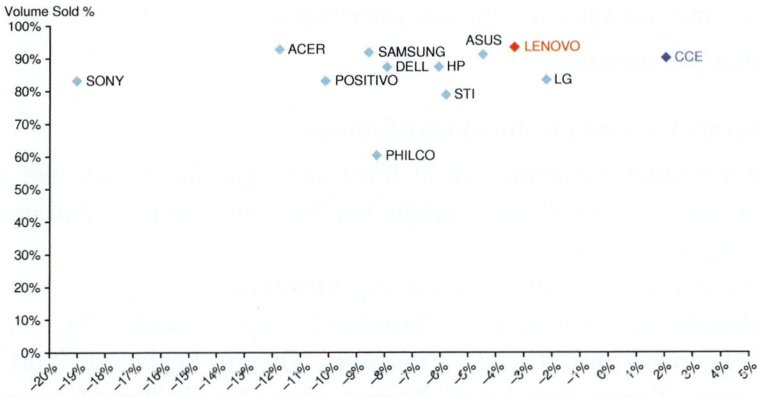

Figure 5: Price erosion and sales volume for 12 brands (10–12 months post-launch)

3.5. Further improvements on analysis conduction

Obviously, Brazil PC analysis was quite successful in terms of detecting the pricing strategies of Lenovo and its competing products. However, there are still improvements to be done.

First, Brazil PC analysis was not efficient in terms of calculation. The analysis was done manually, and was really time consuming and nonreproducible. Besides, it does not analyze lower levels such as price/sales volume pattern in provincial or model levels. What is more, this analysis is more descriptive than predictive. Finally, the graphs are not clearly labeled. Although experienced readers have no problem reading them, improvements can be done.

Compared to Brazil PC analysis, the improvement to be done in this study is to make an automatic, reproducible, and predictive analysis for China's smart-phone market. Additionally, the formats of the graphs could be improved to make them more comprehensible for every user.

4. SOLUTION

4.1. Description of approach

To address the four problems stated in Sect. 2 and achieve the objectives mentioned in the abstract to make the whole analysis more efficient, accurate and user-friendly, following four steps are required:

1) Generate keys for product identification
2) Data cleaning

3) Create metrics: sales volume and price index
4) Dashboard construction

4.2. Generate keys for product identification

Multiple attributes are combined to form composite keys such that a unique product identified via a unique key has only one price and one sales volume at a specific date.

In the dataset, there are the following attributes:

"Telecom Service Operator", "Province", "Type (model)", "System", "Brand", "Launch Time", "Cover", "Processor", "Qwerty-Keyboard", "SIM", "Screen-Size" "Screen-Size Band", "Rear-Camera Pixel", "Rear-Camera Pixel Band", "Front-Camera Pixel", "Front-Camera Pixel Band", "Screen-Resolution", "Screen-Resolution Band", "Thickness", "Region", "Price", "Volume", "Volume Tier", "Price Tier", "Launch Price", "Launch Year (Fiscal)", "Launch Month (Fiscal)", and "Generation"

Initially, the attributes selected to form the composite key are:

"Telecom Service Operator", "Province", "Type (model)", "System", "Brand", "Launch Time", "Cover", "Processor", "Qwerty-Keyboard", "SIM", "Screen-Size Band", "Rear-Camera Pixel Band", "Front-Camera Pixel Band", "Screen-Resolution Band" and "Generation".

"Thickness" is not included into the key because it is highly correlated with the attribute "Type" which has been included: the "Thickness" can be referred via "Type".

"Region", "Volume Tier", "Price Tier", "Launch Year (Fiscal)" and "Launch Month (Fiscal)" are not included in the key because they are derived attributes: "Region" is derived from "Province", "Volume Tier" is derived from "Volume", "Price Tier" is derived from "Price", "Launch Year (Fiscal)" and "Launch Month (Fiscal)" are derived from "Launch Month".

For the continuous variables "Screen-Resolution", "Rear-Camera Pixel", "Front-Camera Pixel" and "Screen-Size", band information rather than the original information are included in the keys. This is because the original information is too detailed and band information is sufficient for identification purposes.

Here is an example to illustrate the current key: "iphone6 plus 16g", "open" (not bonded with any telecom service provider), "Beijing", "08-tdd/fdd" (system), "apple" (brand), "10/01/2014" (launch time), "bar" (cover),

"N" (not a qwerty-keyboard model), "2" (dual-core processor), "ssim" (single SIM card model), "05.> = 5.5" (the 5th kind of screen-size band in the dataset: larger than 5.5 in.), "4.8.0M" (the 4th kind of rear-camera pixel band in the dataset: greater than 5-megapixel but not greater than 8-megapixel), "1.2M" (greater than 0.3-megapixel but not greater than 1.2-megapixel), "02.< = FHD" (resolution is higher than HD but not higher than full HD) and "4G" (generation) together can identify a product.

Without such a key, there would be problems if the price and sales volume of a so-called "product" were searched directly from the dataset, for example, if the model name "iphone6 plus 16g" is treated as a product. It can be found that in August 2014, "iphone6 plus 16g" sold in different provinces have more than one price and more than one sales volume. If this is the case, to determine a unique price and sales volume for this "product" gets confusing. In other words, the model name by itself cannot identify a product. Therefore, the attributes shown above are chosen to form composite keys.

Four very important attributes: "RAM", "ROM", "Battery" and "NFC" are not included in the initial key. This is because all the data of these four attributes from Jan 2014 to Jun 2014 is missing, which accounts for more than 40 per cent of all the data of these four attributes.

The advantage of not including "RAM", "ROM", "Battery" and "NFC" into the key is mainly to save time but this decision may result in disadvantages in that the key is not complete enough to identify products. To decide whether to include these four attributes into composite keys, some data are sampled from the dataset to test whether the current key is complete enough to identify the products.

Using the current key to identify the products, it is found that lots of them either do not have or only have two different "RAM", "ROM", "Battery" and "NFC" information, an empty value and a nonempty value (e.g., "250G" and "-"). In addition, a large proportion of them have several different nonempty values (e.g., "350G" and "400G").

The first situation may result due to the incomplete data input by the data collectors. But it is not difficult to infer that the missing values can be replaced by the nonempty values. For example, "-" can be filled with "250G".

From the second situation, it is obvious that these four attributes should be included into the key else the analysis may suffer too high a risk of treating different products for the same one. Before revising the key, some data cleaning process should be done. This will be illustrated later

Therefore, the finalized key should be:

"Telecom Service Operator", "Province", "Type (model)", "System", "Brand", "Launch Time", "Cover", "Processor", "Qwerty-Keyboard", "SIM", "Screen-Size Band", "Rear-Camera Pixel Band", "Front-Camera Pixel Band", "Screen-Resolution Band", "ROM", "RAM", "Battery", "NFC" and "Generation".

4.3. Data cleaning

Data cleaning is conducted via R programming, first for the duplicate records only one of which is retained.

The dataset also had derived metrics all of which are deleted in order to reduce the size of the dataset. For example there is a column called "Value" for which the values are derived by multiplying the values in the "sales volume" column and "price" column, therefore the "Value" column is dropped.

Records with "NA" or missing values at the key attribute columns were also dropped: price and sales volume. Besides, records older than 12 months are also dropped. This is because the analysis is done for a 12 month-span.

Further, data imputation is necessary for "RAM", "ROM", "Battery" and "NFC" attributes. Following is the key without these four attributes to identify the products:

- If the product records identified by a key have identical nonempty (e.g., "250G") and empty values "-" across all the dates, all the empty values should be filled with the nonempty values (e.g., all the "-" should be replaced with "250G");
- If the product records identified by a key have only empty values, all of them should be dropped;
- If the product records identified by a key have different nonempty (for example, "250G" and "300G") and empty values "-" across all the dates, all of them should be dropped;
- If the product records identified by a key have different nonempty values but no empty values, the records of this key should be divided into different products according to the number of nonempty values

After the data cleaning process, total number of records is reduced from 768,826 to 482,235.

4.4. Create metrics: sales volume and price index

The dashboard aims at visualizing the change of sales volume and price across time in a proper way and, as planned in the beginning, the visualization can be done under two different analytics modes: *prediction analysis* and *comparison analysis*.

Generally speaking, *prediction analysis* helps to consolidate the price information of all selected products into one line and also combines the sales volume of all the selected products into a single bar chart. After that, from all the selected data, a model launched within the recent six months can be chosen for the price prediction, if needed. If there is no product launched within recent six months, prediction will not work. Six months represent the life cycle of a mainstream smart-phone product in China. The price prediction is conducted via capturing the known price erosion pattern of the selected data, which is then applied to a model to get the price of this model for a certain calendar month, by assuming that the price erosion pattern of a single model will be similar to that of the whole brand.

Different from the prediction analysis, *comparison analysis* is more descriptive. It generates parallel lines and clustered bar charts of different colors in a single graph for comparison purposes. There is no prediction analysis to be done under the comparison analysis mode.

Under these two scenarios, different approaches are used to generate the metrics: 1) metrics under prediction analysis mode, and 2) metrics under comparison analysis mode

- **Metrics under prediction analysis mode –**

  Under this mode, the price and sales volume information of all the products selected for the analysis are consolidated into a bar chart with a line chart. Prediction analysis based on newly launched model is available under this mode.

  - **Sales volume**

    For the sales volume, the percentage of monthly sales volume over total sales volume within the recent 12 months are calculated and plotted. For example, if the total sales volume of all the selected products from August 2014 to July 2015 is 250 million pieces and the sales volume of January 2015 is 20 million pieces, the sales volume of January 2015 should be 8 per cent.

- **Price index and predicted price**

  To capture the price erosion trend, price indices are calculated using the methodology below:

Price index of product *i* at *t* months from its launch is denoted as $I_{i,t}$, the sales volume of product *i* at *t* months from its launch is as $V_{i,t}$, and the price of product *i* at *t* months from its launch is as $P_{i,t}$.

Weight $W_{i,t}$ to product *i* at *t* months from its launch is used in the calculation. The weight is calculated as below:

$$W_{i,t} = \frac{V_{i,t} + V_{i,t-1}}{2}$$

The major purposes for using simple moving average method to calculate $W_{i,t}$ is to smooth out short-term and random fluctuations in the sales volume data to highlight longer-term trends of the price erosions.

Further,

$$I_{i,t} = \frac{P_{i,t} - P_{i,0}}{P_{i,0} + 1} \times 100$$

Consolidated price index $I_{T,t}$ for all the *n* selected products is calculated as below:

$$I_{T,t} = \frac{\sum_{i=1}^{n} W_{i,t} \times I_{i,t}}{\sum_{i=1}^{n} W_{i,t}}$$

The advantage of this formula is that it not only consolidates all the products' prices into a single index, it also takes the sales volume of a product into consideration while dealing with the prices, so that extreme sales volumes or prices will not interfere much with the price erosion pattern. The reason why the overall trend should not be interfered by extreme values is that certain products sold at extreme high/low prices for extreme low/high volumes do not represent the overall trend. In other words, the trend line should not be pushed high/low just because of the sale of certain products.

In this way, for every month, a price index for all the selected products is generated.

There are several points worth noting in the calculation:

- The index of the launch month (where $t = 0$) is not calculated. Instead, a value of 100 is assigned to it as a baseline;
- Records which lack price or sales volume information for the current or last month are not considered in the calculation;

The price index prediction is only applicable to those models launched within the recent six months.

The example below is used to better illustrate what kinds of models' prices are predictable and how to predict the prices:

If there is a model called "M" in the dataset, launched no more than six months ago, M's prices will be predictable.

After assuring that M's prices are predictable, if its prices and sales volume information from its launch month to k months post-launch are given, the prediction process can be conducted as below:

Its price indices from its launch month to k months post-launch $I_{M,0}$, $I_{M,1}$, $I_{M,2}$, ..., $I_{M,K}$ can be calculated based on the known price, sales volume and the formula. Then, to predict the price index of the model "M" at $k + 1$ month post-launch, the below formula is used:

$$\frac{I_{M,k+1}}{I_{M,k}} = \frac{I_{T,k+1}}{I_{T,k}}$$

$I_{M,k}$, $I_{T,k+1}$ and $I_{T,k}$ can be calculated via the known data so $I_{M,k+1}$ is solvable mathematically. After $I_{M,k+1}$ is derived, $I_{M,k+2}$ becomes calculable as well. The above process is applied to get the price index of M in all the months.

There is one point worth noting in the calculation:

> If there are missing values between the known data, (e.g., the price/sales volume of January and March are given but February is missing) this methodology is also used to calculate the missing value.

To transform the predicted price indices into predicted prices, a transformation factor is needed. It is set as $P_{M,0}/100$. This is because all the price indices at the launch months are set to 100. To turn the predicted price indices into prices is simply to multiply every predicted price index with the transformation factor.

4.5. Prediction analysis examples

To illustrate more clearly how the above process goes on, some examples based on product records extracted from the dataset are shown below:

Product 1:
Key:
cmcc\anhui\coolpad8021\05-td-lte/t\coolpad\08/01/2014\bar\N\4\512\4096\1500\N\ssim\02.4.0-4.5\3.5.0M\0.3M\06.WVGA\4G

Table 1: Prices and sales volumes of product 1 (7/1/2014–3/1/2015).

	A	B	L	AA	AP	AQ	AT	AU	AV	AW
1	id	time	price	volume	key	months	lastmonthvolume	pricechange	weight	Index
2721	87914	7/1/2014	494	562	cmcc\anh	0	N/A	0	0	0
21359	81288	8/1/2014	480	3551	cmcc\anh	1	562	-0.028340081	2056.5	-58.2814
50679	71344	9/1/2014	462	2414	cmcc\anh	2	3551	-0.064777328	2982.5	-193.198
82754	68445	10/1/2014	401	2706	cmcc\anh	3	2414	-0.188259109	2560	-481.943
114606	62366	11/1/2014	399	2765	cmcc\anh	4	2706	-0.192307692	2735.5	-526.058
145665	56253	12/1/2014	396	2641	cmcc\anh	5	2765	-0.198380567	2703	-536.223
175705	49993	1/1/2015	395	1706	cmcc\anh	6	2641	-0.200404858	2173.5	-435.58
205980	43751	2/1/2015	382	1780	cmcc\anh	7	1706	-0.226720648	1743	-395.174
235123	37532	3/1/2015	373	3238	cmcc\anh	8	1780	-0.244939271	2509	-614.553

Product 2:
Key:
cmcc\anhui\coolpad8017\05-td-lte/t\coolpad\07/01/2014\bar\N\4\512\4096\1650\N\ssim\02.4.0-4.5\1.<=2.0M\N\06.WVGA\4G

Table 2: Prices and sales volumes of product 2 (7/1/2014–3/1/2015).

1	id	time	price	volume	key	months	lastmonthvolume	pricechange	weight	Index
2456	81283	8/1/2014	499	146	cmcc\anh	0	N/A	0	0	0
20949	71339	9/1/2014	455	428	cmcc\anh	1	146	-0.088176353	287	-25.3066
50518	68440	10/1/2014	393	1245	cmcc\anh	2	428	-0.21242485	836.5	-177.693
82507	62361	11/1/2014	384	1600	cmcc\anh	3	1245	-0.230460922	1422.5	-327.831
114360	56247	12/1/2014	369	1947	cmcc\anh	4	1600	-0.260521042	1773.5	-462.034
145413	49988	1/1/2015	367	300	cmcc\anh	5	1947	-0.264529058	1123.5	-297.198
175463	43746	2/1/2015	365	113	cmcc\anh	6	300	-0.268537074	206.5	-55.4529
205738	37527	3/1/2015	364	9	cmcc\anh	7	113	-0.270541082	61	-16.503

Tables 1 and 2 show that 9 months data (7/1/2014–3/1/2015) is available to calculate the sales volumes. The total sales volume of these two products in the shown 9 months is 23913 so that the sales volume at the month of launch is $(562 + 146)/23913 \times 100\% = 2.96\%$. The percentage at one month post-launch is $(3551 + 428)/23913 \times 100\% = 16.64\%$. This process is applied to calculate the sales volume for all the other months.

To calculate the price indices, $I_{1,0}$ and $I_{2,0}$ are assigned the same values of 100 as the baselines.

$$I_{1,1} = 100 \times ((480–494)/494 + 1) = 97.16599$$
$$I_{2,1} = 100 \times ((455–499)/499 + 1) = 91.18236$$
$$W_{1,1} = (562 + 3551)/2 = 2056.5$$
$$W_{2,1} = (146 + 428)/2 = 287$$
$$I_{T,1} = (97.16599 \times 2056.5 + 91.18236 \times 287)/(2056.5 + 287) = 96.4332$$

$$I_{1,2} = 100 \times ((462–494)/494 + 1) = 93.52227$$
$$I_{2,2} = 100 \times ((393\text{-}499)/499 + 1) = 78.75752$$
$$W_{1,2} = (2414 + 3551)/2 = 2982.5$$
$$W_{2,2} = (1245 + 428)/2 = 836.5$$
$$I_{T,2} = (93.52227 \times 2056.5 + 78.75752 \times 287)/(2982.5 + 836.5) = 90.2882$$

The above process is applied to calculate the price indices for other months.

Wherever data is not available for calculating percentages or indices, the line will be broken or the bars will be absent. The bars or lines will resume from where the data is available.

Figure 6 shows the graph generated, a price erosion trend line, and bar chart by consolidating the price and sales volume information of the

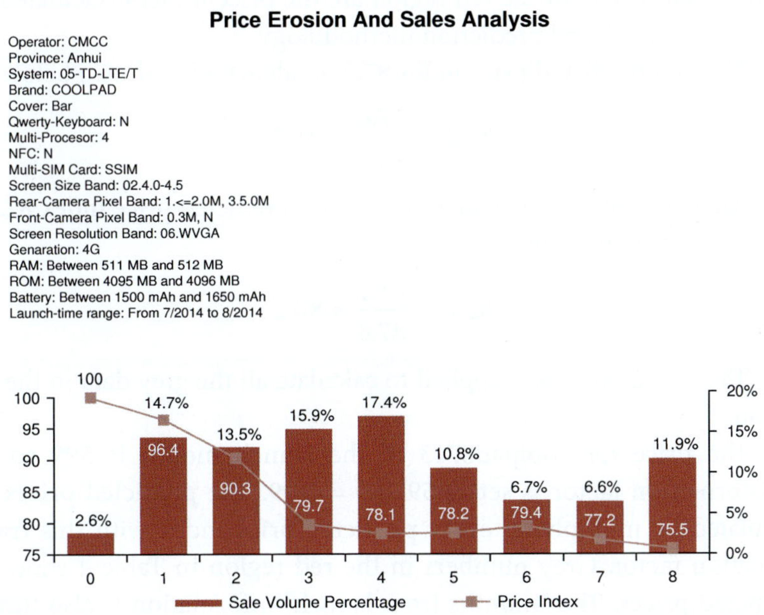

Figure 6: Price erosion and sales volume pattern graph generated manually (zero to eight months post-launch).

two products together. However, neither of the two models selected in Figure 6, coolpad8021 and coolpad8017, is launched within the recent six months so the prediction does not work in this example.

To illustrate how the price prediction process works, two other models launched within the recent six months, coolpad8713 and coolpady75, are selected. The detailed records are shown below in Table 3.

Table 3: Price index prediction for coolpad8713.

Volume	Sale Volume Percentage	Price Index	Months From Launch	Predicted Price
2064	1.0%	100	Jan-15	100.0
23799	11.2%	96.0	Feb-15	97.3
26979	12.7%	94.2	Mar-15	93.7
22770	10.7%	87.6	Apr-15	87.2
30641	14.5%	83.2	May-15	82.7
29558	14.0%	80.7	Jun-15	80.2
25020	11.8%	77.9	Jul-15	77.5
16846	8.0%	74.1	Aug-15	73.7
16681	7.9%	70.9	Sep-15	70.5
8349	3.9%	67.9	Oct-15	67.5
5495	2.6%	67.3	Nov-15	66.9
3015	1.4%	61.6	Dec-15	61.3
658	0.3%	60.0	Jan-16	59.7

In Table 3, the red color numbers in the red region are the price indices calculated via the known price and volume information of coolpad8713. Grey data in the red region are the price indices calculated via previously introduced prediction methodology.

The first predicted price index 87.2 is calculated as shown below:

$$87.2 = \frac{87.6}{94.2} \times 93.7$$

After the data is calculated, the second predicted price index 82.7 is calculated as shown below:

$$82.7 = \frac{83.2}{87.6} \times 87.2$$

The above process is applied to calculate all the grey data in the red region.

The price for coolpad8713 in the launch month is 599 so the transformation factor is set as 59/100 = 5.99. The predicted prices are calculated by multiplying every predicted price index with this transformation factor. Grey numbers in the red region in Table 4 show the predicted prices. The "months from launch" information is also turned into calendar month information to make the whole analysis more easily understandable:

Table 4: Price prediction for coolpad8713.

Volume	Sale Volume Percentage	Price Index	Months From Launch	Predicted Price
2064	1.0%	100	Jan-15	599.0
23799	11.2%	96.0	Feb-15	583.0
26979	12.7%	94.2	Mar-15	561.0
22770	10.7%	87.6	Apr-15	522.1
30641	14.5%	83.2	May-15	495.5
29558	14.0%	80.7	Jun-15	480.4
25020	11.8%	77.9	Jul-15	464.1
16846	8.0%	74.1	Aug-15	441.3
16681	7.9%	70.9	Sep-15	422.4
8349	3.9%	67.9	Oct-15	404.2
5495	2.6%	67.3	Nov-15	401.0
3015	1.4%	61.6	Dec-15	367.0
658	0.3%	60.0	Jan-16	357.4

Figure 7 is the price prediction graph of coolpad8713 generated by plotting the predicted prices from the red region of Table 4.

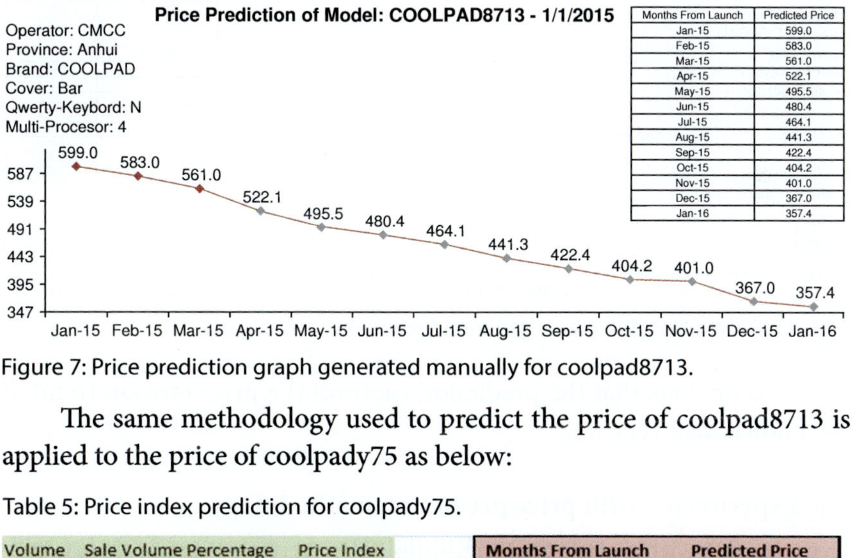

Figure 7: Price prediction graph generated manually for coolpad8713.

The same methodology used to predict the price of coolpad8713 is applied to the price of coolpady75 as below:

Table 5: Price index prediction for coolpady75.

Volume	Sale Volume Percentage	Price Index	Months From Launch	Predicted Price
2064	1.0%	100	Jan-15	100.0
23799	11.2%	96.0	Feb-15	96.0
26979	12.7%	94.2	Mar-15	92.1
22770	10.7%	87.6	Apr-15	85.7
30641	14.5%	83.2	May-15	81.3
29558	14.0%	80.7	Jun-15	78.8
25020	11.8%	77.9	Jul-15	76.2
16846	8.0%	74.1	Aug-15	72.4
16681	7.9%	70.9	Sep-15	69.3
8349	3.9%	67.9	Oct-15	66.3
5495	2.6%	67.3	Nov-15	65.8
3015	1.4%	61.6	Dec-15	60.2
658	0.3%	60.0	Jan-16	58.7

Table 6: Price prediction for coolpady75.

Months From Launch	Volume	Sale Volume Percentage	Price Index
0	2064	1.0%	100
1	23799	11.2%	96.0
2	26979	12.7%	94.2
3	22770	10.7%	87.6
4	30641	14.5%	83.2
5	29558	14.0%	80.7
6	25020	11.8%	77.9
7	16846	8.0%	74.1
8	16681	7.9%	70.9
9	8349	3.9%	67.9
10	5495	2.6%	67.3
11	3015	1.4%	61.6
12	658	0.3%	60.0

Months From Launch	Predicted Price
Jan-15	1060.0
Feb-15	1017.1
Mar-15	976.0
Apr-15	908.2
May-15	862.0
Jun-15	835.7
Jul-15	807.4
Aug-15	767.8
Sep-15	734.9
Oct-15	703.2
Nov-15	697.7
Dec-15	638.4
Jan-16	621.9

Figure 8 shows the manually generated graph for price prediction of coolpady75.

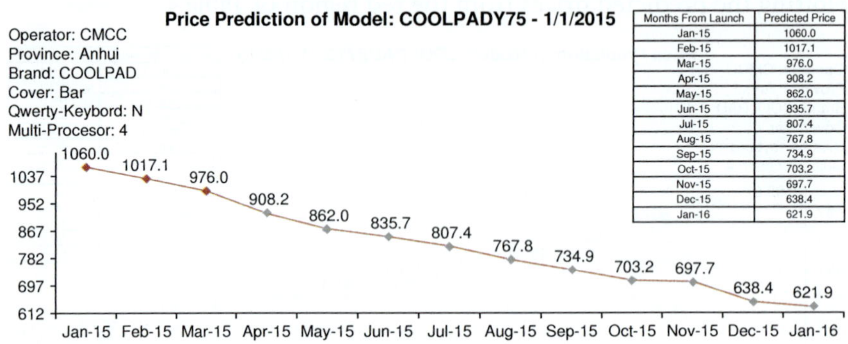

Figure 8: Price prediction graph generated manually for coolpady75.

It is obvious that the prediction captures the price erosion trend of the known data very well.

4.6. Experiments with price prediction methodology

Experiments with some other methodologies were also conducted to predict the price, e.g., time series regression. However, it does not work well because the amount of data available as training dataset for modeling is not big enough.

Another methodology experimented is illustrated below to predict the price.

Assuming the price for model "M" at *A* months post-launch is to be predicted. In order to explain the formula more clearly, some meaningless intermediate parameters are introduced: *Ratio Numerator, Ratio Denominator and Ratio.*

$$Ratio\ Numerator = (|I_{M,A-3} - I_{M,A-4}| \times |I_{M,A-2} - I_{M,A-3}|^2 \times |I_{M,A-1} - I_{M,A-2}|^3)^{1/6}$$

$$Ratio\ Denominator = (|I_{T,A-3} - I_{T,A-4}| \times |I_{T,A-2} - I_{T,A-3}|^2 \times |I_{T,A-1} - I_{T,A-2}|^3)^{1/6}$$

$$Ratio = Ratio\ Numerator/Ratio\ Denominator$$

$$I_{M,a} = [1 + (I_{T,A}/I_{T,A-1} - 1) \times \text{ratio}] \times I_{M,A-1}$$

Price of product M at A months post-launch = $I_{M,A}$ × *the transformation factor*

This methodology undoubtedly has its own advantage in that it incorporates more recent data to predict the future price. However, it is weak in dealing with extreme values.

If there is a scenario where $I_{T,A}$ is too small compared to an $I_{T,A-1}$, the predicted $I_{M,a}$ may become a negative number. So will be the predicted price.

Table 7 shows an example where a negative predicted price –807.6 for the model "Meizu's M463M (16G)" is generated because $I_{T,7}$, compared to $I_{T,6}$, is too small. Figure 9 represents the graph obtained manually for the price of M463M

Table 7: Price prediction for m463m.

Months From Launch	Volume	Sale Volume Percentage	Price Index
0	8944	4.9%	100
1	23671	13.0%	98.9
2	25572	14.0%	99.0
3	29346	16.1%	102.7
4	21224	11.6%	104.8
5	19896	10.9%	102.4
6	18144	10.0%	100.3
7	5171	2.8%	85.8
8	5197	2.9%	77.2
9	7512	4.1%	77.1
10	9388	5.1%	75.8
11	5934	3.3%	77.0
12	2316	1.3%	75.0

Months From Launch	Predicted Price
0	1255.0
1	1173.0
2	1162.0
3	1660.8
4	2045.5
5	1490.3
6	1137.5
7	-807.6
8	157.1
9	154.8
10	123.6
11	147.8
12	101.5

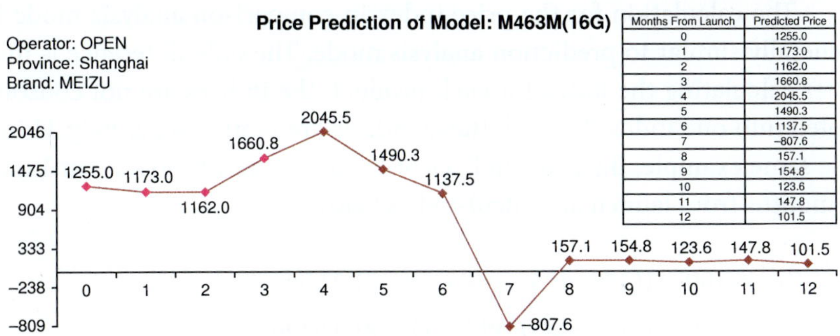

Figure 9: Price prediction graph for M463M generated manually.

However, this methodology is too sensitive to flat prices, for example, if $I_{T,A\text{-}3} = I_{T,A\text{-}4}$, the ratio denominator will become 0 so the whole prediction process becomes mathematically incalculable.

Considering the above two disadvantages, this methodology is rejected as well.

In conclusion, the price prediction methodology adopted is still the first one.

Metrics Under Comparison Analysis Mode – Sales volume and Price Index:

Just as the name implies, there is no need to consolidate the information of two brands together in this mode. Rather, just calculating the sales volume and price indices separately is enough.

1) Sales volume examples

   The examples shown in Tables 1 and 2 are used to illustrate the calculation of sales volume.

   Table 1 contains the detailed data for product 1. The total eight months sales volume for Product 1 is 3782. At the month of launch, the sales volume is 562 so that 562/3782 × 100% = 2.6%. The total sales volume for Product 2 within the shown 7 months is 3196. At the month of launch, the sales volume is 499 so that 499/3196 × 100% = 2.5%.

   The above process is applied to calculate the sales volume of all the other months.

2) Price index and predicted price examples

   The examples shown in Tables 1 and 2 are also used to illustrate the calculation of price indices in comparison analysis mode.

The calculation for the price index in comparison analysis mode is generally similar to prediction analysis mode. The only difference is that after calculating the index for each product, the indices are not consolidated into one index. Instead, those indices are plotted separately. Using the same example, the price indices of Product 1 and Product 2 at 1 and 2 months from launch are calculated as below:

$$I_{1,1} = 100 \times ((480-494)/494 + 1) = 97.16599$$

$$I_{2,1} = 100 \times ((455-499)/499 + 1) = 91.18236$$

$$I_{1,2} = 100 \times ((462–494)/494 + 1) = 93.52227$$
$$I_{2,2} = 100 \times ((393–499)/499 + 1) = 78.75752$$

The above process is used to calculate the price index of all the other months.

Figure 10 shows the price erosion/sales volume comparison between these two models:

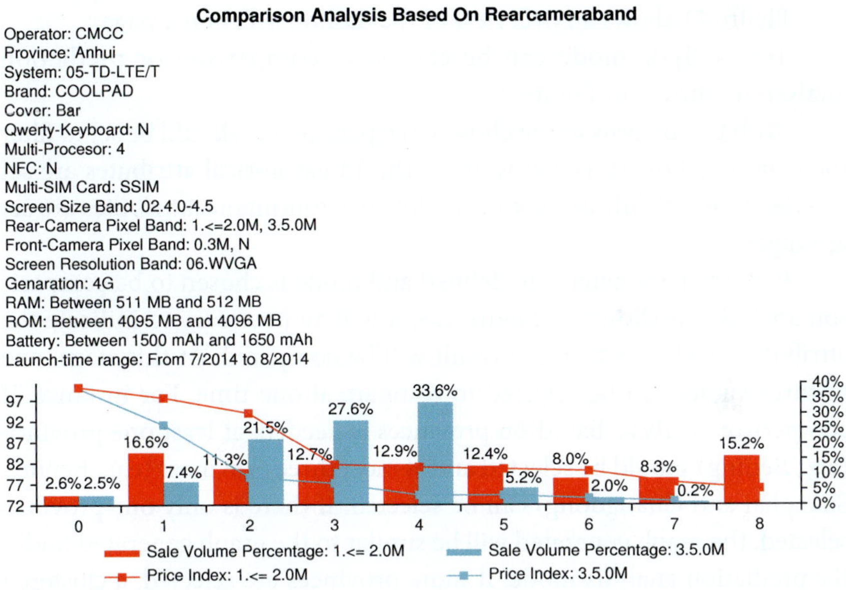

Figure 10: Price erosion and sales volume graph under comparison analysis mode.

4.7. Dashboard construction

It is an Excel-based dashboard built via VBA programming. The reasons to choose this dashboard are listed below:

- Compatibility: Excel is one of the most popular office tools in the world. Everyone using excel can directly download our dashboard and run it without installing any other app/software or re-configuring their own PC/laptop.
- Efficiency and accuracy: The whole process to generate a series of graphs of prediction analysis and comparison analysis takes only about 3 min. What is more, the whole automatic process perfectly avoids manual mistakes or typos which may lead to big mistakes in the final results.

- User-friendly: Once the user is not satisfied with the graph generated or would like to revise the metrics, he/she can choose either to revise the codes or directly change them in the graphs/spreadsheets manually. This is really easy and convenient for the everyday Excel users.
- Low-budget: Unlike other business analytics tools such as SAS or SPSS which require a paid license, this tool is free of charge for both the developers and the internal units in need of this dashboard.

Figure 11 shows an overview of the dashboard's home page:

The analysis mode can be chosen as comparison or prediction analysis as shown in Figure 12.

With the analysis mode chosen, the parameters should be set to filter the data based on 18 key attributes. The 14 categorical attributes are set by selection in the drop-down list while the continuous attributes are set as ranges.

If all the parameters are defined and mode is chosen to be comparison analysis (as shown in Figure 13), it will be necessary to indicate the attribute based on which the result will be compared. At this stage, one to three values can be selected to compare at one time. For instance, if comparison analysis based on provinces is needed, at least one province (e.g., Beijing) should be selected and at most three provinces (e.g., Beijing, Shanghai and Guangdong) can be selected. If there is only one province selected, the graph generated will be similar to the graph generated under the prediction analysis mode. If more provinces are selected, a clustered bar chart and a stacked line chart will be generated. An example will be shown later (refer to Figure 15).

Figure 14 shows that the analysis is 15 per cent completed. The status bar helps to monitor and improve the codes backing up the analysis. For example, at the beginning, if it is found that maximum time was spent between the status of 15–20 per cent completeness, which means that the algorithms executed during these two statuses might not be efficient enough, and the codes between these two statuses can be revised rather than going through all the codes aimlessly. The date placed in the title as shown in Figure 14 represents the "current date". Here, the current date of analysis is set as 1st June 2015.

Figure 15 is a sample graph generated automatically in comparison analysis mode. The scales in the graph fit automatically – the minimum/maximum scale of Y-axis for the price index are set to be the

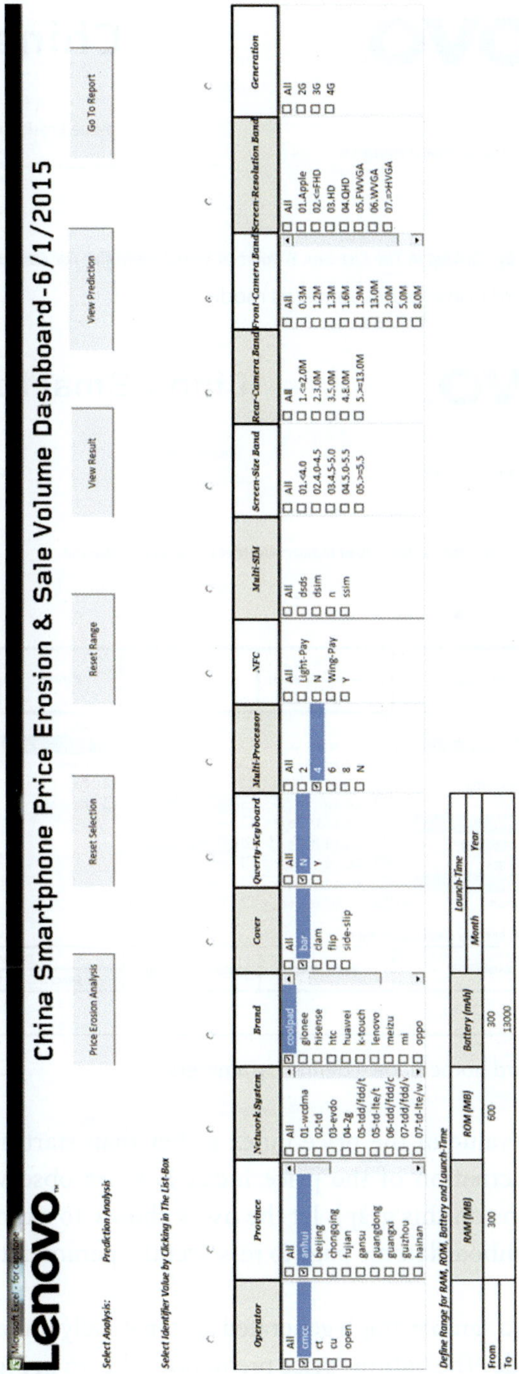

Figure 11: Dashboard home page – overview.

Figure 12: Dashboard home page – analysis mode.

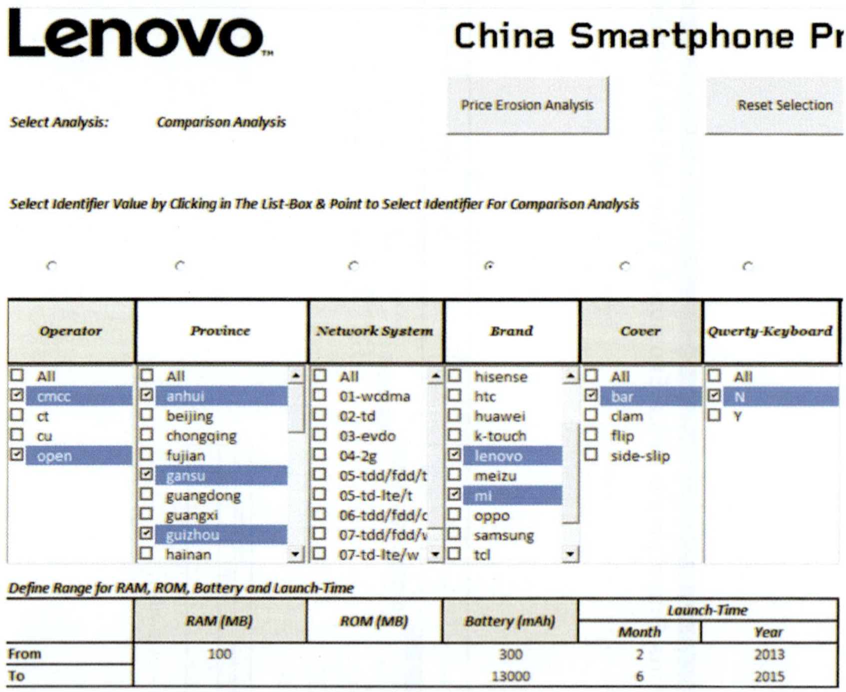

Figure 13: Dashboard home page – define parameters.

smallest/biggest value of the price index rather than starting from 0. In this way, the fluctuation of the price index is more observable for the users. The buttons on this graph let the users choose to export the graph or go back to dashboard home page to re-select the parameters to generate another graph.

Figure 16 is a sample graph generated automatically under the prediction analysis mode. The button "price prediction" shown in Figure 16 helps

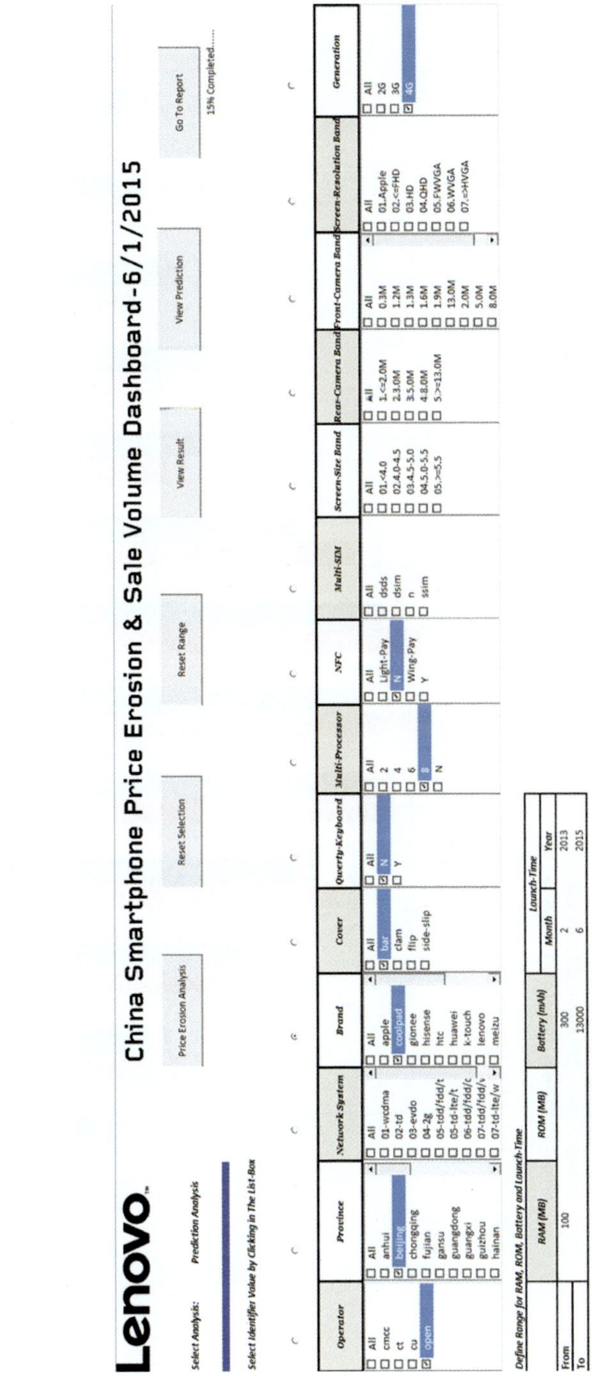

Figure 14: Dashboard home page – status bar.

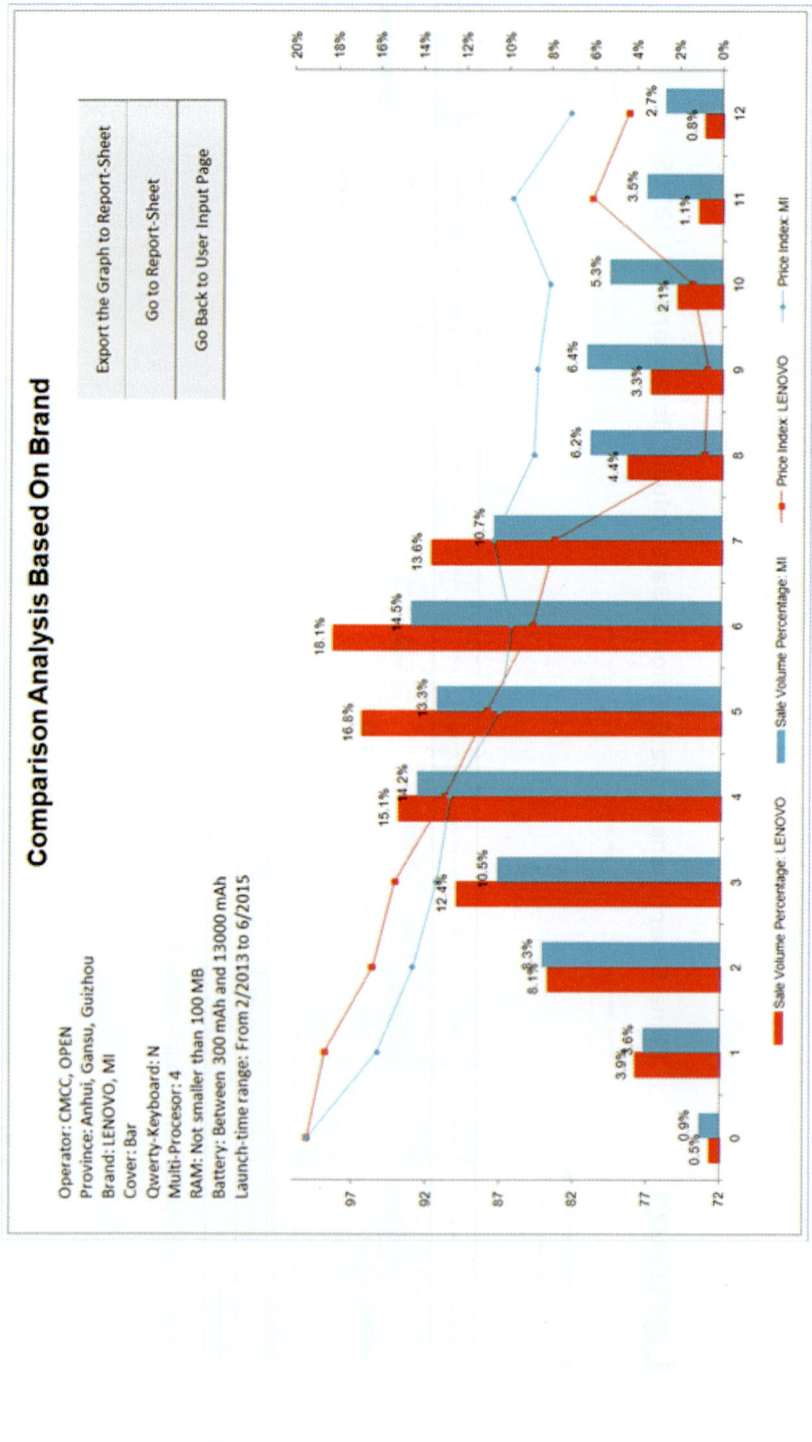

Figure 15: Comparison analysis graph generated automatically.

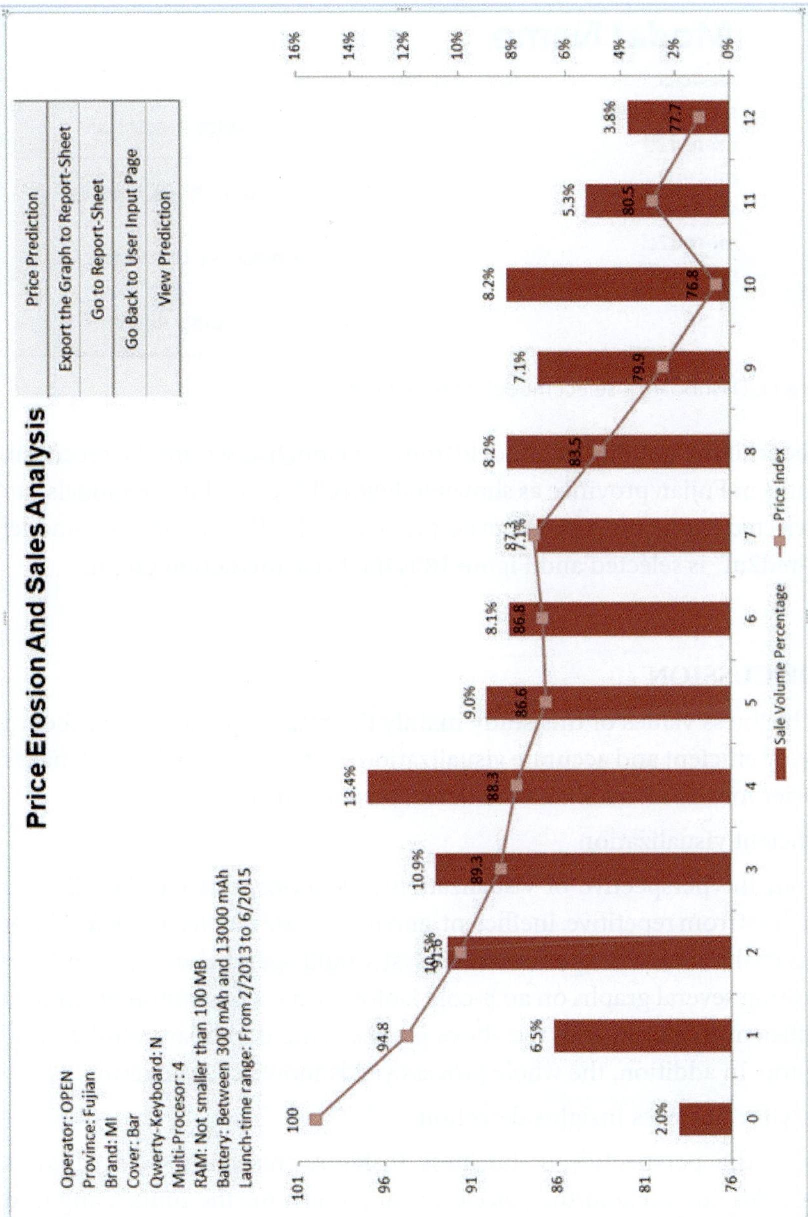

Figure 16: Prediction analysis graph generated automatically.

Figure 17: Dashboard – select model for price prediction.

to show all the unbundled models from MI launched within the recent six months in Fujian province as shown in Figure 17. One of those models can be selected at one time for the price prediction. In this example, the model "mi-red2ul" is selected and Figure 18 is the price prediction graph.

5. DISCUSSION

The business values of this study mainly lie in that it creates a dashboard for very efficient and accurate visualization, and that the dashboard makes it easier for the internal units to detect business insights.

- Efficient visualization

  From the perspective of visualization executions, this dashboard frees analysts from repetitive, inefficient, and inaccurate manual work. Without this dashboard, an experienced analyst would spend about half an hour plotting several graphs on an 8-core laptop, while a maximum of 5 min is sufficient to generate all the above graphs using dashboard on the same laptop. In addition, the whole process yields more accurate results.

- Easy for business insights detection

  From the perspective of business insights, this dashboard captures the sales volume and the price erosion pattern for the units using it to design marketing or pricing strategies. Figures 19–22 illustrate how the dashboard helps to detect business insights.

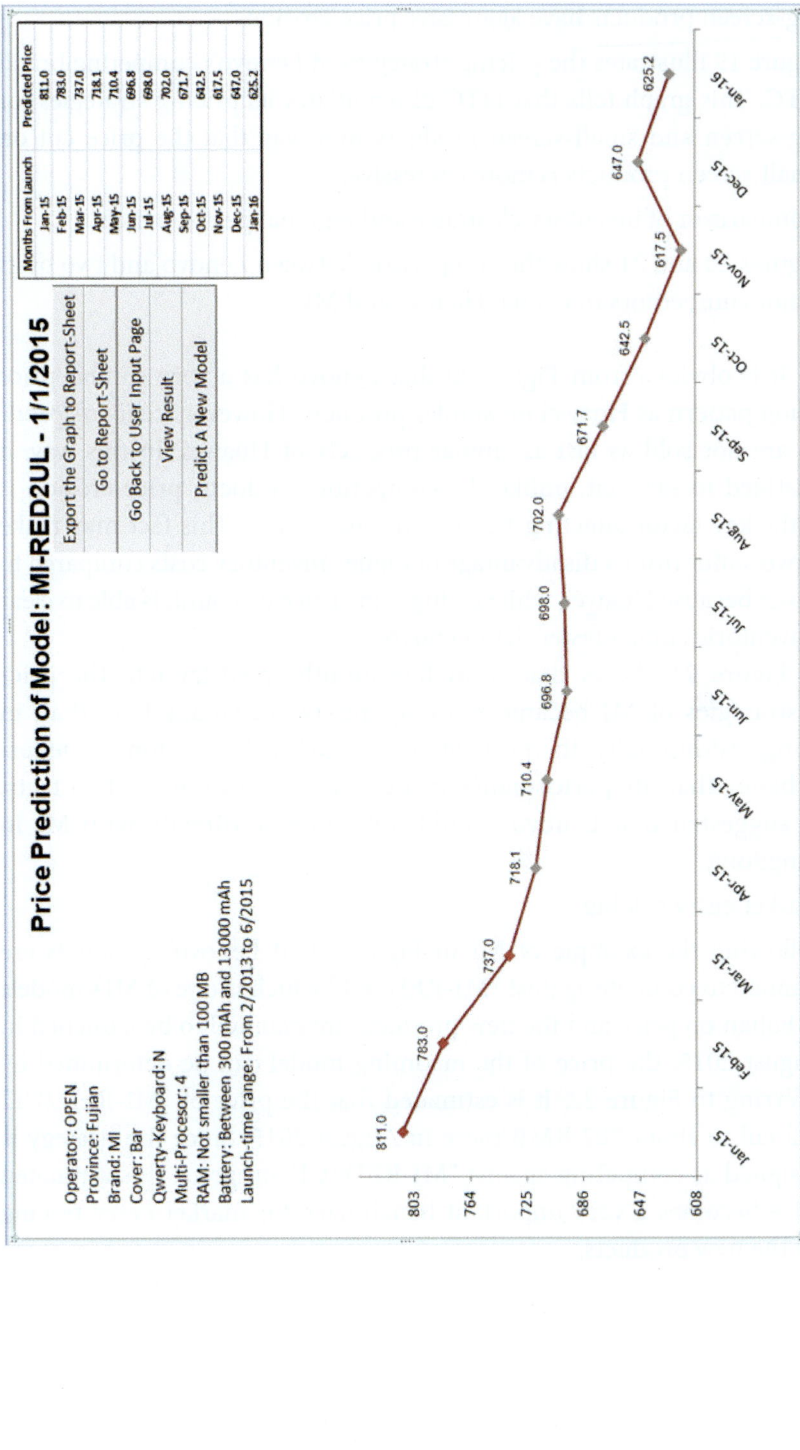

Figure 18: Prediction graph for MI-RED2UL.

- Big-screen products have aggressive price erosion

  Figure 19 illustrates the pricing strategies of Lenovo's competing brand HTC. This graph tells that HTC differentiates its pricing strategies for big-screen and small-screen products in a way that the price cut on small-screen products is more aggressive.

- Comparison of inventory clearance and regional performance

  Figures 20 and 21 show the comparison between Lenovo and two of its major competitors in China, Huawei and MI.

It is obvious from Figure 20 that Lenovo has a very similar price erosion pattern as Huawei on similar products. However, Lenovo's products are not sold as fast as similar products of Huawei. In this way, it is justified to say that, unlike the competing products, price erosion is not the key factor affecting Lenovo products' sales. This fact may make Lenovo suffer from a disadvantage of higher inventory costs compared to Huawei because Huawei, while giving same price discount, is able to clear its inventories much faster than Lenovo.

Figure 21 shows that from five months post-launch, the pricing strategies of MI became more aggressive in Guangdong than in Beijing. Additionally, the performance of MI in Guangdong is generally better than its performance in Beijing. Based on these two facts, it is suggested that Lenovo should not compete directly with MI in Guangdong.

- Market entry pricing

  Following the example of MI in Figure 21, if Lenovo's products are planned to compete against "MI-RED2UL" which is one of MI's models in Fujian on price and the new products are planned to be launched in August 2015, the price of the incoming model can be determined by referring to Figure 22. It is estimated that the price of "MI-RED2UL" will fall to about 702 RMB/piece in August 2015. Since the strategy is designed as competing against "MI-RED2UL" on price, this estimated price becomes a very important benchmark for market-entry pricing for the new products.

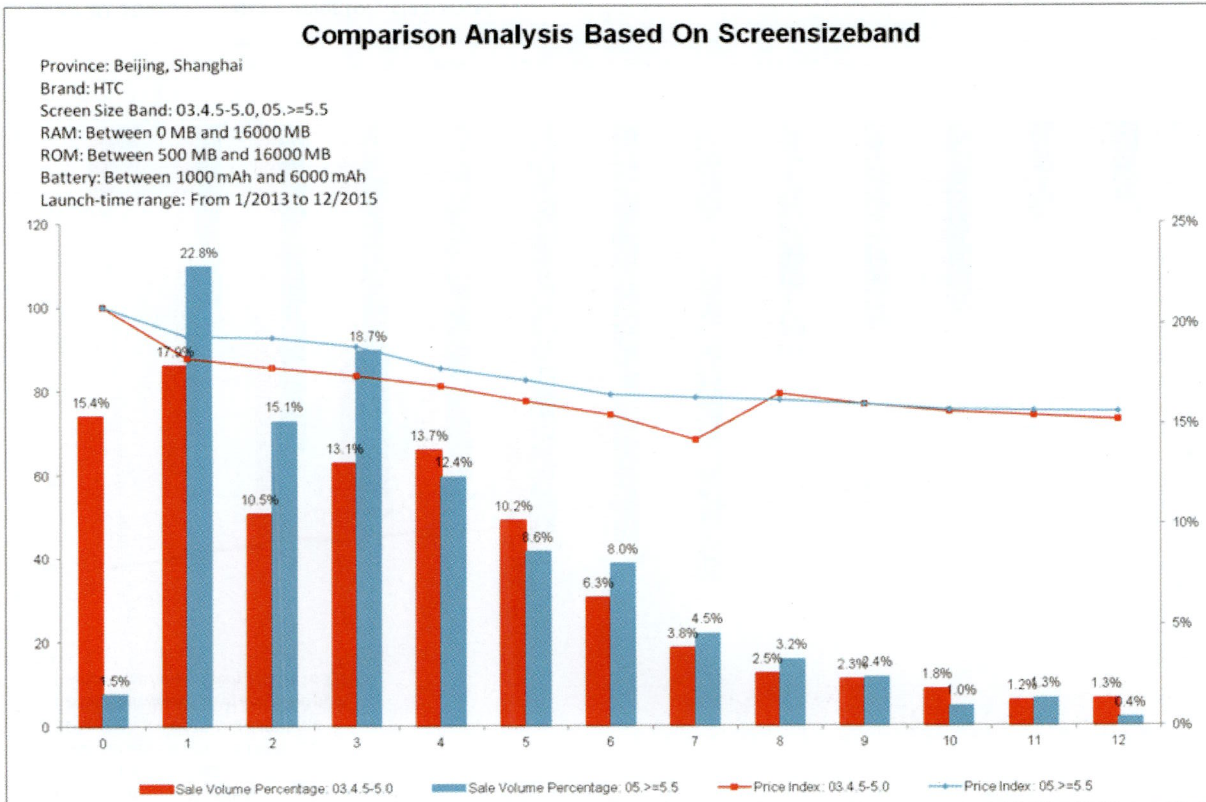

Figure 19: Strategy graph – price cut comparison based on screen size.

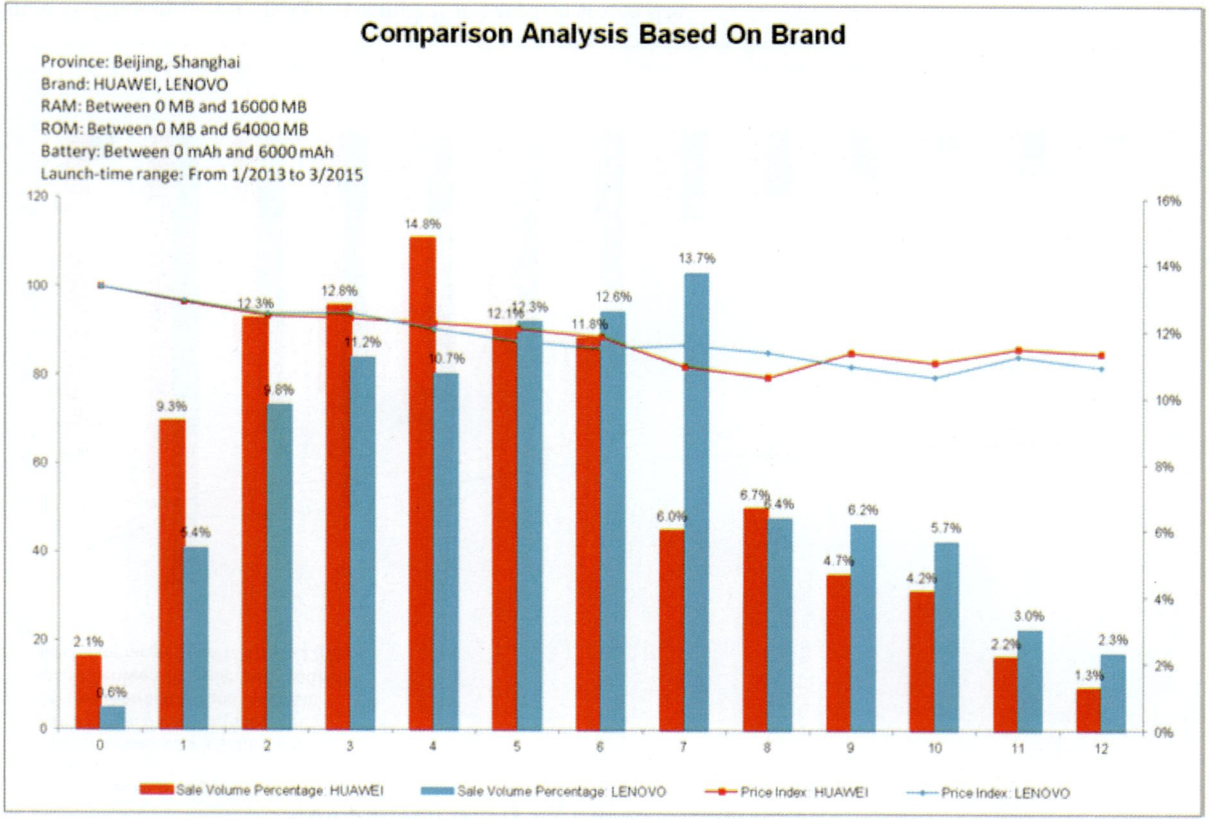

Figure 20: Strategy graph – inventory clearance.

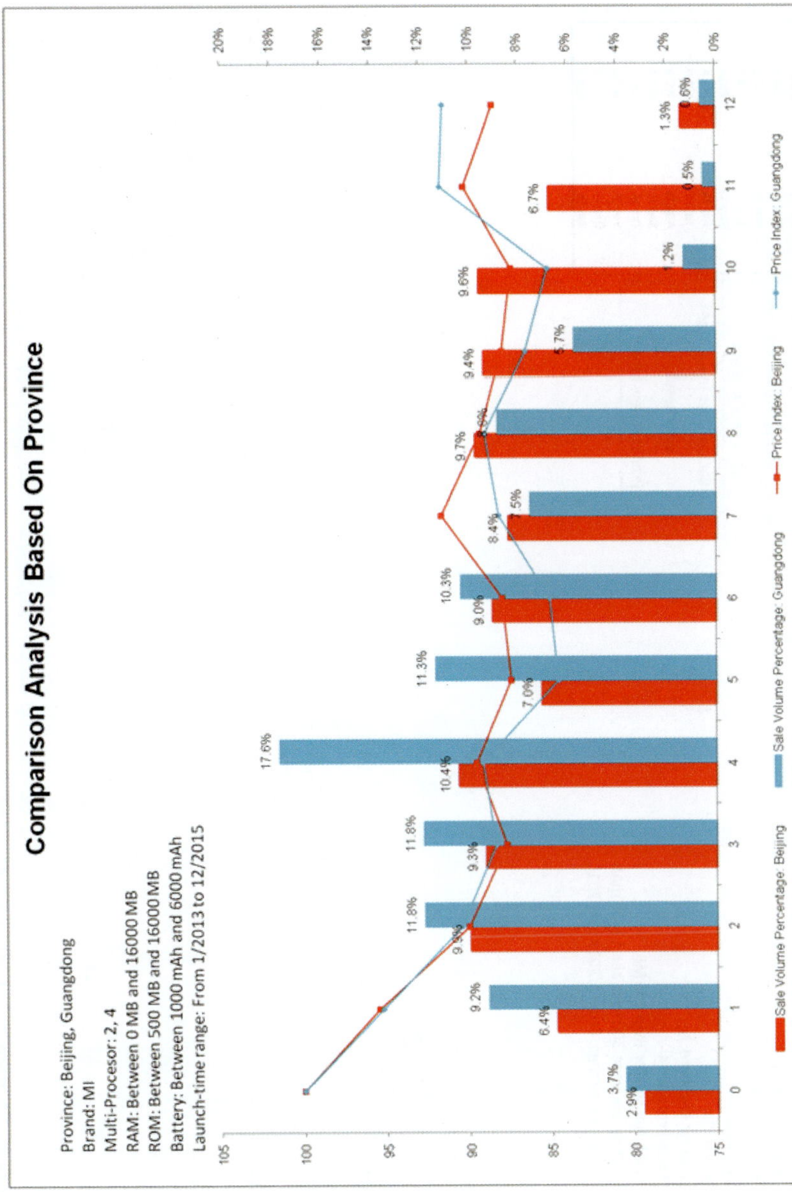

Figure 21: Strategy graph – regional performance.

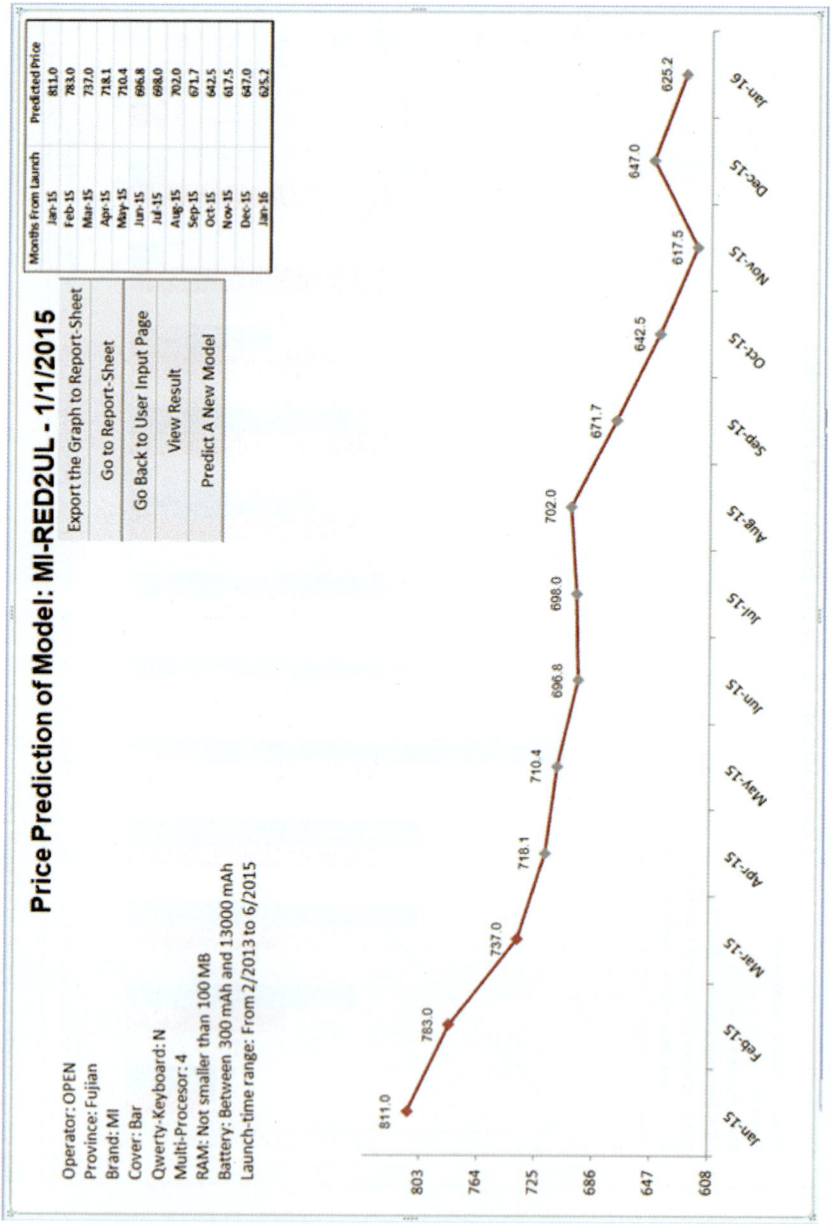

Figure 22: Strategy graph – market entry pricing.

6. CONCLUSION AND FURTHER WORK

Generally speaking, this study satisfied the requirements set by the internal business units of Lenovo.

First, the similar Brazil PC analysis is descriptive, while the current analysis is both descriptive and predictive. It satisfied the internal units' demands for a dashboard not only for descriptive but also for predictive analytics.

To test the prediction accuracy, 15 models are sampled out of 152 from Lenovo's five major competing brands in China for a prediction of prices in May 2015. These 152 models are launched by five brands: Huawei, Vivo, MI, OPPO, and Samsung during November 2014 and April 2015. Those models are also labeled as "smart-phone products" by the brand. Products not labeled as "smart-phone products" are not included in 152 models. Business models from Samsung are typical examples not included in the 152 models. Sampling method for 15 models can be described as below:

1) The internal business units proposing this study suggested the provinces, operators, and brands be selected for the prediction accuracy test. Beijing and Shanghai are among the most developed cities in China, and the quantity of smartphone purchased in these two cities accounts for 11 per cent of the total smartphone purchased in China from 2010 to 2014. In addition, these two cities are the target market of Lenovo's products. Due to these reasons, the prediction accuracy of products sold in these two cities is very important and products from these two cities are sampled for the prediction accuracy test. Regarding the telecom service operator, only products unbundled with any telecom operator are selected for the accuracy test. This is because unbundled products are the mainstream products sold in the market, 59 per cent of the products sold from 2010 to 2014 in China are unbundled products. About the brands – all the five brands selected are similar to Lenovo; they are well-known brands sold in China and they have a full spectrum of mainstream smart-phone products.
2) Using the provinces (Beijing and Shanghai), operators (Open), brands (Huawei, Vivo, MI, OPPO, and Samsung) and launch time (during November 2014 and April 2015) to filter all the 79082

models in the dataset, 152 models are left. These 152 models are denoted as set S. Only products launched during November 2014 and April 2015 are available for the accuracy prediction test because the current date of the analysis is set as May 1st, 2015 and the dashboard is only able to predict prices of models launched within the recent six months dated back from the current date. The life cycle of the smart-phone products in China is commonly deemed as six months. This is why the dashboard in this project is designed to predict the prices of models launched within the time range from November 2014 and April 2015.

3) Among the 152 models belonging to five brands: 41 models belong to Huawei, 15 models belong to VIVO, 19 models belong to MI, 33 models belong to OPPO and 44 models belong to Samsung. The 41 models of Huawei are denoted as set S_{HUAWEI}, the 15 models of VIVO are denoted as set S_{VIVO}, the 19 models of MI are denoted as set S_{MI}, the 33 models of OPPO are denoted as set S_{OPPO} and the 44 models of SAMSUNG are denoted as set $S_{SAMSUNG}$. From S_{HUAWEI}, S_{VIVO}, S_{MI}, S_{OPPO} and $S_{SAMSUNG}$ respectively, three models are sampled randomly for the prediction accuracy test. The models sampled from S_{HUAWEI} are denoted as set $S_0'_{HUAWEI}$, the models sampled from S_{VIVO} are denoted as set $S_0'_{VIVO}$, the models sampled from S_{MI} are denoted as set $S_0'_{MI}$, the models sampled from S_{OPPO} are denoted as set $S_0'_{OPPO}$ and the models sampled from $S_{SAMSUNG}$ are denoted as set $S_0'_{SAMSUNG}$.

Average error percentage is used to measure the prediction accuracy. *i* is used to represent the model of which the price is predicted and there are 15 models in the prediction accuracy test. In this study, the absolute average error percentage is defined as

$$\frac{\sum_{i=1}^{15} \frac{|\text{Predicted Price}_i \text{ at May 2015} - \text{Actual Price}_i \text{ at May 2015}|}{\text{Actual Price}_i \text{ at May 2015}}}{15} \times 100\%$$

Table 8 shows the prediction accuracy based on the selected 15 models.

Table 8: Accuracy table.

Accuracy Table							
Brand	Province	Operator	Model	Launch Month	May 2015 Price - Actual	May 2015 Price -Predicted	Error Percentage
Huawei	Beijing	Open	HUAWEIMT7-TL10	Feb-15	3000	3014	1%
Huawei	Beijing	Open	PE-UL00	Jan-15	2222	2383	7%
Huawei	Beijing	Open	HUAWEIY635-TL00	Mar-15	754	773	3%
Vivo	Shanghai	Open	VIVOX55L	Dec-14	2232	2247	1%
Vivo	Shanghai	Open	VIVOY628	Dec-14	1074	1163	8%
Vivo	Shanghai	Open	VIVO X5MAX*	Feb-15	2809	2708	-4%
MI	Shanghai	Open	MI-REDNOTED	Feb-15	943	920	-2%
MI	Shanghai	Open	MI NOTE 64G	Feb-15	2854	2585	-9%
MI	Shanghai	Open	MI-RED 2 UL	Jan-15	714	746	5%
OPPO	Beijing	Open	OPPO R8207	Jan-15	2204	2267	3%
OPPO	Beijing	Open	OPPO 3007	Dec-14	1273	1407	11%
OPPO	Beijing	Open	OPPO R8200	Mar-15	2212	2242	1%
Samsung	Beijing	Open	SM-A7000	Jan-15	2442	2546	4%
Samsung	Beijing	Open	SM-E7000	Feb-15	1919	1931	1%
Samsung	Beijing	Open	SM-G7200	Jan-15	1672	1752	5%

Based on the error percentages shown in Table 8, the absolute average error percentage of the prediction of the prices at May 2015 for the 15 models is

$$\frac{\begin{array}{c}|1\%|+|7\%|+|3\%|+|1\%|+|8\%|+|-4\%|+|-2\%|\\ +|-9\%|+|5\%|+|3\%|+|11\%|+|1\%|+|4\%|+|1\%|+|5\%|\end{array}}{15}\times 100\% = 4.33\%$$

The same accuracy test shown in Table 8 is also applied to predict the prices for 15 models in April 2015, 15 models in March 2015 and 15 models in February 2015 and the absolute average error percentage for these three tests are denoted as $AAEP_1$, $AAEP_2$ and $AAEP_3$. The 15 models in April 2015 is denoted as set S_A, March 2015 is denoted as set S_M, and February 2015 is denoted as set S_F, S_A, S_M and S_F are sampled from S.

In order to get S_A, S_M, and S_F, nine models are randomly sampled from S_{HUAWEI} and are denoted as S'_{HUAWEI}, nine models are randomly sampled from S_{VIVO} and are denoted as S'_{VIVO}, nine models are randomly sampled from S_{MI} and are denoted as S'_{MI}, nine models are randomly sampled from S_{OPPO} and are denoted as S'_{OPPO} and nine models are randomly sampled from $S_{SAMSUNG}$ and are denoted as $S'_{SAMSUNG}$.

In order to avoid duplicate test, S'_{HUAWEI}, S'_{VIVO}, S'_{MI}, S'_{OPPO} and $S'_{SAMSUNG}$ should satisfy that $S'_{HUAWEI} \cap {S_0}'_{HUAWEI} = \emptyset$, $S'_{VIVO} \cdot {S_0}'_{VIVO} = \emptyset$, $S'_{MI} \cap {S_0}'_{MI} = \emptyset$, $S'_{OPPO} \cap {S_0}'_{OPPO} = \emptyset$ and $S'_{SAMSUNG} \cap {S_0}'_{SAMSUNG} = \emptyset$.

S'_{HUAWEI} is randomly divided into three sets each of which contains three models denoted as $S_1'_{HUAWEI}$, $S_2'_{HUAWEI}$ and $S_3'_{HUAWEI}$.

S'_{VIVO} is randomly divided into three sets each of which contains three models denoted as $S_1'_{vivo}$, $S_2'_{vivo}$ and $S_3'_{vivo}$.

S'_{MI} is randomly divided into three sets each of which contains three models denoted as $S_1'_{MI}$, $S_2'_{MI}$ and $S_3'_{MI}$.

S'_{OPPO} is randomly divided into three sets each of which contains three models denoted as $S_1'_{OPPO}$, $S_2'_{OPPO}$ and $S_3'_{OPPO}$.

$S'_{SAMSUNG}$ is randomly divided into three sets each of which contains three models denoted as $S_1'_{SAMSUNG}$, $S_2'_{SAMSUNG}$, and $S_3'_{SAMSUNG}$.

Finally, $S_A = S_1'_{HUAWEI} + S_1'_{vivo} + S_1'_{MI} + S_1'_{OPPO} + S_1'_{SAMSUNG}$, $S_M = S_2'_{HUAWEI} + S_2'_{vivo} + S_2'_{MI} + S_2'_{OPPO} + S_2'_{SAMSUNG}$ and $S_F = S_3'_{HUAWEI} + S_3'_{vivo} + S_3'_{MI} + S_3'_{OPPO} + S_3'_{SAMSUNG}$.

Models in S_A are denoted as a and

$$AAEP_1 = \frac{\sum_{a=1}^{15} \frac{\left| \begin{matrix}\text{Predicted Price}_a \\ \text{at May 2015}\end{matrix} - \begin{matrix}\text{Actual Price}_a \\ \text{at May 2015}\end{matrix} \right|}{\text{Actual Price}_a \text{ at May 2015}}}{15} \times 100\%;$$

Models in S_M are denoted as m and

$$AAEP_2 = \frac{\sum_{m=1}^{15} \frac{\left| \begin{matrix}\text{Predicted Price}_m \\ \text{at May 2015}\end{matrix} - \begin{matrix}\text{Actual Price}_m \\ \text{at May 2015}\end{matrix} \right|}{\text{Actual Price}_m \text{ at May 2015}}}{15} \times 100\%;$$

Models in S_F are denoted as f and

$$AAEP_3 = \frac{\sum_{f=1}^{15} \frac{\left| \begin{matrix}\text{Predicted Price}_f \\ \text{at May 2015}\end{matrix} - \begin{matrix}\text{Actual Price}_f \\ \text{at May 2015}\end{matrix} \right|}{\text{Actual Price}_f \text{ at May 2015}}}{15} \times 100\%;$$

Finally, AAEP1 = 11%, AAEP2 = 8% and AAEP3 = 13%, which shows that the prediction can maintain an accuracy level of 90 per cent approximately. This accuracy level is much higher than the 75 per cent accuracy level required by the internal units proposing this project.

Besides the advantages of prediction of high accuracy level, this dashboard is costless. The construction of this dashboard is done in Excel via cost-free VBA programming so that it satisfies the low-budget requirements set by the internal business units proposing this project.

Finally, this tool is user-friendly and efficient. A series of needed comparison/prediction graphs can be generated in no more than 5 min.

Admittedly, there are still other modifications to be done in future to make the dashboard better.

Future work

1) Refresh the data.

   As a long-term product rather than a temporary tool, this dashboard should be able to accommodate a new and larger dataset, and to conduct the same analysis without much revision. Currently, data before May 2015 is obtained in our dataset so that all the prices from May 2015 are predicted prices. Once new data is available, they will be cleaned, structured, and put into the dashboard for the analysis.

2) Increase the prediction accuracy.

   From Table 8, it is evident that most of the predictions achieve an accuracy level of at least 90 per cent except the prediction for one model. This result is good but there is room for further improvements. In order to achieve higher prediction accuracy, further revision on the prediction methodologies is needed, for example, as more and more data are incorporated into the dataset, time series regression may be a better way to predict the price. In a time series model, more factors such as seasonality or public holidays per month can be considered as variables so that a more comprehensive prediction can be achieved.

3) Extend the analysis.

   Currently, the analysis is done for China's smart-phone market but the products can be changed, for example, a similar analysis for China's PC market using similar methodologies is also feasible.

Another possible extension may be to conduct the analysis for smartphone markets in other countries. The methodologies to clean data, to form the metrics and to conduct the visualizations will not change very much. From this perspective, the extension of this analysis is generally feasible. Besides, the comparison analysis should be able to accommodate more data. As mentioned previously, the current comparison analysis allows only three values of an attribute to be compared at one time. It will be much better if complete customization can be done, which means that no matter how many values of an attribute are selected by a user, they can be compared at one time.

4) Make the dashboard more dynamic and interactive.

   Currently, all the graphs generated are static, and it would be better to make it dynamic and interactive, e.g., the users should be able to adjust the timeline for the analysis. To be more detailed, the prediction of price is currently based on a 12 months period and the dashboard can be improved further in a way that the user is able to adjust the prediction horizon directly on the graph to shorter terms (eight months) or longer terms (20 months). In addition, some mouse-on effects can be added to the graph: every time the mouse cursor stops on a certain bar, the critical information of this bar appears (show the model of the biggest weight, show the model of the highest price, show the model of the highest sales volume, etc.).

5) Make the dashboard more stable.

   Currently, the instability of the dashboard occurs mainly in its appearance. The size of the dropdown lists, fonts and positions of the buttons may change as the screen resolution alters. One of the further improvements is to make its format more stable.

6) Turn it into an online application.

   To make this dashboard an online available application is important so that it is within reach of everyone in need of it. Besides, there should be a plan to keep refreshing the dataset to make it a long-term product. It is not practical that every time the dataset is refreshed, the internal units using this dashboard have to update the dashboard. So it is necessary to turn this dashboard into an online application which can be conveniently administered.

REFERENCES

1. Zou Deshun, Brazil PC Market Price Erosion and Sales volume Analysis, 2014, Email: dzou1@lenovo.com.

2. Gianluca Fusai; Andrea Roncoroni, Implementing Models in Quantitative Finance: Methods and Cases, 2008, 140–141.

3. Albright, S. Christian, VBA For Modelers: Developing Decision Support Systems With Microsoft Excel, 2001, 81–146.

4. Gerald Knight, Analyzing Business Data with Excel, 2006, 22–39.

5. Steven Roman, Writing Excel Macros, 1999, 401–470.

CHAPTER 3

Heavy Maintenance Profitability Yield Analysis

CHAI Chin Leong

ABSTRACT

Aircraft maintenance is a labor- intensive and complex business where many factors such as capacity resources, turn-around time and contractual details play an important role in impacting the profitability of an aircraft check.

This study was conducted to better understand the factors affecting an aircraft check profitability by examining both operational and financial factors using exploratory data analysis, regression and neural network on data set obtained from two financial year quarters. The findings show a clear difference in the key factors affecting profitability with labor cost-related components now playing a bigger role than past key factors such as labor rate and turn-around time. This finding provides insights to the business stakeholders on potential areas for deeper root cause analysis in the future.

1. INTRODUCTION

Company A is the aircraft maintenance unit for not just Airline B but many other airlines, providing extensive Maintenance Repair and Overhaul (MRO) services of aircraft to more than 80 international airlines worldwide. Company A Group together with its stable of 20 plus global joint ventures and subsidiaries, has several lines of businesses providing maintenance capabilities ranging from line maintenance to aircraft and component as well as fleet management services.

Globally, the commercial air transport fleet stands at nearly 24,000 aircraft with Asia Pacific, China and India having slightly more than a quarter of the world's fleet. The Asian market is expected to enjoy higher growth rates over the next decade [1], representing huge opportunity for the MRO industry. This global airline fleet is expected to triple to 44,000 aircraft by 2035 [2] (Figure 1).

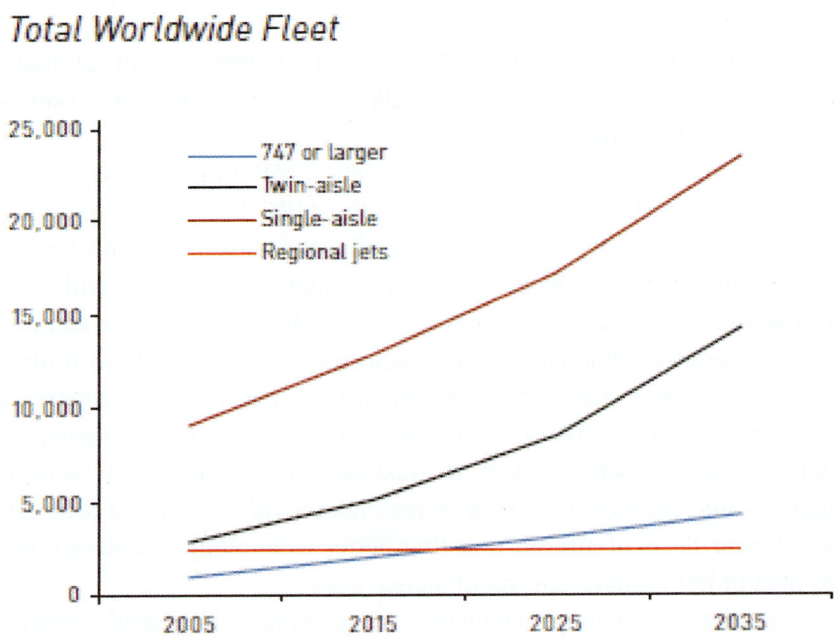

Figure 1: Total worldwide fleet size.

The CAVOK Global Fleet and MRO Market Forecast also puts the MRO spending in 2020 to be $83.2 billion, rising to $100.4 billion in 2025 [3] (Figure 2).

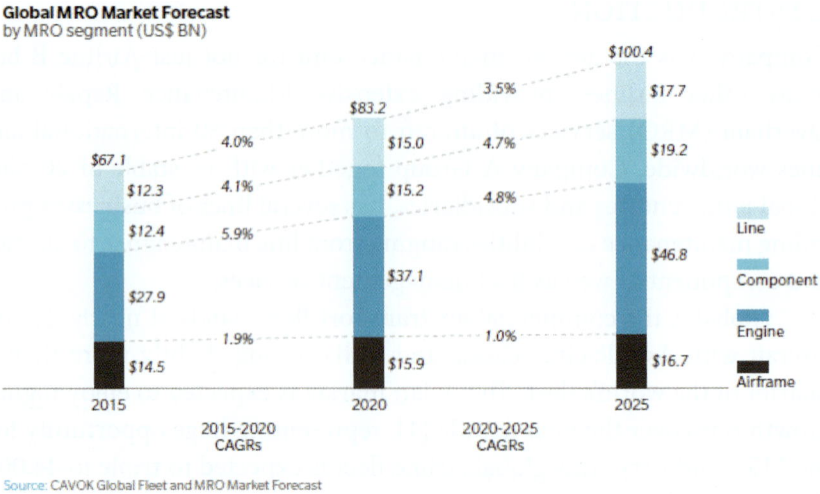

Figure 2: Rising MRO spending.

As of the financial results ending FY14/15, Company A group had a $1.12 billion revenue with the main bulk coming from airframe, component and repair overhaul services.

Though the outlook for business aviation MRO market seems positive for Asia Pacific in the next decade, the MRO business landscape is becoming increasingly competitive, despite the capabilities and branding advantages enjoyed by Company A. Airlines are operating with very slim margins with major cost drivers such as labor, maintenance and fuel expenses greatly influencing their financial performance due to limited leverage over these cost factors. This impact inevitably flows downstream to the labor intensive MRO operators as airlines are relentless in managing maintenance costs while seeking to maximize their flying time to increase their revenue. Moreover, many new regional providers are price competitive. Newer fleets of aircraft boasting better technology and design has resulted in less demand for maintenance works.

Besides facing tough challenges in generating increased revenue, costs have slowly crept up, eroding Company A's profit margins. Aircraft maintenance costs comprise of two major components: labor and spare parts (materials) with the vast majority coming from skilled labor cost, which includes subcontracting, revenue labor and overheads cost. The cost of experienced labor for line and airframe heavy maintenance typically comprises 70–80 per cent of the total maintenance cost [2] as shown in Figure 3 below and Company A is in line with the industry norm based on the current dataset.

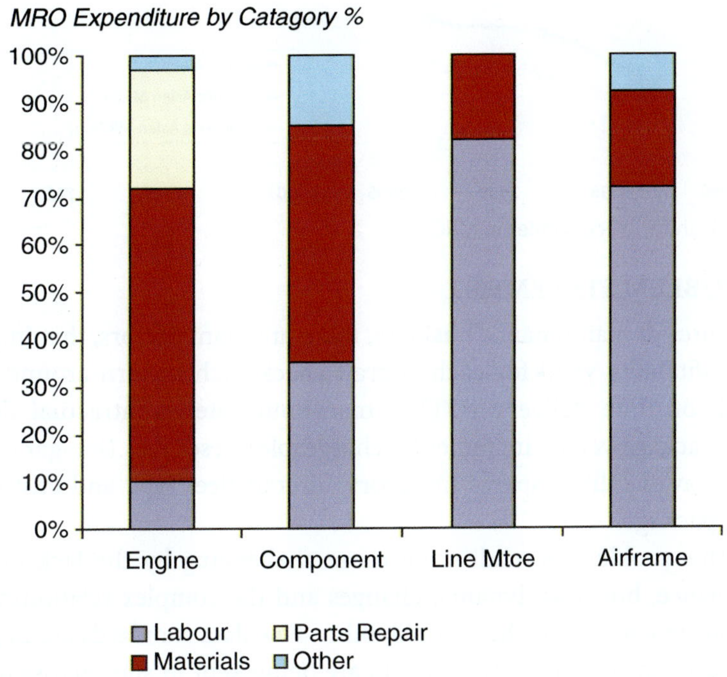

Figure 3: MRO segment cost structure.

The cost advantage enjoyed by Asian MRO companies such as Company A will continue to erode due to wage inflation and a decline in average labor hours per heavy airframe maintenance check as skilled labor shortages in Asia drives up the labor rates [4] (Figure 4).

As the airframe MRO market is a low margin, labor intensive segment, the rising labor cost together with pressure from regional MROs and the business landscape provides an impetus for Company A to better understand its business model and operations to stay ahead of the competition through this project.

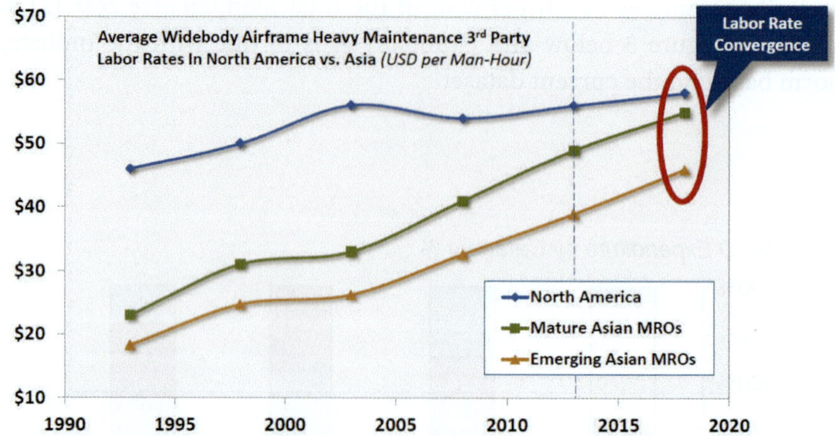

Figure 4: Shifting economies in MRO.

2. PROBLEM STATEMENT

In an aircraft maintenance business, there are many factors, that impacts the profitability yield for each aircraft check such as turn-around time (TAT), on-time delivery (OTD), man-hour rates, contractual details (fixed package versus incremental chargeable), resources (hangar capacity and availability), spares inventory, aircraft fleet type and customers check package.

This problem is made even more challenging by the lack of data governance, business dynamic changes and the complex relationship of the above factors with check profitability. Few data standards are in place to ensure data consistency and data are being kept in silos across disparate systems and multiple manual spreadsheets that support only specific business activities which, in turn, reduces data visibility and integrity. These challenges make it hard to perform MRO operations efficiently and effectively, from scheduling and forecasting to inventory management and replenishment.

The scope of this research project focused on the heavy maintenance arm of Company A. This is one of its core lines of business that provides aircraft and component overhaul services to both the Airline B group and third party customer airlines serviced by its multiple hangars in Singapore.

Heavy maintenance includes regularly scheduled inspections, preventive maintenance and alteration of the entire aircraft which renders the aircraft out of service for a defined period of time. A heavy maintenance check can be broadly categorized into heavy work content such as 'C' or 'D' level maintenance checks which includes detailed inspections and repairs to the airframe and components to restore the aircraft close to its original condition. It can also include lighter work such as de-leasing and aircraft painting services. A typical 'C' level check is conducted every 12–18 months while 'D' level check is conducted every five-10 years.

As shown in Figure 5 below, the revenue from airframe and component overhaul services for Company A group has fallen in FY14/15 compared to the previous financial years. Since it contributes more than a third of the total group revenue, it is of utmost importance for Company A to understand the business model dynamics and arrest the decline of that business so as to improve the company's operating profit.

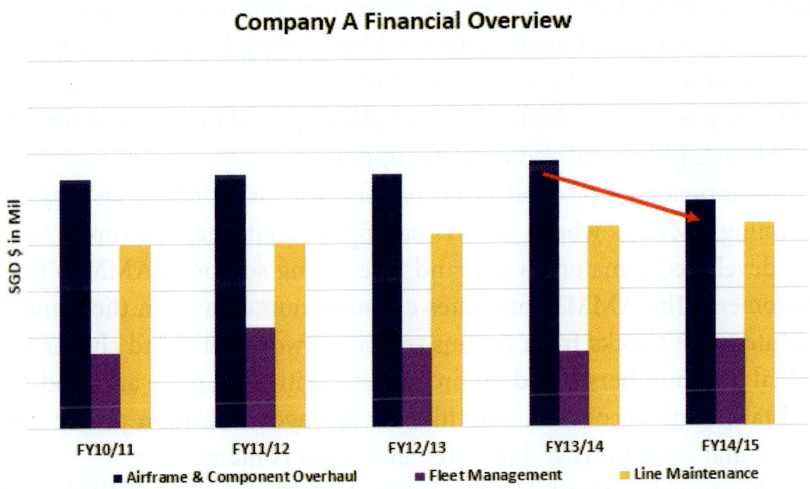

Figure 5: Company a financial overview.

With this in mind, the objective of this project was to better understand the profitability yield of the aircraft checks in the heavy maintenance business. The business structure was modeled and the key contributors in labor profit reduction and their correlation to labor profitability. This helped Company A to identify potential areas of revenue leakages and major cost contributors which the business can then take action to improve its check profitability.

3. STATE OF THE ART

Analytics use in the aerospace industry, particularly in the MRO business, is well established. Indeed, there are applications and detailed research analysis developed by enterprise companies and researchers worldwide to optimize the execution of MRO tasks as well as to study maintenance specific costs and characteristics via event simulations.

The first area where an MRO organization can use analytics to improve operational efficiency is in reducing the delay of aircraft turn-around time (TAT). By ensuring information stored in central data warehouse is consistent, easily filtered and searchable via intelligent search and context awareness such as hyperlink management and aircraft tail number etc. it can be shared with the maintenance engineers and technicians through integrated mobile technology [5].

This ability to access the required information at the right time and place allows business users to overcome common obstacles that can potentially delay TAT such as the tracking of completed tasks and identification of maintenance records for individual aircraft. The reduction in TAT delay also allows better capacity planning and helps to reduce additional costs often incurred by MRO operators.

Another area of application for analytics is in Materials Resource Planning (MRP), where world leading aircraft manufacturer Airbus has developed a materials demand forecasting solution (AMMF) for its customers. The AMMF integrates consumption data from thousands of maintenance checks from Airbus operators worldwide and cluster individual part numbers based on probability, criticality, price and lead-time and takes into account factors like aircraft age, utilization profile, environmental conditions and maintenance work content.

By quickly identifying the spare parts that are most likely to be changed due to wear and tear conditions, the required materials usage can be provided for heavy maintenance checks to reduce the amount of high priority and Aircraft on Ground (AOG) orders. This reaps huge benefits in reducing unnecessary freight cost and TAT delay as 80 per cent of material demands are driven by findings during maintenance event.

More complex cost benefits analysis has been conducted by researchers from Lufthansa Technik AG [6] with data inputs obtained from a particular MRO company. The group used the IATA MRO cost structure to determine event-based costs, which consists of process and operation irregularity expenses. The process costs are defined by labor, material and overheads expenses. Operational charges arise from flat rates defining compensation and opportunity costs of delays such as Aircraft On Ground (AOG) situations multiplied by the corresponding event duration. The results of the study shows a decent savings potential of $66,625 – a cost which could be avoided annually from operational irregularities and non-productive MRO processes which illustrates that there are areas of cost inefficiencies in the MRO line of business that can be avoided to improve profitability.

4. SOLUTION: DESCRIPTION OF APPROACH

To have a better understanding of the business dynamics of heavy maintenance profitability, data for two financial years fourth quarter (FY11/12 and FY14/15) was collected. The data collected were aggregated financial data of major aircraft checks performed during this period and the data source comes from both the MRO ERP (Enterprise Resource Planning) system as well as from spreadsheets maintained by key business users. These two date periods are specifically chosen to illustrate the difference in profitability between a well performing (FY11/12) and underperforming year quarter (FY14/15).

The data consists of both categorical and continuous variables and includes key attributes such as aircraft check type and model, turn-around-time (TAT), labor revenue and cost and customer related details.

Exploratory data analysis was undertaken to provide simple summaries about the data and to identify the key differences in business between the two financial year quarters.

Looking at the volume of aircraft checks performed in the hangars, it was observed that there was a sharp decline (approx. 50 per cent) in heavy checks especially from third party customers, which constitutes roughly 30 per cent of customer base. Though there is a slight decline of approx. 25 per cent of total C checks in FY14/15 Q4, the majority of work from Airline B group remains consistent. This highlights the fact that increasing competition from regional MRO providers in recent years has shrunk the third party customer base for heavy maintenance checks. This reduction in business from third party airlines also resulted in fewer A330 aircraft model being serviced.

From a financial perspective, there was a huge decline of close to 40 per cent in labor revenue due to the reduction in checks but the total labor cost was only a marginal drop of 5 per cent in FY14/15 Q4. The graph below clearly reflects that the labor revenue and cost dominates in check profitability, especially in recent times (FY14/15) as aircraft maintenance is a labor intensive business. Hence, labor profitability will be the focus of this project in subsequent analysis (Figure 6).

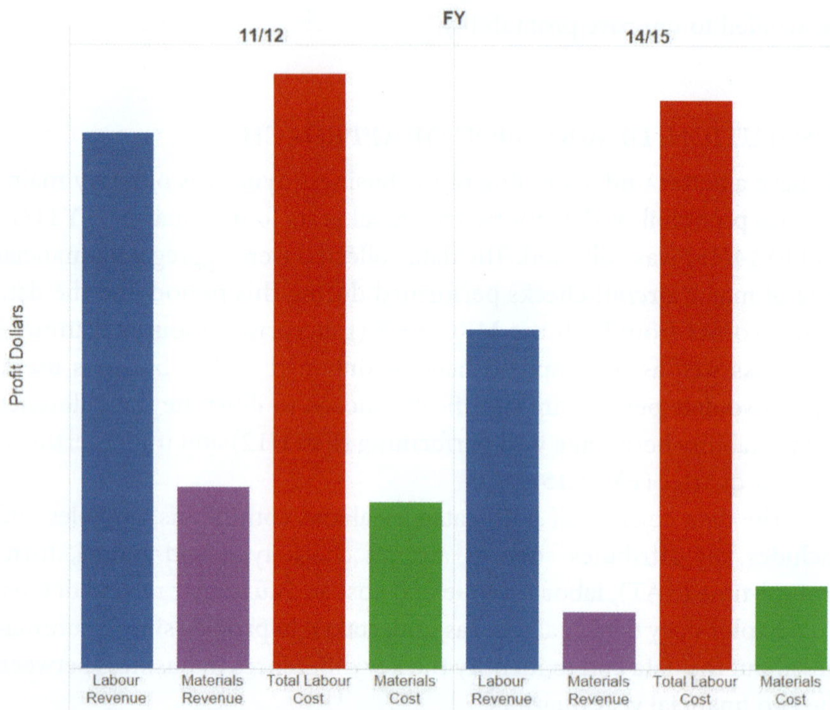

Figure 6: Labor & materials profitability.

A closer look at the different labor cost components reveals that most of the supporting and outsourced labor cost such as sub-contractor services and allocated cost remains relatively close, with the production overheads cost even higher in FY14/15 Q4 by 12 per cent even though the volume of checks reduced. Further analysis showed that the increase in production overheads cost in FY14/15 Q4 came from C checks where the overheads labor cost increased by 30 per cent in FY14/15 Q4 compared to FY11/12 Q4 (Figure 7).

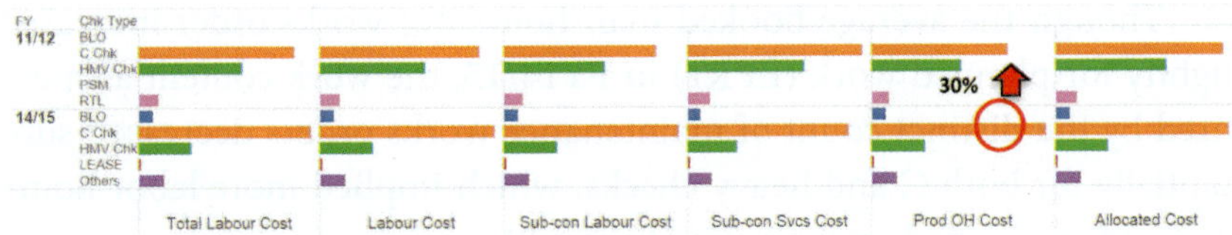

Figure 7: Labor cost breakdown.

This proved that rising labor costs, especially the overheads, eroded the labor profit margin.

The work volume measured by man-hours booked per maintenance works order - where the aircraft engineers and technicians clocked their labor effort in performing the maintenance task activities for the aircraft check - dipped by an average of 3.6 man-hours for unplanned work activities (EWA1). This was due to a decline in the number of C checks undertaken for third party customers and heavy checks from Airline B group.

However, average booked man-hours for planned work (EPR1) increased slightly by 0.9 man-hours, largely due to a surge in C and heavy checks for both third party and Airline B group customers (Figure 8).

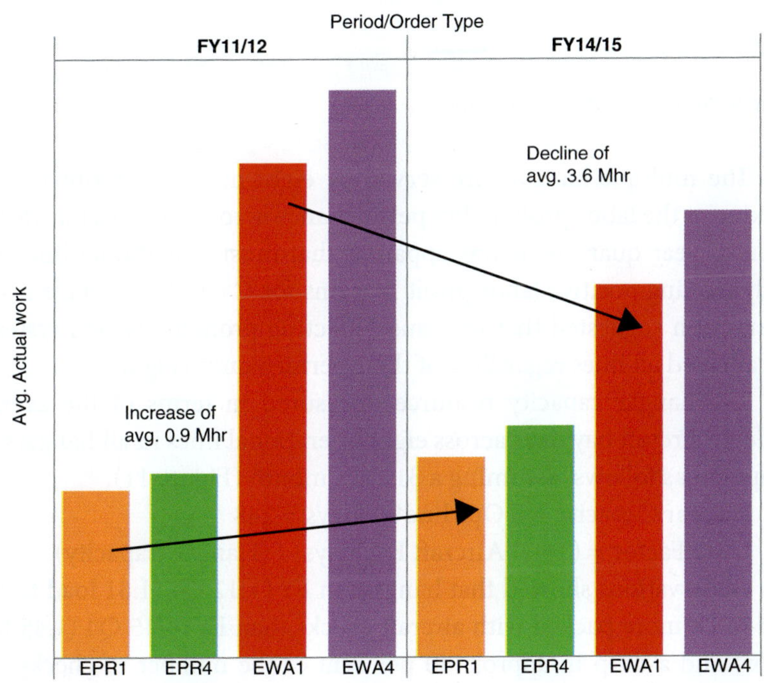

Figure 8: Average booked man-hours.

Though the average booked man-hours per works order increased slightly for planned work (EPR1) in FY14/15, the work content as measured by the distinct count of maintenance works orders decreased substantially for both C and heavy checks, which implied more labor hours booked per planned works order (Figure 9).

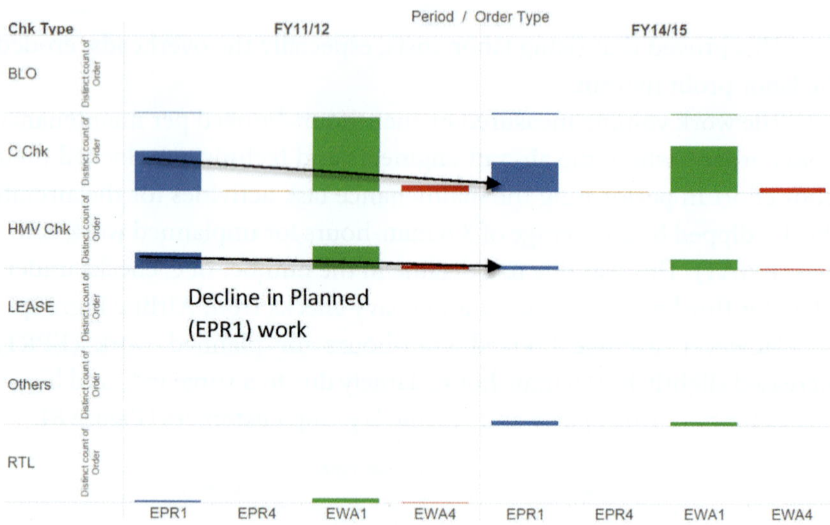

Figure 9: Work content by check type.

The multiple hangars are served by eight major operational lines. Looking at the labor profitability performance across the lines for the two financial year quarters, it was apparent that most operational lines formerly making positive labor profit margins for C checks had fallen. This observation suggested that the cause affecting profitability was systemic as it affected all lines regardless of their performance (Figure 10).

The hangar capacity resource, measured in terms of the average available aircraft bay days across eight operational lines in all hangars are computed as follows, assuming a 31 days month (Figure 11).

Hangar Capacity = 8 Ops line*31 days = 248

Load Factor = (Total Aircraft Bay days) / (Hangar Capacity)

Observations showed that hangars in FY11/12 Q4 (1.81 load factor) used to be more packed with aircraft checks than FY14/15 Q4 (1.45 load factor) and a drop in approx. 40 per cent of the number of checks corresponded to a reduction in approx. 20 per cent of hangar load factor.

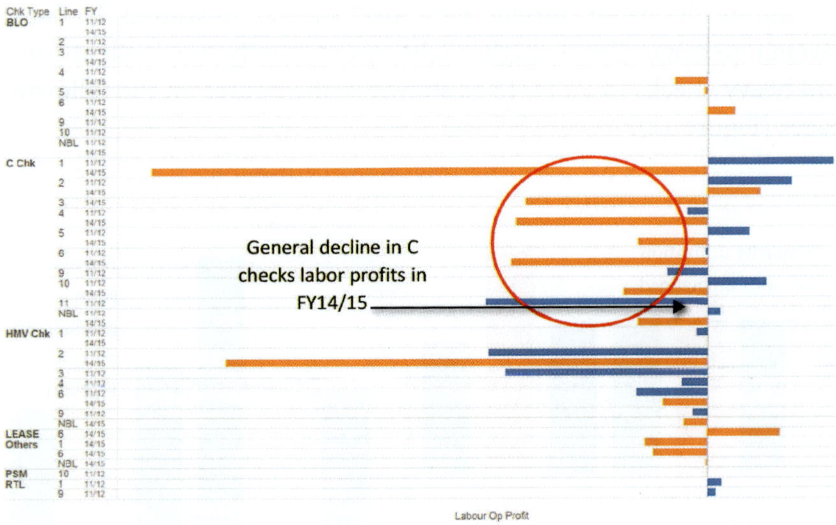

Figure 10: Labor profitability by Ops line.

	FY11/12 Q4			FY14/15 Q4		
Check Type	Jan12	Feb12	Mar12	Jan15	Feb15	Mar15
Light Checks	159	116	154	120	106	147
Major Checks	263	301	310	274	205	172
Others	2	11	32	0	26	28
Total Aircraft Bay Days	424	428	496	394	337	347
Hangar Load Factor	1.71	1.73	2.00	1.59	1.36	1.40
Average Load Factor	**1.81**			**1.45**		

Figure 11: Hangar capacity.

This is despite the fact that the hangars have always been overloaded as the load factor was greater than one.

Though the hangars capacity was frequently being over utilized, it is observed that there is potential hangar capacity wastage as the average labor hours for C checks in FY14/15 were reduced but utilization of hangar capacity remained relatively the same.

From the labor productivity perspective, measured by labor revenue per man-hours, higher labor productivity was evident for C and heavy checks in FY14/15 as shown in the figures on the following pages (Figure 12).

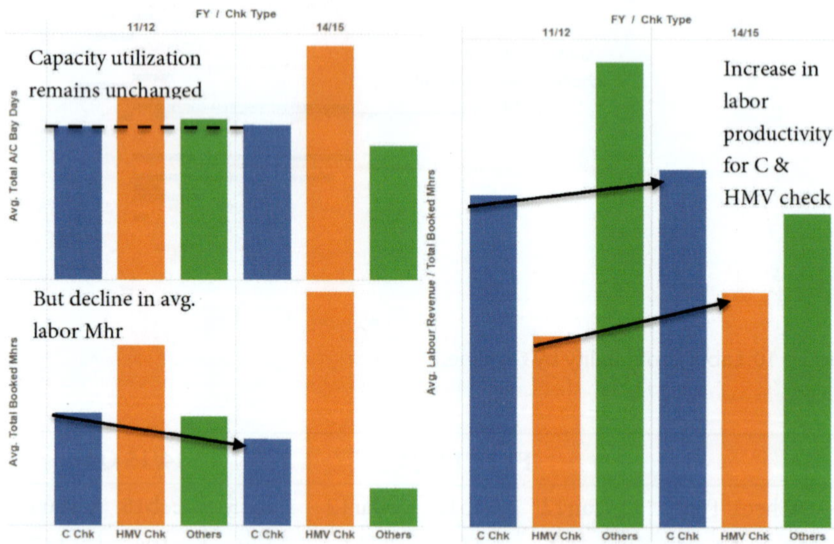

Figure 12: Hangar capacity utilization & labor productivity by check type.

Having a better appreciation of the check differences between the two financial year quarters in terms of financial and operational aspects, regression analysis was used next to determine the overall fit of the model and to better understand the relationship between labor profitability and the various key operational and financial attributes.

As the data was collected in two different time periods, it was appropriate to split the regression analysis. Pre-requisite checks were performed on the two sub-datasets to check for violations of assumptions such as multicollinearity issue and independence of the error residuals. Correlation checks and scatterplots were also performed to inspect the relationship of the key attributes and to spot for significant outliers.

In this exercise, IBM SPSS Statistics software was used for the statistical analysis.

Bivariate Pearson Correlation was performed on some of the key continuous attributes and observed that the labor man-hour rate were negatively correlated with most key attributes except for labor revenue in FY11/12. This behavior was different in FY14/15 where although the labor man-hour rate was positively correlated with the key attributes, it was not statistically significant (Figure 13).

FY11/12	Mhr Rate	Labour Revenue	Actual TAT	Total Accrued Mhrs	Total Booked Mhrs	Total Labour Cost
Mhr Rate	1	0.359	-0.08	-0.326	-0.117	-0.326
Labour Revenue	0.359*	1	0.474	0.659	0.551	0.659
Actual TAT	-0.08	0.474**	1	0.436	0.617	0.436
Total Accrued Mhrs	-0.326*	0.659**	0.436**	1	0.651	1
Total Booked Mhrs	-0.117	0.551**	0.617**	0.651**	1	0.651
Total Labour Cost	-0.326*	0.659**	0.436**	1**	0.651**	1
FY14/15	Mhr Rate	Labour Revenue	Actual TAT	Total Accrued Mhrs	Total Booked Mhrs	Total Labour Cost
Mhr Rate	1	0.325	0.222	0.265	0.305	0.265
Labour Revenue	0.325	1	0.374	0.616	0.615	0.616
Actual TAT	0.222	0.374*	1	0.64	0.75	0.64
Total Accrued Mhrs	0.265	0.616**	0.64**	1	0.932	1
Total Booked Mhrs	0.305	0.615**	0.75**	0.932**	1	0.932
Total Labour Cost	0.265	0.616**	0.64**	1**	0.932**	1

*. Correlation is significant at the 0.05 level (2-tailed)

**. Correlation is significant at the 0.01 level (2-tailed)

Figure 13: Bivariate Pearson correlation.

Another observation was that correlations for those variables at 0.01 level were higher in their Pearson coefficient values in FY14/15. The perfect correlation between accrued man-hours and labor cost was expected as the labor cost is dependent on the accrued man-hours.

Scatterplots of the key attributes were then plotted against labor profitability to spot for significant outliers and obvious relationships between the variables (Figure 14).

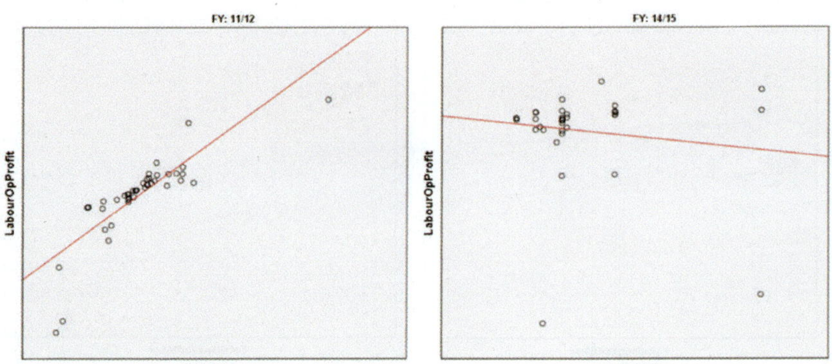

Figure 14: Scatterplot - Labor profit vs. Mhr rate.

Higher labor man-hour rates were positively correlated with labor profits back in FY11/12 but showed a weaker correlation in FY14/15. There were some obvious outliers in F14/15 where the labor profits were very low due to operational issues (Figure 15).

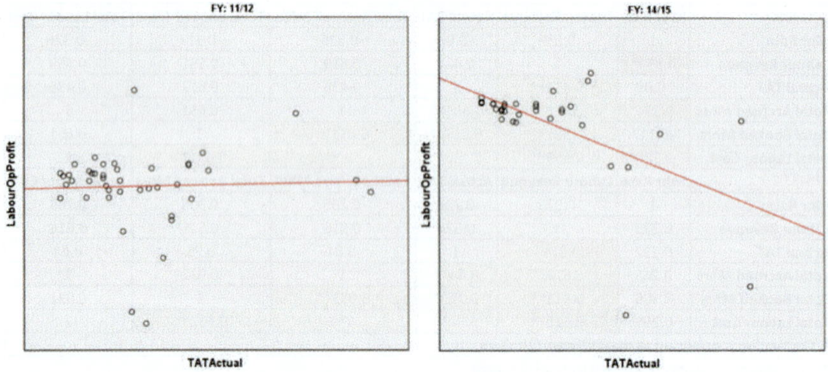

Figure 15: Scatterplot - Labor Profit vs. Turn-around-time (TAT).

Turn-around-time (TAT) showed minimal influence in labor profitability in FY11/12 but in FY14/15, it revealed that long checks were no longer profitable. This could be due to checks taking longer because of delays which require additional manpower or defects found during checks that were not billable to the customer because of contractual terms (Figure 16).

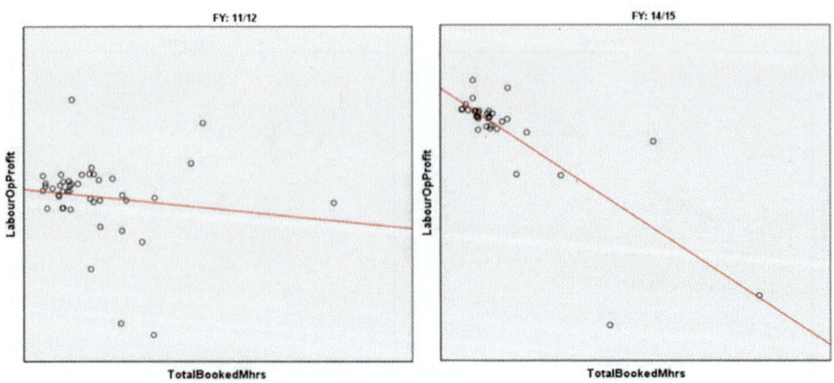

Figure 16: Scatterplot - Labor profit vs. Booked man-hours.

Interestingly, the more labor hours booked by the engineers and/or technicians to the aircraft check, the lower the labor profit especially in FY14/15. This could imply that the contractual threshold for planned work activities was higher in FY14/15 so most of the work fell within the threshold and hence was not billable to the customer (Figure 17).

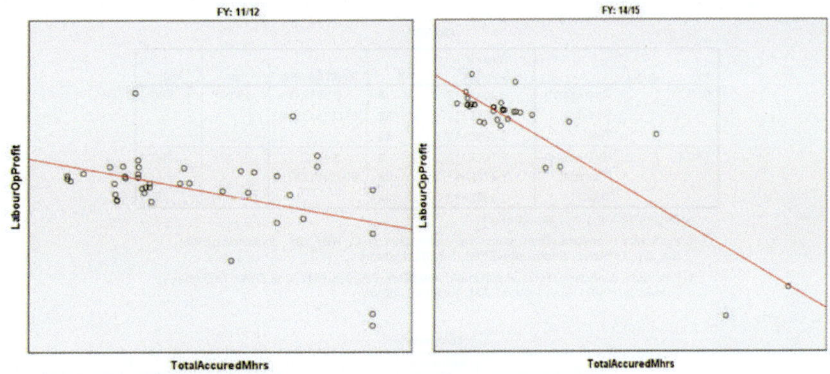

Figure 17: Scatterplot - Labor Profit vs. Accrued man-hours

Similar behavior was also observed in the relationship between labor profits and accrued man-hours. This could mean that the margin per unit labor man-hour rate had eroded significantly due to rising labors costs in FY14/15.

Despite some outliers and weak correlations for some of the attributes, multiple regression using labor profit as the dependent variable was used to better understand whether labor profit could be determined by these variables.

From the regression results below, it was observed that there is no auto correlation issue as the Durbin-Watson test was greater than 1.0 for both financial years' quarters. The R Square value for both models was also high which reflected well on the model's fit. There were a few variables such as total booked labor hours that suffered multicollinearity issues as the VIF value was above 10 based on general guidelines. Moreover, most variables were not statistically significant at 95 per cent confidence level (Figure 18).

There were limitations using regression as some of the independent variables did not have a clear linear relationship with the dependent variable and some of the residuals (errors) of the variables were not normally distributed when verified using the normality test.

Model Summary[b]

FY	Model	R	R Square	Adjusted R Square	Std. Error of the Estimate	Durbin-Watson
11/12	1	.875[a]	.765	.707	255275.5706	2.058
14/15	1	.974[c]	.949	.924	303848.9986	1.293

a. Predictors: (Constant), TotalLabourCostAccuredMhrs, Delta, HMV_Chk, BookedMhrsEWA1, SIA_Grp, TATActual, BookedMhrsEPR1, TotalBookedMhrs

b. Dependent Variable: LabourOpProfit

c. Predictors: (Constant), TotalLabourCostAccuredMhrs, SIA_Grp, HMV_Chk, Delta, TATActual, BookedMhrsEPR1, BookedMhrsEWA1, TotalBookedMhrs

ANOVA[a]

FY	Model		Sum of Squares	df	Mean Square	F	Sig.
11/12	1	Regression	6.804E+12	8	8.505E+11	13.051	.000[b]
		Residual	2.085E+12	32	65165616936		
		Total	8.889E+12	40			
14/15	1	Regression	2.761E+13	8	3.452E+12	37.388	.000[c]
		Residual	1.477E+12	16	92324213978		
		Total	2.909E+13	24			

a. Dependent Variable: LabourOpProfit

b. Predictors: (Constant), TotalLabourCostAccuredMhrs, Delta, HMV_Chk, BookedMhrsEWA1, SIA_Grp, TATActual, BookedMhrsEPR1, TotalBookedMhrs

c. Predictors: (Constant), TotalLabourCostAccuredMhrs, SIA_Grp, HMV_Chk, Delta, TATActual, BookedMhrsEPR1, BookedMhrsEWA1, TotalBookedMhrs

Coefficients[a]

			Unstandardized Coefficients		Standardized Coefficients			95.0% Confidence Interval for B		Collinearity Statistics	
FY	Model		B	Std. Error	Beta	t	Sig.	Lower Bound	Upper Bound	Tolerance	VIF
11/12	1	(Constant)	-101616.902	104551.025		-.972	.338	-314580.372	111346.567		
		TATActual	3309.449	2447.691	.175	1.352	.186	-1676.334	8295.232	.439	2.279
		TotalBookedMhrs	-32.531	34.939	-.649	-.931	.359	-103.700	38.638	.015	66.184
		BookedMhrsEPR1	36.620	39.964	.196	.916	.366	-44.784	118.023	.159	6.270
		BookedMhrsEWA1	45.123	43.367	.576	1.040	.306	-43.213	133.458	.024	41.807
		HMV_Chk	-12602.916	126405.072	-.012	-.100	.921	-270081.622	244875.789	.507	1.974
		SIA_Grp	89110.754	128711.197	.093	.692	.494	-173065.374	351286.882	.403	2.480
		Delta	10573.094	1416.396	.746	7.465	.000	7687.990	13458.197	.733	1.364
		TotalLabourCostAccured Mhrs	-.235	.148	-.284	-1.584	.123	-.537	.067	.229	4.369
14/15	1	(Constant)	1303808.990	282097.054		4.622	.000	705789.951	1901828.029		
		TATActual	-2221.834	3853.630	-.054	-.577	.572	-10391.165	5947.497	.367	2.722
		TotalBookedMhrs	338.566	58.571	2.970	5.780	.000	214.401	462.731	.012	83.202
		BookedMhrsEPR1	-397.298	74.418	-1.180	-5.339	.000	-555.058	-239.539	.065	15.383
		BookedMhrsEWA1	-371.511	79.359	-1.710	-4.681	.000	-539.745	-203.278	.024	42.029
		HMV_Chk	-72882.812	226586.121	-.022	-.322	.752	-553223.930	407458.307	.681	1.468
		SIA_Grp	-381826.327	161044.218	-.159	-2.371	.031	-723224.818	-40427.837	.706	1.416
		Delta	27805.153	14695.757	.138	1.892	.077	-3348.460	58958.766	.593	1.686
		TotalLabourCostAccured Mhrs	-.995	.178	-1.222	-5.586	.000	-1.373	-.618	.066	15.082

a. Dependent Variable: LabourOpProfit

Figure 18: Regression output results.

The artificial neural network method using Multilayer Perceptron (MLP) was chosen for its ability to process complex nonlinear relationships, for being noise tolerant, for not requiring specific assumptions on data distribution and for being able to detect all possible interactions between the predictor variables.

The results of the neural network analysis are shown in Figure 19a. The sum of squares error for the training dataset for both model groups were acceptable as reflected in the predicted-by-observed charts where the predicted values were quite close to the actual data points, though the model tends to underestimate the labor profits slightly for FY14/15.

Model Summary

11/12	Training	Sum of Squares Error	.362
		Relative Error	.022
		Stopping Rule Used	1 consecutive step (s) with no decrease in error[a]
		Training Time	0:00:00.03
	Testing	Sum of Squares Error	.015
		Relative Error	.103
14/15	Training	Sum of Squares Error	1.411
		Relative Error	.149
		Stopping Rule Used	1 consecutive step (s) with no decrease in error[a]
		Training Time	0:00:00.03
	Testing	Sum of Squares Error	.053
		Relative Error	.579

Dependent Variable: LabourOpProfit

a. Error computations are based on the testing sample.

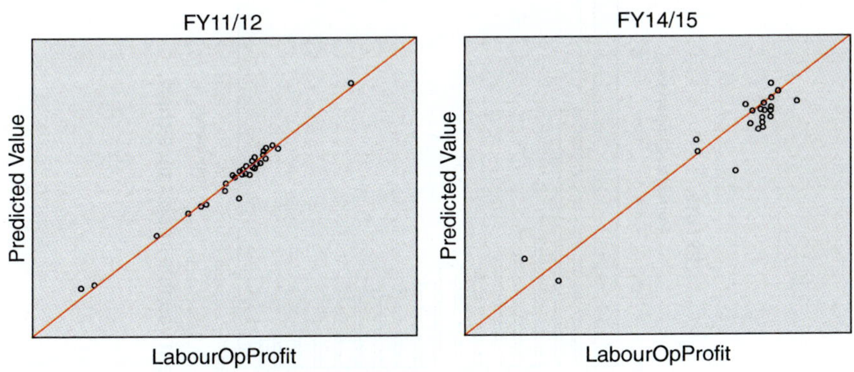

Figure 19: Neural network output results.

The variable importance charts (Figure 20) that measures how much the network's model predicted value changes for different values of the independent variable, show some interesting observations. It appears that man-hour rate and turn-around time (TAT) had the greatest effect in influencing labor profitability in FY11/12 but that

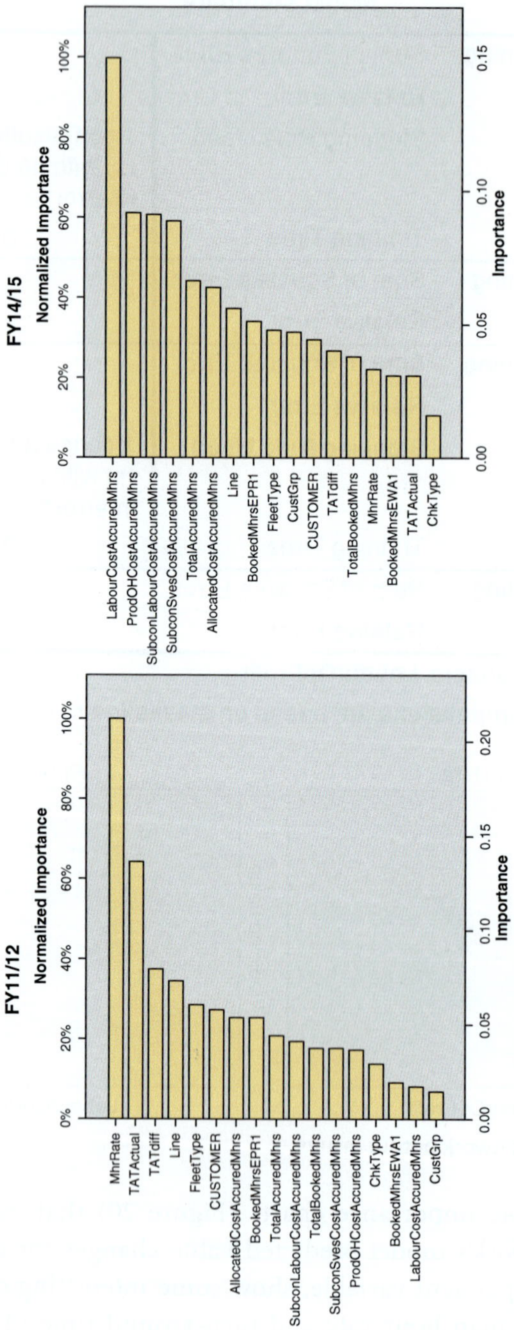

Figure 20: Independent variable Importance chart.

importance changed in FY14/15 where cost attributes dominated instead. The downside of using the neural network is that it was difficult to tell the 'direction' of the relationship between these variables and the target variable, though it can be inferred via earlier regression model results. The findings show the impact and importance of cost components in labor profitability as highlighted earlier in exploratory data analysis.

5. DISCUSSION

The exploratory and statistical data analysis gave the users a better visibility of the heavy maintenance business between two financial years' quarters in terms of operational, productivity and financial performance. The findings also showed the changes in the business dynamics and identified potential areas such as labor productivity, hangar capacity utilization and labor rate etc. where more study can be performed to analyze the root cause as well as laying the foundation for possible optimization work in future.

The neural network analysis also offered a glimpse of the key attributes affecting labor profitability and highlighted the difference between the important variables. This allowed the stakeholders to look at the entire heavy maintenance operations from a more strategic vantage point with a clearer picture of the business profitability.

Through this study, the shortcomings of current analytical capabilities in the organization due to issues such as lack of accurate and detailed data were highlighted, and the findings can be improved by using a larger dataset spanning across multiple full financial years.

6. CONCLUSION AND FURTHER WORK

Though there are limitations in the dataset, this preliminary analysis provides valuable insights and potential areas for further work. A larger dataset across longer time frame could be used to analyze the business performance via time series analysis and forecasting.

It is clear that the importance of an integrated enterprise data repository in a large organization such as Company A (where reliable and detailed data were not easily available for analysis) cannot be underestimated. The organizational analytical capabilities still has much room for improvement and the next step could be to chart out a detailed roadmap to expand its business intelligence capabilities so that Company A can progress from standard reporting and ad hoc analysis to data mining and advanced modelling and optimization.

REFERENCES

1. CAVOK, a division of Oliver Wyman (March 2015). *Global Fleet & MRO Market Economic Assessment.*

2. MSP Solutions (n.d.). *Aircraft Maintenance Repair and Overhaul Market Study. Glasgow International Airport.* STRAIR.

3. Spafford, C, T Hoyland and A Medland (2015). *MRO Survey 2015–Turning the Tide.* Oliver Wyman.

4. ICF International SH&E (2014). *MRO Industry in Asia Pacific.*

5. TerraXML (2013). *Using Big Data to Streamline Aircraft Maintenance.* Retrieved from TerraXML http://www.terraxml.com/community/blog/bid/278922/Using-Big-Data-to-Streamline-Aircraft-Maintenance

6. Kahlert, A, S Giljohann and U Klingauf (2014). Cost-Benefit Analysis and Specification of Component-level PHM Systems in Aircrafts. *Annual Conference of the Prognostics and Health Management Society.*

CHAPTER 4

Supply Chain Analytics

LEE Zhi Hui, Alvin

ABSTRACT

Supply chain costs form a large component of the annual expense of global consumer goods companies. For such businesses to be financially sustainable, as well as environmentally responsible, proper stewardship of their supply chains is essential.

This paper illustrates how an end business user can visually determine the cost component movements of a product category, as well as determine the most cost effective route of product manufacture, via purpose-built dashboards using data visualization software, Tableau, to aid in making better business decisions.

The business context will be briefly discussed, before purpose built data visualization dashboards from a test company's Microsoft Analysis Data Cubes are examined.

1. INTRODUCTION

1.1. The company

A global consumer goods company (henceforth referred to as 'The Company') is one of the world's leading suppliers of fast-moving consumer goods, having its products sold in over 190 countries and used by two billion consumers on a daily basis.

The company is amongst the world's most culturally diverse, and its strong leadership makes it a highly desirable company to work for.

A key differentiator in its business model is a strong focus on growing the business in a sustainable manner.

1.2. Harnessing the power of data

To fulfil its long term business goals, the company needed to do more than simply put more products on the shelves for consumers to purchase; it needed to think and execute on a global scale.

Before 2007, the company operated autonomous entities in nearly 200 countries. This presented numerous challenges in leading the organization as a single global entity.

To be more efficient in its operations, the company consolidated more than 250 enterprise resource planning (ERP) systems into four regionally based SAP ERP systems. This was in contrast to the general practice of adding layers to existing IT infrastructure to prepare for rapid business growth. This allowed the company to be managed as one global platform, maximizing the efficiency of core financial processes and reporting. As a result, the company managed to reduce the time on month-end financial close (from three days to within one day), financial analysis, and product cost forecasting processes.

1.3. The information and analytics team

The Information and Analytics Team was tasked to grow the business by making smarter decisions on a global scale. With over 400 products being distributed, sold and consumed in 190 countries around the world, the company generates massive amounts of valuable data.

The Information and Analytics Team gathered data from over 2,000 sources into a comprehensive data ecosystem (including data generated by retail systems, social media, and internet connected devices), and identifies valuable insights from a vast amount of information.

Such a vast data ecosystem has the potential to be the company's competitive advantage, providing actionable insights into the respective markets.

The strategic priorities of the team were to:

- Bring next phase of digital to life
- Reinvent marketing through technology
- Transform Research & Development via Information Technology
- Achieve greater market share through technology
- Build sustainability

2. PROBLEM STATEMENT

Supply chain costs form a large component of the company's expenses, and proper stewardship is required to manage financial resources effectively, as well as minimize waste to reduce the company's environmental footprint.

The overarching goal of the project was to unlock savings potential in the supply chain domain; small savings cannot be neglected due to the scale of the company's operations (e.g. consider the savings actualized when a frequently used raw material can be procured $0.01 cheaper than its existing rates).

The project encompassed the following domains:

- **Industrial Performance**
  - To be able to identify material and labor inefficiencies at the end of a production batch, and address the issues immediately.
- **Global Product Costing**
  - To provide transparent, comparable costing which will drive international sourcing, thereby increasing asset utilization and reducing capital expenditure.
- **Global Forecasting**
  - To run a faster and globally aligned forecasting solution, enabling sharper gross margin management, with savings in profit and loss statements.

- **Performance Reporting**
  - To enable better performance management through aligned, optimized, interactive, and forward looking information, that will be delivered centrally.
- **Effective Business Partnering**
  - To build a global, supply chain capable of finance organization liberated to drive Gross Margins, Return of Asset, and Risk Management.

For the scope of the project, the business question to be addressed with the aid of data focused on the Global Forecasting domain.

2.1. Key business question to address

"Which factory was / will be the most efficient / cost effective for manufacturing Stock Keeping Units (SKUs) common across factories / countries?

This is a realistic business question to analyze, as it can potentially yield cost savings across the company's vast supply chain.

For example, the company might have the ability to manufacture Product X for the global market from six or seven manufacturing facilities instead of the current 27.

The following questions are also of relevance:

- Which product category experienced a >5% increase in year-on-year manufacturing cost?
- How have cost components involved in the manufacture of a product category changed across the years?
- How have cost components involved in the manufacture of a product SKU changed across the years?
- Which is the most cost effective existing manufacturing facility that produces Product X?
- What are the main contributing factor(s) for Product X being costlier to manufacture in Facility A than Facility B?
- Can the company consolidate the manufacture of a product across their existing facilities?

- What is the forecasted six-month product manufacturing cost that a specific manufacturing plant is expected to incur for the production of Product X?

These questions can be better answered and communicated with the aid of data visualization; helping the business user make better decisions by providing relevant business context simply and powerfully.

Additional business context for this project is stated below:

- **End User of the Project's Deliverables**
  - Supply Chain Operational Centre Hub
  - Project in its advanced phase of development, and scheduled to be completed in 2016.
- **Forecasting**
  - The company has a 20-day forecasting cycle.
  - The company has six quarterly forecasts.
  - Past one-year data is available.
  - Data for (up to) four latest forecast versions is available.
- **Forecast Cycles**
  - Full forecast is done every quarter.
  - In-between a quarterly forecast, a light monthly forecast.
- **Live Data Sources**
  - Forecast data – Costing cockpit
  - Actuals data – Material ledger
- **Data Environments**
  - Development environment (by external vendor)
  - Quality assurance environment (for development team)
  - Pre-production environment (for testing)
  - Production environment (for end business user)

Solution Requirements

- Built off the Global Forecasting Microsoft Analysis Data Cube.
- Must be visually appealing.

- The end-business user must be able to interact with it.
- User queries must yield results in less than two minutes.

3. STATE OF THE ART

This is primarily a data visualization project off a Microsoft Analysis Data Cube with full supply chain data for a specific country of interest. The data in the cube has been cleaned, and is adequately prepared for the end-user. At present, standard Microsoft Excel reports are prepared for end business users (Figure 1).

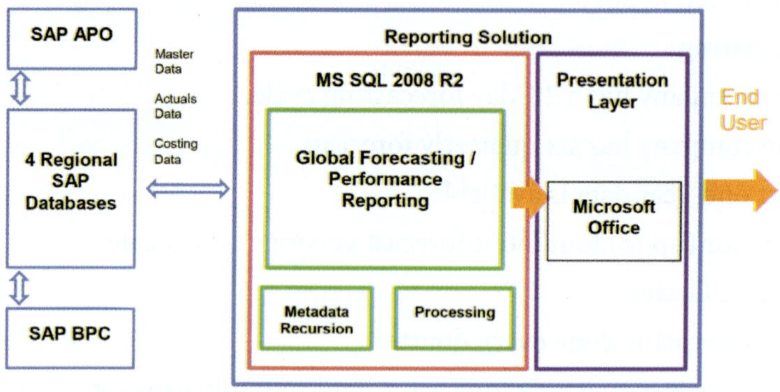

Figure 1: Data architecture.

4. SOLUTION: DESCRIPTION OF APPROACH

4.1. Tableau

Tableau software [1,2] is a data visualization product focused on business intelligence, created by an American software company headquartered in Seattle, Washington.

Tableau combines structured query language for relational databases with a descriptive language for rendering graphics, paving the way for a database visualization language called VizQL (Visual Query Language) [3]. Tableau queries relational databases, data cubes, cloud databases and spreadsheets, generating a number of graph types that can be combined into dashboards and shared over a computer network.

Tableau has won the following awards:

- "Best of 2005 for Data Analysis", PC Magazine [4]
- "2008 Best Business Intelligence Solution", Software & Information Industry Association [5]
- "2015 Magic Quadrant for Business Intelligence and Analytics Platforms; Market Leader" [6]

Tableau was chosen for this project as it yields visually appealing reports, and be easily manipulated by an end- business user.

An important thing to note is that Tableau works best with relational databases. Pertaining to the scope of this project, a Microsoft Analysis data cube is present.

There are certain parameters involved with this project:

- Connecting to a data cube does not allow data extracts, nor data manipulation (as data is pre-aggregated in a cube) [7].
- MDX has to be used for querying a data cube, as opposed to SQL which is used to query a relational data source [8].
- Analysis performed on cubes are different than that from relational data sources (e.g. steps to create data filters to slice and dice) [9].
- Various workarounds are required to allow reports created from a data cube to work like a relational database [10,11].

4.2. Clarity of desired prototype

Which factory will be the most efficient / cost effective for manufacturing SKUs common across factories / countries?

To address this business question, the following prototype was proposed by the Information & Analytics Team:

- **Visualization #1 - Cost to Manufacture SKU Across Plants**
  - User inputs
    - Selects a category / brand
    - Selects SKU of interest
  - Visualization generated
    - X-axis: All existing facilities in which the SKU is manufactured

- Y-axis: The cost (and associated cost components) involved in product manufacture

- ▸ Visually

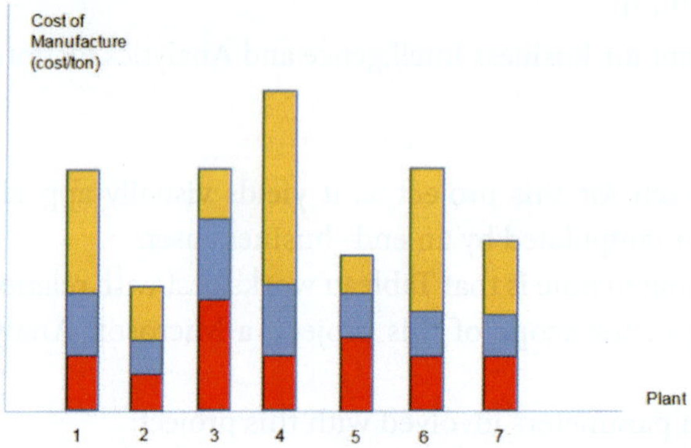

- **Visualization #2 - Actuals and Forecasted Finished Good Costs**
  - ▸ User inputs (an add-on from Visualization #1)
    - Selects a category / brand
    - Selects SKU of interest
    - Selects factory of interest (from Visualization #1)
  - ▸ Visualization generated
    - X-axis: Time (actual finished good costs for the last six months, and forecasted finished good costs for the next six months)
    - Y-axis: Finished goods cost, for the particular factory of interest
  - ▸ Visually

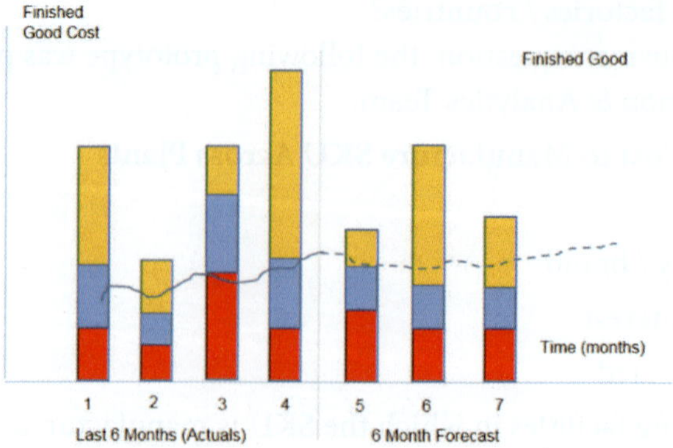

4.3. Building blocks

This section provides an overview of the key visualizations that were purpose built using Tableau. In summary, the visualizations cover the following aspects:

- **Understanding the data**
  - Intended primarily for a business analyst to build foundational understanding of the data set for further builds / analysis.
  - This is essential before further data analysis takes place, as context is critical to bridge the 'reality' that data provides with the real-world business.
- **Analysis #1 - Understanding Cost Component Movements**
  - Intended to illustrate how the cost of goods for a specific product category vary over time (in the granularity of its respective components) to allow a business analyst to quickly identify trends and spot areas of potential concern.
  - In addition, a view illustrating cost component movements of all individual SKUs in a specific product category will allow an analyst to identify trends and spot areas of potential concern.
- **Analysis #2 - Cost Efficient Plants for SKU Manufacture**
  - Intended to aid business analysts in identifying the most cost efficient location to manufacture a specific SKU of interest, in the granularity of its respective cost components.
  - In addition, a six month actual and six month forecast of the finished good rate (i.e. the cost of manufacturing a ton of SKU) is built for each potential manufacturing plant to help forecast upcoming business costs.
- **Analysis #3 - Cost Efficient Plants for Basepack Manufacture**
  - Aimed at helping analysts to identify the most cost efficient location to manufacture a specific basepack of interest, in the granularity of its respective cost components.
  - In addition, a six month actual and six month forecast of the finished good rate (i.e. the cost of manufacturing a ton of basepack) is built for each potential manufacturing plant to help forecast upcoming business costs.

4.4. Understanding the data

Production by Plant Clusters

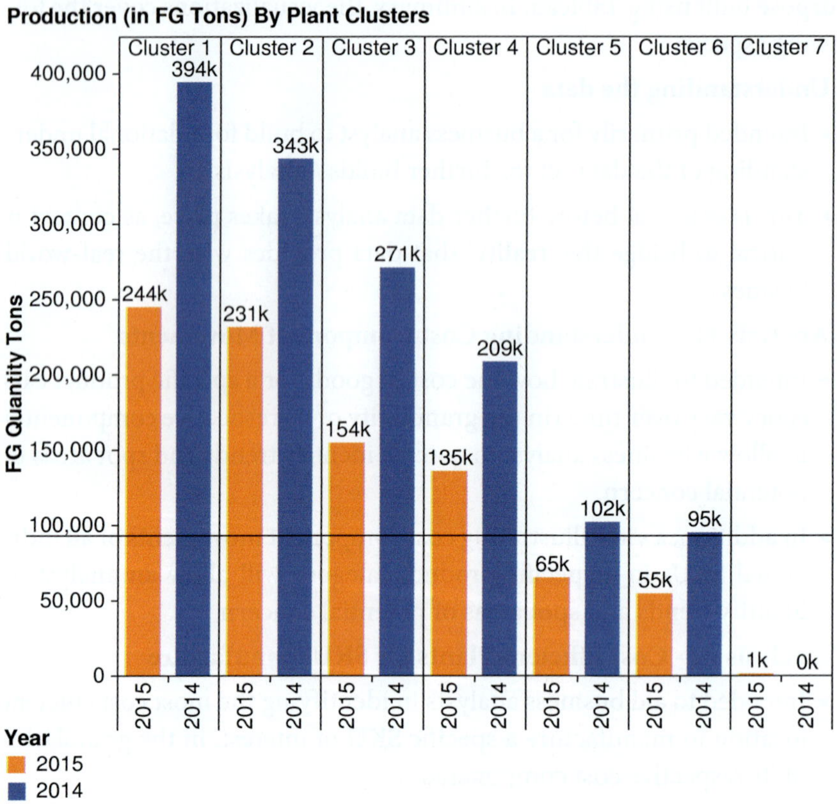

- **Purpose**
  - ▸ To provide an overview of the production plant clusters in the data set, and understand associated production volume trends across the years.
  - ▸ This provides business context when a business analyst examines the production data of specific countries of interest, allowing quick identification of whether there are concerning production trends (e.g. sudden increases / decreases in production volumes).
- **Findings**
  - ▸ 2015's production trend (by volume) closely follows that of 2014.

4.5. Production by product category

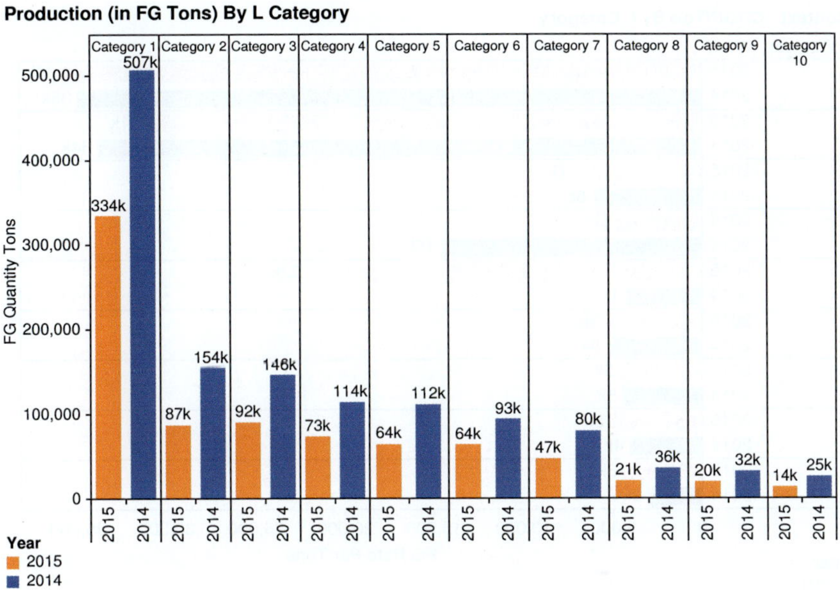

- **Purpose**
  - To rank the production volume (tons) of finished goods by product category in a specific country of analysis.
  - This helps the end-business user gain clarity as to where cost streamlining analysis could initially be performed to yield optimal business impact.
- **Findings**
  - 2015's production trend (by category) follows that of 2014.

4.6. Cost of goods produced/ton (ranked)

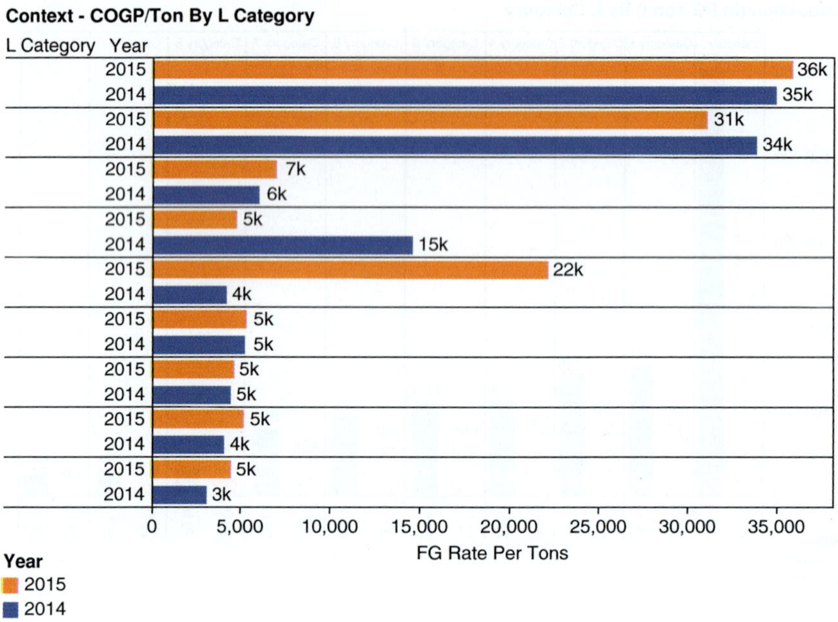

Note: Product categories are removed as they are proprietary information.

- **Purpose**
  - To rank the COGP/Ton of Finished Goods by Category.
  - This ranks the product categories that are the most expensive to produce per ton.
- **Findings**
  - A product category might be costly to produce, but could have low production quantities.
  - It is important to understand the production volume of a specific category in relation to its production cost, to yield tangible results in the event of a cost reduction / streamlining activity.

4.7. Analysis–Visualizing category's cost component movements

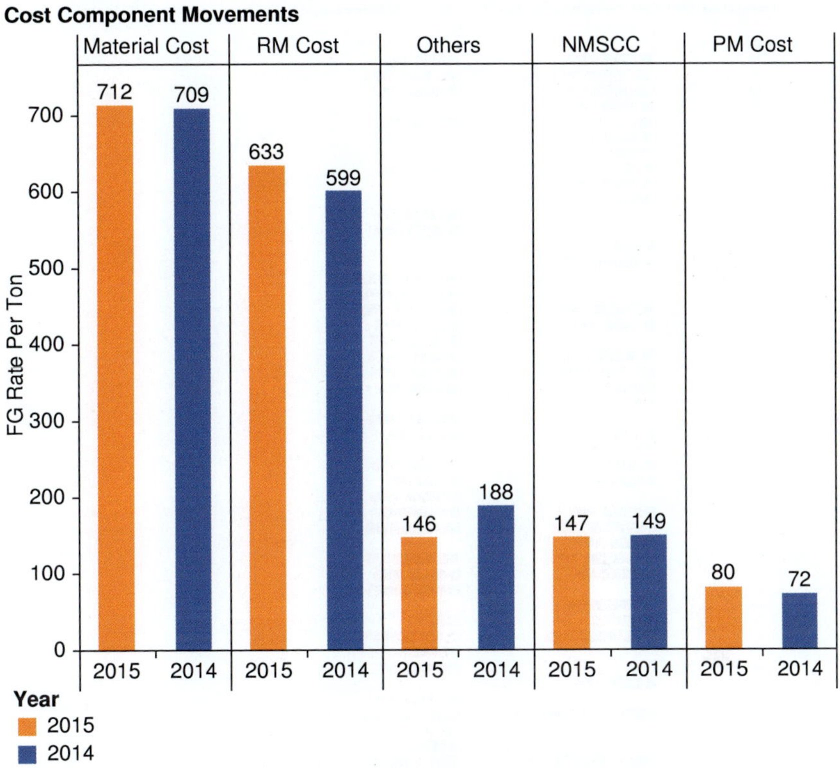

- **Purpose**
  - ▸ To provide the business analyst a quick and easy way to visualize the cost component movements attributing to the COGP/Ton of a product category year on year, aiding in the identification of potential trends that might form upcoming business concerns.
  - ▸ The cost component categories in the analysis (i.e. Material Costs, RM Cost) are predefined across the entire company to aid consistency in supply chain analysis.
- **User Inputs**
  - ▸ A business analyst selects a product category from a drop down menu to view the year on year relevant cost component trends.

4.8. Analysis–Visualizing category's cost component movements

Note: SKU details are removed as they are proprietary information.

- **Purpose**
  - ▸ This visualization ranks a category's SKU production volume (by tons), and overlays its associated cost components.
  - ▸ This allows a business analyst to identify cost component trends per product SKU, per product category year on year.
  - ▸ The visualization is ranked by production volume (in tons) to help an analyst determine which SKU could be further looked at for cost streamlining to yield maximum business impact (due to its large production volume in a product category).
- **User Inputs**
  - ▸ A business analyst selects a product category from a drop down menu to view the relevant cost component trends for all SKUs manufactured (ranked by production volume) in the chosen product category.

4.9. Analysis–Cost efficient plants for SKU manufacture

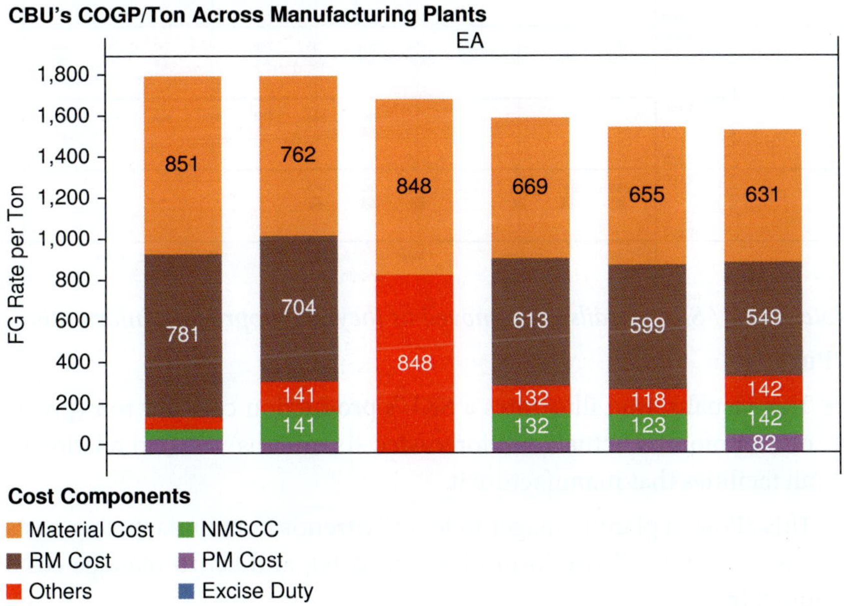

Note: Plant / SKU details are removed as they are proprietary information

- **Purpose**
  - ▸ This visualization ranks a SKU's production cost per ton in relation to all the factories that manufacture it, allowing easy identification of the most cost efficient manufacturing facility.

- Overlaying the visualization with respective cost components allows easy identification of the performance of each manufacturing plant.

- **User Inputs**
  - A business analyst selects a product category from a drop down menu.
  - Then, the SKU of interest is chosen from another drop down menu to view its ranked production cost per ton across all manufacturing locations.

4.10. Analysis–Cost efficient plants for SKU manufacture

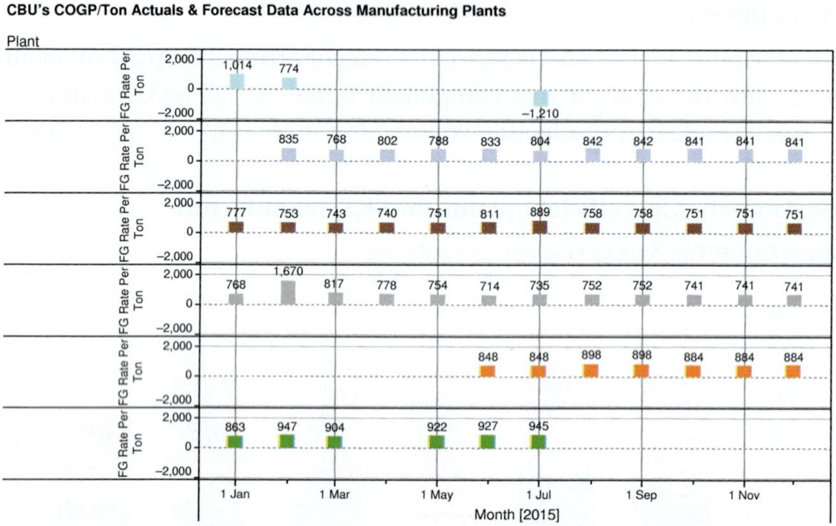

Note: Plant / SKU details are removed as they are proprietary information.

- **Purpose**
  - This visualization illustrates a SKU's production cost per ton (previous six months' actuals and forecasted six months' rates) in relation to all facilities that manufacture it.
  - This allows a plant manager to identify trends in manufacturing costs (e.g. a forecasted rise in production costs), and act to manage costs quickly.

- **User Inputs**
  - A business analyst selects a product category from a drop down menu.
  - Then, the desired SKU of interest is chosen from another drop down menu to view the SKU's previous six months and forecasted six months' production cost per ton across all manufacturing locations.

4.11. Analysis–Cost efficient plants for basepack manufacture

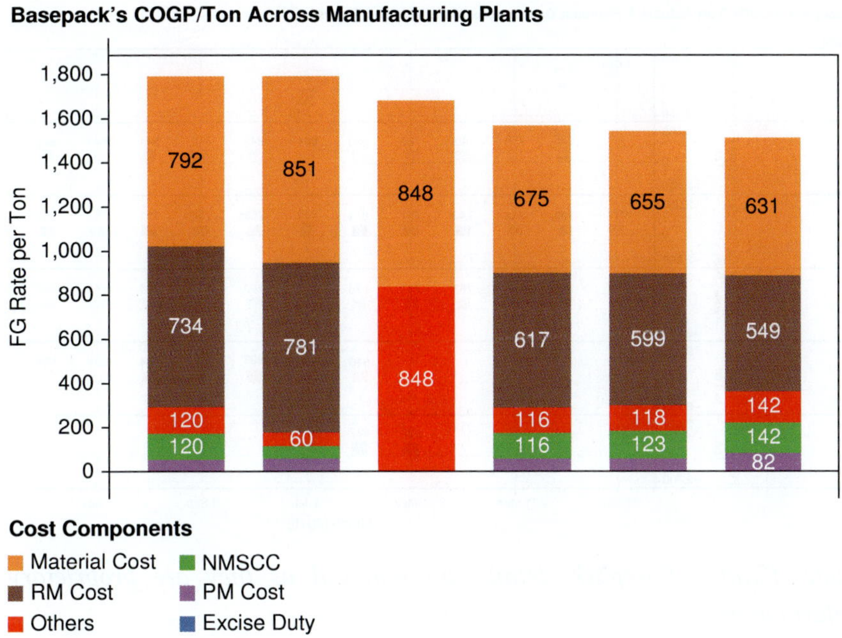

Note: Plant / Basepack details are removed as they are proprietary information.

- **Purpose**
  - ▸ This visualization ranks a basepack's production cost per ton in relation to all the factories that manufacture it, allowing easy identification of the most cost efficient facility.
  - ▸ Overlaying the visualization with its respective cost components allows easy identification each manufacturing plant's capability.
- **User Inputs**
  - ▸ A business analyst selects a product category from a drop down menu.
  - ▸ Then, the desired basepack of interest is chosen from another drop down menu to view its ranked production cost per ton across all manufacturing locations.

4.12. Analysis–Cost efficient plants for basepack manufacture

Basepack's COGP/Ton Actuals & Forecast Data Across Manufacturing Plants

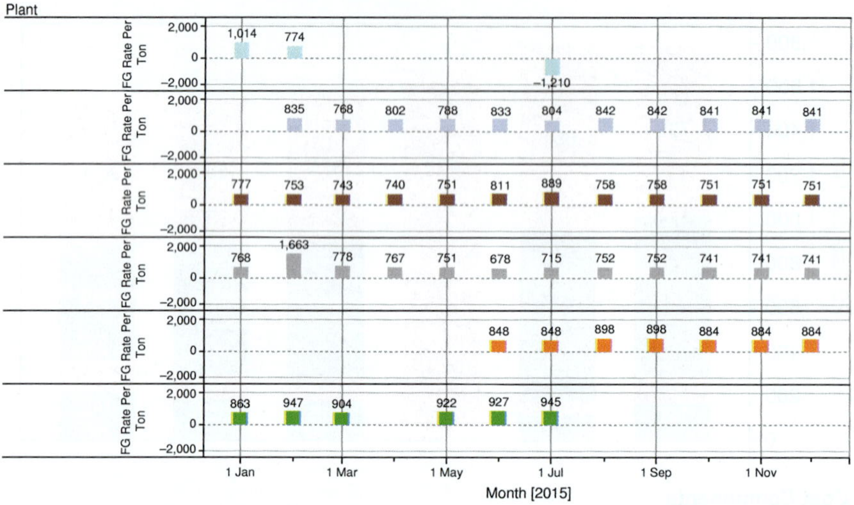

Note: Plant / Basepack details are removed as they are proprietary information.

- **Purpose**
  - This visualization illustrates a basepack's production cost per ton (previous six months' actuals and forecasted six months' rates) in relation to all facilities that manufacture it.
  - This allows a plant manager to identify trends in manufacturing costs (e.g. a forecasted rise in production costs), and act to manage costs quickly.
- **User Inputs**
  - A business analyst selects a product category from a drop down menu.
  - The basepack of interest is then chosen from another drop down menu to view its previous six months and forecasted six months' production cost per ton across all manufacturing locations.

4.13. User dashboards

Four user dashboards were created using the building blocks above to create a seamless, intuitive user experience:

1) Visualizing The Landscape
2) Visualizing Cost Component Movements

3) Visualizing SKU's Cost of Good Produced/Ton (Actual, Forecast)
4) Visualizing Basepack's Cost of Good Produced/Ton (Actual, Forecast)

Interactive User Elements Added:

- Top N Results to Display

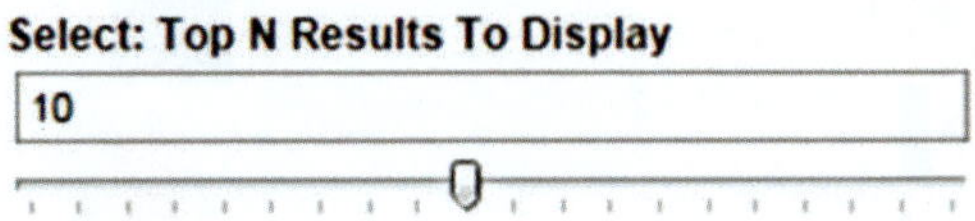

▸ To allow end users to select the number of results to display in a query.

- **Category Selector**

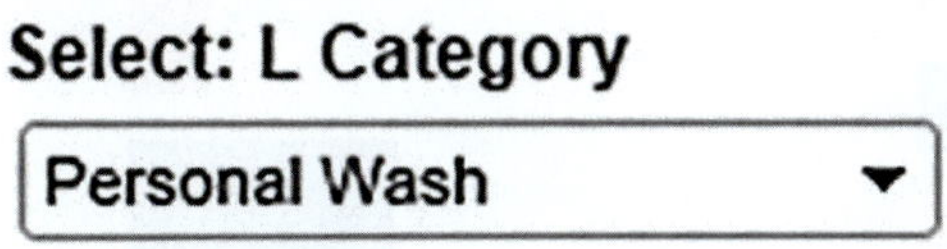

▸ To allow end users to select a category for analysis.

- **SKU Selector**

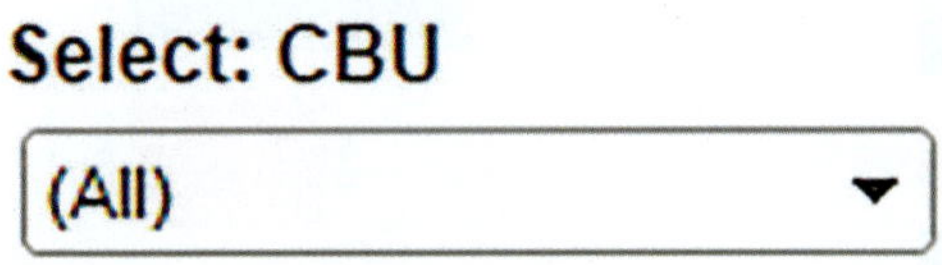

▸ To allow end users to select a SKU for analysis.

- **Basepack Selector**

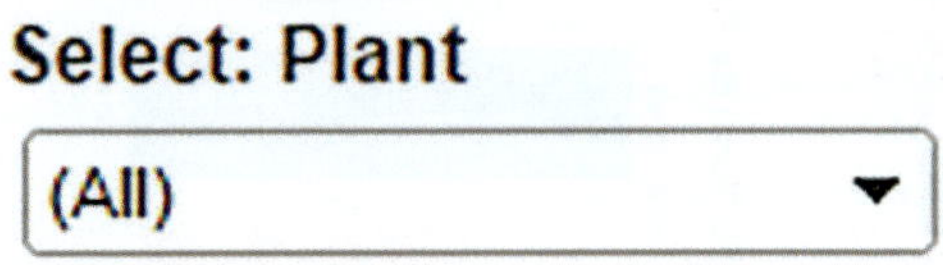

▸ To allow end users to select a basepack for analysis.

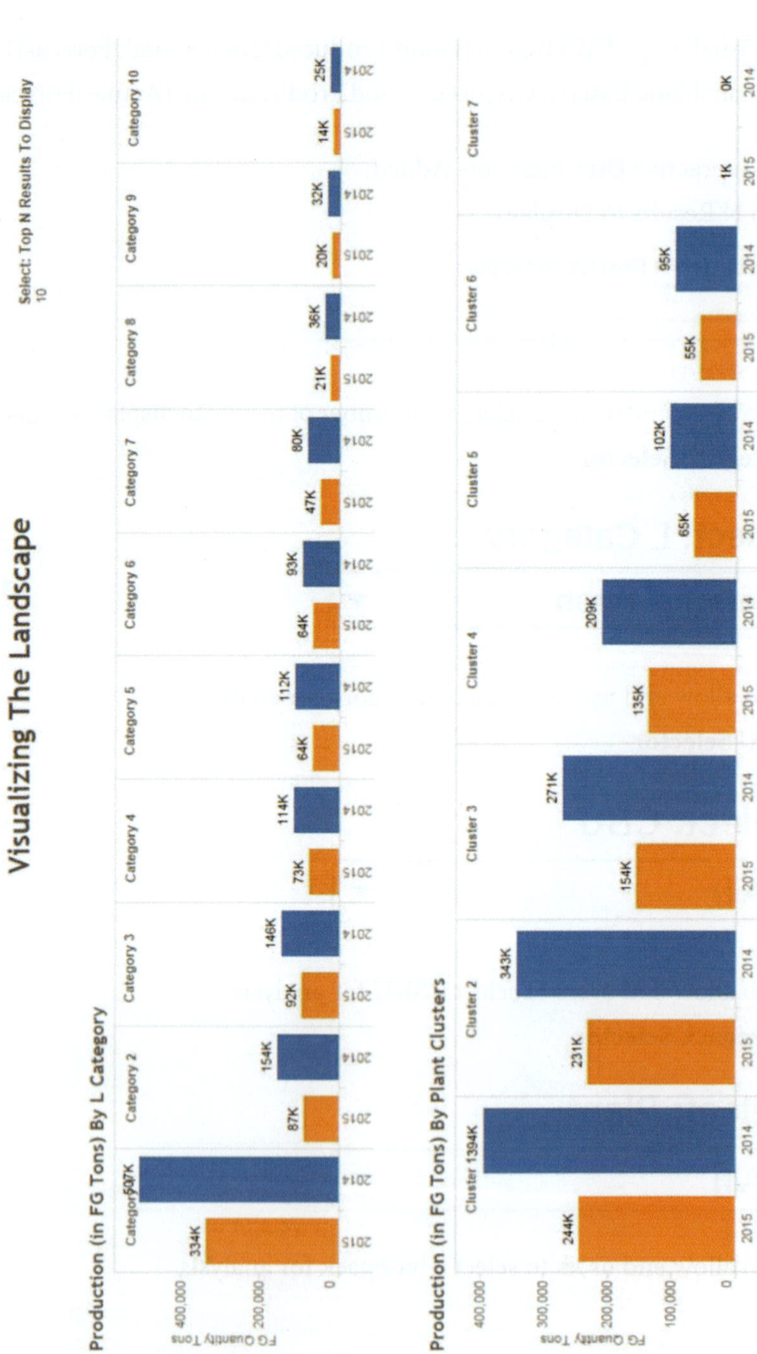

Dashboard #1 - Visualizing The Landscape

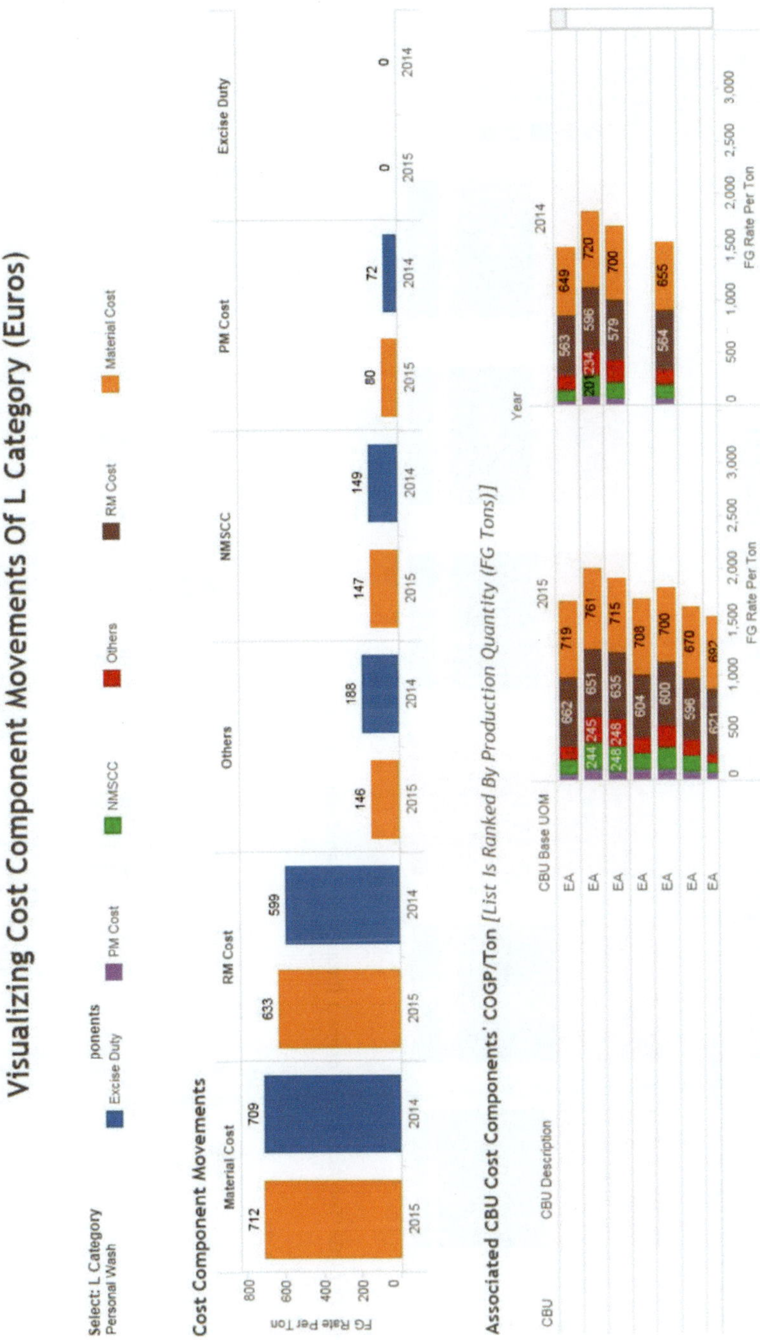

Dashboard #2 - Visualizing Cost Component Movements

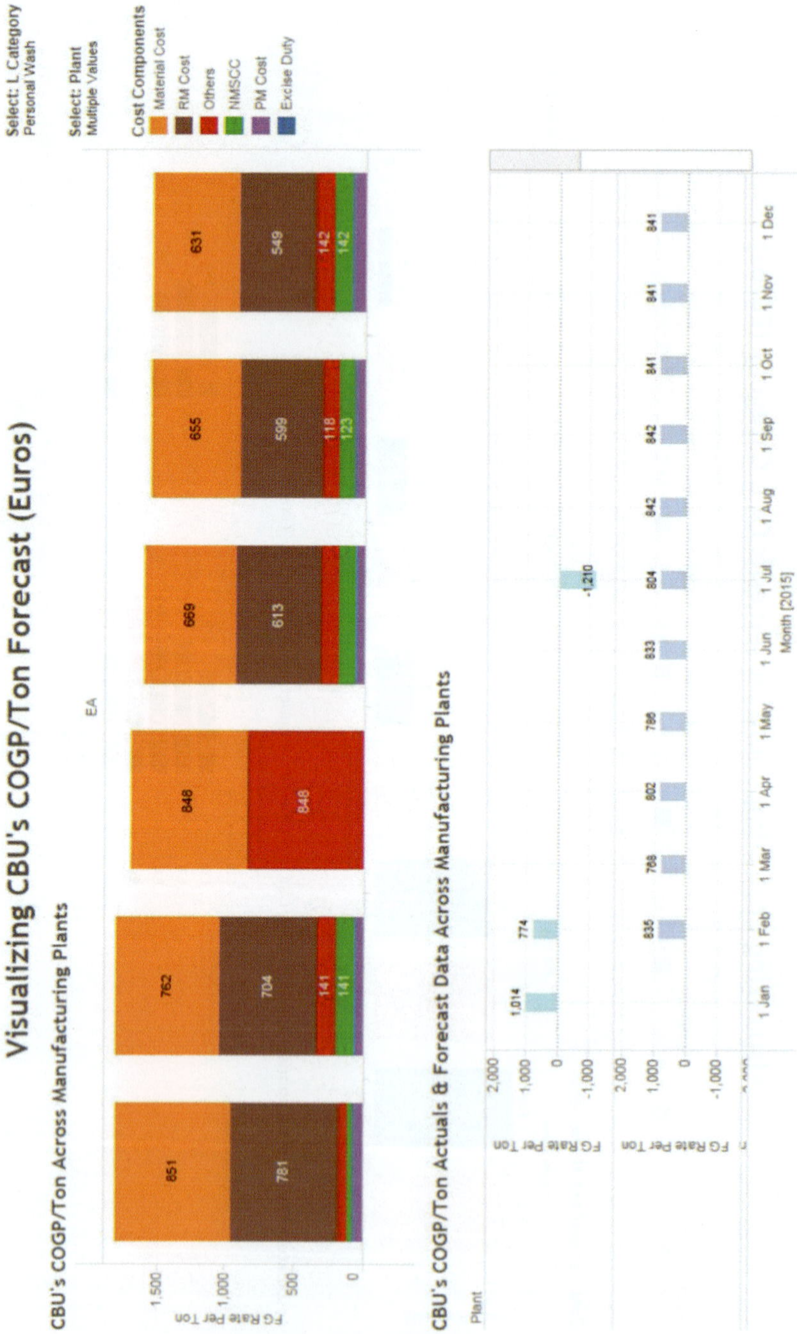

Dashboard #3 - Visualizing SKU's Cost of Good Produced/Ton (Actual, Forecast)

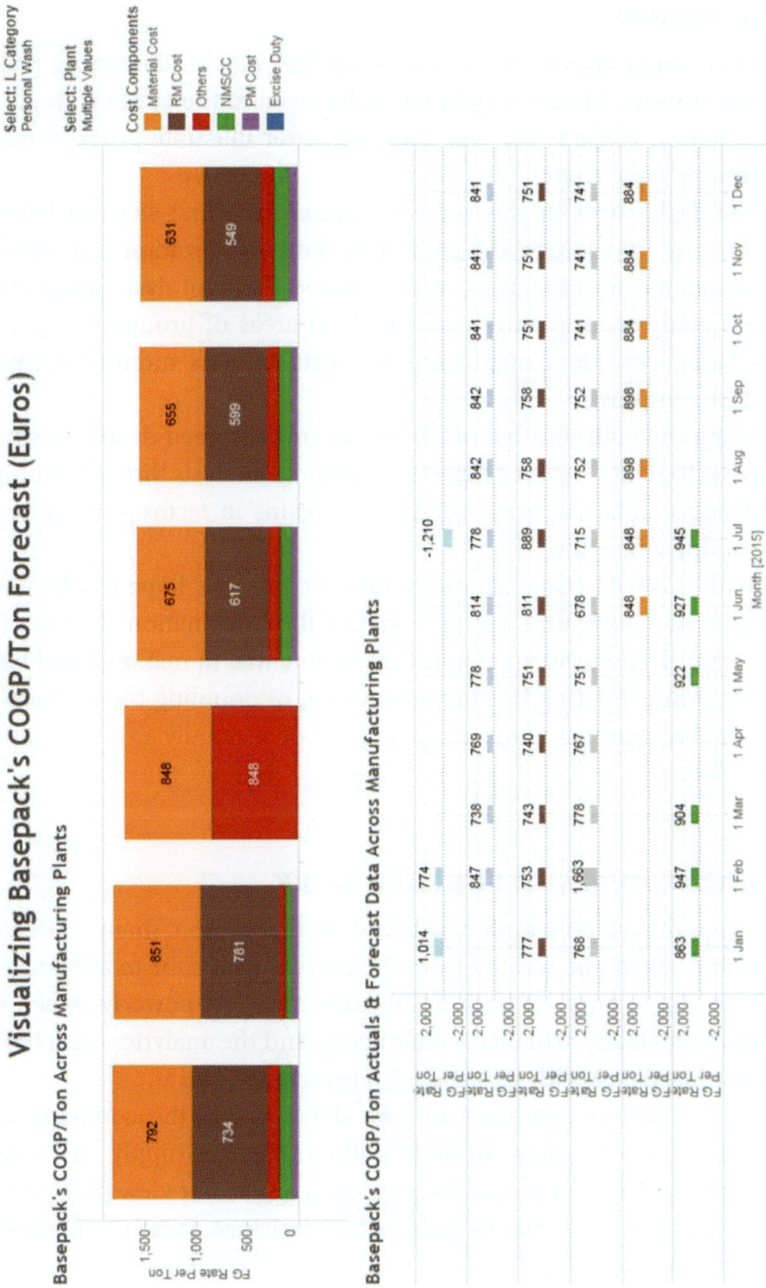

Dashboard #4 - Visualizing Basepack's Cost of Good Produced/Ton (Actual, Forecast)

5. DISCUSSION

Communicating visually with data is a useful way of illustrating reality to business users. Much thought has to be given to the optimal graphical representation of data (bar charts might better illustrate proportions as compared to a pie chart).

The dashboards in this project represent the first steps in helping the company understand the value that data visualization can yield in their respective business units and locations. The built dashboards allow business analysts to identify cost trends in areas of product categories, SKUs, basepacks, plant manufacturing costs, and six month forecasted manufacturing costs.

Using the built dashboards, business analysts need devote less time to 'piecing together' various aspects of a desired analysis through multiple spreadsheets. This will bring productivity gains in terms of man hours and working efficiency.

With this data visualization prototype comes the hope that business users can start to realize the potential of the information they already have on hand, and leverage it to its fullest potential in making good business decisions, fulfilling its long term vision of doubling the business in a sustainable manner upon the backdrop of a rapidly evolving global marketplace.

6. CONCLUSIONS AND FURTHER WORK

Aside from the purpose built dashboards in this project, many more useful dashboards can be created from the current data cube to aid business decisions. These purpose-built dashboards are most powerful when the business user clearly articulates their needs, and the analytics team builds them in accordance with strong design principles [12,13].

As the project continues to take shape across the company, and more offices join the drive to build a global view of supply chain data, the Supply Chain Operational Hub will gain a superior view of the entire company, and harness data to make better decisions, creating substantial value efficiencies.

REFERENCES

1. "Business Intelligence and Analytics | Tableau Software." 18 Aug. 2015 http://www.tableau.com/
2. "Tableau Software - Wikipedia, the free encyclopedia." 2011. 18 Aug. 2015 https://en.wikipedia.org/wiki/Tableau_Software
3. Hanrahan, P. "VizQL - ACM Digital Library." 2006. http://dl.acm.org/citation.cfm?id=1142473.1142560
4. "Tableau - Software: Business - Best of the Year | PCMag.com." 2008. 18 Aug. 2015 http://www.pcmag.com/article2/0,2817,1895722,00.asp
5. "SIIA Codie Awards Past Winners." 2015. 18 Aug. 2015 http://www.siia.net/archive/codies/2015/pw_2008.asp
6. "http://www.gartner.com/technology/reprints.do?id=1 ..." 2015. 18 Aug. 2015 https://www.linkedin.com/grp/post/4919023-5976038509000019968
7. "Connecting to Cubes | Tableau Software." 2015. 18 Aug. 2015 http://www.tableau.com/learn/tutorials/on-demand/connecting-cubes
8. "Analysis with Cubes and MDX | Tableau Software." 2015. 18 Aug. 2015 http://www.tableau.com/learn/tutorials/on-demand/analysis-cubes-and-mdx
9. "Understanding Functional Differences Between OLAP and ..." 2014. 18 Aug. 2015 http://kb.tableau.com/articles/knowledgebase/functional-differences-olap-relational
10. "Tableau: The Cure for the Common Cube - Post-Conference ..." 2015. 18 Aug. 2015 https://tc14.tableau.com/schedule/content/918
11. "Tableau Training and Tutorials." 2015. 18 Aug. 2015 http://www.tableau.com/learn/training
12. "FlowingData." 2007. 19 Aug. 2015 http://flowingdata.com/
13. "Dona Wong." 2009. 19 Aug. 2015 http://donawong.com/

CHAPTER 5

Storage Technologies for Data Reservoir

Balaji Rajamani

ABSTRACT

Enterprises have been continuously studying and exploring data to gain insights and drive business decisions. Large enterprises have business intelligence systems for enabling business analytics. However, with growing competitions in the market, variety of data, and external factors, there is a need to bring in voluminous data into the enterprise and derive intelligence out of it to drive better decision-making. Big data involves managing high volume and variety of data that needs to be processed fast. In the big data world, data related to an enterprise will no longer be limited to ERP and internal systems, but will include internal and external data sources. The nature of the data can no longer be restricted to structured data alone, as the significance of unstructured data is increasing over time to drive business decisions. The data volume will be huge and diverse, requiring a careful design of the IT architecture. This study evaluates and assesses different storage technologies for such large enterprises, with the key considerations of type of storage, performance, security, cost, and big data integration support.

1. INTRODUCTION

The existing architecture in an organization includes a data warehouse system and several independent sources of non-transactional data used by various verticals of business for their independent and focused analysis. The enterprise also receives data from several external systems. The business has many ongoing activities to include additional external data sources over a period of time. The existing architecture needs to be enhanced with the capability to store and process data from both internal and external sources seamlessly.

The objective of this study it to evaluate and assess different technologies for storing internal and external data for analytics, handle variability of the data, and scale to accommodate new sources rapidly. This should also take into consideration the volume of data coming from machine and act as a catchment area, to harness essential information and flush out the irrelevant data once done. The architecture should enable usage of Big Data connectors for analytics.

2. PROBLEM STATEMENT

There are many business requirements especially in marketing/commerce which need to combine diverse data for analytics. Consider the scenario where two datasets are needed for an analytical application, e.g., sales market research data (external data in access DB) and actual sales data (SAP BW). Currently, users manually download the datasets into excel spreadsheet and combine them to arrive at a consolidated dataset, where the process is error prone and lacks global governance. Also, the market research data are specific to regions and each region has different format and vendors to obtain the information, leading to multiple external data sources in different formats to do analytical research.

This human data integration for data preparation process leads to lack of proper governance and carries the risk of wrong data being the source of analytics. These diverse heterogeneous data need to be centrally governed and made available for analytics. This requires more efficient storage architecture to support analytics for different kinds of data. The source and type of data can be categorized as shown in Figure 1:

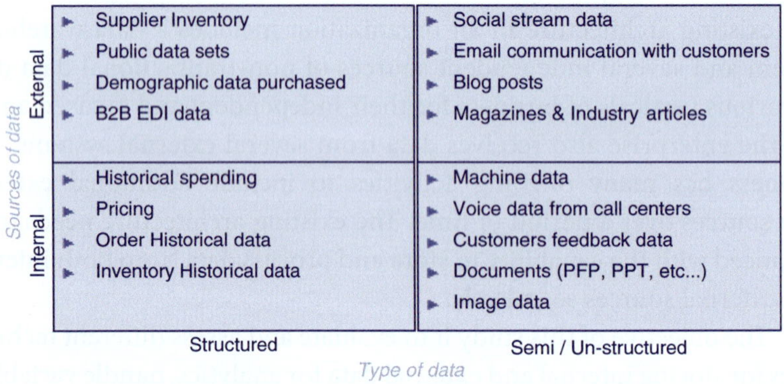

Figure 1: Classification of data.

- **Internal data**
  - Structured: The data from SAP systems, e.g., SAP R/3(ECC), CRM, SCM, etc.
  - Unstructured: Data from Share Point (internal sites), machine data, etc.
- **External Data**
  - Structured: This data includes structured data from external parties, e.g., Nielsen.
  - Unstructured: Information downloaded from specific sites by users and used for analysis (this are very specific cases and not like Twitter feeds or Facebook posts, as these are not the key data source in a B2B business model), emails, blogs/articles (shared drive), etc.

3. STATE OF THE ART

The existing data warehouse (BW) is the single factual source for corporate reporting. However, there are quite a number of DBs maintained by different LoB for specific reporting needs. Though it looks like a simple solution to address a specific need, it leads to several issues. The data is not fully governed as the point of entry is outside the corporate BI. The latency/delay in data updates in these systems can lead to user dissatisfaction, and every system has to be funded separately for maintenance and upgrades. This setup carries the risk of incorrect data being used in business decisions.

One option is to bring all the external data maintained by different LoBs into the existing BW layer. But it leads to too many non-standard (non-SAP) data getting loaded into the BW layer. A few types of data cannot be stored in BW (e.g., unstructured text data), as the cost of storing all in BW will be high. The consistent long-term data (ERP data) fits well into BW, whereas data for short-term analysis/moving data need to reside outside BW. Hence, it is evident that with just SAP BW, all requirements cannot be addressed. Therefore, there needs to be a balanced approach to consolidate the information, and at the same time not to tamper the data quality in the BW layer. This leads to the considering different storage technologies for consolidation purpose.

The storage technology market for analytics is evolving to support the much broader spectrum of data. This creates opportunities in organizations with classical data warehouse setup to augment it with these new datasets paving way for logical data warehouse (LDW) as the long-term path for BI. There is a paradigm shift in the architecture moving from the traditional/operational data warehouse (one system for all analytical needs) to the data reservoir where DW becomes one of the repositories in addition to other sources. The data reservoir can be a combination of different technologies of storage, access, and processing. Hence, the storage technologies for independent elements in the data reservoir becomes more critical as it is expected to support reporting and advanced analytics, along with catchment of data from data sources in the data reservoir. Figure 2 shows the magic quadrant of Gartner[1] for various providers in the data warehouse and data management layer field.

4. SOLUTION: DESCRIPTION OF APPROACH

The solution includes conceptualizing the overall data-flow architecture as part of evaluating the storage technology for analytics. The internal data continues to be in the existing SAP BW and the external data will be integrated in the data reservoir as one or more additional systems.

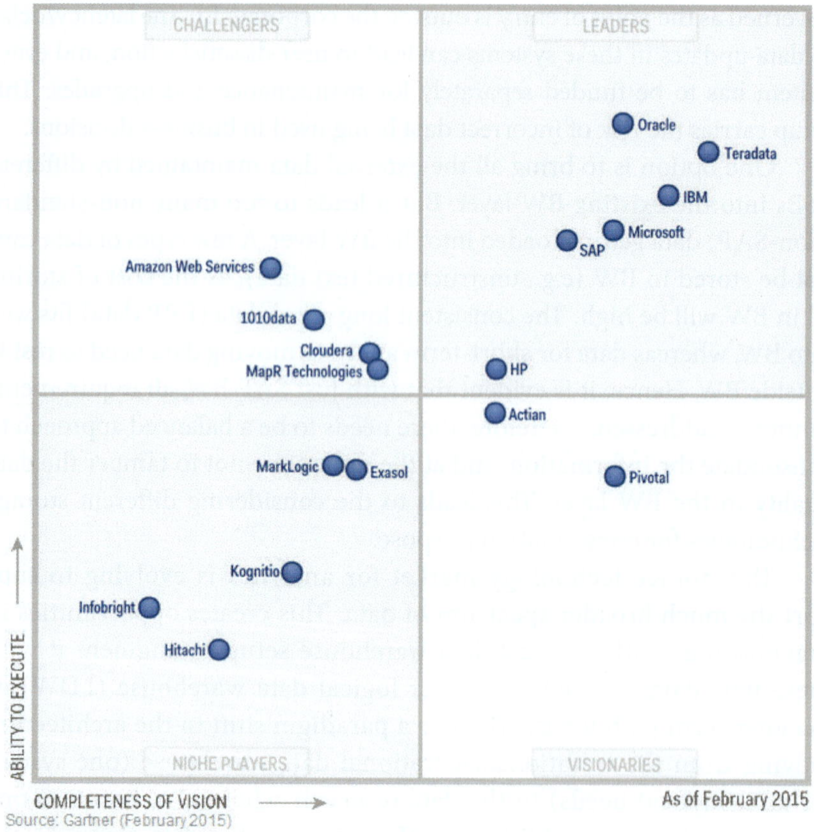

Figure 2: Magic quadrant for data warehouse and data management solutions for analytics.

The number of additional systems is purely dependent on the nature of data, business process relevance, and analytical requirement.

The data reservoir will be the only place where internal and external data meets; and where transactional and non-transactional data will be merged. The existing data warehouse system (traditional BI) will continue 'as is' to support existing services provided to the business.

As part of the overall solution, following steps needs to be addressed:

1) Identify the source of data — internal and external data based on the origin or system of record.
2) Classify the type of data — structured and unstructured.

3) Storage technology evaluation — to fulfil the objective of effective data storage for analytics, the storage needs to be assessed on various factors. As part of this study, following key factors are considered, as these directly affect the TCO (cost)/user experience (performance)/ data sensitivity (security)/ technology (storage)/ big data integration.
   i) Storage — is directly related to the size of DB. This has a big influence on loading and reporting.
   ii) Security — ensures the right person has the access to the right data.
   iii) Cost — includes the initial setup cost, support and upgrade costs, etc.
   iv) Performance — most important of all, the response time to process high volume/diverse data in seconds for agile decision making.
   v) Big data integration — ensure the unprecedented growth in data is leveraged effectively for analytical purpose.
4) Cloud vs. on premise deployment
5) ETL layer definition — cleansing, business rules and merging of diverse data. The merging of data in backend (merging and storing) is more suitable for standard formatted reporting. In this case, the users consume the information with basic navigation such as drill-down on certain fields. The challenge is for any minor change, more efforts are needed to change the backend.
6) Runtime data mash-up — merging diverse data at runtime. The users in this case are supposed to have deeper knowledge of the data and the relationship between them. This is more suitable when data reside in silos and users are trying to perform data discovery activities. The strength of this approach is a higher flexibility provided for data harmonization, whereas the limitation is the restriction to highly skilled users.
7) Analytical tools for reporting

With details of data source (1) and type of data (2) available, this study is focussed on storage technology evaluation (3) and a very brief overview of cloud vs. on site (4). The overall data flow for a typical data reservoir is shown in Figure 3.

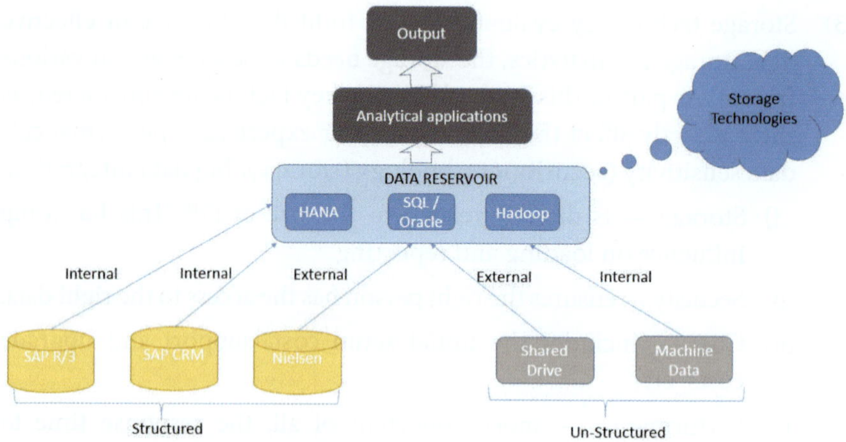

Figure 3: Overall data flow architecture.

4.1. Storage technologies considered

The scope of this study is limited to specific players that include SAP, Oracle, and Microsoft. Teradata is not a supported DB for SAP BW and hence will not be considered. IBM has not been the organization's go-to choice for system, as it is more suitable for IBM host environments.

Oracle: It is the largest market shareholder in data warehouse database (technology independent) supporting big data appliances. Oracle[2] is the major DB enabling SAP for both operational and analytical systems. Oracle DB can also work in conjunction with Oracle Exalytics Business Intelligence Machine to acquire, organize, analyze, and maximize value of big data.

SAP Hana: SAP HANA[3] is an in-memory data platform comprising DB, processing layer with MPP (massive parallel processing) capabilities, advanced analytics (PAL-predictive analytical library), and front-end tools that can support operational and analytical requirements. It is highly advanced in data management with classification of data namely, hot (in memory), cold (in disk, can be loaded to memory), warm (data in near line storage), and very high performance in subseconds for complex queries. SAP HANA supports Smart Data Access, in memory data fabric as part of accessing diverse data (including Hadoop).

Microsoft: SQL Server[4] along with Microsoft Analytics Platforms Systems has the ability to support both in-memory analytical and transactional capabilities. Power Query/Azure (Machine Learning capabilities included) has ability to combine data from multiple sources in Excel with simplified access to unstructured data with HDInsight, a 100 per cent Apache Hadoop based distribution making Microsoft big data technologies, equally noticeable as other market leaders.

Hadoop and Big Data Connectors: While SAP, Oracle, and Microsoft have been key players in structured data, their capabilities for managing unstructured data are still evolving. For big data (unstructured) enterprises prefer the stabilized and mature Apache Hadoop for loading, processing, and analyzing unstructured data. Most of the DBs, in-memory platforms and tools (reporting) provide connectors to Hadoop to support unstructured data.

In order to identify an efficient storage for analytics, these storage technologies will be evaluated on the following key factors:

4.2. Storage

The data storage can be row-based, column-based, or in No-SQL format (i.e., key-value pair, graph, document, column family, etc.) depending on structured or unstructured format. The data is typically stored in data files system in traditional DB approach (RDBMS), in memory or distributed across systems called HDFS (highly distributed file system), making high volume big data transaction viable. The three leading storage are discussed as follows.

4.2.1. Row-based

The data is stored tuple-wise (record-wise) as shown in Figure 4 — easy to insert/update. This is write-optimised and recommended for transactional requirements (access single row/document at a given point of time, no aggregated requirement). Querying all data for a given record is fast. However, querying data at a column level (aggregated)/high volume is expensive.

4.2.2. Column-based

Data is stored as attributes (column-wise) as shown in Figure 5. Retrieving it record-wise is expensive, but drilldown based on attributes is very fast. This is read-optimised and recommended for analytical requirements with very high parallel processing and high compression (requires less DB size compared to row storage). Update of data is not highly efficient and hence not suitable for frequently updated data (transactional).

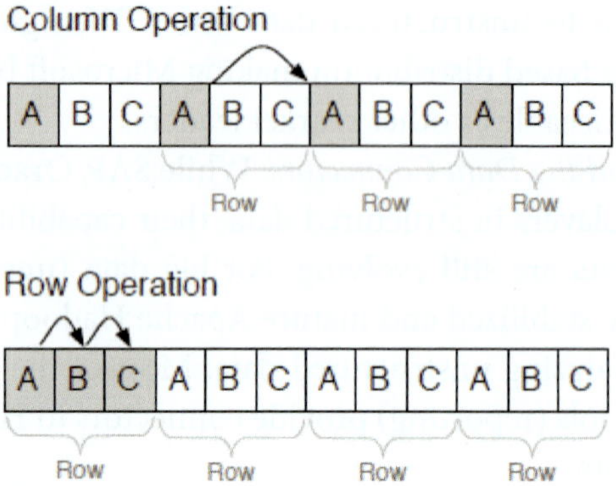

Figure 4: Row type storage.

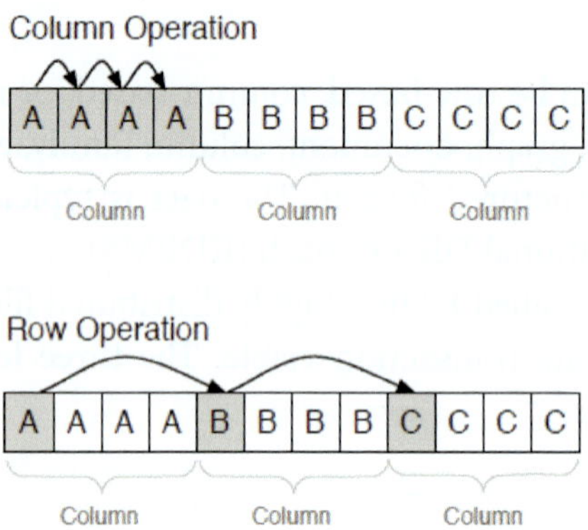

Figure 5: Column-type storage.

4.2.3. HDFS

The data is stored in low cost, easily scalable, and fault tolerant servers in file formats as shown in Figure 6. This is suitable for high-volume, batch-processed requirements and not for real-time, less-volume processing. HDFS stores semi-structured or unstructured data. For example machine data that can run from Terabytes to Petabytes in few weeks/months. The high volume data for example, 100 TB is stored across different servers, i.e., 10 servers of 10 TB each. Hence, the queries can be run in parallel at 10 times the original speed, with a backup mechanism for disaster recovery. The core strength of HDFS is in handling high volume of data for pattern generation, machine learning, and batch-processed analysis.

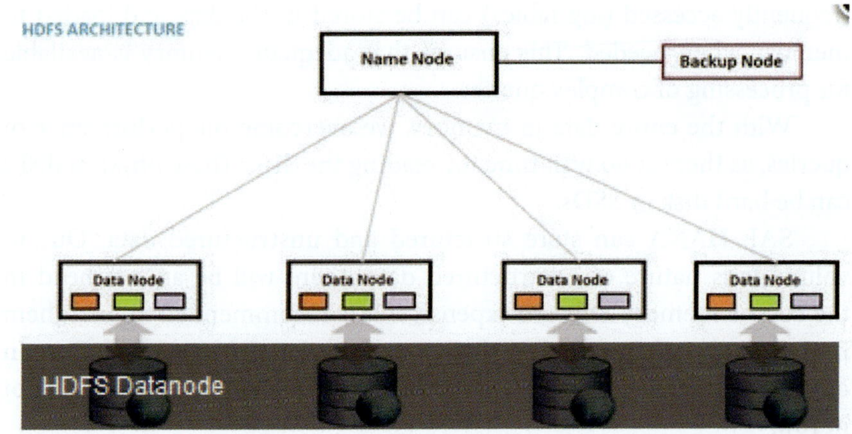

Figure 6: HDFS data storage.

Figure 7 depicts the overall data storage in the reservoir, which can be a combination of row/column with in-memory/disk, in addition to HDFS.

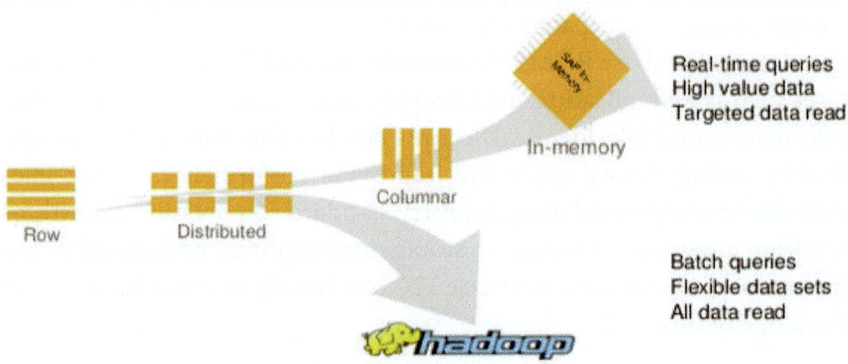

Figure 7: Different storage techniques for data reservoir.

4.2.4. SAP HANA data types

SAP HANA supports both row and column types of data storage. SAP Hana also supports in-memory and disk storage for the underlying data. Disk storage can be used as backup in case of any failure in the memory (for recover purpose) at near zero downtime. Also, the tables that are frequently accessed (log tables) can be stored in the disk and loaded to memory when needed. This ensures that adequate memory is available for processing of complex queries.

With the entire data in memory, we overcome the performance of queries, as there is no wait time for reading the disk. These physical disks can be hard disk or SSDs.

SAP HANA can store structured and unstructured data. Due to voluminous nature of unstructured data, there will be an overhead in the cost as memory DBs are expensive. It is recommended to load them into memory when required than to persist them in memory. Certain data types, namely geospatial, are available only in column tables and not in row.

4.2.5. Oracle data types

Oracle Database RDMS traditionally handles structured data. It has essential data types to handle unstructured or semi-structured data. Oracle 12c comes with Secure Files that provide enhanced LOB-type storage for applications managing all types of unstructured data. Oracle Database 12c has incorporated data types and optimized data structures with operators to analyze and manipulate XML documents, multimedia content, text, and geospatial information.

Oracle Database RDMS, Secure Files have advanced file system features such as Reduplication and Compression. Oracle Database automatically detects multiple, identical Secure Files data and stores only one copy, thereby saving storage space and improving performance. Secure Files data can be compressed using industry standard compression algorithms resulting in significant savings in storage and improved performance. The in-memory functionality of Oracle 12C is relatively new and hence not in the scope of this study.

4.2.6. MS SQL data types

SQL Server stores relational data in the database and non-relational binary large object (BLOB) data in file systems and file servers. In order to reduce cost, BLOBs are usually stored in separate systems and integrity needs to be established in the relational database for access and query.

SQL server has two capabilities to handle BLOB.

- FILESTREAM attribute on var binary column to handle data that are stored on the local file server but is managed and accessed directly within the context of the database. The FILESTREAM column behaves exactly the same as BLOB column, which means full integration of maintenance operations such as backup and restore, complete integration with the SQL Server security model, and full-transaction support are available.
- For cases where BLOBs are stored external to the system, the Remote BLOB Store API in SQL Server provides a way to integrate remote BLOB storage solutions with the relational data, without requiring BLOB store-specific functionality or code.

4.3. Security

Security is a core attribute of any good DB setup. With security, we intend to address the access of data by authorized users. Different storage technologies handle security differently but all ensuring authorized entry and access of data.

4.3.1. SAP HANA

The access is handled via privileges and roles.[5] The privileges can be of following types:

- System-level privilege: Admin, developers-creating/changing schemas, user ID, system admin information, and backup data. The exception is the Database Admin privilege available for only DBA.
- Object privilege: End users/technical users who access object (tables, views, procedures, etc.) with change access (as needed).
- Analytic privilege: End users who view analytic/attribute/calculation views built in HANA.
- Package privilege: Application/content developers who have package level access at repository level in HANA DB.
- Application privilege: Application end users/technical developers specific to SAP HANA XS application.

4.3.2. Oracle

Authorization[6] in Oracle primarily involves two processes: permitting only certain users to access, process, or alter data, and applying varying limitations on user access or actions. The limitations placed on (or removed from) users can apply to objects, such as schemas, tables, or rows; or to resources, such as time (CPU, connect, or idle times).

The access is achieved via following objects:

- Introduction to privileges: right to execute a statement or access another object — can be system, schema, object, table, procedures, etc.
- Roles — managing and controlling privileges for users/DB application is achieved via roles.
- Profiles — collection of privileges, this can be assigned to multiple users.

4.3.3. MS SQL

The entity to be secured is called securable.[7] The entity that receives permission/access to a securable is called a principal. The most common principals are logins and database users. Access to securable is controlled by granting or denying permissions, or by adding logins and user to roles that have access. For information about controlling permissions, use GRANT (Transact-SQL), REVOKE (Transact-SQL), DENY (Transact-SQL), sp_addrolemember (Transact-SQL), and sp_droprolemember (Transact-SQL)

4.4. Cost

Cost of the DB plays a key role in the long-term support and the return of the investment made in the data reservoir. Comparing the three DBs, SAP HANA has the highest cost followed by Oracle and SQL server being the least. However, SAP HANA comes with additional functionalities.

4.4.1. HANA

The licensing cost is calculated in two possible ways:

1) DB volume specific: The cost of hardware (in memory appliance +17 per cent of the cost of hardware/year as software license). Limited functionalities of HANA, all changes need to go through BW DB.
2) Percentage/enterprise license: This can be classified into two further categories:
    i) BW: Hardware cost +8 per cent of overall SAP licensing cost. Any additional memory will result only in hardware cost.

ii) Enterprise: Hardware cost + 23 per cent (15 per cent + 8 per cent for BW) of overall SAP licensing cost. Any additional memory will result only in hardware cost. This includes the licensing of all SAP systems in the enterprise to be moved to HANA (anytime in future as well). However, the hardware cost would be independent for each system.

iii) In addition to this one-time cost (BW at 8 per cent or enterprise at 23 per cent), there will be annual maintenance fee of 17 per cent applicable year on year.

4.4.2. Oracle

The Oracle DB cost is based on number of users (Named user Plus) or processer based.[8] The Named User Plus licensing can be of three types:

- Standard edition one — Minimum five licenses (or total users whichever is higher). Servers with two sockets are supported in this.
- Standard edition — Minimum five licenses (or total users whichever is higher). Servers with four sockets are supported in this.
- Enterprise edition[9] — Minimum 25(or actual number of users) users per processor license. The number of license is product of users (25 or actual) * number of processors.

The processor-based licensing is independent of number of users and is calculated by multiplying the number of cores * the core factor maintained by Oracle.

4.4.3. MS SQL

SQL server is available in three editions: Enterprise, Business Intelligence and Standard. Licensing cost is based on Server/Client Access License (CAL)[10] model or Core (Standard, BI, and Enterprise) model.

The CAL/server based model is for fixed set of users requiring standard functionalities (basic OLTP, basic reporting/analytics, programming tools, and management tools). The cost includes SQL server cost + licensing cost at $209 per user. The server cost for standard and BI editions being $898, $8592, respectively.

The enterprise edition is for organizations with higher computational capabilities and more users. In addition, it has more analytical capabilities (power pivot, power view and advanced analytics), data management (data quality, master data services), in-memory, high availability, etc. The cost includes server cost + core licenses. The core license is \$6874. The number of core licenses is calculated as total number of cores in server * core factor. Microsoft maintains the core factor value based on the processor types.

4.5. Performance

SAP HANA delivers the highest performance as in-memory DB, followed by row-based Oracle DB and SQL Server. The traditional DB (row-based) is more write-optimized and can be tuned for better-read options.

HDFS is more suitable for high volume, unstructured/semi-structured data analysis. However, for performance reasons it is not recommended for online/real time, small volume data processing that could be alternatively handled in Hadoop HBase.

4.6. Big data integration

4.6.1. SAP HANA

SAP Data Services (BODS) is the standard way of accessing Hadoop Data into HANA. There are other options such as Smart Data Access (virtual), SQOOP, Java Connector. The standard way of loading Hadoop data to HANA via data services is shown in Figure 8.

Hadoop data is loaded in SAP HANA as follows:

- Based on target, SAP Data Services translates queries into: Hive Query Language (HQL) or Pig Script.
- Hive/Pig converts queries to Map/Reduce jobs.
- Result data files are generated on the HDFS system.
- SAP Data Services use multiple threads to process data from Hive/Pig.
- Optional transforms: Data quality operations.
- Load results into database.

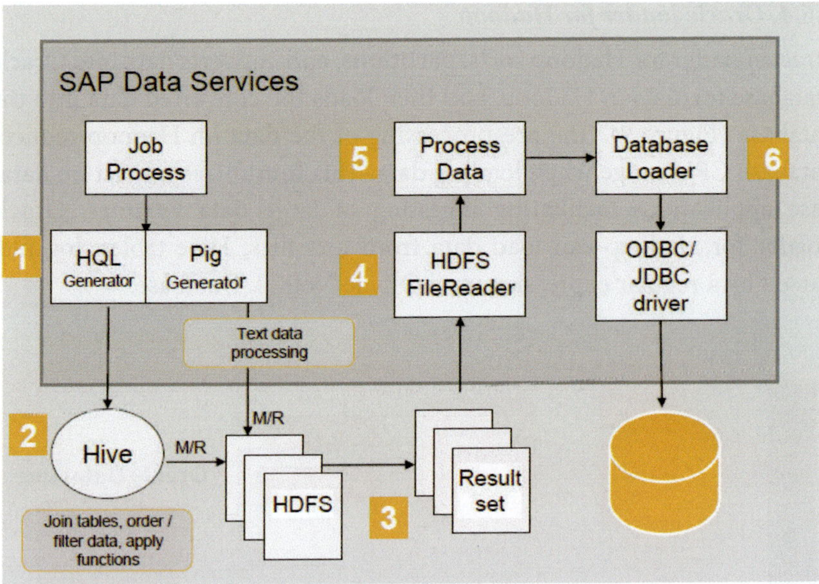

Figure 8: Process of loading Hadoop into a DB.

4.6.2. *Smart data access*

Virtually access any form of external data via HANA at runtime. This eliminates the data load latency time and allows heterogeneous data to be made available for reporting and advanced analytics. The sources can be Hadoop or IQ. Virtual tables are created in HANA, and during runtime, filters and joins are passed to the source system in parallel and results are calculated in individual systems and passed back to HANA for analysis.

4.6.3. *Oracle*

Oracle comes with Big Data Connectors[11] that leverages Apache Hadoop combined with intuitive extensions to existing infrastructure to simplify the development of big data applications. Few of the vital connectors listed below facilitate rapid integration of big data with Oracle database.

- Oracle Loader for Hadoop
- Oracle SQL Connector for Hadoop Distributed File System
- Oracle R Connector for Hadoop

4.6.4. *Oracle loader for Hadoop*

Oracle Loader for Hadoop sorts, partitions, and converts data into Oracle Database formats in Hadoop, and then loads the converted data into the database (Figure 9). The pre-processing of the data on Hadoop reduces database CPU usage when loading data. This minimizes impact on database applications facilitating ingesting of large data volumes. Oracle Loader for Hadoop can load data from text files, Hive tables, log files parsed by a regular expression, and Oracle NoSQL Database.

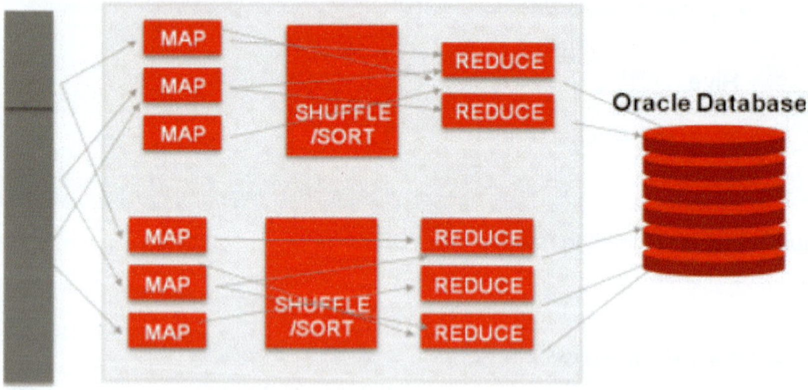

Figure 9: Oracle loader for Hadoop.

4.7. Oracle SQL connector for Hadoop distributed file system

It is an Oracle Direct Connector for accessing data in HDFS directly from Oracle Database. This enables SQL data access on the Hive tables; delimited text files, and Oracle Loader data pump files in HDFS.

4.7.1. *Oracle R connector for Hadoop*

Oracle R Connector for Hadoop is an R package that provides transparent access to Hadoop and data stored in HDFS. It offers users of the open-source statistical environment R the ability to analyze data stored in HDFS (Figure 10), and to run R models efficiently against large volumes of data leveraging Map Reduce. The connector enables R scripts to be run on data in Hive tables and files in HDFS.

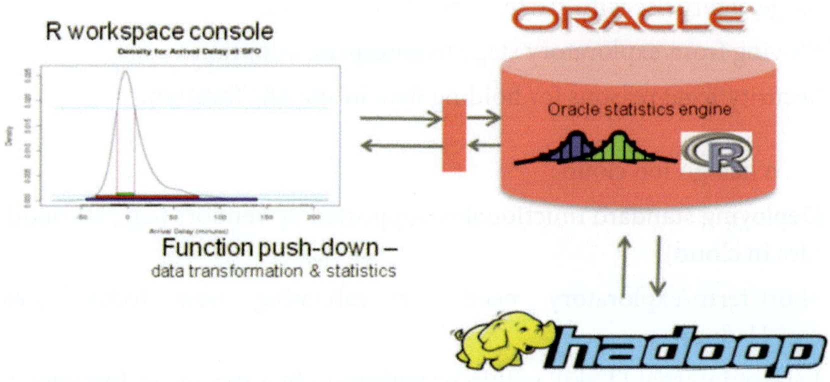

Figure 10: Oracle R connector for Hadoop.

4.7.2. MS SQL

SQL Server connectors for Hadoop[12] enable customers to work with both structured SQL Server data and unstructured data from Hadoop. The two main connectors are:

- Hive ODBC driver that allows customers to move data from Hive directly into either Microsoft Excel or SQL Server BI tools.
- Excel Hive Add-in that enables customers to move data from Hive directly into Excel, or Microsoft BI tools such as Power Pivot, for analysis.

4.8. Deployment options (Cloud/On premise)

The data storage can be either on site or on the cloud. All the three databases discussed above support cloud versions. The differentiators between on site vs. cloud shall help to select the optimal option:

When go for 'on site':

- Complex and custom specific solution to address business requirements, which are not available as standard product functionality.
- Sufficient skillset available in organization to support the technology.
- Sufficient hardware infrastructure can be supported for growth in data volume.

- Large enterprise with strategic need for big data.
- Moving from exploratory stage to enterprise adoption.
- Security/legal reasons for holding data in specific location.

When go for 'cloud':

- Deploying standard functionality supported by vendors (e.g., HR modules in cloud).
- Short-term/exploratory need for validating new technologies, e.g., Hadoop.
- Lack of internal IT skill within organization in a specific technology.
- No major customization needed in hardware to address the requirement.

The following options are supported in cloud:

- SaaS: Software as a Service. Basic form of cloud. SAP HR module Success Factors, RDS, and SAP Business Suite are examples of SaaS.
- PaaS: Platform as a Service. This is more than just consuming the cloud application. The provider supports a middleware/platform to create/deploy applications in the cloud specific to the user.
- IaaS — The detailed level of cloud where entire infrastructure is in cloud including software, servers, network equipment. This has the potential advantage of easy scalability.

For the organization under consideration, there are existing solutions for SaaS for completely out of the box solutions. The focus should be to consider PaaS for integrating the internal content (SAP) into cloud. IaaS should be considered for machine data management (Hadoop), as this is a new technical area in the organization. Pricing details for Oracle/MS SQL can be calculated using AWS calculator or manually as below:

The first year of three-year term rates offer higher discounts.

- Multiply the cost/h of the reserved memory * 720(per month 24*30).
- Add the storage rate cost $0.11 GB/month.
- Add the I/O cost $0.22 per one million requests.

4.9. Comparison

The assessment on key criteria clearly shows that no single storage can fulfil all requirements. The evaluation and trade off (Table 1) with respect to the key criteria need to be considered for selection of the relevant storage technology.

Table 1: Key criteria trade-off comparison table.

Criteria	Data	Evaluation	Trade-off
Storage	Structured Internal data	SAP HANA	High cost "in memory" appliance. Possible mitigation with Near Line Storage (NLS).
Storage	Structured External data	SQL	Master Data needs to be aligned with internal data.
Storage	Unstructured Internal/ External data	Hadoop	Not suitable for often used and high-value data.
Security	Structured Internal data	SAP HANA	No known trade-offs.
Security	Structured External data	SQL	No known trade-offs.
Security	Unstructured Internal/ External data	Hadoop	No out-of-the box security for access control, authentication. Requires add-ons for security.
Performance	Unstructured Internal/ external data	Hadoop	More suitable for batch processing, Data needs to be moved to HANA for high speed processing.
Performance	Structured Internal data	SAP HANA	No known trade-offs.
Performance	Structured External data	SQL	High performance depends on the cache limit.
Cost	Unstructured Internal/ External data	Hadoop	No known trade-offs.
Cost	Structured Internal data	SAP HANA	High cost solution. Mitigated via licensing options, NLS.
Cost	Structured External data	SQL	No known trade-offs.

4.9.1. Capabilities scorecard

The storage technologies has been compared on the capabilities analysed and the scores provided below in Table 2. The scoring ranges from one to five, with five being the best case. SAP HANA emerges as clear winner, except for the cost factor coming into picture. SQL and Oracle are close to each other, but SQL is a better option, due to low cost and ease of support. In case the data volume growth is high, this can be moved to HANA with dynamic data-tiring options.

Table 2: Capability comparison table for storage technologies.

Capability	SAP HANA	SQL	Oracle
Storage	4	3.5	3
Performance	4	3	3.5
Cost	3	4	3.5
Security	4	3.5	3.5
Big data integration	4	3.5	3.5

4.10. Illustration scenario

It is clear that we recognise that not all data are homogeneous and no single tool fits in all requirements. The DB applications shall work seamlessly with data in silos, whereas for analytics the key requirement is to use data across different sources. Consider a scenario, which requires data from two different storage technologies, the requirement (analytics) can be addressed as below. In the case with no consolidation, the complexity of merging the data becomes a user activity leading to risk of error prone incorrect decisions and lack of support for such applications (Figure 11).

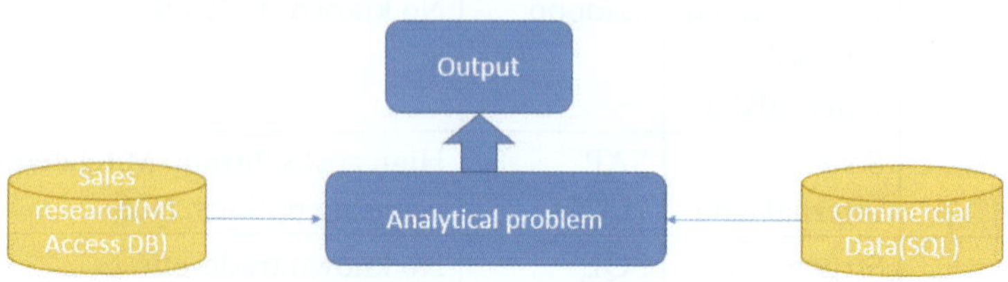

Figure 11: Analytics without consolidation of data.

In this scenario, the sources (sales research and commercial data) are external, low volume data. For storing such external data, SQL will be a better option as per Table 2, than HANA or Oracle. Being low volume, the queries are not expected to have major performance issues. Since there are no risks from security perspective in SQL, it becomes the choice for data consolidation. Pre-populating them for specific business scenarios shall ensure that user can directly start analysing the business problem and not preparing data with consolidation of data using the appropriate storage technology (Figure 12). Applying the capability scorecard above, SQL scores 17.5 on five capabilities or an average of 3.5 overall. However, big data and performance is not a major factor in this scenario and hence considering the rest (storage, cost, and security) the average moves up to 3.7, which can be considered as an optimal score.

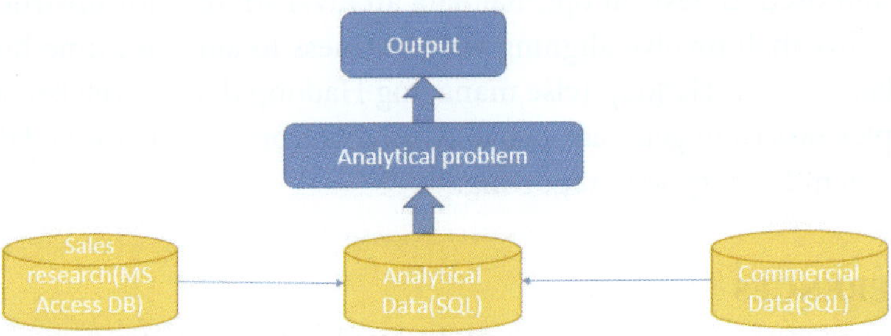

Figure 12: Analytics with consolidation of data.

5. DISCUSSION

The storage technologies for data management compared in this study enable effective analytics considering data with diverse characteristics. This shows that in memory DB of HANA clearly has an edge in terms of performance and in-built analytics library for advanced analytics. This is well aligned with the existing corporate setup and hence is a clear front-runner for the data reservoir. However, this requires strong business case to justify a very high cost of investment. SQL is suitable for handling relatively low/medium volumes of data, whereas Oracle has a high volume performance and high availability. Hence, in case of non-HANA scenario, Oracle stands out for high volume data and SQL for the low volume. Between Oracle and SQL, Oracle scores more in performance and robustness whereas SQL scores high in cost and ease of maintenance skill for the support staff. In all cases, Hadoop fits in as the source of unstructured data. Hence, the study enables decision makers to select the appropriate storage technology with respect to their data source and type of application it is expected to cater.

6. CONCLUSION AND FURTHER WORK

The study evaluated various storage technologies identified, e.g., SAP HANA, Oracle, SQL based on the factors such as storage, security, cost, performance, and support for big data which are key for effective analytics. As part of further work, if the decision is to go for HANA, more user cases need to be explored to provide additional opportunities that company can leverage in HANA to justify the high investment and not limit SAP HANA for effective storage of data (size and volume). With unstructured data growing at a massive rate, the rate of data growth needs to be monitored to have an optimal data archival strategy for unstructured data. This shall involve aligning with business to agree on time horizon for data to be in Hadoop (else managing Hadoop data as well becomes a complex task) and generate valuable insights from unstructured data and store them for corporate reporting.

REFERENCES

1. http://www.oracle.com/us/products/database/big-data-connectors/features/index.html
2. http://www.oracle.com/us/solutions/sap/nl23-db12c-imo-en-2209396.pdf
3. http://help.sap.com/hana/SAP_HANA_Master_Guide_en.pdf
4. http://www.microsoft.com/en-us/server-cloud/products/sql-server/Overview.aspx
5. https://aws.amazon.com/rds/pricing/
6. http://help.sap.com/hana/sap_hana_security_guide_en.pdf
7. http://docs.oracle.com/cd/B19306_01/network.102/b14266/preface.htm#i969250
8. https://msdn.microsoft.com/en-us/library/bb283235.aspx
9. http://sql2014.pl/docs/SQL_Server_2014_Licensing_Guide.pdf
10. http://www.orafaq.com/wiki/Oracle_licensing
11. http://www.microsoft.com/en-sg/download/details.aspx?id=27584
12. http://www.oracle.com/us/corporate/pricing/technology-price-list-070617.pdf

CHAPTER 6

Visualization Tools Assessment and Sustainability Analytics

HUANG Wenchang Alison

ABSTRACT

This project assessed visualization tools and the application of advanced analytics to sustainability data. In collaboration with Unilever's User Experience Team, this work had two main areas namely, the application of Business Intelligence and market research on visualization tools.

The paper also examines sustainability analytics, an improvement based on Unilever's footprint reporting. Advanced analytics was introduced to improve simple data visualization techniques. Moreover, Tableau dashboards provided end-to-end solutions for queries by the end-users in the company, thus delivering a significant advantage to this area of the business.

1. INTRODUCTION

1.1. Introduction of project

Unilever had a huge variety of tools and techniques to create visualizations and dashboards. Different end-users used different tools but there was no standard used for their application. Most of the employees relied heavily on spreadsheets for reporting, but due to well-known limitations they had to repeat the same process daily as a part of routine work. Hence, the objectives of the project were:

- To understand and demonstrate the more sophisticated visualizations available for reporting and analytical purposes and to understand 'what works well, and when'. If information and analytics specialists need to help different end-users create dashboards, which tools and techniques work best? The aim was to create a visualization tools decision-tree. Footprint reporting was used as an example to demonstrate that Tableau may be a useful visualization tool for dynamic dashboard construction.
- The outcomes were a) to improve the footprint dashboards built in Tableau; b) to introduce a new perspective with advanced analytics; c) improved Tableau dashboards; d) to integrate 'R' into Tableau visualization; c) to introduce data modeling into current analysis.

2. PROBLEM STATEMENT

2.1. Problem statement for visualization playbook

Unilever had a large array of tools and techniques as well as trained staff to produce visualizations and create dashboards but wanted to better understand which tool should be used for which problems. It was important to create standard guidelines to recommend the most appropriate visualizations to solve specific business questions. The skills required for this are a working knowledge of visualization tools such as Tableau and other software, a strong BI reporting tool experience and a good understanding of the use of BI in business operations.

Unilever owns licenses for many different BI and visualization tools; for example, Business Objects from SAP is widely used cross countries and departments. Others tools such as, Tableau, was only partially used by different countries or departments. To know how these tools perform in the market, it was important to understand the BI and visualization tools market. Hence market research for BI and visualization tools was performed.

In order to assess the suitability of different options tools, a market research

After gaining an understanding of the whole market, some specific visualization tools were assessed further. The tools selected were 'newer' and 'more niche', some of which were being developed by some start-ups.

To present the results, a tool decision-tree was built.

2.2. Problem statement for sustainability analytics

Unilever aspires to be an industry leader in corporate sustainability, modelling best practices that could be adopted the world over. As a product manufacturer, sustainability is not simply about using less fuel or water but the resources consumed during the entire product life-cycle, including the consumption by a consumer. Unilever embarked on this new initiative to define industry-specific metrics that would realistically standardize and quantify sustainability.

This paper focus on one of the nine areas of interest to the company: 'Reducing Environmental Impact: Waste'.

3. STATE OF THE ART

3.1. State of the art for visualization playbook

Understanding the range of different visualization tools that are available is important for any company using Business Intelligence (BI) or Business Analytics (BA) for its daily business operations.

Since most of the research related to this topic is very business-driven, it was difficult to find suitable academic literature reviews therefore, the findings quoted here are mainly from Gartner,[1] Forrester[2] and other online forums. Gartner and Forrester are two of the largest and most information and technology research companies. Most of the BI platform companies are the customers of Gartner (See Part 4.1)

1 Gartner, Inc. (NYSE: IT) is the world's leading information technology research and advisory company.

2 Forrester Research (Nasdaq: FORR) is an independent technology and market research company that provides advice on existing and potential impact of technology, to its clients and the public.

Figure 1 is a draft of a tools decision tree created with the results of the assessments made of the different BI tools used by the Unilever User Experience Team. This simple chart demonstrates the conclusive but informative result of the BI tools market.

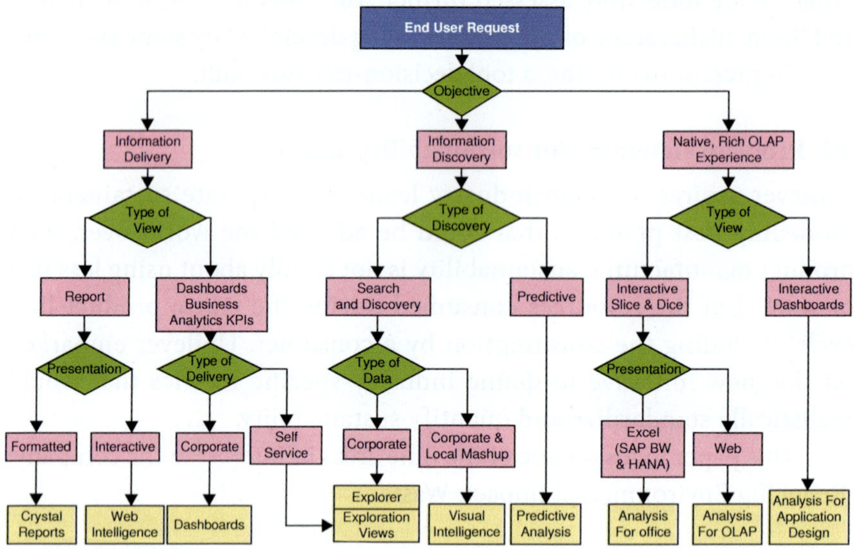

Figure 1: State of the art for project 03.

3.2. Project 01 sustainability analytics

Sustainability is a hot topic in all industries and especially new within the consumer goods industry. Unilever aspires to be at the forefront of it, modelling and leading best practices that the world could follow. However this also means that no examples from other companies can be taken as a reference. At the time when Unilever released the USLP (Unilever Sustainability Living Plan), no other company had measured across the value chain. However, there are signs that others such as Pepsi and Danone are starting to adopt these practices.

PepsiCo Inc.[3] is an American multinational food and beverage corporation with headquarters in Purchase, New York, United States. It has interests in the manufacturing, marketing, and distribution of grain-based snack foods, beverages, and other products. For Pepsi, environmental

3 http://www.pepsico.com/

sustainability means 'finding innovative ways to cut costs and minimize our impact on the environment through energy and water conservation as well as reduced use of packaging material'.[4] This mirrors the business realization of Unilever in sustainability related issues.

PepsiCo anticipated the need to take environmental stewardship to a whole new level at the start of the new millennium, recognizing that environmental sustainability was becoming a core component of sustainable performance.

It began to put in place the systems, processes and metrics needed to drive continuous improvement in energy and water conservation as well as greenhouse gas, packaging and waste reduction. PepsiCo also advanced innovations in packaging and sustainable agriculture, and improved performance in overall productivity and plant efficiency. From the sustainability report in 2013, it can be seen that Pepsi divided its focus of sustainability into energy, water, greenhouse gas, packaging and waste reduction; being more meticulous than the separation of 'waste, water and greenhouse gas' by Unilever.

Danone[5] is a multinational food-products corporation based in the 9th arrondissement of Paris. It has four business lines: Fresh Dairy products, Waters, Early Life Nutrition and Medical Nutrition. Danone's sustainability strategy is set out in 'A Sustainable Food Chain'. As Danone CEO Franck Riboud says in the editorial of the Sustainability Report in 2013, sustainable development is not a virtue or a good deed; it is 'business sense'. "We still firmly believe that for a food group like Danone, reducing our carbon footprint, securing sustainable farming supplies, managing water resources and innovating in recyclable packaging will increasingly contribute to building up competitive advantages".[6]

Figure 2: Summary of Danone's sustainability impact and responsibilities in business.

Figure 2 shows that the method of dividing a value chain in Danone is similar to Unilever (Refer Part 4.2), although Unilever produces a wider range of products besides food. Like Unilever, the numbers in Figure 2

4 http://www.pepsico.com/Purpose/Environmental-Sustainability

5 http://www.danone.com/en/

6 http://downtoearth.danone.com/2014/04/29/danones-2013-sustainability-report-is-available/

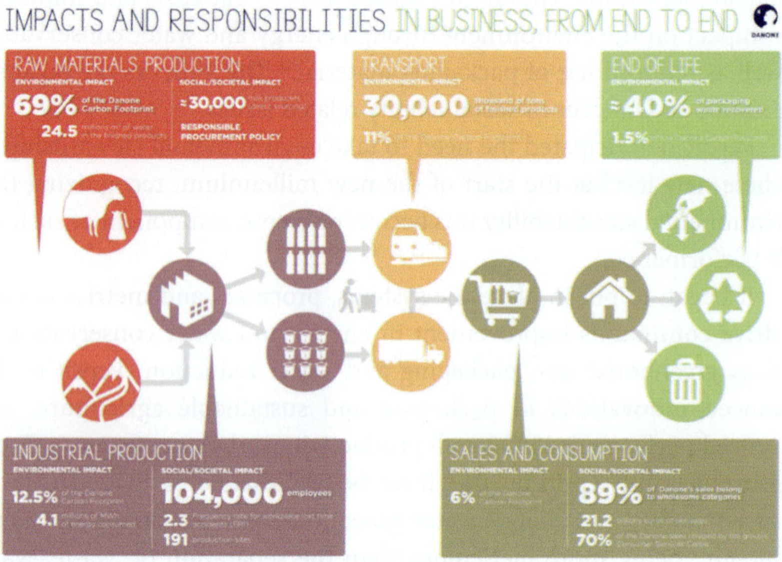

Figure 2: Impacts and responsibilities in business (Danone).

are based on results in 2013. Danone has committed to reducing its greenhouse gas emissions by 30 per cent in five years; a short-term target compared to Unilever's goals.

Having outlined the sustainability practices of PepsiCo and Danone, this papers will now examine the original definition of sustainability measures, metrics and calculations employed at Unilever.

3.2.1. Measure, metrics, and calculation

a) Unit of Core Measure: percentage (%)
   - i) Greenhouse gases (GHG): percentage of reduction of greenhouse gases per consumer use across the product lifecycle in 14 key countries across the product lifecycle.
   - ii) Water: percentage of reduction of water added to the product and water used per consumer use in 14 key countries across the product lifecycle.
   - iii) Waste: percentage of reduction of waste disposed per consumer use in 14 key countries across the product lifecycle.

b) Unit of Subsets Measures:
   - i) GHG: grams of CO_2 equivalents per consumer use

ii) Water: litres of water used per consumer use

iii) Waste: tonnes of waste disposed per consumer use

c) Environmental Metrics

In order to quantify the footprint, it is important to understand the metrics used in the calculations.

Unilever's Sustainability Living Plan (USLP) measures the environmental impact of production across a product's life cycle. There are different life cycles for GHG, Water and Waste e.g. there are three lifecycles in Waste: Primary Packaging, Secondary Packaging and Consumer Use.

i) GHG, water and waste footprints are calculated as 'per Consumer Use' (pCU).

ii) 'Non-Extrapolated Footprint (per Consumer Use)' is calculated based on clustered products. This is because data cannot be collected on all the products, so representative Stock Keeping Unit (SKU)s were analyzed.

iii) Extrapolated Footprint (per Consumer Use) is the extrapolated number based on 'Non-Extrapolated Footprint (pCU)' across the cluster, which uses the total product portfolio, i.e. including un-clustered products.

d) Calculation Description

Calculation formulas cannot be shown here due to confidentiality constraints.

GHG and Waste metrics were measured in 14 countries (Brazil, China, France, Germany, India, Indonesia, Italy, Mexico, Netherlands, Russia, South Africa, Turkey, UK, USA.), representing 85 per cent of global sales (2008). Countries were selected based on growth priority, sales, and specific issues to address.

As per a representative sample of SKU's, product clustering based on consumer habit, pack size, and format represents approximately 80 per cent of sales in top 14 countries.

Methodology peer-review was led by Life Cycle Analysis (LCA) experts and the approach was published in science conference and is awaiting publication.

3.2.2. Footprint reporting dashboard

One example of sustainability analytics is the footprint reporting undertaken by category champions who took charge of a category globally. In 2010, sustainability data was reported in 14 silo Excel spreadsheets. By 2015, when two years (2010 and 2013) data were available, Excel was unable to handle all the data. Hence, they turned to Information and Assistance (I&A) specialists for help in building the reports. Firstly, the I&A specialists combined all the necessary datasets into database systems, and then extracted the data to put into separate Excel spreadsheets. They then use these data to make a visualization in Tableau. The dashboards they built are shown in Figure 3 below:

In dashboard A, the three tables represent the waste per consumer use change ratio in 2013 compared with that in 2010 as show in Table A1:

a) All the bars are green, which represent a decrease in waste pCU in 2013 compared with 2010.
b) The longer the bar and the darker the colour shows greater change in 2013 compared with 2010.

Hence, Category E performed best in 2013 from the perspective of decreasing in waste produced per consumer use.

In dashboard B (shown in Figure 4), there are four Tables: Table B1 and Table B3 represent the performance of different categories; Tables B2 and B4 indicate the performance of different countries.

From Table B1, the absolute value of waste pCU in 2013 by category is provided. Table B3 shows the share of Total Waste by category in 2013, and is separated by country. as per Table B2, shows the information of the share of Waste by country while Table B4 shows share of Total Waste for different countries.

In dashboard C (Figure 5) there are four tables. Table C1 and C2 represent the Top 10 Global Trading Units (GTUs) that produced the most waste pCU in 2013; Table C3 and Table C4 show the GTUs that increase or decrease the most from the perspective of waste change.

In dashboard D1 (Figure 6) there are three tables. Table D1 is a detection of waste outlier; Table D2 and Table D3 are Waste details and GTU details respectively. However, the detection of outlier in D1 suggests a random-walk requiring more advanced analytics or theoretically proved algorithms.

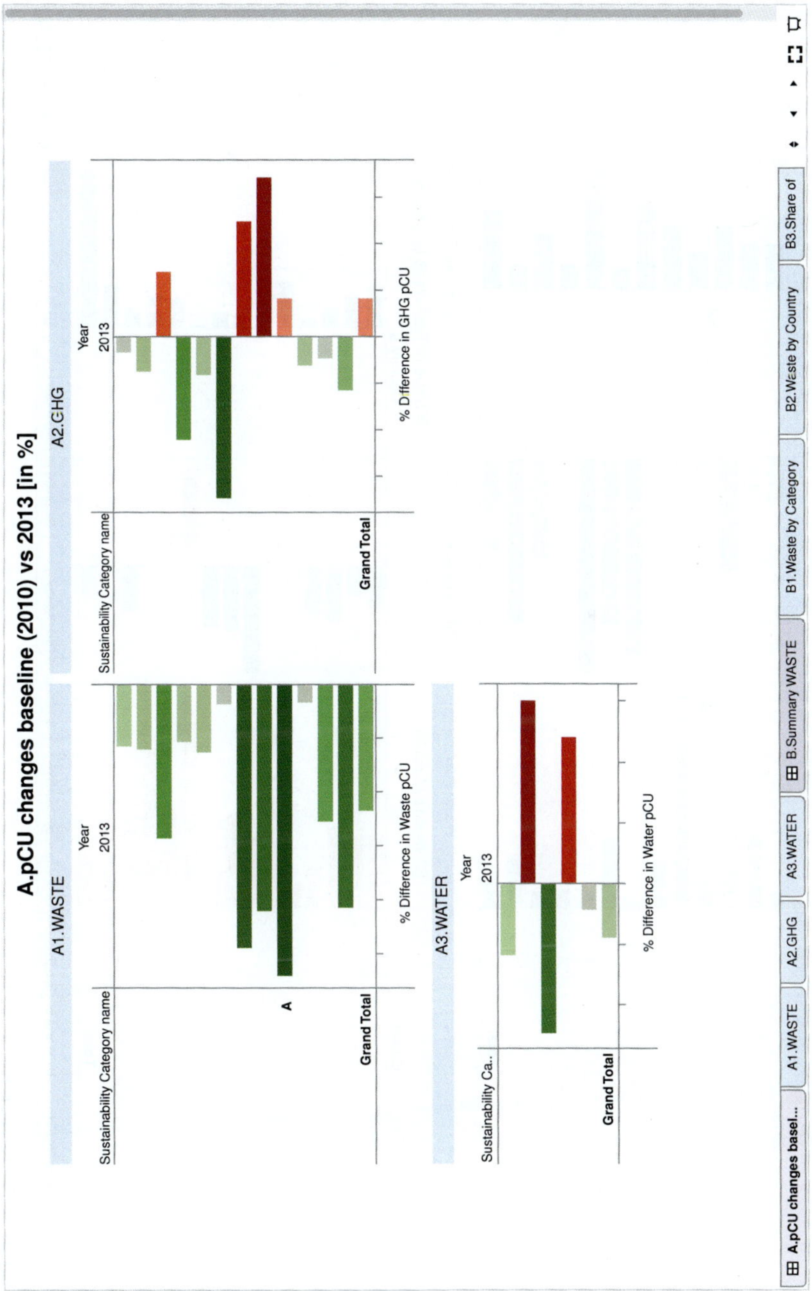

Figure 3: Dashboard A.

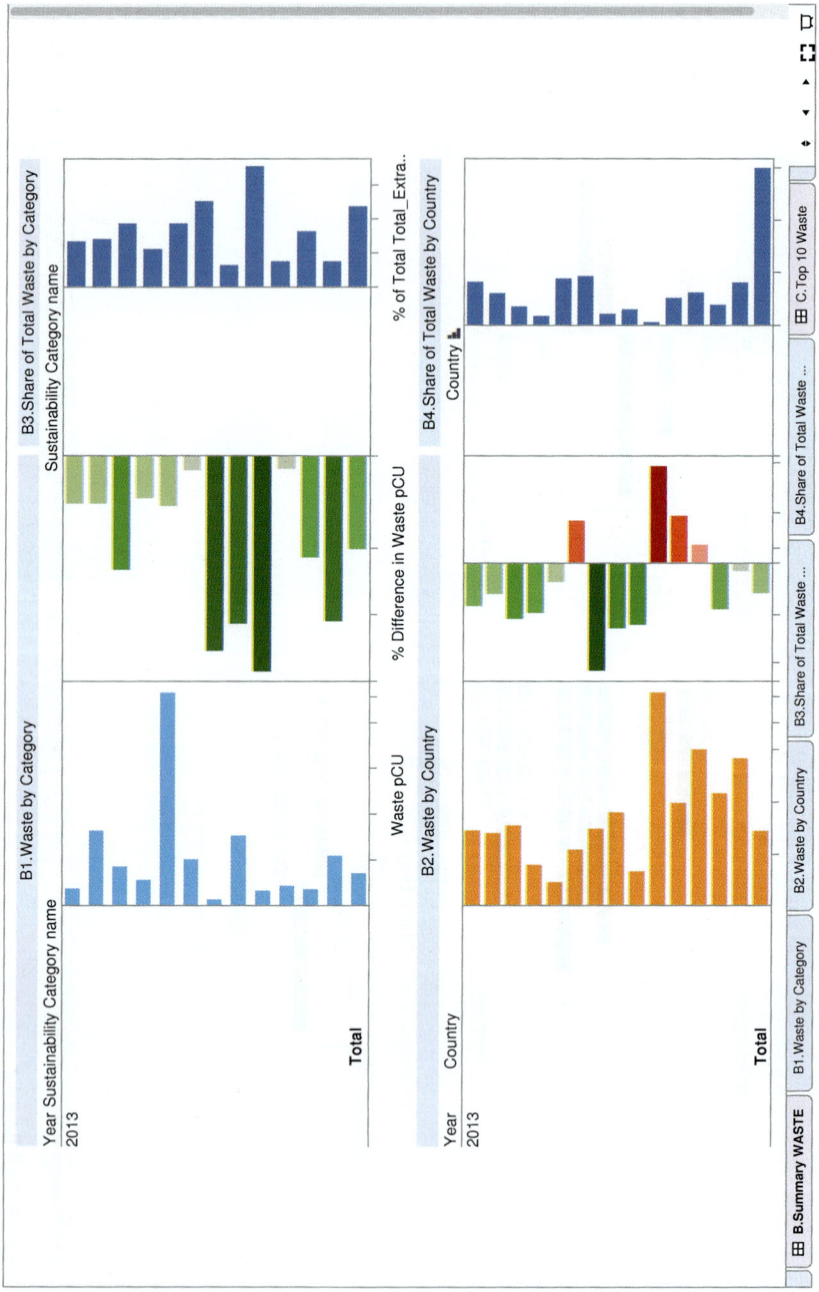

Figure 4: Dashboard B.

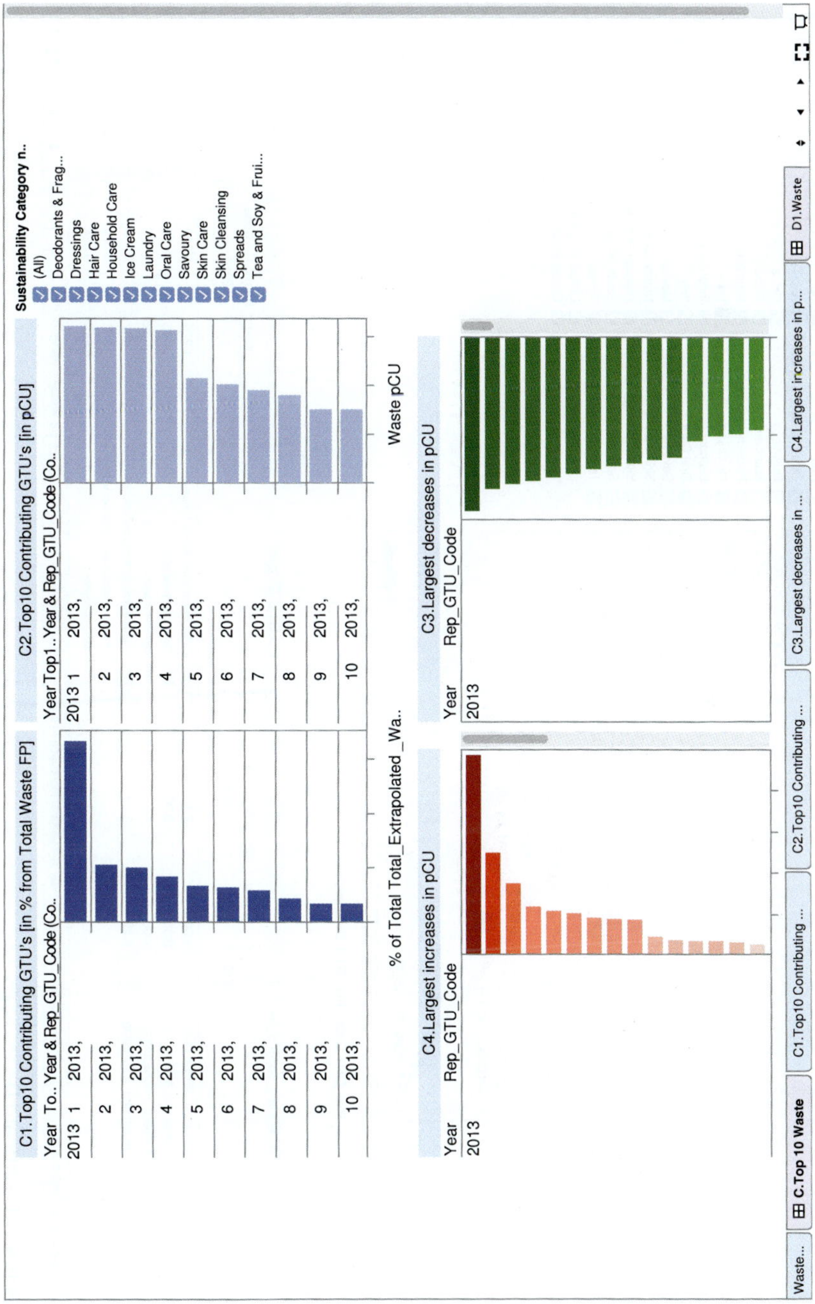

Figure 5: Dashboard C.

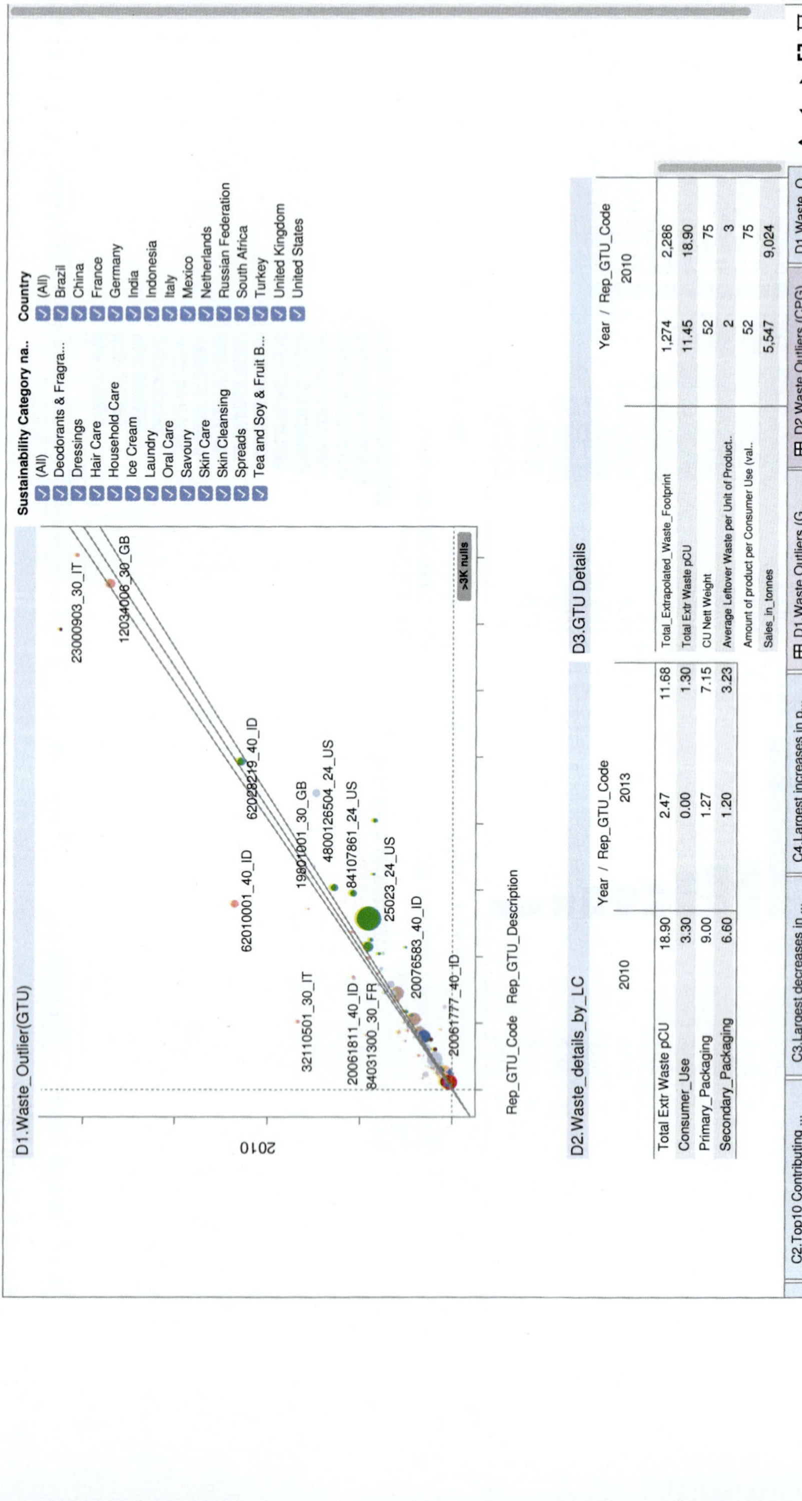

Figure 6: Dashboard D.

4. SOLUTION: DESCRIPTION OF APPROACH

4.1. Project 03 visualization playbook

This part of the project was quite theoretical and the results quoted below are mostly from Gartner,[7] Forrester[8] and some other online forums.

4.1.1. BI and analytics market overview

Gartner defines advanced analytics as the analysis of all kinds of data using sophisticated quantitative methods (e.g. statistics, descriptive and predictive data mining, simulation and optimization) to produce insights that traditional approaches to BI – such as query and reporting – are unlikely to discover.[1]

Most organizations adopt advanced analytics through the use of advanced analytics platforms that provide a full suite of tools for use by data scientists. All modern BI platforms support and promote a single version of actual figures, and minimize operational risk. However, these capabilities carry a hefty price tag of complexity, rigidity, and inflexibility which mean they can be slow to respond to constantly changing customer and business requirements.[2] Moreover, more businesses require the end-users to be 'self-serviced', which in turn requires the use of BI tools and analytics without a very steep learning curve.

The overall positioning of different platforms/tools can be seen in Figure 7. The Magic Quadrant graph was published in February 2015.

Some points to take note:

1) The assessment of different BI and analytics platforms/ tools were performed according to the following 13 critical capabilities:

 i) Enable:

  - Business User Data Mashup and Modeling Internal Platform Integration
  - BI Platform Administration
  - Metadata Management

7 Gartner, Inc. (NYSE: IT) is the world's leading information technology research and advisory company.

8 Forrester Research (Nasdaq: FORR) is an independent technology and market research company that provides advice on existing and potential impact of technology, to its clients and the public.

Figure 7: Magic quadrant for business intelligence and analytics platforms.

- Cloud Deployment
- Development and Integration

ii) Produce:

- Free-from Interactive Exploration
- Analytic Dashboards and Content
- IT-Developed Reporting and Dashboards
- Traditional Styles of Analysis

iii) Consume:

- Mobile
- Collaboration and Social Integration
- Embedded BI

2) Based on the above assessment measures, the positioning of different BI and analytics tools are listed as:
    i) Nine leading vendors (high completeness of vision and high ability to execute): *SAS, SAP, IBM, Oracle, MicroStrategy, Information Builders, Microsoft, Qlik, Tableau*
    ii) Two challengers (low completeness of vision but high ability to execute): *Logi Analytics, Birst*
    iii) Three visionaries (high completeness of vision but low ability to execute): *Tibco Software, Alteryx, Panorama Software*
    iv) 10 niche players (both low completeness of vision and ability to execute): *GoodData, Prognoz, Pyramid Analytics, Targit, Board International, Yellowfin, Pentaho, Datawatch, Salient Management Company, OpenText (Actuate)*

This paper focused on six different tools, listed above:

Table 2: Competitive analysis of features and functions for different products.

	Tableau	Microsoft Power BI	QlikView	MicroStrategy	SAP BusinessObjects	Enterprise BI Server
Vendor	Tableau	Microsoft	Qlik	Microstrategy	SAP	SAS
Platform	Online, On promise, Mobile					
Analysis Features						
Ad Hoc Analysis	✓	✓	✓	✓	✗	✓
Issue Indicators	✗	✗	✗	✓	✗	✗
Online Analytical Processing (OLAP)	✓	✓	✓	✓	✗	✓
Predictive Analysis	✓	✓	✓	✓	✓	✗
Profit Analysis	✗	✗	✗	✗	✗	✗
Trend Indicators	✓	✗	✗	✓	✓	✗
User Friendly Interface	✓	✓	✓	✓	✓	✗
Reporting Features						
Ad Hoc Reorting	✓	✓	✓	✓	✓	✓
Automatic Scheduled Reporting	✓	✓	✗	✓	✓	✗
Customizable Dashboard	✓	✓	✓	✓	✓	✓
Customizble Features	✗	✗	✓	✗	✓	✗
Dashboard	✓	✓	✓	✓	✓	✓
Financial Forecast/Budgeting	✓	✗	✗	✗	✗	✗
Graphic Benchmark Tools	✓	✓	✗	✗	✗	✗
Multiple Languages	✓	✗	✗	✗	✗	✗
Performance Measurements	✗	✓	✗	✓	✓	✗
Support Features						
Email	✓	✓	✗	✓	✓	✓
In Person Training	✓	✓	✓	✓	✗	✓
Online Chat	✓	✗	✓	✓	✓	✓
Phone	✓	✓	✓	✓	✓	✓
Tutorials	✓	✓	✗	✓	✓	✓
FAQ	✗	✓	✗	✓	✓	✓

4.1.2. Tools decision trees & niche tools capability assessment

In addition, Unilever wanted to improve its visualization tools and build better visualization dashboards.

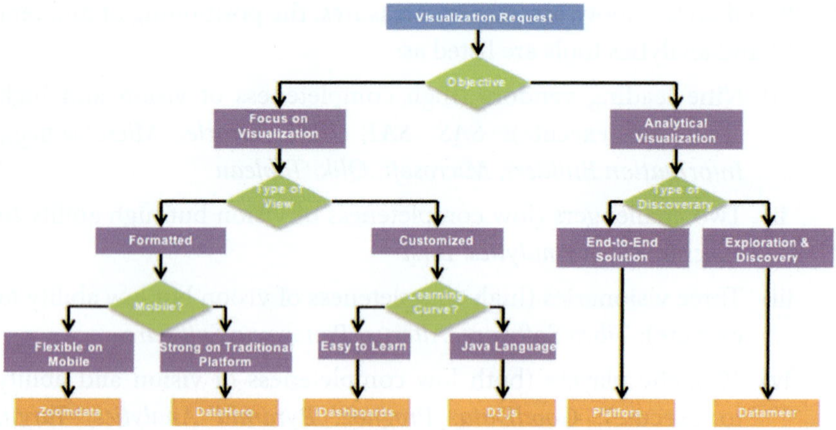

Figure 8: Visualization tools decision trees.

The above chart is the visualization tools decision tree. Depending on the objective of using the visualization, the choice of the platform varies. This can be summarized as follows:

Type of view	Choice of visualization platform
formatted form that can be flexible on mobile	Zoomdata
formatted form but very strong on desktop	DataHero
customized; very easy to learn	iDashboard
customized; steep learning curve, but strong in customization	D3.js
visualize the results from analytics; can answer end-to-end questions directly	Platfora
visualizations during the process of exploration and discovery	Datameer

Some background information on the different visualization platforms used

a) Platfora[9]

The company was founded in 2010, based in San Mateo, CA.

The benefits of using Platfora are: (a) No. one big data analytics platform native on Hadoop. (b) End-to-end platform built for multi-structured data. (c) Self-service, iterative interactive and fast. It is a promising tool to explore as Platfora was selected by Gartner as a 2015 'cool vendor' in big data; Enterprise Strategy Group rates Platfora as a top End-to-End big data discovery. Check where this is from. Looks like blurb from their website, if so, quote properly.

b) DataHero[10]

The company was founded in 2011, based in San Francisco, US. DataHero is a self-service cloud data visualization tool. The benefits of DataHero are: (a) it brings design to the enterprise and emphasis on user-interface (b) Meets demand for ad-hoc data analysis. Many famous bloggers in data visualization domain chose it. The trial version of DataHero is very user-friendly and design-driven; is very easy for first-time users to download and use.

c) Zoomdata[11]

The company was founded in 2012 and is based in Reston, Virginia. Zoomdata is a visualization and analytics platform that: "*Take streaming data, an array of visualizations and a user experience designed for touch screens*". The advantages of Zoomdata is that it is fast and can sharpen billions of records in seconds. It is designed for mobile and 'touch' first and is a pioneer in the area of multi-platform visualization.

d) Datameer[12]

Datameer was founded in 2009 and is based in California. Datameer is a promising startup industry as many of the workers came from Hadoop. As well as having strong end-to-end analytics techniques that support 55 sources, it can also integrate with Tableau. There is a small function 'flip sheet', which is very much like the data exploration

9 https://www.youtube.com/watch?v=4LkKqBXTl40
10 https://datahero.com/
11 http://www.zoomdata.com/en_us
12 https://www.youtube.com/watch?v=lECX8nbpqIU

function in SPSS Modeler. From the perspective of data modeling, this is one of the best ways to have an overall idea of how the data is distributed and correlated.

e) iDashboards[13]

iDashboards was founded in 2003 in Troy, Michigan. It is a pioneer in the data visualization space and recognized for being simple and easy-to-use. The User Interface (UI) is not particularly intuitive but the overall concept is simple and focused as a visualization dashboard. Even for users not familiar with Excel, with simple instructions given, they can quickly master iDashboards.

f) D3.js[14]

D3.js is a JavaScript library for manipulating documents based on data. D3 helps to bring data to life using HTML, SVG, and CSS D3's emphasis on web standards gives the full capabilities of modern browsers without being bound to a proprietary framework, combining powerful visualization components and a data-driven approach to DOM manipulation.[15] The advantages for selecting D3 are: (a) Good Application Program Interface (API) documentation with examples and support via forums (b) performs complicated math operations (c) supports all advanced browsers. The disadvantages are: (a) difficult to learn (b) uses SVG and not canvas, so cannot support billions of data points.

After assessing the tools listed above, Tableau is the one that is most comprehensive having dynamic dashboard building capabilities and integrating with other analytics tools and it is easier to use compared to the others.

4.2. Project 01 sustainability analytics

4.2.1. USLP background information gathering

Unilever has a visible and active strategy on sustainability, which is to "make sustainable living commonplace". The Unilever Sustainability Living Plan (USLP) has an ambitious vision – "To double the size of the

13 http://gallery.idashboards.com/preview/?guestuser=webretail
14 https://github.com/mbostock/d3/wiki/Gallery
15 http://d3js.org

business, whilst reducing our environmental footprint and increasing our positive social impact". The company aims to achieve social and environmental ambitions through the USLP that identified areas of opportunity for brand-led growth, cost savings and future profit.

Launched in 2010, the USLP is a blueprint for sustainable growth. It is a strategic response to the challenges that Unilever faces in doing business in an uncertain and volatile world. The USLP is helping to drive profitable growth for brands, save costs and fuel innovation. The USLP sets out three key goals. Underpinning these goals are nine commitments with targets spanning the social, environmental and economic performance. For each target, there are established objective measurement techniques, including appropriate estimates and assumptions that are listed below:

i) Improving health and well-being: By 2020, Unilever aspires to help more than a billion people take action to improve their health and well-being.
   - Health and hygiene
   - Improving nutrition

ii) Reducing Environmental Impact: By 2020, Unilever's goal is to halve the environmental footprint of the production and use of their products
   - Greenhouse gases
   - Water
   - Waste
   - Sustainability sourcing

iii) Enhancing Livelihoods: By 2020, Unilever aims to enhance the livelihoods of millions of people through:
   - Fairness in the workplace
   - Opportunities for women
   - Inclusive business

Unilever's goal is to halve the environmental footprint of the making and use of their products as the business grows. Hence, the important high-level metric here is footprint. And the construction of Footprint is outlined below:

The environmental footprint calculation can be divided into three different areas: waste, water and greenhouse gas.

i) Waste Footprint:

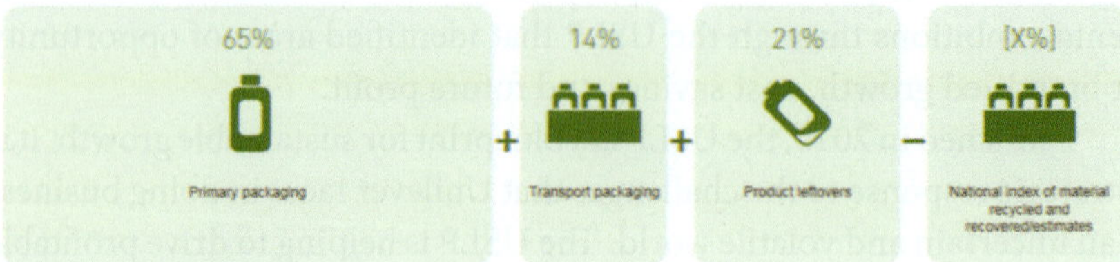

Figure 9: Waste footprint construction.

ii) Water Footprint:

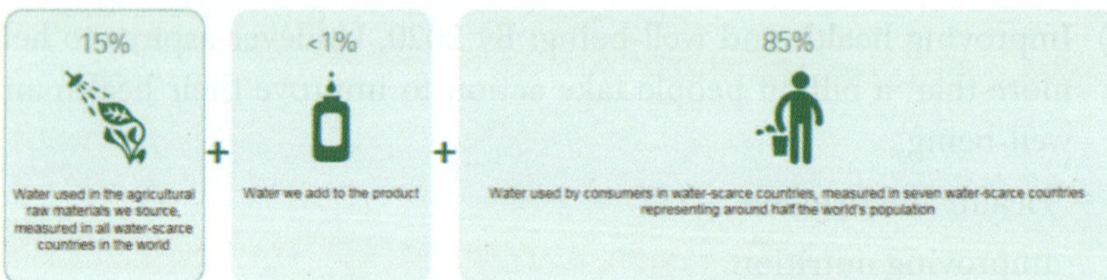

Figure 10: Water footprint construction.

iii) Green House Gas Footprint:

Figure 11: Green house gas footprint construction.

4.2.2. Footprint analytics and dashboard building

One of the first problems experienced with the footprint reporting dashboard was that it did not tell a story. How could end-users with little experience or knowledge of Tableau understand the situation, find and solve problems? Hence, the project required a diagnostic problem solving system/application as well as a reporting dashboard.

The following process helps to understand how to use this Footprint Diagnose System:

A story is made in Tableau and the interface is shown in Figure 12:

With name 'Footprint Diagnose System' on left top corner of each page, the workflow is constructed with six steps. Each page represents a step, with filter area, table area, and instruction area.

Let's first look at the workflow construction as an example:

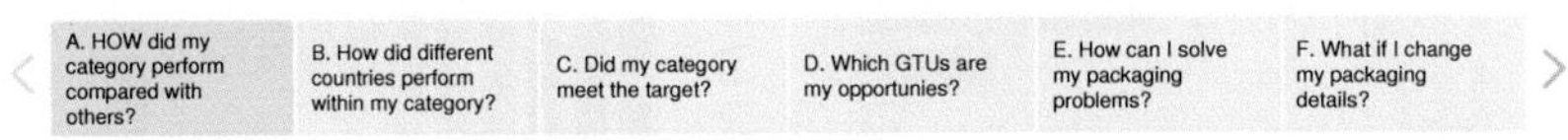

A category manager who is responsible for Category E globally can follow the six stage workflow to first understand the overall situation i.e. 'How did category E perform compared with other categories?' and 'How did different countries perform within my category?'

It is then possible to check whether a category met its specific targets. In order to dive deep into each single Global Treading Unit (GTU) go to workflow D 'Which GTUs are my opportunity?' This step will show which products and which lifecycles of the product caused the increase of waste pCU. Packaging details as lifecycle for waste is: Consumer Use, Primary Packaging and Secondary Packaging can also be examined.

The final step is to perform a "What-if?" simulation that can give the predicted value of waste pCU for the next year if the packaging details are changed. The whole process is an end-to-end user experience, which is easy to use and efficient in problem-solving.

Workflow A, compares performance against categories. To do this

- Step 1 Select your own category.
- Step 2 How did it perform in 2013? (Table A1)
- Step 3 How did it perform in 2013 compared with in 2010? (Table A2).

After selecting my Category E, look at Table A1.

The blue bars represent the share of total sales and the orange bars represent the share of total waste. The reason for putting the share of sales together with share of waste is inspired by the previous footprint dashboard B – it does not make sense to only look at the share of total waste to gauge whether the category performed well or not.

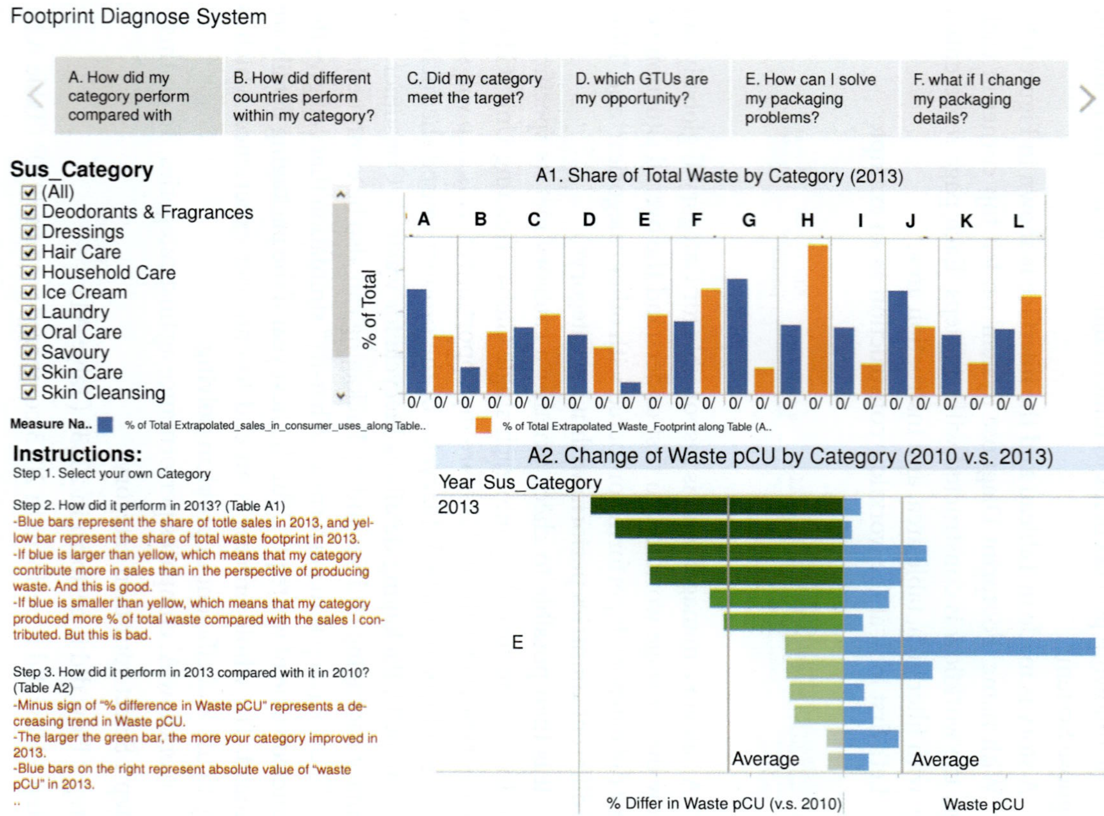

Figure 12: Footprint diagnose system interface.

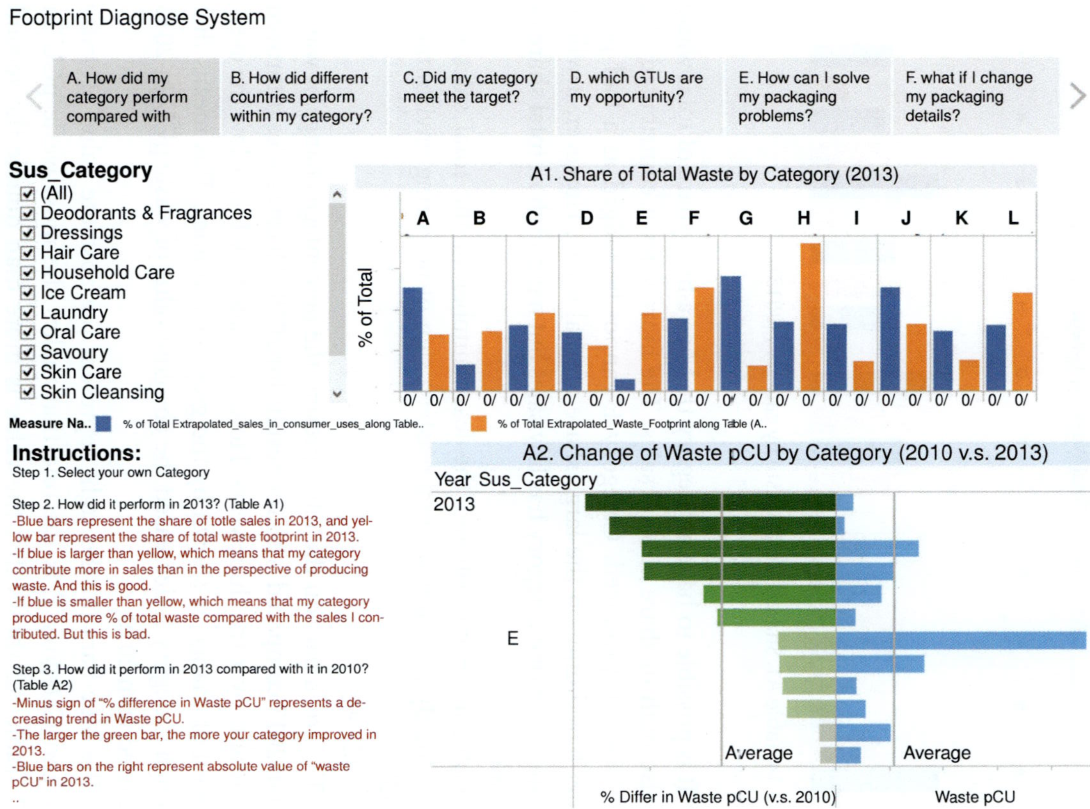

Figure 13: Footprint diagnose system dashboard A.

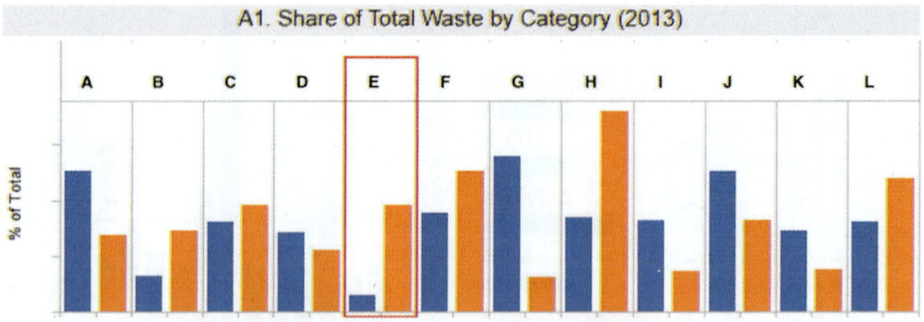

Figure 14: Table A1. Share of total waste by category (2013).

It is possible to have a category that has a high share of total waste but also high in share of total sales. The more sales it contributed, the more waste it produced. Category E cannot be judged as a bad performer based only on the large share of total waste. However, it will is an issue when one category has low sales but has a high in total share of total waste.

Category E contributed the least number to the total sales but scored highly in shares of total waste; a sign of not being environment friendly.

Table A2

The green bars on the left represent the percentage change of waste pCU in 2013 compared with the results for 2010. All categories improved their results over the three years. However, Category E is below the average level of change as shown by the grey vertical lines. This means that although Category E decreased the absolute value of waste pCU in 2013 compared with 2010,

The blue bars on the right represent the absolute value of waste pCU and Category E is the one that makes the most waste pCU in 2013. Table A2 shows that the value is more than double the second ranked category, highlighting an urgent need to improve the results for Category E.

Workflow B looks at how countries compare within a category.

- Step 1 Select your own Category.
- Step 2 How did it perform in 2013 in different countries? (Table B1)
- Step 3 How did the country perform in 2013 compared with in 2010? (Table B2)

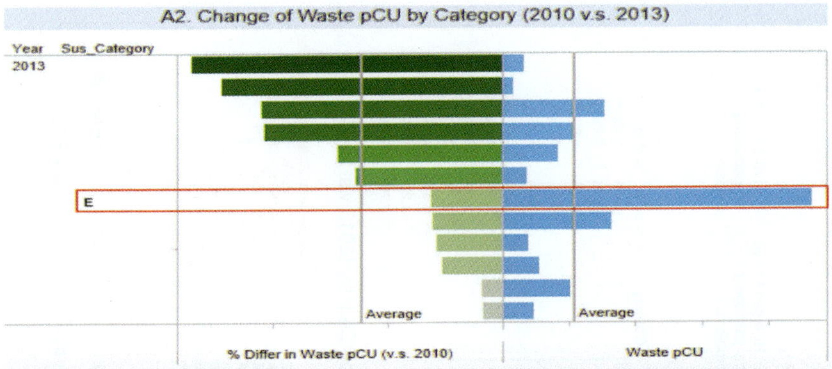

Figure 15: Table A2. Change of waste pCU by category (2010 v.s. 2013).

Besides the traditional filtering, an interactive map was added to act as a filter. By clicking on an area of the map, the corresponding share of total waste, share of total sales, change of waste pCU in 2013 and the absolute value of waste pCU can be shown for this single country. In addition, the color on the map represents the share of total waste by country in 2013; the darker the color, the larger the share.

Selecting Category E from the filter area shows the share of total waste and total sales for all the countries in Sub category in Table B1. Two shares here are fair enough as the number of share of total sales and share of total waste are very close; which means that there are few outliers from the perspective of country.

Table B2 shows the change in 2013 compared with 2010. However, it can be seen that there are countries that experienced increase of waste pCU in 2013 - an urgent issue compared with a large absolute value of waste pCU as this shows an increasing but a "should not happen" situation.

After manipulating the data by country, it is then possible to examine each product for detailed analysis. For example, selecting workflow C would answer the question "Did this category meet its target?"

To use the dashboard:

- Step 1 Select a category.
- Step 2 Set the "Target – Footprint Range" at 75. Compare the size of the box plots in 2010 and 2013 in the category.
- Step 3 Change the "Target – Footprint Range" according to the target for the category, and then select "Outlier Detection" to separate products into "In the range" (meet the target") and "Outliers" (do not meet the target).

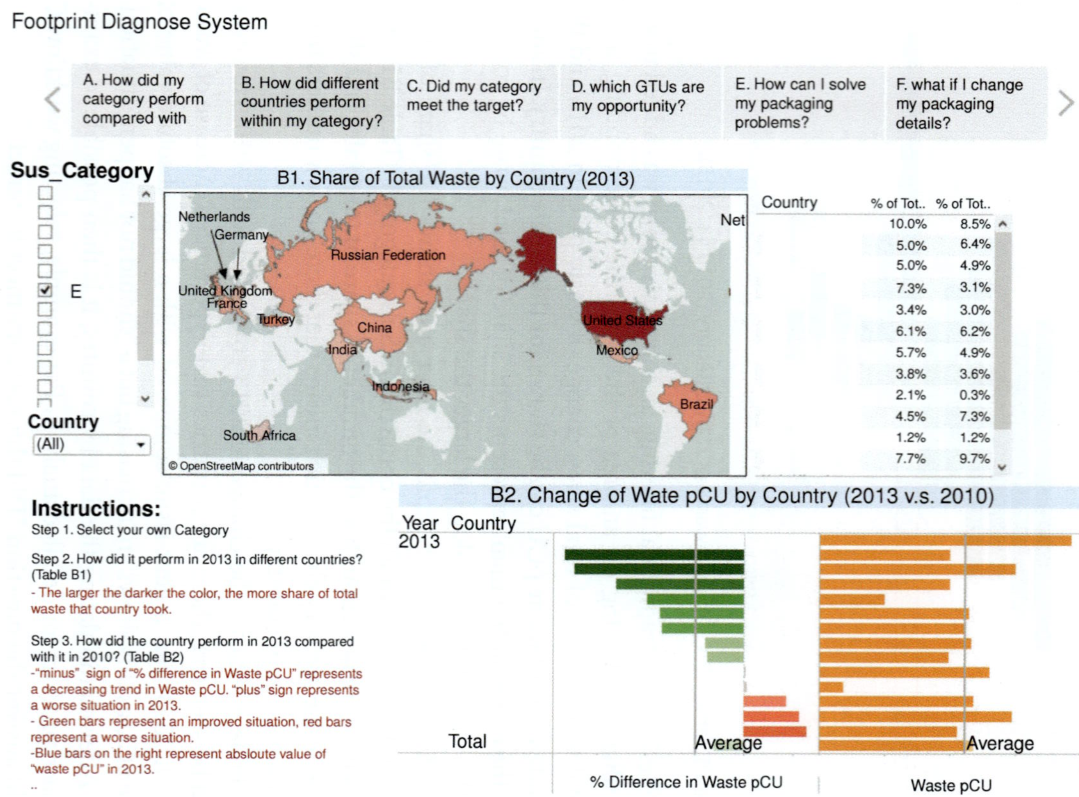

Figure 16: Footprint diagnose system dashboard B.

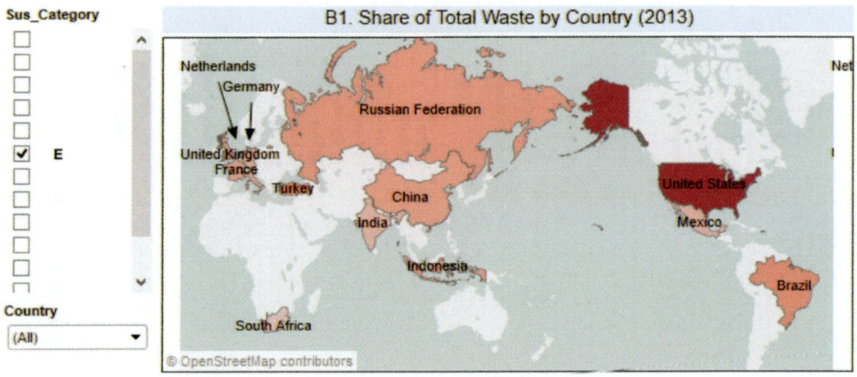

Figure 17: Table B1. Share of total waste by country (2013).

This dashboard is built based on the algorithm of boxplot, which is a good way of showing the distribution of the whole dataset, especially when there are many categorical data with sufficient but not too much data points.

Each dot on the graph represents a unique product, and the box represents the products that produced waste in the majority of the waste range. All dots on the right side of the black vertical line are treated as "outliers" which are not the majority. Each color represents a country.

Then change the "Target – Footprint Range" in the filter area on the right, and the size of the box will change accordingly. Click "In the Range" in "Outlier Detection", to only see all the products that meet the target for Category E set previously.

Clicking "Outliers" will show all the products that did not meet the target of the waste i.e. produced more waste than the target.

For more information in the boxplot for example to detect which product/ GTU is the "outlier" in 2013, put the mouse on the dot and details will be shown.

During the process of information gathering, the boxplot was a little difficult for business users to read / understand.

Boxplots are used to better understand how values are spaced out in different sets of data. To understand the method behind constructing a boxplot, imagine a set of values that are spaced out along a number line.

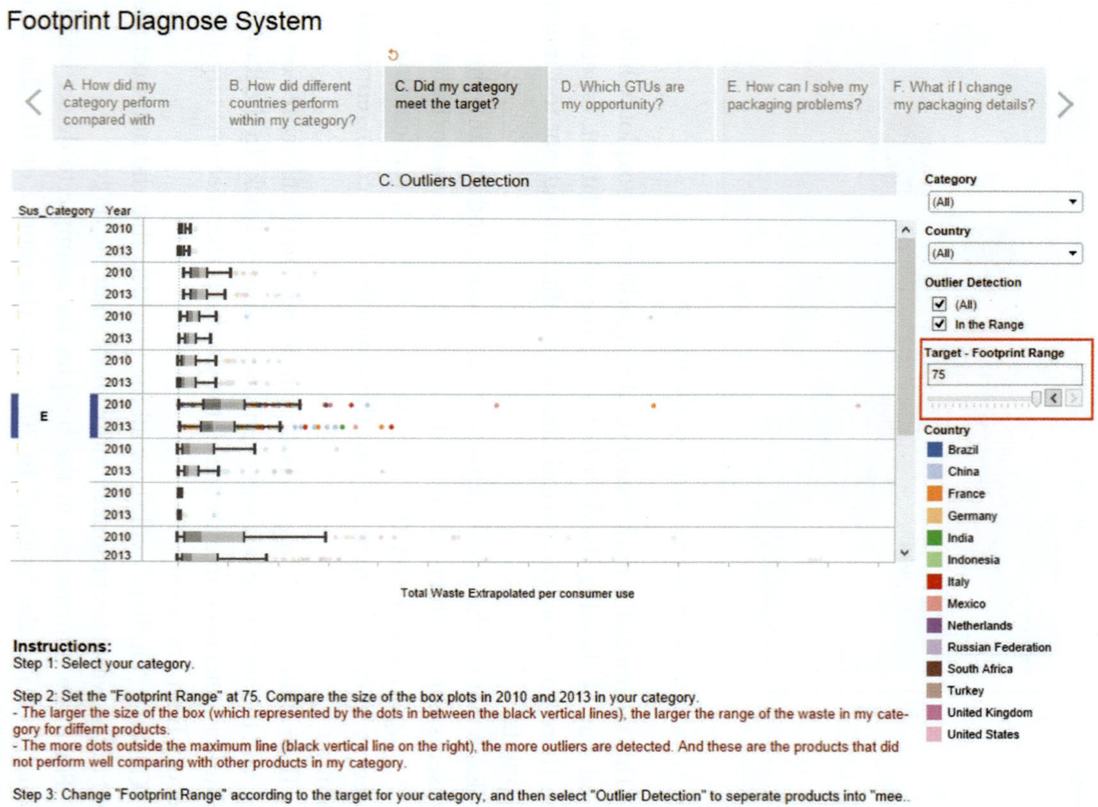

Figure 18: Footprint diagnose system dashboard C.

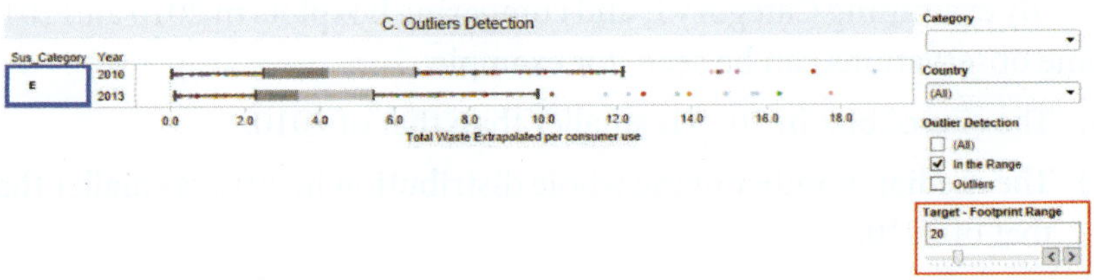

Figure 19: Outliers detection 1.

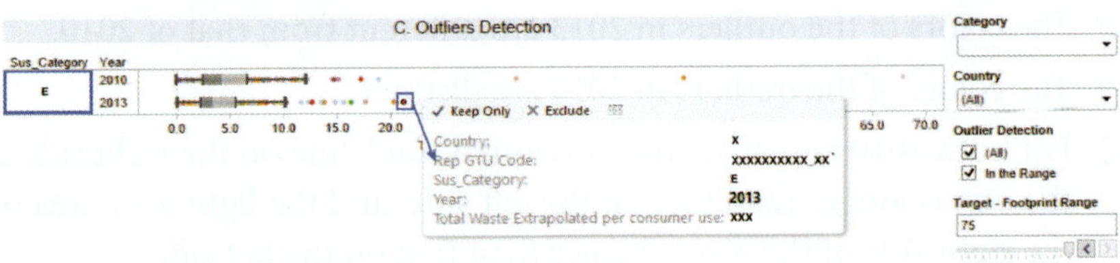

Figure 20: Outlier detection 2.

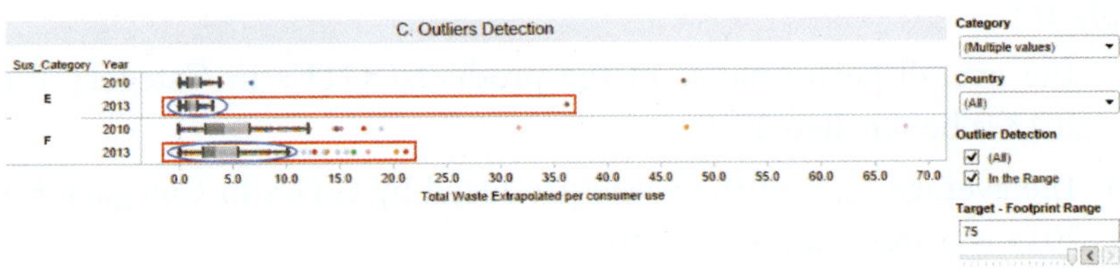

Figure 21: Outliers detection 3.

First, draw a line at the median of the data set — the values in the set that divides it evenly in half, with an equal number of points smaller and larger. If there is an even number of points in the dataset (as in the example below), the median is halfway between the two central points.

Next, divide each half of the dataset in half again, dividing it into four even sets of points. These four sections are called quartiles. The leftmost line marksQ1, the first quartile, while the rightmost line marks Q3 or the third quartile (the median can also be called Q2). Every boxplot has lines at Q1, the median, and Q3. The other major feature of a boxplot is its whiskers.

Usually, boxplots are used to compare multiple different series of data, especially when data is broken up by category. Some examples of data sets to compare are.

Let's use Figure 20 as an example to illustrate how to read a boxplot.

By examining Category F, and comparing boxplots in 2010 and 2013, some observations can be seen, for example

i) The size of box in 2013 is smaller than that of 2010.
ii) The median number of the whole distribution in 2013 is smaller than that of 2010.
iii) There are more outliers (i.e., dots on the right of the black vertical line) in 2013 than that of 2010.
iv) The colors of the outliers in 2013 are different from that of 2010.
v) The colors of the outliers in 2013 are distinct.
vi) For both 2010 and 2013, the horizontal black line on the right side of the box is longer than that on the left side, and the light grey area on the right side of the box is bigger than that on the left side.

The facts and insights drawn from these observations correspondingly are:

i) The overall performance of the products/ GTUs in Category F in 2013 is better than 2010.
ii) The average level of the waste produced by GTUs in Category F in 2013 is better than that of 2010.
iii) Although the overall situation in 2013 is better than that of 2010, there are comparatively more products / GTUs in 2013 than in 2010. This may be because products/ GTUs performing well in 2013 are much better than those which performed badly. Hence the overall level was brought up by those products/GTUs which performed well.
iv) As the color of the dots represents different countries, if the colors are different, it means that the products/ GTUs that performed badly in 2013 are different from those in 2010.
v) As different colors represent different countries, this means that all these outliers belong to different countries. There is no single country with many products taken as outliers, but each country has one or two products that is out of the range of majority waste pCU produced.
vi) A right-skewed distributed boxplot represents the value on the upper side (from median to maximum value) dominating the whole distribution. This means that the waste produced by the products/ GTUs on the right side of the boxplot has a larger impact on the

whole category. If there is a decrease in the waste pCU produced by these products/ GTUs, the overall situation of this category will improve significantly.

If Category E and Category F are compared together (year 2013), there are more observations:

i) The size of box for Category F is much bigger than that of Category E. (Marked with blue cycle on the graph)
ii) The whole range (i.e. with all products/ GTUs considered, including outliers) of Category F is smaller than Category E. (Marked with red rectangle on the graph.) There are more outliers (i.e. dots on the right of the black vertical line) for Category F than that of Category E.

Correspondingly, the facts and insights are:

i) The overall waste pCU produced by Category F is larger than that of Category E, for the size of the box represents the distribution of the majority.
ii) There are more products "out of control" (i.e. not in the range of the majority) in Category F than that in Category E. This means that the products/ GTUs in Category E are more unified and concentrated than that of Category F. This is also a sign that from the perspective of waste, Category E is comparatively easier to manage than that of Category F.

The above are some different understanding of the boxplots.

In workflow D, you would want to know how products/ GTUs in your category perform in detail, and which GTUs did not perform well and can improve further.

Follow the "Instructions":

- Step 1: Select your category.
- Step 2: Table D1 will show you the products that produced much more in waste in 2013 compared with 2010.
- Step 3: Select a single product that you want to understand more (i.e. a product that did not perform well in 2013).
- Step 4: Find which lifecycle went wrong for the product you selected in Table D2. "Waste Details by Lifecycle" are given".

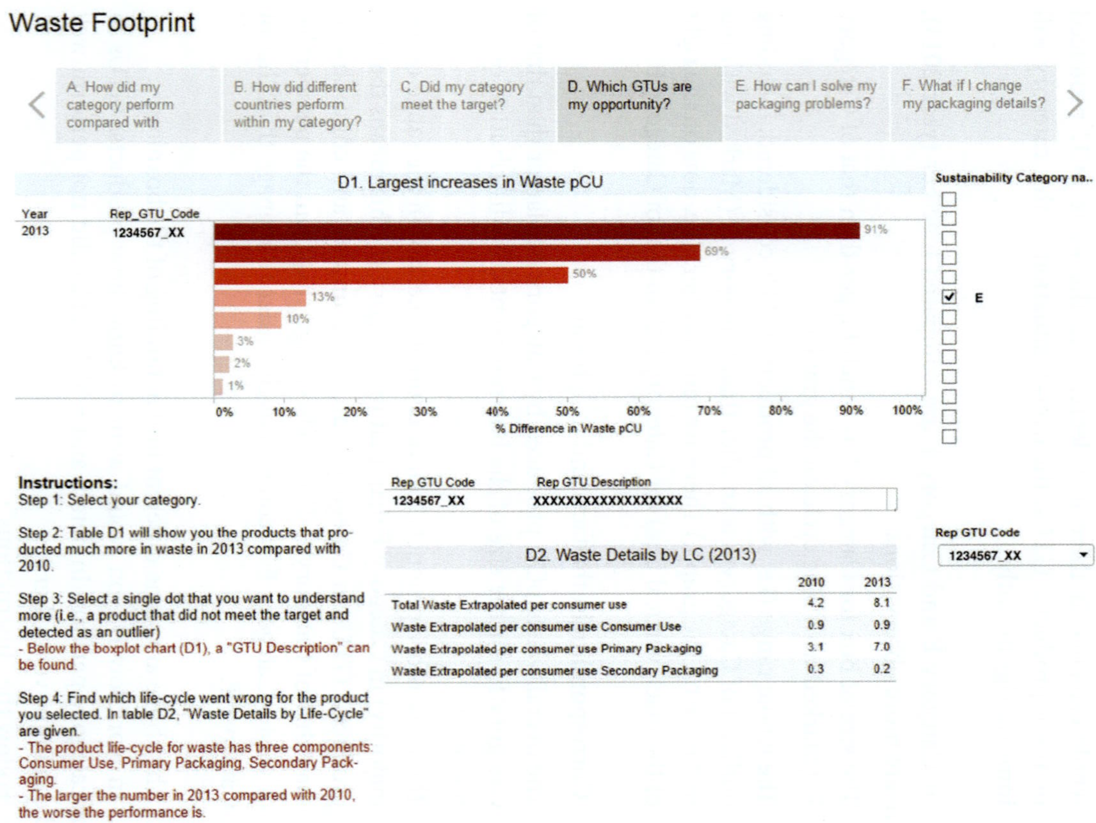

Figure 22: Footprint diagnose system dashboard D.

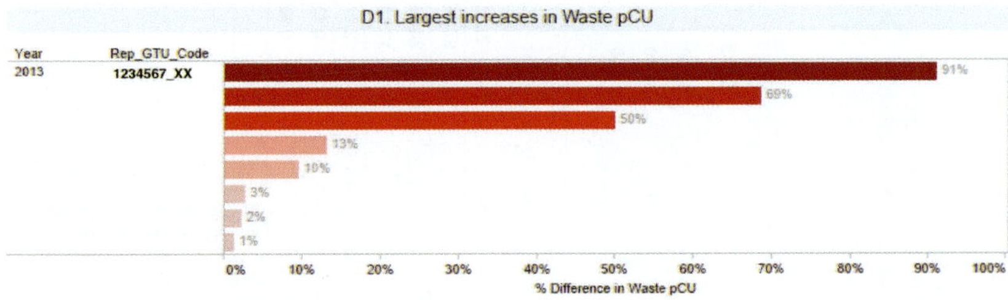

Figure 23: Table D1. Largest increases in waste pCU.

Table D1 shows the GTUs with the largest increase in waste pCU in 2013 in Category E. The graph above shows product with GTU code "1234567_XX" produced 91 per cent more waste pCU in 2013 than that in 2010. This is definitely a problem that needs attention as the waste pCU is almost double when it is supposed to decrease. Hence in Table D2 waste details by lifecycle are listed.

As mentioned previously, product lifecycle for waste can be separated into consumer use, primary packaging and secondary packaging. By examining the lifecycle details it is possible to learn which process went wrong.

For GTU "1234567_XX", total waste pCU increased from 4.2 grams in 2010 to 8.1 grams in 2013, which is almost double. However the waste in consumer use is constant at 0.9 grams while secondary packaging in 2013 even decreased from 0.3 grams (in 2010) to 0.2 grams. But the primary packaging number doubled, from 3.1 grams in 2010 to 7.0 grams in 2013 (the cause of the dramatic increase in total waste pCU in 2013)

At this stage, it was important to know more information about packaging for GTU "1234567_XX" to solve the primary packaging problem as shown in Workflow E below.

In the documentation introducing the calculation of waste, packaging weight and RRI are treated as the most important factors influencing

Rep GTU Code	Rep GTU Description
1234567_XX	XXXXXXXXXXXXXXXXXX

Rep GTU Code: 1234567_XX

D2. Waste Details by LC (2013)

	2010	2013
Total Waste Extrapolated per consumer use	4.2	8.1
Waste Extrapolated per consumer use Consumer Use	0.9	0.9
Waste Extrapolated per consumer use Primary Packaging	3.1	7.0
Waste Extrapolated per consumer use Secondary Packaging	0.3	0.2

Figure 24: Table D2. Waste details by LC (2013).

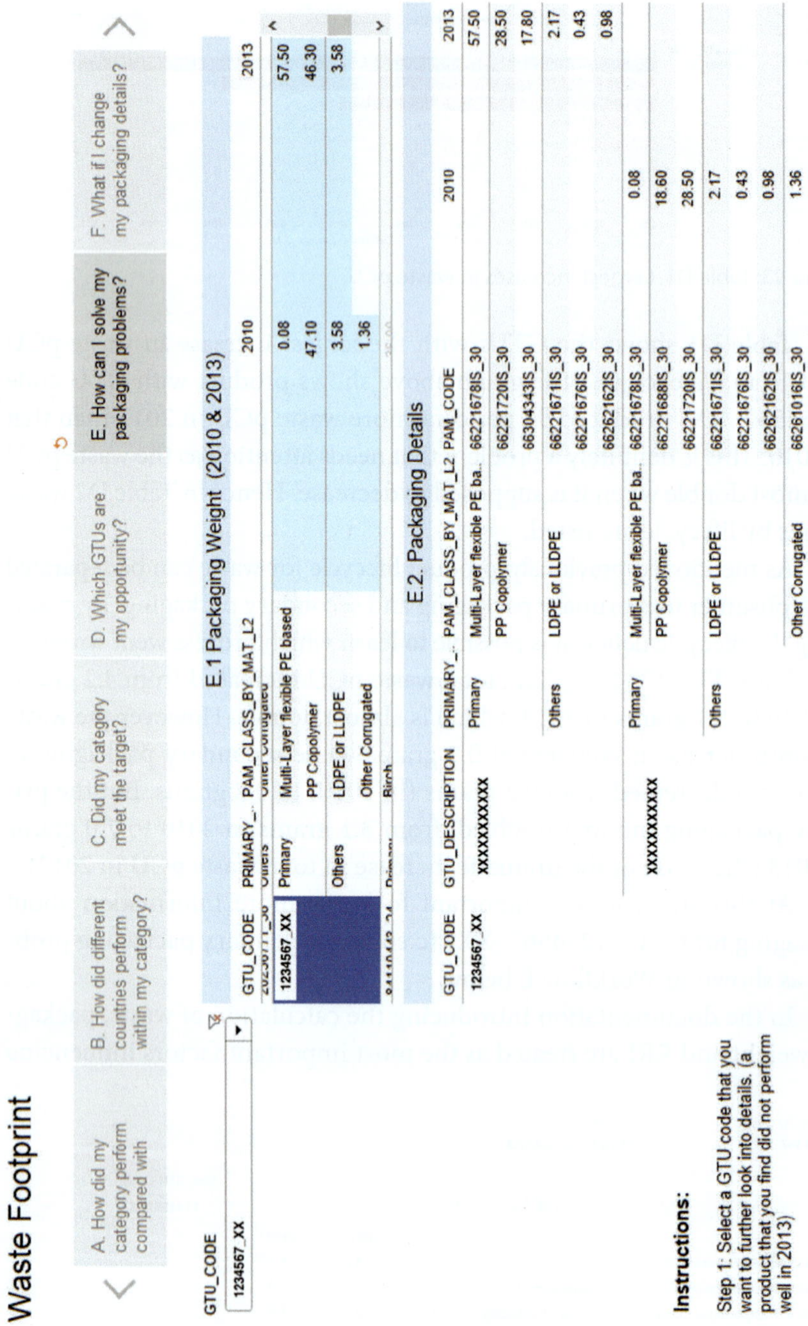

Figure 25: Footprint diagnose system dashboard E.

the production of waste, especially packaging weight which is linearly correlated with waste. Hence only the packaging weight is taken as an example.

The comparison of packaging weight information in two years (2010 and 2013) can be found in Table E1 and material details in Table E2.

Table E1 shows that the biggest change in packaging weight in 2013 is the use of "Multi-Layer flexible PE based". The weight of this material increased from 0.1 grams to 57.5 grams, a significant increase. Another change is the use of "Other Corrugated". The one used in 2010 is no longer used in 2013. These significant changes of material weight can be seen as having an impact on the final waste change. However, considering the importance of RRI rate, further modeling can be made to refine the result further for better accuracy.

After understanding which lifecycle went wrong and which material caused the change, further simulation can be conducted to show the change of the packaging weight, as seen in workflow F below (Figure 26).

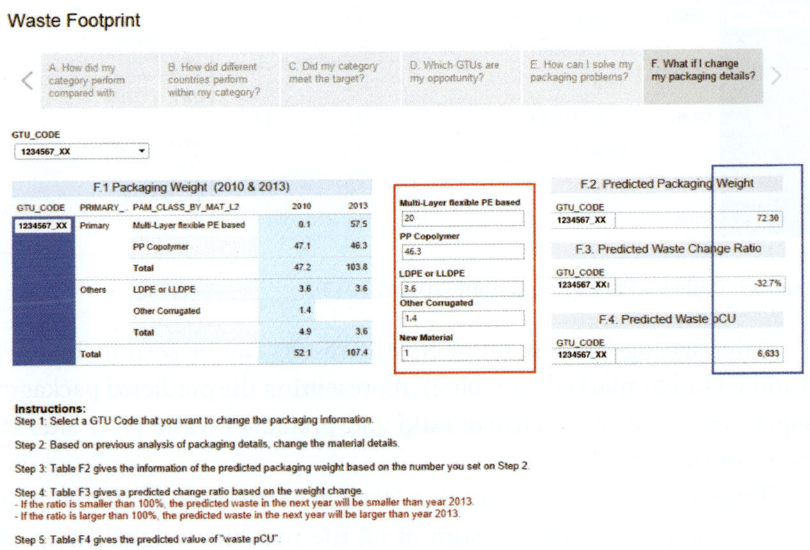

Figure 26: Footprint diagnose system dashboard F.

The objective for this dashboard is to simulate the results after changing the packaging weight for a single product.

Follow the "Instructions":

- Step 1: Select a GTU code that you want to change the packaging information.
- Step 2: Based on previous analysis of packaging details, change the material details.
- Step 3: Table F2 gives the information of the predicted packaging weight based on the number you set on Step 2.
- Step 4: Table F3 gives a predicted change ratio based on the weight change.
- Step 5: Table F4 gives the predicted value of "waste pCU".

The numbers in areas marked red can be changed, i.e. change the number of "Multi-Layer Flexible PE based" weight, "PP Copolymer" weight, "LDPE or LLDPE" weight and "Other Corrugated" weight. New materials can be added in the weight for these materials set.

F.1 Packaging Weight (2010 & 2013)

GTU_CODE	PRIMARY_..	PAM_CLASS_BY_MAT_L2	2010	2013
1234567_XX	Primary	Multi-Layer flexible PE based	0.1	57.5
		PP Copolymer	47.1	46.3
		Total	47.2	103.8
	Others	LDPE or LLDPE	3.6	3.6
		Other Corrugated	1.4	
		Total	4.9	3.6
	Total		52.1	107.4

Multi-Layer flexible PE based
20
PP Copolymer
46.3
LDPE or LLDPE
3.6
Other Corrugated
1.4
New Material
1

Figure 27: Table F1. Packaging weight (2010 & 2013).

After setting all these numbers, the results can be seen in Table F2, F3 and F4 (areas marked with blue), representing the predicted packaging weight, predicted waste change ratio and predicted waste pCU after the change of the material weight

Table F2 "Predicted Packaging Weight" is the sum of all the inputs in red rectangle area i.e. the sum of all the material weight. The packaging weight of "Multi-Layer Flexible PE based" was decreased from 57.5 grams to 20 grams, keep "PP Copolymer" weight the same as 46.3 grams in 2013; "LDPE or LLDPE" weight the same as 3.6 grams in 2013 and change "Other Corrugated" weight back to 1.4 grams - same as that in 2010. A new material with weight 1 gram was introduced. Hence, the predicted packaging weight is 72.3 grams (the sum of all the material weight mentioned above) and as shown in Table F2.

Table F3: "Predicted Waste Change Ratio" is calculated as:

$$\text{Predicted Waste Change Ratio} = \frac{\text{Predicted Packaging Weight Packaging Weight in 2013}}{\text{Packaging Weight in 2013}}$$

As mentioned previously, packaging weight is linearly correlated with waste. Hence, keeping all the others factors constant and changing only the packaging weight, the waste change should be the same as the packaging weight change.

$$\text{Predicted Waste Change Ratio (GTU:1234567\_XX)} = \frac{72.3\text{g} - 107.4\text{g}}{107.4\text{g}} \times 100\% = -32.7\%$$

It shows that after changing the packaging weight for "1234567_XX", the predicted waste in the coming year will decrease 32.7 per cent compared with that in 2013.

Table F4 "Predicted wasted pCU" is calculated as:

$$\text{Predicted Waste pCU} = \text{Waste pCU in 2013} \times \text{Predicted Waste Change Ratio}$$

So the predicted waste pCU for GTU "1234567_XX" is also calculated this way.

A simulation in workflow F for predicted weight was then performed showing waste change ratio and waste pCU after changing the construction of the packaging materials.

Hence, the whole workflow from Step A to F for footprint dashboard (waste) is now completed.

5. DISCUSSION AND FURTHER WORK

The tools assessment project and the sustainability analytics projects had the following benefits:

a) The market research undertaken and the niche visualization tools listed helped the company User Experience Team facilitate their process of understanding the visualization market.

b) The tools decision-trees that were built and the niche visualization tools listed, were by the User Experience team. They have carried out a trial version of some of the tools to better understand their capabilities and functions.
c) In sustainability analytics workflow F, the simulation part that can automatically do prediction when changing the construction of packaging materials, is a creative step that brings a new perspective to visualization and analytics.
d) In sustainability analytics, the construction of a "story" is a benchmark for later "footprint reporting", which helps solve end-to-end business questions, and is more powerful than only using dynamic dashboards.

The outcomes from the tools assessment projects represented an important milestone within a broader journey. Potential continuation of this work may involve trying some additional visualization tools by the User Experience Team in seeking further practical applications.

For the sustainability analytics project, the dashboards built in Tableau and the story constructed were based on partial data and not entire data sets. Further refinement of the sources of data might be advisable.

For second part of the work, only the packaging weight was taken as an important factor for waste analysis. However, RRI is another important variable to be taken into consideration. Lastly, the capability of integrating Tableau with R for predictive analysis would need further assessment.

REFERENCES

1. Herschel, G, A Linden and L Kart (2015). *Magic Quadrant for Advanced Analytics Platforms.*
2. Schlegel, K, et al. (2013). Magic quadrant for business intelligence and analytics platforms. *Gartner RAS Core Research Note* G 239854.
3. Richardson, J, et al. (2008). Magic quadrant for business intelligence platforms. *Core research note* G 154227.

4. Nicolett, M and KM Kavanagh (2011). Magic quadrant for security information and event management. *Gartner RAS Core Research Note (May 2009).*
5. Bernardino, J (2013). Emerging Business Intelligence Technologies for SMEs. *Handbook of Research on Enterprise 2.0: Technological, Social, and Organizational Dimensions: Technological, Social, and Organizational Dimensions*: 1.
6. Reilly, AH (2009). Communicating sustainability initiatives in corporate reports: Linking implications to organizational change. *SAM Advanced Management Journal*, 74.3, 33.

CHAPTER 7

Application of Analytics in Improving Efficiency of Transaction Surveillance

CHAN Chung Ying

ABSTRACT

As regulators in key financial markets tighten regulatory controls on money laundering activities, financial crime risk is a key area for most financial instititutions. Many have invested heavily in purchasing transaction surveillance systems, and taken a conservative approach to flagging suspicious transactions. Although this ensures that the chance of missing any suspicious transaction is minimized, the downside is that it generates a huge number of false positive alerts. This is extremely time consuming for transaction surveillance investigators to eliminate, causing a delay in the identification of genuine alerts. Due to close monitoring by regulators, instituitions are likely to remain conservative and maintain very low detection threholds. This paper proposes an analytical solution to enhance surveillance efficiency by risk-scoring system generated alerts, so that high risk alerts can be prioritized for investigation.[1]

1 Disclaimer: The views and opinions expressed in this article are those of the author and do not necessarily reflect the position of any financial institution or regulatory body.

1. INTRODUCTION

Money laundering is an activity by which criminals disguise the original ownership and control of the proceeds of criminal conduct by making them appear to be derived from a legitimate source. As technology advances, money laundering becomes increasingly sophisticated and harder to detect. Failure to detect money laundering transactions not only poses a serious threat to states and its citizens, but also to the financial institutions processing these transactions.

Due to regulatory requirements and serious consequences of Anti-Money Laundering (AML) non-compliance, almost all international financial institutions have AML solutions in place to detect and alert suspicious transactions. However, most institutions implement AML solutions from an overly conservative approach, resulting in complex and lengthy investigations. For most banks, if a suspicious transaction is detected, the alert will be investigated and escalated to several rounds of investigation. At the highest level of investigation, a Suspicious Activity Report (SAR) will be filed to the regulator if the alert is deemed genuinely suspicious. The investigation hierarchy is exhaustive and painfully time consuming; enhancing the investigation workflow will not only improve operational efficiency, it will also allow risk-based prioritization of alert investigation.

The objective of this project is to present a proof of concept in applying a risk-based solution combining text mining, statistical classification and AML domain knowledge to identify critical AML keywords from historical SAR filing narratives and in turn facilitate risk classification of alerts. During the initial round of alert investigation, if an investigator's narrative on the alert matches any critical AML keyword, the alert will carry a higher risk weight.

This project proposes a solution whereby analytics is applied to transaction surveillance data in order to enhance the investigation workflow. Instead of going through the usual investigation process, alerts that carry higher risk scores can be prioritized for investigation, so minimizing redundancies and expediting investigations on genuine money laundering transactions.

2. PROBLEM STATEMENT

Financial institutions need to comply with increasingly complex and evolving regulations. Recent guidelines from the Financial Action Task Force demonstrate the need for ongoing flexibility and adaptability in

AML strategies. Regulations are both deepening and widening to extend obligations for monitoring. Global banks need to monitor the regulatory landscape constantly, and be flexible when these requirements adapt and change to ensure compliance through the efficient use of a risk based approach (BAE, 2015).

Combating the sophistication and professionalism of today's organized criminals is challenging, especially when banks are managing extremely high alert volumes triggered from the transaction surveillance system. Within the system, many sets of rules are written to establish detection scenarios, and most detection scenarios "catch" suspicious transactions based on volume and amount. The thresholds of detection scenarios are defined in the transaction surveillance system; if a customer's monthly transactional activity breaches the threshold, the system will trigger an alert for investigation.

Given that banks prioritize compliance, it is risky for any bank to lower detection thresholds to reduce the number of false positives. At the same time, banks have limited resources to increase resources in transaction surveillance investigation, and it takes months for a new investigator to acquire the necessary domain knowledge. Given these two constraints, it is critical for institutions to prioritize high-risk alerts. As such, this paper presents a proof of concept by using analytics on readily available data to risk rank alerts.

3. STATE OF THE ART

This section of the document summarizes research work carried out in the course of the project. The most important research area was to understand the investigation process of transaction surveillance, so as to derive a feasible solution in alert prioritization. The research work on transaction surveillance was referenced to an international bank having global business exposures, and handling huge volume of onshore and offshore transactions. Extensive technical research on text mining was also undertaken in order to identify the most frequently used keywords in SAR narratives.

This section briefly describes the classification approach used in the project.

3.1. Money laundering and transaction surveillance

Money laundering is the process that disguises illegal profits without compromising those criminals who wish to benefit from the proceeds. There are two core reasons as to why laundering occurs: either the money trail is evidence of their crime, and/or the money itself is vulnerable to seizure and has to be protected. Regardless of who uses money laundering apparatus, the operational principles are essentially the same. Money laundering follows a dynamic three-stage process, as shown below (UNODC, 2015):

Figure 1: Three-stage process of money laundering.

Transaction surveillance is a core component of AML in any financial institution handling money transfers. With reference to Figure 1 above, multiple money transfers are made in the Layering stage before the funds are integrated for criminal activities. As such, it is critical for financial institutions facilitating money transfers to be vigilant and diligent in screening customers and daily transaction activities, and be responsible for the source and destination of the funds. Due to an increasing focus on regulatory compliance, banks are highly dedicated to a risk based legal and compliance framework, ensuring that AML risk is mitigated in financial services offered to customers.

The framework includes a comprehensive end-to-end process of risk assessment and on-going monitoring. Before a customer account is opened, a highly detailed Know Your Customer (KYC) assessment is performed. This is especially crucial for private bank customers, corporate customers and politically exposed customers. Private bank and politically exposed customers are high-net worth customers that transact in large amounts, while corporate customers usually transact in very large volume. Banks need to ensure that the flow of funds with respect to these customers is legitimate.

Apart from KYC, regular monitoring of customers is performed, with those deemed high risk given annual reviews, transactional activities are monitored and screened, and sophisticated detection systems are programmed and deployed to screen inflow and outflow of funds, making sure that any suspicious transactions are alerted for investigation. Large-scale foreign banks employ investigators to process a huge volume of suspicious alerts every month. These alerts contain valuable information about transactions between the beneficiary and originator. Investigators assess each alert, and escalate any potential money laundering transaction found. The escalated alert will be filed as a case for enhanced assessment, which involves detailed investigations performed by in-house domain experts. Following vigorous assessment, a genuinely suspicious case will be filed as a SAR to the regulators, and the bank may decide to exit the customer involved in the transactions.

As regulation tightens, banks are monitored closely by regulators to ensure compliance in anti-money laundering efforts. Many institutions are also expanding the scope of transaction surveillance, resulting in a drastic increase in the number of SARs filed to regulators. The histogram in Figure 2 shows that the total number of SARs filed to the U.S. regulators increased ten-fold from 2002 to 2011 (FINCEN, 2014).

Figure 2: Number of SARs filed in U.S. from 2002 to 2011.

3.2. Transaction surveillance investigation process

Almost all banks have a comprehensive transaction surveillance process in place. As explained earlier in this section, its scope is expanding and a huge volume of transactions is processed every day. Each of these transactions are screened by the transaction surveillance system. In this system, multiple detection scenarios are implemented to capture all forms of money laundering typologies that can be of interest to investigators (e.g. rapid movement of funds and structuring).

Detection scenarios are logics programmed in the system. They range from the simple logic of capturing round dollar amount transactions, to complicated logic of identifying structuring of transactions to avoid regulatory attention. One example of structuring is that the originator may make multiple transactions at a value less than US$10,000. The Bank Secrecy Act of 1970 requires financial institutions in the United States to assist U.S. government agencies to detect and prevent money laundering (Wikipedia, Bank Secrecy Act, 2015). Specifically, the Act requires financial institutions to report and keep records of daily aggregated cash transactions of more than US$10,000. In such instances, the detection system will collect information of originators and beneficiaries making multiple transactions of value slightly less than US$10,000. If the number of such transactions exceeds the pre-defined monthly threshold, the system will generate an alert for investigation of structuring activity.

Alerts are automatically triggered in this example, and transaction thresholds are usually set low to ensure that the system is capturing the majority of suspicious transactions. On a monthly basis, tens of thousands of alerts can be generated for investigation. Most global banks have a dedicated transaction surveillance workflow in place to ensure that alerts are investigated thoroughly. A typical workflow is shown in Figure.3.

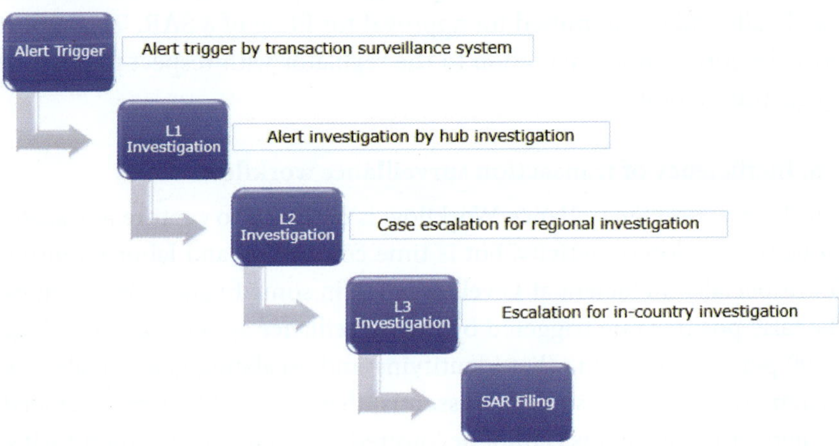

Figure 3: Typical transaction surveillance workflow.

3.3. Level 1 of transaction surveillance (Centralized hub)

Only a fraction of the tens of thousands of monthly alerts are escalated to the next level of investigation – Level 1. The majority of alerts are false positives triggered by the surveillance system, meaning that this stage of the investigation workflow is usually inefficient and prone to delays. Alerts that are not investigated will form a backlog pool pending investigation. This is of concern, as some of the alerts in backlog may genuinely be suspicious. Due to time pressure and an accumulating backlog, Level 1 investigators tend to escalate alerts to the next level which are actually false positives.

3.4. Level 2 of transaction surveillance (Regional)

At Level 2 of investigation, escalated alerts are considered productive. Investigators are trained to perform enhanced investigation on alerts triggered in their assigned region, which involves in-depth assessment on the transactions, counter-parties and countries involved. Upon examining the alert, decisions are made to determine whether the alert is worth further escalation. If it is, a detailed case will be filed and further escalated for Level 3 in-country investigation.

3.5. Level 3 of transaction surveillance (In-Country)

From Level 2, the escalated case will be flagged to the in-country financial crime team. At this stage, investigators will carry out checks to establish and justify the suspicious case. Upon gathering sufficient information, the details will be submitted for approval for filing of a SAR. This report provides formal documentation to the regulator with respect to possible illegal transactions.

3.6. Inefficiency of transaction surveillance workflow

The Transaction Surveillance Workflow is designed to capture any suspicious transaction or activity, but is time consuming and labor intensive. It is especially inefficient at Levels 1 and 2; in some financial institutions, the false positive rate triggered by the surveillance system can be as high as 99 per cent, meaning that identifying and escalating genuine alerts is extremely difficult. As such, it is essential that this workflow be enhanced. As detection thresholds cannot be lowered due to regulatory monitoring, institutions might consider applying statistical risk prioritization on alerts escalated at Level 1, and prioritize these alerts for investigation at Level 2, or even direct escalation to Level 3. This ensures that valuable resources at Levels 2 or 3 can be channeled on high risk alerts. The following histogram (Figure 4) shows the estimated percentage of false positives generated at each level of investigation:

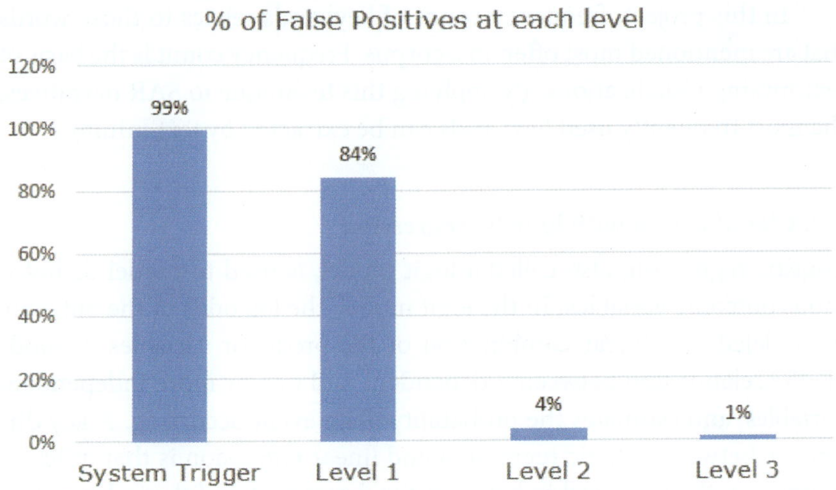

Figure 4: Percentage of false positives generated in workflow.

3.7. Investigation narratives

Any transaction going in and out of the bank carries valuable information that can be used by investigators to establish its legitimacy. As investigators assess the alerts, their findings are logged as narratives that are captured in the transaction surveillance system at each level of the workflow.

The narratives are usually unstructured text, logged by investigators in accordance with certain guidelines. At Level 3, if the in-country investigator deems a case as genuinely suspicious for SAR filing, a SAR narrative will be logged in the transaction surveillance system.

SAR narratives are made up of unstructured text that contains critical descriptions of the SAR filing; as such, they are ripe for text mining. With sufficiently rich SAR narrative data, frequently used keywords can be extracted and deployed to predict potentially suspicious alerts at Level 1.

3.8. Text mining and techniques

At its core, text mining is about discovering patterns and anomalies in sets of text documents. Invariably, the process begins with the creation of a digitized corpus of materials, which can then be cleaned, marked up, and organized, making it easier for computers to read and parse. From there, keywords are identified, counted, and tabulated (Wikipedia, Text Mining, 2015).

In this project, frequency count of keywords relates to those words that are mentioned most often in a corpus. Frequency count is the basis of text mining visualizations. By applying this technique to SAR narratives, the most frequently used keywords can be extracted by text mining.

3.9. Classification with logistic regression

Logistic regression, also called a logit model, is used to model dichotomous outcome variables. In the logit model, the log odds of the outcome is modeled as a linear combination of the predictor variables. It models the relationship between a dependent and one or more independent variables, and estimates the probability of an event occurring. A key difference between logistic regression and linear regression is that in linear regression, the relationship between the dependent and the independent variables is linear, while this assumption is not made in logistic regression (Strathclyde, 2015).

Applying this classification method, the relationship between suspicious alerts and its data attributes can be studied. The data attributes displaying a significant effect on suspicious alerts can be used to derive the probable outcome of the alerts. Specific to this project, the method predicts whether the alert will end up as a Level 3 escalation. As probability of the outcome ranges from zero to one, this range can also facilitate risk scoring of alerts.

4. SOLUTION: DESCRIPTION OF APPROACH

This section describes the technical approach used in proposing the solution. It includes the end-to-end process of executing the proof of concept, tools used in the project, and results of the statistical experiments.

Due to the high sensitivity of data and information security, analysis has to be performed within a controlled environment. This implies that actual statistical results cannot be presented in the paper, and statistical tools available for analysis are limited to those available in the environment.

4.1. Research on availability of data

A sophisticated detection system is used in the transaction surveillance workflow. Alert triggers, escalation information and investigation narratives are captured in the system. The information is stored in the database in a data schema. In this project, Statistical Analysis System (SAS) Enterprise Guide is used as the primary tool for data processing and analysis.

Due to the complex data schema and lack of data guide, extensive research is performed on the schema before useful data can be downloaded for further processing. The data tables identified for project use are shown in Table 1, and data transformation is performed using SAS to create a consolidated alert Level table. This facilitates easy analysis of data.

Table 1: Data tables in project

Table Name	Description	Primary Key	Period
Alert	Capture all system triggered alerts, and typology information	alert_key	2 full years
Case	Capture all cases escalated at Level 2	case_key	2 full years
Alert Case Link	Facilitate linkage between Alert and Case table	alert_key	N/A
Productive	Capture productive information (i.e. escalation, SAR filing)	case_key	2 full years
Alert Detail	Capture Level 1 narratives	alert_key	2 full years
SAR Detail	Capture SAR narratives	case_key	6 full years

4.2. SAR narrative text mining

By identifying the data source of SAR narratives, text mining can be performed on the narratives with the intention of identifying critical AML keywords. A text mining module is available in SAS as a purchasable option, but due to budget constraint, this tool was not available for use in this project. The next best option available is R, with R Studio also installed as an interface for R processing. Research was undertaken on R programming to understand the methods available for text mining in R.

In performing text mining, the process flow illustrated in Figure 5 is applied in identifying the frequently used keywords in SAR narratives. This is also a common approach applied in the industry (WinfWiki, 2014; Feinerer, 2015).

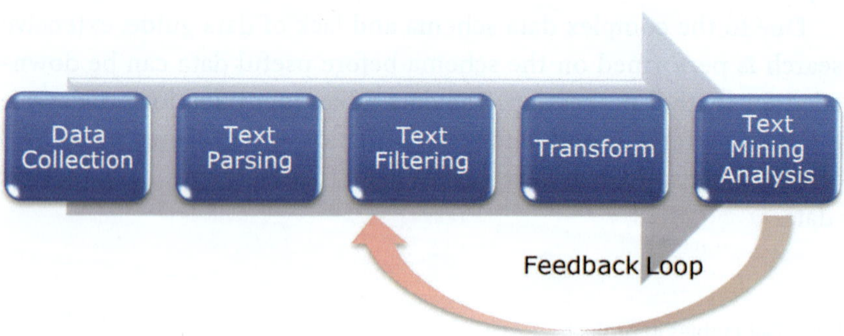

Figure 5: Typical text mining process flow.

4.2.1. Data collection

- SAR narratives collected and each narrative istored as a text file
- Text files imported into a corpus

4.2.2. Text parsing

- Convert all words to lowercase
- Eliminate extra whitespace
- Remove "stop words" (e.g. of, me, you, etc.)
- Remove numbers (e.g. 1, 2, etc.)
- Strip symbols (e.g. #, @, etc.)
- Remove punctuations (e.g. ?, !, etc.)

4.2.3. Text filtering

- Common phrases combined into singular keywords (i.e. new york -> newyork, abc bank -> abcbank, etc.)
- Drop words that are not relevant to the subject (e.g. microsoft)

4.2.4. Transform

- Formation of a Document Term Matrix (DTM) for analysis
- A keyword may appear in one SAR narrative multiple times, but only be counted once in the DTM
- Calculate frequency of word counts, present it in a Word Cloud or Histogram

4.2.5. Text mining analysis

- Review the list of keywords identified
- Combini domain knowledge on the subject, manual review of keywords is performed

Text filtering, transformation and analysis is an exhaustive feedback process. As the list of keywords is analyzed based on domain knowledge, irrelevant keywords are identified, and the process of text filtering has to be performed again. This process can be repeated many times until a final list of useful keywords is identified. In this project, the process was repeated more than ten times before a list of top 200 most frequently used keywords was defined.

The text parsing method of stemming was not used in this instance. Stemming involves the conversion of similar words into a single keyword (for example, 'travelling' and 'travel' can be stemmed into a single word 'travel'). Considering that the objective of this exercise was to identify most frequently used AML keywords, stemming could result in a loss of keyword information or affect the actual frequency count of critical keywords.

Table 2 shows a Document Term Matrix (DTM). For example, if SAR Narrative 1 contained the keywords 'singapore','bank' and 'gambling', one count was shown in the DTM. Specifically for this project, if 'gambling' appeared multiple times in the same narrative, it constituted one count in the DTM.

Table 2: Document term matrix

	Narrative 1	Narrative 2	Narrative 3	Narrative 4	Narrative 5
terrorist	0	0	1	0	0
launder	0	0	0	0	0
iraq	0	0	0	0	0
singapore	1	0	0	0	0
originator	0	0	0	0	0
cheque	0	0	0	1	1
pep	0	0	0	1	0
bank	1	0	0	1	0
states	0	0	1	0	0
gambling	1	0	0	0	0

The following diagram shows a Word Cloud featuring keywords with respect to count frequency. The higher the frequency of a keyword in the DTM, the bigger the keyword will appear in the Word Cloud (Figure 6).

Figure 6: Text-mining word cloud (note: keywords are not related to AML).

After text mining on the SAR narrative data, the top 200 most frequently used keywords are identified. In order to achieve a list highly associated with SAR filing, further review based on AML domain knowledge is performed. Finally, 31 dedicated critical AML keywords are identified.

4.3. Risk classification of alerts

The list of critical AML keywords contains valuable inputs for Level 3 investigators in the process of SAR filing. The list can be used to form a keyword flag, either zero or one, in the Level 1 alert data. For example, if an alert matches with any critical AML keyword, the flag will be indicated as one; if not, it will result in zero. This flag acts as a predictor for classification.

Apart from using the keyword as an indicator, another very useful predictor is the typology of an alert. Each alert triggered on a counterparty can be due to different money laundering typologies. Examples of money laundering typologies are structuring, high risk location and round dollar amount. Each alert can be tagged to multiple typologies, and there are a total of 11 typology flags used in the project.

As mentioned earlier, logistic regression is used as the classification method. Before executing, two years of alert data is divided into 15 months of modeling data and nine months of validation data. In this proof of concept, keyword flag and 11 typology flags are used in the regression, predicting the probability of an alert becoming a Level 3 escalation. Although the ideal solution is to predict SAR filing outcome, the ratio of Level 3 event to Level 1 is very low, and the SAR to Level 1 ratio is even lower. As such, Level 3 escalation is chosen as the dependent variable. Multiple rounds of logistic regression is performed to derive the best model. The validation data is scored accordingly, and results are shown in Table 3.

Table 3: Logistic regression results

Predictors	Estimate	P-Value
Typology 1	–	<= 0.05, significant
Typology 2	N/A	>=0.05, insignificant
Typology 3	N/A	>=0.05, insignificant
Typology 4	–	<= 0.05, significant
Typology 5	+	<= 0.05, significant
Typology 6	–	<= 0.05, significant
Typology 7	+	<= 0.05, significant
Typology 8	N/A	>=0.05, insignificant
Typology 9	–	<= 0.05, significant
Typology 10	–	<= 0.05, significant
Typology 11	N/A	>=0.05, insignificant
Keyword Flag	+	<= 0.05, significant

Establishing the null hypothesis that the predictors has no insignificant impact on the model, a p-value of <= 0.05 rejects the null hypothesis, and vice versa. The final model shows that four typology flags have insignificant effect on the model, while it is important to note the keyword flag is a significant positive estimate in predicting Level 3 outcome. In interpreting the model, Sensitivity refers to true positive rate and one-Specificity refers to false positive rate. Plotting Sensitivity against one-Specificity, this model has achieved an Area Under Curve of 0.82, signifying that the model displays strong capability in discriminating between true and false (Bartlett, 2014). The model successfully incorporates critical AML keywords and alert typologies as variables for risk classification, predicting whether the alert will be escalated to Level 3.

This project leverages the regression odds ratio, ranging from zero to one, as risk score of the alert. Alerts in the validation dataset are sorted in ascending order of odds ratio, and are subsequently divided into ten equal deciles. The lower deciles are made up of alerts with lower odds ratios, while decile 10 stores those with the highest odds ratios. In the validation dataset, 46.1 per cent Level 3 events are classified in the top decile, indicating that odds ratio is an accurate risk measure.

4.4. Refinement by treating each keyword as a predictor

In attempting to refine the model and improve model results, 31 keywords were converted to dummy variables as predictors of the logistic regression model. This approach allowed each of the keyword to be analyzed separately and keywords having p-value of >0.05 were dropped from the model, keeping only keywords of significance to the model output. The refined results are shown in Table 4.

Table 4: refined model results

Predictors	Estimate	P-Value
Typology 1	-	<= 0.05, significant
Typology 2	N/A	>=0.05, insignificant
Typology 3	N/A	>=0.05, insignificant
Typology 4	–	<= 0.05, significant
Typology 5	+	<= 0.05, significant
Typology 6	–	<= 0.05, significant

(*Continued*)

Predictors	Estimate	P-Value
Typology 7	+	<= 0.05, significant
Typology 8	N/A	>=0.05, insignificant
Typology 9	–	<= 0.05, significant
Typology 10	–	<= 0.05, significant
Typology 11	N/A	>=0.05, insignificant
18 keywords	+	<= 0.05, significant
6 keywords	–	<= 0.05, significant
7 keywords	N/A	>=0.05, insignificant

By using the refined model to score the same validation dataset, it emerged that four typology flags and seven keywords had insignificant effect on the model. Moreover, 18 keywords were positive estimates on the outcome, while six keywords displayed negative effect in predicting Level 3 outcome. Plotting Sensitivity against one-Specificity, this model achieved an Area Under Curve of 0.88, signifying that the model displayed strong capability in discriminating between true and false. Using the odds ratio to risk score the alerts, alerts were ranked in ascending order of odds ratio. Upon dividing all alerts equally into 10 deciles, analysis indicated that 58.1 per cent of Level 3 events in the validation dataset were classified in the top decile, once again indicating that the odds ratio provides an accurate risk measure.

After documenting results, the entire technical experimentation was repeated. This provided validation of the experiment to minimize any mistake made in data extraction, text mining, keyword elimination, classification and model interpretation.

5. DISCUSSION

This section highlights the advantages of implementing this solution, and also lists the challenges that may emerge in the execution of this proposal.

5.1. Advantages

- Investigation of alerts in Level 2 backlog pool may take up to three or four months to be completed. This project prioritizes high risk alerts to be investigated first, reducing the lead time for genuine alerts to be flagged.

- Currently there is a huge number of false positives escalated for Level 2 investigation. By prioritizing the higher deciles for Level 2 investigation and leaving lower deciles alerts in the backlog pool, it reduces the number of false positives Level 2 investigators have to deal with.
- Direct Level 3 escalation may be proposed for the top decile of alerts. This ensures that the highest risk alerts are handled by in-country domain experts.

5.2. Challenges

- Even though the number of Level 3 events in the lower deciles is extremely low, there is still a possibility that lower risk alerts may turn out to be a potential SAR filing alert.
- Lowest decile alerts may be proposed for backlog investigation or even hibernation. However much discussion and approval are required to agree on hibernation of low risk alerts.

6. CONCLUSION AND FURTHER WORK

Upon completing the classification model, alerts are risk-ranked and divided into 10 equal deciles. The alerts in the top decile captures close to 60 per cent of all Level 3 events; the top five deciles captures close to 75 per cent of total Level 3 events in the validation dataset. By applying this proposal to the production environment, Level 1 escalated alerts classified in the higher deciles can be given priority during Level 2 investigation. The top decile may even be proposed for direct Level 3 investigation. This ensures that resources are channeled to focus on high-risk alerts because the false positive rate at the top decile is significantly lower than the false positive rate at the lower deciles.

There are two key tasks that could be pursued as the next steps of the project. A possible immediate next step is to perform analysis on the lower deciles of alerts. It is important to study how many low risk alerts eventually end up in SAR filing. If there is minimal number of such alerts, this proposal proves to be a justified prioritization approach, and also shows a strong case for hibernation of low risk alerts.

In the longer term, as more SARs are filed, it is crucial to leverage on the additional SAR narrative information in refining the text mining process.

The more accurate the list of critical AML keywords identified, the stronger these predictors become in the Logistic Regression model.

To conclude, this paper proposes a realistic analytical solution in prioritizing suspicious alerts through text mining and risk classification. The solution does not only offload the Level 2 and Level 3 investigators by channeling resources to high-risk alerts, it also ensures that genuine alerts are quickly flagged out for Level 3 escalation and possible SAR filing.

BIBLIOGRAPHY

1. BAE Systems (2015). *AML Transaction Monitoring.* [Online] Available at: http://www.baesystems.com/what-we-do-rai/financial-crime/financial-crime-solutions/aml-transaction-monitoring [16 August 2015].

2. Bartlett, J (2014). *Area Under the ROC curve.* [Online] Available at: http://thestatsgeek.com/2014/05/05/area-under-the-roc-curve-assessing-discrimination-in-logistic-regression/[16 August 2015].

3. Feinerer, I (2015). *Introduction to the tm Package.* [Online] Available at: https://cran.r-project.org/web/packages/tm/vignettes/tm.pdf [16 August 2015].

4. FINCEN (2014). *SAR Stats.* [Online] Available at: http://www.fincen.gov/news_room/rp/sar_by_number.html [16 August 2015].

5. International Compliance Association (2015). *What is Money Laundering.* [Online] Available at: http://www.int-comp.org/what-is-money-laundering [16 August 2015].

6. Strathclyde, UO (2015). *What is Logistic Regression.* [Online] Available at: https://www.strath.ac.uk/aer/materials/5furtherquantitativeresearchdesignandanalysis/unit6/whatislogisticregression/[16 August 2015].

7. UNODC (2015). *The Money-Laundering Cycle.* [Online] Available at: https://www.unodc.org/unodc/en/money-laundering/laundrycycle.html [16 August 2015].

8. Wikipedia (2015). *Bank Secrecy Act.* [Online] Available at: https://en.wikipedia.org/wiki/Bank_Secrecy_Act [16 August 2015].

9. Wikipedia (2015). *Text Mining.* [Online] Available at: https://en.wikipedia.org/wiki/Text_mining [16 August 2015].

10. WinfWiki (2014). *Analyse Text Mining SAS Text Miner.* [Online] Available at: http://winfwiki.wi-fom.de/index.php/Analyse_Text_Mining_mit_SAS_Text_Miner [16 August 2015].

CHAPTER 8

Predicting Five Year Revenues for Banking Cash Management

LEE Seng Yin Daniel

ABSTRACT

Banks have limited resources to service their clients and thus need to be strategic in deciding how to allocate them. Tradition holds that the bigger the client, the better for the cash management business so it is desirable for banks to select high revenue generating clients to maximize profits.

This project explores how best to predict what a prospective revenue for the bank might be by examining other factors such as industry and company financials by using a multiple linear regression model.

1. INTRODUCTION

In banking, cash management (or treasury services) refers to the broad spectrum of services offered to large businesses to manage their consolidation of cash deposits, payments, and receipts. It is the staple line of business for a corporate and institutional bank that provides reliable assets in the form of cash deposits as well as revenue generation through account and transactional fees.

Asia's cash management market is expected to grow rapidly at about 13 per cent annually, generating revenues of US$280 billion per year by 2015 [1]. While the total pool is attractive, banks in their limited bandwidth can only take on a portion as its clientele. In this competitive space for revenue share, identifying which clients a bank should prioritize sales efforts on becomes key for survival.

2. PROBLEM STATEMENT

Banks place nearly half of their headcount in customer services to on-board and support their clients [2]. In cash management, having more clients is not always better. In a typical bank, as much as 90 per cent of the clientele provide just 10 per cent of the revenue but demand a lot of support from account managers and operations, draining the bank's resources from providing greater dedication to its most important customers – the 10 per cent that provide 90 per cent of the revenue.

To maximize profits, banks try to identify and on-board customers that are high revenue generators and decline the ones that bring little revenue but add additional strain on its system. If the revenue estimates of its clients were not consistently accurate over time, the bank could end up with expensive clients that would be difficult to lose.

This report explores if multiple linear regression would serve as a better predictor of banking cash management revenue over five years than existing methods.

3. STATE OF THE ART

Traditionally, banks have relied on market research and published financial reports to gauge a company's profitability to the bank's cash management business. A company's financial report can be broken down into the balance sheet, income statement, and cash flow statement, and the statistics in each reveal information about the company's size, nature of business, earnings, spending habits, and profitability. Investors and financial analysts also employ a range of financial ratios that describe various aspects of a company's liquidity, debt, profitability, operating performance, and investment valuation. For a cash management service where fees are levied on deposits and transactions, the magnitude of disposable cash and frequency of transactions a client has would determine how much revenue the bank makes from it. Since the net sales of a client generally represent these statistics, banks would normally select clients with the highest sales figures.

4. SOLUTION

4.1. Description of approach

Since actual bank data was unavailable for this report due to confidentiality issues, a suitable proxy for cash management revenue first had to be chosen. Then, a multiple linear regression model was trained using company financial data to predict each company's same-year revenue proxy as a showcase of methodology in which revenue data might be used in if available. One multiple linear regression model was developed to forecast the revenues of each subsequent year, up to five years in the future. Residual analysis was conducted after which the model was tested on its accuracy using a separate set of company data.

4.2. Operating cash flow as a proxy for cash management revenue

Net operating cash flow (Oancf) represents the total cash spent and earned by a company from the daily operation of its business. These cash flows result in transactional and deposit maintenance fees for the bank – the larger the net operating cash flow, the larger the revenue for the bank's cash management service. Operating cash flow is thus chosen amongst other variables to be the proxy of cash management revenue. Accordingly, operating cash flow (revenue) will only be known to a bank for its existing clients and taken to be unknown for companies that are not yet theirs.

4.3. Company financial dataset description, preparation, and architecture

The company financial dataset was obtained from Compustat and contains 372,485 rows of panel data consisting of 31,218 companies' financial statistics over the years ranging from 1950 to 2014. The Customer on Uniform Security Identification Procedures (CUSIP) number is used as a unique identifier of the companies, and the Standard Industrial Classification (SIC) code was also given which indicated which industry the primary business operated in. The SIC codes were mapped to 10 industry categories (referencing siccode.com) and made into nine dummy variables. The data architecture is laid out in Table 1 below.

Table 1: Architecture of company financial data.

ID	Year Dummies			Industry Dummies			Quarter Dummies			Financial Ratios
Cusip	1950	…	2014	Mining	…	Public	Q2	Q3	Q4	…
11A	0	0	1	1	0	0	0	0	1	0.12
232F	1	0	0	0	0	1	1	0	0	3.17
H3V	0	1	0	0	1	0	0	0	1	2.74

…

Balance Sheet Statistics			Income Statement Statistics			Cash Flow Statistics		
Che	…	Csho	Sale	…	Epsfx	Ibc	…	Fincf
0.90	0.95	1.51	0.92	0.48	0.26	3.53	0.33	0.22
0.57	1.95	0.29	0.83	0.84	0.04	0.53	0.14	0.35
2.70	0.21	0.98	0.94	2.07	0.86	0.26	1.92	0.24

4.4. Data cleaning and data split

A lot of variables in the dataset contained N/A values because some companies choose not to report all the variables at such a granular level in their annual reports. However, these missing values can sometimes be derived from other variables that are not N/As. For example, Total Current Assets (ACT) initially had 1245 N/As. But ACT can be derived from:

$$\begin{aligned} \text{ACT} = &(\text{Total Assets}) - (\text{Property Plant and Equipment}) - \\ &(\text{Investment and Advances}) - (\text{Total Intangible Assets}) - \\ &(\text{Other Assets}) \end{aligned}$$

Calculating ACT from the above formula brought the 1245 N/As down to 303. The same approach was used on several other statistics in the dataset to fill out as much N/A values as possible.

Upon cleaning as much as possible, new columns were introduced for key financial ratios which were calculated from the individual financial statistics. Each company's operating cash flow (oancf) from one to fiveyears later were then copied onto each row as shown in Table 2 below.

Table 2: Data extract showing how oancf1-5 were copied onto each row.

cusip	fyear	oancf	oancf1	oancf2	oancf3	oancf4	oancf5
21303	1985	NA	NA	NA	NA	NA	0.178
21303	1986	NA	NA	NA	NA	0.178	−2.122
21303	1987	NA	NA	NA	0.178	−2.122	NA
21303	1989	NA	0.178	−2.122	NA	−1.409	−1.118
21303	1990	0.178	−2.122	NA	−1.409	−1.118	−0.465
21303	1991	−2.122	NA	−1.409	−1.118	−0.465	−1.079
21303	1993	−1.409	−1.118	−0.465	−1.079	−4.288	−0.193
21303	1994	−1.118	−0.465	−1.079	−4.288	−0.193	−1.341
21303	1995	−0.465	−1.079	−4.288	−0.193	−1.341	NA
21303	1996	−1.079	−4.288	−0.193	−1.341	NA	NA
21303	1997	−4.288	−0.193	−1.341	NA	NA	NA
21303	1998	−0.193	−1.341	NA	NA	NA	NA
21303	1999	−1.341	NA	NA	NA	NA	NA

Finally, the data was randomly split into 80/20 portions for training and testing respectively. The companies in the training set represent existing clients of the bank whose revenue (oancf) is known and whose financials are used to build the predictive model. The test set represents the pool of candidate companies whose potential revenues the bank is trying to determine.

4.5. Building the model with multiple linear regression

Correlation matrices and exploratory regressions were first carried out with random subsets of the training data to figure out which ratios or statistics were likely to be significant in predicting oancf (revenue). It was discovered that the raw statistics as explanatory variables tended to be significant but not the financial ratios, even when used exclusively. Thus, it was decided to use only raw statistics and ignore financial ratios for further modeling attempts.

Multiple linear regression was first performed on current year financials against the same year's operating cash flow using all variables except those in the cash flow statement (to avoid a relationship that was too directly derived). Put simply, balance sheet and income statement information were used to predict operating cash flow.

After the initial regression with all variables included, insignificant predictors were removed one by one until all remaining predictors were significant ($p < 0.05$). To ensure independence of predictors, stepwise Variance Inflation Factor (VIF) analysis was then done to remove variables that exhibited too much inter-correlation with the other predictors (threshold of five). After building the regression model predicting same year operating cash flow, the same methodology was repeated using the variables in the training set to predict operating cash flows from one to five years in the future, with the resulting six models and adjusted R^2 given in Table 3 below.

Table 3: Resulting regression output showing the significant variables used, their coefficients, and the adjusted R^2 of each model.

	Oancf	Oancf1	Oancf2	Oancf3	Oancf4	Oancf5
Intercept	−15.2	4.7	0.6	−54.8	−16.8	−27.8
Mining				461.8		
Retail. Trade		96.0				
Yr1999	−22.0				−52.7	
Yr2000					−35.2	
Yr2002	16.7					
Yr2008	33.5	21.1			45.2	77.2
Yr2009	17.9	35.5	25.2			334.9
Yr2011	18.0					

(*continued*)

Table 3: Resulting regression output showing the significant variables used, their coefficients, and the adjusted R^2 of each model. (*continued*)

	Oancf	Oancf1	Oancf2	Oancf3	Oancf4	Oancf5
Yr2012			−113.7			
Yr2014	−306.1					
Che	0.2	0.0	0.1	0.1	0.2	0.1
Recd	0.8	2.6	0.7	−1.6	3.3	0.4
Invrm		−0.2	−0.2	0.4		
Invwip	−0.2	0.1		−0.4		−0.1
Invfg	−0.3	−0.3	−0.1	−0.2	−0.7	−0.4
Aco	0.1		0.1	0.2		
Ppent		0.1				
Dpact	0.1		0.1	0.0	0.1	
Ivaeq		0.0	−0.1	0.0		
Ivao	0.0		−0.2	−0.1		−0.1
Intan		0.0		0.0	0.0	−0.1
Ao	0.0	−0.2	−0.1	0.1	−0.2	
Dlc	0.0		0.1			
Ap			0.0			
Txp	0.2	−0.2	−0.6	0.9	0.2	
Txditc	0.1		0.2			
Lo				0.0		0.1
Mib	−0.4	0.2				
Pstk	−0.3					
Cstk	0.0	0.1	−0.1	0.4	−0.1	−0.1
Caps	0.0		0.0	0.0		0.0
Tstk		0.0	−0.1			0.0
Csho				0.2		
Cogs	0.0				0.0	
Xsga			0.1			
Xrd		0.4		0.4	0.7	1.2
Xint		0.6	0.5	1.2		1.4
Nopi	0.2	−0.6	−0.4	0.3		0.7

(*continued*)

	Oancf	Oancf1	Oancf2	Oancf3	Oancf4	Oancf5
Spi	−0.1	−0.8	−0.6	−0.3	0.0	
Txt			0.4	1.3	0.2	0.6
Mii	0.2		2.4	0.8	1.8	3.7
Ib		0.8	0.6			
Xido	0.1	−0.2	0.1	0.1	−0.3	
Cshtr_f	0.0		0.0		0.0	0.0
Dvpsp_f	12.1	38.8	0.0		157.6	155.3
Mkvalt	0.1	0.0			0.0	0.0
Prch_f			−0.2	1.0		
Adj. R^2	**0.904**	**0.924**	**0.903**	**0.826**	**0.900**	**0.865**

All adjusted R^2 values are relatively high, suggesting that the financial variables are good predictors of operating cash flow. The R^2 values fall as they predict operating cash flow further into the future, which is natural as more distant events are harder to predict reliably.

From Table 3, all six regression models are seen to share the common variables:

- Cash and Short-Term Investments (Che)
- Receivables – Estimated Doubtful (Recd)
- Inventory – Finished Goods (Invfg)
- Common/Ordinary Stock (Cstk)

Cash and short-term investments as well as inventory – finished goods close to the point of sales are straightforward in how it correlates with operating cash flow, but the relationship with estimated doubtful receivables and common/ordinary stock is not easily explained.

4.6. Residual plot analysis of the 6 resultant regression models

The six residual plots in Figures 1a-f look randomly distributed and unbiased, but were slightly skewed and displayed some heteroscedasticity. The six Q-Q plots in Figures 2a-f show that the assumption of normality holds.

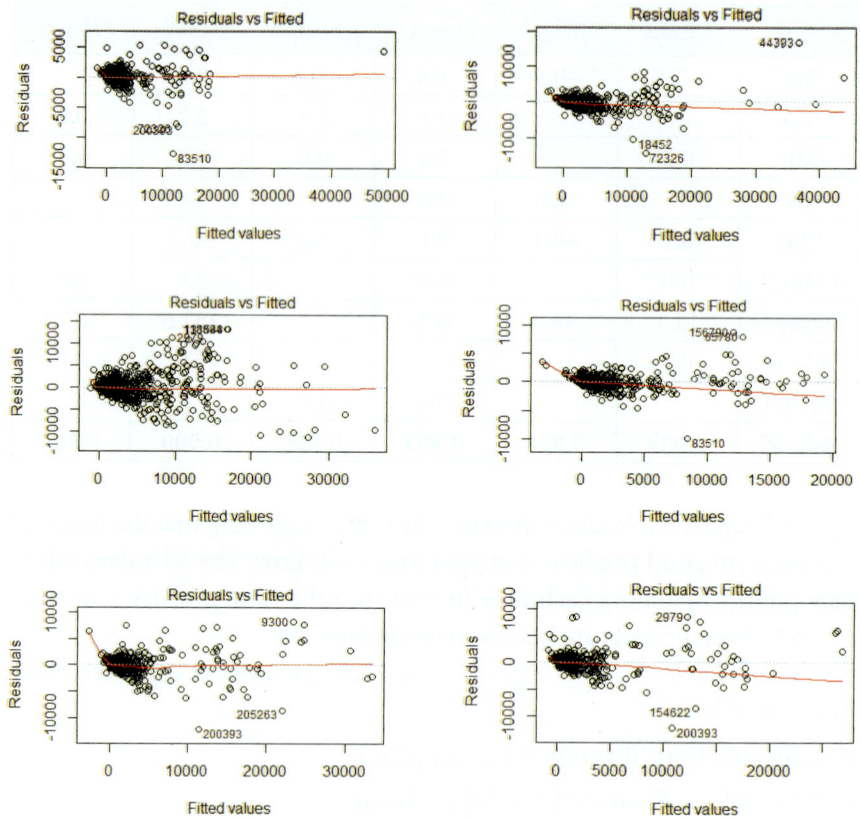

Figures 1a–f: Residual plots against fitted values of the six regression models.

4.7. Testing

The six models were then applied on the test set to generate predictions for the companies' operating cash flow in the current year as well as for each subsequent year up to five years into the future. The overall root-mean-squared error (RMSE) for each year's operating cash flow is given in the following table. The RMSE represents the average magnitude of error made when predicting oancf in each year.

	Oancf	Oancf1	Oancf2	Oancf3	Oancf4	Oancf5
RMSE	311.4	274.2	746.2	625.8	428.9	510.8

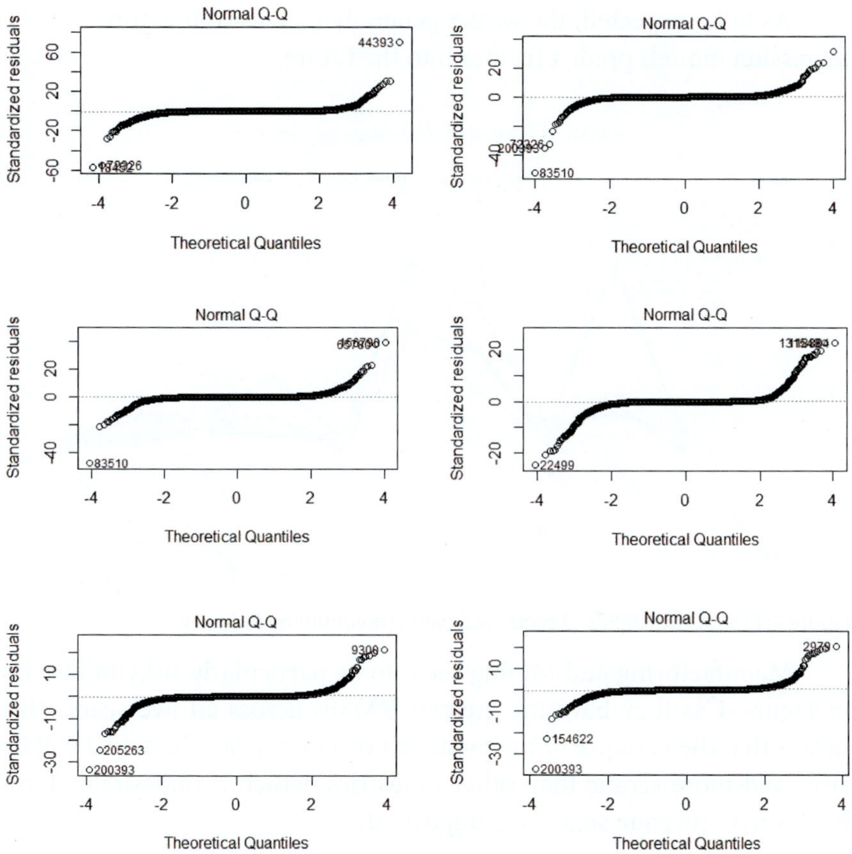

Figures 2a–f: Q-Q plots of the six regression models.

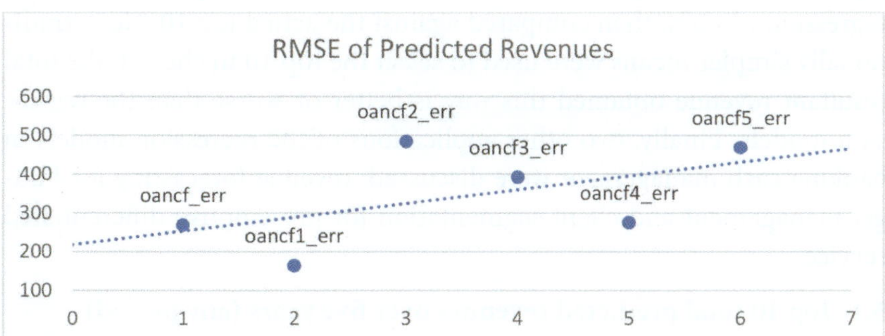

Figure 3: Plot of the RMSEs of predicted oancf (revenue) for years zero to five.

As to be expected, the RMSE generally increases in Figure 3 as the regression models predict further into the future.

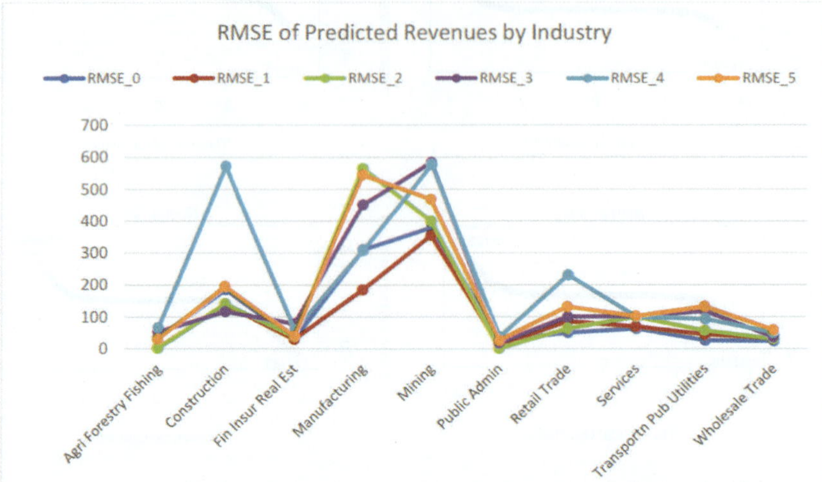

Figure 4: Plot of the RMSEs of predicted oancf (revenue) by industry.

Manufacturing and Mining seem to be particularly risky industries in Figure 4 as they have the greatest RMSEs across all five years. This means that the variance of the predicted revenues from the actual will be large and more erratic than other industries, which is undesirable for a bank where revenue stability is important.

5. DISCUSSION

To determine how effective the regression models were in practice, the top 10 clients were picked based on their revenues as predicted by the regression models, then compared against the actual top 10. Next, traditionally simpler means were used to select the top 10 to check if the total resultant revenue obtained this way is better or worse than the regression models. Finally, two other applications of the regression models in banking cash management were discussed: revenue forecasting for budget management and client segmentation for pre-emptive differentiated service.

5.1. Top 10 total predicted revenues over five years (any period)

For a bank seeking to maximize revenue over a five year period, it should aim to win the business of the companies with the largest five year total predicted revenues. From the test set, the top 10 companies that actually gave the highest five year revenues over any period were identified and they together contributed a sum of $681,957 in revenue to the bank. The 10 highest five year revenues based on the predicted values were then selected and their sum of $668,756 compared with the theoretical top 10. The potential loss of –$8,401 in revenue represents the lost opportunity should the bank have picked ideally (Figure 5).

Theoretical Top 10 Five-Year Revenue (any period)	$681,957
Predicted Top 10 Five-Year Revenuc (any period)	$673,556
Potential Loss	–$8,401

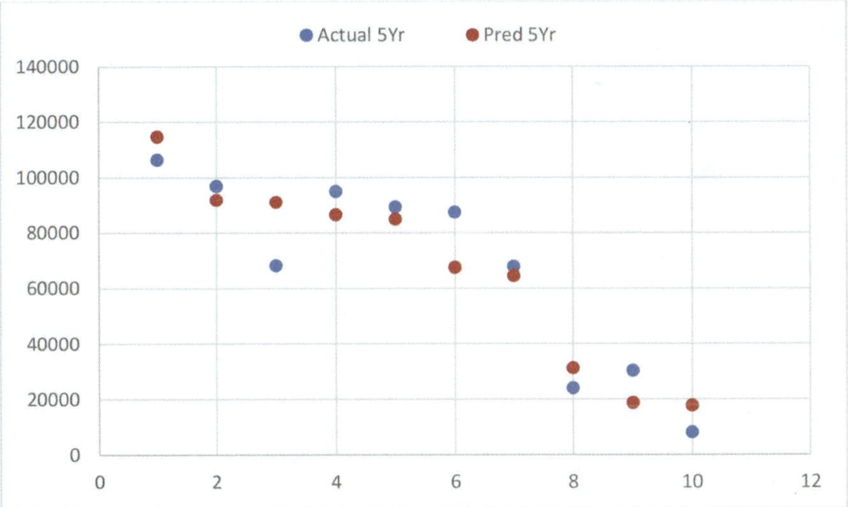

Figure 5: Selected top 10 five-year revenues as predicted over any period and their actual five-year revenues. The difference between predicted and actual represents the error.

The approach mentioned above was able to capture nine of the actual top 10 companies that would have given the highest actual five year revenues. The total error between the predicted and actual revenues of the predicted top 10 is positive $4,800 which means that if the bank had indeed picked this top 10 based on the predictions, it would have earned

$4,800 more revenue in total above what it had initially planned for. However, it would have lost $8,401 in potential earnings if it had selected the true top 10 correctly.

5.2. Top 10 total predicted revenues over five years (Base year 2008)

Next, after verifying that the approach is quite effective in general to identify the top revenue-generating companies, the same method is applied at a fixed point in time. Take for example a scenario where the year is 2008 (fairly recent), and a bank is trying to select 10 clients that

Theoretical Top 10 Five-Year Revenue (base year 2008)	$164,829
Predicted Top 10 Five-Year Revenue (base year 2008)	$161,282
Potential Loss	-$3,547

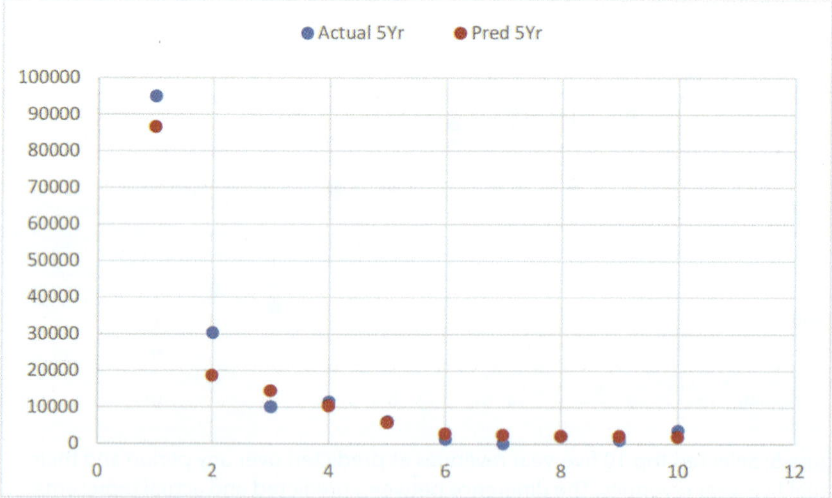

Figure 6: Selected top 10 five-year revenues as predicted in 2008 and their actual five-year revenues.

would generate the highest total revenues over five years. The resulting selection is given below (Figure 6).

With the base year set in 2008, seven out of the actual top 10 were picked by the predictions. If the bank had implemented the predictions, it would have earned $161,282 in revenue, $13,913 above what had been initially predicted, but $3,547 lesser than the true top 10. This is a very positive result, as the bank would have earned significantly higher revenues than it had budgeted for, and it was close to earning the theoretical maximum.

The positive error can be attributed largely to the top two companies that consistently earned significantly higher revenues than predicted for each of the five years, as seen in the breakdown below (Figure 7).

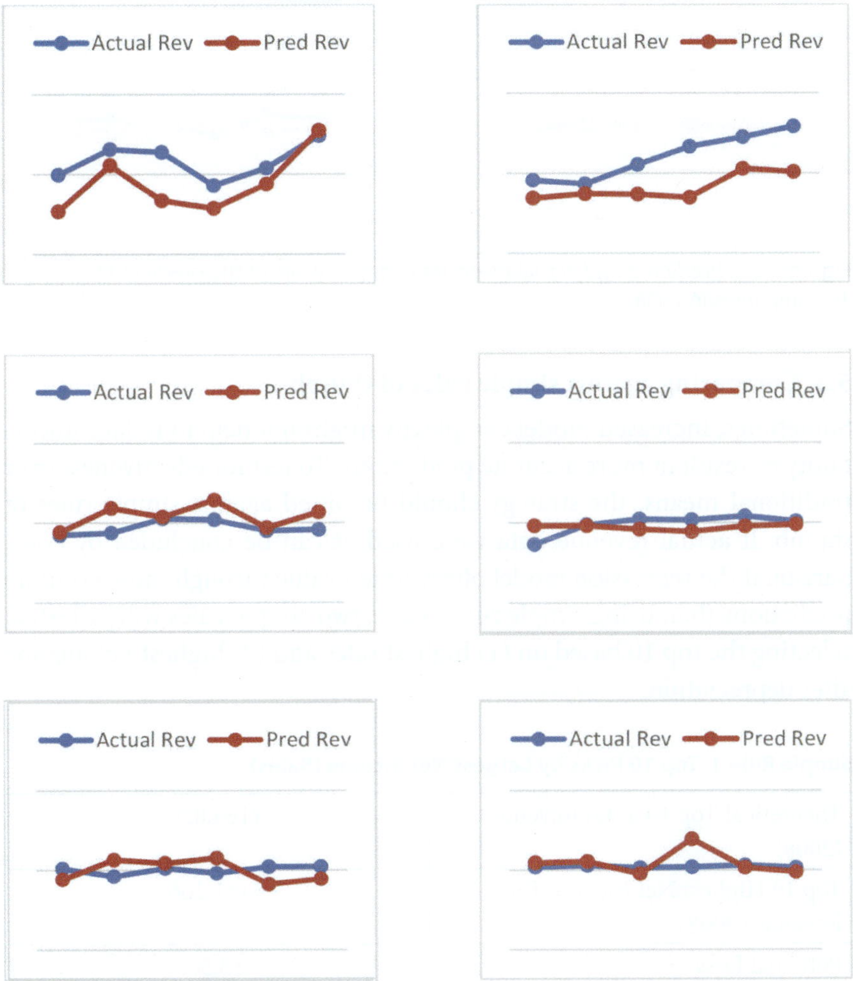

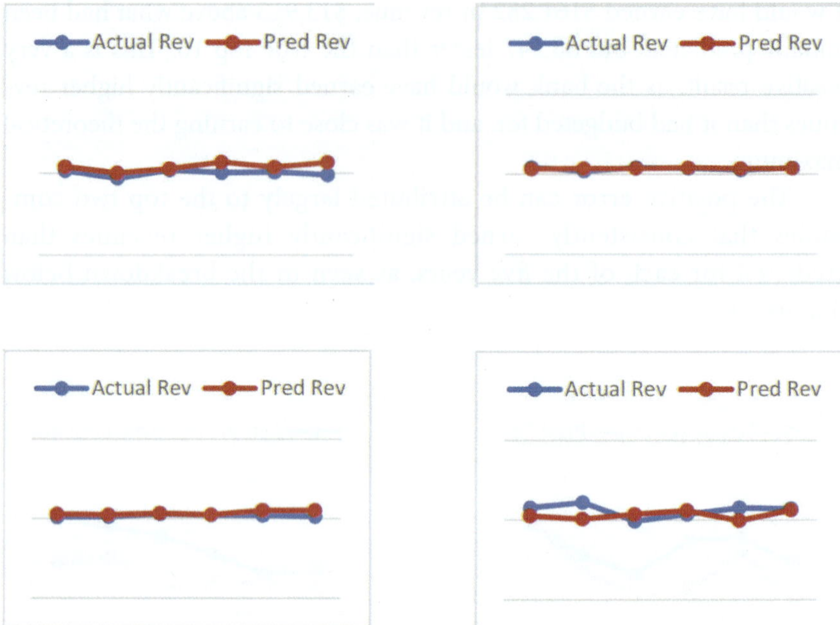

Figures 7a–j: Predicted and actual revenues over five years of the predicted top 10 companies in 2008.

5.3. Comparing against simple rules of thumb

Sometimes, increased model complexity might not help to reduce uncertainty or result in more accurate predictions. To test for effectiveness over traditional means, the strategy should be pitted against simple rules of thumb. If actual revenue data were used, it can be concluded by comparison if the regression model offers added value through more accurate predictions than using simple rules. Here, two simple rules will be tested: selecting the top 10 based on (1) highest sales and (2) highest net income after depreciation.

Simple Rule 1: Top 10 Picks by Largest Net Income (Sales)

Theoretical Top 10 Total Revenue (2008)	$164,829
Top 10 Highest Net Income Total Revenue (2008)	$161,266
Potential Loss	–$3,563

The net income is the total revenue a company makes from its business. Picking the top 10 clients with the biggest net income yields a slightly higher potential loss against the theoretical top 10 than the regression model – our model works better at predicting the top 10 highest revenue generating clients.

Simple Rule 2: Top 10 Picks by Operating Income after Depreciation (Oiadp)

Theoretical Top 10 Total Revenue (2008)	$164,829
Top 10 Highest Oiadp Total Revenue (2008)	$161,677
Potential Loss	–$3,152

Operating income after depreciation is net income subtracting away operating expenses and depreciation. It shows how much revenue is left after the company takes care of its day-to-day operations. Picking the top 10 clients with the biggest Oiadp yields a lower loss against the theoretical top 10 than the regression model. This rule of thumb method worked better than the regression model at predicting the top 10 highest revenue-generating clients.

Because operating cash flow was the dependent variable in this case, it could not be determined conclusively that the regression model or simply selecting the top 10 companies with the highest operating income after depreciation worked better for predicting actual cash management revenue.

5.4. Other applications: Forecast revenue for budget planning and management

Company	Total		2008		2009		2010		2011		2012		2013
1	▲ 5,059	$86,546	$12,666	▲ 2,899	$15,565	▼ 2,219	$13,345	▼ 479	$12,866	▲ 1,513	$14,379	▲ 3,345	$17,725
2	▲ 1,652	$18,675	$2,437	▲ 274	$2,711	▼ 36	$2,675	▼ 201	$2,474	▲ 1,815	$4,289	▼ 200	$4,089
3	▲ 1,248	$14,474	$1,416	▲ 1,500	$2,916	▼ 547	$2,369	▲ 1,052	$3,421	▼ 1,732	$1,688	▲ 976	$2,665
4	▲ 80	$10,386	$1,816	▲ 8	$1,825	▼ 225	$1,600	▼ 142	$1,457	▲ 334	$1,792	▲ 105	$1,897
5	▲ 34	$5,856	$415	▲ 1,244	$1,660	▼ 211	$1,448	▲ 327	$1,776	▼ 1,668	$108	▲ 341	$449
6	▼ 592	$2,778	$467	▲ 81	$547	▼ 775	-$228	▲ 2,184	$1,956	▼ 1,795	$161	▼ 287	-$126
7	▲ 270	$2,441	$400	▼ 383	$17	▲ 263	$280	▲ 414	$694	▼ 314	$381	▲ 290	$670
8	▲ 53	$2,180	$317	▲ 44	$361	▼ 0	$361	▲ 54	$416	▼ 60	$355	▲ 15	$370
9	▲ 225	$2,150	$290	▼ 48	$242	▲ 100	$342	▼ 100	$242	▲ 277	$519	▼ 3	$516
10	▲ 369	$1,881	$258	▼ 192	$66	▲ 300	$366	▲ 230	$596	▼ 629	-$32	▲ 659	$627
Total	▲ 8,399	$147,369	$20,483	▲ 5,426	$25,909	▼ 3,351	$22,558	▲ 3,340	$25,898	▼ 2,259	$23,639	▲ 5,243	$28,882

Figure 8: Forecasted revenue scorecard for 10 hypothetical clients of a bank.

Besides identifying high-revenue clients to pitch to, the regression model could also be used to forecast the future revenues of newly acquired and existing clients of the bank for budget planning and allocation.

The five year forecasted revenue trends for 10 hypothetical clients is shown in Figure 8 above and the overall revenue forecast for the bank is represented in the Figure 9 below.

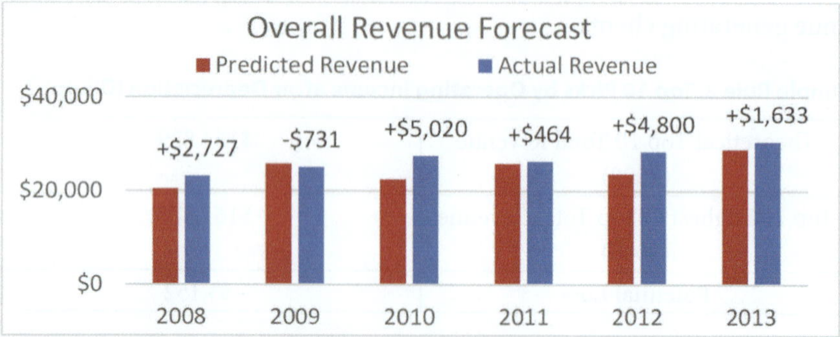

Figure 9: Overall revenue forecast for the bank as predicted by our regression model and the actual revenue and error.

The predictions erred overall on the conservative side and actual revenues outstripped predicted values in five years out of six, or a total sum of +$13,913 over the six years combined.

5.5. Other applications: Client segmentation analysis

One other application of the forecasted revenues was client segmentation. Segments were defined for a bank's existing clientele based on their five year forecasted revenues that determined how the bank continued to treat and service them. Four segments were defined in Figure 10 as follows, where the segment number is ordered in decreasing desirability.

5.6. Pre-emptive differentiated service model for each segment

Once existing clients were segmented based on their forecasted revenues, pre-emptive actions were taken for clients in each segment to attempt to better the situation. For example, clients in the Hi+ segment were appeased to maintain the relationship, whereas clients in Lo- were considered for exiting. Clients in Lo+ were given assistance to boost their businesses in ways that would benefit both the client and the bank's revenues. Clients in Hi- were cajoled into more cash management activities or cross-sold other banking products and services to increase revenue.

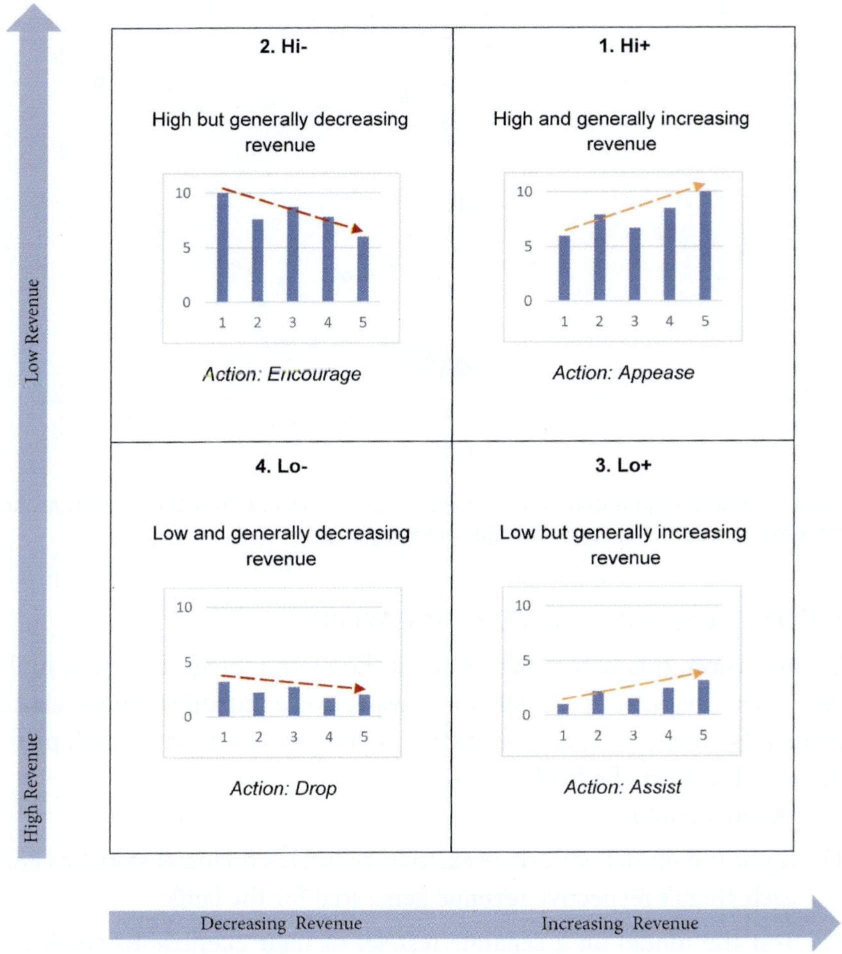

Figure 10: Four client segments and their respective pre-emptive actions.

5.7. Segmentation on test set

From the test set, a subset of the data was taken where all five years of actual and predicted operating cash flows could be calculated for comparison. This subset consisted of 1,609 rows with non-N/A values of actual and predicted operating cash flow across all five years. This subset was classified into the four segments above according to their predicted and actual revenues, with the result summarized in the charts below (Figure 11).

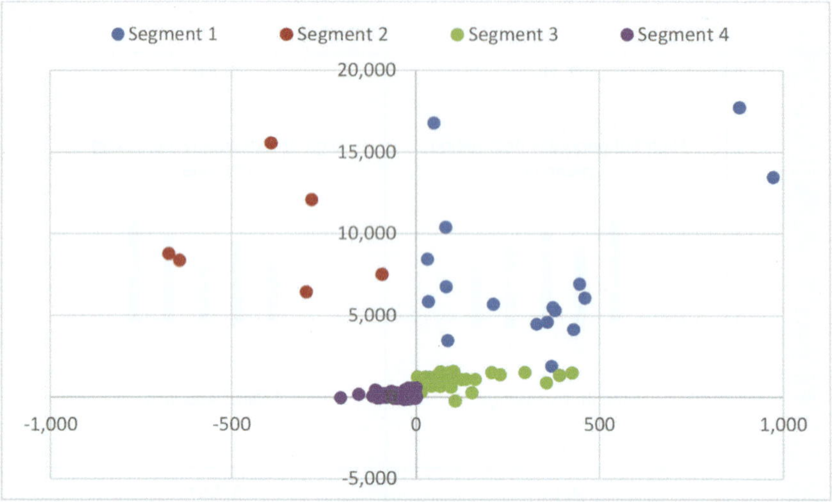

Figure 11: Client segmentation performed on test set, where the *y*-axis is revenue and the *x*-axis represents the total change over five years.

6. CONCLUSIONS AND FURTHER WORK

In conclusion, this report has outlined the methodology for using multiple linear regression models on prospective companies' financials to predict the amount of revenue that would be generated for the cash management business of a bank.

A bank could:

1) Input the model with their existing clientele's financial statistics and each client's respective revenue generated for the bank
2) Test the model on a separate test set of their clientele to check for accuracy
3) Use historical data in the model and compare against their traditional means or other simple rules of thumb to determine if the model is indeed more effective and
4) Apply the model on target companies to gauge if they would be high revenue generating clients or not for a more strategic sales focus.

This report also shows how to test if key financial ratios might play a part in predicting cash management revenues, to analyze residual plots for bias or heteroscedasticity, and check the prediction errors by year and industry to identify particularly risky segments or periods.

Finally, this report demonstrated how a bank could use the revenue forecasting model to forecast the revenues of their existing clients for better budget planning and further to segment their clients for pre-emptive differential servicing to maximize profits. Together, by first identifying and winning the highest revenue generating clients, coupled with revenue forecasting and pre-emptive client servicing, a bank using this model can develop a leading edge over its competitors in the cash management market.

REFERENCES

1. Akash, L, HV Vinayak, N Tommaso, R Raffaela, S Sunghman and C Reet (2012). *Rising to the challenge: Transaction banking in Asia-Pacific.* McKinsey & Company.

2. 30th Annual Cash Management Services Survey 2013 Executive Summary (2013). *Ernst & Young LLP.* http://www.ey.com/Publication/vwLUAssets/EY_-_30th_Annual_Cash_Management_Services_Survey/$FILE/30th_Annual_Cash_Management_Services_Survey.pdf

CHAPTER 9

Big Data Analytics: Implications for an International Reinsurer

LIANG Fang-Yu

ABSTRACT

This study provides a thorough overview as well as examines various ecosystems and analytical capabilities existing in the Asia Pacific region from the viewpoint of an international reinsurer. This is achieved through a combination of (1) high-level market watch and trends analysis and (2) company-specific due diligence in order to explore the potential for a strategic partnership with the reinsurer. Some existing and some potential applications of said data is described in order to evaluate its relevance to the underwriting business in the (re)insurance industry.

The opinions expressed in this article belong exclusively to the author and do not represent the view of Swiss Re.

1. INTRODUCTION

Big Data and other increasingly sophisticated analytical techniques are transforming the (re)insurance industry. With the exponential growth of data,[1] improvements in analytical capabilities and computational power, proliferation of digital/market platforms, and the emergence of "digital disrupters",[2] the reinsurance industry is not only faced with new challenges, but new opportunities as well. As clients and competitors become increasingly sophisticated, reinsurers may be in danger of losing its competitive edge when it comes to risk assessment and selection. Additionally, as primary insurers become better at managing their own risks due to wider access to unconventional information sources, reinsurers' profit margins and premium volumes may be reduced. The latter could be further exacerbated by the entrance of digital market players who use their superior understanding of customers to overturn traditional business models. However, if harnessed appropriately, Big Data can become the new growth engine for the reinsurance industry, which has been characterized by modest but consistent growth.

Since (re)insurance is an information-driven industry, the data avalanche introduced by social media, sensors, smartphones, etc. will have a significant impact on the way it assesses risk. There are two general ways Big Data analytics can add value to the (re)insurance industry. Big Data analytics can be used to add incremental value by improving current internal services. Analyzing large datasets, such as online purchasing behavior or credit card transaction history, could yield correlations and trends that may help generate market or client insight. This information can be used to devise business and customer-retention strategies, provide additional client services, and create customized product offerings. Similarly, by analyzing unstructured data, in the form of notes and surveys, sentiment insights can be gathered and internal operations improved. One of the most mature internal applications of Big Data analytics in the (re)insurance industry is in claims handling and fraud detection. To illustrate, a South Korean insurance company uses 800 different variables, constructed from internal client databases and external information, to detect fraudulent claims. There are also a handful of companies

1 90 per cent of the data today was created in the last two years (SINTEF, 2013).

2 These are internet-related companies that can use their superior knowledge of customers to offer their own insurance products.

offering risk scoring services by processing insurance claimant data via a web application and returning a predictive result generated from wide ranging data across social medial platforms and broader internet. All this information is then cross-referenced with that provided by the claimant and/or derived from publically available online information. Figure 1 presents a visual illustration of Swiss Re's value chain and how Big Data can add incremental value to each of these areas.

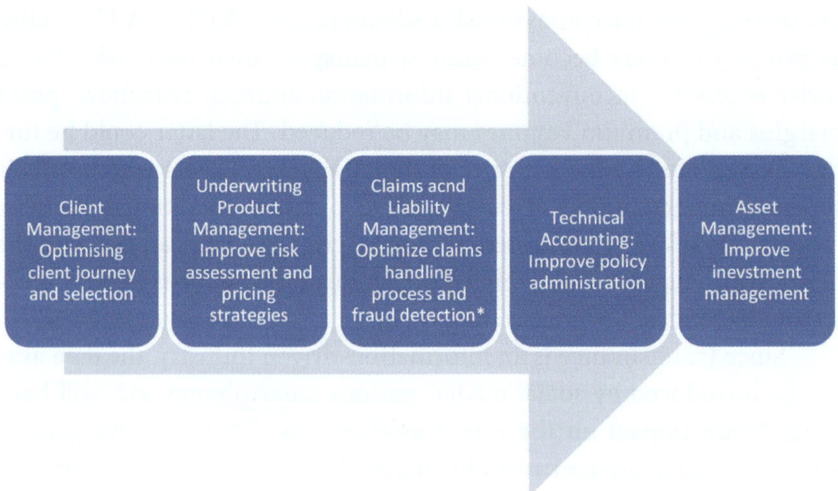

Figure 1: Swiss Re value chain.

While the hypothesis regarding incremental value of Big Data for (re)insurers has been widely tested and confirmed, the jury is still out for the "disruptive role" of Big Data. This may include anything from helping the business tap into new markets to launching new products and creating new distribution channels. A few disruptive mechanisms through which Big Data may transform the (re)insurance industry include Internet of Things (IoT) and cognitive computing.

Internet of Things (IoT): Broadly speaking, IoT pertains to data generated by quantifying variables from the physical world, using technology such as sensors and location trackers. examples could include wearable devices that keep track of heart rate and blood glucose level in order to monitor health conditions, telematics solutions installed in automobiles to capture driving behavior, or sensors installed in manufacturing factories to detect machine breakdown.

Case 1: Telematics Usage-Based Auto Insurance

Unlike traditional auto insurance that attempts to differentiate between "safe" and "high risk" drivers by using historical data, Telematics UBI is a mile-based contract whereby costs/premiums are dependent upon real-time data on mileage, speed, time of day, riskiness of road, and driving behavior. For example, drivers who habitually use their mobile-phones while driving may be charged a higher premium — an incentive structure that encourages drivers to adopt safer driving practices. This information can be captured by onboard telematics devices, smart phones, or GPS devices. Insurance companies that have already adopted this telematics UBI include Progressive and AllState (Karapiperis, 2015).

Cognitive Computing: Through the use of cognitive computing systems[3] that can intelligently read thousands of policies and claims within a short time, (re)insurers can bolster productivity by reducing human errors and operating expenses.

Case 2: IBM Watson in Insurance

IBM Watson Engagement Advisor is an artificial intelligence (AI) system with a key capability in processing natural language. It is currently used in the banking industry. For example it can help relationship managers analyze larger volumes of structured and unstructured data from research reports, customer profiles, and product information; match customers' needs with current investment offerings, and help advisors evaluate different financial options in a streamlined and informed manner.

Data Silos: These are datasets, large or small, from multiple sources that can help (re)insurers gain market insights. This is especially important in developing countries, where data is often of lower-quality, or data centers often exist in silos and are often fragmented.

3 This category of technologies uses natural language processing and machine learning to enable people and machines to interact more organically for the purpose of extending and increasing human expertise. These systems will learn and interact to provide expert assistance to scientists, engineers, lawyers, and other professionals in a fraction of the time it takes for humans to do the same.

For reinsurers and insurers alike, the disruptive role of Big Data represents unexplored territory with vast potential. However, this also requires (re)insurers to tap into increasingly diverse data sources from both internal and external third party sources. Moreover, such data may be structured or unstructured.[4] How will (re)insurers access external third party data from companies that are not necessarily in the insurance industry? Forging new strategic partnerships is the key. Indeed, there is already a wave of strategic partnerships between insurers and independent businesses: AXA with Linkedin, Alibaba with Taiping, etc. The objective of such partnerships is not merely to create new distribution channels, but also to interact more dynamically with clients and better understand their needs. Creating new services is another objective, e.g., American Family Insurance has partnered with Microsoft to order to launch a business incubator for startups focused on smart homes. In fact, 72 per cent of the insurance respondents in Accenture's Digital Innovation survey state that they plan to form new digital partnerships in the near future, or have already done so.

This study will explore the subject of strategic partnership in the context of Asia Pacific, from the perspective of an international reinsurer. It will provide an informative sketch of the data ecosystem in the APAC region and answer the following fundamental questions: What data is available? How can this data benefit the reinsurance business of Swiss Re?

2. PROBLEM STATEMENT

The main purpose of this report is to explore potential strategic data-centric partnerships to help Swiss Re better understand the new ecosystem created by digitalization, and to serve as the foundational enabler for Big Data analytics to be integrated into its reinsurance business. The targeted partners will provide data that can benefit Swiss Re Underwriting and must be relevant to at least one type of risk currently managed by it. The latter includes, but is not limited to, natural catastrophe (NatCat), property and casualty (P&C), and life and health (L&H). At this preliminary stage,

4 Generally speaking, structured data refers to highly organized information that allows for easy inclusion in a relational database. Unstructured data, on the contrary, do not have a defined data model and can include text as well as non-text data (emails, SMS, images etc.).

Swiss Re will not be considering the nature/structure of the partnership model. Instead, the focus will be on the kinds of data that the partner can provide that will benefit Swiss Re's underwriting products. A fictional example follows.

Suppose Swiss Re partners with a bike-sharing company. Unlike transportation services such as public bus or subway, the duration of travel, departure, and arrival position of the shared bikes are explicitly recorded, enabling the bike-sharing system to become a virtual sensor network that can be used for sensing mobility in the city. Hence, it is expected that the most important events in the city could be detected by monitoring these data. Swiss Re could use this data to anticipate events with high casualty risk, which could in turn help them assess the risks and pricing strategies pertaining to the region in question.

3. STATE OF THE ART

This study attempts to address two concerns. First, while there are numerous research papers on the value of Big Data for insurance industry, there are few that shed light on what Big Data means for reinsurers. Second, most of the reports on existing data ecosystems focus on United States and Europe; there are few that provide an in-depth study on the data ecosystems in Asia. This paper will investigate the digital landscape in the Asia-Pacific region, beyond generic statements about "connected things", from the perspective of the reinsurance business. To achieve this goal, the authors will address three main questions: (1) what types of data are available, (2) how can this data benefit the reinsurer, and (3) in cases where the access to data is contingent on the existence of a contractual partnership, how should the reinsurer analyze the viability and ensure the success of the partnership? To answer these questions, the author follows an iterative process, described below. Note that the following procedure is not necessarily performed in chronological order:

- Define a list of criteria factors/framework upon which a successful partnership can be built. This may include the type of data available, factors contingent on geography and culture, the data's relevance to Swiss Re's business model, etc.
- Search possible partners based on the above considerations, with a focus on Asia Pacific, "deep-diving" into those that seem more promising on the basis of available information.

- Iteratively refine the list of potential partners either by pruning or augmenting the targets, based on insights supported by available information and discourses with potential internal and external stakeholders.
- Analyze the business value of said partnerships for Swiss Re and justify the partnership model by a set of relevant KPIs.
- Evaluate the likelihood of developing a proof-of-concept for a specific line of business based on the analysis above.

The main purpose of this research is to generate a list of potential data partners that will enable Swiss Re stakeholders to evaluate each partner on a set of defined factors and prioritize accordingly.

4. APPROACH

A common doubt is whether a strategy to incorporate Big Data analytics into Swiss Re's reinsurance business makes sense in Asia. Indeed, one could argue that such a strategy may be futile due to lack of good quality data in this region. A market-level analysis of the digital ecosystem in Asia will be conducted to address this concern. The results presented in the following section are based on extensive market research, gathered from industry publications, websites, conversations with Swiss Re employees, and dialogues with private businesses, government agencies, and experts.

4.1. APAC digital landscape: Trends and drivers[5]

According to McKinsey Global Institute's 2012 report, world's center of economic gravity has shifted over the past century from the United States and Europe towards Asia. The same can be said of data volume. Consider, for example, the fact that Asian countries have already surpassed its Western counterpart in terms of mobile device usage (McKinsey Global Institute, 2011). In a 2015 study, IDC highlighted the fact that APAC (excluding Japan) will lead IoT with 8.6 billion connected things valued at USD 583 billion by 2020. A wave of investment activities is already being witnessed, especially among big digital disrupters, as well as rapid growth in the number of data-related initiatives in both the public and private sectors, and a proliferation of startups with a focus on IoT and analytics.

5 (Van, APAC Big Data Market Watch, 2015).

Within the last 6 months, 17 innovation labs and analytical centers have been launched, with government and multinational incubators in the ranks of Twitter, Aon, Metlife and Baidu (for examples see Table 1).

Table 1: Examples of Big Data related initiatives in APAC.

Country	Notable activities
Singapore	Twitter also announced the expansion of its Singapore office to be positioned as its APAC headquarter with the launch of #RealTimeLab; Google is building its second data center in Singapore, topping up its total investment in Singapore to be USD 500 million in addition to its USD 600 million center opened in 2013 in Taiwan; AXA launched Data Innovation Lab in Singapore to develop Big Data projects.
Malaysia	IoT Data Centre and Research Lab established in Penang. The participants include Cisco, IBM, Dell, Intel, and Kontron. In 2015, Malaysia signed a deal with SAS to establish a Centre of Excellence that will build and test Big Data proofs-of-concepts for government and commercial use. Malaysia government will also build a Digital Government Lab, one among many activities under its national Big Data and smart cities initiative.
Indonesia	Pulse Lab Jakarta, a partnership between United Nation and Indonesia government, hosted a data innovation mini grants competition in March 2015 with the intention to find innovative solutions to tackle data gaps and address current challenges in the frontline service delivery and protection for the poor and vulnerable.
India	100 smart cities.

Asian governments are also active in smart cities initiatives, which depend on a host of digital technologies, such as sensors and information communication technologies, to improve the quality of public services (transportation, energy, healthcare, etc.), reduce costs and eliminate inefficient resource deployment in order to engage more effectively with city dwellers. Smart cities can help generate a treasure trove of information that (re)insurers can use to evaluate risk exposures, e.g., a comprehensive database on property characteristics such as a building's age, its construction company, whether it is in the middle of a foreclosure, its surroundings and wind fields may help (re)insurers map out and predict the risk of fire without having to physically inspect the sites. According to IHS Technology, the Asia Pacific region will have 31 smart cities by 2025, while the US and Europe may only have 25.

Table 2 lists some of the countries in Asia that have started to build smart cities.

Table 2: Smart cities in Asia.

Country	Smart city initiatives
China	• 200 + initiatives currently. • IoT and connectivity emphasized in its recent 5-year plan. • State Council issues guidelines promoting commercial health insurance development in 2014, encouraging information sharing and the creation of health-related information systems.
South Korea	• Sodongo — world's first smart city due for completion in 2015.
India	• 100 smart cities initiatives announced in Union Budget 2014 with USD 1.1 billion provided, to be launched in 2015.
Japan	• Pilot projects in four cities (Yokohoma, Toyota City, Keilhanna Eco City, Kitakyushu).
Malaysia	• Industry-led IoT data center and research lab setup in early 2015 that focuses on healthcare wearable devices.

Singapore is striving to, and has thus far succeeded in, becoming a smart cities leader in the Asia Pacific region. Building deep analytical capabilities is a key mission of the Singaporean government, which has channeled a variety of resources and funding to meet this objective. Notably, under the partnerships for capability transformation (PACT), the government agency Singapore has partnered with Intel in order to provide support to fledgling start-ups and small to medium enterprises related to IoT. A list of the Singapore government's big-data activities can be found below in Table 3.

Table 3: Singapore government smart nation initiatives.

Name	Organizations involved	Data collected
OneMap	Singapore Land Authority (SLA), Infocomm Development Authority(IDA) Geographic Information System (GIS) National Parks Board	An interactive, multilayered, multi-themed, and customizable smart map that enables easy navigation. Capabilities include a drop-down list of location information on community, health, and environmental services, places of interest, hawker centers, and child care services.
Smart Water Grid	Public Utilities Board (PUB)	Monitor water quality and pressure, and detect pipe leaks in real-time.
Tele-rehabilitation	National University Singapore (NUS) National University Health System (NUHS) Singapore Millennium Foundation	Uses motion sensors to guide stroke patients when they are doing at-home exercises, supported by video footage. Therapists can use this information to monitor the rehabilitation process of stroke patients.
myENV	National Environment Agency (NEA)	Real-time data on water and noise pollution and hazardous substance handling. Provides up-to-date environmental guidelines, construction-noise advice, and immediate feedback on environmental issues such as littering.
Smart Health Assist	Ministry of Communication and Information (MCI)	Uses sensors in a patient's living environment to monitor his or her health. The information is transmitted to medical professionals accurately and regularly. Any deterioration of patient's health can be detected early or anticipated.

(*continued*)

Table 3: Singapore government smart nation initiatives (*Continued*)

Name	Organizations involved	Data collected
PolCam	Ministry of Home Affairs (MHA) Neighborhood Police Post (NPP)	PolCam collects video footage for investigative purposes, while neighborhood police post (NPP) gives citizens round-the-clock access to police services.
Body Worn Cameras and In-Vehicle Video Recording System (IVVRS)	Ministry of Home Affairs (MHA)	Body-worn cameras and in-vehicle video recording systems allow police officers to record encrypted video footages and high-resolution images that can later be analyzed for investigative purposes.
Beeline	Land Transport Authority (LTA)	Online shuttle booking; adaptive and dynamic routes powered by data analytics.
myTransport.SG	Land Transport Authority (LTA)	Bus arrivals, available car parks, traffic conditions (view the latest traffic conditions along expressways and key locations).
Planning for Land Transport Network (PLANET)	Land Transport Authority (LTA)	Collects information of commuters' "journey" to streamline transport planning to understand travelers' behaviors.
Smart Logistics	Infocomm Media Masterplan (IMM)	Uses sensors to improve supply-chain management. Stakeholders can respond to new events during shipment, which will improve cargo and facility security.
Smart Nation Tech Challenges	Infocomm Development Authority (IDA)	Encourage active collaborations among companies and research entities to come up with technological solutions that addresses a real-world problem.

Name	Organizations involved	Data collected
National Cyber Security Masterplan	Infocomm Development Authority (IDA)	Provides the strategic directions to guide Singapore's national efforts to enhance cyber security for public, private, and people sectors.
MyConnection SG	Infocomm Development Authority (IDA)	Gathers usage experience from users' mobile phones, such as broadband speed, latency, and coverage on mobile cellular networks to improve the quality of experience for mobile broad-band users.
Smart Elderly Monitoring and Alert System (SEMA)	Housing and Development Board (HDB)	Motion and door sensors installed at seniorcitizens' home can "learn" the living habits of its residents and alert their caregivers and family members, via SMS notifications, when irregular patterns in behavior are detected.
Smart Urban Tourism w/ Resorts World Sentosa	National Research Foundation of Singapore (NRF) Carnegie Mellon University Resorts World Sentosa	Proof-of-concept for dynamic logistics management in theme parks.
SERC Urban Systems Initiative	A*STAR	Seeks to develop capabilities to: a) address the technological needs of rapidly urbanizing world; and b) enable the development of solutions for complex urban challenges to enhance Singapore's competitiveness.

Another notable development in Asia is the Open Data movement, in which the government releases national databases, with topics ranging from health, industry to the environment, onto an open access platform so that public can use it for research and academic purposes (see Table 4). This is of interest to private industry, such as (re)insurers, as this data is often considered a "free lunch".

Table 4: Open data initiatives in Asia.

Singapore	data.gov.sg currently has more than 8000 datasets. Recently, environmental data gathered from thousands of sensors installed island-wide is added to the database.
China	• In April 2015, the State Council called for further opening of information related to air and water quality, pollutant emissions, and sources of pollution among others. It is seen that opening-up of environment data will foster an environment that encourages innovations in Big Data to help resolve environmental issues. This is also to support and compliment the government's ambition to launch world's biggest carbon market in 2016, a market-based approach to control pollutions by using economic incentives to achieve emission reduction. As the carbon markets become more mature, players will become more sophisticated in pricing carbon securities. This requires a lot of real-time data on environment and energy sector. • Guiyang government is accelerating efforts to develop the city as a base for China's Big Data industries. Last year, the government signed 138 development deals worth 132.61 billion yuan, while additional 61 investment deals valued at 50.64 billion yuan are expected to be finalized before 2017. • China is also working on opendatachina.com.
Hong Kong	Hong Kong is building its open data platform and recently added traffic data and data from other accessible public facilities.
Indonesia	Jakarta opens its data for flooding, crop, and water management via PetaJakarta.org.

Malaysia	Multimedia Development Corporation (MDeC) of Malaysia announced two separate initiatives that will pave the way for open data among Malaysian government agencies: a strategic partnership with Open Data Institute (a non-profit think tank) and the creation of National Data Champions, a select group of data experts who will advise the government on open data strategy and implementation.
Taiwan	Taiwan Open Data (data.gov.tw) currently includes data on social and economic indicators, law and regulation.
Cambodia	Open Development Cambodia provides the public with up-to-date, accurate information about Cambodia and its economic and social development.
Japan	Data go JP.

Given the level of public interest, governmental intervention, and targeted funding, there is ample justification for reinsurers to build Big Data focused strategies in this region.

4.2. How can (Re) insurers benefit from this landscape

To understand how different types of data can benefit Swiss Re's underwriting business, one must first understand the different lines of businesses, what variables are used to assess risks, and how additional information/data can be leveraged to drive value. The key risks covered by Swiss Re are:

Business line (s)	Description
Property and casualty (P&C) and Natural catastrophe (NatCat)	Property casualty insurance pertains to financial losses resulting from being held legally liable for an accident that causes damage to another person or another person's belongings. Swiss Re's Casualty teams underwrite the following lines of business: liability, motor, workers' compensation, personal accident, directors and officers, and professional indemnity. Additionally, there is contingent business interruption (housed under property) due to power outage, machinery breakdown, or natural catastrophes such as floods, hurricanes, forest fires, etc.

(*continued*)

Table 4: Open data initiatives in Asia (*Continued*)

Business line (s)	Description
Property and specialty	Swiss Re property and specialty underwrite across all lines, including property, credit and surety, engineering, aviation, marine, and agriculture.
Life and health (L&H)	Health insurance provides insurance against incurring medical expenses. Life insurance is a contract whereby the insurer promises to pay the policyholder an agreed upon sum of money in the event of his/her death in exchange for a premium.

While it is tempting to organize the list of data providers by line of business, this approach is not always practical, as some risks apply to multiple lines. To illustrate, the 2015 Tianjin explosions triggered losses from multiple lines including: containers; cargo in containers; property; automobiles; and general aviation. Classifying by industry is similarly inefficient as even within a single industry there could be multiple risks. Oil and gas, for example, is susceptible to both cyber-attacks and man-made catastrophes. Given these considerations, the data-providers were grouped based on business logic and customize the relevant dimensions accordingly.

4.3. Business line — life and health

The L&H market has been vibrant in the past year, driven by a competitive start-up environment and favorable regulatory conditions. While investments in the United States and other mature markets has been focused on genomics and telehealth, funding and projects in the APAC region has been directed towards consumer health and wellness, healthcare system navigation, patient-doctor engagement platforms, and patient-friendly sensor technologies.

On the regulatory front, the Insurance Regulatory and Development Authority of India (IRDAI) has proposed to offer reduced premiums for policyholders who acquiesce to third party monitoring of their health. Concurrently, China Insurance Regulatory Commission (CIRC) has also announced that it will open up the Chinese insurance market further and allow for more foreign insurers. The need for more foreign insurance penetration is further intensified by China's volatile stock markets and recent chemical explosion in Tianjin. Both economies, China and India, hold vast untapped potential for L&H (re)insurers given the widening protection gap, driven by growing incidences of non-communicable, lifestyle-related diseases such as diabetes, heart diseases, stroke and cancers.

Researchers have found that the average person in China is exposed to 52 micrograms of PM2.5 per unit of cubed air, dramatically increasing the risk of developing respiratory and heart related problems (Rohde, 2015). According to a recent research conducted by Confederation of Indian Industry, 5.8 million Indians die from life-style related illnesses each year — in other words, 25 per cent of Indians may die of lifestyle diseases before they are 70 (The Times of India, 2015). The severity of the problem is such that numerous initiatives, both government mandated and privately funded, are now sprouting across the country to address it.

Increased lifespan of Asian populations is also driving the age-dependency ratio and creating a sizable demand in cost-effective elderly care. Nowhere is this situation more dire than in Japan, whose elderly population (as defined by those above 65 years of age) is set to increase to 40 per cent of total population by 2055. Given these market trends, it makes sense for Swiss Re to develop an L&H-focused, data-centric strategy in this region.

Reinsurers do not typically have access to insurer's underwriting data. Moreover, claims information is only available on a case-by-case basis. Given that a patient may have multiple policies with the same insurer (or multiple insurers), it will be useful for reinsurers to capture this information in order to have a holistic view of the customer, based on the policies he/she purchased. Specifically, L&H (re)insurers may benefit from having the following information on the patients: health-related spending, hereditary illnesses, industries the patients are in (people in certain industries may be more susceptible to stress-induced illnesses), living/working conditions (including daily commute), and purchasing behavior — in all, information pertaining to the nature (genetic propensities towards certain illnesses) and nurture (lifestyle choices).

Table 5 illustrates a framework for information sources that can potentially improve L&H underwriting. As many insurance companies deploy data inefficiently, due to outdated systems and management issues, a reinsurer may be able to add value if they have access to this data.

Table 5: Useful information for L&H.

Behavioral	Clinical	Drug	Environment	Claims and cost	Financial
Hours of sleep	Imaging and lab results	Drug prescription information	Weather	Historical claims (provided by insurance companies)	Financial data on patient such as income, credit rating, etc.
Serving of fruit/ vegetables each day	Family health history		environment (living and working conditions)	Electronic claims through platform	
Minutes of exercise	Public health data		Profession (which industry the patient works in)		
Intensity of exercise	Genomic data		Commute		
Calories consumed/ burned	Physician diagnosis and treatment information				
Emotional state (stressed, relaxed, etc.)					

How can this data be harnessed to create business value? A few possible applications are illustrated below[6]:

1) **Risk stratification:** This includes a better understanding of how certain demographics (this can include people with specific lifestyles)

6 Some of these applications were adapted based on a conversation with Professor Teo Hock Hai of NUS School of Computing (Hai, 2015).

are more prone to certain diseases, i.e., disease prediction. Based on this information, products can be designed to capture niche markets, such as diabetic patients, and pricing improved. The behavioral data and claims information listed above can also be used to develop KPIs that can be used to monitor health of the workforce, such as monthly/annual sickness frequency, percentage of employees who falls sick per month, percentage of workforce that engages in frequent exercise (and healthy eating), percentage of employees with chronic diseases, number of employees who engage in regular health screening. The latter will increase the success of early detection and reduce the risk of severe illnesses.

2) **Illness trajectory prediction:** Given that a person is already sick, the (re)insurer will be able to predict, based on the person's lifestyle/diet/external environment, whether he/she will get better or worse.
3) **Cost drivers:** What illnesses (common flu, cardiovascular diseases, etc.), external indicators (office environment, mode of transportation, weather, etc.), and (Hai, 2015) factors (wrong diagnosis, drug allergies, etc.) contribute the most to claims costs?
4) **Preventative care:** This can help (re)insurers improve health risks, reduce claims, improve customer loyalty, boost branding, and create differentiation. In fact, (re)insurers are well positioned to drive innovation in the preventative care space. While hospitals rely on sick people for their revenue stream, it is in the interest of (re)insurers that people remain healthy.

The data above can be used to better understand the impact of certain health behaviors and indicators (regular health screening, diet, exercise, body mass index, etc.) on overall wellbeing, as measured by claims, and clinical results. If these health benefits can be quantified, then insurers can offer incentive programs, such as premium discounts, for patients to alter their behavior.

A good example of such programs is BP's "Million Step Challenge", whereby BP provided its 14,000 employees with a fitness device in order to track their physical activity for one year. Employees who have crossed one million steps would be awarded points that can be used to lower their insurance premiums. This program also included other wellness offerings such as onsite general health consultations, biometric health screening, and campaigns targeting physical activity and weight management. The BP example shows that insurers can monetize the concept of preventative care by offering a disease management or lifestyle management program that can potentially change the healthcare cost curve.

5) **Treatment effectiveness:** Diagnostic, prescriptive, and follow-up information can potentially reveal the best and most cost-effective drug/treatment path for a specific disease or illness.
6) **Public policy recommendations:** Public policy, not necessarily related to health insurance, can be driven by "macro" health and medical trends as glimpsed from the data. Theoretically, the government might infer a positive correlation between obesity levels and availability of parks, and decide to channel more funding into building recreational outdoor public facilities.
7) **Product feature comparison and design:** The data can be used to analyze how product features drive behavior, e.g., if copayment is too high, people may choose not to have diagnosis or treatment, potentially resulting in larger claims at the end for higher severity illnesses. If copayment is too low, people may go to the hospital for trivial cases. Data analytics can be used to find the right balance.

   Another possibility could be to study whether a product that incentivizes healthy habits really drives down claims cost by comparing it against a traditional product that does not include an incentive scheme.
8) **Integration of inpatient and outpatient:** Closing the gap between inpatient and outpatient care is important for developing integrated networks that can work together to coordinate care and share accountability for quality, cost, and outcomes.
9) **Research generation:** This is especially important to support certain classes of (re)insurance products and aid product innovation.

But where is this data available? Both in the Asia Pacific region and beyond, the emergence of "connected health" ecosystem can be seen, as illustrated in Figure 2.

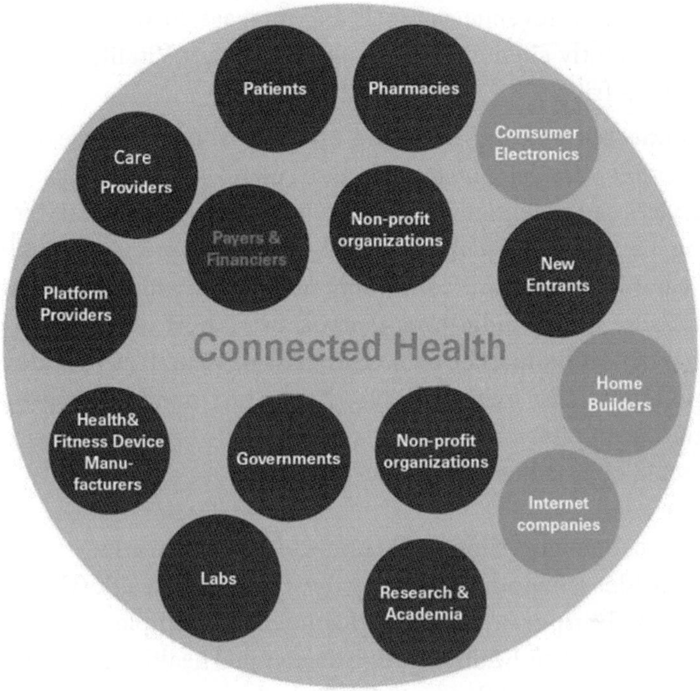

Figure 2: Connected health ecosystem.

In its latest research report, Boston Consulting Group (BCG) dissected the concept of "connected health" into three broad classes:

1) **Segment of one:** Distribution system with personalized and targeted offers, such as products offered under partnership between Tokyo Marine and NTT Docomo.[7]
2) **One-stop-shop:** This is a more advanced version of "Segment of one" whereby the intention is to create a (online) marketplace that aggregates multiple stakeholders and meets different sets of need domains. A key objective of these marketplaces is to create shared-interest communities that encourage more customer loyalty by offering a wide range of services that meet diverse consumer needs along the consumer business cycle. This type of business model will

7 These include one-time overseas traveling insurance or specialized medical insurance packages based on a NTT Docomo's health monitoring technology i-Bodymo (Makino, 2010).

provide new revenue channels and increase customer retention rate. A frequently cited example is the Discovery Vitality program from South Africa.

3) **Connected objects:** These are one-stop-shops that use sensors and wearable devices integrated with platforms and apps. Wearable devices can potentially play a transformative role in L&H underwriting, i.e., the data it collects may become new pricing variable. While wearable devices are commonly associated with digital bands that measure fitness indicators, there is also a host of medical wearables that collect biomarker data. This class of wearables includes glucose monitors, pulse oximeters, blood pressure monitors, smart clothing, muscle monitors, etc. An explanation of the one-stop-shop with connected objects business model follows.

How a one-stop-shop with connected objects works.

Consider a hypothetical company, One Stop Health (OSH). OSH is an integrated corporate health platform whereby employees are incentivized to improve their health through discounted health services/programs, and an interactive mobile app that is linked to a wearable health-tracking device. They have a network of distributors, insurance companies, health providers, physicians, and health-related business vendors.

The idea is that employees can customize their health plan (instead of the company offering the same as health insurance) by channeling their benefits dollars to pro-health activities. Employees are given fixed budget to personalize their premiums and employers can cap rising medical premiums. Recommendation engines will suggest to each employee, based on his/her profiles, the most suitable insurance and medical coverage levels, the rest can be used to spend on OSH's online wellness shop that offer services such as personal training sessions or organic produce delivery. Employees can submit their claims electronically via OSH's platform, and it will be handled by a third party administration. Analytics is used by OSH to track loss and adequacy ratios, evaluate cost effectiveness of existing insurance plans, and encourage corporate health by cohort analysis, which reduces medical claims cost and absenteeism.

Our research yields 111 companies/organizations in the Asia Pacific Region that Swiss Re can potentially partner with. To facilitate faster decision making for management, a set of high-level due diligence factors to enable prioritization and filtering was created. Not surprisingly perhaps, more than one third of the companies in our list are start-ups. As start-ups are notorious for their lack of public information, the factors defined in Table 6 were used to rank them.

Table 6: Factors used to rank L&H start-ups.

Category	Type of business model, i.e., technology provider, one-stop-shop platform operator, commercial databases, research organization etc.
Geographical coverage	Focus was on those with a presence in the APAC region.
Active customer base	This will help approximate the amount of data this organization can provide.
Maturity	This will help approximate the amount of data this organization can provide.
Funding (Angel, seed, Series A, B, C)	Funding level is an indication of the organization's likelihood to success.
Data collection mechanism	The source of data can often determine the reliability and quality of the data collected.
Product	What is the end product — a platform, an app, a database, a wearable device, etc.

Active customer base and maturity are important dimensions to consider when it comes to assessing these start-ups because it indicates the size of the data collected. Table 7 presents some statistics of the list.

Table 7: L&H start-up list statistics.

Variable	Statistics
Customer base	500 users — more than 1 billion users
Maturity/date launched	2000–2015
Funding	Seed (USD 400,000) — Series C (USD 129 million)
Geographical coverage	India, China, Hong Kong, Indonesia, Cambodia, Japan, Thailand, Malaysia, Japan, Philippines, Vietnam, and South Korea

On a cautionary note, sheer data size does not always justify prioritization. Valuable datasets are the ones that link directly to (re)insurance profit factors, such as claims and propensity to purchase. Physical activity data that is not concretely linked to health outcomes or claims activity is therefore not very attractive from a business perspective. Another factor to consider is the data collection mechanism, which can be inferred from the underlying business model and method of monetization, e.g., many technology providers and app developers require users to manually record their diet, psychological well-being, and other health behaviors. As self-reported statistics tends to be biased and dependent on the discipline of the customer to upload his/her information, companies that rely solely on self-reported data may be less interesting for (re)insurers.

Conversely, companies that provide an interactive platform for care providers, insurance companies, pharmacies, and patients can often obtain claims data from insurance partners, clinical data and lab results from the partner hospitals, and prescription data from affiliated pharmacies. Some companies in this region have also successfully integrated other health-related businesses into their platform, such as gyms, nutritional consultants, and super markets. Thus, health behavior can be more accurately captured through customers' purchasing activity.

Finally, some one-stop-shops also analyze customers' online/browsing behavior to determine lifestyle factors. Asia has also seen an entire host of "doctor search" platforms whereby patients may book appointments remotely. This success of this business model is a testament to the fact that in many Asian countries, specifically China and India, seeing a doctor is a time-consuming ordeal that requires waiting in a long queue. Due to the fierce competition in this space, many of these appointment-booking portals have also introduced telehealth capabilities whereby patients can consult doctors online, and health management functions that allow doctors to keep track of patients' medical records, lab results, and patients to follow-up with their preferred doctors. This type of model generates a wealth of potentially valuable data for (re)insurers.

Finally, numerous research reports have shown that the unstructured data in social media platforms can also be mined to predict the spread of contactable diseases ranging from the common flu to severe epidemics. Commute patterns and mode of transportation have also been shown to be good predictors of sickness.

For other private business that are more established, factors such as type of business (whether it is private or public), its size (small, medium, large), and other details regarding its business model and existing partnerships were considered. Lastly, public databases related to hospital administration, electronic health records, medical claims, large cohorts/surveys, and pharmacy records can be useful when it comes to studying the use and outcome of certain treatment paths. However, there is little information on the availability and accessibility of these types of databases in the APAC region. Based on our research, 54 administrative databases were found in this region that includes the following: insurance claims databases, prescription databases, electronic medical records, as well as those which merge some of the above databases. This does not include databases for research purposes such as national health surveys, disease registries, and some unique databases for niche research studies, adding another 20 companies/data vendors to our list. These databases span the following countries: Australia, China, Hong Kong, Japan, South Korea, Taiwan, Malaysia, Cambodia, India, Thailand, and Singapore.

Table 8 lists some of the characteristics considered when evaluating the usefulness of a public database.

Table 8: Framework for analyzing public databases.

Type of database	Hospital administration, medical claims/ reimbursement, pharmaceutical, surveys/ research studies
Data sources	(Depends on the type of database) **Hospital Administration:** Order-entry data, lab results, claims data, receipt data, EMR data, billing data, prescription data, etc. **Medical Claims/Reimbursement:** Electronic claims and health check database. **Pharmaceuticals:** Pharma dispense intramural/ extramural claims. **Surveys:** Primary surveys, anonymized medical records, etc.
Percentage of population represented	This is important for national surveys; the sample size needs to be as representative as possible

(*continued*)

Table 8: Framework for analyzing public databases (*Continued*)

Type of database	Hospital administration, medical claims/ reimbursement, pharmaceutical, surveys/ research studies
Starting year (and ending if applicable)	Tells you the maturity and thus size of the database
Unique patients	Size of database
No. of patients with chronic or severe illnesses	This is important for niche markets such as diabetes and cancer patients
Age distribution	The elderly is an important niche market.
Prescriptions	Prescription code and dosage.
Procedures, surgical operations	Procedure code and date performed.
Hospitalization	Medication during hospitalization and length of stay.
Outcomes	Diagnosis, lab tests, diagnostic data.
Demographic information	Age, BMI, gender, ethnicity.
Insurance information	Type of insurance.
Ease of access	(Discussed already)
Data relevance	Update frequently, latest data.

Just because a database is "public" does not make it readily available. Therefore, a new dimension needs to be introduced,"ease-of-access", to rank these databases accordingly. Some national databases, for example, have stringent requirements that prevent companies from using its databases for private gain.

4.4. Business line — property and casualty

The Property and Casualty (P&C) reinsurance business is characterized by annual renewals and is typically less proactive than its L&H counterpart. While L&H reinsurers work directly with clients to help them create products and portfolios, P&C reinsurers typically take the risk portfolio as submitted to them by cedents. In many cases, P&C reinsurance underwriters are given scant information on the insured. The multiplicity of insured risks under P&C means that customized frameworks are required. However, due to the diversity of risks under P&C and customized nature of coverage, this is not always possible.

Our research yields 84 different organizations that provide data relevant to P&C lines. Examples of the types of data collected and services provided by these companies include: satellite data, telematics solutions and sensor data, unmanned aerial vehicles (UAV)/drones data, video footage and images, social media data, and geospatial maps. The following demonstrates how some of these data sources may help (re)insurers:

Locational/Mobile Network Data: Hypothetically, one can use telecom network data to generate insights on human behavior. A major telecom in Singapore is using GPS data to predict traveling decisions of individuals. Such locational insights could be valuable to (re)insurers, e.g., insurers can find out the exact number of affected people during an extreme event (*ex ante* and *ex post*), this could be a natural disaster or a power outage, or use it to create granular behavioral profiles. This data may also be relevant to political upheaval monitoring, e.g., a huge crowd of people suddenly congregate in one politically significant area, a number of people moving as a cluster through a city (NATO summit protests in Chicago), or a large stationary crowd in a symbolic location (such as the camps set up on Wall Street during the "Occupy" movement).

The ability to monitor and possibly predict social unrest could have important implications for contingent business interruption, supply chain management and also pandemic outbreaks, i.e., the density of crowds in certain locations may cause a virus to spread faster. Additionally, information such as phone calls and texts can be used to map social/business circles and affinity groups.

GIS/Intelligent Maps/Satellite: GIS technology integrates and analyses data from multiple business systems to create a dynamic and interactive map-based view of information, e.g., it may enable law-enforcing entities and governments to quickly identify communities of interest, crime hotspots, uncover trends, and respond to emergency situations (floods, fires, etc.) in the most efficient way possible. It can also help manage the complex planning and construction of oil and gas pipelines by sharing data with the engineers responsible for routing the pipeline.

Social Media: Social media data can be used for the purpose of sentiment analysis (liability insurance), claims fraud detection, and mapping chronic diseases, to name a few applications. Social media platforms can also be used for crowdsourcing. An innovative social media company based in Singapore launched an app whereby users are notified whenever a "task" is available near their current location. The task can range from recording the price of a product at a supermarket, or taking photos and video footages of a car accident. The users are then compensated for their efforts. This is one potential way for insurers to collect information that will help them assess risks or verify claims.

Credit Bureau Data: Credit bureau data has long been used by insurance firms for background checks and fraud detection, i.e., someone who has a low credit rating may be more likely to file fraudulent claims. However, a series of studies are currently being done to study the explanatory power of credit-related data on seemingly unrelated behavioral variables such as driving.

While the list of companies cannot be released, the types of organizations that may supply useful information for the different types of risks traditionally covered by reinsurers are as follows:

Contingent business interruption	• GIS maps inlaid with real-time tracking of objects and people, mapping their locations and building software on top of this data. Clients can utilize customized dashboards to monitor the whereabouts of their assets (trucks, fleets, carriers, etc.). • Water quantity and quality data. Many business processes, e.g., manufacturing and natural gas fracking in particular, are contingent to water supply. Sensor data can also help sewage treatment plants know beforehand if equipment needs to be replaced. • Real-time traffic information and management system that employs sensors to detect the numbers of cars on the road.
Motor	• Telematics subscription service that allows for driving behavior and car-condition monitoring. • Self-driving cars.

Home and property	• Smart security systems that can detect break-ins or suspicious behavior. Nest, a manufacturer of smart gadgets for home security (security camera, smoke and motion detectors) has partnered with home insurance companies to provide discounts for customers who use their gadgets. The program allows home insurers to access user's home information in exchange for a discount. • Sound detection, i.e., if someone in the house screams it will trigger an alarm. • Smart meters to mitigate power outage events. • Up-to-date zip code databases. • Geospatial analysis for crime-density mapping.
Natural catastrophe (NatCat)	• Water gauge datasets for flood prediction. • Climate and weather variables such as sea level, CO_2 concentration, etc. collected using Doppler radar systems, weather satellites, buoy networks and stations, tide gauges, and real-time weather stations. • Survey data to determine a location's resilience to natural disasters, e.g., are the buildings in this area strong enough to withstand a minor earthquake? What is the robustness of water-related infrastructure? • Satellite data for fire detection and hot-spot mapping. • Implanting trackers into animals to collect environmental information (such as ocean data) and study behavioral and genetic changes that could be correlated to extreme events. In a research paper published by Chonnam National University, scientists found that a species of Asian paddle crab is a potential bio-indicator that reflects marine sediment toxicity and can therefore be a molecular marker to monitor marine ecosystems (Park, 2013).
Professional indemnity	• Sensors and measurement systems installed in equipment of high-risk professions, e.g., mining, to monitor operations and performance. • Pulse sensors for long-haul trip drivers to detect sleepiness and therefore prevent accidents. • Sensors that capture physical condition of high-risk factory workers. • Smart glasses and cameras to offer hands-free instruction, real-time data, and workflow-oriented services.

(*continued*)

	• Drones for public-works monitoring and inspection of civil engineering constructions. • Social medial and web analytics to predict the likelihood and outcome of lawsuits. Sentiment analysis on unstructured, real-time data for multinational companies may be used to anticipate costly lawsuits or fines related to environmental, humanitarian, or financial breaches.

4.5. Specialty lines

This paper will examine two business lines under specialty that may potentially benefit from Big Data analytics: agriculture and marine.

4.5.1. Agriculture

In emerging markets, agriculture (re)insurance is usually provided on a parametric basis, as contracts for indemnity generally require direct measurement of the loss or damage suffered by the farmer, and more detailed information to accurately assess potential losses. Field loss assessments can be extremely costly where there are a large number of small-scale farmers or where insurance markets are still nascent.

In its most basic form, index-based agriculture insurance contracts responds to a directly measurable parameter, such as rainfall amount or temperature, during a pre-specified time period. These parameters are chosen because they correlate highly with the loss of a specific crop type suffered by the policyholder. All policyholders in a predetermined area receive payouts based on the same "trigger" and there is no need for in-field loss assessment (the triggers can be different for different crop phases). This kind of weather index is less useful as the risks are more localized, such as in the case of "microclimates" in mountainous areas. Similarly, if the crop yield is impacted by multiple factors (diseases, pests, etc.), accurate loss indexes may be hard to construct. Thus, the three big challenges in agriculture (re)insurance in emerging markets are:

1) **Low spatial granularity of weather-related data:** This becomes a problem when an insured plot is located too far away from a meteorological station for the weather variable to accurately predict loss. Rainfall, an important determinant of yield, is often collected via satellite and gauge station observations. However, the limited number of

stations in China renders spatial interpolation unreliable. Similarly, while gridded satellite data is improving in accuracy and resolution, it is still inferior to gauge data when it comes to capturing rainfall volume. In China, yield and weather data are usually only available at the county level. There are around 750+ weather stations across China installed at different times so it becomes difficult to calibrate the data from different stations into a continuous historical time series.

2) **Hidden risk factors:** The index product may not capture factors such as wind speed during pollination or some undocumented pest damage that impact crop yield. In South East Asia temperature does not always correlate strongly with crop yield.
3) **Incomplete information on crop cycles:** The responsiveness of crop yield to the insured peril usually varies with the crop cycle. Decisions to shift the planting dates based on rainfall forecasts, for example, will alter the growth stages of the crop and cause misalignment with the design of the insurance product, which is based upon assumptions about periods of risks.

Herein lies the value of Big Data. By collecting more information on the farmed areas, be it micro-weather data, or information on soil condition and crop cycles, the exposure can be better assessed and monitored. This could reduce the basic risk of existing parametric products or even allow contracts for indemnity to be written for small farmers.

Examples of applications are as follows:

- **Precision and "Smart" Farming:** Precision farming using drones, sensors, satellites, and automated data collection methods to perform real-time analytics is gaining traction in Asia, particularly in agriculture-driven economies such as India and Indonesia. Drones, or Unmanned Aerial Vehicles (UAV), can monitor crop growth patterns and increase efficiency in loss assessments, while ground sensors can monitor soil conditions (nutrient composition, moisture, etc.) to optimize yield. Furthermore, granular weather data can be made available through the use of weather, climate, and decibel meter sensors. All this information can be used to create crop risk profiles, build yield prediction models and provide continuous risk monitoring (early warning system related to weather and pests, for example). Precision farming equipment can also reduce the overall losses of the farmed area by reducing human errors and ensuring that best-practice protocols are consistently followed, e.g., optimal spacing between each seed sown, composition and volume of fertilizers, etc.

- **More Accurate and Granular Weather Information:** Using satellite technology to measure atmospheric patterns, precipitation and ocean currents can help farmers develop better forecasting and risk management tools. Sensors and other measuring devices in individual farms can be used to capture local meteorological data.
- **Resource Management:** Water availability is an important determinant for crop yield. This is especially true in India, where more than 60 per cent of irrigated agriculture depends on groundwater (The World Bank, 2012). Sensors connected to digital platforms can help to collect and link locally collected groundwater data that is essential to monitor and manage large scale aquifers.
- **ICT Farming Platforms:** There has been a recent push from both private and public sectors to connect farmers in emerging countries to the internet. ICT platforms that allow farmers to access agricultural value chain and interact in an e-community also provide valuable data (such as information on farming practices, which can impact crop yield) and allow greater (re)insurance penetration in these areas. Such technology can also allow agricultural data to be acquired through social incentive apps. With the help of precision farming, one can envision a future where customized and indemnity-based agriculture insurance products can be offered to low-income farmers at a lowered cost.
- **Farming Best Practice:** Some agricultural ICT platforms also collect information on farming practices, either self-reported or from soil sensors. As unsustainable farm practices may result in soil-nutrient damage, and therefore lead to lower yields in the future, it is beneficial for (re)insurers to monitor this risk dimension.
- **Livestock Insurance:** Livestock insurance is nonexistent in most developing countries due to lack of information and difficulty in working with multiple government agencies that oversees animal and livestock regulations. Thailand for example, has a sizeable and growing broiler industry that remains largely uninsured. This is also true of Indonesia's cattle feedlots.

In developed countries such as the US, new technologies are being developed to collect information on livestock. One such example is a sensor that sits in a cow's rumen and uses sonar technology to collect data on heart rate, temperature, rumination time, rumen acidity, and estrogen levels. The information stored on each sensor will be transmitted wirelessly to receivers as cows pass by, and then through the internet to Vital Herd's cloud-based herd management software. This will collate and interpret the data about each animal so it can be viewed by farm managers. The software will send out alerts by text message or email if it appears that any individual animal shows signs that something is seriously wrong. Other innovations include gene banks for livestock to ensure biodiversity and resilience against diseases and weather variability.

- **Leverage Agriculture E-Commerce Platforms:** These can act as new distribution channels for new agriculture insurance products. Browsing activity collected from these platforms can yield behavioral insights, and the transactions conducted via such platforms can serve as a price discovery mechanism, improving current pricing models. It may even be possible to assess crop yield and harvest insights using crop listings.
- **Forest Fires Mapping:** Forest fire is another important source of risk in agriculture. Traditionally, National Oceanic and Atmospheric Administration (NOAA) satellites have been used for regional fire detection and monitoring due to their availability and low costs. However, since NOAA was not originally intended for fire detection and land studies, the number intensity, and the size of a burnt area cannot always be determined precisely. Furthermore, the presence of clouds may also dramatically reduce the accuracy of NOAA images and lead to, an under-estimation of the extent and frequency of burning, and limit the ability to track vegetation parameters. Also, forest canopy fires cannot be detected by NOAA satellites (ASEAN Agreement on Transboundary Haze Pollution, 2015). Other aerial surveillance vehicles can be used to provide higher resolution which will complement information received from NOAA satellites, e.g., some companies offer higher resolution, cloud-free observations, and can provide data on how fast and in which direction fires are spreading. They can also provide information on how a fire may influence the quality of air in urban areas i.e., impact of haze.

- **Natural Catastrophe Prediction:** Flooding, hurricanes, and droughts can all impact crop yields. Take flooding as an example. Historically, water gauge data has not always been readily available. However, given the increased incidences of flood in South East Asia, this is changing. Thai government, for example, released its water gauge data for the first time after the great flood of 2011 so that researchers can build better flood prediction models. In Indonesia, efforts have been made by sending students equipped with GPS devices to manually collect terrain data throughout Jakarta. This data has been the basis of various collaborations, notably one between National University of Singapore and Willis Re.

Based on our research, there are at least 50 companies/organizations that may be able to supply valuable information for underwriting agriculture (re)insurance in Asia.

Table 9 illustrates the assessment framework used to analyze these companies and also some summary statistics.

Table 9: Agriculture strategic partners analysis.

Type	Analytical solutions provider, software provider/ICT, hardware provider (drones, sensors), mobile app provider, research institutions, satellite company, etc.
Geographical coverage	India, China, Indonesia, Thailand, and Australia.
Size	0 (pilot stage) — 4 million + users.
Maturity	Date of inception.
Variables c(accuracy and information if available)	Weather/external environment (daily and location specific), yield, big weather events, and government funds.
Data collection mechanism	Sensors, UAVs/drones, satellite, smart phone apps (GPS and unstructured text data), soil samples, water gauges, etc.
Gridded data (temporal and spatial granularity)	Drones can transmit information almost instantaneously and at higher resolution than even the most advanced low orbit satellites.

4.5.2. Marine

Table 10 demonstrates some of the factors that may impact the risk of a marine portfolio. However, not all of these factors are currently being examined by underwriters.

Table 10: Marine risk variables (Lam, 2012).

Risk Factors	Details	Source
Human factor	• Knowledge and skill of workforce (crew quality)[a] • Safety procedure awareness (port state control)[a]	Insurers
Vessel/ship	• Age of ship[a] • Condition of hull and machinery[a]	Insurers
Cargo	• Cargo attributes • Cargo stacking	Not provided
Port	• Ship berthing and unberthing procedure • Cargo loading and unloading procedure[a]	Insurers (only provided when cargoes are loaded hazardous/dangerous goods)
Environment	• Natural disasters[a] • Extreme weather events[a]	Satellite data and historical weather data
Geopolitical	• Piracy[a] • Political conflicts • Terrorist attacks	Piracy maps created using data on historical attacks

[a]*Currently looked at by underwriters*

Unlike property, marine vessels are nonstationary assets. Thus, a major contributing factor for the basic risk in marine (re)insurance is that neither vessel nor cargo is monitored in real-time. Furthermore, most insurance companies do not systematically keep track of which cargo is loaded on which ship, thereby introducing another level of complexity. As no real-time data is available, marine actuaries use a set of validated assumptions, renewed as needed, in order to build event models and vulnerability curves. Examples of assumptions used to calculate probable, maximum static exposure in a port include trade flows, trade volume transiting in port, average storage period, prevailing sale terms, insurer's market share, etc. A traditional reinsurance costing model uses a top-down approach to calculate the cedent's loss distribution because the exact exposure in an area or single point is unknown. Data is collected from different ports selected for their size, exposure to natural perils, and the nature of the goods traded. Global trade flow assumptions are made by analyzing historical trade flow data and market loss distributions are calculated by proportionally adjusting for cedent's market shares; this is a rough estimate at best.

Natural catastrophes are also a major source of exposure in marine (re)insurance. While the perils themselves might be anticipated, reinsurance companies like Swiss Re often have sophisticated and reliable models when it comes to weather and natural catastrophe prediction, the losses themselves may not be, because marine insurers typically do not know where their insured cargoes and vessels are at any given time, and how long they spend at specific locations (many marine covers provide a limited static exposure, e.g., "up to 60 days at destination"). The latter increases accumulation risks in storage areas. This potential loss accumulation is difficult to determine *a priori* because insurers do not know how much insured value will aggregate in one location at any given time. Another big exposure comes from private yachts and marinas as the insured values of these yachts/pleasure-crafts can be high and geographically concentrated.

Under the regulatory environment created by Solvency II, marine insurers are required to hold capital for their exposure to static risk. It is crucial for (re)insurance companies to be able to manage their capital so as to absorb the escalating risks created by global transport capacities, increased frequency of natural catastrophes, value accumulations, and overall increase in insured values.

Marine underwriters and actuaries can use new technology and data sources to 1) improve existing actuarial assumptions and risk assessments by incorporating real time information beyond traditional trade flow and natural catastrophe parameters, and 2) create new value-added services in order to mitigate potential losses and reduce claims.

The following section will elaborate on these points.

- **Obtain More Information from the Cedent:** When assessing a hull treaty submission, the reinsurance underwriter gets access to a preprocessed document that summarizes the portfolio. These summary statistics may include number of policies involved, estimated number of ships (e.g., fleet of 20 vessels) and net exposure.

For net exposure, the reinsurers generally only see the maximum cover number and not a breakdown of different covers. To illustrate, a standard coverage might include hull and machinery (H&M), total loss/increased value (IV), and loss of hire (LOH). However, reinsurers rarely see exposures disaggregated like this. Suppose the breakdown is $200m, $50m, $20m, accordingly. The reinsurers might only see the maximum total loss of $250m (H&M + IV) or maximum partial loss of $220m (H&M + LOH) (Lee Tookey, 2006). Since reinsurance is done at a portfolio level, the cedents typically do not supply individual policy information. Often this is not practical as there could be thousands of policies in a portfolio. Only in selected cases such as for special acceptances, is this information supplied to reinsurers. With an intelligent language processor such as Watson however, reinsurers can benefit from having policy-level information.

- **Obtain Real-Time Data on Marine Assets:** Marine data is largely reliant on self-reporting and therefore susceptible to human errors and manipulation. By using actual data and activity-based intelligence, reinsurers can assess their risk and exposures in real-time and make better underwriting decisions. Since 2002, all vessels over 300 GT on international voyages are required by the International Maritime Organization (IMO) to fit an AIS transceiver. The Automatic Identification System (AIS) is an automatic tracking system used on ships and by vessel traffic services for identifying and locating vessels by electronically exchanging data with other nearby ships, AIS base stations, and satellites. Shipping companies or third-party service providers track cargoes separately. Theoretically, this information can be linked to create a rich data ecosystem that enables (re)insurers to better understand accumulation risks and maximum probable losses.

23 private and public companies were found that could be considered strategic partners for marine (re)insurers.

Table 11 provides the analytical framework used for marine-related companies.

Table 11: Framework for marine-related companies.

Type	Geospatial, weather data, sea state data, onboard assets monitoring, and analytical provider
Collection mechanism	Terrestrial satellites/AIS base stations, orbiting satellite (low orbit, Inmasat, etc.), floating buoys, sea-surface drones, tide gauges, and onboard sensors
Data update frequency and accuracy	Frequency of data updates (1 min to 12 h, depending on technology), range detection for vessel tracking (30 miles from base station or global)
Main product offering	Services, software, and hardware

Companies are now using commercial and terrestrial satellites to detect AIS signatures at varying levels of spatial and temporal accuracy. Some of these companies also analyze piracy and other illegal marine activities. Three companies were found to study the movement pattern of the vessels and link this to information about a ship's ownership history and country of registration in order to provide real-time information alerting officials to suspicious vessel movements. The commercial micro-satellites used by some of these organizations can also provide granular weather information, which may be useful in predicting disastrous natural events. On the other hand, there is a host of other companies that use mobile sensors installed on on-board assets such as engines, fuel tanks, batteries, or generators in order to monitor the performance of the vessel. When combined with environmental data such as barometric pressure and approaching weather systems, AIS information, this could reveal a lot about the underlying risks of the vessel and its journey.

4.5.3 Offshore Energy

The exposure of offshore energy is similar to that of traditional marine, except that the interests/assets are stationary. Like marine (re)insurance, accumulation and natural catastrophes are considered top exposures and key risks in offshore energy. To that effect, spatially and temporally granular data can help (re)insurer better estimate how much an adverse event (e.g., windstorm, earthquake, etc.) may cost and determine how much capital to hold.

Aggregation, such as accumulation for marine cargo, occurs at different levels — interest, insured, and location — and having full data transparency is the key to its management. On the asset/interest level, there is physical damage, operator's extra expenses, third-party liability, and loss of production income (business interruption). For example, a single blowout can lead to loss of the platform, expenses to extinguish fire and drill a relief well, third-party liability, removal of wreck, and loss of production for a number of days. However, reinsurers often do not have sufficient information on the single installations insured, e.g., two platforms may be bridge-linked, or there could be a clash between a given platform and the drilling rigs operating over or alongside it.

At insured level, it is important for reinsurers to keep track of joint ventures (exploration and production is a risky and capital-intensive business so joint ventures are common), which may lead to another level of complication when calculating exposure, as reinsurers need to know the limits for each of the separate interest insured. Moreover, the same platforms may appear under different names and be insured for different values, depending on how much coverage is bought by the joint venture partner.

The last level, location, is of utmost importance because natural disasters could involve multiple risks in the same location or multiple locations. NatCat analysis involves the following four components, and there is a need for greater data transparency for each:

1) **Hazard:** Where, how often, and with what intensity do events occur? The increasing frequency and severity of events make extreme events much harder to predict.
2) **Vulnerability:** What is the extent of damage at a given event intensity? The lack of data on loss history, available design codes (offshore versus onshore), and asset vulnerability (flowing versus fixed, deep water versus shallow water).
3) **Values Distribution:** Where are the various types of insured objects located and how high is their value? What is the accumulation per region/area? Is there sufficient risk data aggregation? Is it sufficiently accurate? Value distribution is important because the largest

value concentrations are offshore and they are increasing in size. To illustrate, the Gulf of Mexico and the North Sea are considered "hot spots", due to large concentration of high-value assets and frequency of natural hazards, and are often excluded in energy treaties. To illustrate the importance of monitoring values distribution, consider the following example: a typhoon may hit Shanghai, but it could also impact platforms located in the Gulf of Mexico, which is only 12,188km away. This example is illustrative as typhoons are become increasingly common in Asia. Additionally, large completed rigs that are berthed close to one another, sometimes even owned by the same owner, increase total exposure. Beyond knowing the territorial scope, reinsurers should have information on the subsidiaries that are covered, and whether the construction policy includes transport hook-up and commissioning. The location (area or longitude-latitude) for each risk and the unique reference for each installation is also currently unknown.

4) **Insurance Conditions:** What proportion of the loss is insured? What is covered and how? What is the coverage in place? Overlapping policies needs to be disaggregated in order to provide reinsures with clearer information. Moreover, reinsurers should have complete transparency on variables such as interests covered, deductibles, layers, perils covered, policy extensions, limits, etc.

To conclude, reinsurers need to measure, monitor and steer aggregation across interests/assets, insurers, and also per location. But what tools are currently available in the market? Based on our research, there are vendors that offer software products to track locations (field/area/longitude-latitude) of platforms, the unique reference number for all assets, and the interests (property damage/expenses for capping the well/liability insurance and reinsurance obligations, etc.). While aggregation monitoring can be done manually by looking only at key locations and top assets, this is incomplete and may be subject to operational risks. This makes transparency and risk data aggregation fundamental. Additionally, according to the latest IoT report by McKinsey, only 1 per cent of data from an oil rig with 30,000 sensors is examined (McKinsey & Company, 2015). Moreover, this data is usually used for anomaly detection and control, and not optimization and prediction, which may provide the greatest value. A mechanical failure at an offshore platform in Singapore, for example, resulted in USD 85 million of insured losses. Another important dimension is cyber risk, which has grown recently in the energy industry and could result in catastrophic losses. This problem is particularly acute in view of the fact that in many parts of the world, high levels of oil and gas production and infrastructure are in close proximity with politically or environmentally motivated groups.

5. IMPORTANCE OF WORK[8]

Understanding the data ecosystem has significant implications when it comes to closing the protection gap in this Asia Pacific region. A "protection gap" occurs when there is a mismatch between a need for protection and the purchase of insurance or insurance-related products, be it life insurance plans that hedge loss-of-income in the event of death or "cat bonds" that cover part of the loss caused by natural catastrophes such as typhoons and earthquakes. One can also think of protection gap as a measure of underinsurance, i.e., the difference between insured and uninsured losses. Regardless of its interpretation, the undeniable fact is that the protection gap is growing exponentially, triggered by trends such as increased trade flows, the advent of digitalization, growing healthcare costs, and increased frequency and severity of natural disasters; nowhere is this more apparent than in Asia.

Consider the recent earthquake in Nepal, which caused about USD 2 billion in economic losses across the country. However, according to Insurance Information Institute, expected insured losses are only a minimal fraction of the total costs. In 2014, even though Asian natural disasters account for nearly half of the $101 billion global economic losses, total insured losses in Asia stood at a meager 8 per cent compared to the 60 per cent in America.

Another example is the healthcare protection gap — the difference between the levels of healthcare costs which would be required to meet population needs versus the capital available to cover those costs. Swiss Re's study in 2012 showed that the health protection gap in Asia Pacific

8 The author would like to credit Sophia Van (Van, Closing the Protection Gap in APAC, 2015) for the information and research in this section.

could reach USD 197 billion by 2020. It is evident that Asia is severely under-insured and is in dire need of protection.

Big Data and other technological advancements can help the (re)insurance industry address the protection gap problem. As mentioned before, information from social media, mobile phones, sensors, humanitarian drones, and satellites can help (re)insurers design targeted relief efforts to reduce natural disaster-induced losses, and gain a better understanding of, and therefore a greater capacity to control risk exposures. Moreover, new sources of data and innovative ways of capturing them could enable (re)insurers to bridge not only the current protection gaps but also emerging protection gaps that result from the changing risk landscape created by digitization, the IoT, urbanization, and aging population.

The protection gap of interest for many (re)insurers in the APAC region is that of Life and Health (L&H). According to Swiss Re's 2012 report, the L&H protection gap in Asia could reach USD 197 billion by 2020. Big Data can help address this gap in three ways: encourage product innovation targeted at uninsured segments, educate consumers about their protection needs, and create new distribution channels. The number of uninsured people plagued by chronic diseases (diabetes), critical illnesses (cancers), and old age are sizable and growing. One reason for this is because this demographic is costly to insure. Another is that insurers currently do not have enough information available to thoroughly evaluate the risks involved in insuring this segment. Given the increasing availability of health-related data, such as clinical records, behavioral information, and health and nutrition surveys, insurers are now in a better position to evaluate underlying risks and understand customer needs at different stages of life and health conditions.

There is a nontrivial reason why this report chose to highlight the Asian region. Traditionally, actuarial models and assumptions used for evidence-based underwriting in the Asia are often extrapolated from medical studies conducted in Western countries. This is hardly surprising given the historical dearth of similar studies based in Asia. However, due to cultural, genetic, or environmental reasons, same assumptions and statistics drawn from Western studies are not always valid or applicable in the Asian context, e.g., cancer studies conducted in Norway may not be relevant to the Singaporean population.

However, as this study has demonstrated, useful data relevant to the Asian demographic is becoming increasingly available, owing to the digitization of medical records throughout the APAC region, and the increase in data collection from sensors, wearables, broadband internet, and mobile apps. Moreover, the size of data in this region is also increasing exponentially. Previous medical studies were usually conducted on only a few hundred to a few thousand people. This makes it even harder to get a good sampling size for medical trials that involve special patient groups with complicated conditions, such as hypertension with cardiovascular diseases. The growth of Big Data technologies allows global medical databases and real-world data across different population groups to be captured and mined. This allows (re)insurance companies to build predictive models for population segments that could not be modeled in the past.

Finally, traditional actuarial models do not factor in lifestyle choices even though numerous studies, notably one done by World Health Organization (WHO), have demonstrated that lifestyle does contribute significantly to premature deaths. As a result of this, some good risks might be rejected and bad risks accepted. Nonetheless, accurate lifestyle information is notoriously difficult to collect. As wearable devices increase in sophistication and customers move towards online platforms as a means to procure goods and services, (re)insurers can start to price "lifestyle" into their models. To demonstrate, patients with a history of breast cancer used to be strictly excluded from life insurance policies. This exclusion is slowly being relaxed, given the recent emergence of mortality studies on breast cancer patients. These studies have demonstrated that physical activity and healthy diets can contribute significantly to the survival rate of breast cancer patients, and more importantly, certain health-conscious cancer survivors can actually outlive cancer-free people with unhealthy lifestyles. Such findings can drive the creation of new products that not only encourage healthy behavior, but enable (re)insurers to capture some good risks that have traditionally been declined.

Fix the formatting hereWhat about the population that is too costly to insure? Insurers are already using Big Data to develop products that at one point were unaffordable and unavailable. A common misconception is that quality care is always accompanied by expensive treatments. However, studies conducted by Harvard T.H. Chan School of Public Health have shown that "medical inefficiencies", in the form of unnecessary treatments, tests, follow-ups, and operational ineptitude, is a serious problem in the healthcare industry (Gerdeman, 2015). However, such waste of resources can be reduced by using medical predictive analytics, and thus lower overall healthcare costs. For example, more targeted care and early intervention for patients with high risks of decompensation may reduce future complications. Importantly, (re)insurers should help align the care provider's incentive for increased revenues with that of the healthy patient. The values extracted by the (re)insurers would come from the improvement in loss ratios, e.g., Indiana Health Information Exchange delivers quality reports to Indiana primary-care doctors with scores based on clinical and claims data in 26 areas, such as the percentage of diabetic patients getting regular blood-sugar checks. Based on the scores, insurers reward the doctors using QHF's integrated pay-for-performance platform.

As mentioned earlier, wearable technology also represents a promising mechanism for (re)insurers when it comes to preventative care. Non-communicable diseases such as cardiovascular diseases, chronic respiratory disorders, certain cancers, and diabetes, account for 63 per cent of deaths worldwide and are largely the result of unhealthy lifestyle choices. Wearable devices allow people to "measure" their lifestyle and if tied to another service platform, award people for their healthy decisions with benefits such as grocery discounts, gym membership, lower health insurance premiums, airline mileage, etc. Many wearables also include game apps to exploit the competitive streak of human beings and channel that towards healthy behavior. Data generated from these devices and programs will give (re)insurers more insights into patients' needs and risks. This allows for much more meaningful and deeper engagement opportunities that allow insurers to build a more synergetic relationship with its customers. By integrating their products with trust-based services that help people make life-extending changes with multi touch points along the life cycle of policy holders rather than just at the point of purchase and claims, insurers could become consumers' trusted partners.

Finally, the increase in online interactive platforms creates digital distribution channels that can help narrow the protection gap by more efficient distribution of products. The data ecosystem created by such platforms also facilitates the development of new products that meet consumers' specific needs. One example of such a product includes a single year malignant tumor insurance coverage offered on a leading Chinese messaging platform. By paying only 1 RMB, users can choose to share the promotion with his/her friends and earn 1000 RMB whenever a friend clicks on the promotion and pays 1 RMB his/herself. The protection value is capped at 10,000 RMB.

Although the above discussion focuses on healthcare, the value that (re)insurers can create with new sources of data does not end here. There are numerous other global risks that Big Data analytics can help address, from global food security and natural resource management to cyber-related risks.

6. CONCLUSION AND FURTHER WORK

The new digital landscape creates an atmosphere of ambivalence for the reinsurance industry. On one hand, there is a threat of competition and possible destruction of economic rent. On the other, it introduces unique opportunities for reinsurers to better fulfill the mandate to protect society from adverse events while maximizing its business value.

This study demonstrated that Big Data and increasingly sophisticated analytical capabilities have enormous potential for both direct insurers and reinsurers. However, one question remains: How should the reinsurer strategically position itself and most importantly, create value in this digital landscape? Reinsurance companies typically help primary insurers absorb higher-than-predicted losses, for example, those resulting from natural or man-made catastrophes. However, as primaries get more sophisticated at managing their risks, the need for reinsurers may decrease due to reduced volatility in total losses. Should reinsurers then compete directly with primary insurers? This would dramatically change its business model and possibly damage important client relationships. The alternative would be to leverage its access to numerous markets and its deep (and broad) understanding of insurance to play an advisory role that provides best-in-class analytical solutions. The viability of different positioning strategies for the reinsurer has yet to be carefully assessed.

One key point that is not touched upon in this report is the shift of the risk burden given the introduction of telematics, IoT and "smart" technologies. Consider the case of automotive technologies in preventing collisions, such as location tracking and automatic breaking. Mechanical malfunctions will increasingly become the pretext for driving error, thus shifting the liability from driver to auto manufacturers. This could result in new auto insurance products that are packaged with cars that rely on such technologies. The end-consumer of auto insurance will effectively become the auto manufacturer — a change that will alter the entire value chain, from product definition to pricing, distribution, marketing, and claims (Sequeira, 2015). This topic has important implications for existing (re)insurance business lines and should therefore be thoroughly explored.

Returning to the previous discussion on market positioning — What should the reinsurer's strategy be with regards to the digital disrupters? Many of these digital disrupters currently offer, or are planning to offer, insurance products themselves, given their competitive advantage when it comes to accessing direct consumers. Should the reinsurer compete with such players? This may result in reinsurer straying too far from its key competencies and consume too many of its limited resources. This brings us to the question of partnering with these digital disrupters. The question then becomes: What exactly can both parties bring to the table and what form will the partnership take?

This report has been based on existing and many hypothetical uses of Big Data in (re)insurance, since the primary objective is to provide a sketch of the APAC data ecosystems, and drive ideation in the application of these data ecosystems to real-world risks and problems. In reality however, there are numerous regulatory and data privacy concerns. Such considerations are nontrivial as they can stand between the success and failure of implementing an innovative and often valuable solution. To illustrate, a European navigation device maker recently supplied driving behavior data to the local police to help them catch speeding motorists. While this was highly effective, this company was subsequently sued for breach of privacy. The digitalization of traditional business lines introduces complex forms of ownerships that are yet to be studied. Take agriculture for example. With the introduction of precision agriculture and Big Data, a number of questions will arise: Do farms own exclusive rights to the airspace above the farmland? Does the landlord have rights to the agricultural data collected? If a co-op is contracted for soil and fertilizer sampling, does it have ownership rights?

Finally, there is the "elephant in the room" — cyber risk. As more business value and personal information worldwide migrate into open and interconnected digital platforms, the risk of cybercrimes increases exponentially. The economic costs of cybercrimes could easily run into trillion of dollars (McKinsey & World Economic Forum, 2014). This represents the next frontier for risk management; –one that the reinsurance industry cannot easily ignore.

REFERENCES

1. ASEAN Agreement on Transboundary Haze Pollution (2015). *Hotspots*. Retrieved from ASEAN Agreement on Transboundary Haze Pollution: http://haze.asean.org/?page_id=251

2. Asia Insurance Review (15 April 2015). *India: Less than 1/5 of Farmers Insure Crops*. Retrieved from Asia Insurance Review: http://www.asiainsurancereview.com/News/View-NewsLetter-Article?id=32525&Type=eDaily

3. Gerdeman, D (29 June 2015). *Harvard Business School*. Retrieved from HBS Working Knowledge: http://hbswk.hbs.edu/item/consumer-centered-health-care-depends-on-accessible-medical-records

4. Hai, PT (26 May 2015). Head of the Department of Information Systems at the School of Computing, National University of Singapore. (F-Y Liang, Interviewer)

5. Karapiperis, D (2015). *Usage-Based Insurance and Vehicle Telematics: Insurance Market & Regulatory Implications*. Kansas City: NAIC Central Office.

6. Lam, SL (2012). *Rough Set Approach to Marine Cargo Risk Analysis*. Retrieved from International Centre for Maritime Studies: http://www.icms.polyu.edu.hk/ifspa2012/Papers/M26.pdf

7. Lee Tookey (2006). *CARe 2006: Marine Reinsurane*. Retrieved from Casualty Actuarial Society: https://www.casact.org/education/reinsure/2006/handouts/tookey.ppt

8. Makino, T (April 2010). *What's Next: The Search for Disruptive Technologies*. Retrieved from CELENT: http://www.celent.com/system/files/disruptive_innovation_using_mobile_devices_tokio_marine.pdf

9. McKinsey & World Economic Forum (May 2014). *The Rising Strategic Risks of Cyberattacks*. Retrieved from McKinsey&Company: http://www.mckinsey.com/insights/business_technology/the_rising_strategic_risks_of_cyberattacks

10. McKinsey Global Institute (2011). *Big data: The next frontier*. McKinsey & Company.

11. McKinsey&Company (2015). *The Internet of Things: Mapping The Value Beyond the Hype*. McKinsey&Company.

12. MetLife Asia (16 July 2015). *MetLife Launches LumenLab*. Retrieved from BusinessWire: http://www.businesswire.com/news/home/20150716005707/en/MetLife-Launches-LumenLab---First-of-its-Kind-Innovation-Centre#.VcMHIf4cTL8

13. Park, K (2013). Expression of stress response HSP70 gene in Asian paddle crabs, Charybdis japonica, exposure to endocrine disrupting chemicals, bisphenol A (BPA) and 4-nonylphenol (NP). *Ocean Science Journal.*

14. Rohde, RA (2015). *Air Pollution in China: Mapping of Concentrations and Sources.* Berkeley: Berkeley Earth (of UC Berkeley) Press.

15. Sequeira, I (20 June 2015). Fintech Leader (Strategy and Analytics). (F-Y Liang, Interviewer)

16. SINTEF (22 May 2013). *Big Data, for Better or Worse.* Retrieved from ScienceDaily: www.sciencedaily.com/releases/2013/05/130522085217.htm

17. The Times of India (13 August 2015). *25 per cent of Indians May Die of Lifestyle Diseases before They Are 70: Study.* Retrieved from The Time of India: http://timesofindia.indiatimes.com/india/25-of-Indians-may-die-of-lifestyle-diseases-before-they-are-70-Study/articleshow/48460601.cms

18. The World Bank (6 March 2012). *India Groundwater: A Valuable but Diminishing Resource.* Retrieved from The World Bank: https://www.worldbank.org/en/news/feature/2012/03/06/india-groundwater-critical-diminishing

19. Van, S (2015a). *APAC Big Data Market Watch.* Singapore: Swiss Reinsurance Company Ltd.

20. Van, S (2015b). *Closing the Protection Gap in APAC.* Singapore: Asia Insurance Review.

21. Willis Energy Market Review (2014). *Cyber Attacks: Can the Market Respond?*London: Willis Limited.

CHAPTER 10

Consumer Behavior for Credit Card Campaigns

Guillaume Soule

ABSTRACT

This study aims to find a better way to promote the credit card campaigning in collaboration with DBS and the Institute for Infocomm Research.

An approach based on a clean data was designed to use the customers transaction data to discover customer habits in groups. These habits were summarized in terms of frequently visited locations (i.e., cluster of visited locations), particular time of visiting them, type of transactions done there, and any other relevant parameters. A thorough analysis was performed based on a complete set of data to extract precise information to improve the model created. The results of clustering were analyzed using visualization tools.

1. INTRODUCTION

DBS is currently developing datasets that can be leveraged for contextual marketing purposes. To this end, DBS built a conjoint-lab with *A STAR* and *Institute for Infocomm Research* (I2R). It aspires to be the "First bank in Asia to leverage research expertise of I2R to develop new financial solutions". This partnership is part of DBS' ongoing journey to shape the future of banking. With a number of I2R researchers involved, this study of bank data is one of the first of its kind in Asia that will bring a competitive advantage to DBS.

DBS and I2R first explored how to tackle the data and then shared their competences to propose a feasible and interesting collaboration. Once the area of collaboration was determined, I2R analyzed the data provided by the bank.

The study focuses on contextual marketing with the main objective to determine the behavior of a group of customers on the basis of their daily transactions using credit cards, internet, or other methods of payments with respect to their frequent locations, time of visit and types of transactions.

2. PROBLEM STATEMENT

This study analyzed data based on clustering methods and the results were presented using visualization techniques. Generally, a lot of questions can be answered from a certain set of data, and the goal was to design a generic way to answer these questions. This gave an opportunity to work on some challenging issues emerging from different sets of transaction data.

The data comprised a list of transactions made by various customers. Each row represents a transaction defined by its time, location, amount, and customer id. The size of data is quite dynamic, with 50,000 rows, some of them having more than a million transactions.

The most crucial task was to use the available data in the best possible way. Two approaches were adopted for this study.

The first approach was to study one pattern precisely, to identify the behavior of a group of customers on weekdays or weekend. This involved familiarization, visualization, and analytics tools. Next step was to focus on a specific area, such as a unique restaurant, to study the behavior of customers to gain the best possible insights.

The second approach was more generic where the whole set of data was analyzed with analytics tools and some interesting patterns were found. This approach answered the following questions.

"What is the most suitable algorithm for this problem?"

"What are the key issues that must be resolved?"

"What is the best way to represent queries and answers found?"

Above two approaches were somewhat contradictory to each other in terms of handling the data. On one hand, the data had to be dealt rationally and scientifically, while on the other hand it was open to new proposals in line with the purpose of the study. However, the data interpretation was more insightful in this study.

Because of the privacy issues, the data that used for the proposed model is confidential and its characteristics cannot be displayed. Therefore, synthetic data with same parameters but random values was taken into consideration. All the charts and tables presented here are derived from this synthetic data for confidentiality purposes.

3. STATE OF THE ART

3.1. Tools used

As this study involved many steps from data cleaning to visualization, multiple tools were used to optimize the analysis and presentations. R (an open source computer language) along with RStudio were used to handle the data, while Stakoverflow[1] along with some websites was used to find a proper solution to the issues faced.

Data cleaning was done by R, which works via packages that regroup some functions of a certain domain to help create new variables and merge the current ones. For instance, the main functions of clustering are already coded in the package "fpc"[2]. However, there are many other packages available in the market, R was preferred because of a huge variety in the choice of functions and user-friendliness. A feature of R called Shiny package to create an app was predominately used in this study. Apps helped avoiding the repeated running of the same function when results needed to be observed. In addition, effect of any changes made during the study were also displayed. Excel and some other minor tools were also used.

Another tool used for visualization in conjunction with R was Tableau. The advantage of Tableau is the simplicity of usage and the proposed interface. It is just a click and drop tool. It allows to load a map of Singapore[3] (mapping datapoints on google maps) on which the transactions as a function of amount could be represented. The tool enables to change the values of the parameters easily and the changes are reflected almost instantly which in turn allows to understand the changes in the data. Packages such as *ggplot*[4] were also used to plot the data, which gives the possibility to use the results of the clustering in the study, even if the interface is not much user-friendly. These two tools gave the options to work on two levels: directly with the raw data using Tableau or study the results of algorithms using R.

In addition to these tools, a method to define a precise distance function was also needed. With the available latitude and longitude of different transactions, the distance between any two points at a particular time had to be calculated. It was done using Haversine function[5] which calculates distance between two points on the earth surface for smaller areas. However, it is not suitable for places located at the equator such as Singapore because it does not account for the nonspherical shape of the earth, although the changes are quite negligible.

These formulas are as follows:

$$dlon = lon_2 - lon_1$$

$$dlat = lat_2 - lat_1$$

$$a = \sin\left(\frac{dlat}{2}\right)^2 + \cos(lat_1) \times \cos(lat_2) \times \sin\left(\frac{dlon}{2}\right)^2 t$$

$$c = 2 \times a\tan(\sqrt{a}, \sqrt{1-a})$$

$$d = Radius_{earth} \times c$$

Using this function for the latitude and longitude of two points, the distance between these can be obtained in kilometers. A comparison was made between the results obtained with and without using the function, based on which Haversine formula was chosen. The main drawback of using this distance function is the enormous increase in the processing time. Sometimes this increase is simply too huge to be handled by the computer and a simple distance formula had to be used.

3.2. Algorithms used

Standard algorithms already used in the literature were used in this study in conjunction with Stanford Presentation[6] (Rajaraman) to compare the required inputs and outputs. The main methods used are as follows:

- Dbscan that connects only points verified by a density criterion[7] (Gao). Each point was checked for a certain distance from its neighboring points. If the desired number of points were found to be linked together, a cluster was created. To set the methods, two mains parameters had to be defined: ∈ which is the maximal distance between two points of a same cluster; and minPts which represents the minimal number of points required to create a cluster.
- *K*-means clustering is another method where the desired number of clusters needs to be specified first. The algorithm then finds a central vector and assigns the points to the nearest area. Main problem of this algorithm is that the number of clusters has to be specified, which cannot be obtained from the raw data before analyzing it.
- Expectation maximization (EM) clustering is a method based on Gaussian distribution model.[8], which is iteratively optimized until they reach a local optimum. It is one of the drawbacks of the EM as it produces different results on each iteration.

All these methods were compared to find the best fit for this study. On the basis of detailed analysis and models obtained, Dbscan was chosen for the following reasons:

- In Dbscan, variables, e.g., ∈ and minPts have significant values and the inputs are quite simple and relevant. It is also robust against outliers and noise, which is a key criteria in our data since many of the points are not part of any clusters and random behaviors were not observed. Some customers show different behaviors and do transactions in very unusual areas. It creates noise that must be handled by the algorithm. Dbscan does not specify the number of clusters but allows to specify the values of parameters based on which a certain number of clusters can be obtained. Complexity of this algorithm is also quite low hence the processing time is generally less.
- It allows choosing Haversine distance function. As latitude and longitude coordinates were used, Haversine was selected instead of Euclidian distance function.

Dbscan also possess some drawbacks. This algorithm is not really efficient for large dimensions. When there are only a few spatial points, increases in dimension (which is same as the number of parameters considered) have some unwanted consequences. For example, when there are 20 points and only two dimensions, the data can be described quite well, but if there are 20 points and 10 dimensions it becomes almost impossible to get any insights from the data. This increase in dimension with no increase in the number of points ia called the curse of dimensionality. Therefore, creating clusters with a higher number of parameters poses a problem in Dbscan. The decision was taken to focus on clustering the study mainly on the latitude and longitude positions.

Researches to improve the classification and particularly clustering with more parameters are still underway. The most important pitfall that the algorithm will have to avoid is sparsity. An algorithm such as RuleFit[10] focusing more on this issue could be a good project for subsequent studies. Neural network applications and usages also offer a lot of interesting opportunities.

4. SOLUTION: DESCRIPTION OF THE APPROACHES

4.1. Presentation of the data

4.1.1. Creation of synthetic data

All the data and graphs presented in this study are derived from the synthetic data. Same parameters and global distribution were retained from the original data, but all the specific values were changed. To build this set of data, online generators[11] (generate data) were used, but the results were not accurate enough and did not provide any information about the real location of stores in Singapore. Hence, the available data was used. A file was created containing all the points (longitude and latitude) where the transactions occurred, and random numbers of transactions with fake amounts and fake customers were associated to these places.

DBS data was similar to this. However, the biggest difficulty in building a new dataset was to get the latitude and longitude of real places in Singapore. This issue was solved by finding a list of zip codes, and latitude and longitude of the main shops in Singapore, along with a list of places where the customers can pay.

4.1.2. Description of the parameters

Many different datasets obtained from the transaction banking data were taken into account. These datasets were diverse in size depending on the purpose of the study. However, generally these datasets contain the same parameters that will be presented here.

Table 1 is an overview of how the dataset is made presenting only the main parameters.

Table 1: Examples of data.

Customer	Amount	Latitude	Longitude	Date	Source_id
1	32	1.3553	103.42	1/6/2014	absp
1	25	1.3434	103.94	1/6/2014	epsp
1	200	1.2343	103.94	3/6/2014	gcsp
1	150	1.2862	103.56	10/6/2014	epsp
2	49	1.3434	103.34	14/6/2014	absp
2	159	–	–	–	–

A complete description of the main parameters that were worked upon is given below:

- Amount in SGD: Table 2 represents the main characteristics of distribution of amount of transactions. From Table 2, it can be noticed that the range is really large and even if most of the transactions correspond to small amounts (around SGD18.9), some huge transactions up to SGD5000 are also seen.

Table 2: Summary of the variable amount.

Min	First quartile	Median	Mean	Third quartile	Max
0	1.74	17	18.9	75	5000.000

- Source_id corresponds to the method of the transaction, such as NETS (epsp), ATM (absp), or credit (gcsp). The distribution is quite uniform over different datasets, but the ATM withdrawals seem to be of higher amounts and are made in less diverse places.
- Date is given in a standard format along with the time of the transaction. Our time interval starts on the 1 January 2013 and ends on

31 December 2014. The distribution is quite uniform even if there were more transactions in 2014 than in 2013. This is due to the type of data and is not representative of a real trend. The date information was transformed into weekday which was often more useful, or into the year, for the purpose of this study. Specific day of transaction gave too granular information and does not allow an efficient comparison of the behavior of the customer.

- Tableau was used to represent the location data on a map. Latitude and longitude data associated with the zip code gave all the necessary information to plot the data. Figure 1 clearly shows that most of the transactions occurred in the central business district (CBD) of Singapore and along the MRT lines, which is quite expected.

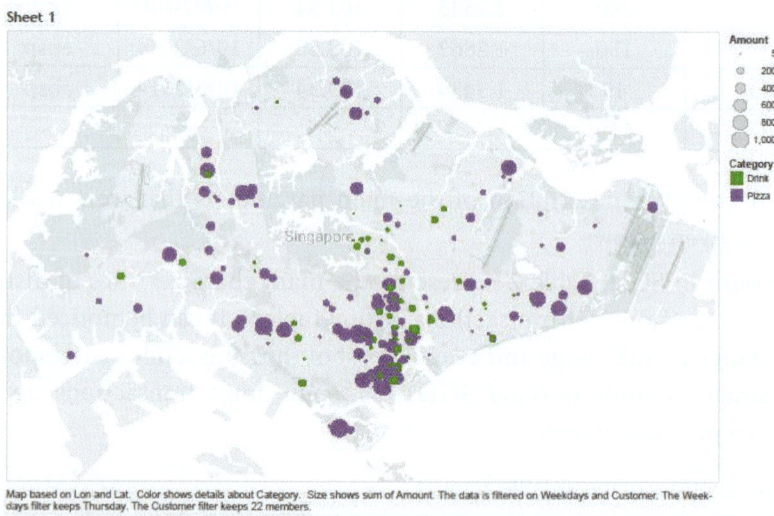

Figure 1: Representation on tableau.

Other parameters that give more accurate information about location are address and postal code of customers with cin and sfx, i.e., customer identity and type of transactions, such as text about the payment terminal, etc., though text mining will be required for all the textual data.

Analysis based on months or days of the week was conducted to see if any insights can be discovered about the trends. Figure 2 shows the monthly expenditure of overall customers. It can be observed that the distribution is more or less uniform, except for a few months when the customers have a willingness to spend more money.

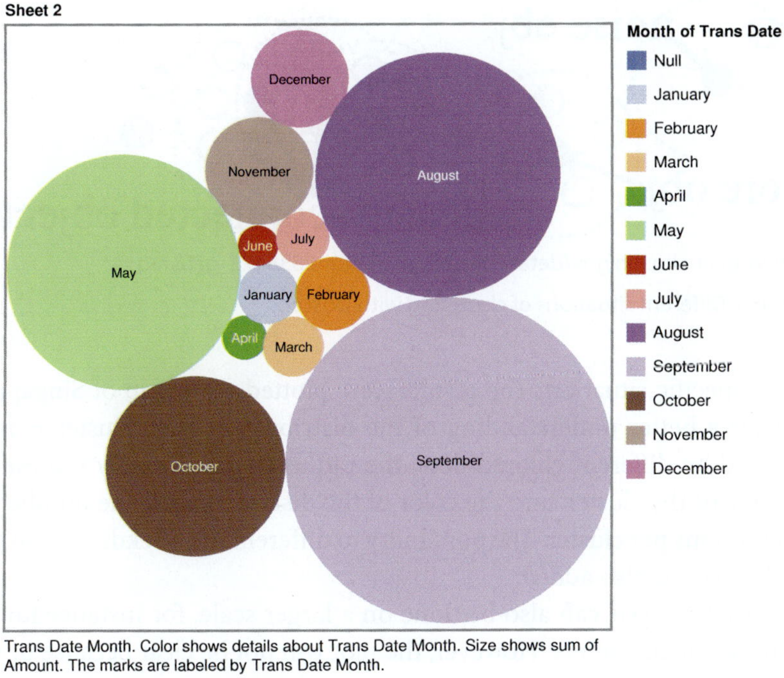

Figure 2: Amount spent per month.

This data is quite diverse and the first analysis gave a lot of basic information. Before performing any deeper analysis, studying the distribution of the parameters is helpful as it brings some insights.

4.2. Different types of analysis

4.2.1. Use of clustering

4.2.1.1. First clustering approach

The data was classified based on the space location. Once the latitude and longitude values for all the transactions are gained, it is easy to plot them on a graph and perform Dbscan algorithm.

This algorithm is based on *K*-mean approach. There are two parameters that must be optimized: minPts which is the minimal number of points that each cluster must have, and $\in$ which is the maximal distance between two points of a same cluster (Figure 3).

First analysis was carried out for a particular group of customers. This analysis consists of finding the more relevant cluster for the group

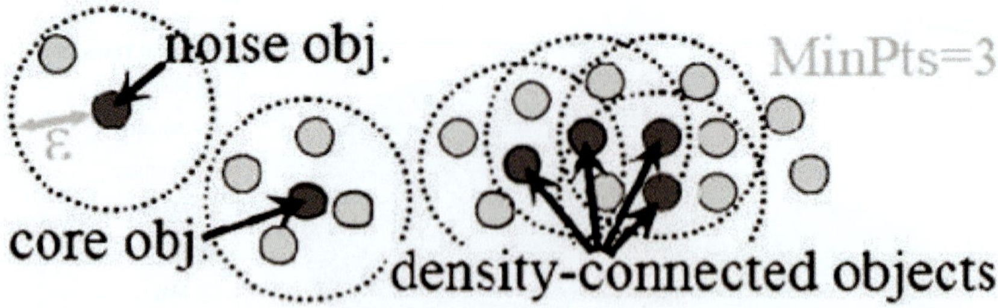

http://openi.nlm.nih.gov/detailedresult.php?img=2838472_gr1&req=4

Figure 3: Different situations of clustering with Dbscan.

and a specific situation. The results were plotted on a map of Singapore to have a better understanding of the distribution. Each cluster is represented by different colored dots; the radius of disk broadly represents the area of the cluster, and the color of the disk represents the number of transactions per cluster. The possibility to differentiate weekdays from the weekends was also added.

This analysis can also be done on a larger scale, for instance for an entire set of customers. However, the plot will not be clear because of the large number of points.

This first try allows us to be familiar with the clustering technics, to discover data distribution, and build a first model which can be further improved.

4.2.1.2. Some representations

Figures 4 and 5 show two plots representing the clustering analysis.

Figure 4: Cluster for a group of customers during the weekends.

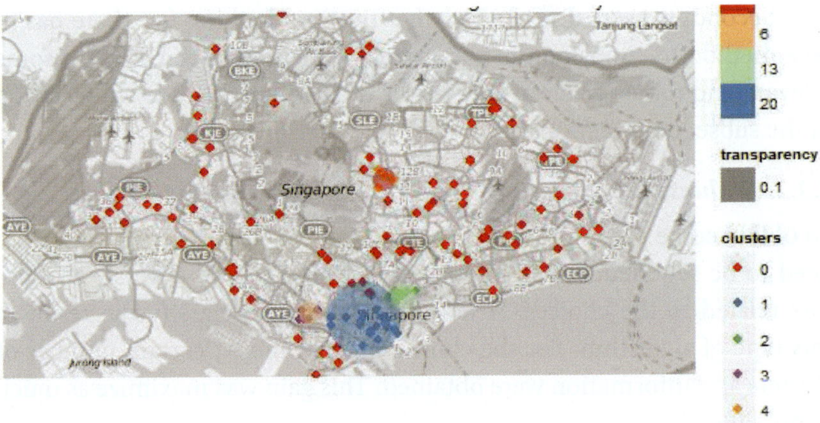

Figure 5: Cluster for a group of customers during the weekdays.

Cluster zero represents all the unclustered data. It can be seen that there is a huge difference in behavior of this group of customers. During weekends, they mainly stay in North near their homes (presumed Cluster one), and sometimes seem to visit some friends or do shopping always at the same place (Clusters two and three).

During weekdays most of their transactions are done in the CBD which could probably be their workplace (Cluster four). The analysis of the clustering behavior gives an insight regarding the propensity of this group of customers to go to certain places.

4.2.1.3. How to use the clustering

Selecting the parameters provides an opportunity to focus on specific questions for example is it better to target weekly clusters more, or find them as a function of the number of transactions or the amount spent?

To answer these questions:

First, if users know the question they seek an answer for, then it is possible to be quite specific about the parameters, e.g., if users want to focus on the weekly walking behavior of one customer, then the parameters can be set: $\in$ must be small because for one cluster it is the radius inside which the customer will walk, so it can be set at 500 m. For the weekly component, there must be at least one transaction a week, so minPoints for one year data will be 52. Sometimes, it is best to focus on certain parameters that are found to be the most relevant for the study. In this case, there was no need to study the distribution of parameters.

Second, if users don't know what they are looking for, there has to be a method to choosing the parameters, which must be based on some relevant and robust criteria. This will be explored in the index description in the subsequent sections.

4.2.2. Evaluate the clustering

To obtain some patterns, the best parameters for the clustering algorithm need to be set. Hence, it is important to find a way to evaluate the factors related to the choices. A few indexes exist to classify the result of this type of algorithm. For the chosen minPts and ∈, certain number of clusters and information were obtained. This gain was maximize as much as possible.

4.2.2.1. Dunn Index

$$DI_m = \frac{\min_{l \le i < j \le m}(\delta(C_i, C_j))}{\max\limits_{l \le k \le m}(\Delta_k)}$$

where m is the number of clusters, $\delta C_i, C_j)$ is the intercluster distance metric, and Δ_k is the max distance intracluster.

For this index, the higher the value is, the better the parameters are. Following graph presents the value of Dunn index as a function of different values of ∈ and minPts (Figure 6).

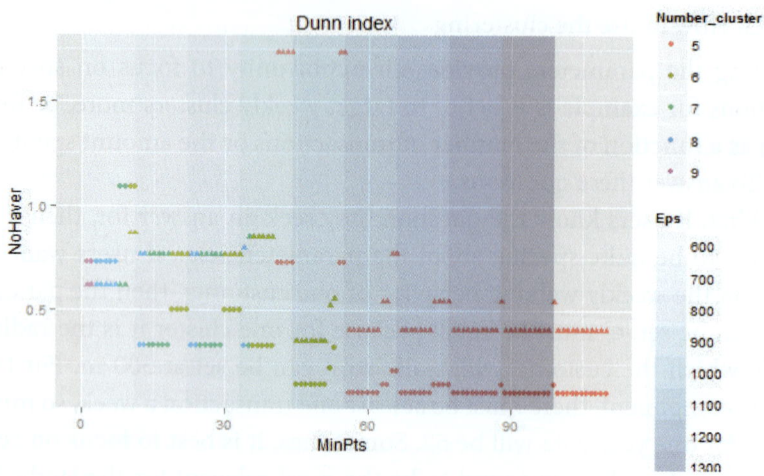

Figure 6: Value of Dunn index as function of ∈ and minPts.

The triangles represent the value of the index using Haversine distance, whereas the circles display the values without it. Color of the points represents the number of clusters which are directly linked with the value of ∈. The more ∈ increases, the more the number of clusters decreases. It wasobserved that the value of Dunn index is higher with the Haversine distance function.

4.2.2.2. Davies-Bouldin index

$$DB=\frac{1}{n}*\sum_{i=1}^{n}\max_{j\neq i}\left(\frac{\sigma_i+\sigma_j}{d(C_i,C_j)}\right)$$

where n is the number of clusters, σ_i is the average distance of the elements of the cluster, and d is the distance between two clusters.

The lower the index value is, the better the parameters are. Following graph represents the values of Davies-Bouldin index as function of different values of ∈ and minPts (Figure 7).

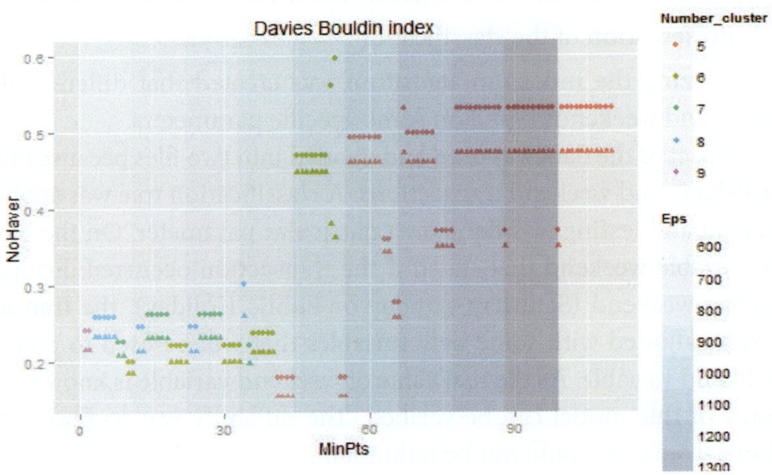

Figure 7: Value of Davies-Bouldin index in function of ∈ and minPoints.

This graph is similar to Dunn index. Value of Davies-Bouldin differs depending on whether the Haversine distance is used or not, and generally is a bit lower for Haversine, which is actually better. The higher the ∈ is, the lower will be the number of clusters and the higher will be the index. In looking for a low index, it is best to use an intermediate value of ∈ that will not give too many clusters.

For both indexes, results of the experiments show different tendencies:

- Haversine distance which is more accurate. There is an average improvement of 11 per cent with the use of this distance.
- Extreme values for ∈ and minPoints lead to outliers for the index value. So intermediate values for these two parameters must be chosen.
- Between the two indexes, Davies-Bouldin seems better. After analyzing the different indexes, the Davies-Bouldin index was chosen as it gave a big range of results that are easier to use. Also, the index emphasized the distance between inter- and intracluster which are our two mains concerns. Intercluster shows some interesting customer movements during the period considered and intracluster gives us a lot of information regarding the size of the cluster and how the points are chosen to be inside this one.

4.2.2. Classification technics to differentiate weekday and weekends

4.2.2.1. Presentation of the classification

After analyzing the index, an algorithm was created that differentiates weekdays and weekends based on some specific parameters.

A subset of the data was used and divided into two files because of its size: weekday and weekend transactions. A classification tree was applied to the data and testing was done on a particular parameter. On the basis of the variable weekend that stated if the transaction occurred during a day of the weekend (Saturday, Sunday or Public Holiday), the transactions were allotted with some new variables that will be used to predict the weekend variable. As the real value of weekend variable is known, the accuracy of this model can be verified. The difficulty was to find some good variables that would not be redundant.

For the selected parameters, some approaches were considered: Dbscan algorithm was applied to both sets of data and this index was used to rate the clustering algorithm. So the minPoints value, ∈ value, and index value were obtained. A Davies-Bouldin index was sought that which is quite low, with more than three clusters and obtained the percentage of values that are classified. Thus for each set of data (weekend/weekdays depending on the customer) some descriptive parameters of the clusters were obtained. Other parameters were also tested — such as the number of transactions per day, frequency of transactions, amount spent, mean, and standard deviation of the amount per day, per week and per month. Since all other parameters did not give good results in the classification process, only the main three were kept, which are presented in the tree plot (Figure 8).

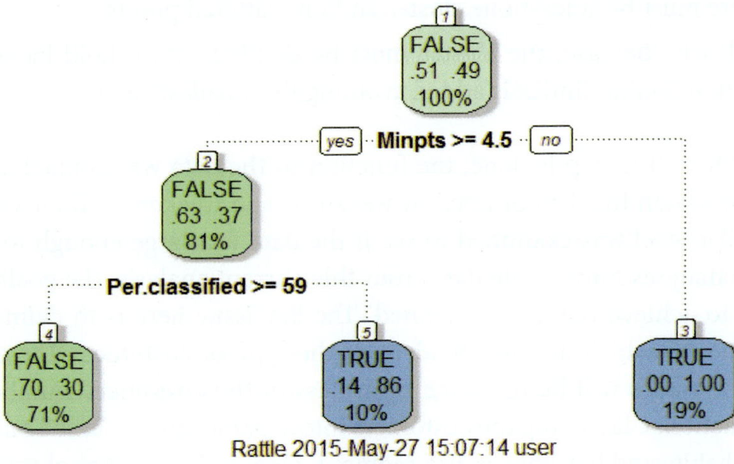

Figure 8: Classification tree to find weekend transactions.

The tree plot shows the most relevant parameters for this classification. As evident from the plot, the number of MinPts is the most important one. It represents the minimum number of points that a cluster can have. If the number of points is less than 4.5, the data represents weekend transactions. Per.classified represents the percentage of points classified into one of the clusters compared to overall data. If these values are greater than 59 per cent, there is a strong hint that the data represents weekday values.

An 85 per cent accuracy prediction model was finally obtained. From the cluster created, the goal was to predict at 100 per cent, or close to a sample of data containing weekend or weekdays. The result obtained was still good and the classification technique was an interesting step to understand the dataset.

4.2.2.2. Results from the classification

This approach gave strong hints to define how to create the final program that will predict if a cluster must be divided into a more granular level or not. Code a function taking in the argument the data, the values of ∈ and minPts, parameters used, and the weekdays being considered. This prediction is based on several steps:

- Checking the number of points is sufficient to apply the algorithm. The number of transactions should be more than the minPts.
- There must be at least one cluster and no scattered points.
- If this is the case, the cluster must be divided. Athreshold based on Davies-Bouldin index is added avoiding the smallest values.

Once this step is done, the function to the data was applied and it was tested on the data ordered by weekdays and weekends. Then a more granular level was examined to see if the data was large enough to perform analyses for a single day. From this current analysis, the goals and ways to achieve them were defined. The key issue here is to define the parameters which are independent of the type of customers The ∈, or minPts values will be the same regardless of the customers' number of transaction. Classifying the customers into separate groups based only on their habits and behavior is also required. Hence, the number of transactions that someone had in one year is also a good indicator.

The final accuracy was still far from 100 per cent and the study did not find any way to improve the 85 per cent accuracy obtained earlier. However, because of this new approach, the importance of the parameters for clustering and the way they should be used for future works was better understood.

4.3. Visualizations of the dataset and of the clustering

4.3.1. First visualizations

4.3.1.1. Classified by weekend behavior

The purpose of the study was to build some models, understand the insights from the data, and present the findings. Thus the importance of visualization using some relevant graphs to show the use of clustering techniques to understand the data was paramount (Figure 9).

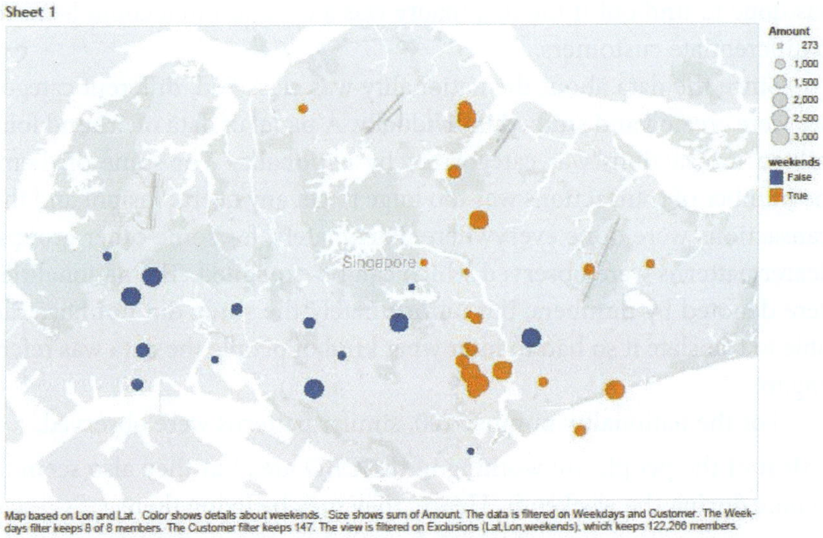

Figure 9: Difference of behavior during the weekends.

All the analyses were carried out in R and Tableau was used to present the results. Two approaches for analysis were used: looking at a group level with group created based on different criterion. First, a group of consumers based on higher number of transactions was studied. Only customers with more than 21 payments per week (which is more than three payments a day) were selected. The next focus was on a group of people classified based on their nationalities. A more complete and larger data was received for this task.

For the data based on the number of transactions, the transaction behavior of the group during weekdays and weekends was presented.

Figure 10 refers to places where the members of that group go spent their weekends along with their preferred locations. The biggest blue bubble shows the place they work, orange and blue the place they live and the two orange bubbles the place they like to go to on weekends, e.g. golf club or mall.

4.3.1.2. Classified by nationality

A new set of data linking the identity of the persons to their nationality was obtained. However, both of these, nationality and identity, were encrypted, and no further details could be accessed. Therefore, a study was done to find out if the nationality was a criterion that could be used to differentiate customers.

Since the data about the nationality was classified, different categories were created and studied individually. A panel of data of around four million transactions was categorized by nationality. For some of them, the number of transactions was too huge to get any useful insight and the transactions were done everywhere. Fortunately, for some other groups, clearer patterns were observed which can be explained. The nationalities were denoted by numbers, but unfortunately the study did not have the table to translate it so had to infer what kind of people the data was referring to.

For the nationality number 700, similar patterns were observed:

- Most of the people are working in the CBD area but they also seem to come during the weekends. Hence, they may be living there.
- Ang Mo Kio seems to be a popular place.
- Some customers go to Sentosa only during weekends.
- The transaction areas seem to cover all the most important places in Singapore.

This group comprises quite a wealthy group of people; maybe lots of expats.

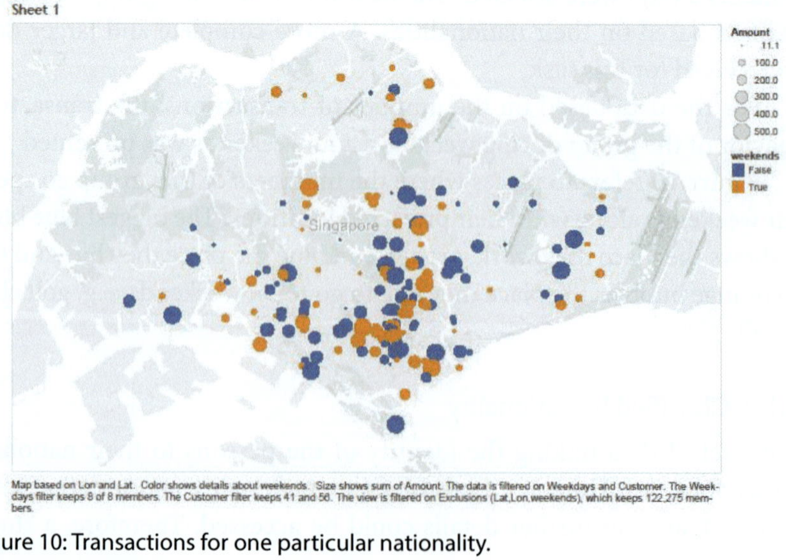

Figure 10: Transactions for one particular nationality.

To perform this analysis, the clustering algorithm was applied to the data, and then how the weekend and weekdays transactions were distributed was studied. Interestingly, working with people of different nationalities gave a lot of comprehension about the data and their behavioral attitudes. This kind of studies with a clear and defined purpose, and can bring a lot of good information to the bank.

4.3.1.3. Prediction of next transactions

As the data received to make these graphs was large including more parameters, some classification was required. One interesting question is: Is it possible to predict how many customers will go to a specific area in the following month?

The first approach was based on the address location, and a classification tree was used. The cluster to which the transactions belonged was added. The most important parameter was the way the subset of people was created, which is logical; the customers showed a tendency to go to same places. The cluster created for the overall data provides general information on the dataset, but not much on the behavior of a group of customers. Therefore, the results based on a cluster classification were lower than with the customer approach.

Unfortunately, besides the previous limit, there was also a limitation for the size of the data. To do some predictions with a high number of parameters, a higher number of transactions were required.

Even if the number of transactions was impressive, when this number was divded by the number of days in a year, it did not generate enough data to create an accurate daily prediction model.

4.3.2. Classify group of consumers

4.3.2.1. Creation of an explanatory data frame

One of the final goals of the study is to understand a customer group's collective behavior. Therefore, a function that applies the clustering algorithm to the transactions of a group of customers was created giving a table as follows: for each group of consumers, there is only one row in the table where the columns represent the relevant parameters to describe the group.

Different parameters were created to allow better understanding of the group. These parameters were divided into three main categories:

- First, the ones that obtained directly from the data such as mean, standard deviation of the amount spent, number of places where the customer did some transactions, and the number of transactions.
- Parameters from clustering obtained after running the clustering algorithms. The most relevant ones are the number of clusters, value of Davis-Bouldin index, and the number of points classified into a cluster.
- Explanation parameters that gave information regarding the panel of customers chosen.

To get this data frame, the function takes as input:

- Data
- List of parameters considered in the clustering
- List of the days on which analysis has to be done
- Value of $\in$ and minPts

In addition to creating the function, improvement on the accuracy of the function was done and the relevant results were obtained. Analysis was done for both real and fake data.

This function is mainly based on some constraints to determine if clustering the input data should be done:

- first, verify if the number of points are sufficient to create clusters
- then check if different clusters can be obtained
- finally, check if the value of the index is sufficient and the clustering really produces useful insights

Tableau was used to analyze the results obtained. Different parameters were plotted, as function of consumer and the fact that clustering was applied to their data.

4.3.2.2. More advanced parameters

Once this first function was created, which was working quite well, it was then applied to different set of available data. As there was no way to verify if the results were good, often the points were plotted to get some insights from the space distribution.

Since the results were different than expected, the parameters were analyzed deeper. A parameter called description, which is generally the name of the shops, was accessed from the available data which revealed more about the transaction. The location data latitude and longitude does not allow us to distinguish among the shops in the same mall. Hence, it was assumed that a transaction carried out in different shops in the same mall is also same, which is true from position point of view but false if consumer behavior is to be understood. Therefore, available text data was analyzed, and some categories such as hobbies or supermarket transactions were built to give more information regarding the type of consumers.

Transactions were differentiated as a function of their type. At that point of time, the focus was more on the analysis of the geospatial clusters, but other parameters were added to the clustering to improve the results. However, using more parameters leads to the problem of the curse of dimensionality that Dbscan algorithm is not able to deal with. Hence, another clustering algorithm robust against these problems had to be found. Research was done on biclustering and max bilclique which are quite recent algorithms[12] but seem to have really good results with any kind of data.

4.3.3. Analyze the clients of a restaurant

This dataset allows for the pursuit of lots of different analysis, some of which are quite global and required to analyze all the customers to find relevant pattern for the whole population; others are more specific. The project focused more on a specific place.

The first part of this study was broad and analyzed behavior as a function of nationality, however, the second part was about the customers of a restaurant.

4.3.3.1. Preliminary study

Dataset containing all the transactions of the clients of the restaurant was obtained and an understanding of the behavior of these customers was made, such as places where they like to go, frequency of their transactions in the restaurant, places where they live. To answer all these questions, different but complementary analyses were carried out.

First, these customers were compared with the overall population of Singapore and the patterns obtained only from the restaurant clients. This was the first step but an interesting one because it gave information on the wealth of the clients and their favorite places compared to general Singaporean population. As it is quite a costly restaurant, most of the clients are from the rich areas around central part of Singapore and Orchard Road.

The area near the restaurant was analyzed. There were two places close by that seemed to be linked with the restaurant (Figure 11). What is interesting is that the two other areas show transactions from VISA and NETS methods of payment. Inside the restaurant they used credit cards, but the ATM outside shows almost similar number of transactions with a higher amount. Therefore, to analyze the transactions in the restaurant, it is important to consider the neighborhood.

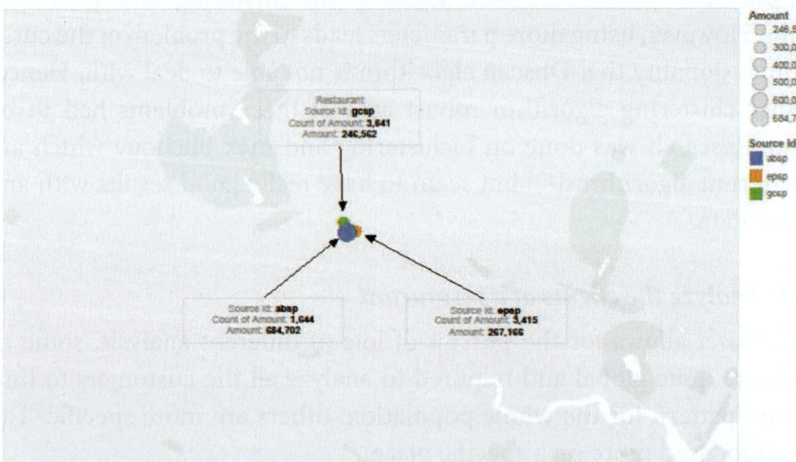

Map based on Lon and Lat. Color shows details about Source Id. Size shows sum of Amount. The marks are labeled by count of Amount. Details are shown for Nassim. The data is filtered on Customer, which keeps 2,201 of 2,201 members. The view is filtered on count of Amount and Inclusions (Lat,Lon,Nassim,Source Id). The count of Amount filter ranges from 1,000 to 9,517. The Inclusions (Lat,Lon,Nassim,Source Id) filter keeps 3 members.

Figure 11: Area near the restaurant.

Then the distribution of the transactions was studied as a function of different parameters. For weekdays, the following information was obtained: the shop is closed on Monday, people like to come during weekends but for other days the number of transactions is almost identical. Similarly, two peaks for particular hour of the days were observed: a bigger one for lunch time and a smaller one for dinner.

The analyses performed focusing on all the parameters except location gave interesting and useful results. Before performing any deep analysis, the simple initial study on the type or the amount of transaction already provided a lot of insight on what to look for.

4.3.3.2 Analysis of the transactions of the clients of the restaurant

Finally, after all these preliminary studies, the clustering algorithm was applied. It is interesting to study the customers as a function of the clusters or areas they like to go. For the customers of restaurant, the Dbscan algorithm was applied to get the clusters based on a fixed number of minimum points, which corresponded to one transaction per month. Different values of the $\in$ value were tried, such as 500 and 1000 m.

Surprisingly, the results obtained showed quite different patterns. First, the smaller clusters were removed so as not to overfill the graphs so that the difference is visible and understandable.

When considering 500m, the clusters will contain only a few places and will underline the specific places where the customers like to go. It seems that it is up to the restaurant.

When consider 1,000m, the results reveal more about the area where people like to go. It will unify different small clusters/places and on average it seems that they finally prefer to go to these places.

To conclude, the most frequent places where the clients like to go depends on the restaurant but after aggregation the most frequent areas are down left of the restaurant.

These results led to some pretty interesting patterns. Of course, deeper analysis can be performed based on the type of customers, sorting them as a function of the number of transactions or amount spent (Figure 12).

Finally, the area near the restaurant was analyzed and the number of clusters located within a radius less than a certain value, i.e., lower than 3 km found to have most of the transactions.

4.3.3.3. Clustering analysis of the clients of the restaurant

The insights obtained from the data were studied further to find what can be done. The size of the data and number of parameters make it a bit difficult to analyze clearly. The percentage of customers that have at least one cluster inside the circle were plotted as a function of the radius of the circle to obtain an excrescent exponential.

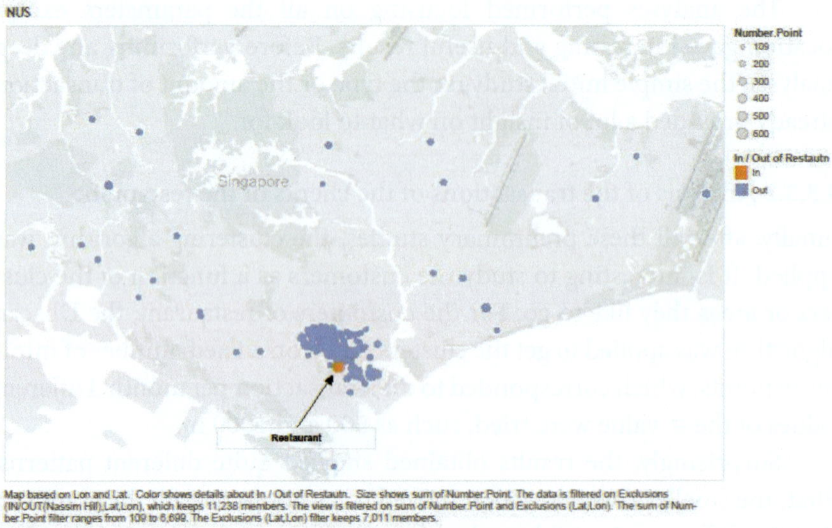

Figure 12: Transactions of the clients of the restaurant.

Thus to analyze the influence of the parameters more precisely, a function was coded that takes the input data, ∈, number of points, and the length of the radius, and gives an output frame with all the information about the customer and their position regarding a precise location.

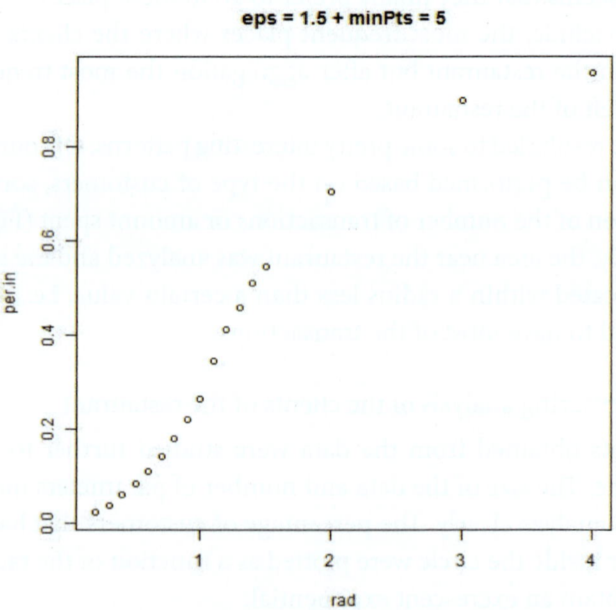

Figure 13: Percentage of customers as a function of the size of the radius.

This was done for a high number of parameters so that more graphs can be produced to best explain the situation of the restaurant.

Figure 13 shows the percentage of customers with at least one cluster inside the radius as a function of the radius. The function looks like a positive tan h function. There is a sharp increase when the radius is low and after that, it reaches a plateau.

This analysis was performed with a great number of combinations of ∈ and minPts. The distribution of the points has always been the same even if there are some small changes in the curvature. These graphs show that with lower values of ∈ a bigger radius is required to reach a high percentage of customers. On the contrary, higher ∈ and lower minPts lead to smaller radius.

To compare them best, a threshold was set so the results could be inferred. A radius linked to 50 per cent of the customers inside the radius is required. Table 3 presents the value of the radius as a function of the other parameters:

Table 3: Radius at 50 per cent as function of parameters of Dbscan.

∈	200 m	500 m	1000 m	1500 m	1500 m	1500 m
MinPts	24	12	8	5	24	12
Radius at 50%	2700 m	1900 m	1600 m	1400 m	2100 m	1800 m

To have a better understanding of the spatial positions of the clusters, a function is created in R that can be used to plot the clusters and highlight the ones located inside the defined radius.

Figure. 14 shows an example of those customers who work at a specific place in the center of Singapore. To know how the clusters are distributed, each point represents a cluster of one customer and the colored one is situated inside the defined area. As function of the number of transactions in one cluster, the color scale and size of the dots are changing.

The study carried out for this specific place taught us how to tackle an entire set of questions and procedures. It was important to find the customers that will be linked to this place (same area, transactions in the neighborhood, etc.). Once this was over, clustering analysis about the transactions and research of the best parameters had to be done.

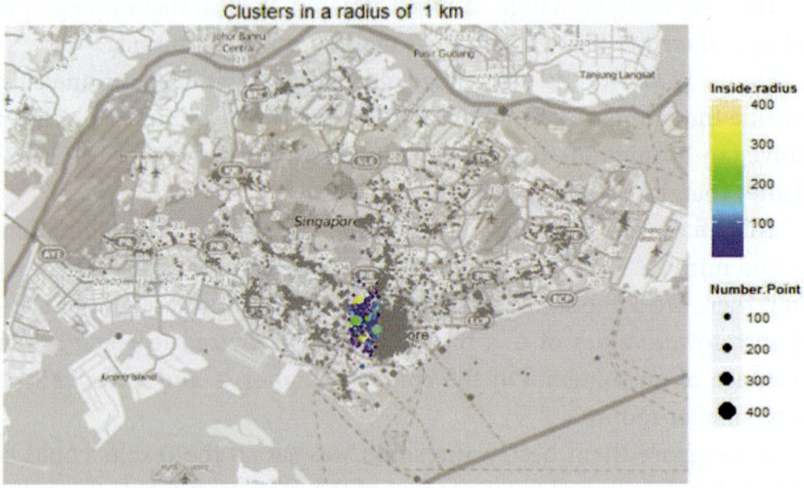

Figure 14: Clusters near a specific place.

4.3.4. Generalization of the work

4.3.4.1 First interrogations

After detailed work was done to understand the behavior of customers of a specific place, it was decided to try to generalize the approach:

- First, the functions and the different ways the data was dealt with were improved, so that this work could be applied to any sort of data. It was important to have a good understanding of the expectations of the company and how this work could be interesting and useful for others.
- To facilitate the understanding of this study, an app was constructed that allows the user to play with different parameters to perform analysis. This app was built with Shiny, a framework available in R and was loaded with two different functions.

4.3.4.2. Representation

The first function gave an idea of the distribution of the transactions for groups of consumers. The transactions are represented as a function of clusters to which they belong. It is possible to change the value of some key variables, such as the number of customers, $\in$, or the number of clusters allowed.

The second function of the app presents the transactions within certain radius of a specific place. For this, the function described in Section 4.3.3 was improved and used. It is possible to change the value of some key variables such as the length of the radius, $\in$, or the number of clusters allowed. It is also possible to choose the place to focus and to differentiate weekdays and weekends.

The user could focus on a group of customers (first part of the app) or she/he could also easily load a place on which he would like to focus her/his study (second part of the app). Once she/he chooses it, only the customers that have already had one transaction in this area will be selected and the analysis proposed will be entirely specific.

Figure 15 is an example of the app for a specific customer.

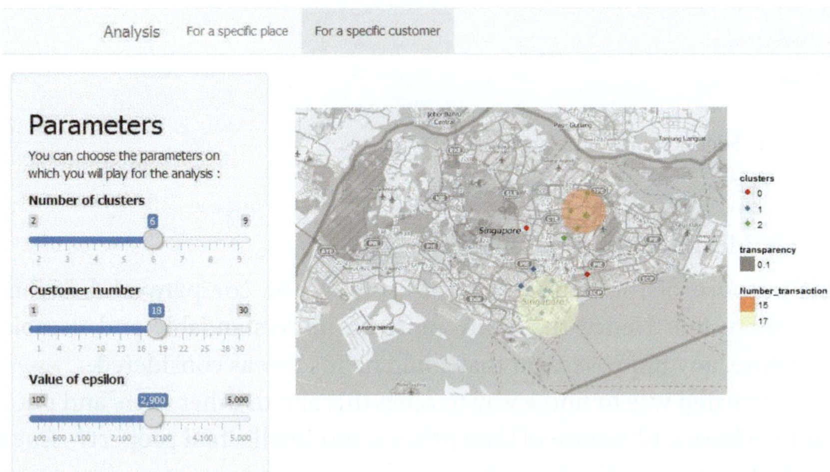

Figure 15: First part of the app.

Goal of this app is to simplify the visualization of the function that was coded. Hence the analysis performed in this study can be used by anyone for different queries.

The app was improved by adding more possibilities such as choosing the dataset on which to perform the study or increasing the accuracy of presentation adding some descriptive charts and tables. However, it was necessary to specify the data required first.

Figure 16 shows the second part of the app presenting the distribution of clusters near a specific place.

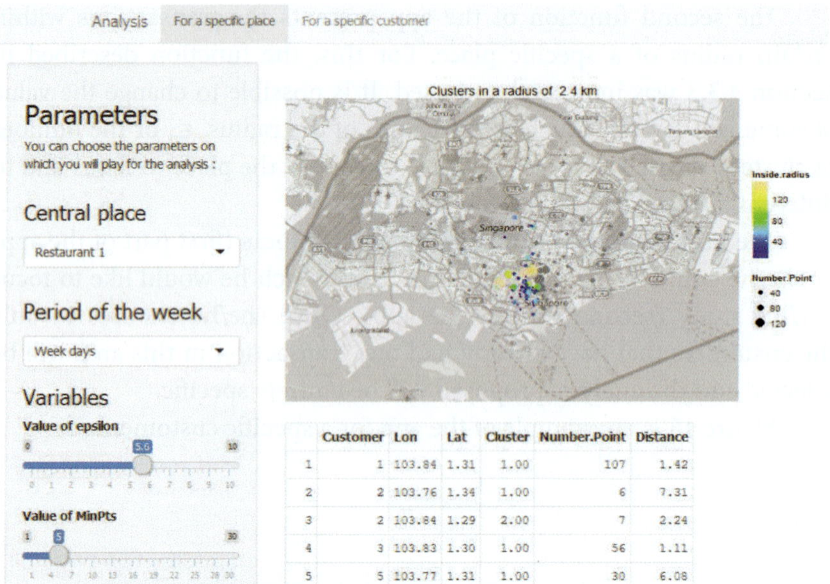

Figure 16: Second part of the app.

4.3.4.3. Meaningful improvements

The purpose of the app is to be useable by the company and anyone else interested. Hence the study must be understandable and useable. Therefore, any improvement that could be made was considered.

First step was to find a way to open this app to other users and put it online. However because of data privacy and intellectual property issues, the study was not placed on internet.

R code that was written for this project, two files ui.R and server.R and to write into the terminal "launchApp('app')" are required to launch the app. However the project still needed to fix the usage of data and see which data could be used and how it must be chosen. The data that will be used must have some specific parameters such as latitude, longitude, and the identity of the customer. The possibility to save the data frame and the image obtained were added.

An optional improvement could be to allow the user to choose any other questions that he might want to solve with the use of the data:

- How do people from the same country behave?

- Could to focus only on the transactions of one place and not on the customers going to this place?
- If focusing only on customers of one place, could they be isolated from the really frequent users from the occasional users?

The final purpose of the work for the app was to propose some easily manageable tools that can be still used at the end of this study.

5. DISCUSSION

The clustering approach was an open and diverse subject. The challenge was to find ways to rank the classification, to be able to understand, and to answer hard-edged questions.

One of the major works was to build a function giving more relevant information about a group of customers. The goal of the function is to help the decision and can be used in a lot of scenarios and will help in future research.

In addition, DBS was helped in presentations or researches based on the data. Some clustering analyses as well as visualizations of the behavior of the customers at a specific place were done for them. The analysis done in this study, based on R and Tableau gave real insights and figures that could be presented quite easily to DBS. Of course, explanation on how it was used was given. It is hoped that the work done in this study can be used again. Indeed, it is easier to compare the result for a particular question than for a broad and general function that can be used in several situations. Author had an opportunity to communicate with the bank and its employees during the study.

It was really a good strategy to adopt two different approaches – one long analysis that took a great part of the time and some punctual questions about some specific issues.

All the issues addressed and solved in this study were real problems. However, if the work done was to be adopted in any other company, it would need to be improvised. That is why each query has been stored and a pattern was built based on them which will allow others to solve the questions quickly. Functions and visualizations that can be used in different situations were created.

6. CONCLUSION AND FURTHER WORK

Following are some suggestions for further work:

- The clustering mainly focused on two parameters — latitude and longitude. Sometimes other parameters were added for particular requests, but the Dbscan algorithm does not deal well with high dimension data. It was necessary to be quite careful using these parameters. To facilitate the future work it is advised to try another algorithm such as *biclustering*. This technique seems really powerful and convenient although there are still two main drawbacks: the processing time is quite slow and the code is not available in R, only in Java. (To build an R-package from Java would have taken too much time.)
- Linked to the previous improvement, work could be done with more parameters such as the ones used here, e.g., amount, nationality, identity of the customers, etc. or sex, age, Singaporean citizen or holder of EP/student pass, etc. To improve the comprehension of the data, some work could be performed on the text parameters. For each transaction, there is a text that gives information about the location. Perhaps more emphasis could be put on the text mining of these data, as these could reveal some different behavior inside some malls with lots of shops and different types of customers.
- Concerning the app built during the project, many improvements can still be done. It is still an alpha version working only for some really specific queries. Further improvements could be made for other options such as the choice of the data, more precise questions, or even the presentation of the graphs.

REFERENCES

1. Blumberg, R and A Shaku (2003, February). The problem with unstructured data. *DM Review*, 42–46.
2. Hennig, C (2014, 10 01). *fpc*. Retrieved from cran.r-project: https://cran.r-project.org/web/packages/fpc/fpc.pdf
3. Baars, H. and HG Kemper (2008, April). Management support with structured and unstructured data–an integrated business intelligence framework. *Information Systems Management*, 132–148.

4. Wickham, H (2015, 03 17). *ggplot2*. Retrieved from cran.r-project: https://cran.r-project.org/web/packages/ggplot2/index.html

5. ASEAN Agreement on Transboundary Haze Pollution (2015). *Hotspots*. Retrieved from ASEAN Agreement on Transboundary Haze Pollution: http://haze.asean.org/?page_id=251

6. Baker, J and M Cameron (1996). The effects of the service environment on affect and consumer perception of waiting time: An integrative review and research propositions. *Journal of the Academy of Marketing Science*.

7. Adobe (n.d.). *Adobe® marketing cloud, clickstream data feeds*. Retrieved from https://marketing.adobe.com/resources/help/en_US/whitepapers/clickstream/clickstream.pdf

8. Verma, R (2009). *Chapter 4 cluster snalysis*. Retrieved from hypertextbookshop.com: http://www.hypertextbookshop.com/dataminingbook/public_version/contents/chapters/chapter004/section004/blue/page003.html

9. Rousseeuw, PJ (1987). *Clustering*. Retrieved from scikit-learn.org: http://scikit-learn.org/stable/modules/clustering.html

10. Stanford (2012, 07 07). *RuleFit*. Retrieved from statweb.stanford.edu: http://statweb.stanford.edu/~jhf/r-rulefit/rulefit3/RuleFit_help.html

11. Anderson, RT, FT Camacho and R Balkrishnan (2007). Willing to wait?: the influence of patient wait time on satisfaction with primary care. *BMC Health Services Research*.

12. Michael Steinbach, LE (2014). The Challenges of Clustering High Dimensional Data. pp. 11–17.

UNCITED REFERENCES

1. Asia Insurance Review (2015, April 15). *India: Less than 1/5 of farmers insure crops*. Retrieved from Asia Insurance Review: http://www.asiainsurancereview.com/News/View-NewsLetter-Article?id=32525&Type=eDaily

2. BAE, S (2015). *AML transaction monitoring*. Retrieved 8 16, 2015, from http://www.baesystems.com/what-we-do-rai/financial-crime/financial-crime-solutions/aml-transaction-monitoring

3. Bartlett, J (2014). *Area under the ROC curve*. Retrieved 8 16, 2015, from http://thestatsgeek.com/2014/05/05/area-under-the-roc-curve-assessing-discrimination-in-logistic-regression/

4. Breiman, L (1984). Classification and regression trees. *CRC press.*

5. Breiman, L (2001). Random forests. *Machine learning.*

6. Choi, YF, TW Wong and CC Lau (2006). Triage rapid initial assessment by doctor (TRIAD) improves waiting time and processing time of the emergency department. *Emergency medicine journal.*

7. Davenport, TH (2015). The Rise of Automated Analytics. *The Wall Street Journey.*

8. Delong, ER-P (1988). Comparing the areas under two or more correlated receiver operating characteristic curves: a nonparametric approach. *Biometrics*, 837–845.

9. Edelman, KD (2015, July). What 'digital' really means. *Mckinsey Insights.*

10. Fan, W, L Wallace, S Rich and Z Zhang (2006, September). Tapping the power of text mining. *Communications of the ACM*, 76-82.

11. Feinerer, I. (2015, 7 3). *Introduction to the tm package.* Retrieved 8 16, 2015, from https://cran.r-project.org/web/packages/tm/vignettes/tm.pdf

12. Fetter, RB and JD Thompson (1966). Patients' waiting time and doctors' idle time in the outpatient setting. *Health Services Research.*

13. FINCEN (2014). *SAR stats.* Retrieved 8 16, 2015, from http://www.fincen.gov/news_room/rp/sar_by_number.html

14. Fitzpatrick, R (2004). Automated dispensing — developing a business case to support investment. *Hospital Pharmacist*, 109–111.

15. Gao, J (n.d.). *clkustering density.* Retrieved from cse.buffalo.edu: http://www.cse.buffalo.edu/~jing/cse601/fa12/materials/clustering_density.pdf

16. Generate data (n.d.). Retrieved from generatedate.com: http://www.generatedata.com/

17. Gerdeman, D (2015, JUN 29). *Harvard business school.* Retrieved from HBS Working Knowledge: http://hbswk.hbs.edu/item/consumer-centered-health-care-depends-on-accessible-medical-records

18. Graban, M (2011). Lean Hospitals: Improving Quality, Patient Safety, and Employee Engagement.

19. Hai, PT (2015, May 26). *Head of the Department of Information Systems at the School of Computing*, National University of Singapore. (F.-Y. Liang, Interviewer)

20. Harris, TH (2007). *Competing on Analytics.* Harvard Business School Press.

21. Hedges, A (n.d.). *Haversine.* Retrieved from andrew.hedges.name: http://andrew.hedges.name/experiments/haversine/

22. Hendricks, D (2013). *whats an email hash anyway*. Retrieved from http://www.clickz.com/clickz/column/2288689/whats-an-email-hash-anyway

23. Hopp, WJ and ML Spearman (2011). *Factory physics*. Waveland Press.

24. Hossain, AB (2013). NoSQL Database: New Era of Databases for Big data Analytics–Classification, Characteristics and Comparison.

25. IBM Knowledge Centre (2015, June 13). *Take tours of the content analytics miner*. Retrieved from IBM Watson Explorer Analytical Components: http://www-01.ibm.com/support/knowledgecenter/SS8NLW_10.0.0/com.ibm.discovery.es.tm.doc/iiyscviewlet.htm

26. ICA, IC (2015). *What is money laundering*. Retrieved 8 16, 2015, from http://www.int-comp.org/what-is money-laundering

27. Joachims, T (1998, April). Text categorization with Support Vector Machines: Learning with many relevant features. *Machine Learning: ECML-98*, 137–142.

28. Karapiperis, D (2015). *Usage-Based Insurance and Vehicle Telematics: Insurance Market & Regulatory Implications*. Kansas City: NAIC Central Office.

29. Kingman, JF (1961). The single server queue in heavy traffic. *Mathematical Proceedings of the Cambridge Philosophical Society, 57*(4).

30. Knowledge Based Systems, I (1994). *IDEF5 Method Report*. Information Integration for Concurrent Engineering (IICE).

31. Lam, SL (2012). *Rough set approach to marine cargo risk analysis*. Retrieved from International Centre for Maritime Studies: http://www.icms.polyu.edu.hk/ifspa2012/Papers/M26.pdf

32. Lee Tookey (2006). *CARe 2006: marine reinsurane*. Retrieved from Casualty Actuarial Society: https://www.casact.org/education/reinsure/2006/handouts/tookey.ppt

33. Leek, T (2012). *Md5 vs Sha*. Retrieved from http://security.stackexchange.com/questions/19705/is-sha1-better-than-md5-only-because-it-generates-a-hash-of-160-bits

34. Lin, D (1998). Using Collocation Statistics in Information Extraction. *Proceedings of the Seventh Message Understanding Conference*.

35. Liu, S, F Liu, C Yu and W Meng (2004, July). An Effective Approach to Document Retrieval via Utilizing WordNet and Recognizing Phrases. *SIGIR '04: Proceedings of the 27thannual international ACM SIGIR conference on Research and development in information retrieval*, pp. 266–272.

36. Makino, T (2010, April). *What's next: the search for disruptive technologies*. Retrieved from CELENT: http://www.celent.com/system/files/disruptive_innovation_using_mobile_devices_tokio_marine.pdf

37. Manzi, ST (2014, December). The Discipline of Business Experimentation. *Harvard Business Review.*

38. Mapping datapoints google maps (n.d.). Retrieved from tableau: http://kb.tableau.com/articles/knowledgebase/mapping-datapoints-google-maps

39. McKinsey and World Economic Forum (2014, May). *The rising strategic risks of cyberattacks.* Retrieved from McKinsey&Company: http://www.mckinsey.com/insights/business_technology/the_rising_strategic_risks_of_cyberattacks

40. McKinsey Global Institute (2011). *Big data: The next frontier.* McKinsey & Company.

41. McKinsey&Company (2015). *THE INTERNET OF THINGS: MAPPING THE VALUE BEYOND THE HYPE.* McKinsey&Company.

42. MetLife Asia (2015, July 16). *Metlife launches lumenlab.* Retrieved from BusinessWire: http://www.businesswire.com/news/home/20150716005707/en/MetLife-Launches-LumenLab—-First-of-its-Kind-Innovation-Centre#.VcMHIf4cTL8

43. Missikoff, M, P Velardi and P Fabriani (2003). Text mining techniques to automatically Enrich a domain ontology. *Applied Intelligence 18*, 323–340.

44. Moe, WW (2003). Buying, Searching, or Browsing: Differentiating Between Online Shoppers Using In-Store Navigational Clickstream.

45. Park, K (2013). Expression of stress response HSP70 gene in Asian paddle crabs, Charybdis japonica, exposure to endocrine disrupting chemicals, bisphenol A (BPA) and 4-nonylphenol (NP). *Ocean Science Journal.*

46. Rajaraman, JL (n.d.). *Clustering.* Retrieved from web.stanford.edu: http://web.stanford.edu/class/cs345a/slides/12-clustering.pdf

47. Rao, R (2003, November-December). From unstructured data to actionable intelligence. *IT Pro*, 29–35.

48. Rohde, RA (2015). *Air Pollution in China: Mapping of Concentrations and Sources.* Berkeley: Berkeley Earth (of UC Berkeley) Press.

49. SAS Institude (2015, June 20). *SAS text miner.* Retrieved from SAS Knowledge Base - Products and Solutions: http://support.sas.com/software/products/txtminer

50. Sequeira, I (2015, June 20). Fintech Leader (Strategy and Analytics). (F.-Y. Liang, Interviewer)

51. SINTEF (2013, May 22). *Big data, for better or worse.* Retrieved from ScienceDaily: www.sciencedaily.com/releases/2013/05/130522085217.htm

52. Stackoverflow, R (n.d.). Retrieved from Stackoverflow: http://stackoverflow.com/

53. Strathclyde, UO (2015). *What is logistic regression*. Retrieved 8 16, 2015, from https://www.strath.ac.uk/aer/materials/5furtherquantitativeresearchdesignandanalysis/unit6/whatislogisticregression/

54. The Times of India (2015, August 13). *25% of Indians may die of lifestyle diseases before they are 70: Study*. Retrieved from The Time of India: http://timesofindia.indiatimes.com/india/25-of-Indians-may-die-of-lifestyle-diseases-before-they-are-70-Study/articleshow/48460601.cms

55. The World Bank (2012, March 6). *India groundwater: a valuable but diminishing resource*. Retrieved from The World Bank: https://www.worldbank.org/en/news/feature/2012/03/06/india-groundwater-critical-diminishing

56. UNODC (2015). *The money-laundering cycle*. Retrieved 8 16, 2015, from https://www.unodc.org/unodc/en/money-laundering/laundrycycle.html

57. Van, S (2015). *APAC Big Data Market Watch*. Singapore: Swiss Reinsurance Company Ltd.

58. Van, S (2015). *Closing the Protection Gap in APAC*. Singapore: Asia Insurance Review.

59. Vemuri, S (1984). Simulated analysis of patient waiting time in an outpatient pharmacy. *American Journal of Health-System Pharmacy*.

60. Weiss, U (2015). Uwe weiss on predictive analytics. *interview by Lutz Finger*.

61. Wikipedia (2015). *Bank secrecy act*. Retrieved 8 16, 2015, from https://en.wikipedia.org/wiki/Bank_Secrecy_Act

62. Wikipedia (2015). *Text mining*. Retrieved 8 16, 2015, from https://en.wikipedia.org/wiki/Text_mining

63. Willis Energy Market Review (2014). *Cyber Attacks: Can the Market Respond?*. London: Willis Limited.

64. WinfWiki (2014). *Analyse text mining SAS text miner*. Retrieved 8 16, 2015, from http://winfwiki.wi-fom.de/index.php/Analyse_Text_Mining_mit_SAS_Text_Miner

65. Yang, Y and X Liu (1999). A Re-examination of Text Categorization Methods. *Proceedings of the 22nd annual international ACM SIGIR conference on Research and development in information retrieval*, pp. 42–49.

66. Yu, Q and K Yang (2008). Hospital registration waiting time reduction through process redesign. *International Journal of Six Sigma and Competitive Advantage*.

CHAPTER 11

Exploring Accuracy and Efficiency of Preventive Maintenance Prediction with Machine Learning Techniques

LIM Wei Bin Kelvin

ABSTRACT

This study discusses various machine learning techniques that were explored to improve accuracy and efficiency in predictions. A variation of different categories of methods such as dimension reduction, features scaling, hyperplane optimization, other machine learning classifier, and ensemble learning on the dataset were carried out to understand the difference in performance on a set of metrics.

The results show that the Gradient Boosting Machine (GBM) model is robust and effective in tackling this problem. In addition, information on the tradeoff between accuracy and efficiency, and suggestions to the challenges faced during the implementation, were also made.

1. INTRODUCTION

DBS has over 1100 Automated Teller Machines (ATMs) and 280 Cash Acceptance Machines (CAMs) in their network in Singapore. It has successfully implemented a proprietary solution to reduce ATM out-of-cash incidents, to increase the efficiency of its ATM Network and thereby customer satisfaction.[1] These can be further improved by preventive maintenance to ATMs and CAMs thus reducing the occurrence of unexpected failures.

DBS and I2R initiated a project to develop a solution for this problem by developing a Joint Lab's predictive maintenance model (JL model) using historical data to predict the occurrence of failure in each of the three components of their machines, namely dispenser, card reader, and Bunch Note Acceptor (BNA) each have their own model and prediction requirements. Features used in these models came from analyzing the machines log, transaction data, and profile of machines. With these predictions, DBS will be able to schedule and perform necessary preventive maintenance so that downtime and disruption are both minimal, thus improving customer satisfaction.

However, given the large number of machines and transactions, it is difficult to produce these predictions accurately and in a timely manner. Hence, the main contribution of this study is to perform various machine learning techniques to achieve an improved accuracy from the JL model as baseline and also to make the model more efficient. These techniques will include dimension reduction, features scaling other machine learning classifier, ensemble learning, and hyperplane optimization which will be discussed in more details later. These techniques are generic and can be applied to other similar machine learning problems to improve accuracy and efficiency.

2. PROBLEM STATEMENT

2.1. Objective

At the end of this study, the accuracy of various methods explored would be produced together with findings on any reduction in duration. The evaluation metric for accuracy to be used would be area under curve (AUC) of the receiving operating curve, Precision at 20 per cent recall (P20) and 50 per cent recall (P50). An increase in these evaluation metrics will give a more accurate prediction of faulty machines for preventive maintenance which will in turn lead to the DBS' goal to improve its ATMs and CAMs availability.

The JL model for various machines gives following accuracy:

	BNA	Dispenser	Card Reader
AUC	0.723	0.701	0.635
Precision at 20% recall	0.779	0.392	0.156
Precision at 50% recall	0.733	0.244	0.103

The above accuracy is computed using one year of data to train and one month of data to test. It is computed by taking average of three periods of training and testing. This accuracy will act as a baseline for comparison with the various techniques to be explored.

2.2. Exploratory data analysis

After performing exploratory data analysis, the quality and quantity of the data format were found to require significant efforts before the various methods to improve accuracy and efficiency were explored. This is because the exploration would require using other less robust and more computationally intensive method, a function is needed to be built to process the data into an easily "ingestible" format which could be used for various R packages. For each JL model, there were around 400 K observations by 400 variables.

A summary and structure of a *mock-up* data is presented in Table 1 to illustrate the need for the transformation of the data.

Table 1: Mock-up data: summary and structure.

##	X	ID	Date	VARIABLE0
##	Min. : 1	ABCD : 683	2014-11-10: 1114	Min. : 108947
##	1st Qu.:101821	KFOK : 676	2014-10-26: 1113	1st Qu.: 229835
##	Median :203825	NVIE : 358	2014-11-06: 1113	Median : 510254
##	Mean :204088	LEPD : 358	2014-08-24: 1112	Mean : 440993
##	3rd Qu.:306025	KOED : 358	2014-09-18: 1111	3rd Qu.: 628492
##	Max. :409395	IJIE : 358	2014-06-11: 1110	Max. : 976281
##			(Other):388254	(Other) :384372

##	VARIABLE 1	VARIABLE 2	VARIABLE 3	VARIABLE 4
##	Min. : 0.00	Min. :0	Min. : 0.00	Min. : 0.00
##	1st Qu.: 1.00	1st Qu.:0	1st Qu.: 0.00	1st Qu.: 1.00
##	Median : 2.00	Median :0	Median : 0.00	Median : 1.00
##	Mean : 2.66	Mean :0	Mean : 0.68	Mean : 1.25
##	3rd Qu.: 4.00	3rd Qu.:0	3rd Qu.: 1.00	3rd Qu.: 2.00
##	Max. :57.00	Max. :0	Max. :38.00	Max. :13.00
##	NA's :102521	NA's :102521	NA's :102521	NA's :102521

##	VARIABLE 5	VARIABLE 6	VARIABLE 7
##	TEXT1 : 74440	C1 : 26091	TEXT6 : 66502
##	TEXT2 : 53332	C2 : 23479	TEXT7 : 56208
##	TEXT3 : 50957	C3 : 23211	TEXT8 : 47261
##	TEXT4 : 43535	C4 : 21667	TEXT9 : 38485
##	TEXT5 : 38113	C5 : 21240	TEXT10 : 37539
##	(Other) :121175	(Other) :265864	(Other) :111080
##	NA's : 9493	NA's : 9493	NA's : 33970

##	VARIABLE8	VARIABLE9	VARIABLE10	VARIABLE11
##	Min. : 0	Min. : 0	Min. :9999	Min. :9999
##	1st Qu.: 9999	1st Qu.: 9999	1st Qu.:9999	1st Qu.:9999
##	Median : 9999	Median : 9999	Median :9999	Median :9999
##	Mean : 10337	Mean : 10615	Mean :9999	Mean :9999
##	3rd Qu.: 9999	3rd Qu.: 9999	3rd Qu.:9999	3rd Qu.:9999
##	Max. :186982	Max. :290960	Max. :9999	Max. :9999

##	LABEL
##	Min. :0.0000
##	1st Qu.:0.0000
##	Median :0.0000
##	Mean :0.1234
##	3rd Qu.:0.0000
##	Max. :1.0000

The mock-up data above illustrates various kinds of data that exist in 400 variables. Missing and insufficient information are indicated separately in different variables. Some were indicated as "NA", while others as an arbitrary large number such as "999" or "9999" (e.g., variables five and eight). Many variables have more than 75 per cent of their observation not available (e.g., variable 3). Some have no variation (e.g., variable 11). Some exist as factor labeled as text (e.g., variable 6). Some are totally correlated (e.g., variable 10 and 11). Data pre-processing will be done to the dataset to transform them into a format which all, if not most, of the R existing functions could ingest. These data processing steps will be elaborated later under Solution (see Section 4).

3. STATE OF THE ART

There are some documents about machine learning to predict fault and ways on improving accuracy. The works documented came mainly from scientific papers, textbooks, blogs written by R package owners and interview with Kaggle winners — a platform for predictive modeling and analytics competition. Although, none of them is directly applicable to the specific problem this study is dealing with, the steps performed can be a good starting point to explore.

The methods mentioned could be broadly categorized into five categories — dimension reduction, features scaling, using other machine learning classifier, hyperplane optimization, and features engineering. These possible new steps and GBM from the baseline JL model will be briefly explained in this section and a combination of them will be performed.

3.1. Dimension reduction

Dimension reduction is a possible step in producing a good accuracy. It is the process of reducing the number of random variables under consideration and can be divided into feature selection and feature extraction. This is a widely recommended step to improve accuracy.[2–4] Furthermore, this is also important to this study too, because there is an overwhelming number of variables. Using the entire set not only takes longer time but is also likely to worsen the performance.[3,5–7]

Features selection can be categorized into filter and wrapper approaches.[4,5] The type of feature selection method chosen to be tested is called the filter method. Filter methods select variables regardless of the model. They are based on general features such as correlation with the variables to predict. Filter methods suppress the least interesting variables. The others variables will be part of the model classification. The main reason for choosing the filter method for feature selection is that it is faster and is robust compared to overfitting.[7] Pearson correlation ranking is used through the naïve Bayes classifier. However, filter methods tend not to consider the relationship between variables.

The wrapper method which considers the relationship between variables takes much longer time and is therefore dropped in this discussion.

The typical steps to a filter selection method could be summarized as follows:

- Providing set of all features.
- Selecting the best subset using correlation with dependent variable.
- Fitting it into a learning algorithm.
- Evaluating the performance.

3.2. Features scaling

Feature scaling is used to standardize the range of independent variables or features of data. This is also widely recommended and performed in many of the machine learning works.[2] This is important in our context since the range of values or raw data vary widely, causing many machine learning algorithms to fail because majority of the machine learning classifier calculate the distance between two points. By scaling it, methods like gradient descent would converge much faster with feature scaling than without it. The kind of feature scaling chosen would be to rescale it to [−1, 1].

3.3. Gradient boosting machine

GBM is the machine learning classifier used by JL model. It is an ensemble learning method for improving the predictive performance of classification or regression procedures, such as decision trees. Gradient-boosted models (GBM) can handle interactions, automatically select variables, are robust to outliers, missing data and numerous correlated and irrelevant variables.[8] GBM is also one of the most used algorithms by top Kaggle winner because of its accuracy, convenience, and efficiency.[9] One of the drawbacks of using GBM would be that there are commonly four parameters needed to be tuned for the classifier to work at its optimum condition. By having four tuning parameters, number of possible combinations to achieve optimum accuracy increase exponentially and require significant amount of time and effort to tune. These four tuning parameters are learning rate, number of trees, minimum number of observations in a leaf, and interaction depth.

3.4. Random Forest

Random Forest is an ensemble learning method for classification, regression, and other tasks that operate by constructing a multitude of decision trees at training time, and outputting the class that is the mode of the classes (classification) or mean prediction (regression) of the individual trees. Random Forests classification use a modified tree learning algorithm that selects, at each candidate split in the learning process, a random subset of the features. This process is sometimes called "feature bagging".

Random Forest is another relatively accurate machine learning method adopted by many Kaggle winners.[2] There is also a previous study performed for predicting fault using statistical and machine learning model. The result of the study shows that Random Forest performed the best among the few other models tested.[10]

3.5. Other machine learning classifier: ensemble learning

Ensemble learning methods use multiple learning algorithms to obtain better predictive performance from any of the constituent learning algorithms. Ensemble learning is important method used in many Kaggle competitions.[2,11–13] A good combination of models would be one that is fairly uncorrelated and have similar average accuracy.[14,15] The ensemble learning method to be used in this project will be a greedy optimization which will create a simple linear blend of models. The greedy algorithm is based on the work of Caruana *et al.* (2004).[15]

3.6. Tuning parameter search

Hyper-parameter optimization includes choosing a set of hyper-parameters for a learning algorithm, usually with the goal of optimizing a measure of the algorithm's performance on an independent dataset.[16]

There are plenty of methods to perform a hyper-parameter optimization, and the two commonly known ones are grid search and random search.

A grid search is performed to identify a better set of parameters which improve the accuracy. It is simply an exhaustive searching through a pre-specified subset of hyper-parameters space of a learning algorithm, e.g. with GBM, the tuning parameters are the number of trees, shrinkage, and minimum number of observation at each leaf and interaction depth. A coarse resolution of the search will be performed due to the time constraint to this project.

3.7. Summary of methods to explore

In summary, Table 2 gives the possible methods from literature review used in predicting fault through machine learning models, and ways to improve accuracy and efficiency for machine learning predictions. These methods will be explored both independently and in combination.

Table 2: Summary of methods used.

Features selection/ extraction	Feature scaling	Other ML model	Parameter Search
Univariate Filters	Standardization and Centering	Random Forest and Ensemble Learning	Grid Search

4. SOLUTION: DESCRIPTION OF APPROACH

4.1. Data preparation

As mentioned in problem statement, significant efforts will have to be taken in pre-processing the data into a manner that most R functions could ingest. The key processing steps carried out include:

- Recoding the arbitrary large numbers which indicate unavailable information to "NA".
- Explicitly converting categorical variables to dummy variables.
- Removing variables with zero variance.
- Recoding target variable from "1" and "0" to "Yes" and "No".

Tables 3 shows the variables before and after pre-processing the data.

Table 3: Data pre-processing

Before			
Response	**Variable1**	**Variable2**	**Variable3**
1	North	9999	9999
1	South	9999	9999
1	South	4	9999
0	East	5	9999
0	West	9	9999

After				
Response	**Variable1 North**	**Variable1 South**	**Variable1 East**	**Variable2**
Yes	1	0	0	NA
Yes	0	1	0	NA
Yes	0	1	0	4
No	0	0	1	5
No	0	0	0	9

Several things can be observed in the above data pre-processing:

- Responses are re-coded from "1" and "0" to "Yes" and "No".
- Categorical variable is recoded to dummy variables from having "North" in variable named "Variable1" to having "1" in variable named "Variable1.North".
- The first two observations in "Variable 2" which have arbitrary large numbers indicating unavailable information are replaced with "NA".
- Variable three is dropped due to lack of variance.

Figure 1 shows the modeling flow for various techniques.
Figure 2 shows implemented parameter search for GBM.

4.2. BNA — Dimension reduction

The JL model used 391 features for BNA model. A univariate feature selection was conducted over each of the three months before feeding back into the JL model. The univariate feature selection eventually suggested

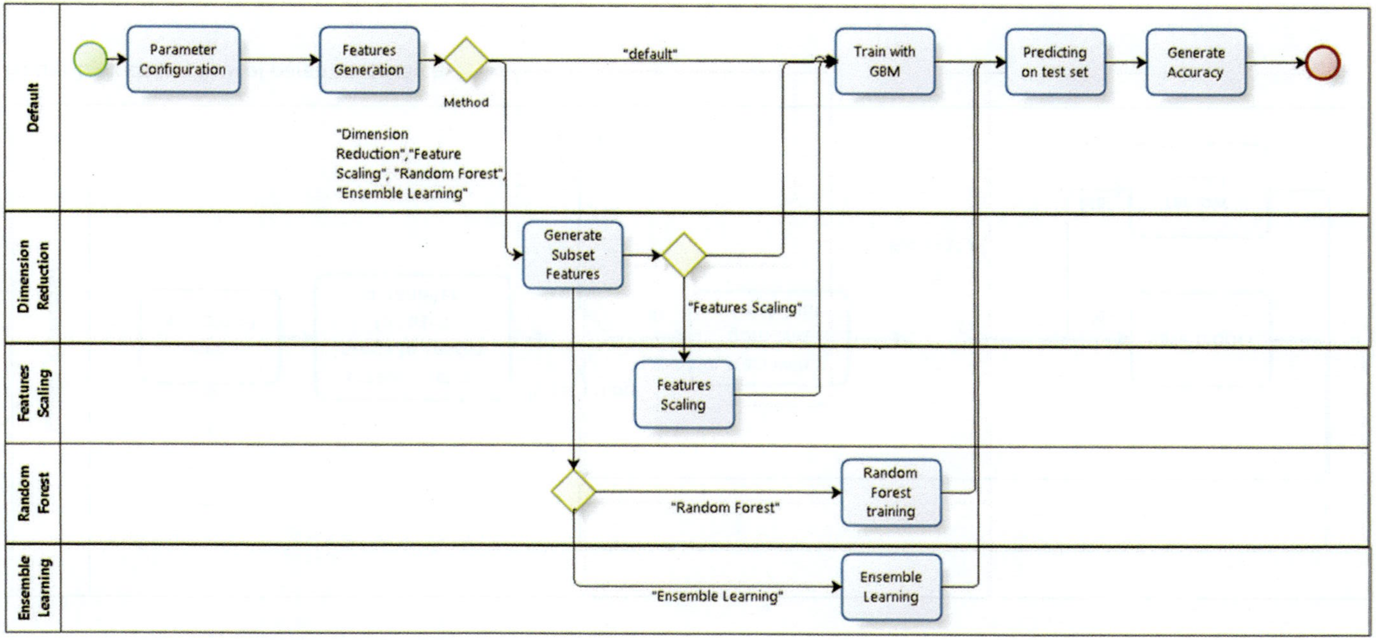

Figure 1: Modeling flow of techniques explored.

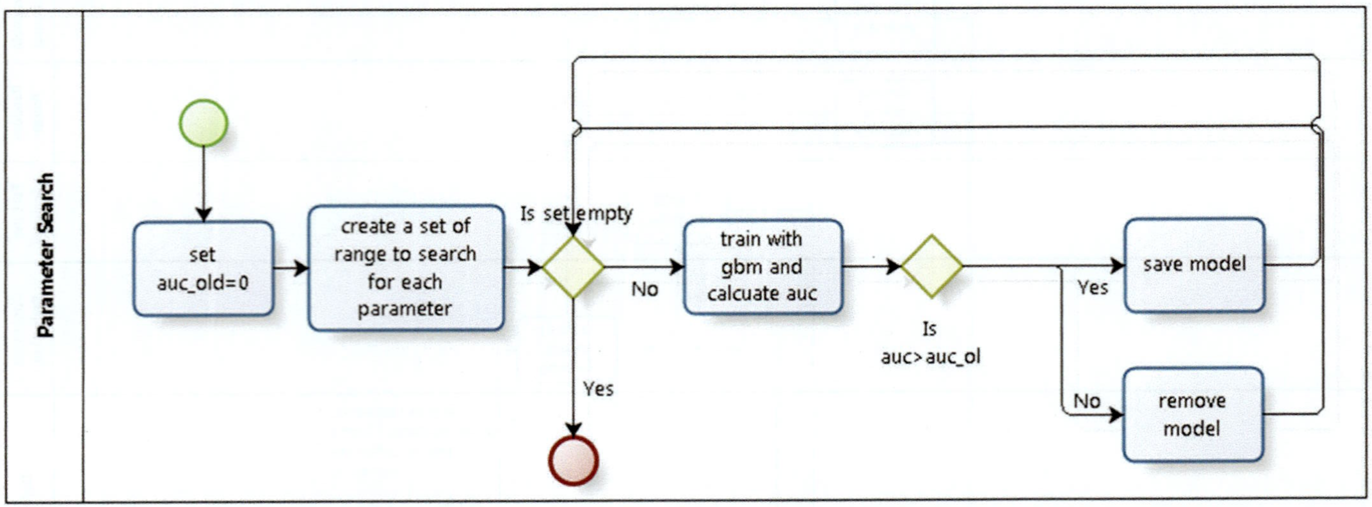

Figure 2: Modeling flow of parameter search

a subset of 47 features for 1st month, 49 features for 2nd month, and 51 features for 3rd month. The union of the subsets of 55 features is taken to perform training with the original GBM model.

Row Labels	Dimension Reduction	Baseline	% Change
AUC	0.720	0.723	−0.4%
P20	0.768	0.779	−1.3%
P50	0.733	0.733	0.0%

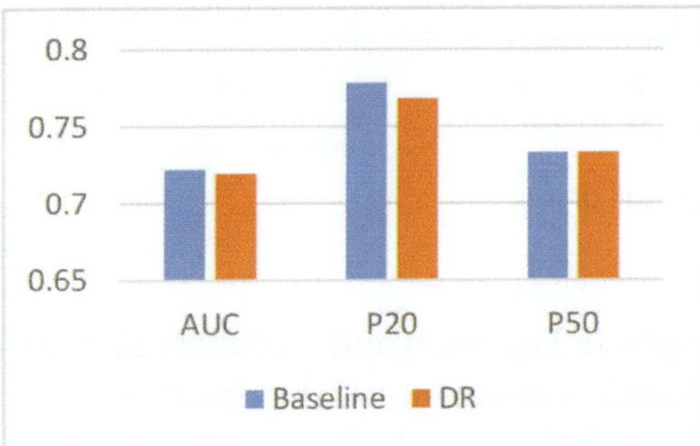

Figure 3: Baseline against dimension reduction accuracy.

From Figure 3, shows that there is not much reduction in accuracy (0 per cent to −1.3 per cent) after a features selection prior to running the JL model.

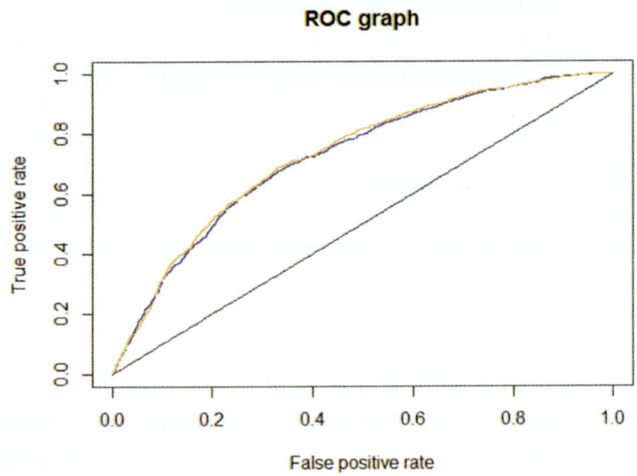

Figure 4: ROC graph.

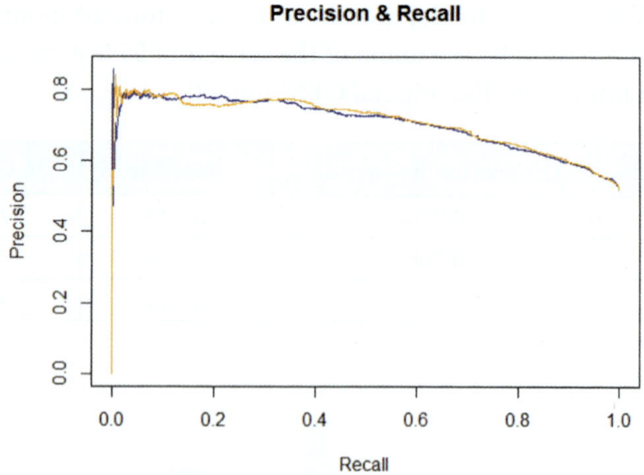

Figure 5: Precision–recall graph.

The two graphs in Figures. 4 and 5 confirm that there are not much changes to the overall performance of the classifier.

In terms of speed, the chart in Figure 6 below shows the number of features and the speed of performing only the training, before and after performing features selection.

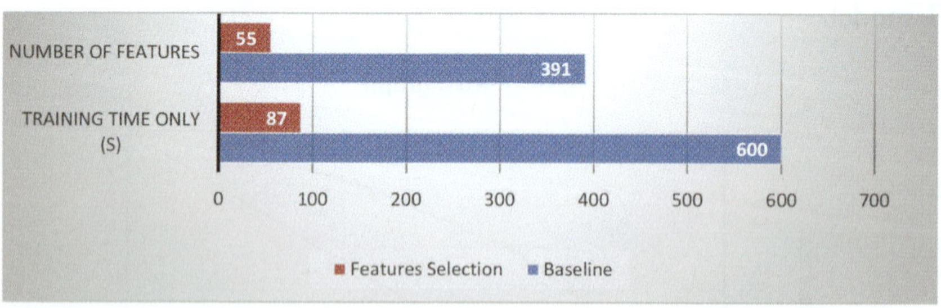

Figure 6: Number of features and training time comparison for baseline model and post features selection.

By using approximately 15 per cent of the original number of features the time taken to train the model was significantly reduced from 600s to 87s. This represents an 85.5 per cent reduction in training time. Approximate duration of 2 h needed to generate all 391 features is believed to have a significant reduction too.

4.3. BNA — Features scaling

As mentioned in the earlier section, the operations performed for features scaling include imputing "NA" with median value of the variable, and also centering and scaling it to [−1,1].

Row Labels	Scale	Baseline	% Change
AUC	0.718	0.723	–0.6%
P20	0.767	0.779	–1.5%
P50	0.729	0.733	–0.5%

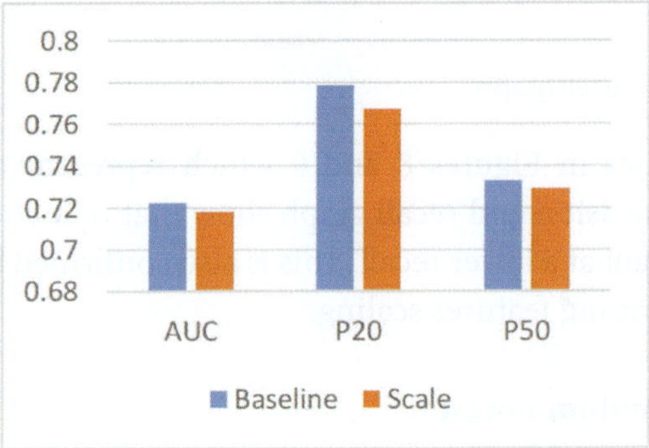

Figure 7: Baseline against features scaling accuracy.

From Figure 7 demonstrates that centering and scaling the features led to a reduction in accuracy, which is more significant at precision at 20 per cent recall.

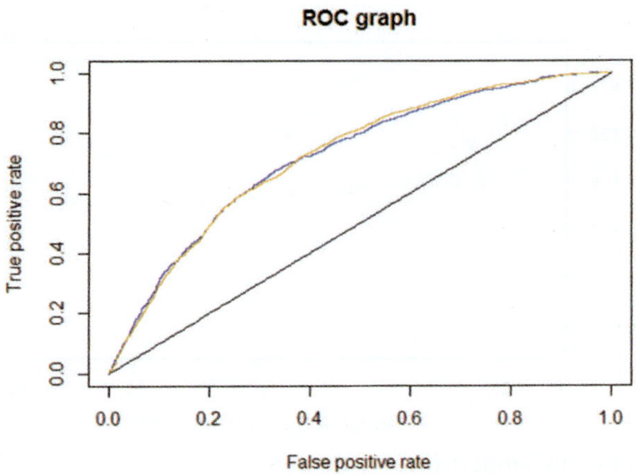

Figure 8: ROC graph.

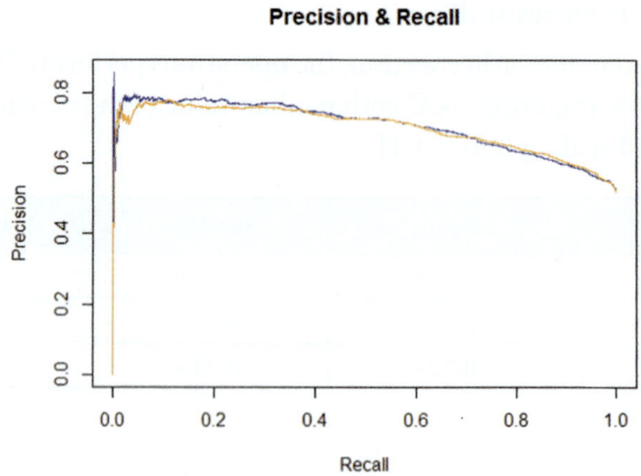

Figure 9: Precision–recall graph.

Orange lines in Figures 8 and 9 which represent the baseline JL model in the precision and recall graph show that reduction in precision is more significant at a lower recall. This is also confirmed by reduction in P20 after performing features scaling.

4.4. BNA — Random Forest

A Random Forest parameter tuning was performed before training. The number of variables available for splitting at each tree node was heuristically searched from 8 to 100, and found to be best at 35 with a training accuracy of 0.8213 for BNA model. The number of trees is fixed to be at default 500 which is supposedly of little value to tune (Figure 10).

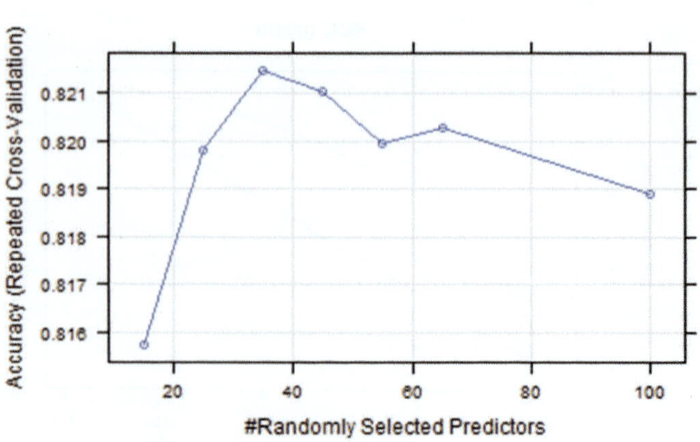

Figure 10: Accuracy vs Random Forest parameter.

Row Labels	RF	Baseline	% Change
AUC	0.666	0.723	–7.9%
P20	0.687	0.779	–11.8%
P50	0.663	0.733	–9.6%

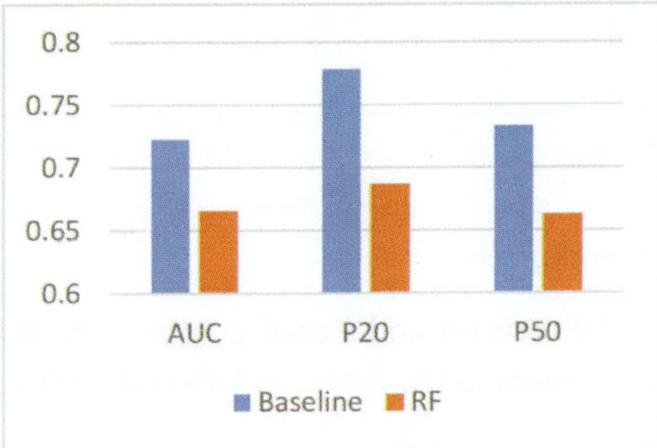

Figure 11: Baseline against Random Forest accuracy.

Figure. 11, shows that Random Forest classifier led to a significant reduction in accuracy, which is more significant at precision at 20 per cent recall with an 11.8 per cent change.

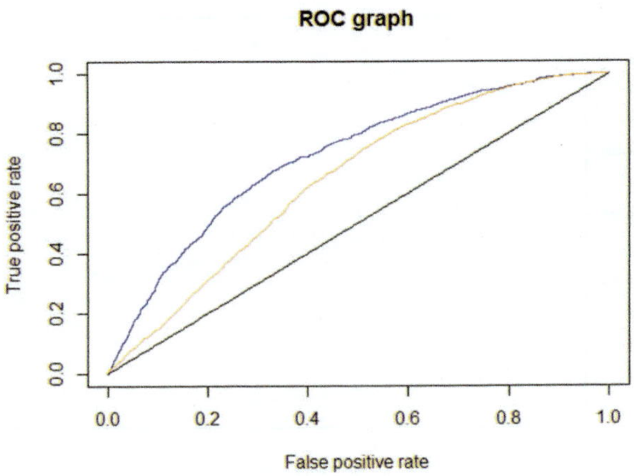

Figure 12: ROC graph.

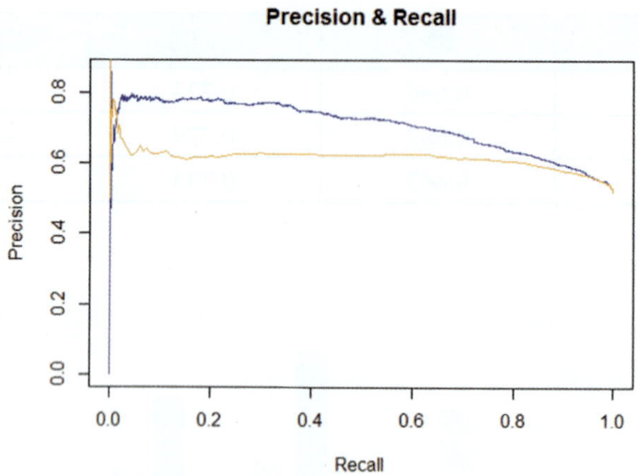

Figure 13: Precision–recall graph.

The ROC and Precision and Recall graphs show that at almost all cutoffs, JL model dominated the Random Forest classifier (see Figures 12 and 13).

4.5. BNA — Tuning parameter search

The JL model has parameter fixed as number of trees = 300, interaction depth = 12, minimum number of observation at each = 5 leaf, and shrinkage = 12. These parameters were searched at a coarse level. The parameter found to be more sensitive to the accuracy performance was the interaction depth.

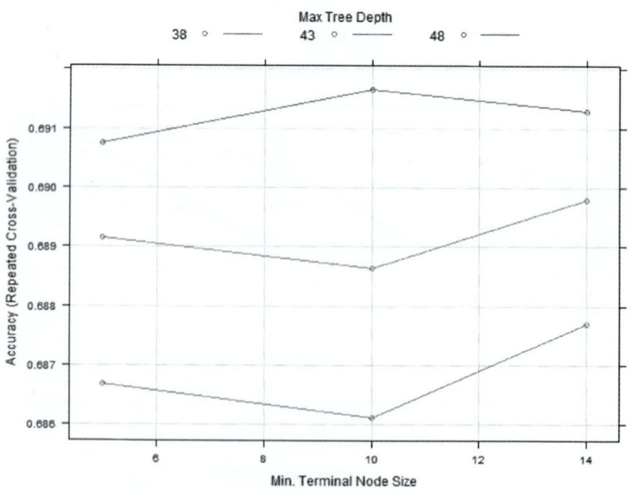

Figure 14: Max tree depth and min terminal node against accuracy.

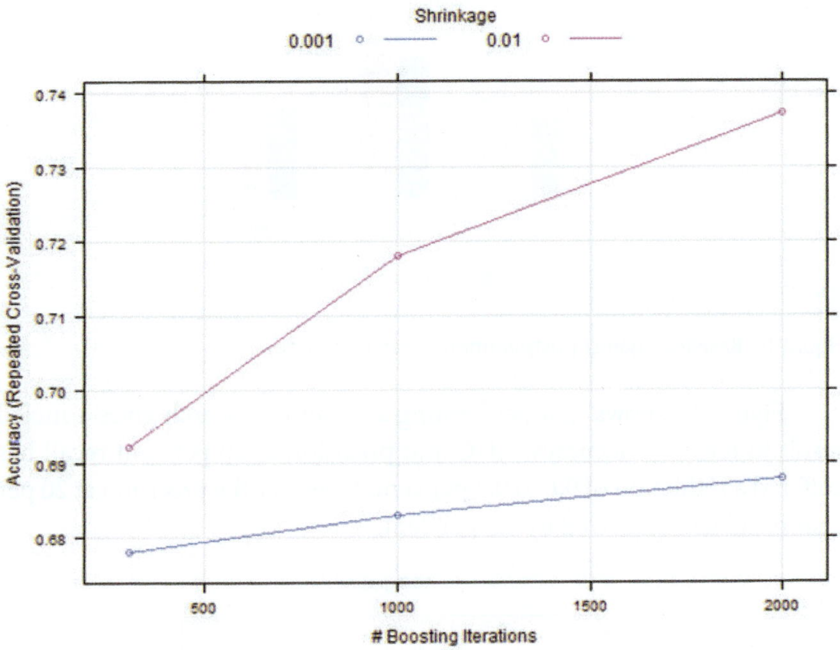

Figure 15: Shrinkage and boosting iteration against accuracy.

The graph in Figure 14 shows that increasing max tree depth leads to a more significant improvement in accuracy. Min terminal node size has almost no improvement on accuracy. The graph in Figure 15 shows that increasing boosting iterations will lead to higher accuracy. Shrinkage at 0.001 with a boosting iteration less than 2000 will be worse off than the current 0.01 with 300.

These insights lead to the adjustment of increasing interaction depth to a higher number. Reducing shrinkage will require way above 10 times the baseline boosting iteration for any probable improvement to be observed (Figure 16).

Row Labels	PS	Baseline	% change
AUC	0.717	0.723	−0.7%
P20	0.783	0.779	+0.5%
P50	0.729	0.733	−0.6%

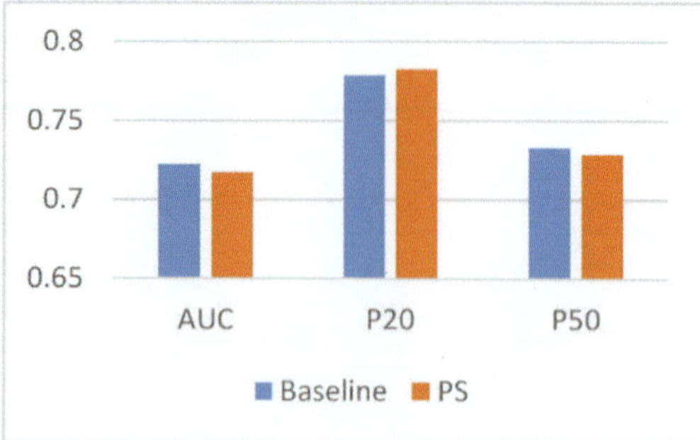

Figure 16: Baseline against postparameter search accuracy.

Figure 16 shows that performing a parameter search gives a mixed result in terms of accuracy. AUC and precision at 50 per cent recall has suffered a reduction of 0.6 to 0.7 per cent. However the precision at 20 per cent recall has improved by 0.5 per cent.

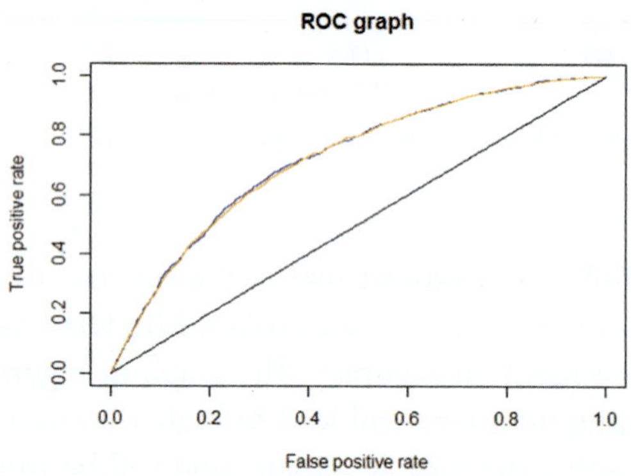

Figure 17: ROC graph.

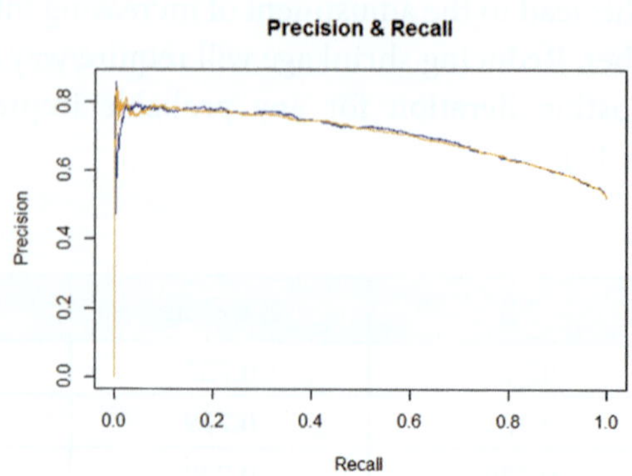

Figure 18: Precision-recall graph.

From precision and recall graph, it confirms that by using a higher interaction depth over the baseline JL model in blue, precision will improve at lower recall (see Figures 17 and 18).

4.6. BNA — Ensemble learning

R package called "caretEnsemble" was used to evaluate the performance of ensemble learning on the BNA data. An ensemble of GBM and generalized linear model (GLM) was tried out. The reason for choosing GLM to ensemble with GBM is because of GLM's speed and that it performed better on linearly separable data which could complement GBM.

```
> modelCor(resamples(cl))
       gbm1        glm
gbm1   1.0000000   0.8797392
glm    0.8797392   1.0000000
```

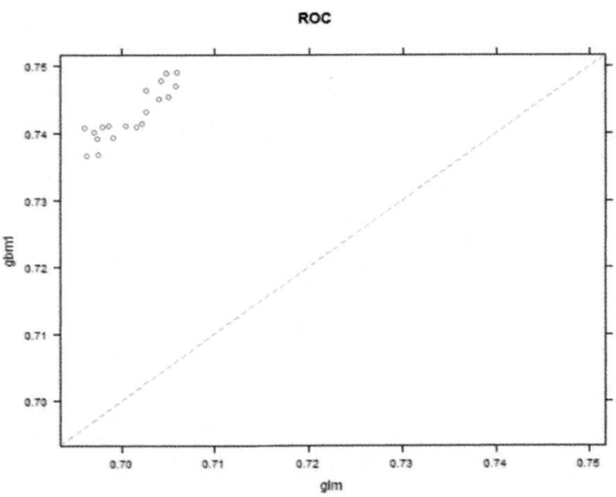


```
> greedy_ensemble <<- caretEnsemble(cl)
> summary(greedy_ensemble)
The following models were ensembled: gbm1
They were weighted:
1
The resulting AUC is: 0.7423
The fit for each individual model on the AUC is:
metricSD gbm1   0.742336   0.003790882
```

The above output shows that the accuracy of GBM and GLM was highly correlated. The GLM model also produced a much worse off accuracy as compared to GBM at every sample. This results in a weight of one for GBM and zero for GLM which will produce the exact same prediction as having GBM alone. The duration needed to run an ensemble learning of GBM and GLM is also significantly longer as training would need to be performed on two machine learning classifiers instead of one.

4.7. BNA — Results

Table 4 presents a summary of outcomes from the various methods.

Table 4: summary of results

Method	Metric	Month 1	Month 2	Month 3	Average
Benchmark	AUC	0.730	0.722	0.716	0.723
	P20	0.763	0.776	0.797	0.779
	P50	0.736	0.726	0.737	0.733
Dimension Reduction	AUC	0.718	0.714	0.727	0.720
	P20	0.751	0.799	0.756	0.768
	P50	0.732	0.731	0.735	0.733
Scale	AUC	0.715	0.715	0.724	0.718
	P20	0.748	0.797	0.756	0.767
	P50	0.723	0.739	0.726	0.729
Random Forest	AUC	0.685	0.655	0.656	0.666
	P20	0.708	0.684	0.670	0.687
	P50	0.691	0.658	0.639	0.663
Parameter Search	AUC	0.718	0.714	0.720	0.717
	P20	0.760	0.818	0.770	0.783
	P50	0.732	0.731	0.723	0.729
Ensemble Learning	AUC	0.730	0.722	0.716	0.723
	P20	0.763	0.776	0.797	0.779
	P50	0.736	0.726	0.737	0.733

Figure 19 shows the summary of percentage difference of explored techniques as compared to JL model.

	Dimension Reduction	Scaling	Random Forest	Parameter Search	Ensemble Learning
AUC	−0.4%	−0.6%	−7.9%	−0.7%	0.0%
P20	−1.3%	−1.5%	−11.8%	0.5%	0.0%
P50	0.0%	−0.5%	−9.6%	−0.6%	0.0%

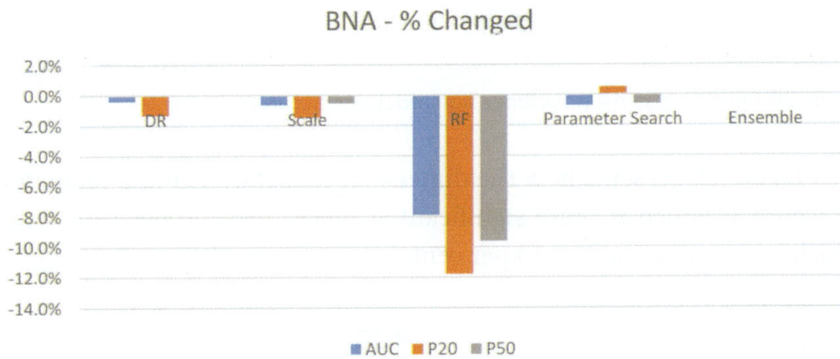

Figure 19: Summary of performance for BNA JL model.

4.8. Dispenser

4.8.1. Dispenser — Dimension reduction

The original model contains 328 features for BNA. A univariate feature selection was conducted over each of the three months data before feeding back into the original model. The univariate feature selection eventually suggested a subset of 32 features for January, 35 features for March, and 39 features for April. The union of the subsets of 39 features is taken to perform training with the original GBM model.

Row Labels	Baseline	DR	% Change
AUC	0.710	0.702	−1.0%
P20	0.427	0.383	−10.2%
P50	0.248	0.235	−5.4%

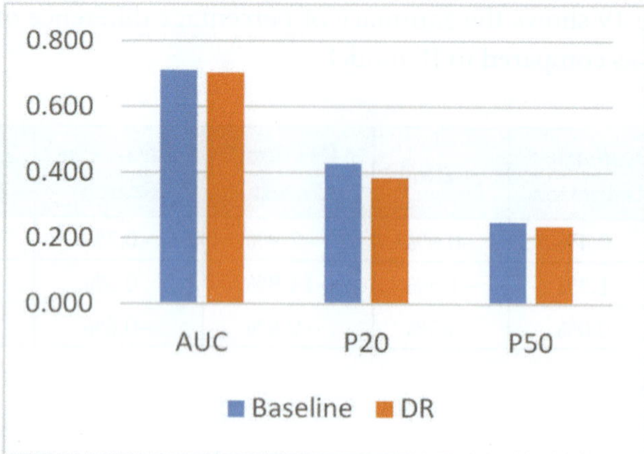

Figure 20: Baseline against postdimension reduction accuracy.

Figure 20 presents how the dimension reduction led to a reduction in accuracy, which is more significant at precision at 20 per cent recall which has a reduction of −10 per cent.

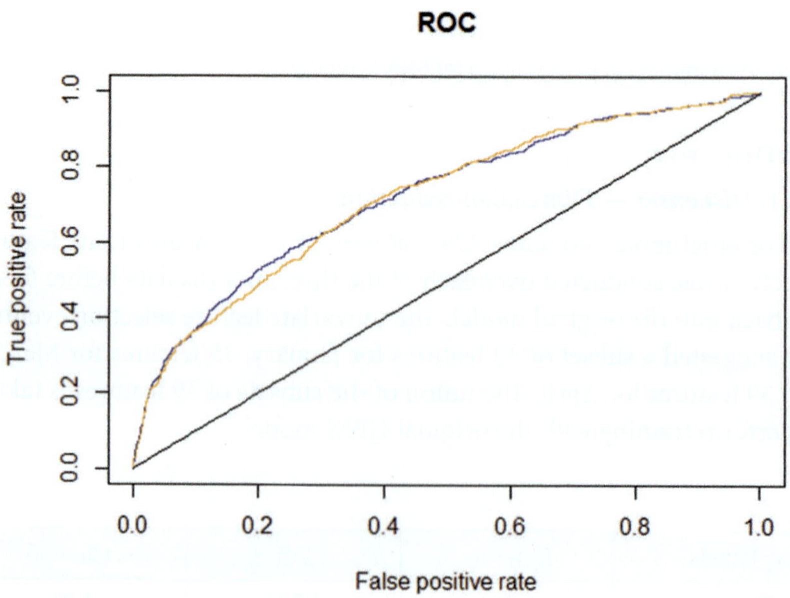

Figure 21: ROC graph.

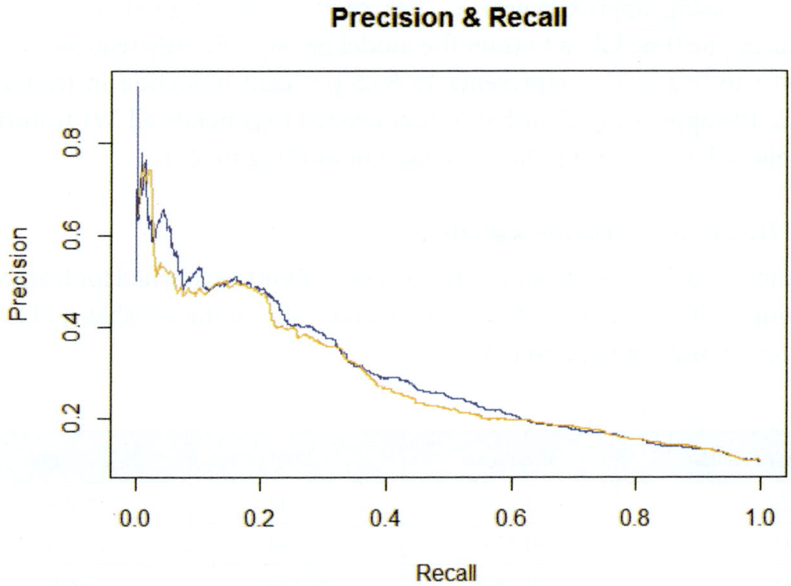

Figure 22: Precision–recall graph.

The blue lines which represent the baseline JL model in the ROC and precision and recall graphs (Figures 21 and 22) shows that the reduction in precision is more significant at a lower recall. This is also confirmed in the reduction in P20 after performing features scaling.

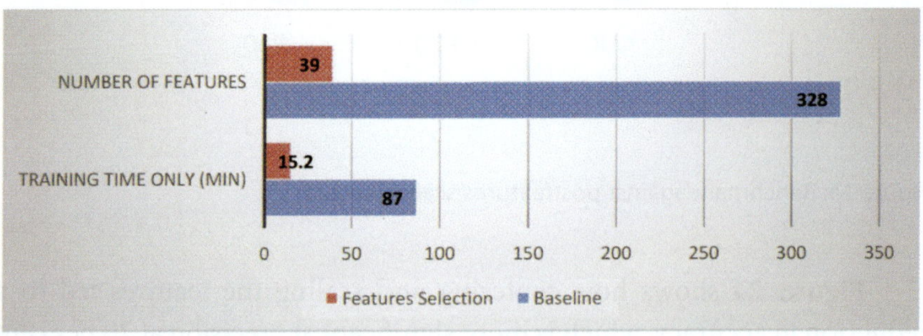

Figure 23: Number of features and training time comparison for baseline model and postfeatures selection.

By using approximately 12 per cent of the original number of features, the time taken to train the model has significantly reduced from 5200 s to 912 s. This represents an 85.5 per cent reduction in training time. The approximately 6-h duration needed to generate all 391 features is believed to have a significant reduction too (Figure 23).

4.9. Dispenser — Features scaling

As mentioned in the earlier section, the operations performed for features scaling include imputing "NA" with median value of the variable, and also centering and scaling it to [−1,1].

Row Labels	Baseline	DR	% Change
AUC	0.710	0.702	−0.9%
P20	0.427	0.383	−14.3%
P50	0.248	0.235	−3.6%

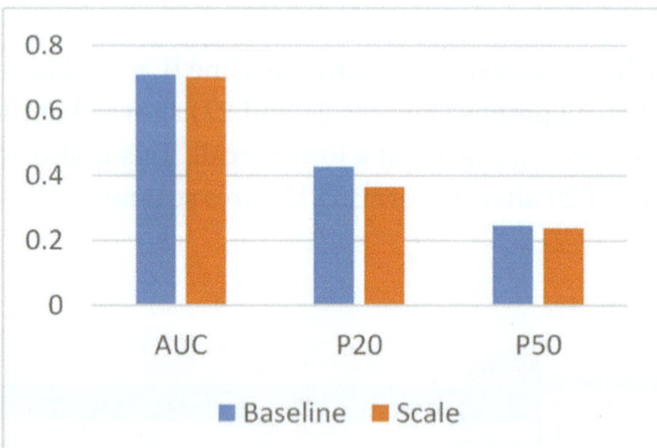

Figure 24: Benchmark against postfeatures scaling accuracy.

Figure. 24 shows how centering and scaling the features led to a reduction in accuracy, which is more significant at precision at 20 per cent recall with a −14.3 per cent change.

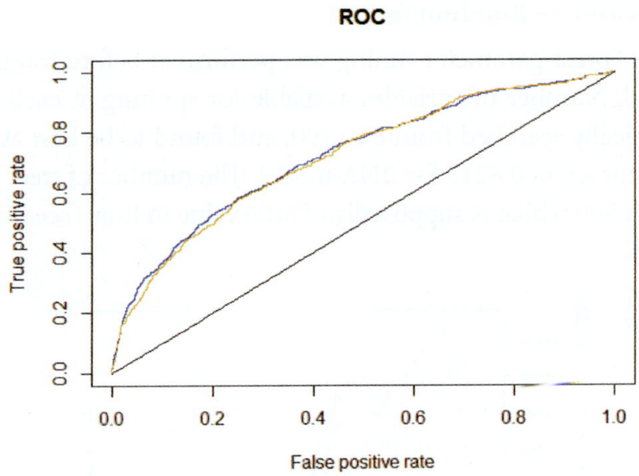

Figure 25: ROC graph.

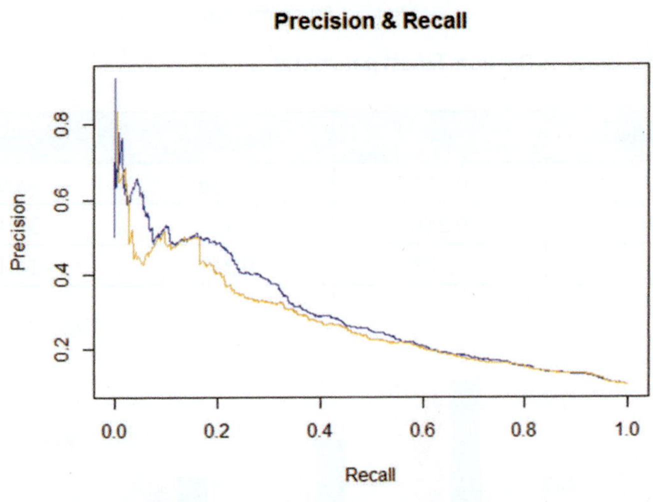

Figure 26: Precision–recall graph.

The blue lines which represent the baseline JL model in the precision and recall graph shows that the reduction in precision is more significant at a lower recall. This is also confirmed in the reduction in P20 after performing features scaling (see Figures 25 and 26).

4.10. Dispenser — Random forest

A Random Forest parameter tuning was performed before training as per BNA model. Number of variables available for splitting at each tree node was heuristically searched from 8 to 100, and found to be best at 35 with a training accuracy of 0.8213 for BNA model. The number of trees is fixed to be at default 500 which is supposedly of little value to tune (see Figure 27).

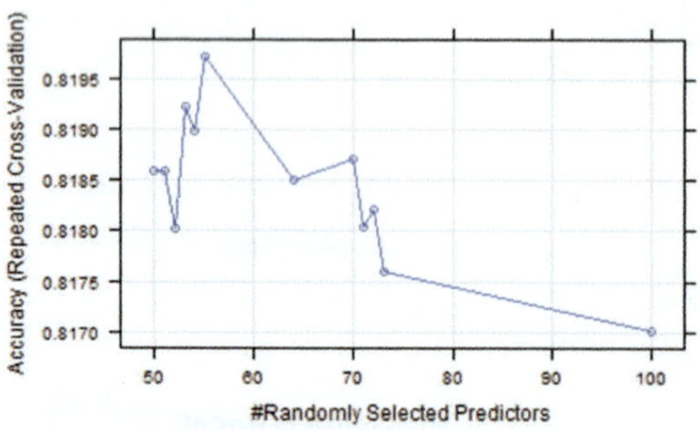

Figure 27: Accuracy vs Random Forest parameter.

Row Labels	RF	Baseline	% Change
AUC	0.675	0.710	–4.9%
P20	0.286	0.427	–33.1%
P50	0.208	0.248	–16.1%

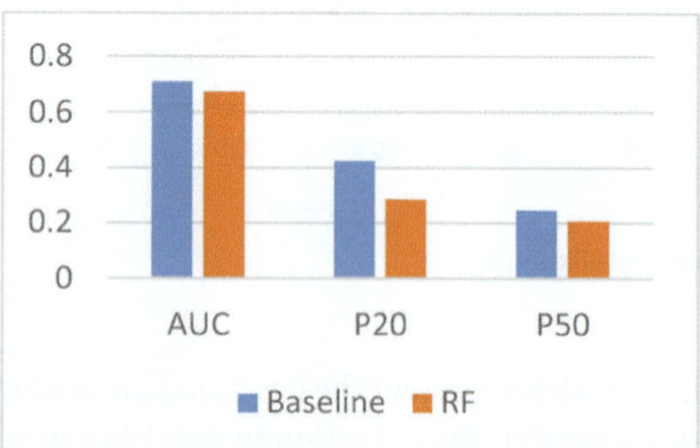

Figure 28: Baseline against Random Forest accuracy.

Figure 28 shows how the Random Forest Classifier led to a significant reduction in accuracy, which is more significant at precision at 20 per cent recall with a 33.1 per cent change.

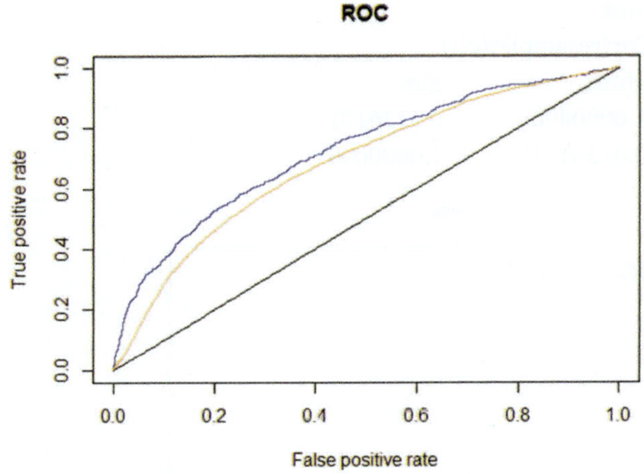

Figure 29: ROC graph.

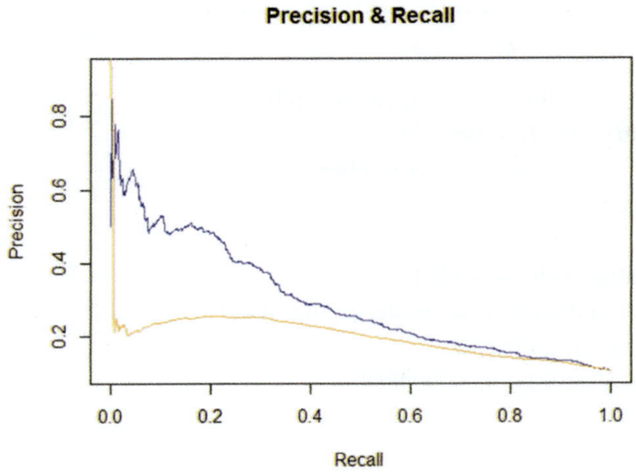

Figure 30: Precision–recall graph.

The ROC graph and precision and recall graph (Figures 29 and 30) shows that at almost all cutoff, the JL model in blue dominated the Random Forest classifier in orange.

4.11. Dispenser — Ensemble learning

As per BNA model, an ensemble learning of GLM and GBM is performed using "caretEnsemble" package.

```
GLM - GBM
> modelCor(resamples(cl))
        gbm1        glm
gbm1    1.0000000   0.3726171
glm     0.3726171   1.0000000
```

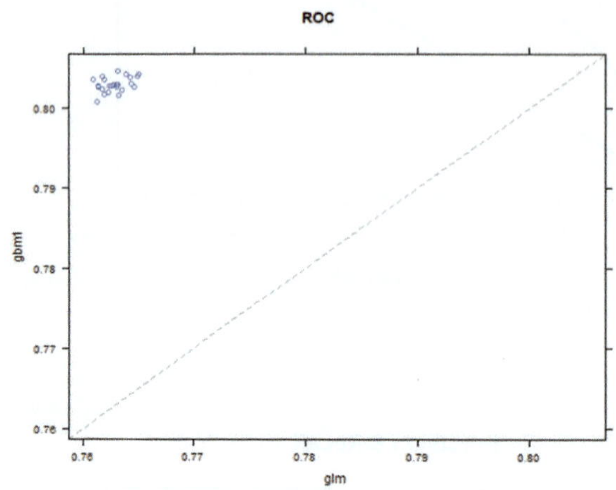


```
> greedy_ensemble <<- caretEnsemble(cl)
> summary(greedy_ensemble)
The following models were ensembled: gbm1
They were weighted:
1
The resulting AUC is: 0.8024
The fit for each individual model on the AUC is:
method metric metricSD
gbm1   0.8024031   0.0009048895
```

The samples accuracy from GLM and GBM show that they are fairly uncorrelated at R = 0.373 which is good to perform ensemble learning. However, the scatterplot of the individual accuracy shows that the accuracy from GBM dominated GLM. Expectedly, this resulted in a weight allocation of one to GBM which gives the training accuracy of what GBM alone would provide. Other mix of machine learning classifiers were explored such as GLM, Decision Trees, and Random Forest but they were either not feasible or did not perform better than the benchmark accuracy.

4.12. Tuning parameter search

As per written in BNA portion of parameter search, the JL model has parameters fixed at Number of trees = 300, interaction depth = 12, minimum number of observation at each = 5 leaf, and shrinkage = 12.

These parameters were searched at a coarse level. The parameter found to be more sensitive to the accuracy performance was interaction depth.

The graphs in Figures 31 and 32 below show the performance of the model when a combination of parameters was run.

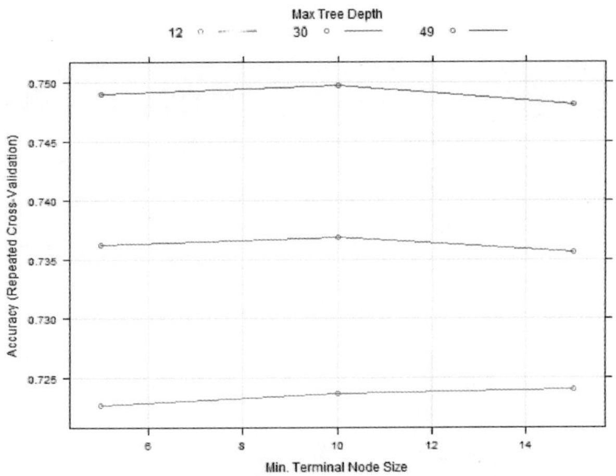

Figure 31: Max tree depth and min terminal node against accuracy.

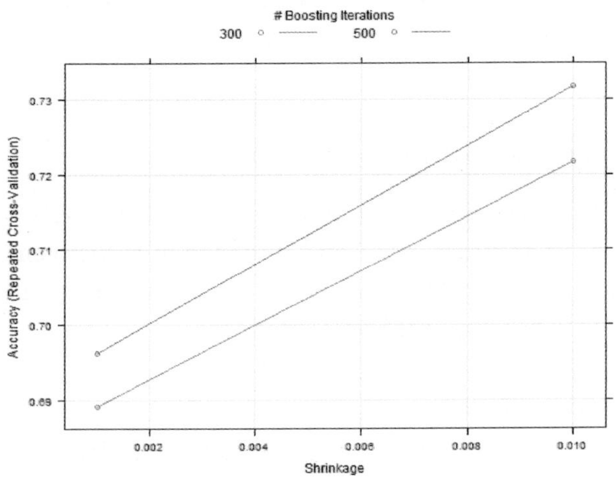

Figure 32: Shrinkage and boosting Iteration against accuracy.

The parameter search for dispenser model gives a similar finding as the BNA model. To reiterate, the graph in Figure 31 shows that increasing max tree depth leads to a more significant improvement in accuracy. Min terminal node size has almost no improvement on accuracy. The graph in Figure 32 shows that increasing boosting iterations will lead to higher accuracy. Shrinkage at 0.001 will need a boosting iteration of greater than 500 for it to be better than the current 0.01 with 300. These insights led to the adjustment of increasing interaction depth to a higher number. Reducing shrinkage will require almost double the boosting iteration for any improvement to be observed.

Row Labels	PS	Baseline	% Change
AUC	0.713	0.710	+0.5%
P20	0.429	0.427	+0.5%
P50	0.253	0.248	+1.8%

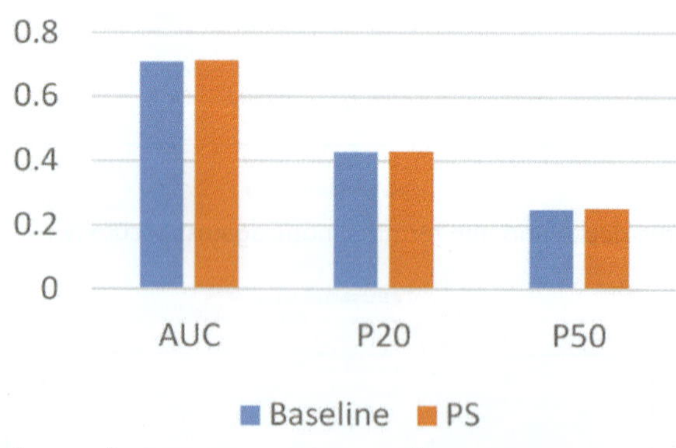

Figure 33: Baseline against post parameter search accuracy.

Figure 33 shows how performing a parameter search gave a mix result in terms of accuracy. AUC and Precision at 50 per cent recall has suffered a reduction of 0.6 to 0.7 per cent. However the precision at 20 per cent recall has improved by 0.5 per cent.

4.13. Dispenser — Results

Table 5 presents a summary of percentage differences for various techniques.

Table 5: summary of percentage differences.

Method	Metric	Month 1	Month 2	Month 3	Average
Benchmark	AUC	0.701	0.702	0.725	0.710
	P20	0.408	0.392	0.481	0.427
	P50	0.253	0.244	0.248	0.248
Dimension Reduction	AUC	0.695	0.699	0.722	0.705
	P20	0.354	0.378	0.473	0.402
	P50	0.231	0.245	0.223	0.233
Scale	AUC	0.696	0.694	0.719	0.703
	P20	0.354	0.338	0.405	0.366
	P50	0.238	0.254	0.226	0.239
Random Forest	AUC	0.659	0.679	0.687	0.675
	P20	0.310	0.289	0.258	0.286
	P50	0.202	0.217	0.206	0.208
Parameter Search	AUC	0.705	0.707	0.728	0.713
	P20	0.413	0.401	0.474	0.429
	P50	0.261	0.248	0.250	0.253
Ensemble Learning	AUC	0.701	0.702	0.725	0.710
	P20	0.408	0.392	0.481	0.427
	P50	0.253	0.244	0.248	0.248

Figure 34 shows the summary of percentage difference of explored techniques as compared to JL model.

	Dimension Reduction	Scaling	Random Forest	Parameter Search	Ensemble Learning
AUC	−1.0%	−0.9%	−4.9%	+0.5%	0.0%
P20	−10.2%	−14.3%	−33.1%	+0.5%	0.0%
P50	−5.4%	−3.6%	−16.1%	+1.8%	0.0%

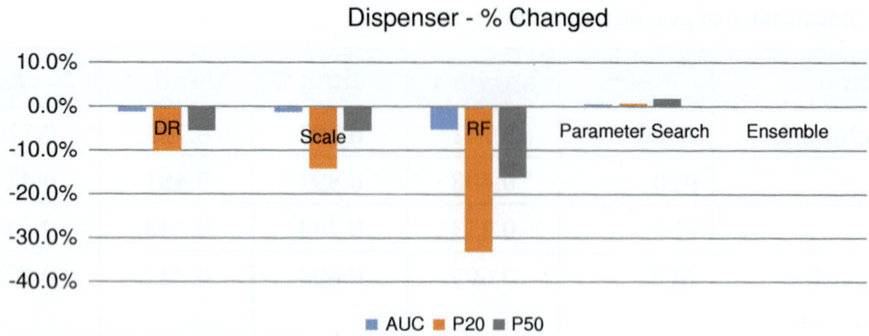

Figure 34: Summary of performance for BNA JL model.

4.14. Card reader

4.14.1. Card reader — Parameter search

After testing and understanding the performance of dimension reduction, features scaling, random forest, and ensemble learning approach for BNA and Dispenser, and due to lack of time to duplicate these run in card reader, effort was made in identifying the optimum parameters for card reader as a priority.

Row Labels	Baseline	PS	% Change
AUC	0.635	0.634	–0.1%
P20	0.156	0.143	–8.6%
P50	0.103	0.100	–2.9%

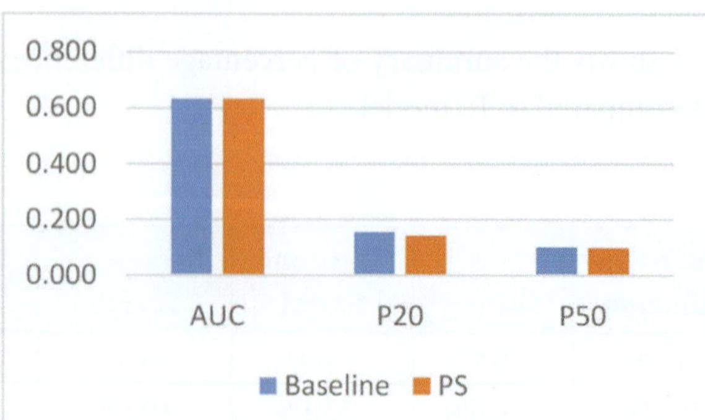

Figure 35: Baseline against postparameter search accuracy.

Figure 35 shows how performing a parameter search gave a mixed result in terms of accuracy. AUC and precision at 50 per cent recall has suffered a reduction of 0.6 to 0.7 per cent. However, precision at 20 per cent recall has improved by 0.5 per cent.

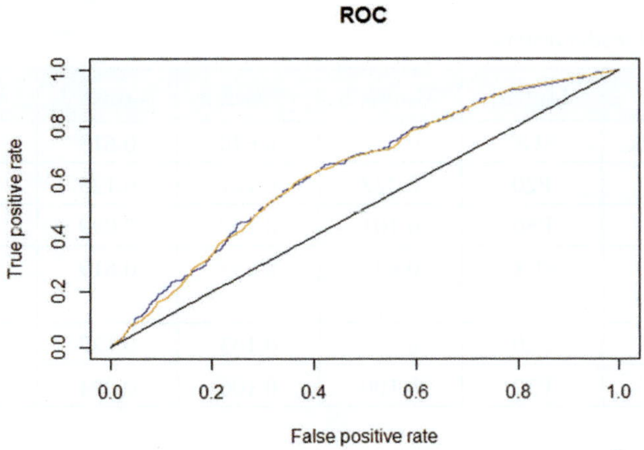

Figure 36: ROC graph.

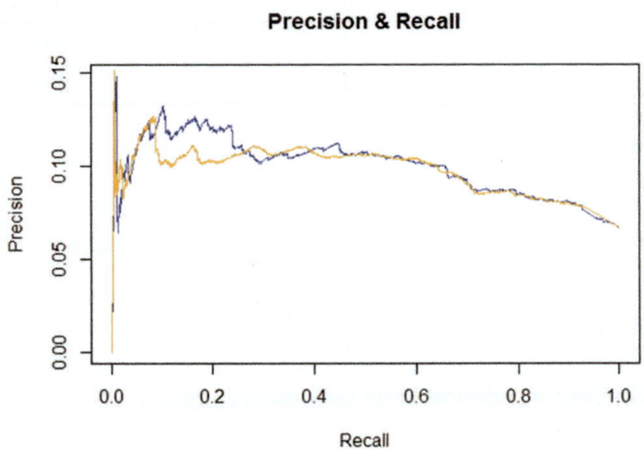

Figure 37: Precision-recall graph.

The blue lines which represent the baseline JL model in the precision and recall graph shows that the reduction in precision is more significant at a lower recall. This is also confirmed in the reduction in P20 after performing features scaling (see Figure 36 and Figure 37).

4.14.2. Card reader — Results

Table 6 presents the card reader results

Figure 38 shows the summary of percentage difference of explored technique as compared to the JL model.

Table 6: card reader results

Method	Metric	Month 1	Month 2	Month 3	Average
Benchmark	AUC	0.652	0.640	0.613	0.635
	P20	0.222	0.121	0.125	0.156
	P50	0.101	0.107	0.099	0.103
Parameter Search	AUC	0.647	0.637	0.619	0.634
	P20	0.197	0.103	0.127	0.143
	P50	0.100	0.106	0.094	0.100

	Benchmark	Parameter Search
AUC	0	–0.1%
P20	0	–8.6%
P50	0	–2.9%

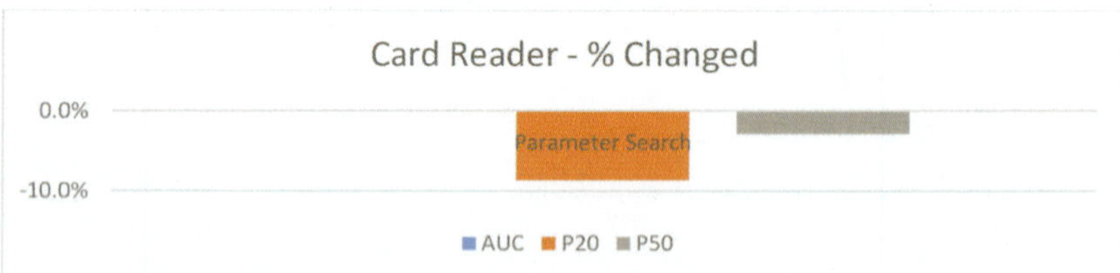

Figure 38: Summary of performance for card reader JL model.

5. DISCUSSION

From this study to explore various ways to improve the accuracy of machine fault prediction work, it can be seen that the JL model used as benchmark has two striking values: robust in accepting various kinds of data structure and being fairly accurate without requiring to perform various transformation.

However, the GBM package in JL model is inconvenient in tuning its parameters. JL model uses the same set of tuning parameters for all BNA, dispenser, and card reader. The same set is also used for any time period without considering if there is any major change to the data. Intuitively, in the long run there would be changes to the data such that JL model set of tuning parameters would be far from being accurate anymore. These changes are expected because in future, DBS would be actively servicing the machines and machine faults would be less likely occur. It would be recommended to follow a process, manually or automatically, to ensure that the set of tuning parameters is still optimum for data and its purpose.

One way to ensure this set of tuning parameters will still be optimum would be to incorporate a loop to search in a predefined set of tuning parameters. The value of this approach would be that it will thus require little human intervention. However, the problem in this case would be that, depending on the number of predefined set of tuning parameters, it would take up much more time to train the model than what it originally is doing already.

Alternatively, to prevent incurring more time in training the model each month, a periodic search for an optimum tuning parameter could be conducted. However, this would require someone to take ownership to ensure that this search is carried out.

Another point to highlight would be the reduction of training and accuracy when training the model with a smaller subset of the features. It was found that by using just about 15 per cent of the variables, the training time could be reduced to about 15 per cent of the original duration. This was at the expense of a reduction of accuracy of 1.5 per cent for BNA and 10.2 per cent for Dispenser. An evaluation on the cost and benefits to this reduction in training time and accuracy could be conducted to determine if it is worth the change in number of features.

6. CONCLUSION AND FURTHER WORK

6.1. Conclusion

In this paper some of the commonly known methods that could possibly improve the accuracy of various models were investigated. A comparison of different methods explored was reported

This study searched extensively on best practices in an attempt to improve their accuracy and this was discussed in Section 3: These categories of method were dimension reduction, feature scaling, other machine learning classifiers, and ensemble learning. Due to time constraint this and the purpose of this study, some of the more promising methods were chosen and selected in each of these categories. A loop was also created to perform a parameter search around the existing model to improve the models' accuracy and robustness.

There were many challenges faced in the study even before the various methods were tried out. These challenges and how they were overcome was discussed in Section 4: Solution: Description of Approach.

The key challenges were explained to be the data format and volume. The data format challenge was handled by transforming the data into a universal format which is acceptable by most packages. The data volume challenge was overcome by saving and re-using data as much as possible so that they need not be regenerated. The various results obtained from the categories of methods were produced too in Section 4. The method found to have value over the baseline model was to create a parameter search before using the model. The result of this was −0.1 to +0.5 per cent change for AUC, +0.5 to +1.8 per cent improvement for P20, and −0.7 to +0.5 per cent change for P50. These changes could be obtained by almost no additional step and time. It was also shown that by training the model with about 15 per cent of the variables, only 15 per cent of the time was required. However this is at the expense of a reduction of accuracy to the baseline JL model.

In Section 5: Discussion, the pros and cons of performing a tuning parameter search on a regular basis and also the reduction in training duration if a subset of features were used was discussed. A regular search on a set of optimum tuning parameters would enable the model to be robust but at the expense of longer training time. On the other hand, using a subset of features would reduce the training timing but at the expense of a dip in accuracy.

6.2. Further work

The tuning parameters were mostly searched in a bivariate way which means changing only two tuning parameters at a time. A more optimized set of tuning parameters could have been found if the searches were done in a combinatorial way. However, this would mean exponentially more number of tests would be required. To illustrate this, assuming there could only be five options for each of the four variables, a total of 5^4 = 625 set of tuning parameter would need to be tested as compared to 20, if carried out in an univariate way.

There are many ways to perform ensemble learning method which may improve accuracy, other than the greedy optimization approach. More work can be done to evaluate the suitability and performance of other ensemble learning methods such as weighing, averaging, rank averaging, stacked generalization, blending, stacking with logistic regression, stacking with non-linear algorithm, and more. However as ensemble learning usually requires the training of more than one classifier, the overall time required to train and predict should be of utmost importance.

Further work can also be done in the area of feature engineering which is the process of using domain knowledge of the data to create features that make machine learning algorithms work better. It is often the most important part to achieve significant improvements in accuracy.[8] This is mainly because there is a limitation to how many tools and libraries can be accessed to improve the accuracy. To further improve it, subject matter experts would need to provide domain knowledge such that these advanced models can be applied to it.

REFERENCES

1. DBS newsroom. *DBS-SAS network efficiency and customer satisfaction.* https://www.dbs.com/newsroom/DBS_awarded_most_innovative_use_of_infocomm_technology retrieved on 1 June 2015.

2. Triskelion. *Profiling Top Kagglers: KazAnova, Currently #2 in the World.* http://blog.kaggle.com/2015/05/07/profiling-top-kagglers-kazanovacurrently-2-in-the-world/ retrieved on 1 June 2015.

3. KNIME. *Seven Techniques for Data Dimensionality Reduction.* https://www.knime.org/blog/seven-techniques-for-data-dimensionality-reduction retrieved on 1 June 2015.

4. The Caret Package. *Feature Selection Overview.* http://topepo.github.io/caret/featureselection.html retrieved on 12 July 2015.

5. Kuhn, M and Johnson, K (2013). *Applied Predictive Modelling.* ISBN: 9781461468486 Springer.

6. Silvia, C, V Marco and C Valentina (2012). *Variable Selection and Feature Extraction through Artificial Intelligence Techniques. Chapter 6.* http://cdn.intechopen.com/pdfs-wm/41752.pdf

7. Isabelle, G and E Andre (2003). *An Introduction to Feature Extraction.* http://clopinet.com/fextract-book/IntroFS.pdf

8. Hastie, TJ, R Tibshirani and J Friedman (2009). *The Elements of Statistical Learning,* 2nd Ed. New York: Springer.

9. NYC Data Science. *Featured Talk: #1 Kaggle Data Scientist.* http://nycdatascience.com/featured-talk-1-kaggle-data-scientist-owen-zhang/ retrieved on 1 June 2015.

10. Ruchika M and J Ankita (2012). *Fault Prediction Using Statistical and Machine Learning Methods for Improving Software Quality.* http://jips-k.org/dlibrary/JIPS_v08_no2_paper03.pdf

11. No Free Hunch. *Learning from the Best.* http://blog.kaggle.com/2014/08/01/learning-from-the-best/ retrieved on 1 June 2015.

12. Kuncheva, L and C Whitaker (2003). Measures of diversity in classifier ensembles. *Machine Learning,* 51, 181–207.

13. Sollich, P and A Krogh (1996). Learning with ensembles: How overfitting can be useful. *Advances in Neural Information Processing Systems,* 8, 190–196.

14. Zach M. (2015). *A Brief Introduction to CaretEnsemble.* http://cran.r-project.org/web/packages/caretEnsemble/vignettes/caretEnsemble-intro.html retrieved on 1 June 2015.

15. Caruana et al (2004) *Ensemble Selection from Libraries of Models.* http://citeseerx.ist.psu.edu/viewdoc/download?doi=10.1.1.60.2859&rep=rep1&type=pdf

16. James B, B Remi, B Yoshua and K Balazs. *Algorithms for Hyper-Parameter Optimizaion.* http://papers.nips.cc/paper/4443-algorithms-for-hyper-parameter-optimization.pdf

CHAPTER 12

Estimation of Queue Length and Analysis of Reneging Effects in a Bank Branch Setting

Puneet Goyal

ABSTRACT

Understanding waiting lines or queues and learning how to manage them are one of the most important areas in operations management. In the service economy, people wait in line every day, from driving to work to checking out at the supermarket or opening a new account in a bank. It is basic to create schedules, job design, inventory levels, and so on. In short, waiting lines are pervasive. It is important for a bank to estimate the number of customers arriving in a branch at a given point in time to manage the resources wisely, and at the same time help customers with the onerous process of waiting.

This study attempts to look at the problem of long queues in bank, and how each different customer behavior (e.g. reneging: when a person, who has entered a line, later decides to leave it without being served) affects the arrival rate and overall service performance of the branch.

Queuing theory is a well-studied form of operations research that answers these questions. In this paper, customer arrivals in a bank branch is studied along with the effects of reneging for one of the largest bank in Asia using techniques like stochastic models and regression analysis.

1. INTRODUCTION

Banks are a major component of the financial system, and retail banking in Asia is on the cusp of a new era of amazing growth and opportunities, but also one that will see downward pressure on returns. These opportunities are not easy to capture. The major problem is the difficulty of the banks to match their service facilities to the needs of customers promptly. Rapidly shifting consumer behavior calls for a potential revamp of traditional operating models—roles of the branches may change; new channels will need to be introduced, and new capabilities will need to be built [1].

In order to tap this growth opportunity and to handle the unpleasant experience of waiting in a queue, DBS incorporated an SMS 'Q' system across its branches [2] along with its traditional ticket queue system where a customer takes a ticket from a self-service counter and then proceeds to a waiting area. With this new system, a customer can request for a queue number via SMS prior to visiting a branch, and can receive notification on the number of customers ahead of him in the queue. The ticket prints out a letter and number combination indicating the service type and service order of the customer. A display panel flashes the ticket number and indicates the counter where customers will be served.

An interesting feature of almost all ticket queues is that the ticket number is hidden until the ticket is issued to a customer. While such a design might be intuitive, it has the advantage of recording complete information of customer arrivals, including any reneging customers. Larson and Katz et al. (1991) [3] argue that customers' attitudes toward queueing can be strongly influenced by many attributes other than the waiting time, such as the waiting environment and social justice. Katz et al. (1991) demonstrate, via several case studies, that a change in the queueing environment, such as installing a news board or a TV set in the waiting area, makes the waiting experience a positive one and tends to increase customer satisfaction. They also show that customers may become infuriated if they experience social injustice, especially when the first-in, first-out (FIFO) service rule is violated. In both regards, the ticket-queue arrangement provides a better waiting experience to customers. Compared to the physical queueing arrangement, the ticket queue liberates people from physical discomfort and mental boredom of standing in crowded queues, and gives them freedom to make more productive use of the waiting time.

This paper summarizes a comprehensive analysis of operational data from the queue system of a DBS branch in Singapore. The data spans five months during the year 2014–2015, and was collected at an individual level of transaction for a customer. It includes data for more than 80,000 transactions of customers covering all cash, non-cash as well as investment services. Every customer that arrives in a branch passes through two stages, each of which generates distinct data. The first of these stages is arrival stage, which is triggered when a ticket number is raised for an arriving customer and generates a record of arrival time. If no counter is available for service, the customer then waits in the waiting area. The second stage is the service stage, with data capturing the start and end of the service time for the customer. In addition to these time stamps, each record includes a categorical description of the type of service requested and the counter that served the customer.

To facilitate the analysis, a simple, single-server ticket queue was initially considered in which customers arrive according to a Poisson process and service times are independently and identically (i.i.d) distributed. It was difficult to measure the balking rate (when a person, who would otherwise have entered a line, decides not to enter it), in a queue ticketing system, hence reneging customers are considered in the latter part of the analysis.

In the first part of this study, a Markov chain model was formulated for the ticket queue. Here, the states of the Markov chain were aggregated, and the infinite state space reduced to a finite one by taking different granularities of time slots. The resulting Markov chain has the structure of a quasi-birth- and death (QBD) process that admits a matrix product form solution of the steady-state distribution. Then, the aggregated states were disaggregated into individual states to obtain their steady-state probabilities. After obtaining the steady-state distribution, it is possible to evaluate key performance measures of the ticket queue: in particular, the queue length and a customer's expected waiting time for a given ticket position.

The second part of this paper looked at how reneged customers who returned back for service in the branch influenced the overall arrival rate using cox inhomogeneous Poisson process and Kaplan Meier survival analysis.(Returning customers were defined as those who initially left the queue without getting served and returned later during the day or the next day.) For this analysis, the probability of a customer returning was calculated, and that probability was used to estimate the overall arrival rate of customers, and the influence of the returning customers at different hours of a day using regression analysis.

2. PROBLEM STATEMENT

Waiting for services is part of daily life. Unfortunately, waiting cannot be eliminated without incurring inordinate expenses. In fact, all that can be achieved is to reduce the adverse impact of waiting to acceptable levels. In a traditional non-queuing environment, customers can be left confused as to which line to stand in and which counter to go to when called, and can also be distracted by noisy crowded environment.

In situations where facilities are limited and cannot satisfy the demand made upon them, bottlenecks occur which manifest themselves as a queue. When customers wait in queue, there is the danger that waiting time will become excessive, leading to the loss of some customers to competitors [4]. Bank operators can confidently tell when the first customer will enter the banking hall the minute the bank opens to the public. Intermittently, as customers enter and leave banking halls, processors have no idea of the expected time the next customer will enter, join the queue, wait in queue, be served or leave. The obvious cost implication of customers waiting range from idle time spent when queue builds up (which results in man-hour loss) to loss of goodwill (which may occur when customers are dissatisfied with a system). Thus, management should evaluate the performance of different queuing structures and strike a middle ground between cost on one hand and benefits of improved service on the other hand, which is the main thrust of this study.

This paper is concerned with ticket queues in which the physical queue is effectively invisible and a customer's queueing position can only be inferred from their ticket position. The following issues are of specific interest: (1) Estimate the queue length at a given point in time, considering the case when an impatient customer might leave the queue in between, and (2) Estimate the effect on customer arrival when impatient customers drop from a queue and returns back for service later.

3. STATE OF THE ART

One of the earliest works on queuing with reneging was firstly studied by Haight [5], who studied how to make a rational decision while waiting in a queue and the probable effects of this decision. Ancker and Gafarian (a) [6] carried out an early work on Markovian reneging with Markovian arrival and service patterns, and analyzed the M/M/1/N queuing system with balking and reneging. For steady state analysis, they obtained the steady state probabilities, mean number in queue and system, probability of balking, waiting, reneging, acquiring service and customer loss rate. Ancker and Gafarian (b) [7] also obtained results for a pure balking system (no reneging) by setting the reneging parameter equal to zero.

Multi server queueing systems occur in many real life situations such as hospitals, retail stores etc. Xiong and Altiok [8] studied multi-server queues with deterministic reneging times with reference to the timeout mechanism. Gavish and Schweitzer [9] also considered a deterministic reneging model with the additional assumption that arrivals can be labeled by their service requirement before joining the queue, and arriving customers are admitted only if their waiting plus service time does not exceed some fixed amount. Kapodistria [10] studies a single server Markovian queue with impatient customers and considers the situations where customers abandon the system simultaneously. He considers two abandonment scenarios: in the first one, all present customers become impatient and perform synchronized abandonments;, while in the second scenario, the customer in service is excluded from the abandonment procedure. He extends this analysis to the M/M/c queue under the second abandonment scenario.

The impact of information as provided to queueing customers is discussed in Larson and Richard [11] and quantified in a controlled experiment by Katz et al (1991). Analytical modeling studies were done by Whitt (1999) who conducted a comparison study of two M/M/s/r systems, in which one system provided no information to waiting customers and the second system gave the system state and the queueing time information. He developed algorithms to compute important performance measures. In particular, he used numerical studies to show that the first model has higher customer balking rates than the second.

Another body of literature that focuses on the study of survival models was carried out by Edward L. Kaplan and Paul Meier when they collaborated to publish a seminal paper on how to deal with incomplete observations [12]. Subsequently, Kaplan-Meier curves and estimates of survival data have become a familiar way of dealing with differing survival times (times-to-event), especially when not all the subjects continue in the study. Examples of when times-to-events may be important end-point variables include cancer survival times and many other applications in medical science. As illustrated by these examples, survival times need not relate to actual survival with death being the event; the event may be any event of interest. Kaplan-Meier analyses are also used in non-medical disciplines.

These queuing systems deal with customer impatience and customer balking in different queueing setups. They offer different extensions of customer impatience in single-server and multi-server queues. Furthermore, customer impatience has a highly negative impact on the business of any firm as it leads to loss of potential customers, and hence business. Keeping in mind the negative impact of customer impatience, this paper examines arrival rates whilst analyzing the impact of returning customers over the arrival rate.

4. SOLUTION: DESCRIPTION OF APPROACH

4.1. The queuing system

Ticket-queue technology operates as follows:

- each customer is issued a ticket on arrival which bears a number that runs in ascending order.
- the number being served is broadcast on a display panel.
- when the service of the customer with the displayed number is completed, the system calls for the next number if it is not the last number issued; otherwise, the system infers that there are no waiting customers and displays the next number to be issued to avoid delays.

It is assumed that the technology makes the service provider constantly aware of the last number issued. Another assumption is that neither the service provider nor the customers know which customers have already walked away with their tickets, until their numbers are called. The basic structure of a queueing model is as follows:

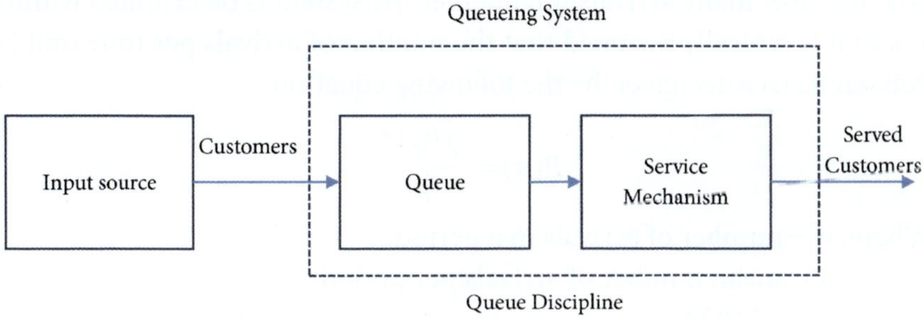

Figure 1: Basic queuing model.

4.2. Customer arrivals

According to Kendall (1953) [13], waiting line models assume that customers arrive according to a Poisson probability distribution. The Poisson distribution specifies the probability that a certain number of customers will arrive in a given time period.

Also, the arrivals at a service system may be drawn from a finite or an infinite population. The distinction is important because the analyses are based on different premises.

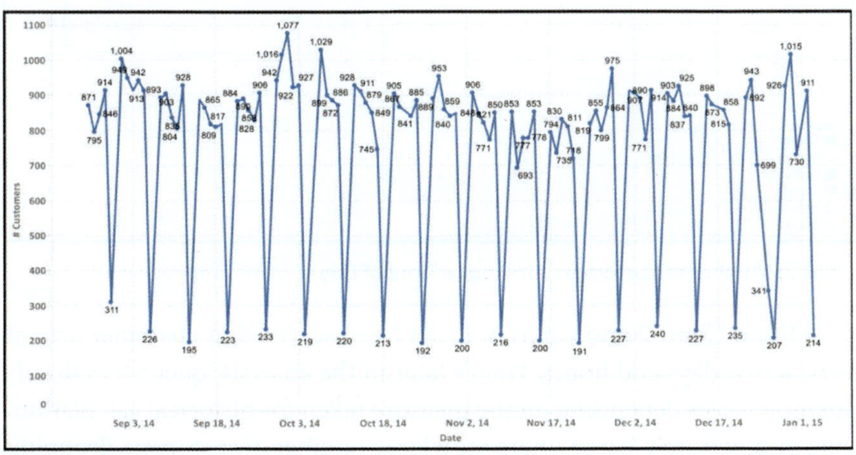

Chart 1: Number of Customers Arriving vs Time

When describing a waiting system, the manner in which customers or the waiting units are arranged for service must be defined. Waiting line formulas generally require an arrival rate, or the number of units per period (such as an average of one every six minutes). A constant arrival distribution is periodic, with exactly the same time between successive arrivals. How many arrivals might enter the system is determined within T, and it is typically assumed that the number of arrivals per time unit is Poisson distributed given by the following equation:

$$P(n) = \frac{\lambda^{n} e^{-\lambda}}{n!}$$

Where; n = number of arrivals in a period

λ = mean number of arrivals per period

e = 2.71828

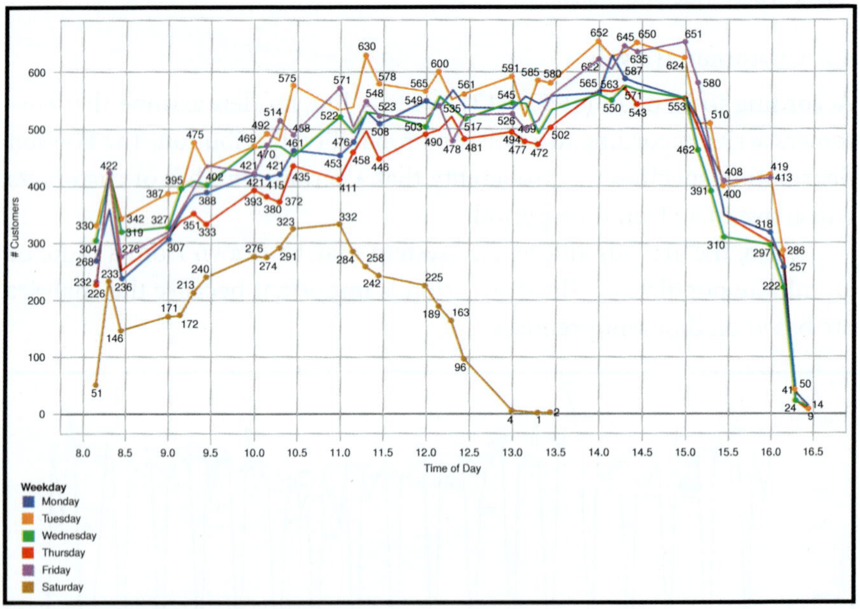

Chart 2: Number of Customers Arriving vs Time of Day

From Chart 2 and Chart 3, it can be observed that customer arrival vary across days and hours. Hence later in the analysis, queue length calculation varies depending on the measure taken for historical calculation. Specifically from Chart 3, there are a large number of customers dropping off from the queue since November 2014 and less customers being served.

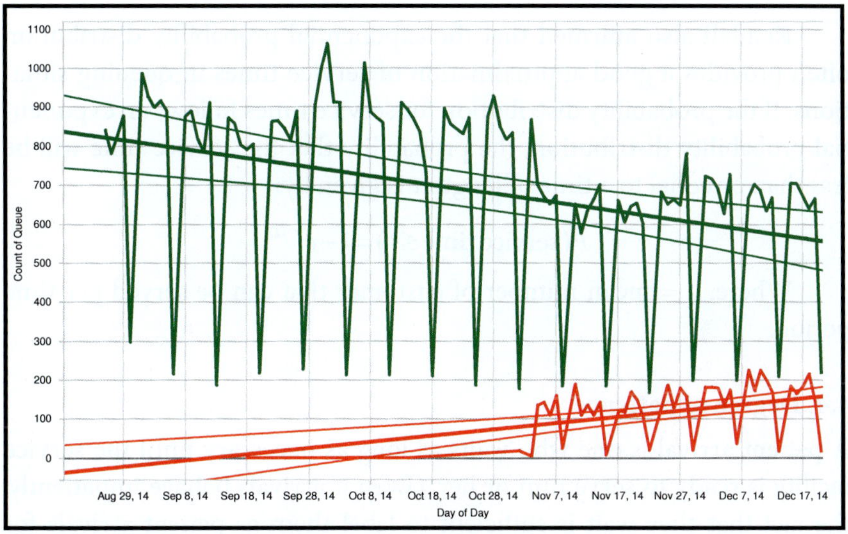

Chart 3: Number of Customers served & dropped vs Time of Day

4.3. Service time

Kendall, in 1953, stated that service times are described by an exponential distribution where the probability that a particular service time will be less than or equal to a given amount of time. The service time is the time the customer spends at the service facility once the service has started. Service time normally varies according to the individual situation. In this study, there are different service times during different hours of day and weekdays as well.

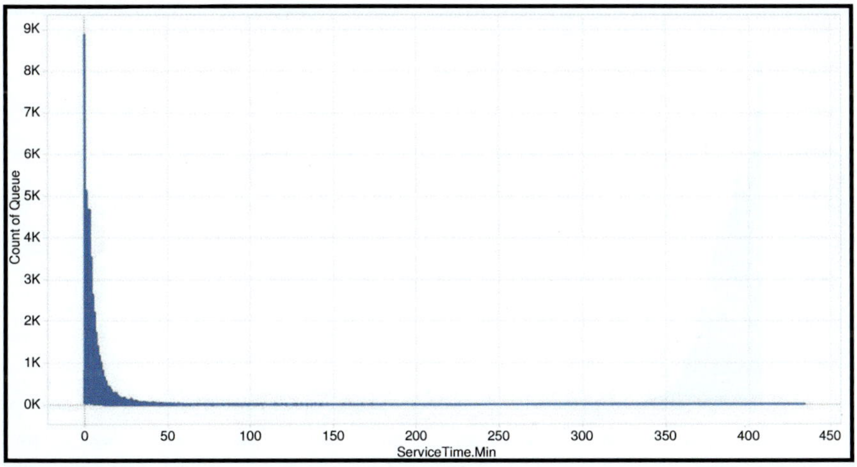

Chart 4: Service Time Distribution (Avg.: 6.6 min)

Kendall also affirmed that the exponential probability distribution often provides a good approximation of service times in queuing situations. If the probability distribution for service times follows an exponential probability distribution, the probability that the service time will be less than or equal to a time of length t is given by:

$$P(\text{service time} \leq t) = 1 - e^{-\mu t}$$

Where: μ = mean number of customer that can be served per time period.

4.4. Degree of patience

A patient arrival is one who waits as long as necessary until the service facility is ready to serve him or her. (Even if arrivals behave impatiently, the fact that they wait is sufficient to label them as patient arrivals for purposes of waiting line theory.) There are two classes of impatient arrivals. Members of the first class arrive, survey both the service facility and the length of the line, and then decide to leave. Those in the second class arrive, view the situation, join the waiting line, and then, after some period of time, depart. This study only considers cases of reneging customers (Class 2). The patience of customers that stay in the queue is the actual wait time, while for the customers who renege, the offered wait time was calculated [14] by assessing the average wait times of two chronologically adjacent customers who do not abandon the queue.

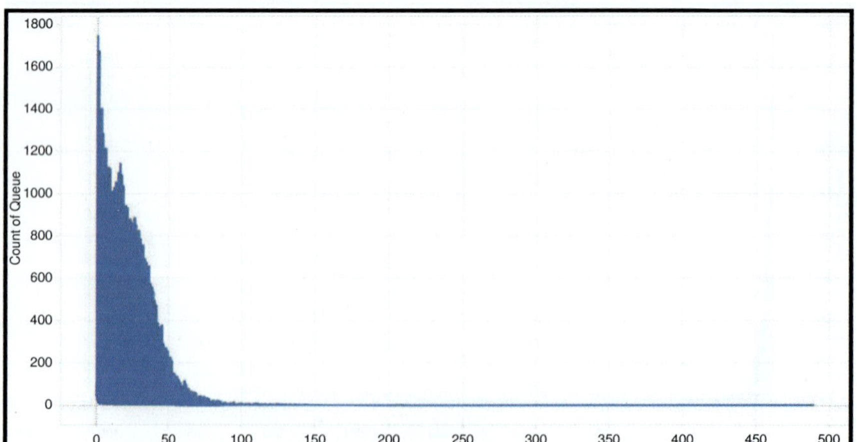

Chart 5: Wait Time Distribution (Avg.: 23.6 min)

4.5. Stochastic model

In this section, the Markovian is formulated, based on the following assumptions:

1) The study considers a single-server queuing system in which the customers arrive in a Poisson fashion with a rate that depends on the number of customers present in the system at that time i.e. $\frac{\lambda}{n+1}$
2) Service times are independently, identically and exponentially distributed with parameter μ.
3) Customers are served in order of their arrival.
4) Upon joining the queue, each customer will wait a certain length of time for service to begin. If it does not begin within that allotted time, they will get impatient (renege) and may leave the queue without getting service with some probability p, and may remain in the queue for service q (=1−p). The reneging times follow the exponential distribution.

4.6. Kendall's notation

In queueing theory, a discipline within the mathematical theory of probability, Kendall's notation is the standard system used to describe and classify a queueing node. In this analysis, the following notations have been used frequently to denote a queuing model:

Symbol	Name	Description
M	Markovian or memoryless	Poisson arrival process
M	Markovian or memoryless	Exponential service time
c	Number of service channels	

4.7. Markov birth and death process

Birth-death processes: General A birth-death (BD process) process refers to a Markov process with a discrete state space, the states of which can be enumerated with index I = 0,1,2,... such that state transitions can occur only between neighboring states, $i \rightarrow i + 1$ or $i \rightarrow i - 1$

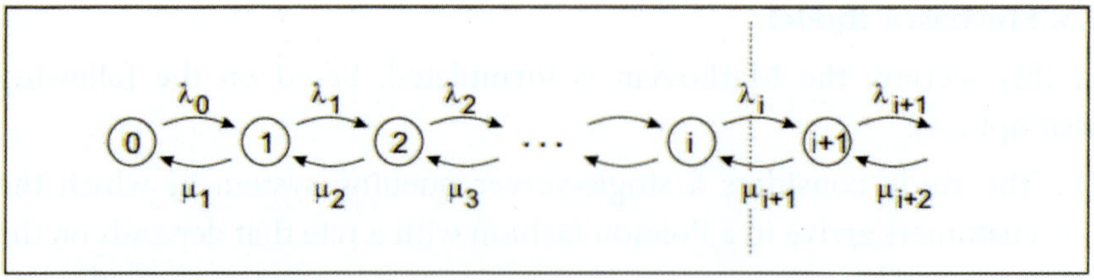

Figure 2: Graphical representation of QBD process.

Where λ is the arrival rate

μ is the service rate

4.8. M/M/1 queue:

The above Markov chain represents the number of customers on a given time stamp. The following assumptions are taken in order to calculate the steady state probabilities of the number of customers:

$\lambda 1 = \lambda 2 = \lambda 3 \ldots = \lambda(n + 1)$

$\mu 1 = \mu 2 = \mu 3 = \mu(n + 1)$

In order to reach a steady state probability, it is necessary that the ratio ($\rho = \frac{\lambda}{\mu}$) should be less than one. If not, then the queue length will tend to infinity.

Some basic formulas that are useful to understand performance measures in the queueing theory are:

Average Utilization of Counter: ρ

Ls (Average number in the System) = $\frac{\rho}{(1-\rho)}$

Lq (Average number in the Waiting line) = Ls – ρ

Ws (Average Waiting time in system) = Ls/λ

Wq (Average Waiting time in queue) = Lq/λ

To begin the analysis, the standard M/M/1 queue is modelled with the dataset, and the queue length for Dec 1st is estimated using the historical averages of arrival and service rate.

Only one service (i.e. Cash Services – Personal account) and one counter (Counter 2) were considered. The result of the analysis is as shown in table 1.

Table 1: Result of analysis for M/M/1 queue

Time	Arrival rate	Service rate	Estimated queue	Actual Queue
8	2.7	5.3	1	2
9	4.2	5.3	3	1
10	4.3	5.3	3	4
11	4.6	5.6	4	10
12	4.6	6.4	4	16
13	5.1	4.8	23	13
14	5.4	5.5	4	6
15	6.1	4.7	23	0
16	3.3	4.2	2	0

Based on the data, a simulation is performed for the first hour of 1st Dec illustrating the actual queue formation.

From Chart 6, it was observed that the mean queue length using simulation is 1.55 ~ 2, which is very close to the actual queue length 2. The variation between actual and predicted queue length is shown in chart 7.

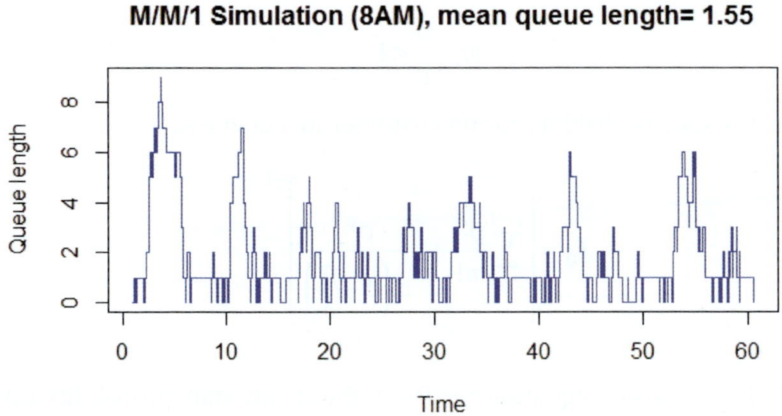

Chart 6: Simulation for M/M/1 queue

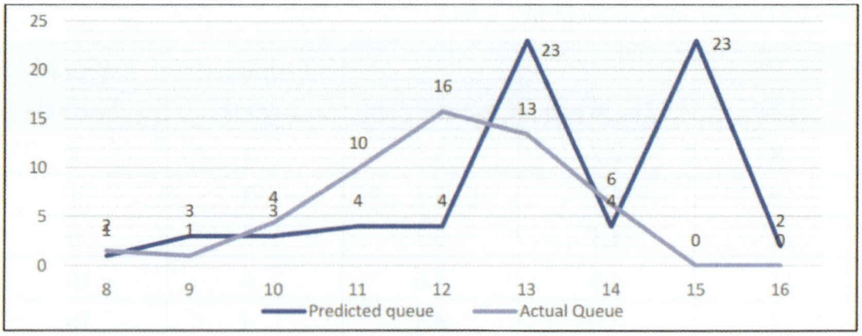

Chart 7: (M/M/1) Actual & Predicted Queue Length vs. Time

4.9. M/M/C queue

M/M/C is a variation of the classic queue, assuming that the service is provided by c servers operating independently of each other. This modification is natural if the mean arrival rate is greater than the service rate, then the system will not be stable; hence the number of servers should be increased. However, in this situation there are parallel services and the study is concerned with the distribution of first service completion.

In this multiple counters model, the assumption of server utilization (ρ) is somewhat different from the case of M/M/1 queue system seen in the previous scenario:

$$p = \frac{\lambda}{c^{*}\mu} < 1$$

$$or, \ \frac{\rho}{c} < 1$$

The steady state probability for no customer in a queue is:

$$P_0 = \left[\sum_{0}^{c-1} \frac{\rho^n}{n!} + \frac{\rho^c}{c!\left(1 - \frac{\rho}{c}\right)} \right]^{-1}$$

Using the above equation for *P* (0), the steady state probability can be calculated for 1, 2… n customers in the queue by the equation that follows. Since in this case there are c servers, to obtain the distribution of Pc two cases must be distinguished accordingly, as μ depends upon c:

$$\sum_{k=0}^{inf} p_k = 1$$

$$Pn = \frac{\rho^n}{n!} p_0 \text{ where}; n < c$$

$$Pn = \frac{\lambda^n}{c! \mu^n c^{n-c}} p_0 \text{ where}; n \geq c$$

The steady state Length of queue is calculated as:

$$L = \sum_{n=c}^{\text{inf}} (n-c) p_n$$

$$= \frac{\rho^{c+1} p_0}{(c-1)!(c-\rho)^2}$$

Data similar to the previous analysis was modeled, and following are the results obtained:

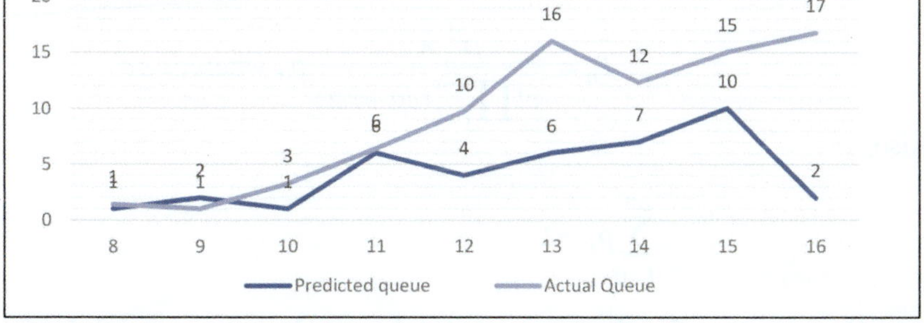

Chart 8: (M/M/c) Actual & Predicted Queue Length vs. Time

The results are superior to the previous analysis, but a high variation in actual and predicted queue length remains, where dropping off /reneging customers are not taken into account. Hence for the same 1st December data, the reneging rate is incorporated to perform the prediction.

4.10. M/M/C queue with reneging

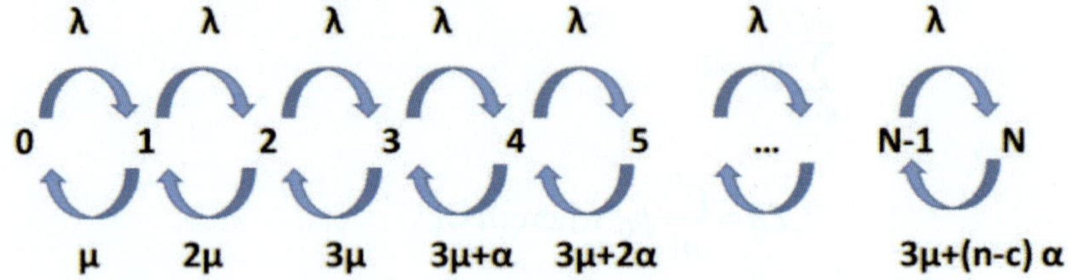

Figure 3: Graphical representation of QBD process with reneging.

The above is the Markovic state for customers in a queue at any given hour when there are three counters. Note that the only additional parameter in this chain from the standard MMC model is α. This is defined as the patience level of a customer. In this model, the patience of dropping off customers is defined as half the average wait time of non-dropping customers. The steady state formulas for the above chain can be derived as follows:

Similar to the case of M/M/C queue, two cases are modeled to deal with multiple counters. Therefore,

$$P_n = \frac{\rho^n}{n!} p_0 \text{ where}; n < c$$

$$P_n = \frac{\rho^n \lambda^{n-c}}{c! \prod_{r=1}^{n-c} (c\mu + r\alpha)} p_0 \text{ where}; n \geq c$$

Also,

$$\sum_{k=0}^{\text{inf}} p_k = 1$$

Hence, using the above equations, the steady state probabilities for no customer in the system is calculated.

$$P_0 = \left[\sum_{j=0}^{c} \frac{\rho^j}{j!} + \frac{\rho^c}{c!} \sum_{j=1}^{\text{inf}} \frac{\lambda^j}{\prod_{r=1}^{j} (c\mu + r\alpha)} \right]^{-1}$$

Finally, the steady state length of queue at any given hour is given by:

$$L = \sum_{j=0}^{\inf} j\lambda^{j-1} * \left(\frac{p_0\, \rho^c\, \lambda}{c! \prod_{r=1}^{j} (c\mu + r\alpha)} \right)$$

Once the steady state probabilities are calculated, similar analysis as before is carried out to estimate the queue length for 1st December using historical arrival and service rates.

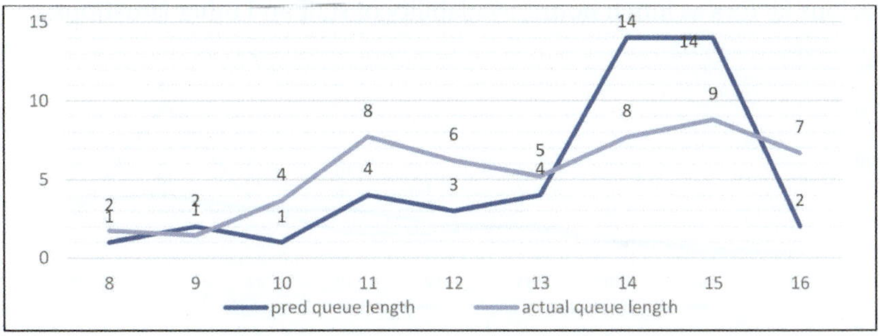

Chart 9: (M/M/C reneging) Actual & Predicted Customers vs. Time

Table 2: Result of analysis for M/M/C (reneging) queue

Hour	Arrival rate	Service time	Predicted queue	Actual queue
8	44	6.6	1	2
9	77	6.9	2	1
10	102	6.0	1	4
11	126	6.0	4	8
12	135	5.4	3	6
13	129	5.0	4	5
14	137	5.2	14	8
15	125	5.8	14	9
16	68	7.1	2	7

The result of queue length when reneging behavior of customers is taken into account is better than the previous analysis as seen in Chart 9. But to improve this result, the methodology to calculate historical average is modified. This is done by taking the last and first two days of previous months (moving window) to calculate the historical average and estimate the arrival rate on Dec 1st.

From Chart 10 below, it can be observed that there is a good estimation of the queue length up to 12.00 pm but there are some shocks after that. These shocks are because of the incorrect estimation of number of counters open as in the real world, setting the number of counters open depends on various factors as lunch hours, availability of staff and other situations.

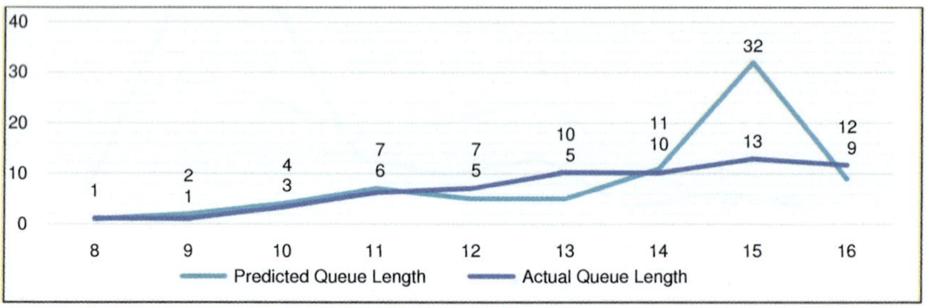

Chart 10: Actual & Predicted Customers vs. Time using moving window

The results from the above analysis were improved by increasing the granularity of time stamps. All the previous analysis is based on one hour time stamps, but in the further analysis a 15 minute time stamp is used.

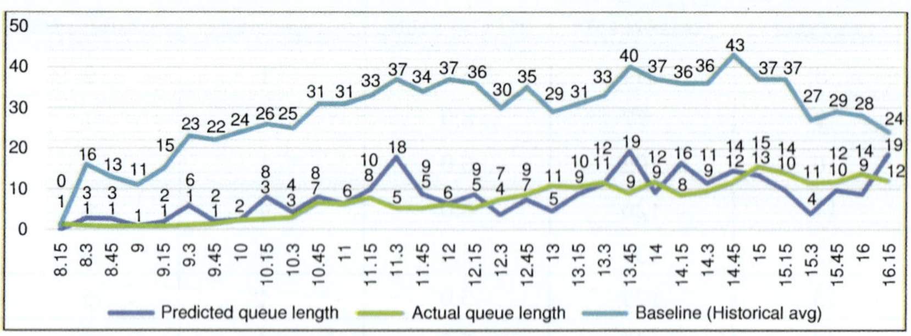

Chart 11: Actual & Predicted Queue Length vs. Time

From the results in Chart 11 it was observed that there is quite a high improvement in accuracy of queue length estimate for December 1st using moving window historical data. In the next section, results are extended for all of December.

4.11. Prediction of queue length

To test the model's accuracy, queue length is estimated using M/M/C queue model considering a customer reneging. The following split of training and testing data set is considered:

Training data = August 2014-Nov 2014

Testing data = Dec 2014

Two different approaches are taken, and then the is compared with both approaches against the benchmark accuracy. These two approaches and benchmark accuracy are described as follows:

Benchmark Accuracy: The benchmark model is the historical arrivals lcss number of counters at a given time stamp (Benchmark = Historical average –Number of counters open)

Approach 1: The best accuracy for the model is with a moving window average for the arrival rate. The moving window is taken as three days for each of the previous months. For instance, to predict the queue length for 15th December, 14th, 15th and 16th of the previous months was used to calculate the average arrival rates. The scatter plot for the predicted and actual values can be seen in Chart 12 (a).

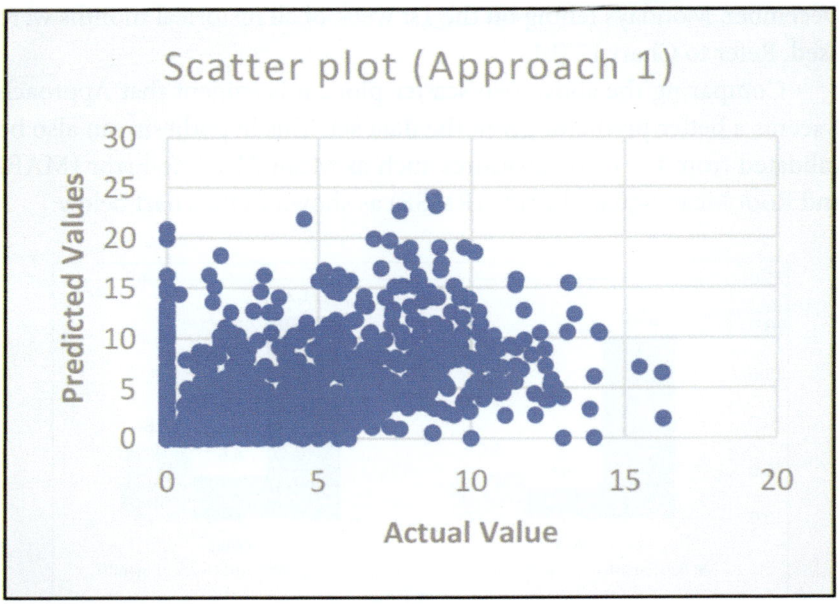

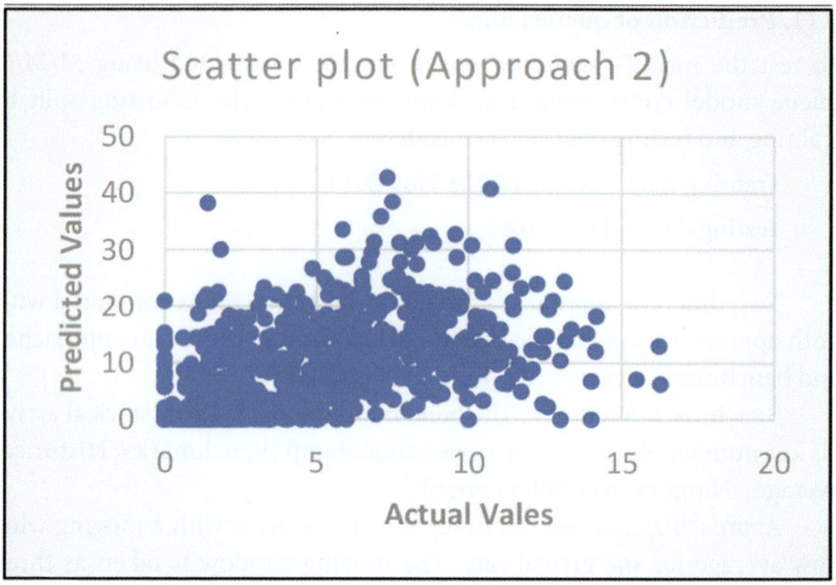

Chart 12 (b): actual vs. Predicted values for different approaches

Approach 2: In this second approach, the arrival rate was calculated using week of the month and day of the week split; for instance, to calculate the arrival rate at different hours on Monday in 1st week of December, Mondays falling on the 1st week of all historical months were used. Refer to Chart 12 (b).

Comparing the above two scatter plots, it is evident that Approach 1 seems a better predictor given the data set. This hypothesis can also be validated from the error measures such as Mean Absolute Error (MAE) and Root Mean Squared Error (RMSE) as shown in the chart below:

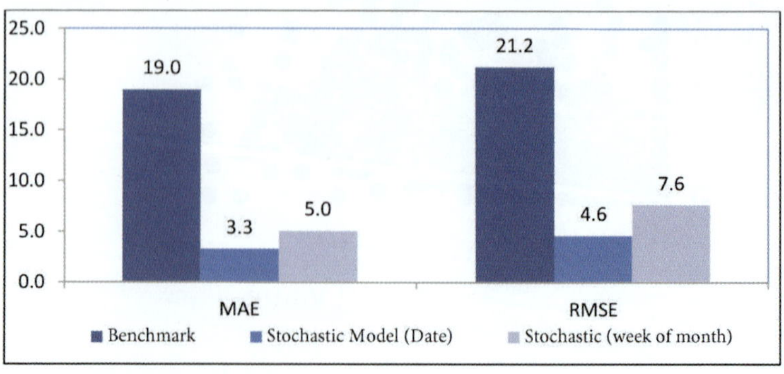

Chart 13: Accuracy measures Vs. Values

Hence to conclude, it is asserted that a moving window estimates the length of queue more accurately then other calculation measures. In the next section, the effect of reneging over the arrival rate will be examined.

4.12. Effects of reneging:

Compared to the stochastic analysis, this analysis is more intuitive in terms of economic theory and involves econometric analysis. Before examining model, it is worth analyzing some variables of interest that might affect the demand of customers in a branch bank.

To analyze the change in demand of customers due to reneging behavior, the distribution of customers returning once they leave a queue was addressed. To formulate this, a subset of customers was extracted, as per Chart 14.

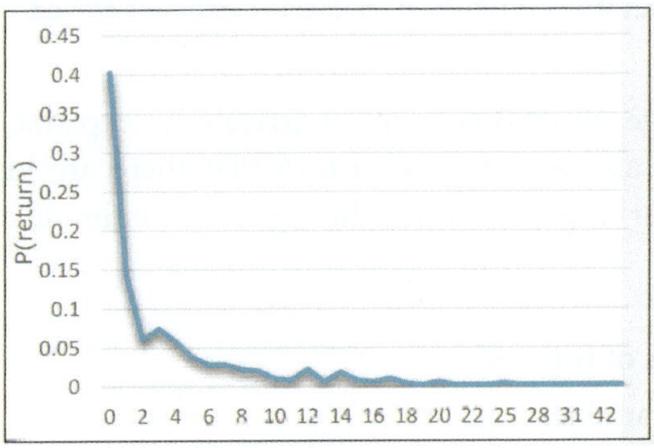

Chart 14: Probability of return vs number of days

It can be observed in Chart 15 that the return of customers follows a decreasing exponential distribution, with most that leave a queue return within four hours the same day. It is observed in Chart 16 that the kink between 22–26 hours shows that there is a relatively high probability of customers returning the next day once they drop from a queue.

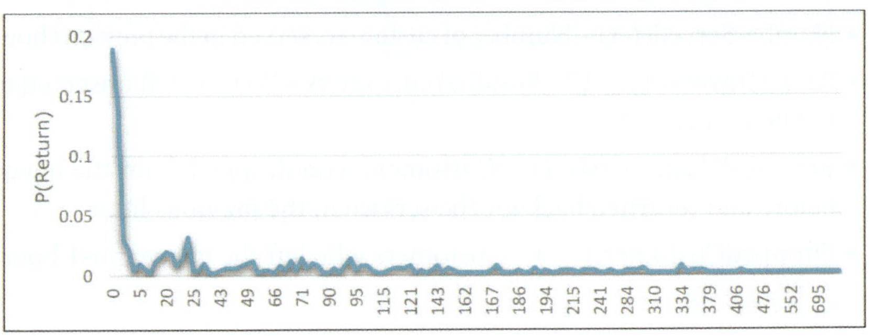

Chart 15: Probability of return vs number of hours

A major question is: How much of the total arrival rate can be explained by the returning customers?

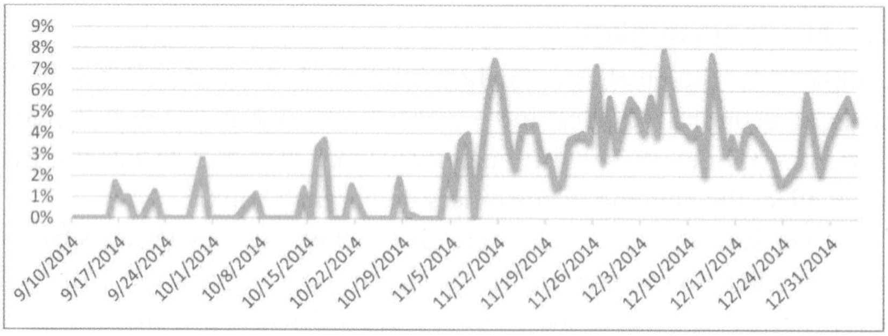

Chart 16: Date vs Customers returned relative to customers arrived

On average, about 3 per cent of arrivals are explained by returning customers. It can be seen in Chart 16 that there are high number of customers returning for service during the months of November and December.

4.13. Variables of interest

- Dependent variable:
  - Demand(t) – Defined as total customer arrivals
- Independent variables:
  - Hour fixed effect
  - Day fixed effect
  - Service ID
  - Demand (t-1) – Customer arrival in previous hour
  - NumberServed(t-1) – Number of customers served in the previous hour
  - ArrivalInventory(t-1) – Residual customers who were left unserved in the hours before t-1
  - ReturnedCustomers(t-1) – Customers who dropped from the queue before and returned back for the service in the previous hour
  - DroppedCustomers(t-1) – Customers who left the queue in t-1 hour

Validating assumptions for regression:

1) Normality: QQ Plot

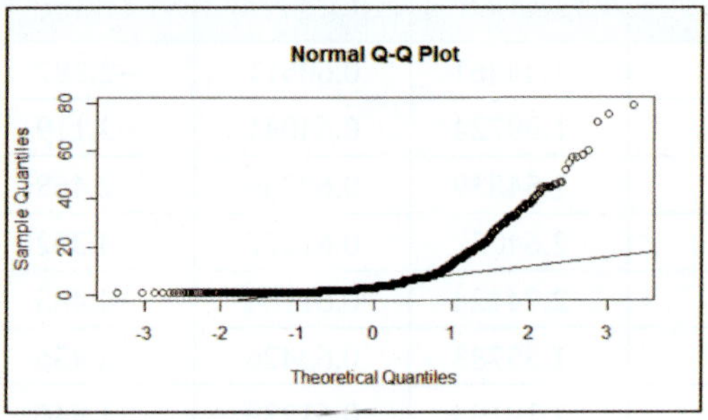

Chart 17: QQ plot for dependent variable

2) Linearity: Scatter plot

The y variable (Demand(t)) has high positive correlation with the independent variables except for Dropped customers (t-1)

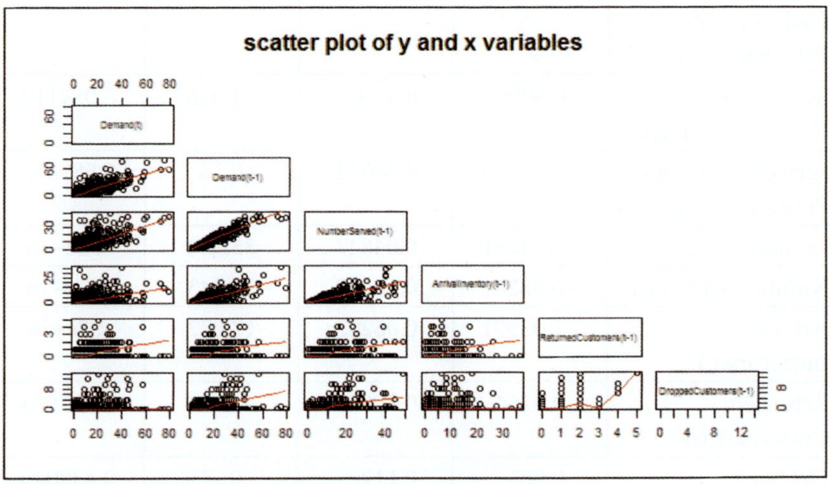

Chart 18: Correlation between dependent and independent variables

To perform the model, validation divided the data into test and training. The training set has data from Aug '14 to Nov '14, while the model was tested on Dec '14 to Jan '15.

4.14. Result of regression

Table 3: Output of regression (training)

Variable	Estimate	Std. Error	*t* value	Pr(>|t|)
(Intercept)	−1.44461	0.60511	−2.387	0.017127
hour9	1.99724	0.64041	3.119	0.001861
hour10	1.54839	0.62735	2.468	0.013722
hour11	2.6405	0.61377	4.302	1.83E−05
hour12	2.74424	0.61184	4.485	7.99E−06
hour13	1.55783	0.63426	2.456	0.014187
hour14	1.19193	0.61239	1.946	0.051849
hour15	1.83828	0.61982	2.966	0.003079
hour16	−2.45746	0.6819	−3.604	0.000327
Service Description Account Opening - Personal Account	0.13861	0.44437	0.312	0.755143
Service Description Cash Services - Personal Account	2.41965	0.43225	5.598	2.70E−08
Service Description Non-Cash Services	0.80969	0.42001	1.928	0.054119
Service Description Personal Loans	−2.34179	4.34034	−0.54	0.589615
Demand.t.1.	1.74261	0.04847	35.954	< 2e−16
Number Served.t.1	−0.88242	0.06239	−14.143	< 2e−16
Arrival Inventory.t.1	−1.05971	0.06207	−17.072	< 2e−16
Returned Customers.t.1	−0.6264	0.30097	−2.081	0.037623
Dropped Customers.t.1	0.085	0.112	0.759	0.448046
Residual standard error: 4.314 on 1180 degrees of freedom				
Multiple R-squared: 0.8139, Adjusted R-squared: 0.8107				
F-statistic: 258 on 20 and 1180 DF, *p*-value: < 2.2e−16				

Day fixed effects are removed from the model as *P* value for dummy variables for day fixed effect is not significant. Result for the regression model over testing data is as follows:

Table 4: Output of regression (testing)

Variables	Estimate	Std. Error	*t* value	Pr(>|t|)
(Intercept)	−3.38857	1.17858	−2.875	0.004178
hour9	2.19064	1.14877	1.907	0.056991
hour10	4.59469	1.13934	4.033	6.20E−05
hour11	3.9098	1.18412	3.302	0.001016
hour12	5.27357	1.15955	4.548	6.52E−06
hour13	4.2869	1.2261	3.496	0.000505
hour14	3.90055	1.18105	3.303	0.001013
hour15	1.25179	1.19217	1.05	0.294123
hour16	−4.51798	1.25973	−3.586	0.000362
Service Description Account Opening - Personal Accou	0.88589	0.83185	1.065	0.287307
Service Description Cash Services - Personal Account	10.15028	1.08031	9.396	< 2e−16
Service Description Non-Cash Services	3.6497	0.8298	4.398	1.28E−05
Demand.t.1.	1.67852	0.05108	32.862	< 2e−16
Number Served.t.1	−1.08093	0.06572	−16.448	< 2e−16
Arrival Inventory.t.1	−0.73813	0.07368	−10.018	< 2e−16
Returned Customers.t.1	−0.84202	0.31969	−2.634	0.008653
Dropped Customers.t.1	0.11442	0.12337	0.927	0.354076
Residual standard error: 5.671 on 618 degrees of freedom				
Multiple R-squared: 0.8935, Adjusted R-squared: 0.8908				
F-statistic: 324.1 on 16 and 618 DF, *p*-value: < 2.2e−16				

4.15. Analysis of the results

From the result of regression model, it was observed that the customer's arrival is highly fluctuated at different hour of day. Also it appears that the arrival of customers during previous hours has a very high positive impact over demand in the current hour, while other variables have a negative impact.

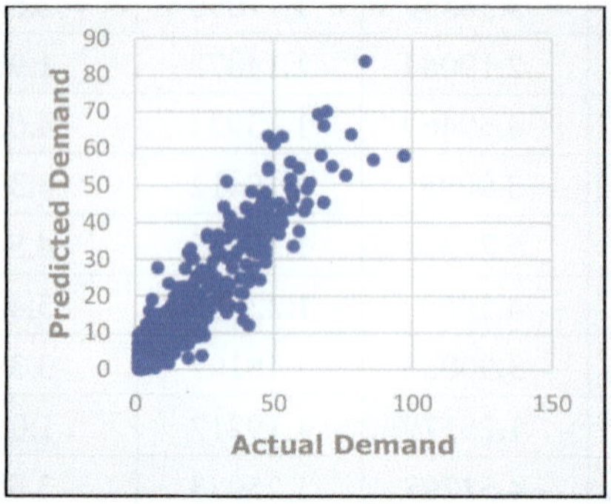

Chart 19: Scatter Plot for Predicted Vs Actual Arrivals

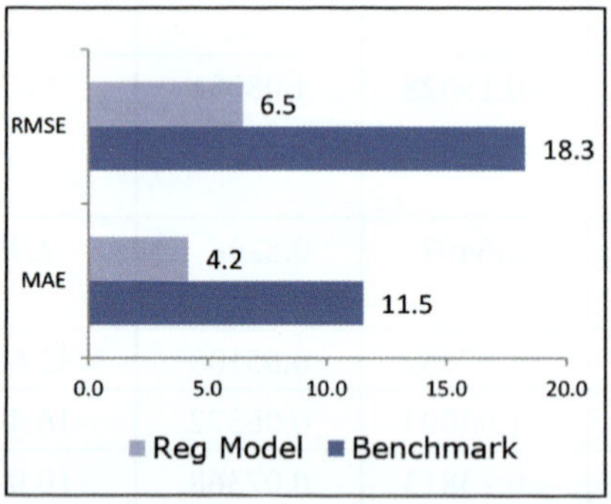

Chart 20: Comparison of Model Accuracy with Benchmark Model

In the previous analysis, returning customers are considered, assuming they will directly influence the overall customer arrival rate. Though the accuracy seems to be within acceptable limits, it is not necessary that all returning customers influence the arrival rate with equal probability. As seen from the charts before, the probability of customers returning at different hours follows the exponential decay function. Thus it is important to estimate the probability of returning customers first, and then use that probability to estimate the overall arrival rate. Survival analysis models factors that influence the time to an event. Survival analysis is generally defined as a set of methods for analyzing data where the outcome variable is the time until the occurrence of an event of interest. The event can be death, occurrence of a disease, marriage, divorce, etc. The time to event or survival time can be measured in days, weeks, years, etc. In this case, an event is a customer returning for a service.

Unlike ordinary regression models, survival methods correctly incorporate information from both censored and uncensored observations in estimating important model parameters. Ordinary least squares regression methods fall short because the time to event is typically not normally distributed, and the model cannot handle censoring (very common in survival data) without modification. In survival analysis, subjects are usually followed over a specified time period and the focus is on the time at which the event of interest occurs. Nonparametric methods provide simple and quick looks at the survival experience, and the Cox proportional hazards regression model remains the dominant analysis method.

The dependent variable in survival analysis is composed of two parts: one is the time to event and the other is the event status, which records if the event of interest occurred or not. One can then estimate two functions that are dependent on time: the survival and hazard functions. The survival and hazard functions are key concepts in survival analysis for describing the distribution of event times. The survival function gives the probability of surviving (or not experiencing the event) up to that time. The hazard function gives the potential that the event will occur, per time unit, given that an individual has survived up to the specified time.

A number of models are available to analyze the relationship of a set of predictor variables with the survival time.

Parametric: Exponential, Weibull and Lognormal Distributions

Non Parametric: Kaplan Meier method

Semi parametric: Cox regression model

Parametric methods assume that the underlying distribution of survival times follows certain known probability distributions. Popular examples include the exponential, Weibull, and lognormal distributions.

The description of the distribution of survival times and change in their distribution as a function of predictors is of interest. Model parameters in these settings are usually estimated using an appropriate modification of maximum likelihood.

A nonparametric estimator of the survival function, the Kaplan Meier method is widely used to estimate and graph survival probabilities as a function of time. It can be used to obtain univariate descriptive statistics for survival data, including the median survival time, and compare the survival experience for two or more groups of subjects. To test for overall differences between estimated survival curves of two or more groups of subjects, such as males versus females, or treated versus untreated (control) groups, several tests are available, including the log-rank test. This can be motivated as a type of chi-square test, a widely used test in practice, and in reality is a method for comparing the Kaplan-Meier curves estimated for each group of subjects.

A popular regression model for the analysis of survival data is the Cox proportional hazards regression model. It allows testing for differences in survival times of two or more groups of interest, while adjusting for covariates of interest. The Cox regression model is a semiparametric model, making fewer assumptions than typical parametric methods but more assumptions than those nonparametric methods described above. In particular, and in contrast with parametric models, it makes no assumptions about the shape of the so-called baseline hazard function. The Cox regression model provides useful and easy to interpret information regarding the relationship of the hazard function to predictors. While a nonlinear relationship between the hazard function and the predictors is assumed, the hazard ratio comparing any two observations is constant over time in the setting where the predictor variables do not vary over time. This assumption is called the proportional hazards assumption and checking if this assumption is met is an important part of a Cox regression analysis.

In this scenario, the event is when a customer returns back in 48 hours. The assumption has been that if a customer returns after 48 hours (two days), they are considered as new customers. Hence the survival function gives the distribution of customers not returning to the branch. The hazard function provides the distribution of customers returning back to the branch. Following are the two distributions:

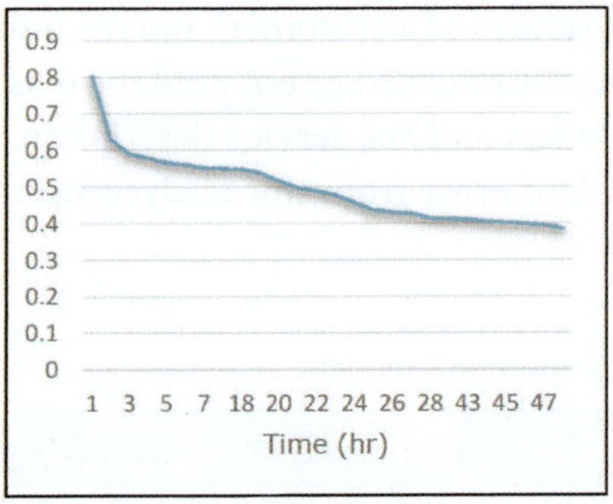

Chart 21: Survival function with respect to Time

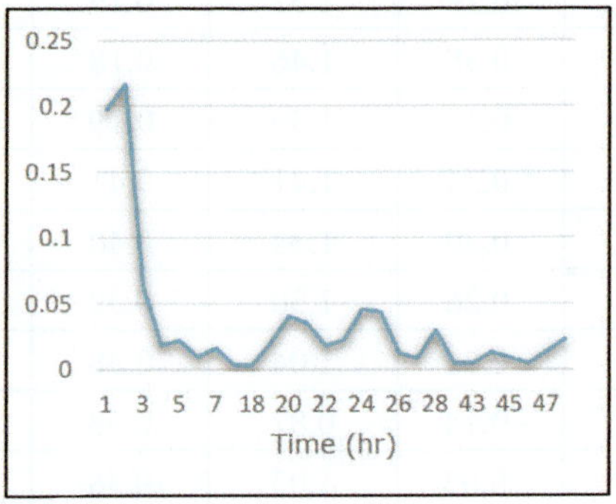

Chart 22: Hazard function with respect to Time

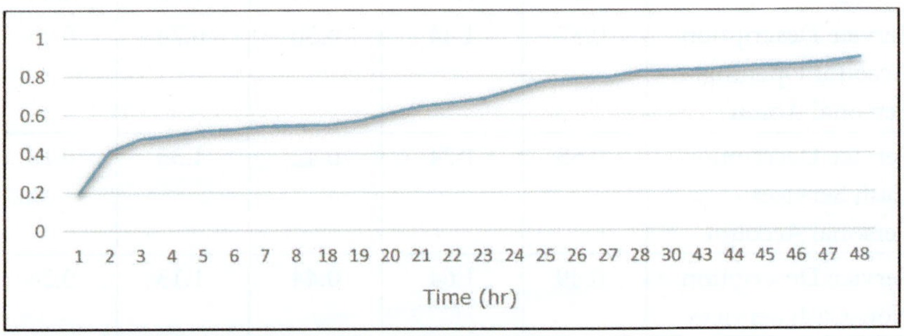

Chart 23: Cumulative Hazard function with re Time

To model the data set as a survival model, only those observations with hashed phone numbers were taken in order to uniquely identify a customer's journey. The dataset includes 345 events with total of 553 cases, and each returning customer uses cox regression model. The dependent variable is the event (return of a customer) and the independent variables are time after a customer returned or not until the maximum of 48 hours, hour and day fixed effect and the service description. Table 5 shows the coefficient and standard error from this analysis using cox proportional model:

Table 5: Output of cox proportional model

Variable	coef	exp(coef)	se(coef)	z	Pr(>|z|)
weekDayMonday	0.36	1.43	0.17	2.09	0.04
weekDaySaturday	−1.07	0.34	0.60	−1.79	0.07
weekDayThursday	0.28	1.32	0.19	1.46	0.14
weekDayTuesday	0.38	1.46	0.18	2.13	0.03
weekDayWednesday	0.33	1.39	0.19	1.70	0.09
hour_start9	0.34	1.41	0.41	0.84	0.40
hour_start10	0.29	1.34	0.40	0.74	0.46
hour_start11	0.26	1.30	0.39	0.66	0.51
hour_start12	0.04	1.04	0.38	0.11	0.92
hour_start13	−0.14	0.87	0.38	−0.36	0.72
hour_start14	0.03	1.03	0.38	0.07	0.94
hour_start15	−0.39	0.68	0.39	−1.00	0.32
hour_start16	−0.34	0.71	0.44	−0.77	0.44
Service Description Account Opening - Personal Accou	0.37	1.44	0.50	0.74	0.46
Service Description Cash Services - Personal Account	0.55	1.74	0.42	1.33	0.18
Service Description Non-Cash Services	0.49	1.64	0.44	1.13	0.26
Concordance = 0.582 (se = 0.019)					
Rsquare = 0.057 (max possible = 0.999)					
Likelihood ratio test = 32.23 on 16 df, ***p*** = 0.009345					
Wald test = 29.13 on 16 df, ***p*** = 0.02307					
Score (logrank) test = 30.18 on 16 df, ***p*** = 0.01711					

From the results in the Table 5, it was observed that only day of the week seems to be a significant variable with a very low R2 value. This is because of small sample size and the noise in the data to identify returning customers correctly. Hence to calculate the probability of returning customers at different hours, the non-parametric Kaplan-Meier model is used. With the non-parametric model, it is possible to calculate the probabilities of returning customers at each hour which can be used to estimate the overall arrival rate and analyze the effect of returning customers at different time of day.

Table 6: Output of Kaplan Meier model

Time	n.risk	n.event	survival	std.err	Lower 95% CI	Upper 95% CI
1	553	109	0.803	0.0169	0.77	0.837
2	444	96	0.629	0.0205	0.59	0.671
3	348	22	0.59	0.0209	0.55	0.632
4	326	6	0.579	0.021	0.539	0.621
5	320	7	0.566	0.0211	0.526	0.609
6	313	3	0.561	0.0211	0.521	0.604
7	310	5	0.552	0.0211	0.512	0.595
8	305	1	0.55	0.0212	0.51	0.593
18	304	1	0.548	0.0212	0.508	0.591
19	303	6	0.537	0.0212	0.497	0.58
20	297	12	0.515	0.0213	0.475	0.559
21	285	10	0.497	0.0213	0.457	0.541
22	275	5	0.488	0.0213	0.448	0.532
23	270	6	0.477	0.0212	0.438	0.521
24	264	12	0.456	0.0212	0.416	0.499
25	252	11	0.436	0.0211	0.396	0.479
26	241	3	0.43	0.0211	0.391	0.474
27	238	2	0.427	0.021	0.387	0.47
28	236	7	0.414	0.0209	0.375	0.457
30	229	1	0.412	0.0209	0.373	0.455
43	228	1	0.41	0.0209	0.371	0.454

(*continued*)

Table 6: Output of Kaplan Meier model (*continued*)

Time	n.risk	n.event	survival	std.err	Lower 95% CI	Upper 95% CI
44	227	3	0.405	0.0209	0.366	0.448
45	224	2	0.401	0.0208	0.363	0.444
46	222	1	0.4	0.0208	0.361	0.443
47	221	3	0.394	0.0208	0.356	0.437
48	218	5	0.385	0.0207	0.347	0.428
49	213	5	0.376	0.0206	0.338	0.419

In Table 6, time in the above output is the number of hours after which a customer will return. These probabilities of returning customers are then used and aggregated to calculate the demand of overall customer's arrival. The variable of Internet to look for is "Exp_prob_return" with different time lags. But the only significant result for this variable is with "Exp_prob_return.t.". The results of our regression model is shown in Table 7:

Table 7: Regression Output

Variables	Estimate	Std. Error	*t* value	*P* Value
(Intercept)	−0.6929	0.7687	−0.901	0.367731
hour10	0.437	0.77709	0.562	0.57408
hour11	1.8483	0.75276	2.455	0.014349
hour12	3.08835	0.76606	4.031	6.24E−05
hour13	1.46767	0.85162	1.723	0.085319
hour14	0.12753	0.8472	0.151	0.880399
hour15	1.39159	0.8084	1.721	0.085679
hour16	−5.88517	0.91533	−6.43	2.57E−10
Service Description Account Opening - Personal Account	0.55999	0.67521	0.829	0.407228
Service Description Cash Services - Personal Account	7.28781	0.78781	9.251	< 2e−16
Service Description Non-Cash Services	2.51899	0.65748	3.831	0.000141

Variables	Estimate	Std. Error	*t* value	*P* Value
Exp_prob_return.t.	4.01203	0.90379	4.439	1.07E−05
Demand.t.1.	1.67609	0.05969	28.08	< 2e−16
Number Served.t.1	−1.20853	0.06898	−17.52	< 2e−16
Arrival Inventory.t.1	−0.76539	0.08306	−9.215	< 2e−16
Residual standard error: 4.659 on 616 degrees of freedom				
Multiple R-squared: 0.849, Adjusted R-squared: 0.8456				
F-statistic: 247.4 on 14 and 616 DF, ***p***-value: < 2.2e−16				

The accuracy of the model has improved from 81.39 per cent to 84.9 per cent R2 when returning customer's probabilities are included in the model. Looking at the *p* value of the hour fixed effects, it is observed that 11.00 am, 12.00 am and 4.00 pm are the most significant hours. To analyze the effect of returning customers over the total demand, these variables are regressed for the individual hour. The result of this analysis is seen in Table 8:

Table 8: Regression Output for Individual Hours

11 AM				
Variables	**Estimate**	**Std. Error**	***t* value**	**Pr(>|t|)**
(Intercept)	−0.33016	1.10974	−0.298	0.767
Service Description Account Opening - Personal Accou	0.60273	1.33209	0.452	0.652
Service Description Cash Services - Personal Account	0.02774	1.74228	0.016	0.987
Service Description Non-Cash Services	0.88129	1.32095	0.667	0.507
Exp_prob_return.t.	3.82418	2.53375	1.509	0.135
Demand.t.1.	2.16896	0.14837	14.618	< 2e−16
Number Served.t.1	−0.82911	0.19736	−4.201	6.65E−05
ArrivalInventory.t.1	−1.37087	0.23795	−5.761	1.38E−07
Residual standard error: 3.489 on 83 degrees of freedom				
Multiple R-squared: 0.8981, Adjusted R-squared: 0.8895				
F-statistic: 104.5 on 7 and 83 DF, ***p***-value: < 2.2e−16				

12.00 pm				
Variables	**Estimate**	**Std. Error**	***t* value**	**Pr(>|t|)**
(Intercept)	0.1087	1.3177	0.083	0.93442
Service Description Account Opening - Personal Accou	1.0907	1.7177	0.635	0.52707
Service Description Cash Services - Personal Account	8.9263	2.1314	4.188	6.60E–05
Service Description Non-Cash Services	4.5539	1.7075	2.667	0.00909
Exp_prob_return.t.	20.0506	3.2669	6.138	2.28E–08
Demand.t.1.	1.651	0.1933	8.541	3.35E–13
NumberServed.t.1	–1.1679	0.225	–5.191	1.31E–06
ArrivalInventory.t.1	–0.8801	0.3095	–2.844	0.00553
Residual standard error: 5.069 on 89 degrees of freedom				
Multiple R-squared: 0.8765, Adjusted R-squared: 0.8668				
F-statistic: 90.26 on 7 and 89 DF, ***p***-value: < 2.2e–16				

4.00 pm				
Variables	**Estimate**	**Std. Error**	***t* value**	**Pr(>|t|)**
(Intercept)	1.06137	0.96105	1.104	0.2757
Service Description Account Opening - Personal Accou	0.63416	1.46546	0.433	0.6674
Service Description Cash Services - Personal Account	1.13891	1.3301	0.856	0.3967
Service Description Non-Cash Services	–0.02852	1.11573	–0.026	0.9797
Exp_prob_return.t.	0.58166	0.99871	0.582	0.5634
Demand.t.1.	1.23033	0.0742	16.58	< 2e–16

4.00 pm				
Variables	**Estimate**	**Std. Error**	***t* value**	**Pr(>|t|)**
NumberServed.t.1	−1.07936	0.0858	−12.58	7.78E−16
ArrivalInventory.t.1	−0.23049	0.0903	−2.553	0.0144
Residual standard error: 1.918 on 42 degrees of freedom				
Multiple R-squared: 0.9229, Adjusted R-squared: 0.9101				
F-statistic: 71.83 on 7 and 42 DF, ***p***-value: < 2.2e−16				

4.16. Impact of returning customers

In the previous section it was assessed that 11.00 pm, 12.00 pm and 4.00 pm are the hours that returning customers a have significant impact on the overall demand of customers. To analyze the economic impact of the returning customers, data for these hours was aggregated, and the wait time of customers analyzed. There was a high correlation (0.45) between wait time and returning customers. Table 9 shows the result of the regression analysis:

Table 9: Regression Output

Variables	**Estimate**	**Std. Error**	***t* value**	**Pr(>|t|)**
(Intercept)	13.78582	2.98186	4.623	1.32E−05
Demand	0.0846	0.03787	2.234	0.0281
Returning.Customers	1.15317	0.49472	2.331	0.0221
Balked.Customers	−0.10118	0.1225	−0.826	0.4111
service.time	−0.32665	0.21862	−1.494	0.1388
Queue.Length	0.93766	0.17054	5.498	3.87E−07
Residual standard error: 9.298 on 86 degrees of freedom				
Multiple R-squared: 0.4884, Adjusted R-squared: 0.4587				
F-statistic: 16.42 on 5 and 86 DF, ***p***-value: 2.38e−11				

From the results in Table 9, it was observed that the coefficient of returning customers is 1.15, which can be interpreted as when each renege customer returns for a service, that person will have to wait for

13.78 + 1.15 = 14.93 min. Also since the standard deviation of returning customers is 2.68 ~ 3, the economic impact of the returning customers over wait time is 3 × 1.15 = 3.45 min. Also there is a 7.04 min increase of wait time because of the variation in the returning customers.

4.17. Prediction of total demand:

The model is now validated using testing data for December. The scatter plot for the actual and predicted values is seen in Chart 24.

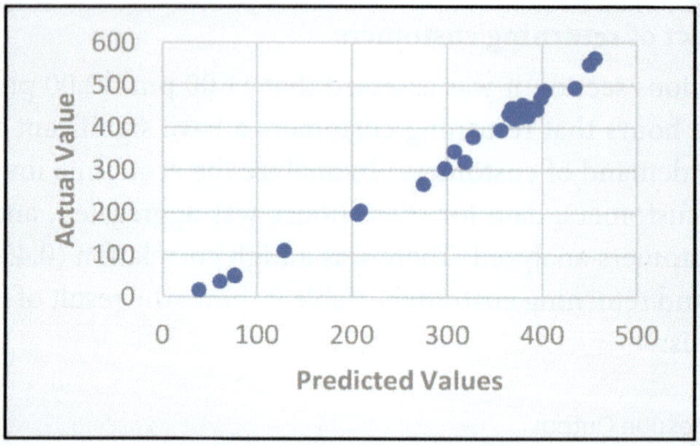

Chart 24: Scatter plot for predicted vs actual values

From the above scatter plot there is a high correlation between predicted and actual values and the R2 for the testing dataset to be 89 per cent.

This is validated from the following time series chart for daily customer arrivals:

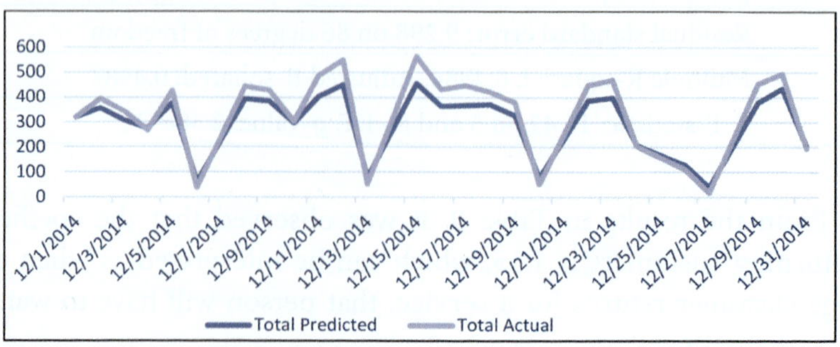

Chart 25: Actual & Predicted values vs. Time

5. DISCUSSION

From the study it was observed that queues in the DBS banking hall are time consuming. From the descriptive analysis, it was analyzed that people spend more time waiting in a queue then the time required to get served. Also as time passes, the wait time keeps increasing. However, from some studies in the US banking ecosystem, it was found that customers rarely queue, while other research showed that queuing in Africa can be attributed to poor queuing systems and their management.

It is unsurprising that this study confirms Wang (2000) by realizing a huge cost incurred by customers as they wait in long queues in the bank. In alignment with Wang, it was also found by Gronroos, (2007) [15] that the time wasted in the bank by the customers could be channeled into profitable ventures. The issue of time wasted while waiting for customer transactions could be due to many reasons - from the queue systems management to disproportionate distributions of transactions (which have for a long time made processors (humans and machines) appear overloaded or dormant and slowed down the processing). Operational levels functions are less managed and this creates pressure, especially on frontline operators. For instance, as found in Nigeria, when a system breaks down, it becomes very hard for the banks to restore confidence and customers queue without knowing who will serve them. In many studies, it is also realized that the effects of processor challenges are exercised on the customers and the expected breaking and recovery times of processors (human or machine) are less considered by the majority of banks for management. This situation directly or indirectly leaves customers stranded in the middle of their transactions.

The nature of customer transaction is an important factor in determining the queue length and the dropping off behavior of customers. Transactions have their own characteristics; for example, the time spent making deposits is different from that spent making withdrawals. Branches in different locations handle customers differently. In some branches, all services can be met at the same counter while in certain other branches, there are designated counters for particular services.

5.1. Model risks

Models are simplified representation of reality. This simplification is inevitable given the complexity of the relationship between variables. In any case, it is a source of risk that needs to be identified, analyzed and

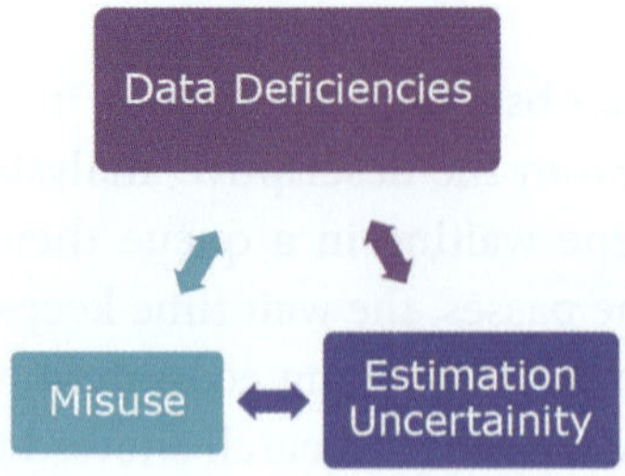

Figure 4: Model risk framework.

managed like any other risk in an institution. With both models examined here, stochastic Markov chain and deterministic survival analysis, there are specific model risks. Model risk can basically be defined as "potential for adverse consequences based on incorrect or misused model output and reports" [16]. Model risk falls into the following three categories.

- **Data deficiencies** in terms of both availability and quality, including data errors, lack of historical depth, errors in feeding of variables or insufficient sample size. Some of the specific cases of data deficiencies in this paper's model are:
  - Lack of data to estimate unique identification for customers
  - Seasonality is not properly addressed because of small sample size
  - Difficult to identify a customer dropping off from a queue because of manual error in data collection
- **Estimation uncertainty** or model error in the form of simplification, approximations, flawed assumptions or incorrect model design. Any of these can occur at any point in the model development, from design to implementation, which can lead to erroneous results that are not consistent with the purpose and intended use of the model. They include estimate uncertainty (reflected in confidence interval, which are often calculated but tend not to be used), and also the use of unobservable parameters, the lack of market consensus on the model's functional form, among others. The following are the some of the model errors that might occur in our case:
  - Steady state probabilities for Markov chain process is calculated for continuous time; this might affect the model accuracy as in this case, it was calculated for a discreet time event

- ▸ Calculating the reneging rate is difficult to calculate accurately because of the same reason as above

– **Model misuse**, which includes using the model for purposes other than those for which it was designed, and not re-estimating or re-calibrating the model in a long time.

6. CONCLUSION AND FURTHER WORK

In this paper, the theory of queuing with reneging has been reviewed, with multiple situations relevant to the bank ticket queue system. Since reneging is a commonly observed phenomenon, results presented in this work will be of use to practitioners of queuing theory. The different situations take into account various scenarios of queue formation as M/M/1 and M/M/c (with and without reneging). The success factor for each of the situation is the accuracy of prediction against actual length of the queue. Results of the traditional M/M/c/c models can be obtained by substituting $\alpha = 0$ in our results. It is also possible to derive steady probabilities of the queuing system using birth and death model. Graphs of the descriptive statistics are presented to understand the distribution of parameters and validating the assumptions of theory.

This paper also analyzed how the arrival rate is influenced by customers who renege and return later for the service. Findings present efficient and effective evaluation tools that can help management quantify service performance, accurately predict the queue length based on their ticket positions, benchmark the performance gap with the physical queue, and implement an improvement when it is called for. Ticket-queue technology opens a new area for researchers to explore. Given its widespread adoption in government agencies and commercial service organizations, research interests in this subject can be expected to grow. There are several possible research directions for ticket-queue management, such as:

- Effect of reneging across branches: It is important to study the effect of reneging and arrival rate in nearby branches and how these reneged customers interact with the bank branches close by. This study helps to understand customer loyalty and gives a better estimate of performance of the service for a branch
- Modelling and performance evaluation of ticket queues: In order to manage the queues effectively, management needs tools to estimate key

performance measures accurately. These Markov models can serve as the starting points from which to study more complex networks of service facilities. Some of the performance measures that need to be correctly evaluated are effective queue length, mean reneging rate, proportion of customers lost (due to reneging and finite buffer) among others.

- Improving customer service: In this paper, it is assumed that a customer's reneging decision is based on expected delay in the system/patience level. In reality, a customer's decision may depend on other attributes of their anticipated delay. Indeed, providing guarantees for quality of service (QoS) has become a critical issue for many service providers. Efficient methods to estimate those measures pose an interesting future research topic. If reneging becomes a significant concern, then providing customers with dynamic waiting time information may be an effective means to discourage abandonment. For instance, some companies use handheld electronic devices to communicate with the customers in their virtual queue, while some restaurants issue beepers to arriving customers, allowing restaurant staff to alert customers when service becomes ready. This not only enhances customers' comfort level in the virtual queue, but also allows management to gain full information on the number of waiting customers in the virtual queue, because reneging customers return their beepers to the system before departing.

REFERENCES

1. 'Retail banking in Asia: actionable insights for new opportunities' by McKinsey & Company

2. https://www.dbs.com/newsroom/DBS_POSB_First_bank_in_Singapore_to_introduce_SMS_queue_system_in_all_full_service_branches

3. Katz, LK, BM Larson, RC Larson (1991). Prescription for the waiting-in-line blues: Entertain, enlighten, and engage. *Sloan Management Review*, 4, 44–53.

4. Kotler, P (1999). Marketing Management, the New Millennium Edition. Michael, K. (2001), "Service on Call" in Banking Technology News Service Network http/www.fineos.com/documentation/features/bankreach.com.

5. Haight, FA (1959). Queueing with reneging. *Metrika*, 2, 186–197.

6. Ancker Jr., CJ and AV Gafarian (1963). Some queuing problems with balking and reneging I. *Operations Research*, 11, 88–100.

7. Ancker, Jr., CJ and AV Gafarian (1963). Some queuing problems with balking and reneging. II. *Operations Research*, 11, 928–937.

8. Xiong, W and T Altiok (2009). An approximation for multi-server queues with deterministic reneging times. *Annals of Operations Research*, 172, 143–151.

9. Gavish, B and PJ Schweitzer (1977). The markovian queue with bounded waiting time. *Management Science*, 23(12), 1349–1357.

10. Kapodistria, S (2011). The M/M/1 queue with synchronized abandonments. *Queuing Systems*, 68, 79–109.

11. Larson, RC (1987). Perspectives on queues—Social injustice and the psychology of queueing. *Operations Research*, 35, 895–905.

12. Kaplan, EL, P Meier (1958). Nonparametric estimation from incomplete observations. *Journal of the American Statistical Association*,53, 457–81.

13. Kendall, DG (1953).Stochastic processes occurring in the theory of queues and their analysis by the method of the imbedded markov chain.*The Annals of Mathematical Statistics*, 24(3), 338.

14. Robert JB and C Terwiesch (2013). Waiting patiently: An empirical study of queue abandonment in an emergency department, *Management Science*

15. Gronroos, C (2007). *Service Management and Marketing: Customer Management in Service Competition*, 3rd Ed. Chichester: John Wiley and Sons Ltd.

16. http://www.managementsolutions.com/PDF/ENG/Model-Risk.pdf

CHAPTER 13

Customer Insights for Insurance Companies

Shishir Jain

National University of Singapore

ABSTRACT

A Singapore-based insurance giant wanted to have a 360-degree view to know more about its customers. This study performed the review which helped the company (alias "the Insurance Company") analyze things for the first time, both from traditional policy as well as customer point of view. Actionable insights were provided to the company from the created customer view. The whole analysis was broken down into following four parts: (1) to find the evolution of customers in company over the year; (2) to determine the characteristics of the customers who leave within two years of their interactions; (3) to determine the characteristics of the customers who leave after five years and those who stay; and (4) to determine the characteristics of home insurance customers who also buy car insurance policies. These analyses revealed some interesting patterns about customer behavior.

1. INTRODUCTION

"The Insurance Company Group" is a leader in the insurance and asset management sector, serving millions of customers across the globe. It offers a wide range of products, catering to the needs of individuals and companies.

All the previous analyses of the Company were based on the policies but not on the customer viewpoint. In an attempt to better understand the behavior of its customer, the company wanted to know the customer views.

This study provided the company with a customer view and found interesting insights from the data. To emphasize the relevance of customer view in financial industry, an excerpt from the study [1] by Experian is given here:

> The benefits of achieving a single customer view are many and they are felt right across the business. Customers will enjoy better service levels, leading to greater loyalty. Better targeted marketing efforts will deliver long-term improvements in profitability. As such, a single customer view should be seen as the foundation of customer service excellence.

2. PROBLEM STATEMENT

The first problem to deal with was "Who are the Insurance Company's customers?" To answer this, various descriptive and predictive analytical techniques were used on customers and policies data. The main challenge was to obtain a customer view from the policy transaction data. The purpose of the study was to have a better understanding of the customer behavior and to analyze things from customer perspective.

This study used only retail customers, those who buy policies as individuals and not as a group or industry. Though group health customers were also added in the study to get a more holistic view from a large number of customers, due to limitations of available data for group health customers they were not used in the subsequent analysis. Only exclusively retail customers were included in the records.

3. STATE OF THE ART

State-of-the-art techniques related to problem statement were studied from three different points of views. Firstly, in terms of techniques prevalent in the industry to solve similar problem; secondly, in terms of the process employed in the industry; and finally, research done in the related fields for solving a similar problem. These three points of views are discussed in detail in the following sections.

A) Techniques

The techniques studied and used in this paper for descriptive and predictive modeling are (1) rule fit ensemble, (2) decision tree, and (3) random forest.

Rule Fit Ensemble [2,3]: In this technique, regression and classification rules are derived from a linear combination of simple rules obtained from the data. Each rule is a conjunction of a small number of simple statements. It differs from other methods in the fact that all the learners in this method use all the variables but different weights on these variables to arrive at the rules. Rules generated from this model are thus more interpretable than other models with the same prediction accuracy.

Random Forest [4]: This is an ensemble-based learning method for classification and regression, and works by building many decision tree models. It corrects the over-fitting done by single decision tree by taking into account different variables in different iterations to construct a collection of decision trees with controlled variance. Random forests can be used in a natural way to rank the importance of variables in a regression or classification problem. The first step in measuring the variable importance in a dataset is to apply a random forest to the data, during which the out-of-bag error for each data point is recorded and averaged over the forest.

To measure the importance of a particular feature "x" after training, the values of x are permuted among the training data and the out-of-bag error is again computed for this dataset. The importance score for x is computed by averaging the difference in out-of-bag error before and after the permutation over all trees. The score is normalized by the standard deviation of these differences. Features which produce large values for this score are ranked more important than features which produce small values.

B) Data Mining Process

Different process models are used in industry for data mining and finding insights from the data, such as SEMMA (sample, explore, modify, model, and assess) [5], CRISP-DM [6] (cross-industry standard process for data mining) are used. This study uses CRISP-DM model of analysis.

Cross-industry standard process for data mining comprises following phases (1) business understanding, (2) data understanding, (3) modeling, (4) evaluation, and (5) deployment as shown in Figure 1.

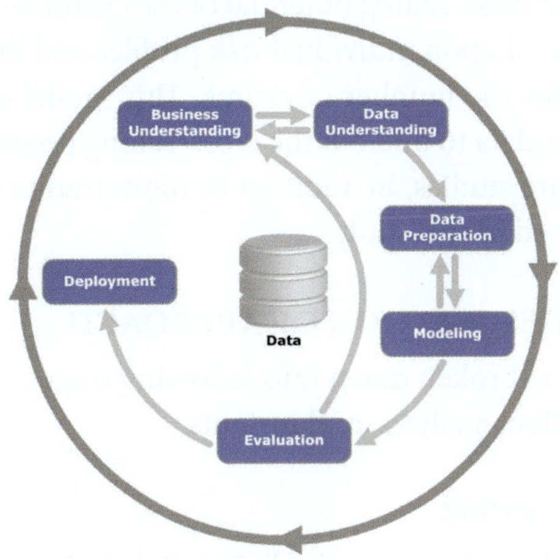

Figure 1: Cross industry process for data mining.

C) Related Work in Academia and Industry

Various methods developed in academia and industry regarding customer segmentation, lifetime value, and cross-selling potential were considered for the purpose of this study. Su-Yeon Kim, Tae-Soo Jung, Eui-Ho Suh, and Hyun-Seok Hwang in their paper *Customer Segmentation and Strategy Development Based on Customer Lifetime Value: A Case Study* [7] talk about lifetime value-based segmentation of the customers into different bands. They defined lifetime value as the sum of the revenue gained from the customers minus the total cost of attracting, selling, and servicing customers, and based upon that define marketing strategies to retain high-value customers. Phillip E. Pfeifer Robert L. Carraway in their paper *Modelling Customer Relationships as Markov Chain* [8] talk about modeling the lifetime value of customer as Markov Chain of interactions between the customer and the industry, and based upon stochastic process, finding the probability of the customer being in any state. In Insurance industry, this can be modeled by having different lines of business (LOBs) as active and inactive states, and finding the probability of transitioning from one state to another for all customers. This will give us the probabilities of cross-selling different policies, customer leaving the insurance company in next few years. Similarly, for cross-selling, Fredrik Thuring in his paper *A Credibility Method for Profitable Cross-Selling of Insurance Products* [9] talks about using credibility theory to determine the cross-selling potential of the customers. He models the customers based upon individual risk profiles and by using a Poisson distribution for the number of claims. This model can be applied to the company's data to find out the cross-selling potential of every customer in future studies, in addition to more traditional classification techniques used in this study.

4. SOLUTION: DESCRIPTION OF APPROACH

The solution can be broken down into following stages: data understanding, data preparation, analysis, and insights.

4.1. Data understanding

Data comprised last 20 years of all the policy transactions and client details which are captured from production system (AS400) as follows. (1) Policy transaction: It captures all the transaction on the policy in terms of actions, LOB, contract type, GWP, and date of transactions. (2) Customer mapping: It captures demographic information of the customers such as nationality, date of birth, and postal address. (3) Claim transaction: It captures when a claim occurred and how much did it cost. (4) External data: Other data from external sources provided customer segmentation based upon the postal code of customer mapping table.

Finally, these sources were combined to get (1) customer information and (2) customer transaction database.

Customer information: This table contains the demographic data of the customer along with the external data captured from external vendor. Based upon postal codes, the customers of the company were segmented into different socio-economic groups with different features through this data.

Customer Transaction: This table contains the transactions (action initiated by the customer) by the customers. Each row defines a particular transaction done by the customer in the form of action taken. Policy Transaction table was used to get customer transaction table as shown in Figure 2.

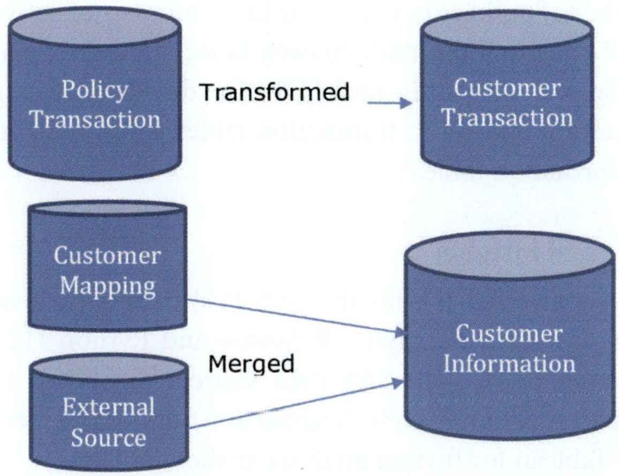

Figure 2: Transformation of production system tables.

The Customer transactional view was then finally changed to customer view to get various insights from the data.

4.2. Data preparation

The customer transaction data had all the transactions done by the customer, but it didn't give the information as to what stage the customer is at in his lifetime with the company. To extract this information from the transactions, the customer transaction table was transformed into (1) Customer View and (2) Customer View Transactional.

Customer View Transactional: Sliding window of one year was used to capture the status of the customer at the end of one year period and transform the data into customer view at the end of each period. This table was made with respect to each LOB and each distribution channel, which means that the status of the customer was calculated with respect to each LOB/distribution channel, captured using category field. For example, if category is one the information was captured with respect to Motor LOB and so on. The status of the policy can be following types: (1) in-force, (2) lapsed, (3) lapsed-all, (4) in-force-other, and (5) NA.

This table helped determine the yearly transaction made by the customer and his evolution in the company with respect to each LOB/distribution channel in terms of lapsed, new, existing and win-back.

Customer view: Each row of this table defines the full view of different customer. NRIC is the unique key for this table. It captures information such as number of policies in particular LOB, number of active policies in a LOB, GWP contribution made to each LOB, number of claims in each LOB, total claimed amount in each LOB. The details were extracted from policy transaction and claim transaction tables, and finally merged with customer information table.

4.3. Analysis and insights

Tableau [10] connected it with the SAS [11] data source was used for analysis. For descriptive analytics R Studio and Python [12] were used after connecting them with SAS data sources as shown in Figure 3. The data tables, customer view (transaction) and customer view, were imported in Tableau for further analysis as shown below.

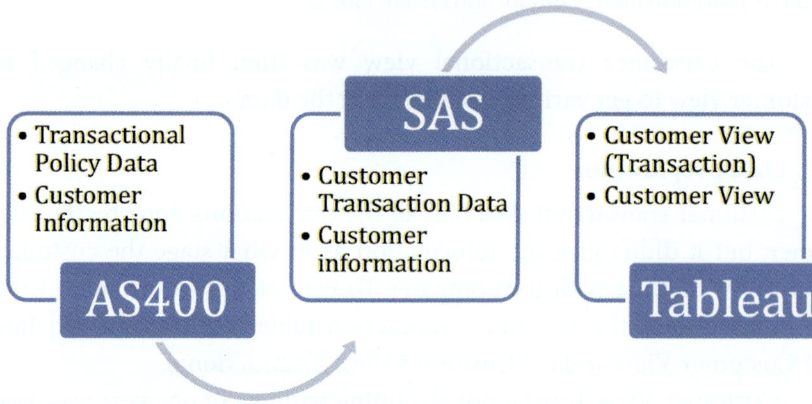

Figure 3: Database tables across different systems.

In Tableau many features were extracted to show in the form of Reports and Dashboards.

A) Year on year analysis (lapsed, existing, win-backs, new)

In this analysis, the year on year changes in the number of new, lapsed, win-back, and existing customers.

These analyses were further drilled down by LOB and distribution channel. Here, Period is defined as the period of study with respect to which lapsed, new, existing and win-back were calculated. Lapsed customers were defined as those who have lapsed all of their policy in the period and have left the Insurance Company. New customers are those who have joined for the first time in the company.

Existing customers are those who are in-force both at the start and end of the periods. Win-back are those customers who lapsed all of their policies previously in some period but are joining back again.

The overall analysis as shown in Figure 4, shows the number of new customers joining the company is decreasing but the number of existing customers is increasing. This indicates that although retention of the customer is good but Singapore insurance market has now become saturated. Also, interesting to see is the number of win-backs that increased steadily. These are the customers who came back after leaving the company.

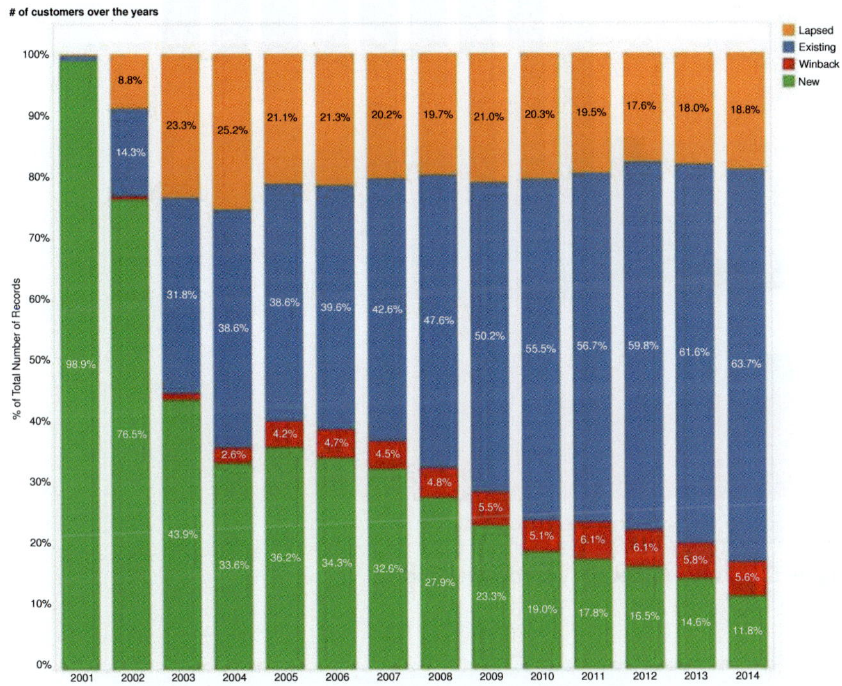

Figure 4: Number of lapse, win-back, existing, and new customers.

A further drilling down the LOB provided following insights.

In case of Motor policy, as shown in Figure 5, the number of win-backs is higher than any other LOB. This indicates that (1) motor comprises majority of the portfolio and (2) those coming back are the customers whose COE expired and they bought a new car.

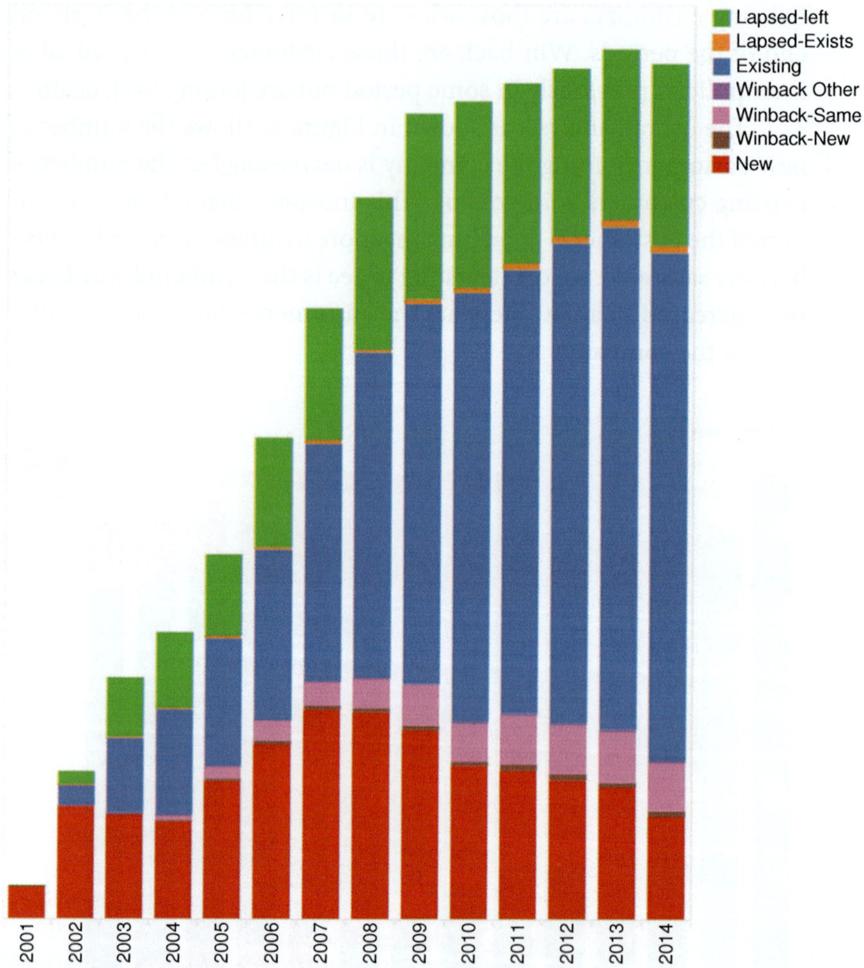

Figure 5: Number of people year on year–motor.

When compared with customers from home insurance segment, as shown in Figure 6, an apparent change in the behavior of the customers can be seen. Home insurance customers tend to be more loyal and have higher retention rate when compared to other LOBs. But in terms of win-backs, most are *win-back–new*, i.e., they come in this LOB from other lines. On further analysis, it can be seen that motor customers are the ones who start to cross-sell in home insurance LOB.

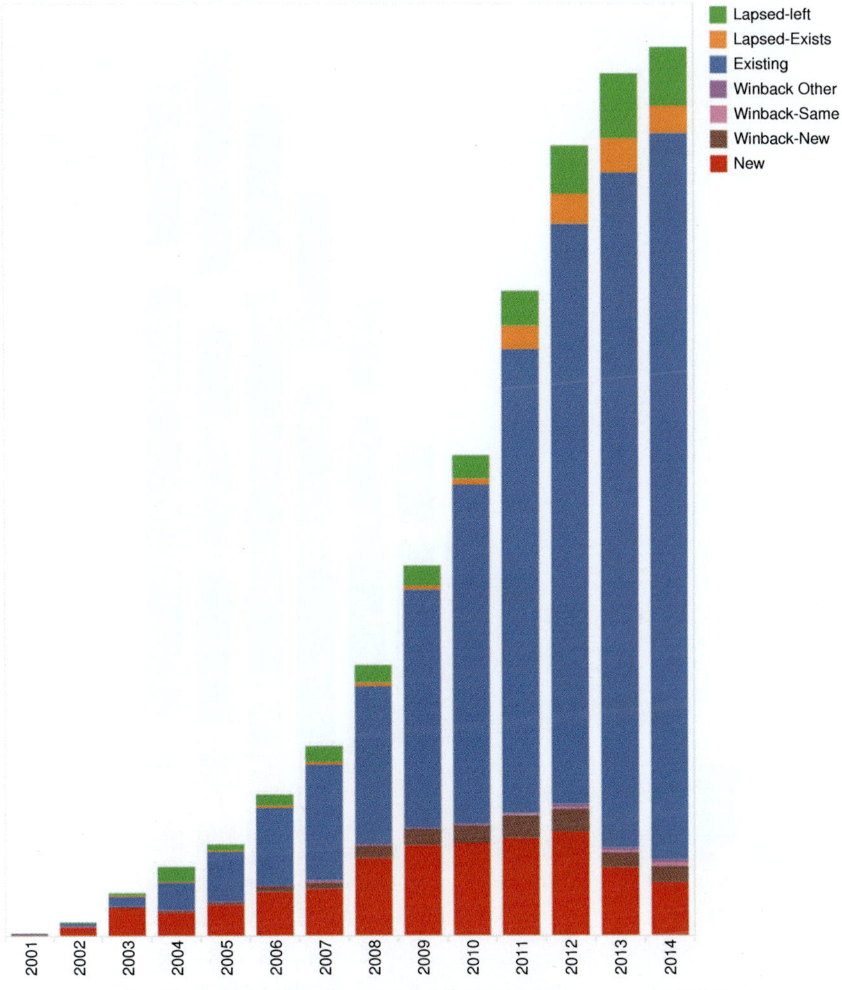

Figure 6: Number of people year on year–home insurance.

Similarly as shown in Figure 7, customers who lapsed travel-annual but still continue are significant than other businesses. travel-annual customers are those who have propensity to cross-sell with other LOBs.

In drilling down by distribution channel (as shown in Figure 8), the fact that majority of the customers come from agents can be verified, but what is interesting to note is that the number of new customer joining through agents is decreasing, whereas the number of customer joining through the partner bank is increasing (Figure 8).

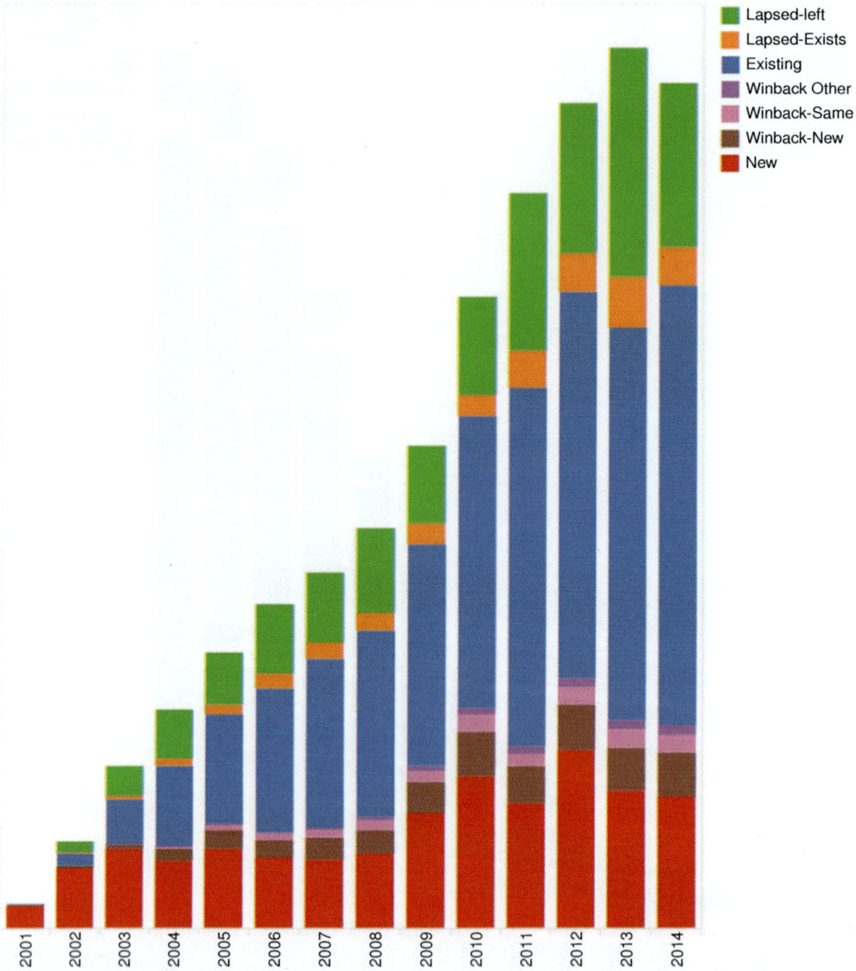

Figure 7: Number of people (lapse, win-back, new, existing) travel-annual.

Similarly, the number of customers coming through direct channel is increasing. What was also interesting to find is that the number of customers lapsing through private banks lower compared to other businesses.

B) Analysis on the new customers joining the company

In this analysis, only the new customers joining the company each year is studied.

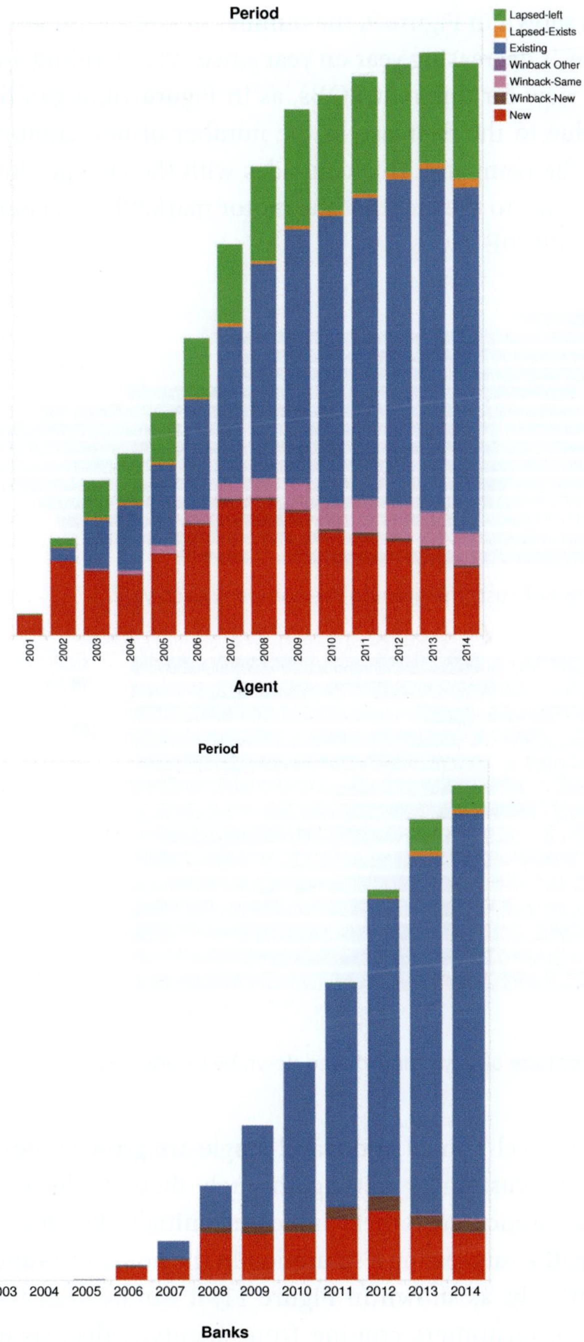

Figure 8: Number of people through agents and partner banks.

As shown in Figure 9, the number of new customers joining the company is decreasing year on year since 2008. Drilling down further on this view for different LOBs, as in Figure 10, it can be seen that this is due to the decrease in the number of new motor customers joining the company. This coincides with the changes in COE laws, which points to the fact that the motor market has become saturated because of COE laws.

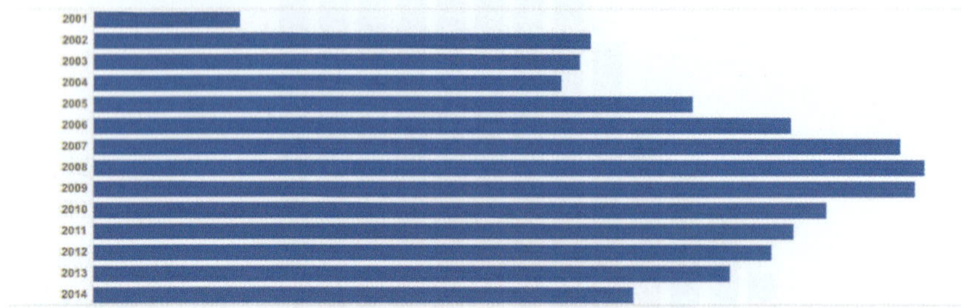

Figure 9: Number of customer joining the company each year.

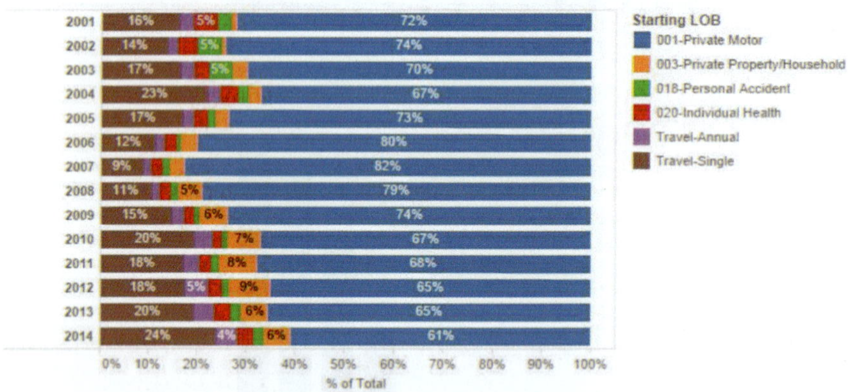

Figure 10: Percentage of customers drilled down by businesses.

The travel-annual and travel-single are growing portfolios and number of customers joining through these LOBs is increasing. Home insurance customers increased initially but have started to decrease, this suggesting a saturation in the home insurance markets.

Similarly, as shown in Figure 11, it can be seen that the percentage of customers coming from agents is decreasing whereas percentage of customers coming through partner banks and direct

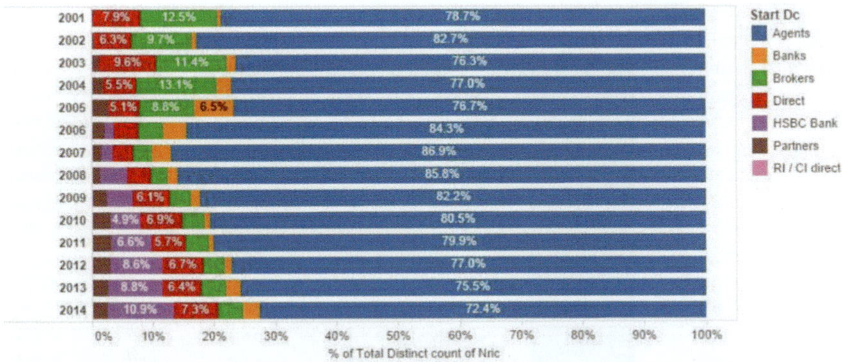

Figure 11: Percentage of customers drilled down by DC.

channel are increasing. Direct channel, including those coming through online, has shown a steady growth and will continue to grow in near future as more and more customers, with the help of internet, will buy policies online.

Upon further analysis of where these new customers are coming from, by using segmentation groups, it can be seen that most of the customers come through segmentation groups G and F, as shown in Figure 12.

Figure 13 shows that the customer group B is more likely to buy individual health policy than other groups. Thus marketing campaigns can target customer segment B for individual health policies. Similarly, customer segment B is more likely to buy travel-single

	Start Date					
Mosaic Group	2010	2011	2012	2013	2014	2015
A	3.06%	3.21%	3.67%	3.25%	2.99%	2.60%
B	6.02%	6.22%	6.23%	6.62%	6.31%	6.13%
E	7.92%	8.05%	8.24%	8.45%	8.61%	9.45%
C	9.86%	10.87%	11.38%	9.74%	9.52%	7.96%
I	11.28%	10.37%	10.19%	10.32%	9.80%	10.22%
D	11.90%	11.86%	11.79%	11.75%	11.64%	12.02%
H	13.10%	12.75%	12.57%	12.70%	12.26%	12.21%
G	16.70%	16.51%	16.21%	17.15%	17.32%	17.22%
F	20.15%	20.16%	19.71%	20.02%	21.56%	22.19%

Figure 12: Number of people joining the company by segmentation group.

		001-Private Motor	003-Private Property/ Household	018-Personal Accident	020-Individual Health	Travel-Annual	Travel-Single
A	2010	60.13%	17.51%	0.76%	3.90%	7.71%	9.99%
	2014	62.28%	10.62%	0.40%	4.12%	9.03%	13.55%
B	2010	47.27%	14.32%	0.77%	12.53%	7.40%	17.71%
	2014	43.58%	8.05%	1.26%	12.58%	10.88%	23.65%
C	2010	64.51%	10.29%	1.27%	2.72%	4.94%	16.27%
	2014	53.84%	6.84%	1.04%	4.67%	7.21%	26.40%
D	2010	63.45%	13.10%	0.98%	2.03%	4.68%	15.76%
	2014	61.18%	7.74%	0.82%	2.97%	4.98%	22.32%
E	2010	62.75%	5.16%	0.66%	1.33%	3.72%	26.38%
	2014	59.56%	4.65%	2.16%	1.57%	4.24%	27.82%
F	2010	72.98%	4.54%	1.14%	0.67%	2.30%	18.36%
	2014	65.64%	3.37%	3.02%	1.49%	2.56%	23.93%
G	2010	75.13%	3.49%	0.94%	0.75%	2.08%	17.60%
	2014	65.50%	3.83%	2.86%	2.15%	2.20%	23.46%
H	2010	75.89%	3.72%	0.67%	0.36%	1.54%	17.84%
	2014	65.44%	3.69%	2.69%	2.17%	2.11%	23.91%
I	2010	67.23%	5.50%	0.90%	0.59%	2.87%	22.90%
	2014	59.64%	4.98%	2.31%	1.99%	3.89%	27.19%

Figure 13: Number of people joining the company by segmentation group in each LOB.

policies than travel-annual policy and hence should be targeted when campaigning for new travel-single schemes/policies.

When analyzing the customers on the basis of their age and starting LOBs, Figure 14 shows that among all the LOBs except travel-single more than 50 per cent of the customers are in the age

	Start Lob					
Age (bin)	001-Private Motor	003-Private Property/ Household	018-Personal Accident	020-Individual Health	Travel-An..	Travel-Si..
10	0.04%	0.05%	1.26%	1.15%	1.75%	3.86%
20	18.04%	6.03%	19.17%	27.37%	18.66%	27.09%
30	34.23%	33.76%	29.07%	38.23%	30.64%	25.07%
40	26.32%	30.70%	29.12%	20.99%	22.94%	17.02%
50	16.55%	17.77%	17.29%	9.76%	14.40%	13.89%
60	4.44%	7.68%	3.98%	2.43%	7.91%	8.38%
70	0.35%	3.05%	0.11%	0.08%	3.19%	3.81%
80	0.03%	0.90%			0.49%	0.82%
90	0.00%	0.07%			0.01%	0.05%

Figure 14: Age vs starting LOB.

group of 30–50 years, but in travel-single more than 50 per cent of customers are in the age group of 20–40 years. This means that compared to older people younger people tend to buy travel-single policies. Travel–single are one-time travel policies and hence this is intuitive as mostly young people who travel less, buy one time travel policy for single trips.

Similarly, when drilling down by gender with respect to LOB as in Figure 15, it reveals that mostly men buy Motor and home insurance policies but in case of travel-single, more females than males buy the policies. This is due to traditional reasons that motor and home insurance are generally in the name of husbands/fathers.

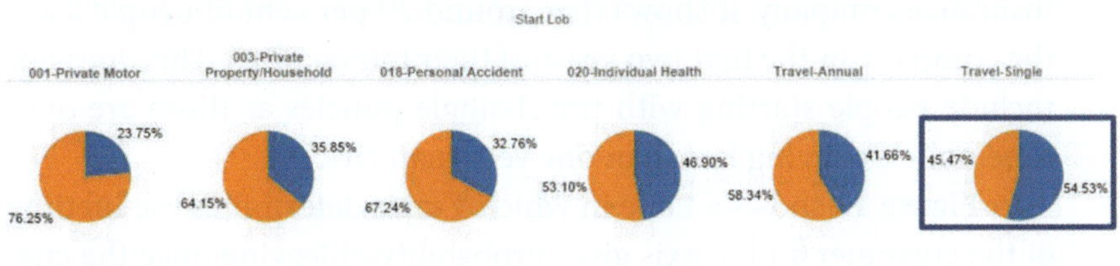

Figure 15: Gender vs starting LOB.

Age (bin)	Cltsex	001-Private Motor	003-Private Property/ Household	018- Personal Accident	020- Individual Health	Travel-An..	Travel-Si..
				Start Lob			
10	F	9.23%	28.57%	48.18%	61.33%	53.95%	55.36%
	M	90.77%	71.43%	51.82%	38.67%	46.05%	44.64%
20	F	20.09%	34.65%	44.78%	54.06%	52.33%	57.91%
	M	79.91%	65.35%	55.22%	45.94%	47.67%	42.09%
30	F	25.14%	32.41%	34.61%	45.64%	39.94%	51.19%
	M	74.86%	67.59%	65.39%	54.36%	60.06%	48.81%
40	F	25.48%	35.36%	26.80%	42.73%	33.19%	52.60%
	M	74.52%	64.64%	73.20%	57.27%	66.81%	47.40%
50	F	23.64%	39.21%	26.80%	40.31%	39.49%	55.93%
	M	76.36%	60.79%	73.20%	59.69%	60.51%	44.07%
60	F	18.41%	40.72%	26.44%	42.41%	47.13%	54.48%
	M	81.59%	59.28%	73.56%	57.59%	52.87%	45.52%
70	F	20.45%	43.43%	20.00%	30.00%	45.78%	54.50%
	M	79.55%	56.57%	80.00%	70.00%	54.22%	45.50%
80	F	27.66%	53.79%			45.31%	57.35%
	M	72.34%	46.21%			54.69%	42.65%
90	F	40.00%	63.64%				68.57%
	M	60.00%	36.36%			100.00%	31.43%

Figure 16: Analysis by age, gender and LOB.

This makes travel-single policies unique as they are bought by more females than males across all age groups.

Similarly, young people health, travel and personal accident policies are also bought by females. This is due to lifestyle changes, as Females are becoming more independent and buying policies for themselves apart from traditional ways through their husbands or parents. Also, Females buying more travel and personal accident policy tends to indicate that they are more responsible than their male counterparts for safety and security.

C) Analysis on the basis of leaving Company

When analyzing the lifetime after which the customer leaves the insurance company, it shows that around 29 per cent of people leave the company in the first two years of their interactions. This does not include people starting with travel-single policies as those are one-time policies having less than one year maturity.

Figure 17 shows a table in which *Y*-axis determines the lifetime of the customer and *X*-axis gives probability of leaving once the customer has stayed in the company for more than *y* number of years, i.e., each row defines the probability of leaving for a customer who has survived *y* years. For example, the table shows that if a person survived for two years (given by *Y*-axis) in the insurance company, his probability of leaving will be 18.7 per cent in the next year, and 12.59 per cent in the next year, and so on.

If narrowed to these particular LOB, Figure 18 and Figure 19 show that home insurance customers have the lowest probability of leaving in contrast to travel-annual customers who have the highest probability of leaving of around 60 per cent. Also, Individual health customers have above average probability of leaving.

	0	1	2	3	4	5	6	7	8	9	10	11	12	13	14
0	4.73%	25.20%	11.48%	7.72%	5.12%	3.72%	2.67%	2.00%	1.44%	1.08%	0.78%	0.52%	0.30%	0.06%	0.00%
1	27.77%	12.84%	8.51%	5.64%	4.10%	2.94%	2.20%	1.59%	1.19%	0.86%	0.58%	0.33%	0.07%	0.00%	
2	18.71%	12.59%	8.35%	6.07%	4.35%	3.26%	2.36%	1.76%	1.28%	0.85%	0.49%	0.11%	0.00%		
3	16.83%	11.16%	8.11%	5.82%	4.36%	3.15%	2.35%	1.71%	1.14%	0.66%	0.14%	0.03%			
4	14.67%	10.66%	7.65%	5.73%	4.14%	3.09%	2.25%	1.50%	0.67%	0.18%	0.00%				
5	13.73%	9.85%	7.38%	5.33%	3.97%	2.89%	1.93%	1.12%	0.24%	0.01%					
6	12.71%	9.52%	6.67%	5.13%	3.73%	2.49%	1.44%	0.31%	0.01%						
7	12.78%	9.23%	6.88%	5.01%	3.34%	1.94%	0.41%	0.01%							
8	12.31%	9.18%	6.60%	4.45%	2.59%	0.55%	0.01%								
9	12.72%	9.26%	6.17%	3.58%	0.78%	0.02%									
10	13.58%	9.05%	5.25%	1.12%	0.03%										
11	13.36%	7.76%	1.85%	0.04%											

Figure 17: Probability of leaving the company in next *N* years if person has survived *x* years.

	0	1	2	3	4	5	6	7	8	9	10	11	12	13
1	11.49%	25.32%	11.02%	6.06%	3.69%	2.86%	2.09%	1.80%	1.28%	1.19%	0.94%	0.65%	0.39%	0.14%
2	30.40%	13.22%	7.27%	4.44%	3.43%	2.51%	2.16%	1.53%	1.42%	1.12%	0.78%	0.47%	0.17%	
3	20.94%	11.52%	7.02%	5.43%	3.97%	3.43%	2.43%	2.25%	1.78%	1.24%	0.74%	0.27%		
4	15.84%	9.66%	7.48%	5.47%	4.71%	3.34%	3.10%	2.45%	1.71%	1.01%	0.38%			
5	12.47%	9.65%	7.06%	6.08%	4.31%	4.00%	3.16%	2.21%	1.31%	0.49%				
6	11.72%	8.57%	7.39%	5.24%	4.86%	3.83%	2.68%	1.59%	0.59%					
7	10.257%	8.840%	6.266%	5.819%	4.588%	3.208%	1.902%	0.709%						
8	10.852%	7.692%	7.143%	5.632%	3.938%	2.335%	0.870%							
9	9.556%	8.874%	6.997%	4.892%	2.901%	1.081%								
10	10.811%	8.524%	5.960%	3.534%	1.317%									
11	11.031%	7.713%	4.574%	1.704%										

Start I

Figure 18: Probability of leaving for people starting health.

	0	1	2	3	4	5	6	7	8	9	10	11	12
0	2.37%	37.03%	9.74%	5.32%	3.11%	2.27%	1.58%	1.38%	0.83%	0.62%	0.66%	0.48%	0.24%
1	42.13%	11.08%	6.06%	3.54%	2.58%	1.79%	1.58%	0.94%	0.71%	0.76%	0.54%	0.27%	0.07%
2	21.96%	12.00%	7.01%	5.12%	3.55%	3.12%	1.87%	1.40%	1.50%	1.08%	0.53%	0.14%	
3	16.98%	9.92%	7.24%	5.03%	4.42%	2.64%	1.98%	2.12%	1.53%	0.75%	0.20%		
4	13.24%	9.66%	6.71%	5.89%	3.52%	2.64%	2.83%	2.04%	1.00%	0.27%			
5	12.39%	8.61%	7.56%	4.52%	3.39%	3.62%	2.61%	1.29%	0.35%				
6	11.33%	9.94%	5.95%	4.46%	4.77%	3.43%	1.69%	0.46%					
7	12.51%	7.48%	5.61%	6.00%	4.32%	2.13%	0.58%						
8	9.477%	7.108%	7.598%	5.474%	2.696%	0.735%							
9	8.969%	9.588%	6.907%	3.402%	0.928%								
10	12.24%	8.82%	4.34%	1.18%									
11	12.38%	6.10%	1.66%										

Figure 19: Probability of leaving for people starting travel-annual.

D) Cross-selling potential and segmentation analysis

When analyzing people in a particular LOB in terms of their lifetime with the insurance company, it can be seen that when they start to cross-sell with other LOBs gives the following results.

In terms of percentage, people starting with a home insurance policy (Figure 20) tend to cross-sell more than people starting with

Years in AXA	%Health-..	%Motor-H..	%TravelS..	%Travela-..	%pa-HOM..	% of Home Cross S..
1	6.2%	74.9%	2.6%	15.2%	6.7%	5.8%
2	5.7%	79.9%	2.8%	13.2%	6.0%	7.6%
3	4.9%	81.9%	3.6%	12.5%	5.8%	9.2%
4	4.9%	81.7%	4.3%	13.1%	6.2%	10.7%
5	4.1%	82.3%	5.6%	14.1%	6.8%	11.5%
6	3.7%	84.4%	6.0%	15.4%	7.2%	12.6%
7	4.7%	80.1%	7.5%	15.8%	8.5%	14.6%
8	4.5%	79.2%	9.4%	14.7%	9.8%	15.3%
9	7.7%	78.7%	9.8%	15.3%	13.7%	18.6%
10	5.1%	76.8%	9.4%	13.8%	13.8%	20.6%
11	3.8%	86.1%	3.8%	12.7%	19.0%	18.9%
12	10.3%	79.3%	10.3%	24.1%	10.3%	24.0%
13	11.1%	66.7%	22.2%	22.2%	11.1%	25.0%

Figure 20: Home insurance cross-seller.

other lines of business, and they cross-sell mostly with motor policy. Those starting with personal accidents policy, tend to cross-sell more with health policy in early days of their lifetime, but in the later stages they cross-sell more with motor policy.

Similarly, percentage of people starting with motor policy and then cross-selling is less in the initial years, due to the fact that there are more motor customers. So the percentage of motor customer is low (Figure 21).

When analyzing the cross-sellers with respect to customer segmentation as in Figure 22, it shows that customer segments A, C, P have higher percentage of cross-selling and can be used further for targeting.

When analyzing on the geography of Singapore from where customers are coming from, Figure 23 shows that the home insurance customers are mostly concentrated in central Singapore. They are generally well-to-do high-class families or expatriates. Whereas

Years in AXA	%Health-PA	%Home-PA	%Motor-PA	%TravelS-..	%Travela-..	cross sellers t..
1	41%	12.6%	38.0%	4.6%	12.0%	8.4%
2	27%	17.1%	50.6%	5.7%	8.7%	9.9%
3	22%	18.0%	55.2%	6.2%	10.5%	11.4%
4	19%	20.4%	55.0%	6.7%	10.9%	12.2%
5	17%	22.9%	55.8%	4.8%	11.9%	13.1%
6	15%	24.4%	58.2%	5.1%	10.2%	13.4%
7	16%	23.8%	57.9%	5.6%	9.3%	13.4%
8	16%	24.7%	55.2%	5.7%	10.3%	13.4%
9	15%	22.9%	59.0%	6.3%	9.0%	12.1%
10	11%	22.3%	61.5%	6.9%	9.2%	12.1%
11	12%	21.4%	62.5%	5.4%	10.7%	11.8%
12	13%	29.8%	57.4%	4.3%	14.9%	14.6%
13	29%	57.1%	42.9%	0.0%	0.0%	19.4%

Figure 21: PA cross-seller.

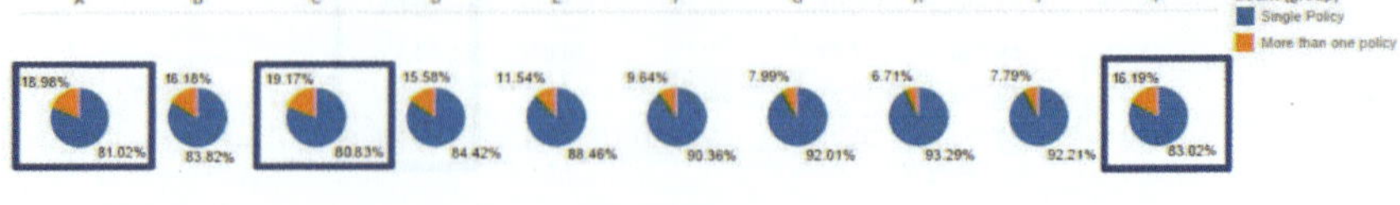

Figure 22: Customer segments vs number of policies.

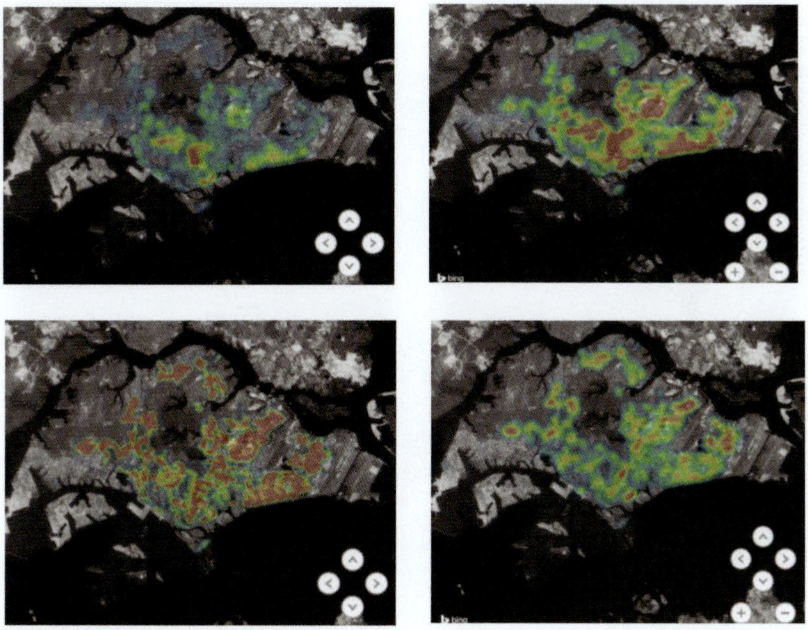

Figure 23: Heat map of customers in different LOBs.
(a) Home insurance customers heat map
(b) Travel-annual customer heat map
(c) Motor customers' heat map
(d) PA customers' heat map

in case of personal accident, customers are concentrated more on the periphery of Singapore in the east, west, and north. These are the customers who travel to the central business district often for work. Travel-annual customers on the other hand are more concentrated in the central, north-eastern and east Singapore. They are generally those customers who travel offshore frequently, for example, expatriates or business people.

Motor customers on the other hand are unique and spread throughout the Singapore in various areas. They cover majority of the company's portfolio and are concentrated throughout Singapore.

When further analyzing different LOBs by the customer segmentation group, the penetrations of different LOBs in each segmentation groups can be seen. For example, when conducting a narrow down to central Singapore where most of the customer segment A and C live, Figure 24 shows that home insurance customers are mostly situated

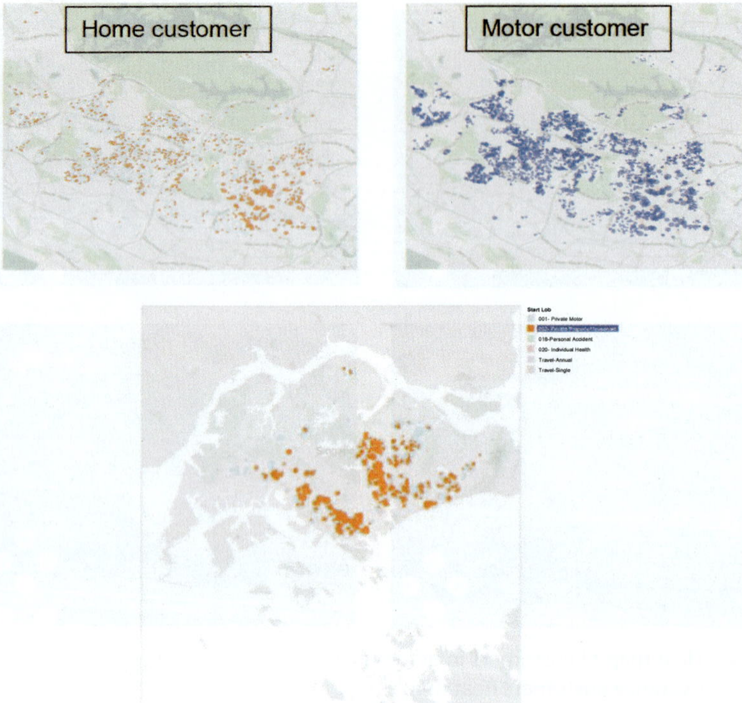

Figure 24: (a) Customer penetration of home insurance and (b) motor in central Singapore. (c) Customer penetration of household customers in segment C.

in the central right whereas motor customers are concentrated more to the central left. It can be argued that more aggressive campaigning should be done for the customers in central right for motor policies and for motor customers on central left for home insurance policies.

Similarly, Figure 24 shows the penetration of household customers in the customer segment C. Though all the segment C customers are similar in their characteristics, the penetration of home insurance customers is low in east and north east of Singapore, and in the future, campaigns for the agents to sell more home insurance policies in those areas could be devised.

E) Home Insurance Cross-sellers with Motor Policy

In this analysis, active home insurance customers were used and tried to find inherent rules which differentiate customers who cross-sells home insurance policy with motor policy, and those who do not.

Here active customers are those who as on 31 May 2015 hold a policy with the company.

The following descriptive analysis was used to see the effect of various variables. The effect of lifetime (time spent with the company), as evident from Figure 25, shows that the percentage of people cross-selling home insurance policy with motor policy increases along with the loyalty. Figure 26 shows that the customer having

	%Health-..	%Motor-H..	%TravelS..	%Travela-..	%pa-HOM..
1	6.2%	74.9%	2.6%	15.2%	6.7%
2	5.7%	79.9%	2.8%	13.2%	6.0%
3	4.9%	81.9%	3.6%	12.5%	5.8%
4	4.9%	81.7%	4.3%	13.1%	6.2%
5	4.1%	82.3%	5.6%	14.1%	6.8%
6	3.7%	84.4%	6.0%	15.4%	7.2%
7	4.7%	80.1%	7.5%	15.8%	8.5%
8	4.5%	79.2%	9.4%	14.7%	9.8%
9	7.7%	78.7%	9.8%	15.3%	13.7%
10	5.1%	76.8%	9.4%	13.8%	13.8%
11	3.8%	86.1%	3.8%	12.7%	19.0%
12	10.3%	79.3%	10.3%	24.1%	10.3%
13	11.1%	66.7%	22.2%	22.2%	11.1%

Figure 25 Home insurance cross-sellers by lifetime.

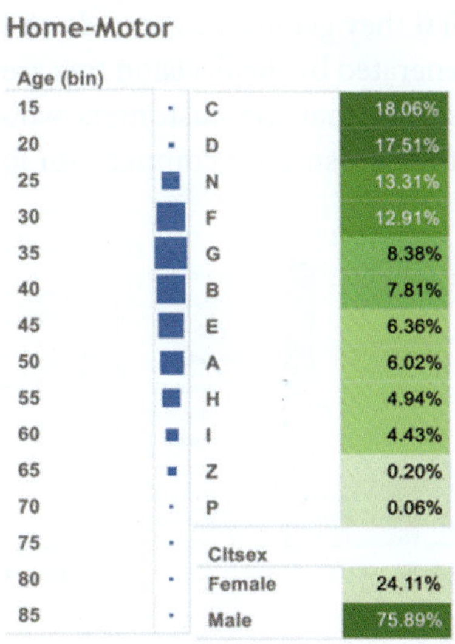

Figure 26: Home insurance cross-sellers by age, sex, and segmentation group.

home insurance and motor policies are in the age group of 30–45, and come from customer segmentation group C and D. Most of them are males because traditionally these policies are bought by males in the households.

Along with those discussed above, the following variables were taken for the classification model: (1) Total GWP contributed/year: This is total yearly GWP given by a customer to the insurance company. (2) Loyalty: This is the number of years the customer remained active. (3) Age group: This defines the year span the customer fits in. (4) Customer segmentation: This defines the customer segmentation group for each customer. (5) Number of policies in different LOBs. (6) Starting distribution channel.

Using Random Forest and Rule Fit, it was possible to find the importance of variables in determining the classification. Figures 25 and 26 show the most important features which determine whether or not a person will cross-sell with motor policies are: (1) yearly GWP contribution, (2) loyalty, and (3) segmentation group.

This means that more premium a customer gives to the company, more loyal she is, and if she belongs to certain segmentation group then she is more likely to buy motor policy along with a home insurance policy. Also, starting distribution channel was significant, which points to the fact that agents and brokers can help the company to cross-sell if they get incentives to do so (Figure 27).

The rules generated by the decision tree are as follows:

Figure 28 shows that the customers who have higher GWP and who stay with the insurance company for longer are more likely

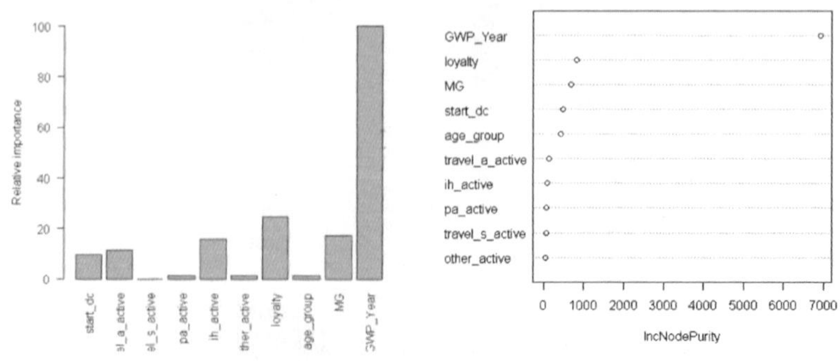

Figure 27: Importance of the variables.

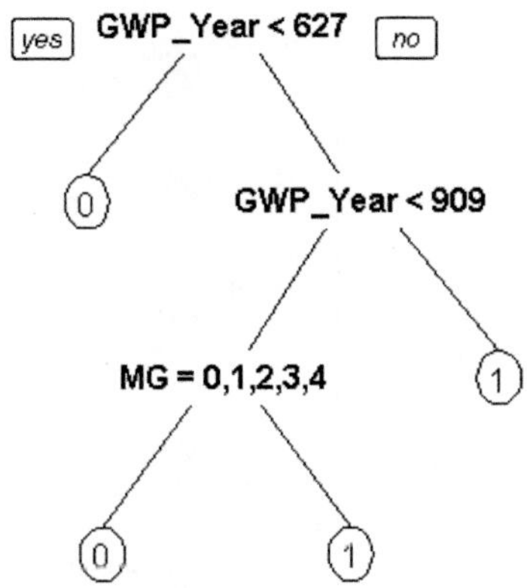

Figure 28: Decision tree for cross-selling.

to cross-sell, as well as those who come from customer segments 0, 1, 2, 3, 4.

Drawbacks: These variables are only able to explain 45.65 per cent of the variance and hence new features needs to be identified to explain more variance in the data. In addition, since GWP is on two nodes, it indicates a linear relationship, and that a linear model like GLM would yield better results.

Future studies should analyze the claims taken by the policy holder before cross-selling which might be another significant factor in the analysis.

Customers who leave within first two years

A large number of customers leave the insurance company within the first two years. To see what affects this behavior, several factors were analyzed.

Data used in this model was the policy and claims transaction data of all customers in the first two years of their interaction. All the customers who joined after May 2013 were removed from the data. For other customers only the first two years of policy and claims transaction data was taken into account.

To see which factors might play an important role in the classification, following descriptive analysis was done on the variables.

As shown in Figure 29, when analyzing gender vs LOB of the customers who stayed vs those who left, it can be seen that few LOBs

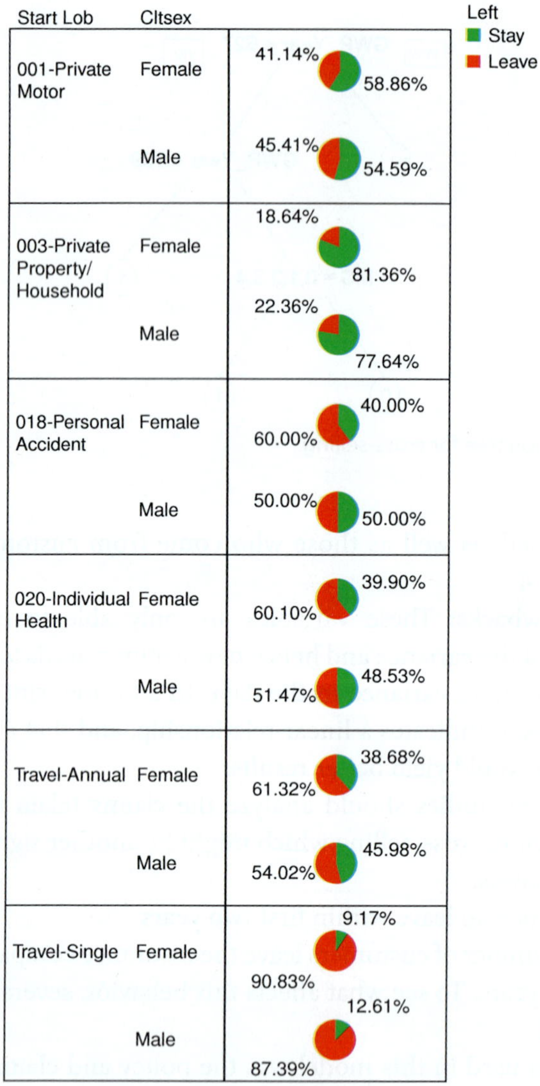

Figure 29: LOB vs gender vs probability of leaving.

such as home insurance are very stable whereas people joining from travel-annual and travel–single have very low retention. Females seem to be more stable in private motor and household, i.e., they are less likely to leave compared to males in general. Whereas an opposite trend is seen in personal accident policy, in which females are more likely to leave than males.

When examining the effect of age on the probability of a person leaving, as shown below, it shows that younger and older people have higher probabilities of leaving than middle-aged people. This implies that young people buy those policies which have lower retentions like travel-single, or this might be due to the fact that they are cross–shoppers and buy insurances from various different outlets. The probability of a person leaving also increases with the age. This might be due to the fact that they die during the policy term and are not actually leaving the company (Figure 30).

When the effects of age, gender, and LOB are combined as in Figure 31, it can be seen that home insurance customers have higher

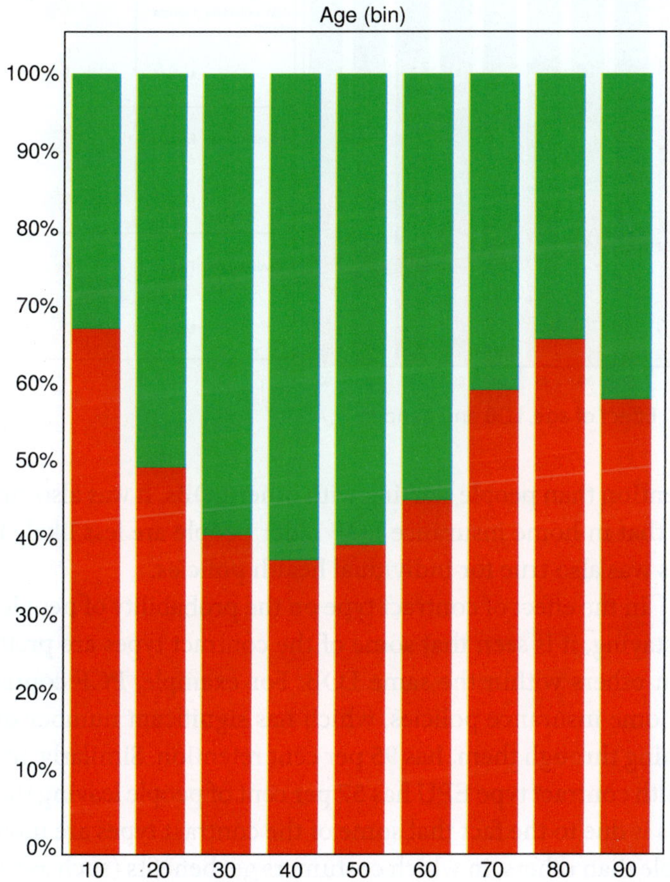

Figure 30: Effect of age on probability of leaving.

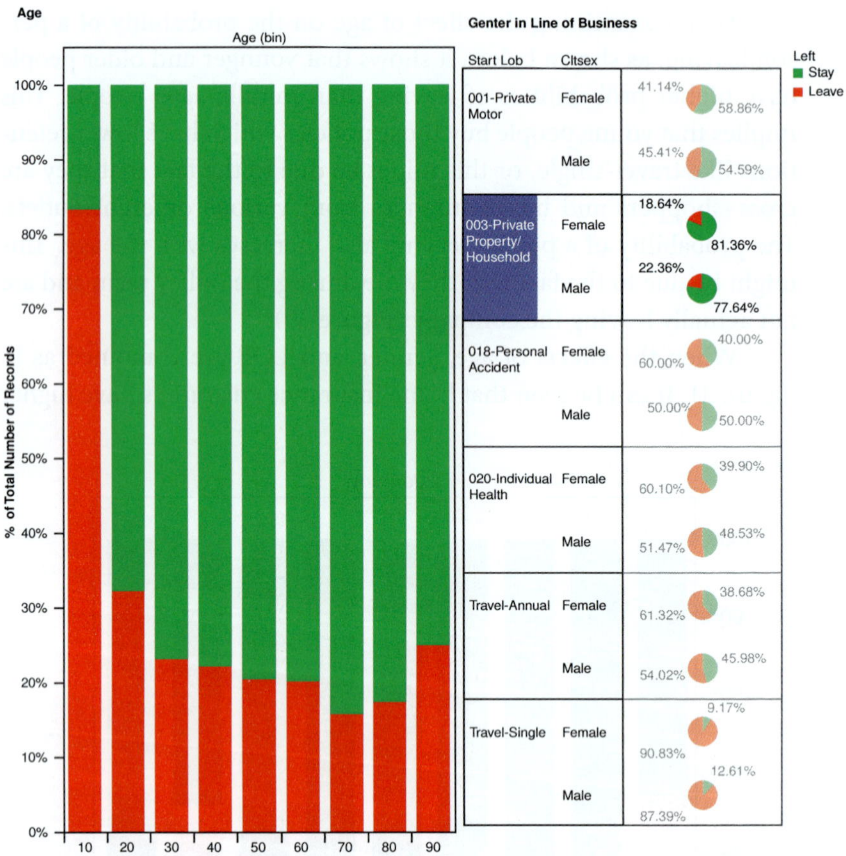

Figure 31: Effect of age, LOB and gender.

retention than people starting with other LOBs. It was also striking to see that in home insurance LOB older people are less likely to leave. This was also true for individual health policies.

In the effect of contract type on the probability of people leaving or staying, it is seen that some of the contract types are pretty stable than others within the same LOB. For example, PCF contract type in home insurance policies, which has significant number of people joining through them, has 95 per cent retention. Similarly, individual health contract type EPU has 57 per cent of people leaving through it. This is due to the fact that some of the contract types are intrinsically stable than others, in which costumers get benefits (such as reduction in GWP) if they stay long term with the policy (Figure 32).

Start Lob	Start Cnttype	Left: Stay	Left: Leave
001-Private Motor	VA1	98.02%	1.98%
	VA2	97.96%	2.04%
	VA3	98.31%	1.69%
	VMO	57.07%	42.93%
	VMX	53.64%	46.36%
	VMZ	54.05%	45.95%
	VPA	62.62%	37.38%
	VPB	58.74%	41.26%
	VPC	54.62%	45.38%
	VPX	66.05%	33.95%
003-Private Property/ Household	PBA	58.33%	41.67%
	PBP	25.00%	75.00%
	PCF	94.32%	5.68%
	PFF	85.00%	15.00%
	PFM	100.00%	
	PFO	100.00%	
	PMZ	66.67%	33.33%
	SH1	53.66%	46.34%
	SHD	87.80%	12.20%
	SHH	68.00%	32.00%
	SHL	100.00%	
	SHO		100.00%
	SHP	68.70%	31.30%
	SHQ	72.25%	27.75%
	SHT	93.95%	6.05%
018-Personal Accident	ACI	67.68%	32.32%
	APE	60.78%	39.22%
	APG	66.67%	33.33%
	ASP	92.80%	7.20%
	ASS	95.65%	4.35%
	SAG	100.00%	
	SAO	71.62%	28.38%
	SAP	64.24%	35.76%
	SAS	62.35%	37.65%
	SAT	57.14%	42.86%
020-Individual Health	500	80.00%	20.00%
	AHL	100.00%	
	AHO	100.00%	
	AHP	42.86%	57.14%
	AHQ	87.50%	12.50%
	AVA	100.00%	
	EOC	58.42%	41.58%
	EPU	43.46%	56.54%
	ESC	51.79%	48.21%
	HAP	50.11%	49.89%
	HBP	56.39%	43.61%
	HCA	60.00%	40.00%
	HCH	85.71%	14.29%
	HIG	36.54%	63.46%
	HOC	58.95%	41.05%
	HPC	54.84%	45.16%
	HPE	45.80%	54.20%
	HPJ	66.67%	33.33%
	HSP	76.68%	23.32%
	HSS	100.00%	
	IPR	77.78%	22.22%
	IPU	58.33%	41.67%
Travel-Annual	ST1	100.00%	
	STA	63.77%	36.23%
	STB	49.60%	50.40%
	STT	100.00%	
Travel-Single	ATP	31.70%	68.30%
	STC	32.95%	67.05%
	STS	56.93%	43.07%

Figure 32: Effect of contract types.

Similarly Figure 33 shows the effect of claim on the probability of customers' leaving or staying: those who received a claim have less chance of leaving than their counterparts. This is due to the fact that they have already been exposed to the services of the company and hence are less likely to leave.

Along with the factors listed above, various other features were captured and used in decision tree classification to determine the inherent rules that significantly define the people who leave the insurance company within first two years. Some of the features that were extracted are as follows: (1) number of policies in various LOBs, (2) number of claims taken in different LOBs, (3) age group, (4) segmentation group, (5) total GWP gain each year, and (6) GWP_R–A flag which captures whether the customer contributed to a raise in GWP in last two years (this raise might be due to addition of covers), and (7) GWP_D–A flag which captures whether the customer have faced a decrease in GWP.

Importance of Variables: The most important variable in determining whether a person leaves or stay in the insurance company include: (1) number of motor policy, (2) raise in GWP, (3) total GWP contribution yearly, (4) joining LOB, (5) number of home insurance policies, and (6) segmentation group (Figure 34).

Decision Tree:

If the customer has gained a raise in GWP, he won't leave the company. The Raise in GWP in the same policy is generally due to addition of covers to the policy, i.e., in the case of upselling. So if the same policy is upselled, the customers are less likely to leave. Hence, the suggestion that the company upsells more in the initial stages of the customer lifetime, as it not only increases the retention but eventually leads to profitability. Also, if the customer has bought more than one motor or home insurance policies, she is less likely to leave. The customers having more than one motor and home insurance policies

Claim	Stay	Leave
No Claim Taken	56.00%	44.00%
Claim Taken	63.77%	36.23%

Figure 33: Effect of claims.

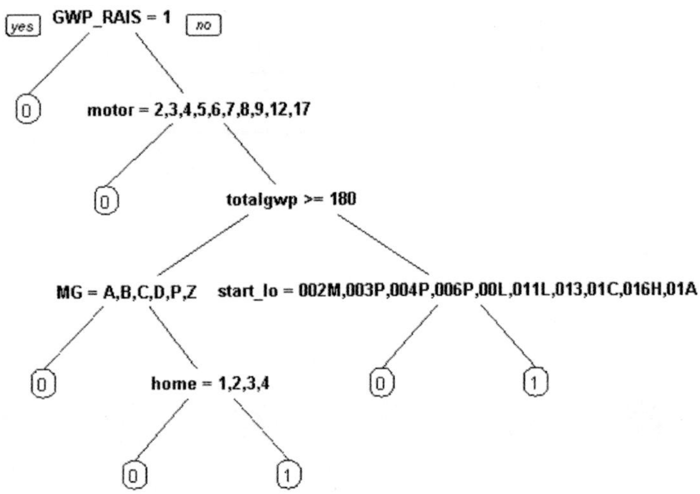

Figure 34: Decision tree for customers who leave within two years.

are special customers as they are generally more well-to-do and can be targeted to cross-sell other policies along with their initial policies.

F) Customers who stay for more than five years and those who left after five years

For analyzing these customers, only those who stayed within the company for more than five years were used, i.e., if the customer leave in between his/her sixth year then she is classified into one class and if she completes her sixth year then she is classified into another class.

When the people leaving after five years were analyzed, the percentage of people leaving is less than those for two years. People starting with home insurance and personal accident policies have 90 per cent retention as opposed to 87 per cent average retention for other polices and are less likely to go (Figure 35).

When analyzing this further by age of the person at the time of leaving, it can been seen that middle aged people are less likely to leave after five years compared to younger or elder people. Younger people might be potentially shopping from other shops (Insurance Company; Figure 36).

When analyzing by the number of polices a person holds across different LOBs, the probability of leaving remains the same, as shown in Figure 37. Hence, number of policies is not a good indicator of

Start Lob	Stayed	Left
001-Private Motor	85.56%	14.44%
003-Private Property/House..	90.40%	9.60%
018-Personal Accident	90.37%	9.63%
020-Individual Health	88.63%	11.37%
Travel-Annual	86.86%	13.14%
Travel-Single	87.71%	12.29%

Figure 35: Effect of LOB.

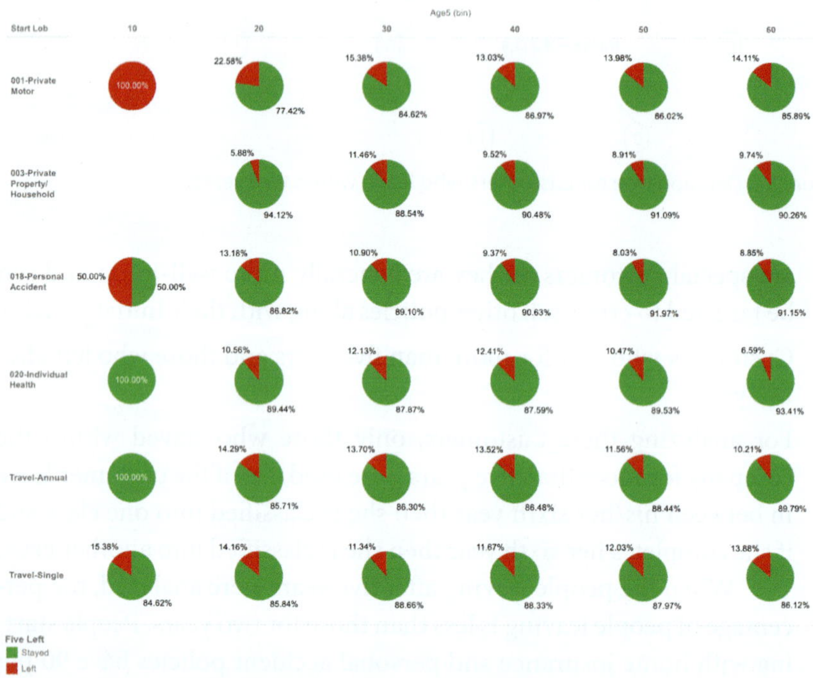

Figure 36: Effect of age and LOB.

whether the person will leave the company or not after five years. This is due to the fact that in five years the customer have had enough interactions and opportunities for cross-selling, and hence it does not have a significant effect on whether a person will leave or stay with the company if he has more than one policies. Something that might be overlooked is the fact that people starting with different LOBs might behave differently.

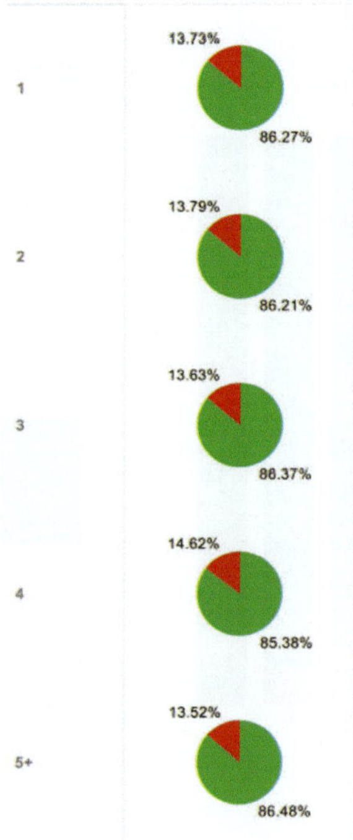

Figure 37: Effect of number of policies.

As shown in the Figure 38, the people in customer segment A and C are far less likely to go than the people in customer segments H and I. Customer segments A and C live in Central Singapore and generally belong to high class or expatriate families. These rich customers tend to shop around less than their counterparts.

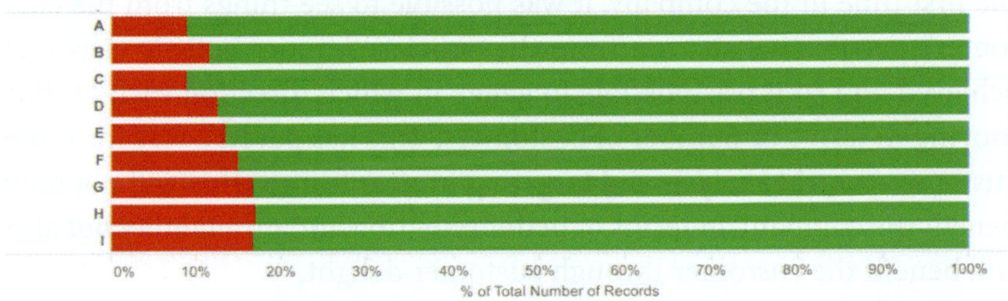

Figure 38: Effect of customer segmentation groups.

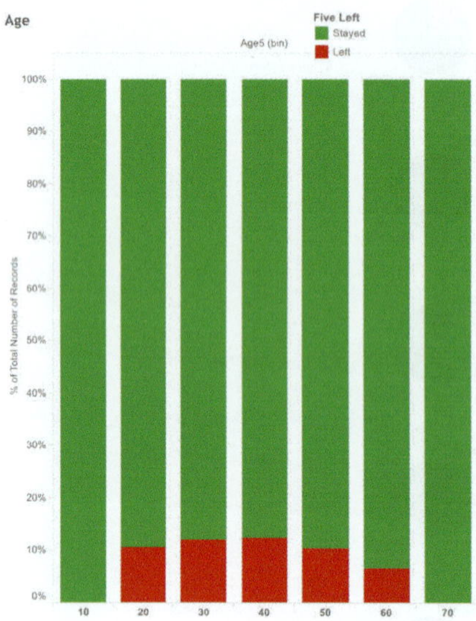

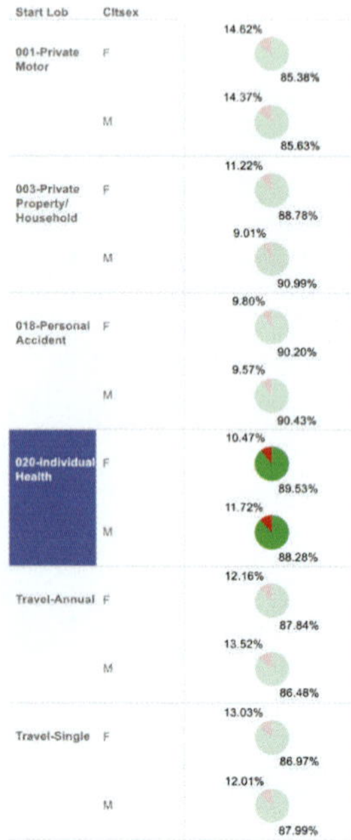

Combined effect of LOB and age on the people who are leaving shows that in individual health more people leave the company in the middle of age groups than in the earlier or later stages. Similarly in the private property/home insurance policy customers the reverse trend can be seen in which middle aged people are less likely to leave than their other counterparts.

5. DISCUSSION

This was the first step in a series to put customer first in the company. For the first time in the company, it was possible to see things from the customer's perspective and not from the policies. A more holistic view was achieved and so it was possible to gauge in which direction each LOB is moving in terms of number of customers. This has paved a way for more customer-centric analysis and targeting in near future. This will not only benefit the company in terms of better retention and profitability but also will benefit the customer through customer delight.

6. CONCLUSION AND FURTHER WORK

Through this analysis it was possible to dive deep into the customers of Insurance Company. The research revealed that the new customers joining the company are decreasing year on year though the overall customer portfolio is increasing. This indicates that the insurance market in Singapore is saturated but the retention of the Insurance Company is good. Some of the LOBs such as home insurance have better retention than other LOBs such as travel or individual health. This is mainly due to the type of contract types in home insurance which have higher time period of renewal than others. The analysis was also able to find that the home insurance customers are concentrated mainly in Central Singapore. The term Win-Back customers was coined for those who come back again to the Insurance Company after lapsing all their policies. These customers tend to be more loyal than their counterparts, and hence in future the company should campaign more to win-back its lost customers. Yearly gross written premium contributed by a person plays a significant role when cross-selling home insurance policies with motor policies. One of the key insights from the study was that upselling or adding of covers to an existing policy plays a significant role in determining whether a customer will leave or stay with the insurance company after initial few years of interactions. Hence the suggestion that the company upsell more for achieving better retention rates which will lead to better profitability and customer delight.

In the further work, the company should analyze the customer cross-selling potential through the use of credibility theory as mentioned in the "state-of-the-art" section. The company should also try to model customers as Markov chains to find the lifetime value of the customers and segment the customers on this basis. It will also help in gauging the new business values of the customers which will increase the profitability and lead to higher retention rate in the near future. Also, an analysis of win-back customers will determine the factors which affect to win them back.

REFERENCES

1. http://www.experian.co.uk/assets/about-us/white-papers/single-customer-view-whitepaper.pdf

2. http://statweb.stanford.edu/~jhf/ftp/RuleFit.pdf

3. http://statweb.stanford.edu/~jhf/R_RuleFit.html

4. https://www.stat.berkeley.edu/~breiman/RandomForests/cc_home.htm

5. http://recipp.ipp.pt/bitstream/10400.22/136/1/KDD-CRISP-SEMMA.pdf

6. ftp://public.dhe.ibm.com/software/analytics/spss/documentation/modeler/14.2/en/CRISP_DM.pdf

7. http://www.sciencedirect.com/science/article/pii/S0957417405001934

8. http://web.stanford.edu/class/msande121/Links/crmmodelingmarkov.pdf

9. http://www.actuaries.org/ASTIN/Colloquia/Madrid/Papers/Thuring.pdf

10. http://www.tableausoftware.com/learn/whitepapers

11. https://support.sas.com/training/

12. https://docs.python.org/2.7/

CHAPTER 14

Establishing the Liquidity Profile of Non-Maturity Demand Products

Vijayalakshmi Mulakalapalli

ABSTRACT

The Market Risk Management-Asset Liability team at OCBC wanted to develop an empirical methodology to establish the liquidity profile for non-maturity demand deposits. This study proposes to establish the weighted average maturity (WAM) and hence liquidity premium for non-maturity products in the OCBC commercial book. The existing methodology uses two different approaches based on balance trend while assuming normality to balance movements. Stochastic modeling of the historical balance data using Johnson distribution (to accommodate non-normality) and entropy optimization (to achieve global maxima) was used in the improved approach to correct these shortcomings. These two approaches, along with qualitative overlay for a few portfolios, form a robust alternative to the existing method.

1. INTRODUCTION

1.1. Objective

The OCBC Bank group of businesses comprises a family of companies owned by Singapore's longest-established local bank. OCBC Bank is the longest established Singapore bank, formed in 1932 from the merger of three local banks, the oldest of which was founded in 1912. It has been ranked by Bloomberg Markets magazine as the World's Strongest Bank for two years, 2011 and 2012. OCBC Bank operates its commercial banking business in 18 countries and territories. Its key markets are Singapore, Malaysia, Indonesia, and Greater China.

This project is centered on sound liquidity management practices to be implemented to strike the right balance between deposit behavior and lending/investment horizons. Liquidity refers to the ability of an institution to meet demands for funds. Liquidity management means ensuring that the institution maintains sufficient cash and liquid assets to satisfy client's demand for loans and savings withdrawals, and to pay the institution's expenses.

Asset-liability management (ALM) is continuously engaged in the process of monitoring asset and liability volumes, maturities, and rates in order to minimize interest rate risk and maintain an acceptable profitability level.

One of the main objectives of the bank is to avoid liquidity crunches so as not to fail on obligations, without incurring reputational or other significant losses. In order to achieve this goal, a sound risk management system needs to be in place. In particular, the focus of this study, non-maturity deposits play a major role in influencing the cash reserves of the bank. While bank balance sheets have a lot of flexibility to plan their investment horizons based on their liabilities payment cycle, this option is not available with non-maturing deposits (checking accounts, savings accounts, and money market accounts) which do not have a contractual maturity. On the other hand, these deposits constitute majority of the banking book balances, putting them on the forefront of liquidity management tasks. To add further to this complexity, behavior of account holders cannot be assumed to be the same across all types of accounts. They can be segmented based on multiple criterions such as customer size (individual, small and medium Enterprises, and large corp), sensitivity to interest rate (rate sensitive and insensitive), relationship with the bank, and so on.

The effect of these factors can manifest in different forms, such as:

- Individual customers can have an erratic deposit/withdrawal pattern, leaving the bank vulnerable in case of stressed market scenarios.
- Interest rate increments would drive more customers to withdraw from their accounts and invest in alternate channels.
- When the local market is competitive — competition usually reduces the margin between the interest rate charged on loans and the rate paid on deposits. In a competitive environment, the institution may not be able to increase rates earned on loans or lower the rate paid on deposits without affecting client demand and profitability of the institution.

The objective of this study is to suggest a suitable methodology to establish the liquidity runoff profile of non-maturity accounts to better understand and arrive at liquidity premium. By assuming 95 per cent confidence, this study aims to attain the maximum possible assertiveness in future cash reserves contributed by non-maturity deposits. This will also ensure conformity to the core calculations (done at 95 per cent confidence).

The extended scope of the study is as follows:

1) Customer segmentation into various cohorts. These cohorts are believed to behave from both a liquidity and interest rate perspective in a similar manner.
2) Establish a liquidity profile for each of these cohorts and translate it into a liquidity premium profile.

Data Availability: (see Table 1)

Table 1: Classification of data gathered.

Data granularity	Estimated data points	Issues
Every account end of day balance, going back three years	4.9 billion	No machine in MRM-ALM powerful enough to manage the data.

(continued)

Table 1: Classification of data gathered. (*continued*)

Data granularity	Estimated data points	Issues
Every account month end balance, going back three years	222 million	Not enough computational power to perform any calculations.
Cohorting approach (proposed)	69,000	Breaking up current and savings accounts (CASA) by: family/account_type/ segment/ currency, etc. This produces 585 possible permutations of "cohorts" into which CASA products could be placed. A combination of these 585 permutations was then agreed with each business.
Current core calculation methodology	396	Current core calculation methodology is based on 11 "cohorts" viewed over 36 month ends. $11 \times 36 = 396$.

Issues to achieve pragmatic outcomes: (see Table 2)

Table 2: Issues and narratives.

Issue	Narrative
Group similar customers together into a "cohort"	These customers are believed to statistically behave from both liquidity and interest rate perspectives in a similar manner.
Be agreed with the CFS/ GCB businesses	To be periodically updated to reflect the changing business nature over time, and how the different businesses view their customer relationships. This includes adapting the methodology to take account of balance sheet growth trends which might otherwise give "false volatility".

Issue	Narrative
Balance opposing factors	Qualitatively and quantitatively consider highly granular approaches (with associated high complexity and data intensity) with wider portfolio approaches (which are simpler to understand, but less defensible at the individual account level).
Ensure consistency	Ensure cohorts are treated in a coherent and consistent way between different risk reports, such as interest rate gaps. Pv01's economic value of equity sensitivities, etc.
Be flexible and practical	Ensure that the approach is able to accommodate likely specific circumstances and changes over time, and allow risk managers scope to agree practicalities with business managers
Be pragmatic and defensible	In terms of ease of understanding, audit trials, and statistical defense of outcomes

1.2. Existing methodology

The current methodology follows the approach given below to obtain liquidity profile of non-maturity deposit customers.

1) **Establishing cohorts of data**

- In order to establish the optimum approach to the liquidity analysis of CASA accounts, several practical aspects need to be considered:
  - Granularity of the data (account level/summarized)
  - Complexity of the calculation (highly complex, defensible at the account level/simplified approach).

  The study aims to balance these factors by collating CASA type products into "cohorts".
- First, review customer account breakdown by: position in GL, family (CFS/GCB), account type, product subtype, segment and currency
- Cohorts were created by grouping together customers who are believed to statistically behave from both liquidity and interest risk perspectives in a similar manner.

- This is a qualitative mapping exercise, bringing together similar accounts/segments/account types where their behavior is felt to be consistent, and/or no single pool of accounts dominates another in terms of volume.
- Splitting CASA: CASA and other non-maturity demand deposits were broken into three buckets:
  1) Noncore: Volume which could not be considered to be stable with the bank over an extended period of time.
  2) Core, rate sensitive: Volume which although stable over an extended period, was considered to be wholly price sensitive to changes in short-term wholesale rates.

These resulting cohorts were further validated with the business.

2) **Translating cohort volatility into a liquidity premium profile:** This is done as follows:
   - Calculate a simple standard deviation of the cohort and last observation to be used as the mean.
   - Discuss any clear volume trends over the last three years with the relevant business, and agree on removal of trends in calculating sigma (likely using a linear trend analysis over the full period, but not necessarily so).
   - Two different portfolio scenarios are examined in the existing methodology:
     - No observable trend in the monthly balances
     - Observable trend in the monthly balances
     - To accommodate these scenarios, based on the historical trend, two different sigma values (standard deviation) are observed:
     - the normal standard deviation
     - standard deviation assuming a linear trend over a representative period (means some qualitative judgment overlay)
   - The standard deviation is assessed at 95 per cent confidence interval. This is consistent with the core calculations for business as usual (BAU) cash flows. Hence, liquidity premiums will be consistent with both liquidity and interest rate risk reports.

- Using the last observed volume (mean) and monthly standard deviation (SD) for each cohort, a cash outflow profile for the cohort under the BAU runoff scenario can be built.
  - In Scenario 1, where portfolio balances do not follow any particular trend, standard deviation of the balance series and last observed monthly balance are used to arrive at a liquidity profile.

    Using 95 per cent confidence, LP balance for month "*n*" (i.e., *n*th forecast month):

    Mean = Last observed actual balance and

    Standard deviation = SD of the balance series * SQRT (n)

    LP balance for month n = Mean − 1.96*SD
  - In scenario 2, where portfolio balances display a trend, first and last points of the balance series are used to identify the slope of the balance trend. This slope is used to obtain a linear trend line for the balance. Using the residual values from actual minus linear trend balances, standard deviation for the portfolio is obtained. By following the same method as scenario 1 (with last available balance as mean) and normal distribution calculations, LP for the portfolios with significant trend patterns was obtained.

Given that there will always be a tail volume running out to perpetuity, the cash flow profile can be truncated at 5 per cent of the initial volume (mean value).

3) **Weighted average maturity calculation**

- Weighted average maturity (WAM), in the current problem, refers to the average number of years taken by the portfolio (or cohort) balance to reach 5 per cent of its initial value (or reference value at time $T = 0$) with 95 per cent confidence.

$$\text{WAM} = \frac{\left(\sum_{i-1}^{n} \text{balance}_i \times i\right)}{\sum_{i-1}^{n} \text{balance}_i}$$

- In case of cohorts with liquidity beyond 100 months, balances till 100th month are only considered in the WAM calculation which is in line with the business decision for a WAM limit of 8.5 years.

4) **Qualitative judgment**
   - The analysis is necessarily dependent on some key assumptions; most notably the performance of the two major cohorts, and application (and usage) of trend analysis.
   - Standard deviation calculations have to incorporate trend and anomaly removal for portfolios which are still growing.

1.3. Results (existing methodology)

Results: CFS

- The CFS non-maturity demand product portfolio was broken down into 15 cohorts. The weighted average liquidity maturity profile for CFS is 6.2 years. Results of the analysis for CFS are largely driven by three key cohorts, all of which have material qualitative judgments applied to them, which had a partial impact on the overall result.
- The analysis does show a clear differentiated liquidity value of some products over others. As products continue to mature, this approach would be expected to capture the lost growth in products' early stages, and hence WAM/LP could be expected to decline.

Results: GCB

The GCB non-maturity demand product portfolio was broken down into nine cohorts. The weighted average liquidity maturity profile for GCB is 2.9 years. GCB's approach to cohorting differs from CFS in that it is not driven by product, but rather by segment, and also by including the interest rate offered to them (see Figure 1).

1.4. Proposed revised methodology

The revised method follows four major steps to model the LP curve.

1) Month-over-month (MoM) difference of log balances. This would be more aligned with the definition of normal distribution as its domain extends from (−Inf, Inf).
2) Obtain a least square regression line for the data from above step by regressing it against time (month number). This would take care of any significant growing/declining trend in our data.

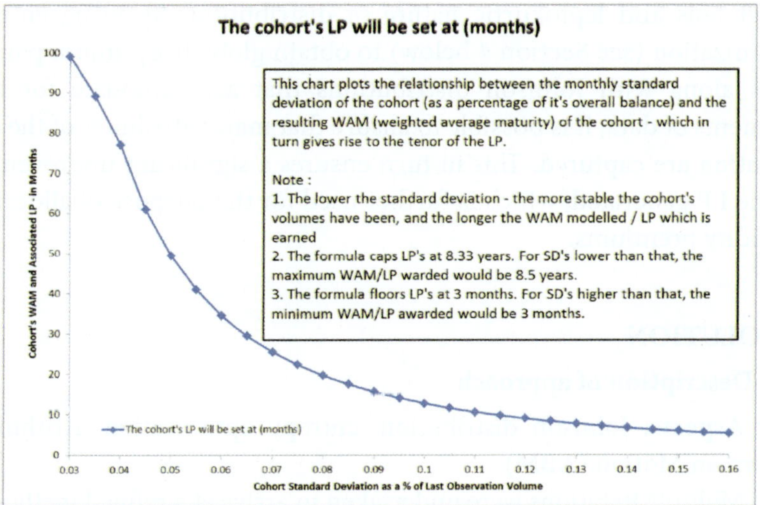

Figure 1: Monthly standard deviation and resulting WAM of the cohort.

3) Extract residuals by subtracting numbers in the above step from actual monthly balances.
4) Apply Johnson distribution to the residuals to obtain parameters for location (mean), scale (variance), skewness, and kurtosis. Using 95 per cent confidence, these parameters were used to obtain LP for each portfolio.

2. PROBLEM STATEMENT

The market risk management — asset liability management team sets out to establish a practical approach to the establishment of the liquidity profile of CASA (for the purpose of allocating liquidity premiums) on an empirical basis using historical position data, identifying a "follow the dollar" approach in each CASA account.

3. STATE OF THE ART

The solution for this problem plays a key role in efficiently managing the liquidity risk of the bank while striking the right balance between positive and conservative treatments. In this case, the distribution assumed for the historical data plays a key role in capturing phenomenon such as fat tails and leptokurtic nature of distribution. By using entropy optimization (see Section 4 below) to obtain globally optimum parameters along with Johnson distributions that accommodate for four moments of data, it is possible to ensure that major attributes of the distribution are captured. This in turn ensures a significant improvement in the LP generated, which is further used for the purpose of allocating liquidity premiums.

4. SOLUTION

4.1. Description of approach

Key Aspects: Johnson distribution, entropy optimization, Arithmetic Brownian Motion (ABM)

Multiple iterations were undertaken to arrive at a refined methodology used in the final solution. Johnson distribution has been used across all these iterations since it accommodates for nonnormality of data by using four moments to capture skewness and kurtosis along with mean and variance.

Entropy optimization technique is used to obtain the Johnson parameters which accurately represent the distribution of data in consideration. In addition, one of the iterations uses time varying Johnson parameters by borrowing from the concept of ABM. Both Johnson distribution and entropy optimization will be elaborated in the next parts of this section.

4.2. Johnson distribution

Normal distribution had played a dominant role in both theoretical and applied statistics. Properties and behavior of this distribution are well understood by an average user. It is, however, evident that the normal curve will not be able to represent many of the distributions encountered in statistical practice. Particularly, when quantifying risk, tail probabilities, and asymmetry play an important role in arriving at reasonable values. In view of the importance and widespread use of normal curve, it is natural to consider the possibility of relating observed distributions to the standard form.

An added advantage would be the fact that functions associated with the normal curve were well tabulated. In particular, significance testing and associated probability distributions were worked out thoroughly for normal distribution cases.

In the above circumstances, Johnson distribution serves as a useful way to depart from normality. Johnson system covers four classes of distributions, which are able to model a wide variety — some say all — of empirical distributions. Using a different nonlinear transformation for each kind of non-normal variable, it is transformed into a normal form. While the original distribution retains all the four moments with fat tails and non-symmetric nature, the transformed variables can use all the assumptions of a normal distribution.

By writing a transformation of a variable x to normality in the formal manner.

$$z = r + \delta f\left(\frac{x - \xi}{\lambda}\right),$$

where z is a unit normal variable and the function applied can be customized based on the range of possible values of x.

By writing $y = (x - \xi) / \lambda$, it follows that the distribution of x will be of the same shape as that of y with the standard deviation of x being λ times of y, and ξ will affect only the expected value of the distribution of x. It follows that the parameters r and δ determine the shape of the distribution of x, with λ as the scale factor and ξ as location factor. In general, r affects skewness and δ affects kurtosis. The two parameters λ and δ are taken by convention to be positive.

In the Johnson transformation family, there are four distributions whose variates can be transformed into normal variates: lognormal (S_L), bounded (S_B), unbounded (S_U), and normal (S_N).

Using $z = r + \delta f(y)$, $y = \left(\frac{x - \xi}{\lambda}\right)$

S_L: $f(y) = u$ the lognormal, $x \in (\xi, +\infty)$

S_U: $f(y) = u + \sqrt{1 + u^2}$ an unbounded distribution, $x \in (-\infty, +\infty)$

S_B: $f(y) = u/(1 - u)$ a bounded distribution, $x \in (\xi, \xi + \lambda)$

S_N: $f(y) = \exp(u)$ the normal, $x \in (-\infty, +\infty)$

A number of methods can be used here for estimating the parameters of these distributions, including moment matching (MM), method of percentile points, least squares, and maximum likelihood. Moment matching method was selected as it yields better estimates using moments of data, which is in line with our goals to capture tail probability numbers. In the moment matching method, the actual parameters of the chosen distribution are obtained by equating the sample moments to the moments of distribution taken as a function of the parameters, from which the parameters may be solved.

Entropy optimization is the technique used to obtain the best fitted parameters (based on moment matching).

4.3. Entropy optimization

The term entropy was coined by Rudolf Clausius around 1865 as a measure of the amount of energy in a thermodynamic system as a function of temperature of the system and the heat that enters the system. With E. T. Jaynes' *maximum entropy principle* and its variations, Shannon's entropy to select a probability distribution that complies with known observations about an unknown distribution and yet remains most noncommittal has penetrated a wide range of disciplines. Various entropy optimization models have proven their usefulness with successful applications in image reconstruction, pattern recognition, statistical inference, queuing theory, spectral analysis, statistical mechanics, transportation planning, urban and regional planning, input-output analysis, portfolio investment, information analysis, and linear and nonlinear programming, etc.

The concept of entropy is closely tied to the concept of uncertainty contained in a probability distribution. In particular, entropy can be defined as a measure of probabilistic uncertainty. Suppose the probability distribution for the outcome of a coin-toss experiment is (0.01, 0.99), with 0.01 as the probability of having a tail. One is likely to notice that there is much more "certainty" than "uncertainty" about the outcome of this experiment and hence about the probability distribution. In fact, it is almost certain that the outcome will be a head. If, on the other hand, the probability distribution governing that same experiment were (0.5, 0.5), there is much less "certainty" and much more "uncertainty", when compared to the previous distribution. Generalizing this observation to the case of n possible outcomes, it is possible to conclude that the uniform distribution has the highest uncertainty out of all possible probability distributions. This implies that, if a probability distribution had to be chosen for a chance experiment without any prior knowledge about that distribution, it would seem reasonable to pick the uniform distribution.

In the absence of any information about the probability distribution, the best course of action is to choose the distribution that maximizes the uncertainty. In the absence of any information, this problem is relatively easy because the uniform distribution is the one with maximum uncertainty. However, with the information about some of the moments of the distribution, it is not clear what distribution maximizes uncertainty while satisfying the moment constraints. By mathematically describing uncertainty in terms of entropy, this reasoning can be generalized and it is possible to choose the distribution that maximizes uncertainty subject to the given moment constraints. In this way, full use of all the information given is used but any assumptions about information that is not available are avoided. Such reasoning leads to the maximum entropy principle, which says:

Out of all possible distributions that are consistent with the moment constraints, choose the one that has the maximum entropy.

The distribution determination problem according to the principle of maximum entropy can be formulated as the following mathematical problem (for a discrete distribution):

$$\text{Maximize } S = -\sum_{j=1}^{n} p_j \ln p_j$$

$$\text{s.t. } \sum_{j=1}^{n} p_j = 1,$$

$$p_j \geq 0,\ j = 1,\ldots,n$$

This is a concave optimization problem where more constraints can be applied. To summarize, the least biased distribution parameters given as a set of known constraints will be obtained (first four moments of the data).

4.4. Research an applied work done

Multiple iterations were undertaken with a goal to identify the best-fit Johnson parameters to the given distribution. Taking the last available monthly balance of a cohort as mean and assuming 95 per cent confidence, these Johnson parameters were further used to model the liquidity runoff profile. The current and following sections provide the detail flow of analysis to arrive at the final approach. Additionally, justification for each section plugged into the final solution is also given in detail.

4.5. Using Johnson's SU transformation

Johnson provides four different transformations to obtain the normal form of a variable. This would mean that the transformation used should be aligned with the domain of variable under interest. As the log balance differences were utilized here, Johnson SU would be the ideal fit.

Johnson-SU distribution is closely related to normal distribution. Consider a Gaussian distribution. Its probability distribution function (PDF) for properties of hyperbolic functions can be written as:

PDF of normal distribution:

$$f(x) = \frac{1}{\sqrt{2\pi}} e^{-0.5z^2}, \text{ where } z \text{ is standardized } x,\ z = (x-\mu)/\sigma$$

PDF of Johnson SU distribution is:

$$g(x) = \frac{\delta}{\lambda\sqrt{z^2+1}} \frac{1}{\sqrt{2\Pi}} \exp\left[-\frac{1}{2}\left(r + \delta \sinh^{-1} z\right)^2\right],$$

$$\text{where } z \text{ is transformed } x, z = \left(\frac{x-\xi}{\lambda}\right)$$

From the above equations, it can be said that J-SU is approximated normal distribution controlled by the four parameters as follows:

By use of inverse arc sine function (i.e., arcsinh), J-SU guarantees it is asymmetric-type normal distribution

r determines intercept of $g(x)$

δ determines weight of arcsinh. As δ grows, $g(x)$ approaches $f(x)$

As μ and σ determine location of x on $f(x)$ in normal, ξ and λ determine location of x on $g(x)$ in J-SU.

To reiterate, in view of our effort to transform an unconstrained variable (MoM log changes domain is $(-\infty, +\infty)$), SU transformation is the most sensible choice in the current scenario.

4.6. Closed form solutions for Johnson SU moments

In the optimization scenario, while maximizing entropy/other choice factor, additional constraints have to be levied so as to ensure that the transformed distribution still retains the same moments of the actual distribution. The constraints are set such that actual data moments calculated should equal the Johnson values from the closed form.

With, *r* moments for Johnson *y* can be obtained by:

$$\omega = \exp\left(\frac{1}{\delta^2}\right)$$

$$\Omega = \frac{r}{\delta}$$

$$d_0 = 3(2\omega + 1) / 8$$

$$d_2 = \frac{1}{2}\omega^2(\omega + 2)$$

$$d_4 = \omega^2\left(\omega^4 + 2\omega^3 + 3\omega^2 - 3\right) / 8$$

Moment 1: $\mu_1 = -\sqrt{\omega}\sinh\Omega$

Moment 2: $\mu_2 = (\omega - 1)\left(\omega\cosh(2\Omega) + 1\right) / 2$

Moment 3: $\mu_3 = -(\omega - 1)^2\sqrt{\omega}\left\{\omega(\omega + 2)\sinh(3\Omega) + 3\sinh\Omega\right\} / 4$

Moment 4: $\mu_4 = (\omega - 1)^2\left\{d_4\cosh(4\Omega) + d_2\cosh(2\Omega) + d_0\right\}$

Using moment transformations,
*N*th moment of X = *N*th moment of $Y^*\,(\lambda)^N$

4.7. Time varying Johnson Parameters

By assuming that the log difference of balances follows an ABM and equating ABM's normal terms with the normal ones of SU Johnson transformation, the following was obtained:

$$r = a\sqrt{dt},\ \delta = b / \sqrt{dt},\ \xi = c,\ \lambda = d$$

Then the further set of non-time dependent parameters were optimized (*a*,*b*,*c*,*d*) with *dt* as 1/12 (due to month level balance data).

4.8. Arriving at the final approach

This section provides an overview of all the approaches tested before arriving at the final solution. Different optimization criteria such as squared error minimization, maximum likelihood estimation along with time varying/invariant Johnson parameters are tested before using entropy optimization. Due to the presence of nonlinear constraints, simulated annealing and nonlinear constrained optimization routines could only be used to achieve global optima.

With squared error minimization (time varying Johnson parameters)

1) Using Johnson closed form solutions for moments and actual data moments
   - In this iteration, squared difference between moments of the data computed through two methods is used to obtain the best fitted Johnson parameters. MoM difference of log balances are used here to obtain liquidity runoff profile.
   - Closed form solutions for Johnson moments and actual data moments (four moments) are calculated. As mentioned earlier, an optimization routine which minimizes the squared difference between the Johnson moments and data moments is used to find the best fit Johnson parameters (by iterating the moment values in the closed form solutions using Johnson parameters).
   - Convergence: Due to possible presence of local optima, the optimization routine didn't converge to a single value from different starting points.

With entropy optimization (time varying Johnson parameters)

1) Using actual data moments and moments using probability distribution
   - In this iteration, entropy optimization (maximizing $-\Sigma(p^*\log p)$) while imposing moment constraints on the data is used to obtain the best fit Johnson parameters. MoM difference of log balances are used here to obtain liquidity runoff profile.
   - Using the actual standard deviation of log Differences, a possible range of values is created with:
     - Lower Limit = −5*SD
     - Upper Limit = +5*SD

- Next, cumulative density function of Johnson distribution is estimated using the four parameters (*a*, *b*, *c*, and *d*):
  - CDF of Johnson SU: $\Phi\left(r + \delta \sinh^{-1}\left(\frac{x-\varepsilon}{\lambda}\right)\right)$, where Φ is the CDF of standard normal distribution
- To simplify entropy optimization problem, CDF values obtained are discretized by subtracting one from the other. On the two extremes of the distribution, leftmost point value is used as it is and the rightmost value is obtained by $1-p$ value.
- An optimization routine which maximizes entropy for the distribution obtained in the above step constrained for the moments of data is used. This routine makes use of nonlinear optimization (higher moment constraints are nonlinear) to achieve this.
- The constraints imposed try to equate the actual data moments with the moments calculated from the discrete probability distribution (*p* values).
- Convergence: Due to possible presence of local optima, the optimization routine did not converge to a single value from different starting points. As there could be information loss due to the discretization of probability distribution, the next iteration makes use of Johnson closed form equations to calculate moments instead of using the probability distribution.

2) Using actual data moments and Johnson closed form moments (Converged)
   - This iteration is similar to the prior one except the constraints used in the entropy optimization
   - As mentioned earlier, due to the discretization of the probability distribution there could be some information loss while trying to calculate the moments for the data. Instead, the closed form moment solutions for Johnson-SU distribution were applied and were equated with actual data moments. This led to the convergence of solution while obtaining same set of Johnson parameters from different starting points.

   LP using time varying Johnson parameters:
   LP is obtained from the best fit Johnson parameters as follows:

- Using the below notations, gamma and delta are calculated for each month (from the last available actual balance) by an increment in *dt* by 1/12 (a month expressed in years).

$$r = a\sqrt{dt},\ \delta = b\ /\ \sqrt{dt},\ \xi = c,\ \lambda = d$$

- While this accommodates for random walk using Brownian motion, the LP obtained was extremely conservative at 95 per cent confidence.
- In addition, this method is not suitable for certain portfolios which exhibit a trend pattern in their balances. In such cases, the standard deviation along with skewness and kurtosis could be overestimated.
- One such scenario is plotted below (see Figure 2).

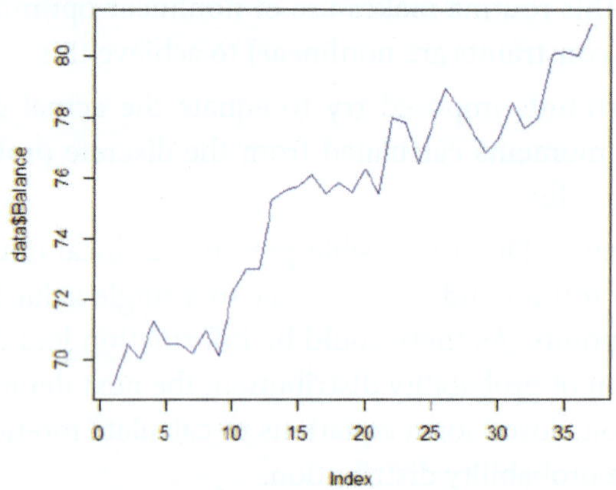

Figure 2: Monthly balance plot for portfolios with trend pattern.

This plot clearly indicates an upward trend. By calculating log differences and moments directly from this, more randomness in the system was assumed.

Removing drift and using time invariant parameters:

This iteration focuses on removing the trend component from the balance data to identify the most suitable Johnson fit parameters.

- This iteration retains all steps of the previous iteration while normalizing the drift component in the data.
- MoM difference of log balances are used here to obtain the liquidity runoff profile. Mean value of the log difference series is subtracted from the original series to obtain normalized data series.

- This normalized data is used further in entropy optimization to identify the best set of Johnson parameters.
- Results: This iteration did not improve the results by a significant margin since the new series is just a parallel shift from the original one. This calls for a more pragmatic approach to identify the parameters while removing the trend component in the data.

Final approach using regression residuals

This iteration focuses on forming a unified approach (regardless of the series trend) to identify the Johnson parameters to capture data variation, while discarding the effects of balance trend due to portfolio increase/decrease effects.

- First, a best fit regression line is obtained with dependent variable as MoM difference of log balances explained by the month.
- The original series is normalized by subtracting it from the best fit line to obtain regression residuals. This will take care of the trend component in the data with the residual capturing of other significant movements in the data.
- In this way, every series can be broken down to expected (trend) and unexpected (residuals) components which can be used for the LP calculations. This method is particularly useful due to its flexibility to accommodate series with no particular trend in the data.

4.9. Architecture of the final solution

This section provides a detailed overview of the solution to create the LP for a particular portfolio. A final summary of results for all the portfolios is also provided.

Solution walkthrough for a single cohort (portfolio):

The solution compares the existing and Johnson methodologies while charting the LP and obtaining the WAM for the portfolio. Here the application of both methods for GCB-SME, EMB, EB, NonIntPaying Customers portfolios are presented.

This is one of the Key portfolios with volume around 50 per cent of the total GCB book. A significant increasing balance trend across time for this portfolio can be observed (see Figure 3).

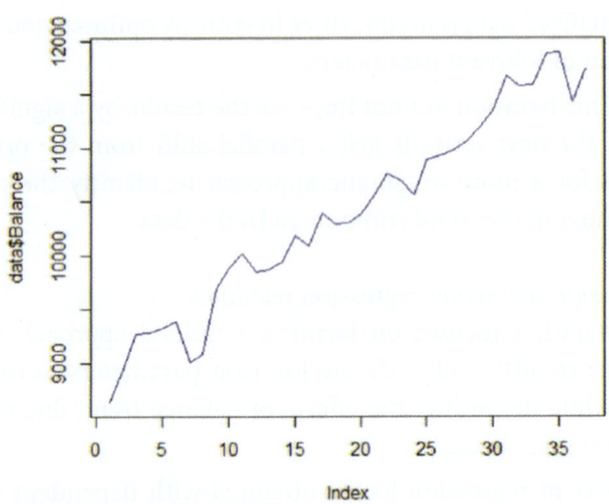

Figure 3: Balance Series for GCB-SME portfolio.

LP using existing methodology:

As mentioned earlier, this methodology uses two different portfolio scenarios in analyzing the LP for a portfolio:

- Scenario 1: No observable trend in the monthly balances
- Scenario 2: observable trend in the monthly balances

As the portfolio in consideration clearly exhibits a trend in monthly balances, Scenario 2 is used to calculate the standard deviation, applying normal distribution with 95 per cent confidence to it.

- Create a trend line by joining the first and last points of the balance series. A deviation number for each actual balance point from the trend line is calculated. Standard deviation of this deviation series and last available balance are used in the LP calculations at 95 per cent confidence.
- Using 95 per cent confidence, LP Balance for month "n" (i.e., nth forecast month) = Mean − 1.96 * SD * SQRT(n)

LP using revised methodology:

- As mentioned earlier, this method uses the residuals of regression for monthly log balance difference data w.r.t time. These residuals are plugged into an entropy optimization routine to obtain the best fit Johnson parameters.

- The inverse probability distribution using these Johnson parameters at 95 per cent confidence gives the required critical value.

  LP Balance for month "n" (i.e., nth forecast month) = Balance for month "$n - 1$" * exp (critical value)

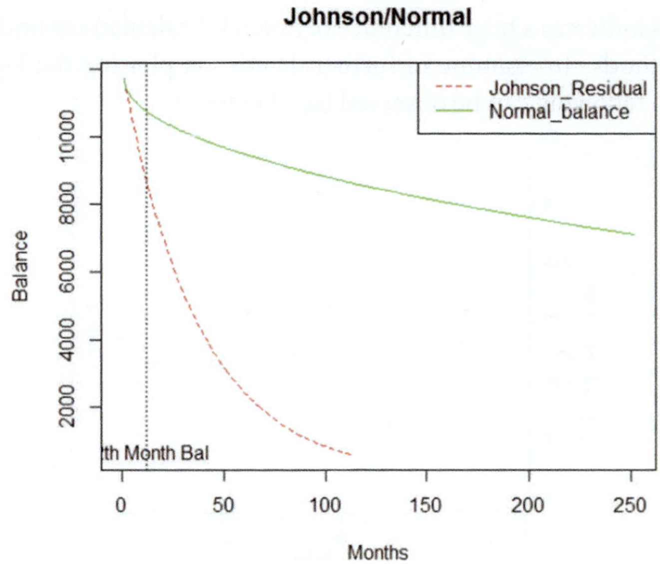

Figure 4: LP using Johnson/Normal method.

From the above graph (see Figure 4), it can be observed that the rate of balance decline is under-estimated by the Normal method due to various reasons (explained in the following sections).
WAM calculation:

- WAM, in the current problem, refers to the average number of years taken by the portfolio (or cohort) balance to reach 5 per cent of its initial value (or reference value at time $T = 0$) with 95 per cent confidence.

  - $$\text{WAM} = \frac{\left(\sum_{i-1}^{n} \text{balance}_i * i\right)}{\left(\sum_{i-1}^{n} \text{balance}_i\right)}$$

- In case of cohorts with liquidity beyond 100 months, balances till 100 month are only considered in the WAM calculation which is aligned with the business decision for a WAM limit of 8.5 years.
  - WAM using Balances with normal distribution – greater than eight years
  - WAM using Johnson residuals method – 2.7 years

This indicates a huge difference between LP calculations undertaken for 2 methods. To examine in further details, on plotting the log differences the following can be observed (see Figure 5):

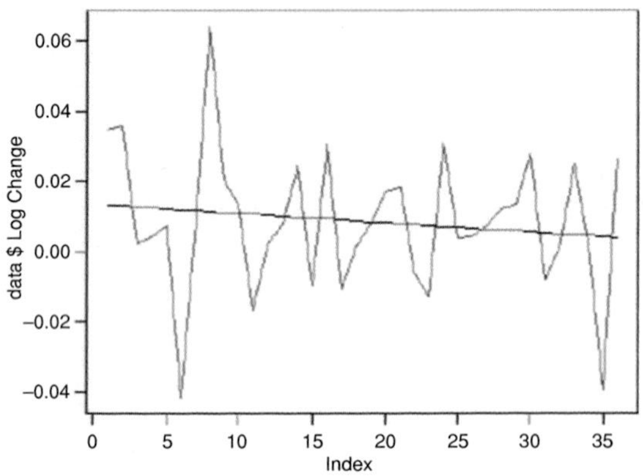

Figure 5: Log difference of monthly balance.

This portfolio is a test case, while looking at monthly balances alone would be misleading. Log difference of monthly balances indicates another story despite the almost linear growth shown in balance graph.

Qualitative overlay

Further judgment is exercised initially before applying any numerical calculations to the balance data. Cases such as new portfolios with insufficient data to backtest and anomaly in the balances due to an external event stimulus (Ex: IPO) were smoothened to obtain a better profile.

Summary of results for all cohorts:

WAM of major cohorts obtained from Johnson and Normal is compared (see Table 3).

Table 3: Comparison of WAM of major cohorts obtained from Johnson and Normal distribution.

Cohort Name	WAM normal in years (with qualitative overlay)	WAM — Johnson distribution in years
CFS-01-360A	8.5	0.4
CFS-02-AW	5.1	4.3
CFS-03-B+/D+	1	1.2
CFS-04-CDA	8.5	3.6
CFS-05-Corp	0.75	0.4
CFS-06-CFPSRS	4.3	1.6
CFS-07-Easycredit	1.8	1.1
CFS-08-ES	5	2.5
CFS-09-ESPP	0.25	0.15
CFS-10-FRANK	5	2
CFS-11-MSA	5	0.5
CFS-13-NIBCA	5	1.7
CFS-14-PB/STMT	8	8
CFS-15-PLUS	1.3	3.4
GCB-01-SME, EMB, EB, NonIntPaying	5	2.7
GCB-02-LargeCorp, NonIntPaying	1.7	0.5
GCB-03-BK+NBFI, NonIntPaying	0.25	0.25
GCB-01-SME, EMB, EB, IntPaying	1.64	0.9
GCB-02-LargeCorp, IntPaying	0.82	0.5
GCB-03-BK+NBFI, IntPaying	0.25	0.4

Qualitative Judgment could mean:

- Business decision for new portfolios instead of mathematical calculations.

- Normalization of anomalies to capture events such as IPOS, significant interest rate movements.

Case-by-case analysis for cohorts with significant difference (greater than four years WAM difference between two methodologies):

Cohort:
CFS-01-360A

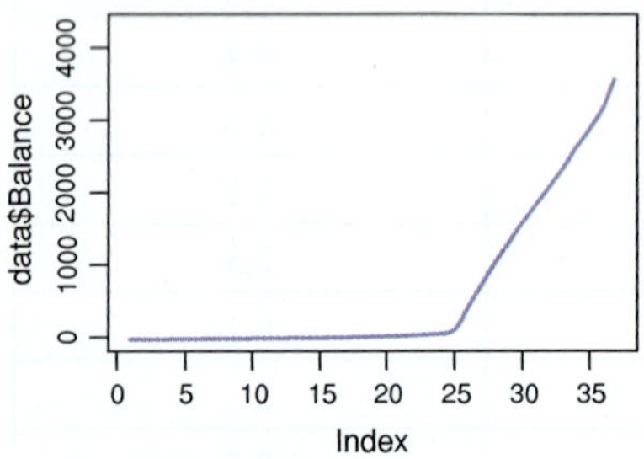

Figure 6 (a): Data trend.

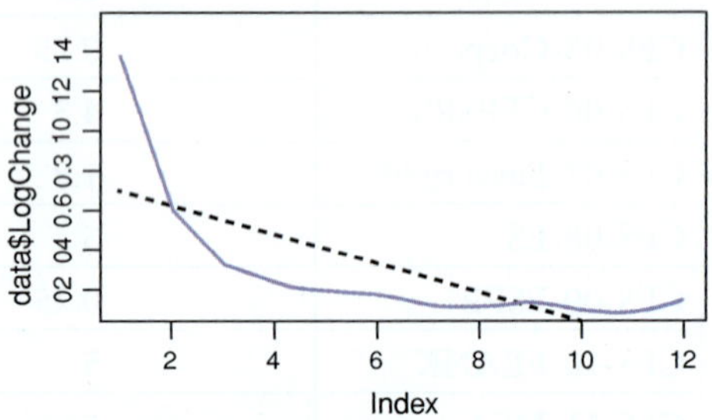

Figure 6 (b): MoM difference of log balances (with best fit regression line).

Comments:
MoM differences of log balances vary from 0.07 (7 per cent) to 1.14 (114 per cent) which shows that the portfolio has yet to stabilize (see Figure 6). In this scenario, careful re-examination of the data has to be carried out before applying Johnson to the residuals as it might yield misleading results.

LP: Considering balances from March 2014 (see Figure 7)

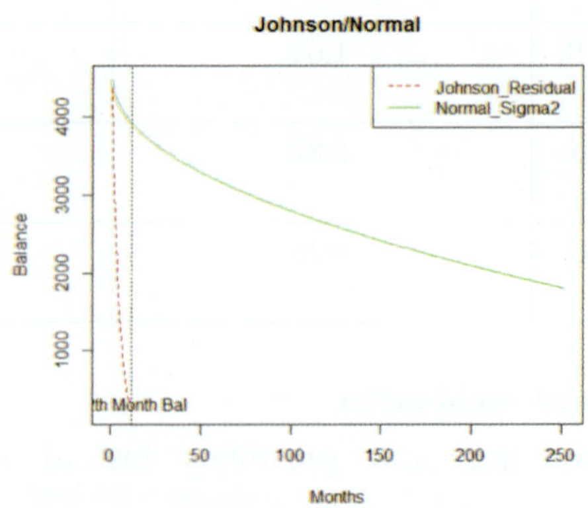

Figure 7: WAM for balances as on March 2014. Portfolio is effectively only one year old and needs more data to backtest. WAM numbers should be reviewed again.

Cohort:
CFS-04-CDA

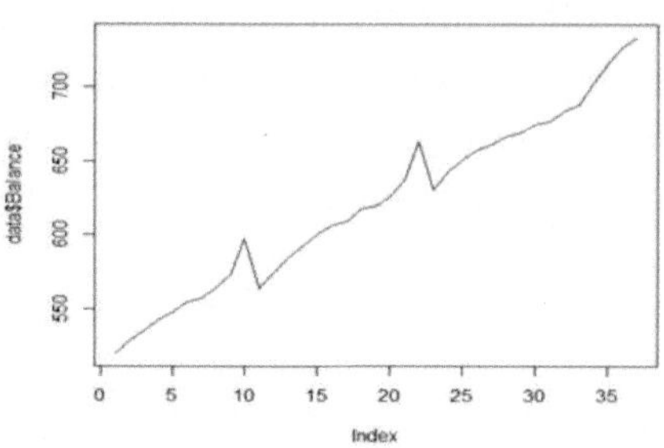

Figure 8: (a) Data trend.

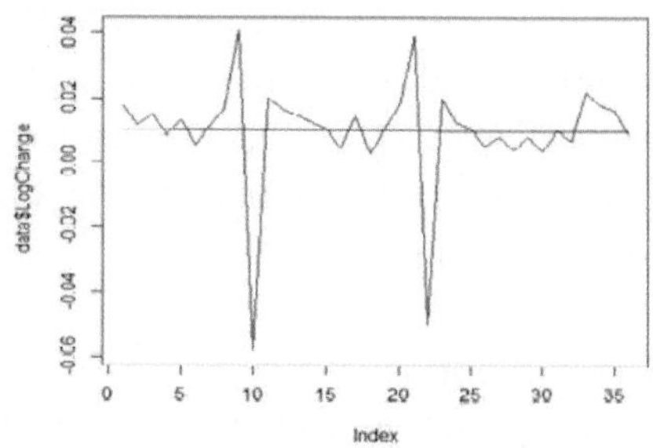

Figure 8: (b) MoM difference of log balances (with best fit regression line).

Comments:
Product has clear linear growth trend when the balance trend is observed. However, the two major fluctuations in MoM log differences will be captured by Johnson and lead to a more conservative estimate compared to normal (using the balance series instead of the log difference series) (Figure 8).

In this case, Qualitative judgment becomes instrumental in determining the WAM value since the two data points are clearly anomalies to be normalized.

Cohort:
CFS-10-FRANK

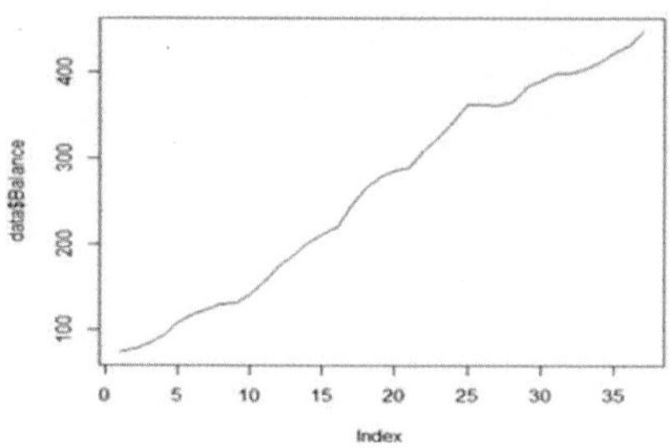

Figure 9: (a) Data trend.

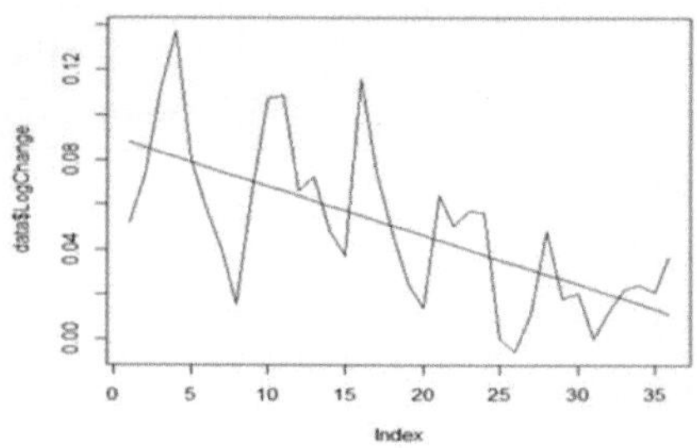

Figure 9: (b) MoM difference of log balances (with best fit regression line).

Comments:
Clear linear growth of a new portfolio over three years gives rise to a material difference in quantitative results — similar to the case with 360A accounts. On the other hand, MoM log difference values clearly show a volatile trend which has been captured by Johnson distribution calculations (Figure 9). In this scenario, careful re-examination of the data has to be carried out before applying Johnson to the residuals as it might lead to misleading results.

Other cohorts:
Cohorts such as CFS-11-MSA, CFS-13-NIBCA also face similar issues like those highlighted from the previous test cases. Data anomaly smoothening or qualitative judgment had to be incorporated in all these cases to balance mathematical robustness and business impact.

Robustness check:
The monthly balances for the recent three months have been used to compare the performance of revised methodology with the existing one. Data for CFS cohorts was sourced from Fermat using SQL queries. However, GCB data summaries were obtained using an available list of accounts as no clear data filters were in place. Owing to this complexity, robustness check has been performed for CFS cohorts only.

By comparing the actual balances with the 95 per cent confidence values obtained from existing and revised methodologies, the number of exceptions were counted (if, any) in the recent three months (i.e., April, May, and June 2015) (see Table 4).

Table 4: Comparison of actual balances of cohorts for three months.

Cohort name	No. of exception from existing methodology	No. of exceptions from revised methodology
CFS-01-360A	0	0
CFS-02-AW	0	0
CFS-03-B+/D+	0	0
CFS-04-CDA	0	0
CFS-05-Corp	0	0

Cohort name	No. of exception from existing methodology	No. of exceptions from revised methodology
CFS-09-ESPP	0	0
CFS-10-FRANK	0	0
CFS-11-MSA	0	0
CFS-14-PB/STMT	0	0

There are no exceptions encountered through both methodologies. Interestingly, the balance of majority of these portfolios is following an increasing trend. As the market situation had held stable for the past three months, this check had not provided any significant insights with respect to the robustness comparison of the two methods. Their stability could be put to test when stressed economic situations are encountered.

5. DISCUSSION

5.1. Business value of the solution

The ability of a banking institution to meet demand for deposit withdrawals and other cash outflows is a major indicator of its stability. If it cannot meet depositor withdrawal requirements and general creditor expenses, or if it is forced to significantly limit new lending, it will result in customers loosing confidence. Loan horizons and maturity of other lending units have to be carefully planned to avoid any such liquidity crunches and reputation losses.

On the other hand, there is enough flexibility to suitably plan investment decisions due to the presence of huge variation in customer behavior. They can be individuals with random deposit/withdrawal behaviors, large Corporations with visible seasonality in the cash management cycle, and interest rate sensitive/insensitive customers, etc. At the same time, providing a prudent cushion for unforeseen liquidity needs is also important.

All the above points indicate the need for an effective approach which can be customized based on customer behavior, while being conservative to avoid any stressed market scenarios. The revised LP analysis, with its significant improvements, therefore holds a key importance in the risk management perspective.

5.2. Justification for using Johnson distribution

In everyday business problems, Normal curve will not be able to adequately represent all the properties of the data. It has no provision to accommodate skewness or kurtosis which are extremely important to capture phenomenon such as asymmetry and fat tails. In the above circumstances, Johnson transformations serve as a useful way to depart from normality.

As our current problem is centered on finding tail probability (95 per cent confidence means 5 per cent area at tail), skewness which indicates the likelihood of negative events over positive (or vice versa) and Kurtosis which measures the thickness of tails are especially significant.

5.3. Sample fitting of log residuals

In the graph below (see Figure 10), log residuals data (after removing the trend component) for a sample cohort has been fitted using both normal and Johnson distributions.

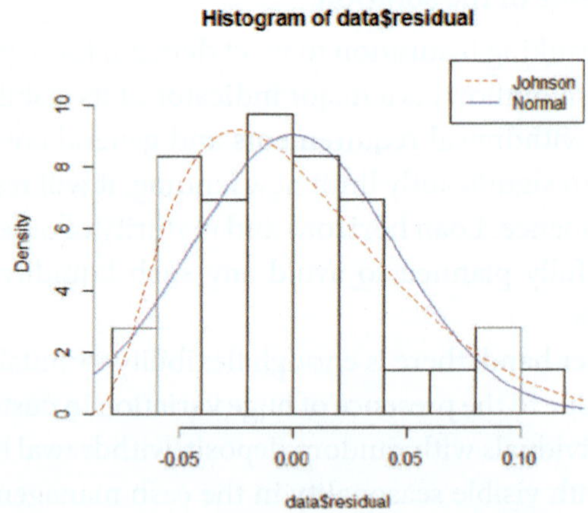

Figure 10 Log residual data for Johnson and normal distributions.

As it can be observed from the plot, positive skewness of data and thickness of the tails are captured by Johnson distribution unlike Normal which is only concerned with mean and spread of data while assuming symmetry.

5.3.1. Improvement achieved using revised methodology

Revised method differs from the earlier version in three key aspects:

- *Using log difference of monthly balance vs using the monthly balance as it is*

  As the distribution properties of normal distribution were utilized in these calculations, the variable of interest should adhere to the domain (possible values) of normal distribution. However, taking balance as it is will violate this principle. While the domain of normal distribution is (–Inf,Inf), balance of a cohort cannot fall below 0. In addition, the distribution of balances will be highly skewed (see graph in Figure 11 below — plotted with Normal fit to the data).
- *Residuals obtained using least squares regression instead of a slope from two extreme points*
- *Utilizing the capabilities of Johnson distribution to factor in asymmetry and fat tails into the liquidity profile calculations*

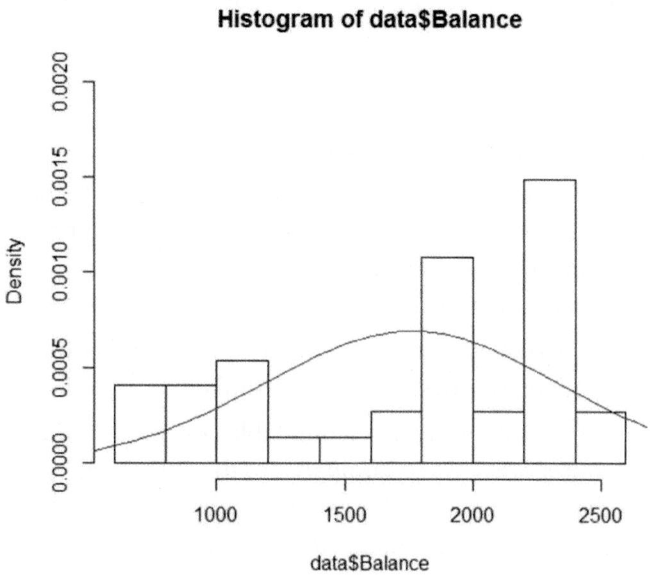

Figure 11: Histogram of data balance.

5.4. Incorporating qualitative judgment

Qualitative overlay had a significant impact in defining the LP of many portfolios. Certain default measures were taken to tackle each kind of data anomaly such as:

- New portfolios with no established behavior and insufficient data to backtest were assigned a default WAM value of five years irrespective of the calculations.
- Portfolios with declining balances in recent years, potentially due to the cannibalisation of the product to other cohorts, were assigned a default WAM of five years. Potential to review if the declining trend continues.
- Balance spikes due to special events (e.g., IPOs) are normalized to ensure that average user behavior is captured.
- For a few portfolios with drastic growth, only the stabilized series is used for WAM and LP calculations.

For new portfolios, qualitative judgment beats the mathematical methods employed. In case of portfolios with one-off balance anomalies, some data normalization has to be done before applying Johnson methodology.

6. CONCLUSION AND FURTHER WORK

This study proposes an empirical approach to establish the Weighted Average Maturity (WAM) and hence liquidity premium for non-maturity demand deposits in the OCBC commercial book.

The key conclusions are:

- While the approach establishes a framework for derivation of theoretical WAM, a qualitative overlay must be applied.
- As can be observed from the results table, Johnson numbers are significantly conservative when compared to the existing approach. This is driven by the usage of log balance differences instead of pure balances and inclusion of further moments to calculate the critical points.
- CFS propose 15 cohorts, however one of them (passbook/statement accounts) represents nearly half of the entire CFS non-maturity deposit portfolio. For this particular cohort, both Johnson and normal yield

similar results, therefore narrowing down the gap between results of two approaches.

- GCB propose nine cohorts, however one (SME customers with no interest paid to customers) represents around 46 per cent of the entire GCB non-maturity deposit portfolio. For this particular cohort, Johnson and normal approaches yield significantly different results (five years — Normal, 2.7 years — Johnson)
- The analysis is necessarily dependent on some key assumptions — most notably the performance of two major cohorts (as they have the highest impact on WAM) and the application of trend analysis.

Possible further Improvements:

- While the analysis takes care of extreme movements through skewness and kurtosis, it is still based on the historical data of the past three years. The Singapore market had been relatively stable in this time period which might not be an accurate representation of the future.
- The two large cohorts in GCB and CFS (passbook/statement accounts and SME customers with no interest paid to customers) account for almost half of these portfolios. There is a scope for presence of different subcohorts in these cohorts due to huge volume of customers in them.
- In few cases, customer behavior could be endogenic e.g., business decisions affecting pass through rate will affect customer withdrawal behavior in the presence of a competitive market.

REFERENCES

1. Johnson, NL. (1949). Systems of frequency curves generated by methods of translation. *BiometrIka*, 36(1/2), 49–176.
2. Shu-Cherng, F. et al (1997).*Entropy Optimization and Mathematical Programming.* New York: Springer.
3. Shenton, LR and KO Bowman (1975). Johnson's SU and the skewness and kurtosis statistics. *Journal of the American Statistical Association*, 70(349), 220–228.

CHAPTER 15

Finance Net-Interest Margin Analysis with Qlikview

ZHENG Arthur

ABSTRACT

This study aimed to deliver a proof of concept (POC) using Qlikview to prepare Net Interest Margin (NIM) dashboards to analyze the data. Current data inputs and process flows were reviewed and a new data model proposed, as well as areas where data flows and manual processes can be streamlined or automated were reviewed. Data integration and modeling were developed in Qlikview to replace the existing Excel-based analysis. The POC was developed to demonstrate the feasibility of using Qlikview to prepare NIM data, and to provide a more interactive and effective analysis with significantly shortened timeframe and effort. A robust data model and design architecture were also proposed.

1. INTRODUCTION

DBS is a leading financial services group in Asia, with strong presence in Southeast Asia, Greater China Region and India. DBS provides a full range of services in consumer, SME, and corporate banking activities across Asia. DBS' finance department wants to expand the use of business intelligence tools such as Qlikview for quick, effective, and interactive ways to analyze and drilldown financial data, which can be used by multiple finance groups, thus streamlining the data flow and standardizing data definitions, since all are accessing the same pool of processed data.

NIM analysis was chosen as the focus for this study. This study also reviewed the business process flow with an aim to streamline and automate manual processes, and reduce the number of manual spreadsheets used to prepare the NIM analysis dashboard. Qlikview was chosen as the analytics tool to monitor movements in Net Interest Income/margin (NII/NIM) and deliver insightful analysis for decision support. The deliverable of the study was a proof of concept (POC) of the Qlikview NIM Dashboard, with suggestions to bring it to production mode.

2. PROBLEM STATEMENT

NIM is a measure of the difference between the interest income generated by banks and amount of interest paid out to their lenders, relative to the amount of their interest-earning assets. DBS has huge business in loans and deposits that incur interest income and expense, as well as many other types of financial products that involve lending and borrowing of capital. NIM analysis thus is essential for the profitability of core banking business and is one of the key performance indicators for management review as well as for public financial reports.

Figure 1 illustrates the net interest income and NIM snapshots reported in DBS 2014 Annual Report (p. 31) and net interest income by different asset and liability classes in 2013 Annual Report (p. 124).

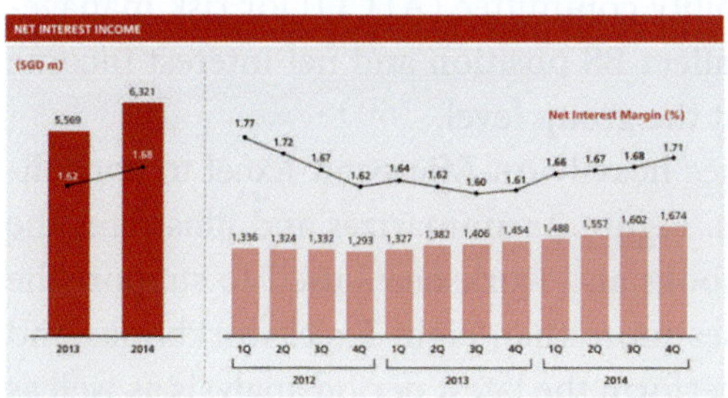

In $ millions	The Group 2013	The Group 2012
Cash and balances with central banks and Due from banks	**460**	496
Customer non-trade loans	**4,710**	4,341
Trade assets	**1,458**	1,303
Debt securities	**1,358**	1,481
Total interest income	**7,986**	7,621
Deposits and balances from customers	**1,926**	1,782
Other borrowings	**491**	554
Total interest expense	**2,417**	2,336
Net interest income	**5,569**	5,285

Figure 1: Net interest income/margin-DBS annual report 2013, 2014.

Definitions and formulas for NIM related financial terms and acronyms:

IBA: Interest bearing assets — e.g., loans

IBL: Interest bearing liabilities — e.g., deposits

IR: Interest income or revenue — interest earned from interest bearing assets

IP: Interest expense — interest paid for interest bearing liabilities

NII: Net interest income = Interest income − Interest expense

Average rate = Interest income/Interest bearing assets (also referred to as asset yield by asset class) or Interest expense/Interest bearing liabilities (also referred to as funding cost rate by liability class)

NIM: Net interest margin = Net interest income/Interest bearing assets

IBA and IBL come from bank's balance sheet (BS). IR and IP come from bank's income statement, also called profit and loss (P&L) statement. Average rate is calculated to gauge performance of different assets, liability classes, value is converted to equivalent annualized rate.

In line with current business understanding, NIM movements can be linked to movements in BS and profit loss financial reporting components, which require further division into various types of assets, liabilities, interest income, and expense. The division involves various dimensions, such as account type, product type, and country view. Apart from these internal divisions, there are two other external factors considered for NIM analysis — market interest rates and foreign exchange rates. Market interest rates affect pricing policy (asset side) and funding cost (liability side). Interest rate risk exposure and management is an important part of the asset-liability committee (ALCO) for risk management. Foreign exchange rates affect BS position and net interest income reported in Singapore dollars at the group level.

Current NIM process relies heavily on Microsoft Excel to consolidate data and perform analysis. Figure 2 summarizes and illustrates the complexity of the Excel workbooks and worksheets used to support the NIM analysis. This analysis uses more than eight Excel workbooks and over 300 active worksheets to perform the latest period analysis as well as to maintain a certain level of historical trend analysis.

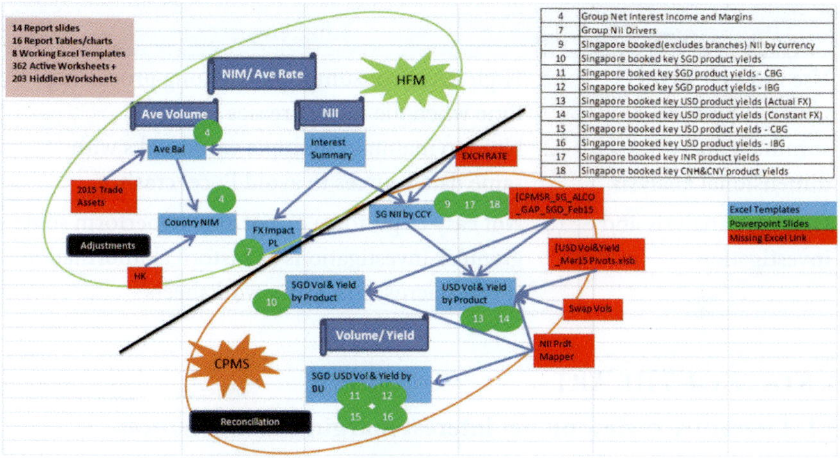

Figure 2: Current Excel-based NIM analysis overview.

While performing NIM analysis, many challenges were presented at each process steps during working with Microsoft Excel.

Process steps	Challenges
Depend on upstream finance teams for report consolidations	1. Sequential rather than parallel processing, which slows down data compilation and analysis
Consolidate various spreadsheets into report review	2. Too many files to manage 3. Too many levels of depth for calculations, not easy to investigate and troubleshoot 4. Need to be very cautious with formulas with lookup function or relative row, column positioning 5. Difficult to audit or detect data errors, formula errors, and break links
Maintain manual user mappings within worksheets	6. Various customization by different finance teams 7. Difficult to synchronize with related system trees and their frequent changes
Maintain manual adjustments within spreadsheets	8. Manual data not corrected at source 9. Lack of synchronization, which relies on communication 10. Potential varied 'truth' further downstream

Process steps	Challenges
Use multiple pivot tables to provide summary and dimensional analysis	11. High RAM consumption and long processing time when file size increases 12. Need to maintain multiple workbooks with same data sources to avoid Excel crash
Granular analysis and investigation	13. Not easy to perform or not able to perform some granular investigations as historical information spreads across too many worksheets

3. STATE OF THE ART

3.1. Literature review on net interest margin decomposition

Ho and Saunders (1981) argued that there were four main factors which affect the "pure spread" of NIM: degree of risk aversion, market structure, average size of bank transactions, and variance of interest rates on loans and deposits. They analyzed NIM with a dealership model, where a bank was treated as a dealer between lenders and borrowers. Angbanzo (1997) extended the model to include credit risk as well as liquidity risk. Maudos and Fernandez de Guevara (2004) incorporated the operating cost into the model and used Lerner and Herfindahl indexes to measure market structure.

Loans as a primary credit service are sensitive to credit risks and the degree of risk aversion affects bank's pricing policy on loans, rates to be charged, and deposit rates to be paid. Market structure can influence bank's behavior beyond policy pricing. Banks in competitive markets are expected to have relatively lower margins compared to uncompetitive markets. Volatility of interest rates can directly affect loan income and deposit expense, and indirectly affect bank's assets and liabilities structure. Primary source of interest rate risk is the timing differences in the re-pricing of bank assets, liabilities, and off-balance-sheet instruments. These re-pricing mismatches are fundamental to the business of banking and generally appear either due to borrowing short-term to fund long-term assets or long-term to fund short-term assets.

Central bank lending rates and interbank rates also affect the bank's funding cost. DBS has a strong regional presence in Singapore, Hong Kong and China, thus three major interest rates are considered, which include ABS SOR (Singapore Swap Offer Rate), HIBOR (Hong Kong Interbank Offered Rate) and PBoC (People's Bank of China) lending rates.

As the banks diversify their product offerings, bank portfolios that generate revenue not only consist of primary loans, but other interest-bearing assets and fee income activities. This suggests that NIM analysis can investigate customer view performances (e.g., customer segmentation by institutional banking group and consumer banking group) as well as product specialization view performances (e.g., loan, bonds, money market, swaps, etc.).

Christoph and Andrea (2011) examined German banks' NIM with relation to bank rates as well as BS compositions. They suggested that (i) Changes in market-wide bank rates have greater impact on and explain more of the variation in NIMs than those in BS compositions. (ii) Changes in bank rates and BS compositions affect the NIM changes less strongly for derivative users than for nonusers. On an average, banks employ interest rate derivatives to reduce on-balance risk. (iii) When risk-taking becomes more lucrative, banks tend to increase their on-balance exposure. This effect is more pronounced for derivative users than for nonusers.

3.2. Literature review on enterprise business intelligence

According to Forrester Research by Evelson (2008): "Business intelligence is a set of methodologies, processes, architectures, and technologies that transform raw data into meaningful and useful information used to enable more effective strategic, tactical, and operational insights and decision-making".

Business intelligence will require an empowered workforce to be armed with timely data and enable them to navigate through self-service and data discovery environments. As a result, business intelligence can empower users to create new analytics solutions that improve business processes and to leverage data sources in new combinations that could not be analyzed before.

According to Berson *et al.* (2002), business intelligence architecture includes several stages for extraction, transformation and loading (ETL), data warehousing, database query and reporting, and subsequent developments also include stages for on-line analytical processing (OLAP) data analysis, data mining, and visualization.

Among various Business intelligence platform vendors, Qlikview provides a unique solution in intuitive and spontaneous data exploration and discovery. It is widely recognized in the industry and ranked in Leaders category in Gartner's Magic Quadrant in 2015.

4. SOLUTION: DESCRIPTION OF APPROACH

4.1. Understanding current situation: Data sources, reports, and users

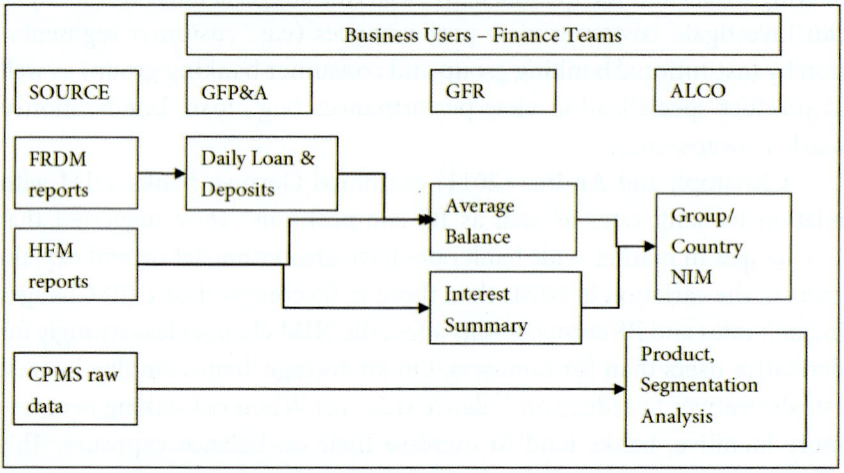

Figure 3: Current process flow.

In current process flow, there are three finance teams involved in preparing relevant information and reports that contribute to NIM analysis (see Figure 3). ALCO is our target business user, who will perform NIM reporting and analysis as well as net interest income (NII) simulation on a monthly basis. Group financial reporting (GFR) is the finance team who performs month-end financial consolidation and generates standard financial reports such as BS, and profit and loss statements. Group finance planning and analytics (GFP&A) is responsible for Group MIS reporting including daily reporting of loans and deposits balances. There is a high level of reporting dependency from upstream to downstream finance teams which allows only sequential process flow rather than a parallel one.

The three main source reports come from three key finance systems: HFM, FRDM, and CPMS.

- HFM is a financial consolidation system, which offers benchmark figures for finance teams for monthly financial reporting.
- FRDM is the finance data mart, which contains granular financial data and balances at instrument level, integrating data from various sources. Daily loan and deposit balances are generated from FRDM. The scope for daily balance report is being expanded to cover other asset and

liability products. During this POC stage, BS components will be taken from a combination of both HFM and FRDM reports. In planned production stage, all BS components will be taken from the FRDM daily reports.

- CPMS is a monthly processing system that offers more detailed information by product, customer segmentations for the bank's cost, and profitability analysis. It also includes FTP (fund transfer pricing) information, which is used by ALCO for credit and liquidity management.

A comparison of the three systems as data source is listed in Table 1.

Table 1: Data source system comparison.

System	HFM	CPMS	FRDM
Frequency	Monthly	Monthly	Daily
Benchmark/ usage in NIM	Yes for monthly balance sheet and interest income/ expense components	No, only for breakdown analysis	Partial — Daily loans and deposits balances
Granularity	Low	Medium	High
Granularity details	Account, product, affiliates	Account, product, customer segmentation, transaction currency, FTP	Customer segmentation, transaction currency, affiliates, geography, deal, maturity
Direction	Needed for monthly consolidation engine and benchmark financial reporting: balance sheet, profit loss, intercompany etc.	To be replaced by FRDM in the long run	Daily balance sheet components

With the above understanding of finance systems' offerings and limitations, the team has agreed to streamline current data sources for a POC Qlikview application and determine more strategic data sources for production Qlikview application. With a timeline of three months, this POC development will use a set of detail reports (Excel workbooks) to replace current user-produced intermediary reports (aggregated Excel workbooks), because these detail reports are system-generated and contain more granularity than user-produced intermediary reports. To build the dashboard reports from these detail reports, reporting rules are extracted and maintained in separate rules table, which will then be used by Qlikview to perform summation calculations. These detail reports also serve better for data consolidation and reduce downstream variations of "source" reports, the number "source" spreadsheets for NIM analysis thus is reduced from 12 to 9.

To expand Qlikview application to production mode, the team has proposed more strategic data sources based on the above review. The proposed production Qlikview will create a common data layer with integration of multiple strategic data sources. This core data layer contains granular data directly queried from databases, and can support both the NIM analysis as well as other reporting and analysis needs within the Group Finance. It will help to remove dependency on upstream intermediary reports and a different finance team will be able to perform parallel processing and achieve a shared 'truth' with the same processed data sources.

1) Use FRDM generated flat data dump for BS statement (SQL query into FRDM database).
2) Use HFM generated flat data dump for P&L statement (underlying raw data after financial consolidation, query into HFM database).
3) Streamline and build accounting business rules to apply on flat raw data.

On top of these raw data, there are other reference trees and mapping tables to support various dimension analysis listed in Table 1. They will facilitate Qlikview applications to drill up and down with respect to these dimensions, such as account type, product type, and country view. Reference trees include account roll-up tree, product roll-up tree, and entity roll-up tree. Roll-up trees follow a hierarchy structure. By drilling down through the hierarchy tree, it will provide further granularity with respect to this dimension.

1) Account tree represents the type of transactions and can be classified into one of the asset, liability, revenue, and expense accounts.

Asset and liability classifications illustrated in Figure 1 come from this account tree, e.g., customer loans can split into bills receivable, loans, and advances to customers in next account level.

2) Product tree is the classification of products offered by DBS. It provides various levels of product specialization view, e.g., loans may consist of housing loans, personal loans, and term loans, etc.
3) Entity tree contains the hierarchy of subsidiary companies and bank branches. Country viewpoint is also directly linked to this tree.

Additional mapping tables facilitate business users to create customized viewpoints on product group and currency group that are different from those reference trees. These additional dimensions are essential to perform variance analysis and to provide perspectives on the potential causes of periodic movements with respect to account type, product type, and country view.

4.2. Manual adjustments data management and improvements

NIM reporting and analysis is part of a large finance closing process, illustrated in Figure 4. Data from various finance systems are fed into general ledger, which is a central repository to keep organization's financial transactions and accounting data. Accounts reconciliations are performed by accounting professionals to ensure accuracy and validity of financial information. Then, a consolidation process will be performed within HFM to produce relevant financial statements and reports.

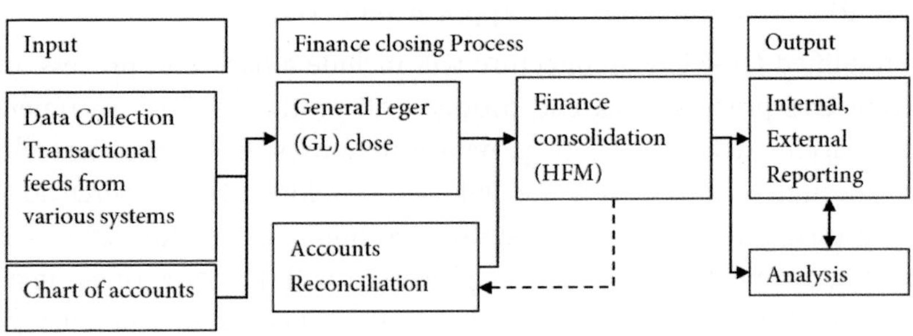

Figure 4: Typical finance close process work flow.

In the current NIM process flow, there are three areas where manual adjustments are performed within Excel workbooks, which are not timely reflected in accounts reconciliations into HFM system. These adjustments are necessary due to:

1) Late adjustments (reconciliations) to finance consolidations. Instead of refreshing a chain of reports, manual adjustments are performed with Excel workbooks and worksheets.
2) Reconciliation inputs into system are on a higher level, which need manual breakdown to ensure proper allocation to revenue and expense classifications.
3) Account and product combination that need to be picked out for special reclassifications in reports.

Different approaches were used to manage these manual adjustment data during POC and production stages. In the POC design, manual adjustment data are managed in separate Excel worksheets as user data inputs, Excel templates are created to capture the manual data in a more structured and governed manner. In the production design, efforts have been taken by finance teams to streamline the data process and ensure reconciliation data being uploaded into source systems at proper granular accounting levels. Special case three was streamlined by creating additional account to cater for these accounting entries, which will be processed with standard system trees. As data is corrected at source, Qlikview applications that built on these sources will be able to achieve simultaneous update and synchronization across finance teams.

4.3. Qlikview architecture and application design

A simplified Qlikview architecture will include a back-end process and a front-end process. back-end process will produce source documents from various data sources (e.g., data warehouses, Excel files, text files, etc.) through scripting using the Qlikview Developer. Those source documents are highly compressed and stored as binary data within QVD files. Source documents can be further processed with business rules, aggregation, and summation within Qlikview Publisher for enrichments that support business needs.

Front-end process is where end-users interact with the documents and data that they are authorized to see via the Qlikview server. It contains the Qlikview user documents that have been created at the back-end. All communication between the client and server occurs here and is handled via HTTPS. Within the front end, QVS is responsible for client security. End-users can only access Qlikview documents that exist at the front end. Authentication can be applied at various levels: server folder, QVW file, and even application sheets, thus enabling better security control for enterprise deployment.

Figure 5 illustrates Qlikview infrastructure architecture for enterprise setup. Qlikview infrastructure is split between two servers, so that horizontal scaling is feasible to meet future requirements.

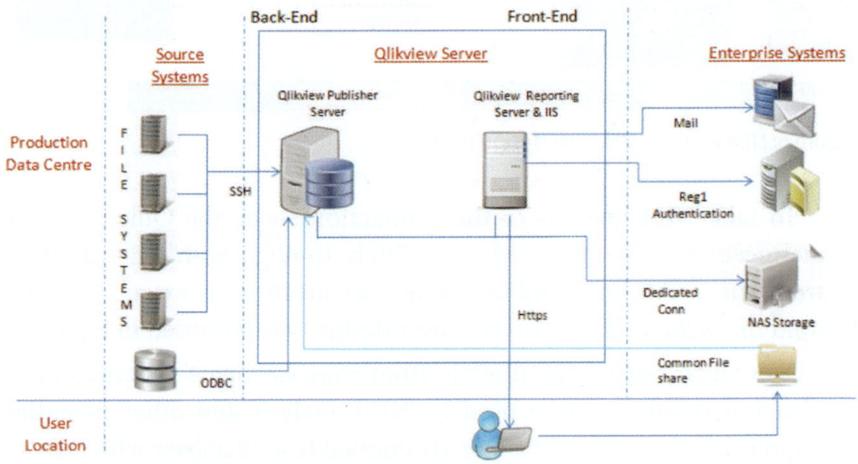

Figure 5: Finance Qlikview infrastructure architecture.

Built on this infrastructure, NIM analysis Qlikview application is thus designed as seen in Figure 6. Back-end process will perform data loading and enrichment processing. Various data source Excel worksheets are ingested into Qlikview through scripting. Further enrichments with reference to system trees and customized mapping tables were performed in Qlikview Publisher to achieve intermediary output, which has been aggregated for final presentation dashboard. On the front end, eight Excel workbooks analysis were recreated and integrated in presentation layer in a single Qlikview Publisher.

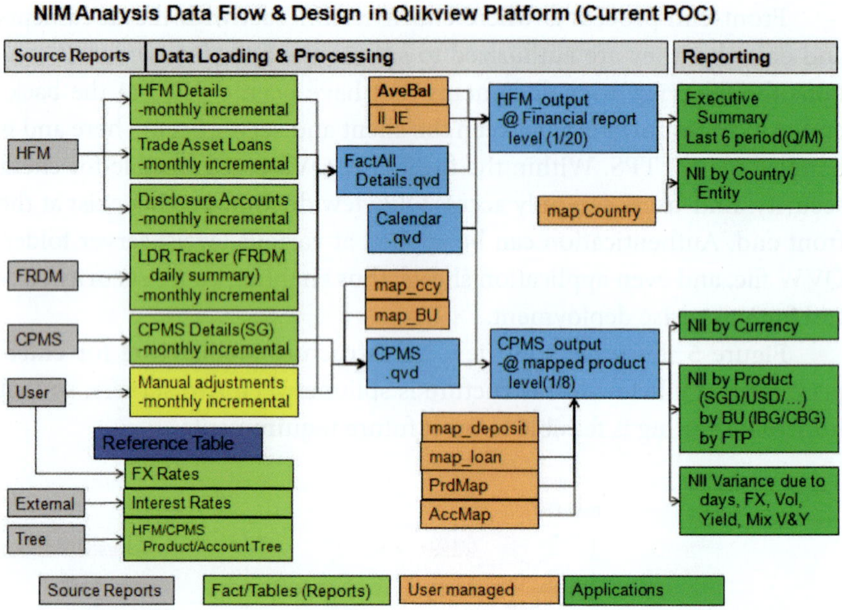

Figure 6: NIM analysis Qlikview design (POC).

To take NIM analysis to the production stage, the Qlikview data model needed to be improved accordingly to align with strategic data sources and create more robust design architecture to extend support beyond the NIM analysis. A three-layer design was proposed in Figure 7.

1) Data layer: Ingest data directly from sources; create generic binary documents that can be used by NIM analysis and other potential applications. Data will be directly queried from database with ODBC connections and exported to Qlikview server.
2) Business layer: Enrich data with business rules and requirements needed for NIM analysis. Business rules were discussed with multiple finance teams to seek consensus. Business rules mapping tables will be managed and updated by respective process owners. System trees are all managed within FRDM system, thus to ensure a single version fact to be used across finance teams.
3) Presentation layer: Dashboard and analysis to fulfill NIM analysis needs. With this design more Qlikview presentation applications can be built based on data, either from data layer or business layer, thus extend support to other finance teams or analysis functions.

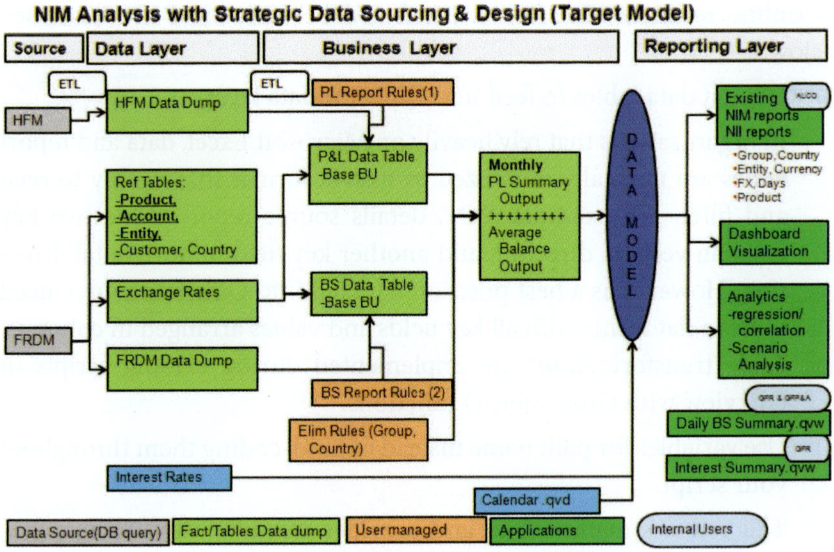

Figure 7: NIM analysis Qlikview design (Production Target Model).

The most critical improvements from the POC to production design include:

- More strategic and granular flat data table used which was queried directly from the source systems rather than structured reports generated from the source systems.
- Detail design extended to include daily processing data sources, data frequency can increase from monthly to daily.
- Master reference data (trees, rates, etc.) processed from centralized FRDM rather than ad-hoc sources.
- Streamlineed process workflow, business rules and eliminated manual adjustments.
- Followed Qlikview design best practice with Star Schema data model and three layer design architecture.

4.4. Qlikview development: Challenges and best practices

During POC Qlikview development, best practices were adopted and a number of challenges were solved through internal experts as well as online resources. Lessons learned and best practices are discussed below:

1) Use flat data tables to feed into Qlikview data layer.

   In organizations that rely heavily on Microsoft Excel, data and report tables are normally organized in matrix format that is easy to read and filter. For example, POC details source reports have two key fields in vertical direction and another key field in horizontal direction. However as a best practice, data fed into Qlikview source need to be in flat forms with all key fields and values arranged in columns. Table transformations are implemented during loading scripts in Qlikview with CrossTable () functions.

2) Use variables for path name instead of hard-coding them throughout your script.

   This reduces maintenance and provides a simple way to find paths, and general practice is to put them in the first tab to make it easy to find. Recommended structure includes folders that contain applications, raw data, QVD, rules, etc. Use relative path instead of full path for variable declaration to facilitate easy migration from location to location.

3) Data load optimization

   After table transformation loading, value fields can be cleaned up by filtering out zero, empty or null values and redundant fields can be removed.

4) Clean up data fields and field values before applying mapping, join or use as key field.

   Data ingested from Excel worksheets may contain undesirable characters, e.g., empty space or break lines at both ends of a cell value, which needs to be trimmed or truncated. Fields with a mixture of string and numeric values may fail to join exactly due to numeric approximations, which can be fixed by converting field values to string. Fields from Excel columns may contain multiple attributes that need to be split with string functions. Column names need to be standardized across tables and aligned to organization naming conventions.

5) Incremental loading and enrichments

   POC data sources come in on a monthly basis, best practice is to load only the latest month's records to improve loading efficiency especially when datasets become large. Reference trees and mapping tables may have new changes from month to month, thus enrichments scripts need to match period between incremental data, new trees and maps. As a result, incremental aggregation and fact table outputs are preserved with respect to business requirements for each historical period.

6) Data value transformation in data layer

   During POC design, our data source values are reported as YTD (year-to-date) in Excel worksheets. However for presentation needs, analysis viewpoints are in monthly, quarterly, and yearly views. So data value is best to be organized in MTD format to reduce complexity of expressions in the presentation layer. This transformation is performed in data layer.

7) Auto generation of calendar and enrichments

   User maintained tables should be minimized. Calendar is auto-generated with reference to existing periods inside fact data tables and enriched with pre-calculated columns. Presentation layer expressions' complexity is significantly reduced by introducing these pre-calculated columns, e.g., past months sequence, current year to date flag, last year to date flag and number of days within each month, quarter, and year.

8) Reduce complexity of user managed mapping tables

   Some large customized user mapping tables can be derived from existing system trees and enriched with a smaller customized table. In this case, Qlikview will take in only the key and common smaller user tables and enrich them with system trees in scripts. This is necessary to ensure a more smooth business process management and synchronization with latest system trees.

9) Separation of data layer and presentation layer as illustrated in both Figures 6 and 7.

   When the complexity of the project increases, especially of data loading and enrichments, the best practice is to adopt three-layer design architecture. Data and business layers run at the back-end and perform all sorts of data extraction, transformation, loading, enrichments, and some aggregations. This setup is aligned with the two-server architecture and to ensure reporting layer is more light-weighted to optimize user-front performances.

10) Use set analysis (Qlikview tool) in presentation expressions

    To improve performance in the presentation layer, Set Analysis tool is recommended for expressions rather than using "if conditions". Set Analysis is much faster because it takes advantage of Qlikview's selection engine to simply exclude all of the rows that don't match; however IF conditions need to check through all rows of data to match field value, which takes longer time.

11) Maintain robust data models for presentation layer

    Synthetic keys have a bad reputation. The consensus is that they cause performance and memory problems; thus best practice is to avoid synthetic keys. If there are multiple key fields to match between tables, these can be extracted to a link table. Final data model should reduce snowflake tables and consolidate them in business layer, star schemas are generally the best solution for fast and flexible Qlikview applications.

12) Data validation

    It is essential to build data validation checkpoints throughout data delivery journey. There were three checkpoints with Qlikview applications. First checkpoint is to validate incremental loading being processed successfully and adequate number of rows added to optimized QVD documents. Second checkpoint is to validate that there is only a single corresponding match between account and respective business rules. This checkpoint ensures that business logic and aggregation are performed correctly. Third checkpoint is the user acceptance test (UAT) on presentation layer whereby Qlikview outputs should align with current manual processed Excel outputs. This checkpoint collaborates the efforts among Qlikview developer, business analyst, and business users.

4.5. NIM reporting and analysis framework

Current NIM analysis focus is to identify movements and investigate the potential causes. In a typical financial analysis cycle, three types of periodic analysis will be performed: month-on-month, quarter-on–quarter, and year-on-year analysis. Current NIM reporting and analysis framework can be simplified and summarized as in Figure 8. The POC Qlikview design enables business users to view dashboard reports and perform analysis in a single integrated application. Business users only need to navigate within the same Qlikview application and will be able to perform analysis in a much faster, more interactive and effective manner.

Reporting & Analysis

Group Movements: IBA, IBL, IR, IP, NII, Yield, NIM	Country Movements: IBA, NII, NIM, Adjusted values w.r.t Days within period	Country & Product & Customer Movements: NII by Accounting currency, Product Group, Product type, Customer segmentation, etc.
Contribution analysis: Assets, Liabilities classifications	Contribution analysis: Days impact, Exchange Rate impact, Others	Contribution analysis: Balance change impact, Yield change impact, Mixture of Yield and Volume change

Delivered Analysis Insights & Summary

Days adjusted NII, Exchange Rate impact, market shocks, and provisions	Impact from market interest rates, cost of funding, changes in balance sheets composition (volume change, product mixture change, etc.)

Figure 8: Current NIM reporting and analysis framework.

Two user cases are discussed here to illustrate how Qlikview NIM analysis can help answer business questions and support decisions to take actions.

4.5.1. Dashboard and Insights delivery

Figure 9 below illustrates the generic overall summary of DBS Group NIM performance with artificial figures. Period-on-period movements are analyzed and can be further drilled down with respect to various dimensions according to analysis framework in Figure 8. Impact of various factors and dimensions is calculated in terms of net interest income. Further insights and discoveries are then summarized for management review. Qlikview application is able to deliver much faster from data collection and integration to dashboard representation. Business users are able to investigate and analyze more granular data in a more interactive and effective manner, which cannot be easily achieved with Microsoft Excel.

	20xx			20xx			Movements (YoY)		
	Balances	Interest Revenue /Expense	Yield	Balances	Interest Revenue /Expense	Yield	Balances	Interest Revenue /Expense	Yield
Customer loans	67.53	1.82	2.69%	64.94	1.56	2.40%	2.60	0.26	0.29%
Interbank assets	11.69	0.16	1.33%	12.99	0.13	1.00%	-1.30	0.03	0.33%
Securities	20.78	0.39	1.88%	19.48	0.34	1.73%	1.30	0.05	0.14%
Interest Bearing Assets	**100.00**	**2.36**	**2.36%**	**97.40**	**2.03**	**2.08%**	**2.60**	**0.34**	**0.28%**
Customer deposits	77.92	0.52	0.67%	83.12	0.47	0.56%	-5.19	0.05	0.10%
Other borrowing	16.88	0.13	0.77%	12.99	0.10	0.80%	3.90	0.03	-0.03%
Interest Bearing Liabilities	**94.81**	**0.65**	**0.68%**	**96.10**	**0.57**	**0.59%**	**-1.30**	**0.08**	**0.09%**
Net Interest Income		1.71			1.45			0.26	
Net Interest Margin			1.71%			1.49%			0.22%

Figure 9: Group NIM summary report (artificial figures).

NIM analysis will help to answer business questions related to movements in net interest income (NII) and NIM. Summary of insights can be illustrated by remarks on NII/NIM in 2014 Annual Report (p. 31). "Net interest income increased 14 per cent to SGD 6.32 billion as loans grew and NIM improved. NIM for the full year increased six basis points to 1.68 per cent as trade loan pricing was higher and yields on securities and interbank assets rose. Deposit and other funding costs were stable. NIM progressively increased during the course of the year and reached 1.71 per cent in the fourth quarter, the highest in 10 quarters". "Net interest margin (Customer Segmentation: CBG) also improved from better housing loan pricing". These statements illustrate the summary on movements and underlying cause analysis with respect to various dimensions.

4.5.2. Insights to actions

Analysis of China's performance has pointed to high correlation between market interest rate and NIM; thus actions have been taken to improve NIM in China Region by improving loan to deposit ratio (LDR). More loans on assets side of the BS will help to generate higher interest income, thus improving NIM.

Quote from 2013 Annual report (p. 40) on China's performance: "With further interest rate liberalization during the year, NIM came under pressure, especially in the first half of the year. Against this backdrop, steps were taken to improve the loan-deposit ratio and our deposit mix". Figure 10 illustrates the trend of interest rate, NIM, and LDR. NIM has increased with the improvement in LDR, however, was offset by further decline of interest rates in the following periods. These observations are aligned with research findings in literature review.

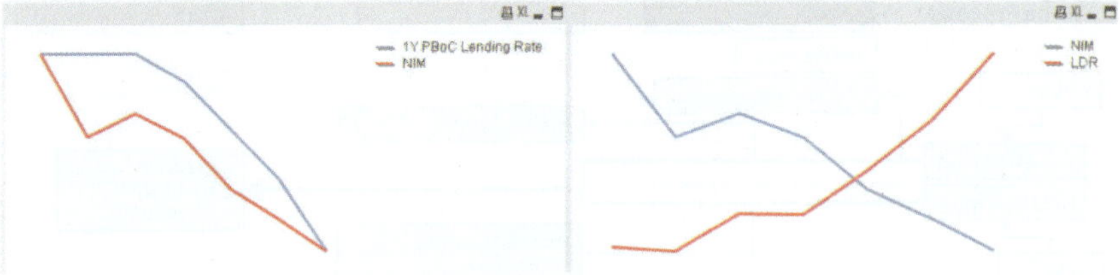

Figure 10: China analysis — NIM, interest rate, LDR.

5. DISCUSSION

As for a POC Qlikview design, it is most critical to deliver and demonstrate the functionality, usability, flexibility, and capability of new applications that will help transform current reporting and analysis practices. The benefits that stem from Qlikview application projects and implementations include:

- Strategic data sources and common references shared across finance teams
- More centralized data sources in one place to support financial reporting and analysis
- Automated process for data ETL (extract, transform, load) and quality check, not having to wait for an analyst to deliver it or the IT department to be involved
- Automated process for data enrichment and consolidation, without performing complex functions and formulas in multiple Excel workbooks
- Better governance for manual adjustment of the data. Data is reconciled and corrected at source rather than at user-front, and simultaneously synchronized across all supporting Qlikview applications
- Streamlined business rules and consensus between upstream and downstream finance teams, as well as streamlined data flows and business process flows (Figure 11)
- Removed dependency on upstream report consolidation and enable simultaneous processing by multiple finance teams
- Faster delivery from data to reporting

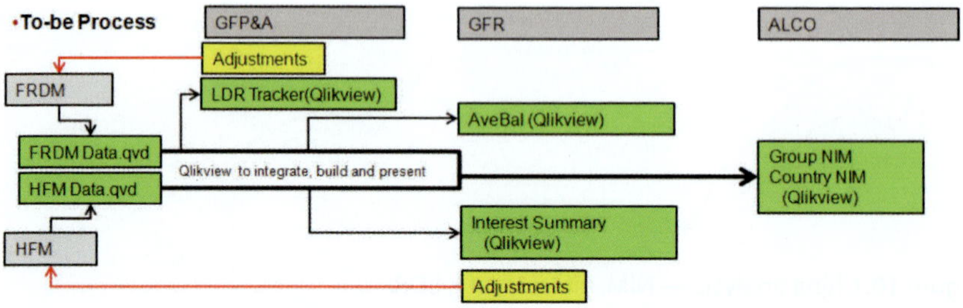

Figure 11: To-be process flow with integration of Qlikview applications.

6. CONCLUSION AND FURTHER WORK

Building functioning Qlikview applications is a first step to adopt business intelligence in operations. Following the application implementation, organizations, including both project team and business users, need to further incorporate the value creations into their business process management. In this project, a great deal of effort was focused on improving data sources and building Qlikview applications to fulfill current business needs and delivered a POC Qlikview application. Management has agreed to bring this application to production. More strategic data sourcing and architecture has been discussed and planned for Qlikview production design. With the production design, new analysis viewpoints can be explored to enhance NIM analysis for further insights and new Qlikview applications can be created to support beyond NIM analysis and current business users.

Qlikview supported process has enabled business users to better answer what has happened and why it happened in the past. Strategic data sources can extend the support to view what is happening on a daily basis rather than conventional monthly financial close. To further drive from insights to actions, business users can adopt more analytical capabilities within Qlikview as well as other analytics tools (SAS, SPSS, R, etc.) to enhance predictive analytics and prescriptive analytics. Though there is a Group Research team that performs more analytical work within the organization, the new Qlikview framework can also encourage more collaboration between operations and research.

REFERENCES

1. Ho, T and A Saunders (1981). The determinants of bank interest margins: theory and empirical evidence. *Journal of Financial and Quantitative Analysis*, 16, 581–600.

2. Angbanzo, L (1997). Commercial Bank net interest margins, default risk, interest rate risk and off balance sheet activities. *Journal of Banking and Finance*, 21, 55–87.

3. Maudos, J and J Fernandez de Guevara (2004). Factors explaining the interest margin in the banking sectors of the European Union. *Journal of Banking and Finance*, 28, 2259–2281.

4. Christoph Memmel and Andrea Schertler (2011). Bank's management of net interest margin: evidence from Germany. *Deutsche Bundesbank Discussion Paper*, 13/2011.

5. Gerald Hanweck and Lisa Ryu (2005). The sensitivity of bank net interest margins and profitability to credit, interest-rate and term-structure shocks across bank product specializations, *FDIC conference paper*, 2015.

6. Evelson, B (2008). Topic Overview: Business Intelligence. https://www.forrester.com/report/Topic+Overview+Business+Intelligence/-/E-RES39218 Forrester

7. Berson, A, S Smith and K Thearling (2002). *Building Data Mining Applications for CRM*, New York: McGraw-Hill, 3, 41–53, 236.

CHAPTER 16

Online Visitor Classification and Unified Creation With Clickstream Data

Gopala Raju

ABSTRACT

In a traditional store environment, it is possible for sales people to differentiate serious shoppers from window shoppers by simple observation. 'Serious' shoppers are very focused on looking for a specific product or two, whereas 'window' shoppers look at many different products and categories. Sales personnel can identify and decide to help serious shoppers and ignore window shoppers. However in a virtual environment, there are no sales people, and customers use multiple devices such as computers, smart phones, and tablets to browse websites and make purchases.

This study explains how clickstream data can be retrieved, processed, and used to classify customer visits into categories such as buying, browsing, searching, and knowledge building. It also explains a way to create unified user profiles by combining their visits through multiple devices. By using Adobe clickstream data of a telecom company's website, some measures are derived and used in a clustering analysis to group visitors into a few categories. Such a categorization of visits helps marketers to identify likely buyers, design more effective and customized promotions, and build more effective web content.

1. INTRODUCTION

In consumer analytics, it is often a requirement to identify and classify consumers, so that they can be tracked to understand their interaction with website, their behavior and to offer products/services and promotional content suitable for them. The user identification is straightforward for authentic websites. However for websites such as e-commerce, the identity is anonymous until the final steps of purchase. In addition, considering that a consumer uses multiple browsers, computers and mobile devices to browse a website, it is a challenge to create a unified profile to understand the overall customer behavior.

Companies rely on web analytics platforms such as Google Analytics, Adobe SiteCatalyst, and WebTrends to collect user information and interaction from their websites. These platforms include JavaScript in designated pages, which collects some parameters from the browser once a page is loaded, and sends information to the tracking server. The script often receives a single pixel image as a response. It is also a common practice to collect information at a particular movement, e.g., a click or hovering over a link. The parameters typically include basic browser details, device details, cookies, shopping cart contents, custom tagging, and user information, etc.

Clickstream tracking activity creates a large number of records on the tracking server, depending upon the size of the website, ranging from few thousands to millions per day (see Figure 1.)

With easy and huge availability of smart phones and tablets, about 50 per cent of traffic is reported to come from smart devices when a telco's website data was analyzed. It is common for a consumer to browse different products and gather information from mobile devices at first and later on might use a personal computer to make a purchase. This sort of browsing fragments clickstream data, it results in multiple user profiles. When data is analyzed, it may appear that the user purchased a product directly from a device, but in reality she/he might have spent more time browsing, comparing, and reviewing product(s) from another device.

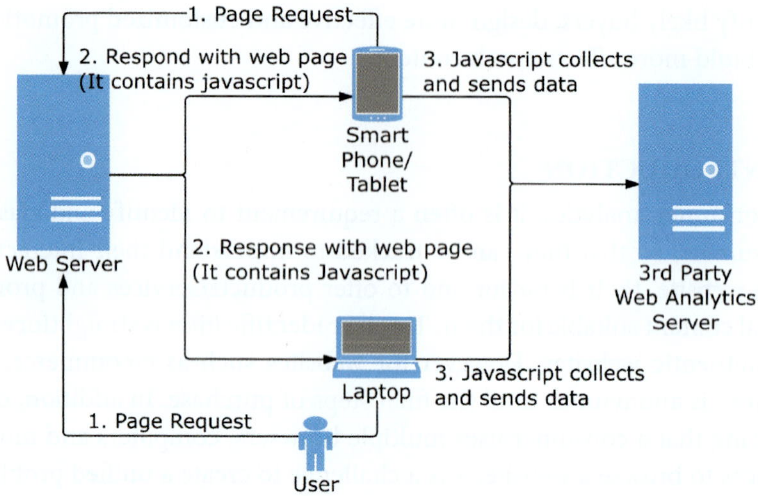

Figure 1: Clickstream tracking.

Anonymous user data is not very useful for an organization to generate leads or customize offers. Organizations like to reduce ratio between anonymous and known profiles by attaching some identity to a user, or using third-party or social media data. There are many companies, which create and sell user profiles via real-time bidding. When it comes to financial institutions, due to confidentiality of data, usage of third party or social media is not commonly practiced.

One of the companies in Singapore (called DS in this study), is trying to build a platform for its customers. The platform fetches click-stream data from adobe SiteCatalyst servers, performs some cleansing, stores data in a big-data store, and more importantly helps its customers to build analytical models with the data. The platform also addresses defragmented visitor profiles problem by creating a mechanism to create Unique User Identification (UUIDs). This study was done for DS to build the platform and solve their customer problems.

This study specifically focuses on analyzing clickstream data of a Singapore-based telecom company (a customer of DS), with a website having both informative content and a wide range of products and services that can be purchased or subscribed by customers.

This study focuses on addressing platform as well as analytical requirements of a telco customer.

2. PROBLEM STATEMENT

Organizations would like to understand how their websites are being accessed, who their customers are, and how their customers make purchase decisions. Such understanding helps companies to offer customized services, conduct marketing campaigns, present promotional content, and improve their websites, products and service offerings.

One of the telecom companies in Singapore would like to categorize its website visitors, identify them, reduce anonymous visits, and create unified user profile by combining user identities from multiple devices, so that whole behavior can be understood instead of fragmented user activity.

The overall business objectives of the telecom company are:

- Classify website's visitors into categories
- Perform descriptive analysis on the data and combine user visits from multiple devices after creating unified user profiles
- Model the attribution to explain the causes of behavior and events
- Understand customer behavior holistically, instead of analyzing device-specific data which may provide only partial information

However, for DS the project-specific objectives are:

- Create a platform which allows customers to generate unique customer identity (UUID) based on their email addresses
- Identify and design a data store for storing semi-structured data from web analytics and other sources
- Import web analytics raw data from SiteCatalyst
- Import other data collected through forms or surveys
- Clean and transform data for analytics and reporting purposes
- Build required analytics models
- Feed data from data store to Tableau reporting tool

3. STATE OF THE ART

Many researchers in the past, both practitioners and academics have studied consumer search behavior. Some of these addressed inter-store comparisons across multiple online retailers while others examined intra-store behavior.

One paper in particular (Moe, 2003) explained about how clickstream data can be used to classify visitors into categories. The current study uses similar dataset as the one used by Moe (2003) to derive classifications. Moe categorizes customer visits into two types: directed-buying visits and search/deliberation visits. Directed-buying visitors already have sufficient knowledge about products they are interested to buy, so they spend more time on browsing fewer products before purchasing them, whereas in search/deliberation visits, visitors focus on information gathering about products and services, so they look at various products and categories, and may not buy anything in the end but they might purchase on later visits. The study ultimately classified visitors into five categories, knowledge building, hedonic browsing, directed buying, search deliberation and shallow. Similar categorization was attempted in the current study.

Another study (Hossain, 2013) is related to the technology aspect. Since the volume of clickstream data is so huge, various NoSQL databases were analyzed and good analysis of the technological details and alternatives are suggested.

To come up with a mechanism to create UUID, some websites were referred (Hendricks, 2013; Leek, 2012) which helped to understand hashing email addresses and different encryption alternatives.

Clickstream data is complex in nature and contains hundreds of variables, so Adobe clickstream documentation was referred. The paper also explains how certain key measures can be calculated based on raw attributes.

4. SOLUTION: DESCRIPTION OF APPROACH

The telecom company in Singapore offers a range of services from broadband to cable television to mobile network. It serves both corporate and personal consumers. The company has a large website which provides lot of informative content about its services, as well as an e-commerce section where consumers can purchase mobile and tablet devices and subscribe to mobile network services. This paper attempts to understand how visitors browse the e-commerce section and make purchases.

The website has been tagged extensively for web analytics using adobe SiteCatalyst services. For majority of pages, JavaScript submits data to Adobe servers on page load, but for e-commerce pages, data is also submitted whenever a product is searched, viewed, and added to or removed from shopping carts.

SiteCatalyst servers are recording about 400,000 entries a day on an average for the Telco website.

4.1. Data sources/extraction

Adobe SiteCatalyst provides basic reporting to satisfy operational needs but does not have capability for modeling and in-depth analysis, so it has to be performed outside of SiteCatalyst platform. Currently, SiteCatalyst provides two types of data exports, by using data warehouse and external data feeds. Sample data was extracted initially using data warehouse feature. It was found that some of the raw variables like timestamps are not included in the export. Also data warehouse exports are huge in size and require very high computing resources to process them. A day worth of exported data was about 30GB in size and very difficult to process.

Later SiteCatalyst documentation identified that raw data can be delivered as regular feeds. So a request was submitted to SiteCatalyst for data feeds to deliver it on a daily basis to a FTP server. Data feeds provide clickstream data in raw format, which include many common attributes, but some of the required attributes are missing which can be derived from raw attributes. The daily feed contains clickstream data in tab delimited format, multiple lookup files which help to assign labels for some data properties such as operating system, and a summary file explaining total records in a feed file. Adobe's documentation explained well the various attributes and how some of the frequent measures can be computed from dataset.

Clickstream data feed is the main data source used in this paper. An artificial data feed to mimic unique customer ids (UUIDs) for some customers is used as a secondary source.

4.2. Overall design

In this study, SiteCatalyst data feed is used as main data source and is combined with other sources such as online application forms data and user identity feeds, and stored in a NoSQL database called DSE Cassandra.

SiteCatalyst servers send the data to an FTP on a daily basis. A scheduled job retrieved files from FTP location and processed by application.

Some cleaning, explained later, is performed on the data before it is submitted to data store, DSE/ Cassandra. Data related to an organization is stored together in a single keyspace/database.

A sample set for a week worth of data is used for analysis and model building in R. Cleaning rules and new variable creation logic was identified in R initially and later implemented in application using Clojure.

New variables are created and data is aggregated to create measures in java. The aggregated data is stored in a separate table in DataStax Enterprise Edition (DSE).

Clustering is performed using R script, which gets invoked by a scheduler after data load is completed. The script runs k-means clustering algorithm and results are merged back to aggregated data in data store.

Aggregated data along with UUIDs, clustering information, and other data is fed to a Tableau server for reporting. When there is a reporting requirement, data is pulled out of DSE using Tableau's import data wizard (see Figure 2).

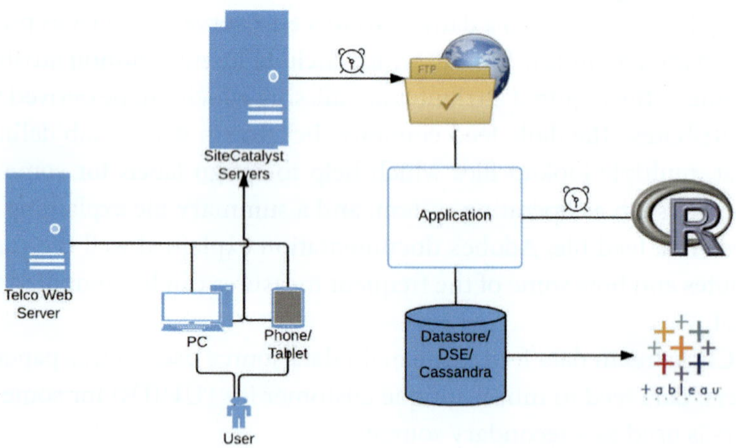

Figure 2: Overall architecture.

4.3. Technical design

An application platform is being built in Java for DS to:

- collect data feeds from Adobe SiteCatalyst servers
- perform some cleaning on the data
- store cleaned data into a NoSQL data store

- send data to a R Script for model development
- aggregate data and to make it available for reporting using Tableau

The platform helps DS's customers to enhance their reporting of clickstream data, understand visitor interaction with site from multiple devices, and build analytical models with data.

SiteCatalyst servers constantly record clickstream data generated from visitors' computers and smart devices. On an average, servers recorded four million entries for the website. Partially aggregated data is available for basic reporting on SiteCatalyst reporting platform. SiteCatalyst also provides raw data as data feeds for the client for their own analysis and reporting. Data feeds contain very basic properties from which new variables and measures can be calculated.

Data feeds are retrieved from FTP site by loading module and some cleaning is performed based on URLs to reduce junk and irrelevant data. Cleaned version of data is stored in a NoSQL database. Cleaning and Loading Modules are written in Clojure, which is a functional programming language that runs on Java Virtual Machine (JVM).

DSE was selected as a main data store as it offers Cassandra along with other relevant technologies to make a true enterprise solution that covers store, search, and analytics use cases. It includes NoSQL database Cassandra for storage, SOLR for search, and Hadoop and Spark for analytical use. DSE offers a linearly scalable solution for the enterprise and supports almost all big-data uses. Cassandra supports wider and flexible tables, even up to thousands of columns and all records in a table do not need to have same columns. This is important as data feed attributes vary frequently and database has to accommodate such changes.

Cassandra/DSE supports key spaces, which are equivalent to database in relational terms. Separate data are stored in separate key space. Whole raw data is stored in a single table, since larger tables do not create any performance issues when stored in Cassandra. Three attributes *visitor_id*, *visit_number* and *date* make partition key, so that data for a customer's visit is stored in a single node within a multi-node cluster.

Apart from two application platform modules, data loading and cleaning which are written in Clojure, others are written using Spring framework in Java.

Cleaned data is aggregated after every data load and stored in a separate table, and aggregated data is sent for model development in R on a daily basis using a scheduler. Once R script is executed, result file is loaded and merged back with aggregated data in data store.

Aggregated data is retrieved by Tableau server for reporting using a database connector, since Cassandra does not have a connector for Tableau, DSE's hive data connector was used. Hive reads data from underlying storage of Cassandra called Cassandra File System or CFS (see Figure 3).

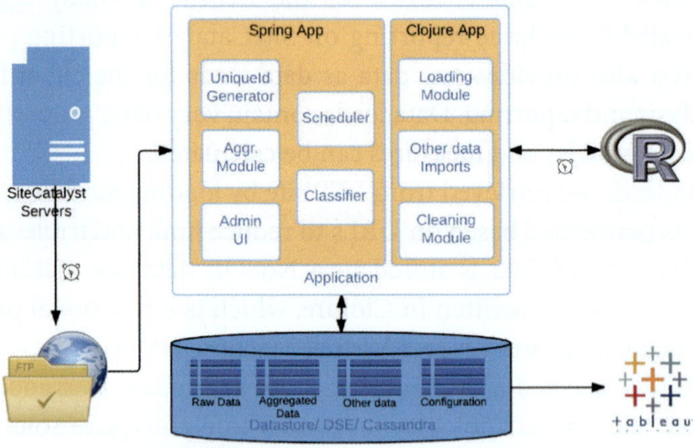

Figure 3: Technical design overview.

4.4. Assumptions and limitations

The following assumptions were made relating to data, model, and platform:

i) The model developed here can be applied to DS's other customers as well with minor changes customizations.
ii) For Telco, online visits may not result in online purchases as they have physical stores throughout Singapore, so analysis of in-store purchases is out of scope of this study.
iii) For unique identifiers, a mock dataset was used created by randomly selecting some visitor ids. It may not be complete real world representation.
iv) The solution is built using a trial version of DSE, since they offer free licenses for startups. It offers a good complete solution for large volumes of data that organization will have in future.

v) Page visit duration is limited to 3 min with an assumption that a page does not require more than 3 min to read; user probably left a page idle if the duration is more than 3 min.

vi) It is assumed that marketing emails containing UUID are read from multiple devices and user clicks on website links at least once over few days or months. User remains anonymous until an UUID is assigned on a device

4.5. UUID creation

With increased number of smart devices and data services usage in Singapore, clickstream data has also increased significantly over the past few years. Users increasingly browse websites from their mobile devices, e.g., while they are commuting, and they may also use a different device, to purchase a product or service. This results in multiple profiles (visitor ids) in clickstream data, and analyzing such data to understand overall interaction is always partial.

To overcome this limitation, UUIDs were created based on user's email address. A HashKey based on secure hashing algorithm 1(SHA1) encryption is generated for user's email address and pushed to user's computer or mobile device at appropriate time. This is then stored in a UUID cookie and is available for SiteCatalyst tracking.

The encryption based on SHA1 generates almost unique same HashKey for every email address (see Figure 4). However, the algorithm is case-sensitive, so the email address should always have consistent casing of all the letters.

Figure 4: Example of UID generated based on email address.

Following are some opportunities for telco to send UUID HashKey and subsequently create user cookies.

- Any marketing emails, containing a hyperlink to website, sent to users is a good opportunity to send UUID. Hash keys should be generated and included in such mass emails. The website should have application logic to generate UUID cookies when UID parameter includes URL.

- Html form filled on website is another opportunity to create UUID cookie.
- Service emails containing confirmation links, information content, Thank You messages is another opportunity to push UUID cookies to client browser.

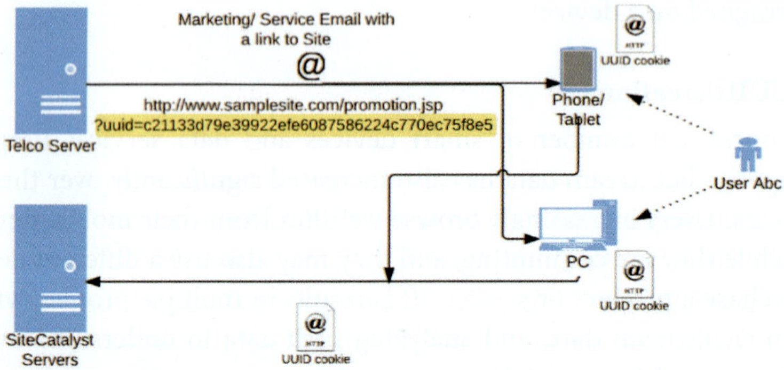

Figure 5: UUID tracking using marketing emails.

Once UUID cookie is stored in user's devices, tracking JavaScript retrieves the cookie and sends it to SiteCatalyst servers. The server extracts the cookie and new attribute/variable cust_uuid is created. Once the attribute appears in data feeds, it is possible to aggregate multiple visitor ids using UUID for reporting and analysis purposes (see Figure 5).

4.6. SiteCatalyst data feed contents

SiteCatalyst servers send data feeds on a daily basis using FTP and each feed contains following files:

- *Manifest File*: containing following details about each file from uploaded dataset:
  - File name
  - File size
  - MD5 hash
  - Number of records contained in the file
- *Lookup Files*: it does not contain hit data but are supplemental files that provide column headers for the hit data, and translate the IDs found in the data feed to actual values e.g., a value of "497" in the

browser column indicates that the hit came from "Microsoft Internet Explorer 8".

The lookup files are delivered together in a compressed zip named according to the following:

<report_suite_id>_<YYYY-mm-dd>-<HHMMSS>-lookup_data.<compre._suffix>

- column_headers.tsv (customized for this data feed)
- browser.tsv
- browser_type.tsv
- color_depth.tsv
- connection_type.tsv
- country.tsv
- javascript_version.tsv
- languages.tsv
- operating_systems.tsv
- plugins.tsv
- resolution.tsv
- referrer_type.tsv
- search_engines.tsv
- event_lookup.tsv (customized for this data feed)

- *Hit Data Files*: Hit data is provided in a hit_data.tsv file. The amount of data in this file is determined by the delivery format (hourly or daily, single or multiple files). This file contains only hit data. The column headers are delivered separately with the lookup files. Each row in this file contains a single server call.

4.7. Important variables in data feeds

The raw dataset has about 652 variables in total, out of which about 230 have data on daily feeds, while others have missing values. The variables with missing data are ignored, neither stored in database nor used in model building.

Appendix 1 in the appendix shows some of the important variables in the dataset used during cleaning, to derive newer variables and to perform aggregation.

4.8. Data cleaning

A week's worth of data is considered for analysis, model building, and reporting. Iit is loaded into R for basic understanding and generating descriptive statistics. The cleaning rules, logic to create new variables, and aggregation process is identified in R initially and then implemented in Java/ Clojure application.

Following cleaning is performed on the raw data. Some of the rules are mentioned in the feed reference document from Adobe.

i) Excluded records, which have flag *exclude_hit* > zero.

ii) Excluded records with *hit_source* as five, eight, and nine.

iii) Filtered rows with *page_url* variable containing the following:

   a) *Word blocked*

   b) Empty strings

   c) Having words such as *bet, poker, casino*, and other *obscene* words

iv) Website user profile pages.

Finally, there are many variables in the dataset, which do not have any data. Such variables are ignored, and the final cleaned dataset contained about 240 variables. Total dataset has about 2,726,909 records.

4.9. Derived variables

Many of the raw variables have a lot of missing data and too many categories. To perform classification, some key measures need to be calculated using the raw data.

derived_visitorId: This variable is a standard visitor identity variable in SiteCatalyst reporting, but in data feeds it is not available. It is computed by concatenating *visid_high* and *visid_low* with "_" as a separator.

derived_post_prop1: This variable represents page category and it is computed based on raw variables *post_prop1* and *page_url*. First it is assigned to *post_prop1*, but since it contained a lot of missing data, page_url is parsed based on the below logic and values computed for derived_post_prop1 (see Table 1).

derived_page_category: This variable is used to group pages into categories and these categories are required to compute some of the key

Table 1: Page URL parsing to create categories.

***page_url* contains**	***derived_post_prop1***
search.starhub.com	Search
personal/mobile	mobile
personal/store/mobile	mobile
personal/hubbing	hubbing
/broadband	broadband
/about-us	company information
/support	support
/rewards	rewards
/business	corporate
Promotion	promotion
Voice	voice
tv/	tv
Cartsummary	checkout
Orderconfirmation	checkout
Billing	checkout
store.html	products

measures used for visitor classification. The variable *derived_post_prop1* is used to compute page categories, grouped into, home pages, search pages, product related pages, promotional pages, information related pages, and checkout pages.

Appendix 2 gives the grouping of *derived_post_prop1* values to page categories.

derived_page_duration: This is an important variable, which explains how much time (in seconds) a user has spent on a page and is computed by sorting based on *derived_visitor_id, visit_num and post_cust_hit_time_gmt* (timestamp). For some rows, this value is not set as there is no subsequent page record or it's the only page visited by during particular visit.

In reality a user may open a page but never read the contents or opened another page simultaneously, in such cases, this field can have a really huge duration. Hence, the need to set a high value of 180 s for it, if its higher than 180, it is assumed that a page does not take more than 3 min to read.

derived_visitor_class: This variable explains whether a visitor is interested in business or personal products. If class cannot be determined, value is set to *don't know* class.

derived_customer_type: This variable is computed to determine whether the visitor is an existing or new customer.

derived_product_type: This variable explains what type of product or service a visitor is interested in. The categories include *broadband*, *mobile*, and *TV*.

derived_brand: This variable explains what kind of brand a visitor is interested in, e.g., Apple, Samsung, LG, etc.

derived_product: This variable explains what kind of product the visitor is interested in, e.g., IPhone 6, Samsung Galaxy S5.

Page Category Count Variables: The variables below are computed to represent page counts per visit related to five page categories

derived_home_page_visit_cnt	*No of home pages viewed per visit*
derived_products_page_visit_cnt	*No of product pages viewed per visit*
derived_search_page_visit_cnt	*No of search pages viewed per visit*
derived_promotions_page_visit_cnt	*No of promotional pages viewed per visit*
derived_inforel_page_visit_cnt	*No of information related pages viewed per visit*
derived_checkout_page_visit_cnt	*No of checkout pages viewed per visit*

4.10. Aggregation/creation of measures

In clickstream data, each record represents visit to a single web page, typically a full interaction includes multiple pages, e.g., if a checkout process is considered on any e-commerce site, there will be multiple pages such as shopping cart page, billing page, shipping page, and order confirmation page. Each of these pages will have rows in clickstream data. Analyzing individual rows is not useful to understand what happened during visits.

To overcome this limitation, data is aggregated at visit level; some key measures are computed per visit and are subsequently used for analysis and model building. *derived_visitor_id* and *visit_num* variables are used to group rows together and following variables are computed.

visitor_class_business_count:	Sum of visit counts to business related product pages per customer visit.
visitor_class_personal_count:	Sum of visit counts to personal products related pages per customer visit.

visitor_class_business_count: A sum of visit counts to business related product pages per customer visit.

visitor_class_personal_count: A sum of visit counts to personal products related pages per customer visit.

brand_visit_count: Number of brand related pages browsed per visit.

brand_unique_visit_count: Number of unique brand related pages browsed per visit.

percent_diff_brand: Concentration of brand page visits computed by dividing *brand_unique_visit_count* by *brand_visit_count.*

product_visit_count: Number of product related pages browsed per visit.

product_unique_visit_count: Number of unique product related pages browsed per visit.

product_diff_brand: Concentration of product page visits computed by dividing *product_unique_visit_count* by *product_visit_count.*

pages_visited: Total number of pages browsed per visit.

percent_home_visits: Number of home pages browsed per visit, which includes categorical and sub-sectional home pages.

percent_product_visits: Number of product related pages browsed per visit.

percent_promotion_visits: Number of promotional pages browsed per visit.

percent_search_visits: Number of search pages browsed per visit.

percent_inforel_visits: Number of information related pages browsed per visit, this measures covers articles, news, general services, and support pages.

percent_checkout_visits: Number of checkout related pages browsed per visit, though a visitor has browed shopping cart and checkout pages, he/ she may not purchase something in the end, hence this measure is computed.

The aggregation at visit level reduced the size of dataset significantly from 2,726,909 records to 882,699 records. Total sample size for purchase is 139.

4.11. Classification model in R

Aggregated data is used for classification in R, to group visitors into some categories. Two types of classifications are tried in R, Decision Trees and K-means clustering.

There are 139 records representing purchase class in aggregated dataset, remaining 882,560 rows represent nonpurchase class. Since the ratio is very high, a sample set was created and used in classification analysis.

All 139 rows are included in the sample set from purchase class, and 417 rows were selected randomly from nonpurchase class, so the ratio in sample set has become 25–75 per cent.

a) **Decision Trees**: Decision trees classification was tried initially in R, with all the variables from aggregated dataset. The result was satisfactory and was able to classify some of the cases successfully but not all.

   Variables used:

   Decision variable: purchased

   Independent variables: visitor_class_business_count, visitor_class_personal_count, customer_type, product_type, viewed_support_pages, brand_visit_count, brand_unique_visit_count, percent_diff_brand, product_visit_count, product_ unique_visit_count, percent_diff_product, max_product_viewed, pages_visited, percent_home_visits, percent_product_visits, percent_promotion_visits, percent_inforel_visits, percent_search_visits, avg_page_time

The resulting plot is shown in Figure 6 below.

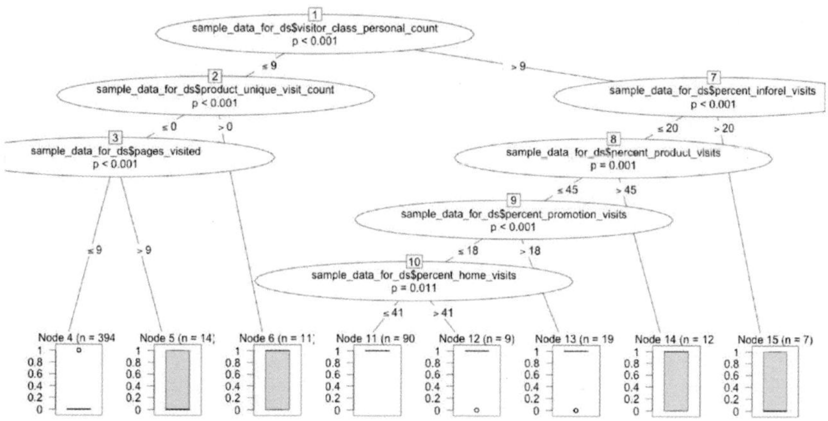

Figure 6: Decision tree plot 1.

The same classification tree using simple plot 2 (see Figure 7):

b) **K-Means Clustering**: A sample set with 25–75 per cent ratio of purchase to nonpurchase, was also used for clustering using K-Means algorithm. Initially, all aggregated variables were used for the model, but later some variables were excluded to get a better fit.

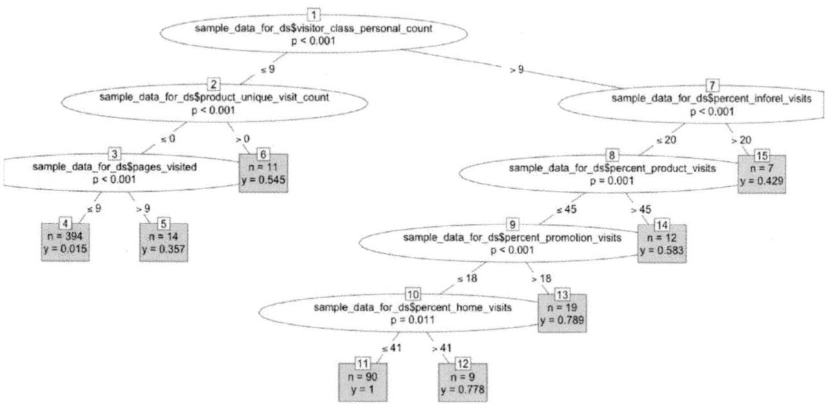

Figure 7: Decision tree plot 2 (simple type).

Variables used:
percent_diff_brand, percent_diff_product, max_product_viewed, percent_ home_visits, percent_product_visits, percent_promotion_ visits, percent_ inforel_visits, percent_search_visits, avg_page_time

Number of clusters to be used is determined by using a scree-plot (see Figure 8).

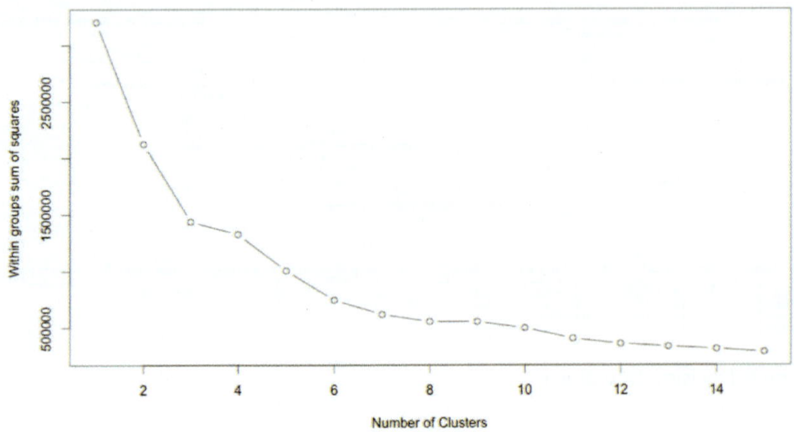

Figure 8: Scree-plot.

As the scree-plot suggested, around six, the line flattens off, so the K-means is tried for four, five, six, and seven clusters, and validated each of the resulting loading with purchased variable. With six clusters, number of purchases are loaded more into cluster two (Figure 9).

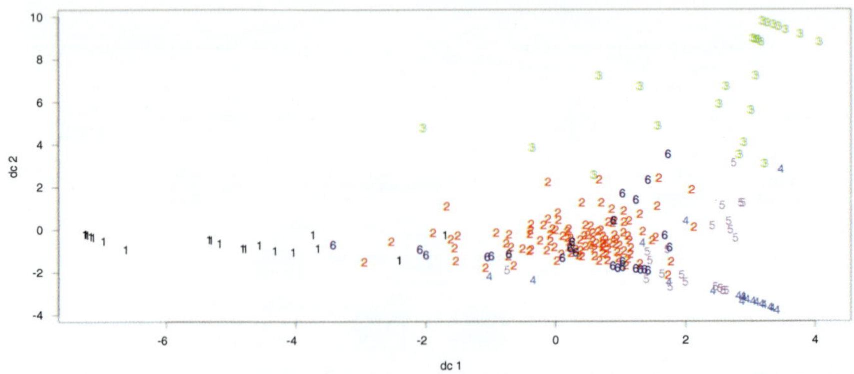

Figure 9: Clusters (two represents purchase class).

Shown below (Table 2) is the loading of purchased category responses into six clusters:

Table 2: Loading of purchase class into six clusters.

		Clusters						
		1	**2**	**3**	**4**	**5**	**6**	**Total**
Purchased	0	104	14	45	49	156	49	417
	1	0	135	2	1	0	1	139

4.12. Analysis based on unique user IDs

Though it is possible to create a UUID practically based on customer's email addresses, it is a huge time-consuming process to implement and have some sample data to understand how it helps with analysis and understanding of user interaction with website. For this reason, a dummy dataset was created to mimic UUIDs for this study.

A dataset for UUIDs was prepared based on the cleaned data used for cluster analysis. Total 100,000 unique visitor ids were taken into a separate data frame in R and each visitor id was assigned a random number between 1 and 100,000, encoded using SHA1 encryption algorithm to generate hash keys. These hash keys are considered as UUIDs for analysis. The visitor ids with hash keys (UUIDs) were merged back to cleaned dataset. The merged dataset was loaded into Tableau to perform further analysis.

Table 3 below shows the summary of this generation process.

Table 3: Summary of UUID dataset.

Original number of rows in cleaned dataset	2,726,909
Number of unique users in cleaned dataset	444,396
Number of unique users taken for Hashkey generation	100,000
Total number of unique random numbers (and hash keys) generated for 100,000 users	63,259

4.13. Device and operating system traffic analysis

Telco would like to understand how much traffic was generated from mobile devices. Original operating system variable *os* is a numeric data type, so new variable was created by using lookup files, which were included in the data feeds. Since our dataset was based on one week of clickstream data, it was required to combine seven files to create a single *os* lookup file. The *os* variable was joined with consolidated lookup file to create *os_name*. The variable *os_name* is parsed further to create *os_type* based on the following keyword mapping (Table 4). Figure 4 below shows the results for the top 25 items.

Table 4: Keyword mapping of OS name to device.

iOS	Mobile
Android	
Mobile	
Phone	
RIM	
Nokia	
Asha	
Symbian	
Bada	
Samsung	
LG	
Others	PC

4.14. Analysis of purchase activity based on UUIDs

Telco would also like to understand how UUIDs would help us understand purchase activity across devices. It's an assumption that a customer may use his mobile or smart device to browse products or services on the website, in reality he might use different devices to make purchase. With the introduction of UUID in the dataset, this analysis seemed possible.

To test the assumption, a dataset was prepared with purchase activity attached at UUID level. All UUIDs, with any purchases in the cleaned dataset were extracted and then filtered.

The resulting dataset has nicely loaded purchase data into UUIDs, meaning some of visitor ids do not have purchases except one. There is a

	Derived Os Type	
	Mobile	**PC**
Windows 7		660,066
Android 4.4.2	403,369	
Mobile iOS 8.3	300,854	
Windows 8.1		202,322
Android 4.4.4	191,027	
Android 5.0	145,582	
Android 4.3	96,156	
OS X 10.10		65,755
Android 5.0.1	57,125	
Android 5.0.2	55,235	
Linux		53,743
Android 4.2.2	48,013	
Mobile iOS 8.2	43,776	
Windows XP		40,062
Mobile iOS 7.1.2	31,623	
Mobile iOS 8.1.3	29,851	
Mobile iOS 8.1.2	28,282	
Android 4.1.2	25,366	
OS X 10.10.2		24,480
Windows Vista		21,148
OS X 10.9.5		20,786
Windows 8		18,401
Mobile iOS 8.1	13,278	
Mobile iOS 7.1.1	10,229	
Mobile iOS 8.1.1	9,908	

Figure 10: Device share of Traffic.

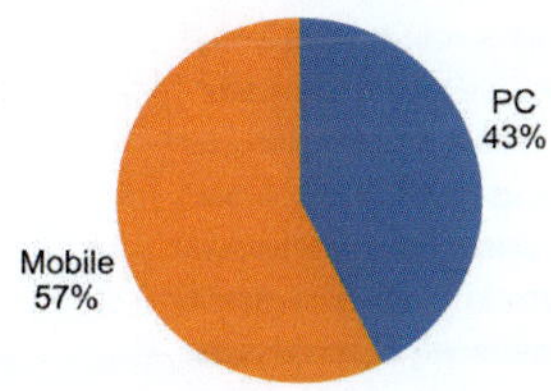

Figure 11: Traffic from different OS and device type (Top 25).

maximum loading of seven visitor ids to one UUID, which theoretically means a user used seven devices to browse the websites but used one to make a purchase (Figure 12).

Note: Please note that in the table above, there is repetition of one visitor_id when displayed in No and Yes (purchased) columns. It is due to the nature of data and visualization, e.g., 1st row has only seven visitor ids in dataset, but in the chart, it appears to be eight.

	"Purchased"	
UUID	No	Yes
"83b4400a05c5332152c29bb463147c60b558e3c7"	7	1
"3f4b208246304085efaed47b2d84967f5dbf9946"	5	1
"4c6661ce782fa8a20935a0fe5693fe8da6889b0c"	4	1
"0bfc05c356dac1b6f8b1b518e7d4e9150838741d"	3	1
"5cb86201125dca53d1a2f93b832f9461b9f6b05c"	3	1
"8d23f00622f59a4357be5a78276c4c1ed020d073"	3	1
"1cef1f9b6cfa42ccdd5c8635337ea57c460eaf70"	2	1
"f937c9a58cedd457deb2358f9d5f4f174f1f4f08"	2	1
"cec1b91c7aec9c6e522d13e67df5c43fffd06f95"	2	1
"f16d81b4ed0b7e0e0142ac1216fed8383d2d6a96"	2	1
"ae0aad2bcca00d7a447c3547abb8c14a7973b47f"	2	1
"8c200c0afde318b3c823d38e5782c987ee06379b"	2	1
"52d69f508f7ca1eb1bcef3e14be6fa751798c81a"	2	1
"454ca57f94cc83a16e030955b3c7c61e7a7e7820"	2	1
"d6242e143c52d980ee45a97da2c40a0ecc763abc"	2	1
"e28df6962ebd70806bd9d56d8b6fc2f947307c8d"	2	1
"a909fe0d6d1fc26491f1c349ad347f402ca600c9"	2	1
"fa4e9ad5cc791470ca2d12e9cfd53754804d8e01"	2	1
"2273e65ca6b33ed0aec476ae4a962c376b65a6ed"	2	1
"15aff1af9fe2c461365d3e126e3ea7501beff15b"	2	1
"9e38d70e2faf56933d8be6d4c52073b52672fc5f"	2	1
"54dc904e03f2c0977f315def9ec1ca5a15ca3e6d"	2	1
"2b8aa24c32d3f68cbce5c3aab54866e37a3da928"	1	1
"20a56dfbef0aca736ac9402ce0080fa13aaf32eb"	1	1
"66b5a1dc82c8b94c57784a4ce2b2fed45a9650e8"	1	1
"faffb8a587c825dfdc5152fdb6dcf84ca0d42ebd"	1	1
"abef86ccaab048d64ff029e92bb893a270a6f14e"	1	1
"a5a0042530432cfbd9cc51c87f5f4fdfeebfc92b"	1	1
"24358e54c6354406070d7c3c51b6594e866ceccf"	1	1
"99decb02723dd4f8aeef566fd94f3b3b8636853c"	1	1
"07659a1d5cec03757e448af1ce3a9dd08bf05c8b"	1	1
"da936a64b251874dafded727c92ed2a6ed569346"	1	1
"5ae16003a607bb0f19dfe9c05113a2f433a55a3e"	1	1

Figure 12: UUID to Visitor ID Loading

Table 5 gives the detailed listing of visits from multiple operating systems; majority of mobile tracking is from Android and IOS devices. The results are grouped in the table below:

Table 5: UUID based visits from OS and devices.

	Mobile		PC		
UUID (First 5 digits)	Android 4.1.2–5.0.1	IOS 8.1.2–8.3	NA	OS X 10.7.5–10.10	Windows XP, 7, 8
0bfc0	0	1		0	72
1cef1	0	0		4	25
2b8aa	34	0		0	0
3f4b2	2	2		0	61
4c666	0	13		0	46
5ae16	0	0		433	0
5cb86	0	0		0	172
8c200	0	0		0	46
8d23f	610	14		0	14
9e38d	63	0		0	81
15aff	0	109		0	4
20a56	36	0		0	0
52d69	7	0		0	40
54dc9	15	0		0	1140
66b5a	0	0		0	36
83b44	17	5		3	38
99dec	0	0		0	104
454ca	0	3		0	44
2273e	0	1		0	111
07659	0	0		166	0
24358	0	0		0	99
a5a00	0	0		0	82
a909f	52	0		0	46
abef8	0	0		48	0
ae0aa	2	0		0	43
cec1b	1	0		0	29
d6242	2	0		0	53
da936	0	0		0	202

(*continued*)

Table 5: UUID based visits from OS and devices. (*continued*)

	Mobile		PC		
UUID (First 5 digits)	**Android 4.1.2–5.0.1**	**IOS 8.1.2–8.3**	**NA**	**OS X 10.7.5–10.10**	**Windows XP, 7, 8**
e28df	0	0		0	73
f16d8	0	0	1	0	32
f937c	2	0		0	27
fa4e9	0	0		0	98
Faffb	0	0		0	42

A summary of visit classification into six different categories is shown in Table 6.

More complex analysis and reporting based on UUIDs is possible. However due to confidentiality of data and time constraints, only basic ones are shown in this study.

Table 6: Page categories by UUIDs.

	Page Category					
UUID	**Home**	**Info. Related**	**Products**	**Promotions**	**Search**	**Checkouts**
0bfc0	19	1	13	26		14
1cef1	7	3	5	1		13
2b8aa		8	18			8
3f4b2	22	13	12	4		14
4c666	19	11	9	16		4
5ae16	95	32	261	22		23
5cb86	43	12	59	3		55
8c200	6		17	5		18
8d23f	186	36	182	136	6	92
9e38d	38	7	44	4		51
15aff	26	4	36	6		41
20a56	12		7	9		8
52d69	19		11	5		12
54dc9	393	84	276	150	3	249
66b5a	9	3	10	1		13

	Page Category					
UUID	**Home**	**Info. Related**	**Products**	**Promotions**	**Search**	**Checkouts**
83b44	27	1	3	16		16
99dec	24	8	25	6		41
454ca	4	5	8	6		24
2273e	36	2	46	1		27
07659	42	6	36	6		76
24358	20	1	32	3		43
a5a00	24	2	26	1		29
a909f	29	10	11	31		17
abef8	14		15	2	3	14
ae0aa	14		10	2	2	17
cec1b	10	7	5	4		4
d6242	7	3	20	15		10
da936	30	11	97	19		45
e28df	21	17	17	5		13
f16d8	7		13			13
f937c	6		3	5		15
fa4e9	31	2	15	17		33
Faffb	7		18	2		15

5. DISCUSSION

In this paper, it was explained how clickstream data can be retrieved from web analytics tracking servers; how it can be cleaned, stored, and aggregated to create some measures which are used for analysis and reporting. It also addressed some of technical details from the solution and analytics point of views.

Since the volume of clickstream data is huge, traditional databases are not a good fit to satisfy scalability, search and semi-structural data storage requirements. DSE is proposed as a main data store as it supports common big data use-cases such as storage, search, scalability, and batch-based processing. It is important for a startup company to choose a big data solution proposed in this paper to handle such huge clickstream data feeds to support their customer's analytical requirements.

The methodology used to create UUIDs is very important for companies as web traffic from smart devices is increasing with advancements in technology. Even with artificial dataset used in this study to mimic UUIDs, valuable insights are drawn from the data. Due to confidentiality and time constraints, some insights are not included in this study.

The UUID solution is very useful for financial institutions, e.g., a bank can identify a customer who browsed loans section of their website, their sales person can contact the customer to offer some negotiation related to the loan.

The classification model derived in this study is helpful for the Telco Company to understand their customer's browsing behavior. As explained by Adobe (n.d.) and also shown in this study, a serious shopper behaves differently from a casual and information–gathering one. This sort of classification is applicable and valuable for e-commerce websites as well. When serious shoppers are identified on the website, they can be shown relevant content and promotional messages to help them purchase some goods or services.

6. CONCLUSION AND FURTHER WORK

The methodology used in this study to retrieve, process and store clickstream data is practical in nature. Organizations can choose similar solutions shown in this study depending on their needs. A big data solution is more suitable to handle such data feeds. However if an organization has existing traditional infrastructure, it can be leveraged as well with a little more effort. If DES license is an issue, it can be replaced with fully open source technologies, which offer similar capabilities.

The UUID solution proposed in this paper is possible to implement practically. However success depends on the nature of business and how well it is implemented. For some organizations the solution is very useful, while for others it may not be so relevant. Such UUID solution can be combined with other data sources, e.g., CRM data that an enterprise might already have to make the solution more powerful and usable.

The classification achieved in this paper with customer segments may not be very convincing as the distance between clusters is not optimal and there is no clear segregation of clusters. The solution can be further enhanced, for example, by structuring their website content better – certain measures such as product, brand variety, and search page visit count can be improved. Any improvements in measure computations increase classification results significantly.

Appendix 1: Important variables in dataset.

Column name	Column description	Data type	Example lookup
browser	The browser ID (has lookup table) actually used for the hit. See pre_browser.	32-bit unsigned integer	
campaign	The campaign value passed in on the hit. May not end up being the value that gets passed to the interface (see post_campaign).	String (255 chars)	1123
channel	Custom traffic variable for site sections (channels).	String (255 chars)	Corporate or Personal
connection_type	Connection type ID (has lookup table).	8-bit unsigned integer	0
cookies	Specifies whether JavaScript session cookie is accepted.	string (1 char)	Y
country	Country ID (has lookup table).	32-bit unsigned integer	Country Lookup Key
cust_hit_time_gmt	(timestamp-enabled report suites only) The timestamp sent with the hit. This "timestamp" is in Unix time (number of seconds since 1, January 1970).	32-bit unsigned integer	1102750716
cust_visid	A visitor ID passed in with the hit to be used as the visitor ID for the next hit (instead of using visid_high and visid_low).	String (255 chars)	UserID123ABC
daily_visitor	A flag to determine if current hit is a new daily visitor.	8-bit unsigned integer	0

(*continued*)

Appendix 1: Important variables in dataset. (*continued*)

Column name	Column description	Data type	Example lookup
date_time	Time in readable format in Time Zone specified by Report Suite ID, set by Adobe servers. Adobe servers combine post_cust_hit_time_gmt and report suite's time zone to create date_time. hit_time is in the timezone of the report suite	datetime	YYYY-MM-DD HH:MM:SS (this is not in Unix time.)
exclude_hit	Hit excluded by client rule.	8-bit unsigned integer	Hits that have a value other than 0 for this column are not used by Analytics reports
geo_city	City from Digital Envoy.	String (255 chars)	los angeles
geo_country	Country from Digital Envoy.	String (255 chars)	usa
hit_source	A flag for the back-end processing to know what type of hit the data is.	8-bit unsigned integer	
hit_time_gmt	Set by Adobe servers, this is the timestamp used for non-timestamped report suites. "Timestamp" is in Unix time (number of seconds since 1 January 1970).	32-bit unsigned integer	1096614122
ip	IP address for user's computer, from users ISP.	String (255 chars)	1. 112.89.14
ip2	A second IP address to be used by VISTA to determine validity of hits.	String (255 chars)	
language	Language ID (has lookup table).	32-bit unsigned integer	See Languages Lookup Key: FK

Column name	Column description	Data type	Example lookup
new_visit	A flag that determines if the current hit is a new visit.	8-bit unsigned integer	0
os	Operating system ID (has lookup table).	32-bit unsigned integer	See Operating Systems Lookup Key: FK
page_type	Page type variable (only used for error page).	String (255 chars)	errorPage
page_url	URL of the page view,. address of the page in address bar of the browser.	text	htp:/www.adobe.com/search/search_results.htm
pagename	Name of the page (if set).	String (255 chars)	search_results
post_prop1-75	Custom traffic variables 1–75.	String (255 chars)	[Custom]
prev_page	The page id of the previous page. This is an internal identifier and not useful to the customer.	32-bit unsigned integer	0
prop1-75	Custom traffic variables 1–75.	String (255 chars)	[Custom]
purchaseid	Unique identifier for a purchase. Identifies a duplicate purchase (see duplicate_purchase).	String (255 chars)	1584A9646G
user_agent	User agent as found in the HTTP header sent from the browser.	text	
user_hash	Hash on the report suite ID.	32-bit unsigned integer	3757249664
user_server	Custom traffic variable for servers.	String (255 chars)	[Custom]

(*continued*)

Appendix 1: Important variables in dataset. (*continued*)

Column name	Column description	Data type	Example lookup
userid	The numeric ID for the report suite ID (normally seen in the name of DW files).	32-bit unsigned integer	644614
username	Report suite ID.	String (255 chars)	adobe
visid_high	Part 1 of the visitor ID. Combination of two visitor IDs (visid_high and visid_low) creates a unique visitor ID.	64-bit unsigned integer	1. 70E+18
visid_low	Part 2 of the visitor ID. Combination of two visitor IDs (visid_high and visid_low) creates a unique visitor ID.	64-bit unsigned integer	1. 21E+17
visid_new	Indicates whether this is a newly generated visitor ID. Only available if visid_type=3 (Example: a new s_vi cookie was generated).	string (1 char)	
visid_time-stamp	If the visitor ID was generated by us (visid_type=3), this is the timestamp for when the ID was originally created.	32-bit unsigned integer	
visid_type	Integer that specifies how the visitor ID was calculated (based on a lookup).	8-bit unsigned integer	0 = Custom VisitorID (A custom visitor ID was set in the code using s.visitorID)
visit_key-words	Keywords used to find the site.	String (255 chars)	my keyword
visit_num	Number of current visits (Incremented each time a visitor returns to the site).	32-bit unsigned integer	visit_num is not incremented for excluded hits

Column name	Column description	Data type	Example lookup
visit_page_num	Page sequence number in the current visit.	32-bit unsigned integer	17
visit_referrer	Referrer to the visit.	String (255 chars)	http://www.google.com
visit_search_engine	Search engine used to find the site.	32-bit unsigned integer	00
visit_start_page_url	Start page for the visit.	String (255 chars)	http://www.adobe.com
visit_start_pagename	Page name the visit started at.	String (255 chars)	homepage
visit_start_time_gmt	GMT timestamp of the first page view in this visit.	32-bit unsigned integer	1102750716
weekly_visitor	A flag to determine if current hit is a new weekly visitor.	8-bit unsigned integer	[Custom]
yearly_visitor	A flag to determine if current hit is a new yearly visitor.	8-bit unsigned integer	0
zip	Zip code (i.e., 84604, 85381) passed in by JavaScript, or populated by GeoSegmentation data.	String (255 chars)	84604

Appendix 2: Page categorization.

derived_post_prop1	***derived_page_category***
subsection homepage	Home
section homepage	
Homepage	
Search	search

(*continued*)

Appendix 2: Page categorization. (*continued*)

derived_post_prop1	***derived_page_category***
voice	Products
Tv	
products services	
products	
product-vas	
product-plans	
product listing	
product details	
mobile	
compare products	
broadband	
rewards	Promotions
promotions	
product-packages	
viewhistory	InfoRelelated
support	
starhub apps	
sonic-roi	
sonic-brochure	
sonic-booking	
newsroom	
legal notifications	
legal notices and terms	
forms	
follow starhub	
error pages	
corporate sustainability and responsibility	
corporate	
contractors corner	
company information	
careers	
articles	
NA	
BLANK	

derived_post_prop1	***derived_page_category***
order summary	Checkout
order configurator	
checkout	
cart summary	

REFERENCES

1. Adobe (n.d.). *Adobe® Marketing Cloud, ClickStream Data Feeds.* Retrieved from https://marketing.adobe.com/resources/help/en_US/whitepapers/clickstream/clickstream.pdf

2. Hendricks, D (2013). *whats an email hash anyway.* Retrieved from http://www.clickz.com/clickz/column/2288689/whats-an-email-hash-anyway

3. Hossain, AB (2013). NoSQL Database: New Era of Databases for Big data Analytics — Classification, Characteristics and Comparison.

4. Leek, T (2012). *Md5 vs Sha.* Retrieved from http://security.stackexchange.com/questions/19705/is-sha1-better-than-md5-only-because-it-generates-a-hash-of-160-bits

5. Moe, WW (2003). Buying, Searching, or Browsing: Differentiating Between Online Shoppers Using In-Store Navigational Clickstream.

CHAPTER 17

Business Analytics for Price Optimization

CHUA Hui Xiang

ABSTRACT

This project examined how a fashion retailer can use its massive wealth of transactional data to optimize pricing decisions for two of its franchised brands. The main challenges faced by fashion retailers include pricing and predicting demand for products for each department within the store. The project set out to create a demand prediction model to understand the factors that affect demand and determine the extent to which prices and discounts can impact demand. The differences between customers holding membership with the retailer and non-members were examined and the how seasonal promotions impact customer demand.

1. INTRODUCTION

This research focused on two franchised fashion retail brands, Topman and Topshop, under Wing Tai Retail Pte Ltd. Operating in a highly competitive market with dynamic competitive environmental shifts, the ability to optimize price in response to market changes within a short time frame is critical. In the fashion retail industry, one of the key drivers behind consumption is price.

Demand models were used to perform the price optimization for different departments under each brand. These models aimed to provide a model for Wing Tai Retail Pte Ltd to be more flexible with pricing, promotions and forecasting. The aim was to develop technology that would allow them to react more quickly to market conditions, that could monitor customer demand by measuring how a price is perceived by consumers (members versus non-members) for different departments under different outlets, promotions, and seasons.

The primary goal of this research was to develop a demand model with both good explanatory and predictive power to formulate a price optimization algorithm. Data on sales of members and non-members from April 2014 to March 2015 for Topman and Topshop were provided.

2. PROBLEM STATEMENT

A recent survey by Software Advice, a Gartner subsidiary and point-of-sale research firm, Software Advice, examined how retail technology adoption, especially pricing strategy, can help a retailer stay afloat in today's make-or-break market (Schrantz, 2015). The report confirmed that retailers face a number of important decisions when determining how to price their goods and services for example, to discount, price below the competition, or bundle. Setting prices correctly can attract customers, drive sales, burnish a retailer's reputation, while incorrectly-set prices can have a profoundly negative impact on sales and customer loyalty. Sales forecasting, in addition to revenue management, is important in highlighting problematic troughs in the retailer's liquidity and profitability so that corrective actions can be taken early.

Compared to other retailing service industries, it is well argued that sales forecasting is a very difficult task in fashion retail because the demand for fashion products is highly volatile, with the ever-changing taste of the consumers and the product life cycle being very short. In addition, the sales of fashion products are strongly affected stochastically by seasonal factors, fashion trend factors, and many tricky variables such as weather, marketing strategy, political climate, item features, and macroeconomic trends (Liu et al., 2013), of which some are unpredictable. In order to achieve economic sustainability in a highly competitive environment, a company should adopt a consumer-demand driven 'pull' operational strategy. Hence understanding what drives demand becomes a critically important task.

3. STATE OF THE ART

The objective of price optimization is to maximize revenue under the assumption that demand is a function of price. The demand model determines the shape of the objective function and therefore is one of the most important inputs.

Econometric models with price as an explanatory variable have been popular for forecasting market level demand. One reason for the popularity of these demand functions as an input to price optimization is their set of properties, such as linearity, concavity and increasing differences, that leads to simpler, tractable optimization problems that can provide managerial insights (Lee, 2011). With the sales data provided by Wing Tai, various functions were explored, such as a log linear regression model and a Poisson regression model, which are namely linear panel models and non-linear panel models, assuming fixed effects (FE)/ random effects (RE).

FE explores the relationship between the predictor and outcome variables within an entity e.g. a person. Each entity has its own individual characteristics that may or may not influence the predictor variables. When using FE, it was assumed that something within the individual may impact or bias the predictor or outcome variables and this needed to be controlled e.g. being male or female, or a member versus a non-member and what could influence the response towards different seasons - the Great Singapore Sale or Christmas. FE controls for the effect of time-invariant characteristics were used to assess the net effect of predictors on the outcome variable. Another important assumption of the FE model is that those time-invariant characteristics are unique to the individual and should not be correlated with other individual characteristics. If the error terms are correlated, then FE is not suitable and instead RE should be assumed. The Hausman test is performed to assess whether FE or RE is more appropriate (Wooldridge, 2010).

The model that could provide the highest predictability and interpretability was chosen as the eventual demand model using criteria such as the log-likelihood as well as the Akaike Information Criterion (AIC) and the Bayesian Information Criterion (BIC).

Statistical time series models such as ARIMA and SARIMA are also widely employed in sales forecasting. Despite being popularly used for their simplicity and speed they do not usually lead to very promising results in terms of performance and are usually worse than other more sophisticated methods (Liu *et al.*, 2013). Also, such techniques simply analyze the demand data themselves to identify temporal patterns that emerge and persist. They ignore factors that could possibly drive demand and in this context, such time series models are not useful for managerial insights to increase demand.

Furthermore, the approach used by pricing and revenue optimization must be tailored to the specifics of the underlying market structure. From the point of view of the retailer, the key concept is what type of customer commitment is required in each market. Different types of customer commitments require different analytic approaches. Segmenting customers based on their willingness to pay and finding ways to charge different prices to different segments is a critical piece of pricing and revenue optimization (Philips, 2005). Hence, the flexibility of econometric models in incorporating membership also supports our choice of employing these models in demand prediction.

The model would help us in understanding how changes in price affect the sales of a certain product. The slope and elasticity of the objective function (price-response function) indicates the price sensitivity at a particular price. The slope of the price-response function measures how demand changes in response to a price change, while price elasticity (defined as the ratio of the percentage change in demand to the percentage in price) measures the sensitivity of demand to price (Philips, 2005).

4. SOLUTION: DESCRIPTION OF APPROACH

The first dataset provided contained sales transactions across different stores of Topman and Topshop from 1 April 2014 to 31 March 2015. When a basket is paid for, a transaction receipt number is recorded, along with the store ID and date. Items are categorized according to a product category, where at the top of the hierarchy is the Department, followed by Class, with the very specific Style of the product at the bottom of the hierarchy. For example, there are 20 Departments and 6,205 Styles for Topman and 35 Departments and 14,901 Styles for Topshop. For each record, the Transaction value, Discount, Cost and Unit per transaction were also provided. Sales transactions made by members were provided in another dataset, of which matching of datasets by the unique internal receipt number (namely a combination of transaction receipt number, date, and store) were performed. Records with negative quantity (approximately 2 per cent of all records) were removed as they reflected refunds.

The one-year data allowed us to look at the possibility of seasonal effects, such as the Great Singapore Sale in June/July, Christmas (late December) and Chinese New Year (early February). 210,741 transactions and 369,710 transactions were made in the year for Topman and Topshop respectively. To have a better understanding of the trend of Topman's and Topshop's sales and transaction history, as well as the relationship between demand and price, the research first looked at how the number of transactions/ sales/ units transacted varied with discounts.

4.1. Topman

For Topman, approximately 3,000 to 4,000 transactions were made in a week at non-peak times while the number of transactions peaked near Christmas and Chinese New Year, hitting approximately 8,000 transactions per week (see Figure 1). It was also observed that roughly

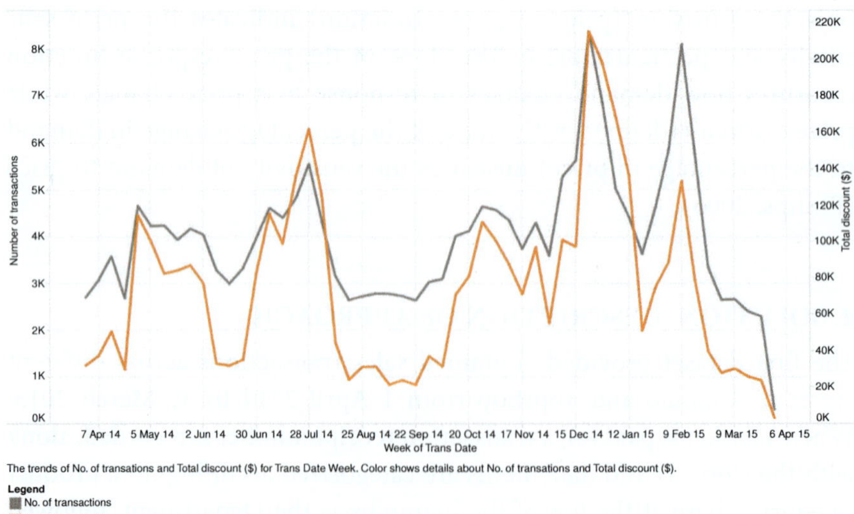

Figure 1: Total number of transactions against total discount ($) within the week for Topman.

6,000 transactions per week were made towards the end of Great Singapore Sale in July. While large variations in total discounts occured across the year, the number of transactions, total sales (see Figure 2) or total units transacted (see Figure 3) reacted with equivalent or similar magnitude. For example, total discounts increased by about three and a half times at

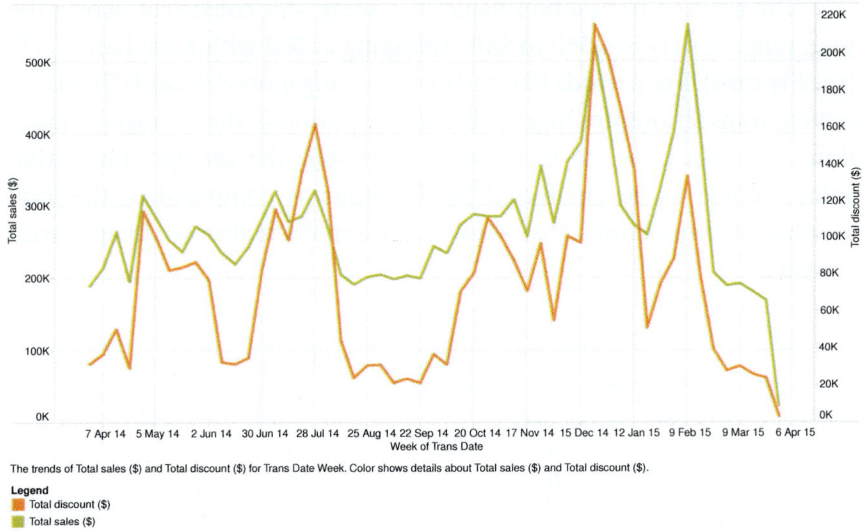

Figure 2: Total sales ($) against total discount ($) within the week for Topman.

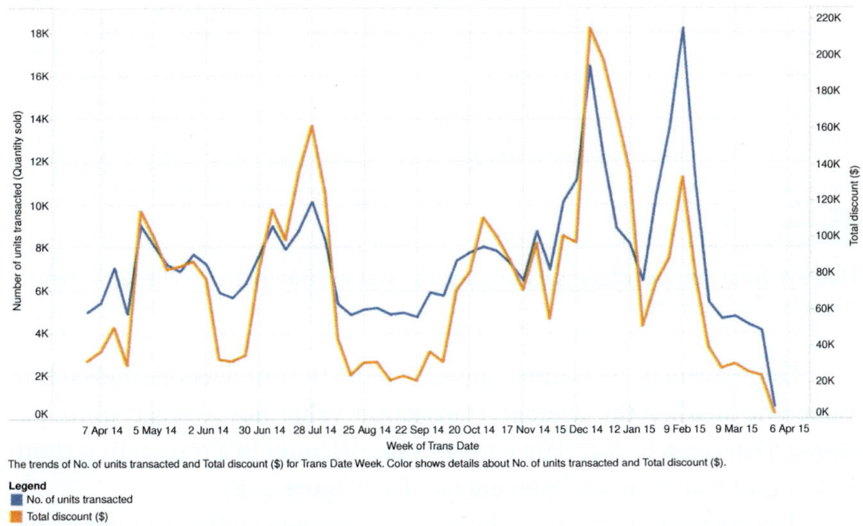

Figure 3: Total quantity sold against total discount ($) within the week for Topman.

the end of June but the total number of transactions improved by only one and a half times. In another case, total discounts fell by approximately eight times, but the total number of transactions dropped by two times near the end of August. For some weeks, discounts given could be high but this did not increase total sales nor number of transactions. Hence, discounts offered might be excessive.

The average transaction value in a week was consistent across the year, ranging between \$60 to \$80, averaging at \$68 with a median of \$55 (see Figure 4). For periods like end of Great Singapore Sale and Christmas (where transactions are higher than other periods), the average transaction value was closer to the low range of \$60. The average transaction value seemed to be unaffected by discounts as compared to the total number of transactions that showed greater fluctuations/ changes with discounts.

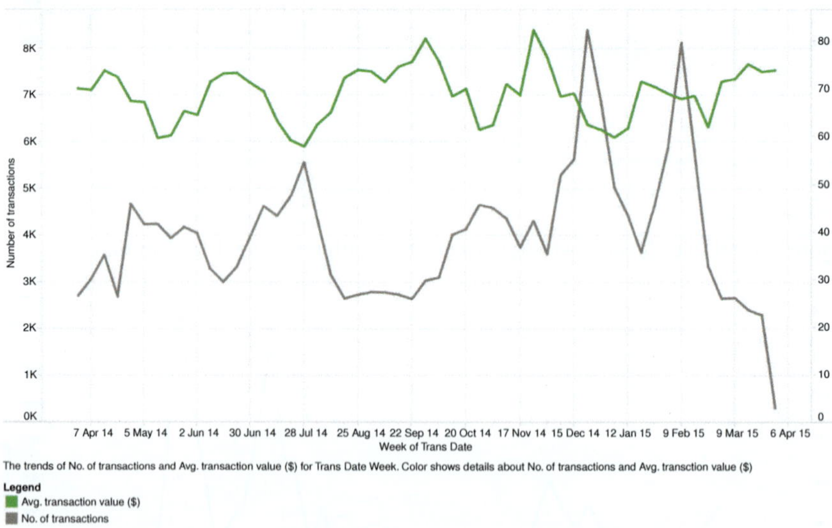

Figure 4: Total number of transactions against average transaction value (\$) within the week for Topman.

Large average discounts caused a reduction in average transaction value and neither the average transaction value nor average units per transaction seem to correlate with average discount in a transaction (both in terms of \$ amount and percentage) (see Figure 5–8).

The correlation between the average percentage discount per transaction in a day and average gross margin of the transaction was strong.

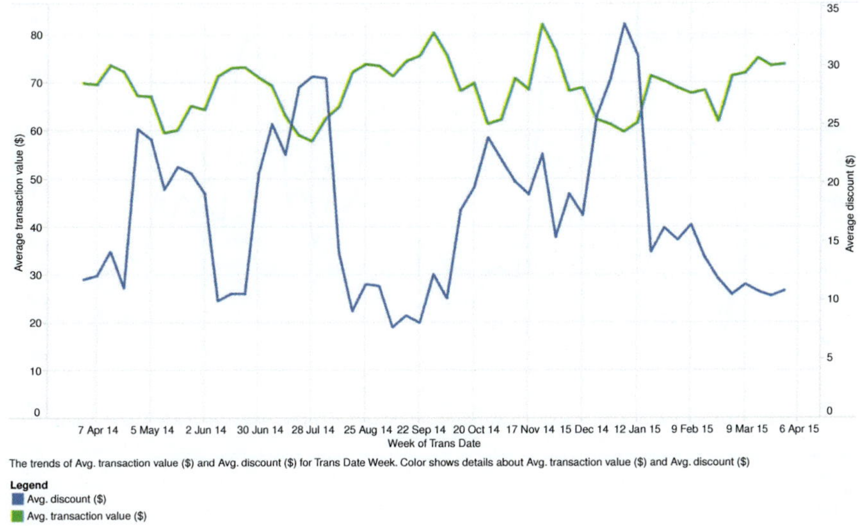

Figure 5: Average transaction value ($) against average discount ($) per transaction within the week for Topman.

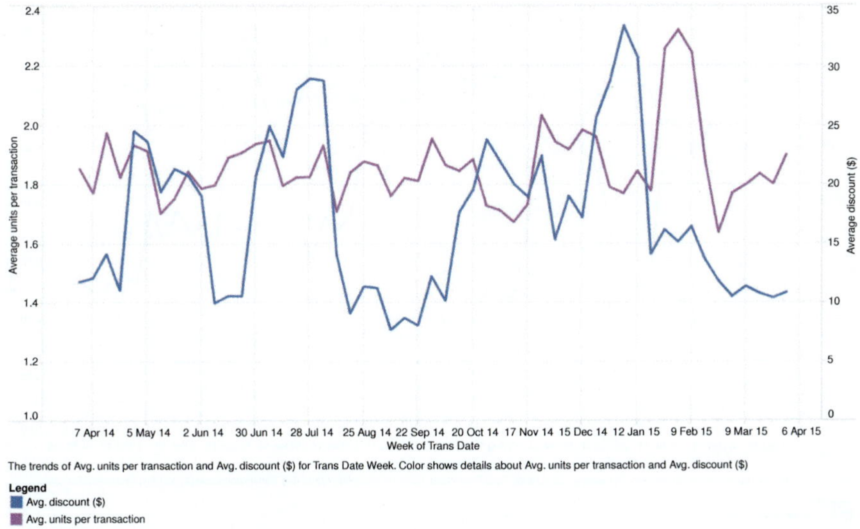

Figure 6: Average units per transaction against average discount ($) per transaction within the week for Topman.

The rest of the variables e.g. average transaction value, average total retail price, and average unit per transaction in a day, however, did not appear to have a strong relationship with average percentage discount (see Figure 9).

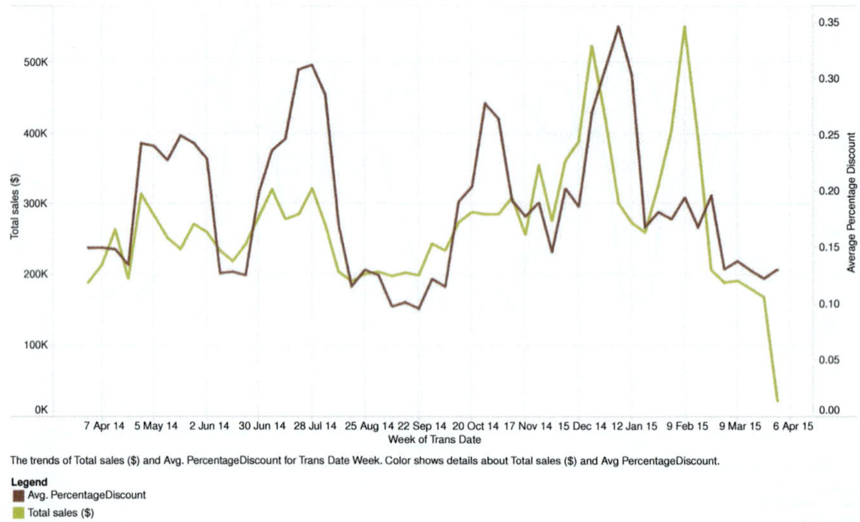

Figure 7: Total sales ($) against average percentage discount per transaction within the week for Topman.

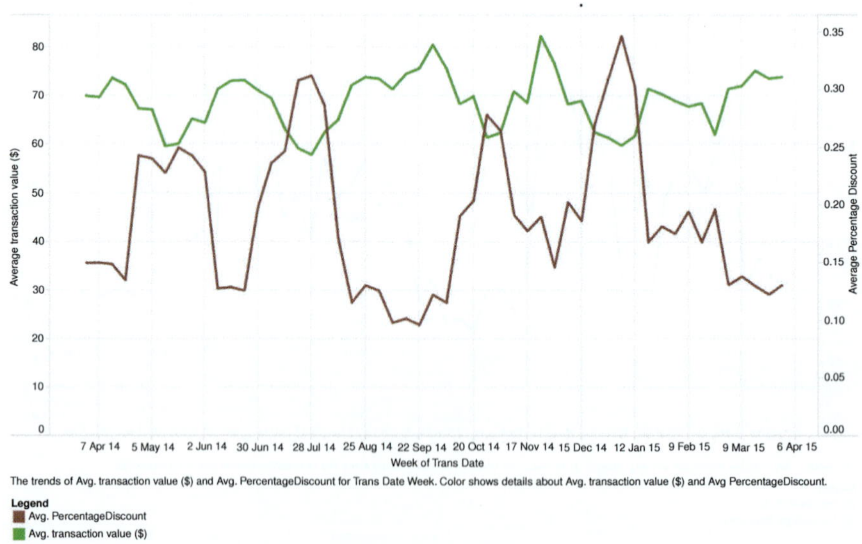

Figure 8: Average transaction value ($) against average percentage discount per transaction within the week for Topman.

The number of transactions made by non-members was significantly more than those made by members. Members only contributed to 28 per cent of total transactions made in the year and 34 per cent of total

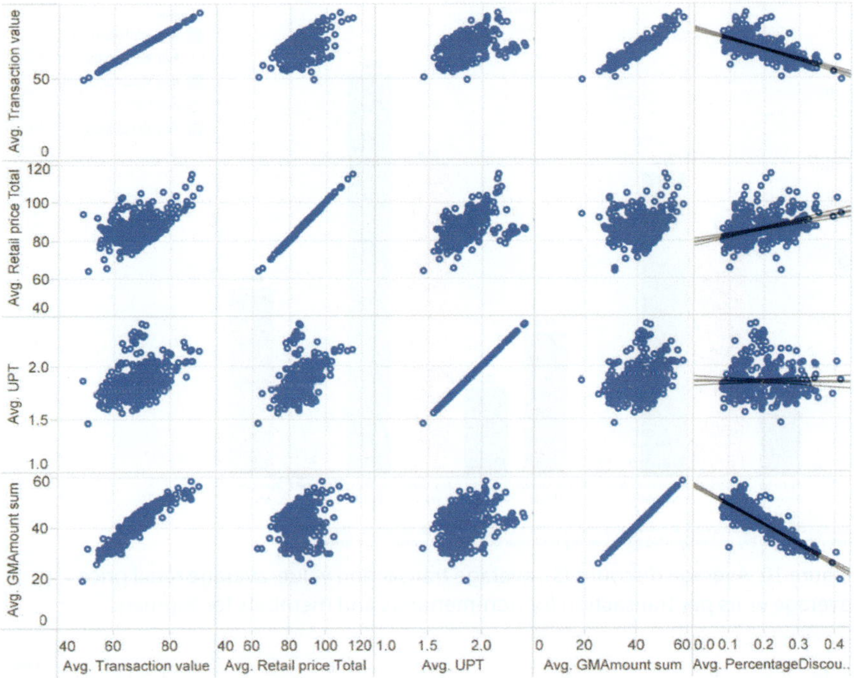

Figure 9: Scatter plot of average transaction value, average total retail price, average UPT, average gross margin against average percentage discount per transaction in a day for Topman.

sales for Topman. On average, members spent more than non-members (see Figure 10).

4.2. Topshop

For Topshop, the number of transactions peaked in week of 28 April, 27 October and 22 December 2014 (Christmas) (see Figure 11). Unlike Topman, the variations in both the number of transactions, total sales (see Figure 12) and number of units transacted (see Figure 13) seemed to follow the total amount of discounts given more closely. In addition, the peak periods observed in terms of number of transactions were different to that of Topman. The surge in number of transactions late April was due to a clearance sale where off-season products were marked down while the surge in late October was due to members taking up loyalty promotions sent to them to introduce the cross-brand promotions.

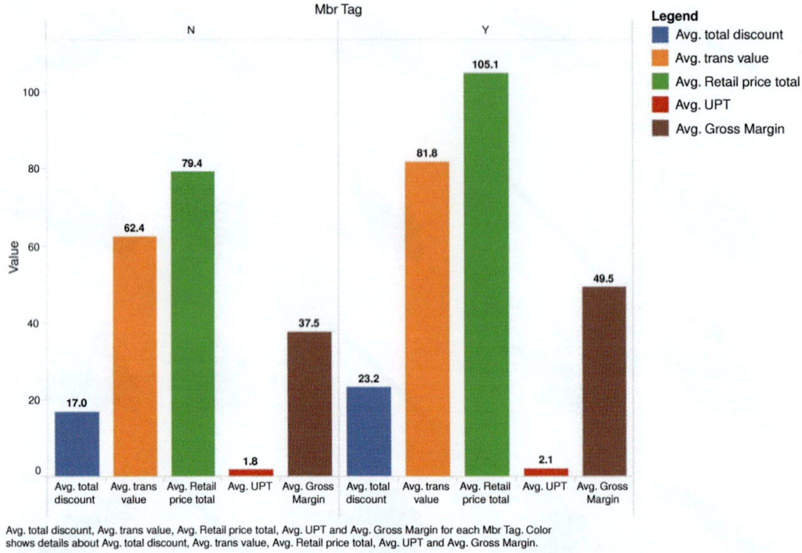

Figure 10: Average discount ($), average transaction value, average retail price, average units per transaction for non-members and members for Topman.

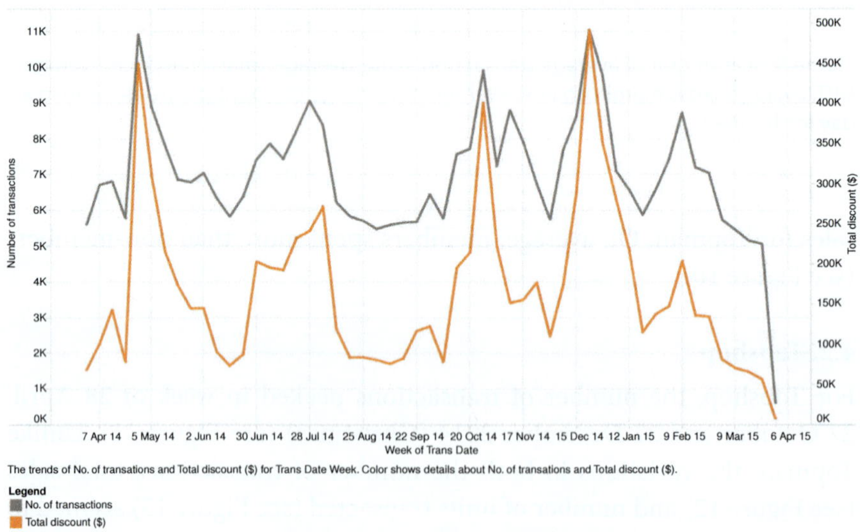

Figure 11: Total number of transactions against total discount ($) within the week for Topshop.

In contrast, the number of transactions/ total sales/ units transacted for the week of 9 Feb 2015 (Chinese New Year) was also relatively high even though the discounts were not. This was an interesting observation

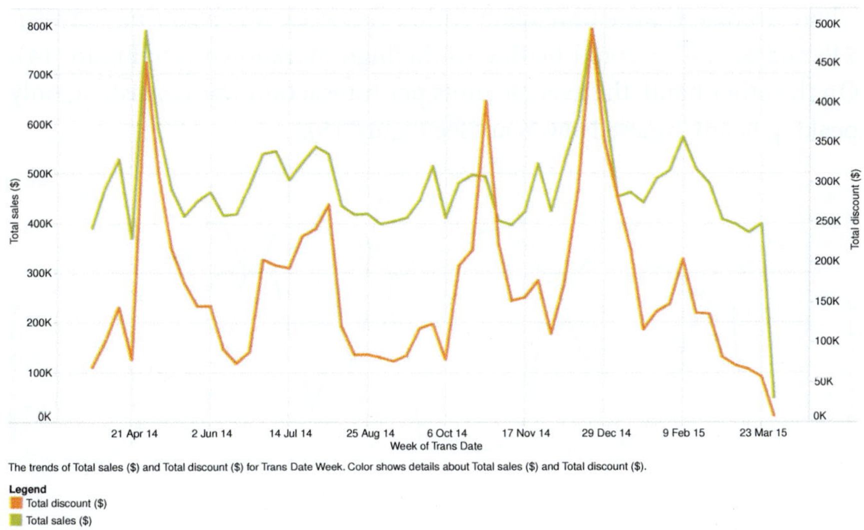

Figure 12: Total sales ($) against total discount ($) within the week for Topshop.

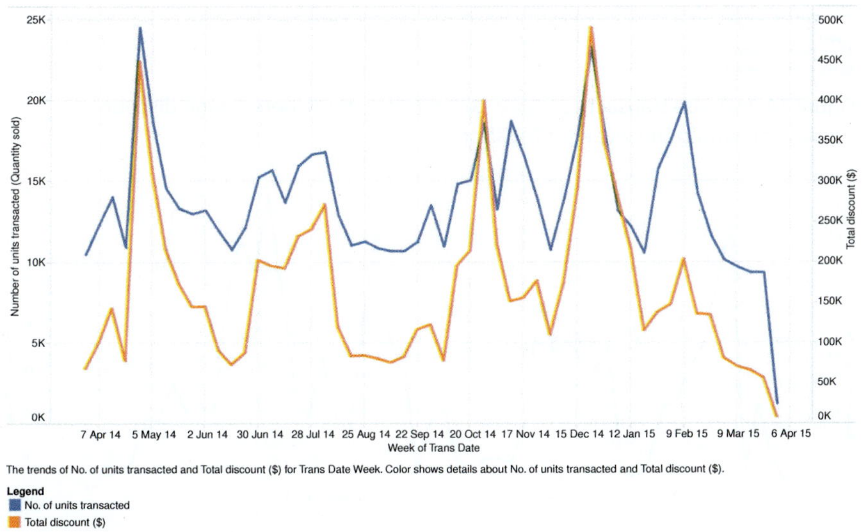

Figure 13: Total quantity sold against total discount ($) within the week for Topshop.

as this could indicate that consumers tend to spend more during festive seasons regardless of the amount of discounts given.

The average and median transaction value for Topshop was $68 and $50 respectively. Mid-October to mid-November showed exceptions where average transaction value within the week was hovering between $45 and $60. This could be due to the high markdown (see Figure 14). On the other hand, the average units per transaction was consistent, only peaking near Chinese New Year (see Figure 15).

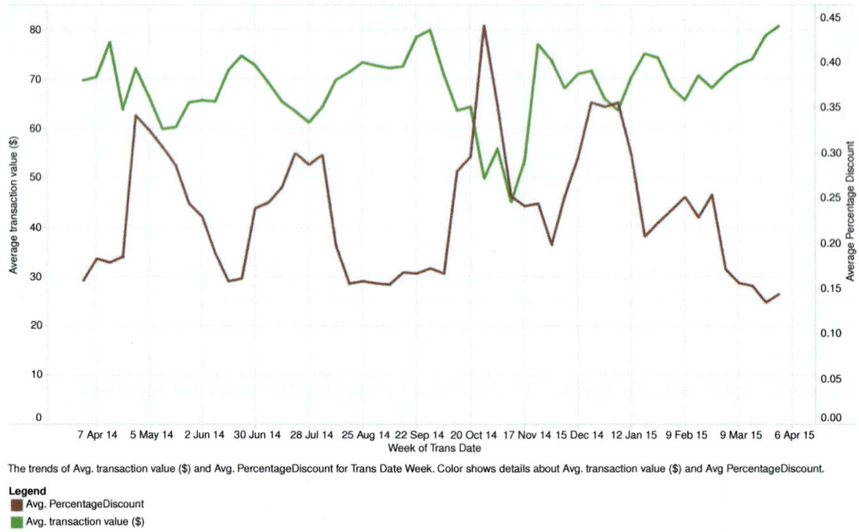

Figure 14: Average transaction value ($) against average percentage discount per transaction within the week for Topshop.

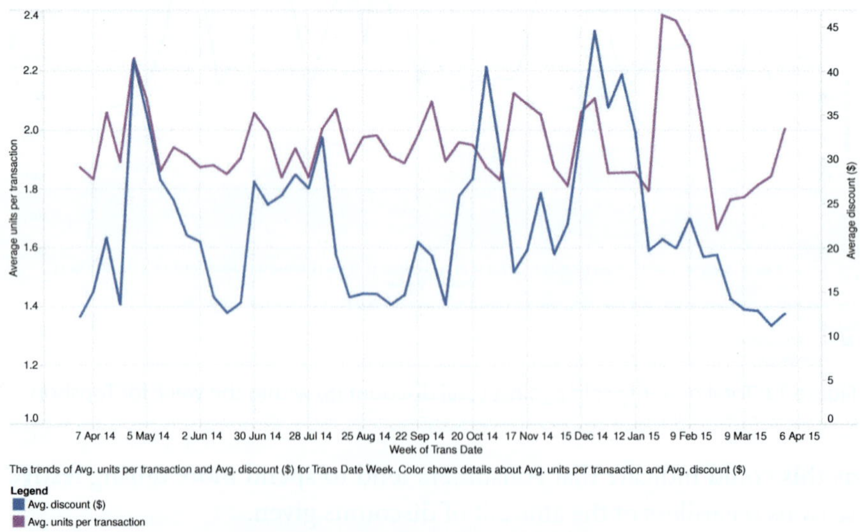

Figure 15: Average units per transaction against average discount ($) per transaction within the week for Topshop.

Similar to Topman, the correlation between average percentage discount per transaction for Topshop in a day and average gross margin of the transaction was strong. The rest of the variables eg. average transaction value, average total retail price, and average unit per transaction in a day, however, did not appear to have a strong relationship with average percentage discount (see Figure 16).

Members contributed 40 per cent of total transactions and 47 per cent of total sales made in the year for Topshop. Similar to Topman, on average, members spent more than non-members (see Figure 17).

4.3. Demand prediction model

Pricing strategies were typically determined at the department level and hence demand was aggregated at the department level in a transaction as well as predicting the units per transaction of a particular

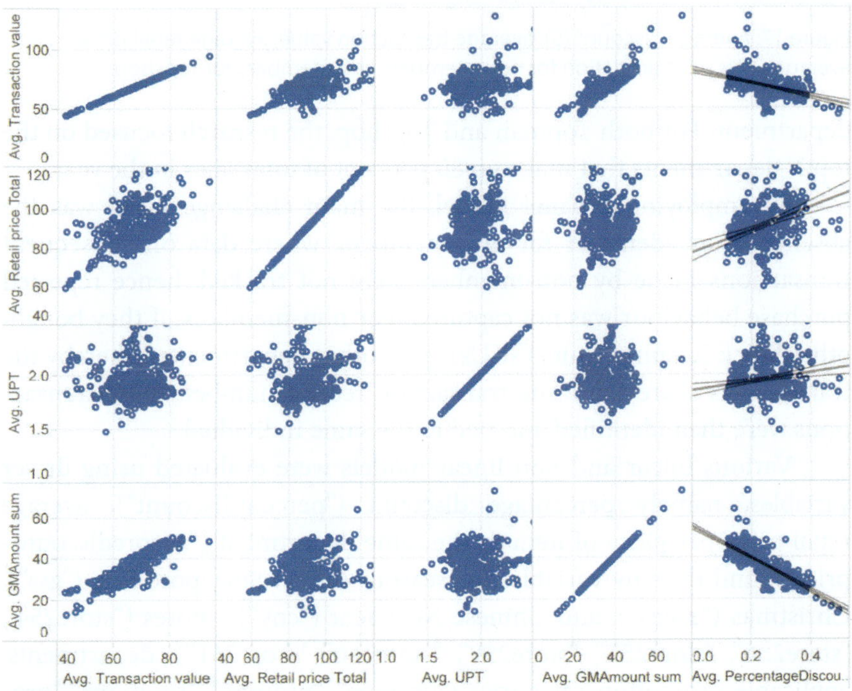

Figure 16: Scatter plot of average transaction value, average total retail price, average UPT, average gross margin against average percentage discount per transaction in a day for Topshop.

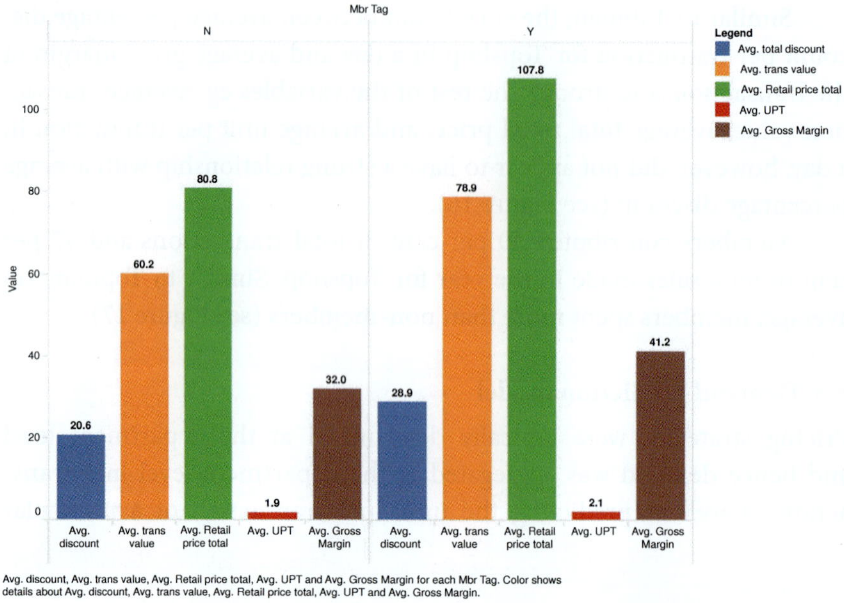

Avg. discount, Avg. trans value, Avg. Retail price total, Avg. UPT and Avg. Gross Margin for each Mbr Tag. Color shows details about Avg. discount, Avg. trans value, Avg. Retail price total, Avg. UPT and Avg. Gross Margin.

Figure 17: Average discount ($), average transaction value, average retail price, average units per transaction for non-members and members for Topshop.

department. For both Topman and Topshop, the research focused on the top *N* departments that make up 80 per cent of total sales in the year.

By employing a panel model, the main challenge faced was the absence of an identifier for non-members, where data on subsequent transactions made by non-members were not tracked, hence repeated purchase behaviour was not captured. For non-members, if they bought other Stock Keeping Units (SKUs) from other departments, whereby the transactions share the same transaction receipt number, these transactions were then identified and tied to the same individual.

Various linear and non-linear models were evaluated using driver variables, namely percentage discount ("percentdiscount"), average retail price per piece of item in the same department ("aveprediscount-price"), and dummy variables for seasons (Great Singapore Sale ("gss"), Christmas ("xmas"), and Chinese New Year ("cny")), stores ("store254", "store256", "store257", "store259", "store260", "store261"), departments, applicable promotion categories ("promoa", "promoc", "promom", "promos") and membership ("mbrtag"). Then the best fit for the different demand models were examined. The Hausman test was also performed to assess whether fixed effects or random effects was an appropriate assumption for the panel model. In the fixed-effect model, membership was controlled as it is time-invariant.

Stata 12.0 was used to develop the models.

A fixed-effect Poisson demand prediction model was most appropriate model and worked best for Wing Tai. The Poisson distribution was selected as it is a discrete probability distribution (the nature of the outcome variable is discrete) and expresses a probability for events occurring in a fixed interval of time with a known average rate and independently of the time since the last event (similar to how the event of consumers buying occurs).

In summary, the Poisson rate of the Poisson-like demand was specified with the following equation for consumer *i* at time *t*:

$$\lambda_{it} = \exp(\beta_1 K_{it} + \beta_2 \mathrm{RP}_{it} + \beta_3 \mathrm{gss}_{it} + \beta_4 \mathrm{xmas}_{it} + \beta_5 \mathrm{cny}_{it} + \sum_{k=6}^{11} \beta_k \mathrm{store}X_{it} + \beta_{12} \mathrm{promoa}_{it} + \beta_{13} \mathrm{promoc}_{it} + \beta_{14} \mathrm{promom}_{it} + \beta_{15} \mathrm{promos}_{it} + \sum_{k=16}^{15+N} \beta_k \mathrm{deptrank}Y_{it})$$

where K is the percent markdown, RP is the retail price, i.e. pre-discount price, X refers to the store code, Y refers to the rank of the department in terms of total sales, and N refers to the top N departments making up at least 80 per cent of total sales.

For Topman, $N = 8$ while for Topshop $N = 12$. The list of departments and their sales rank can be found in Appendix A.

Given the demand prediction model, the profit function for consumer *i* at time *t* is as follows:

$$\mathrm{profit}_{it} = \lambda_{it}(\mathrm{RP}_{it}(1 - K_{it}) - C_{it})$$

where C is the cost of the item sold and $\mathrm{RP}_{it}(1\text{-}K_{it})$ captures the price after the discount.

Table 1 summarizes the results for the equation mentioned above.

Table 1: Coefficients of variables for the fixed-effect Poisson demand prediction model.

Variables	Topman	Topshop
Percentmarkdown	−0.9892277**	−0.5335035**
Aveprediscountprice	−0.0041592**	−-0.0024707**
Gss	−0.0061755	−0.0031733
Xmas	0.0136291	−0.0027465
Cny	0.0497616*	0.1273443**
store254	−0.014777	−0.0085765
store256	0.0011777	−0.0170269
store257	0.0197448	−0.0078127
store259	0.0134248	−0.0076965
store260	−0.0067217	0.0304727**
store261	−0.0022799	−0.0072003
Promoa	0.2119348*	0.394483**
Promoc	0.0768303**	0.3361373**
Promom	0.2209572**	0.4010516**
Promos	0.694497**	0.7877955**
Deptrank1	0.132632**	−0.2689227**
Deptrank2	−0.0334247**	−0.310769**
Deptrank3	−0.0345707**	−0.3512838**
Deptrank4	−0.0344961*	−0.3653749**
Deptrank5	−0.0651971**	−0.2412319**
Deptrank6	−0.052842**	−0.3487876**
Deptrank7	−0.1116273**	−0.40081**
Deptrank8	0.2834587**	−0.3948696**
Deptrank9	–	−0.3329784**
Deptrank10	–	−0.4373099**
Deptrank11	–	−0.4445731**
Deptrank12	–	−0.444691**
No. of observations	138,822	319,248
Log-likelihood	−86784.952	−244930.18
AIC	173615.9	489914.4
BIC	173842.2	490202.5

* denotes that coefficient estimates are significant at 10 percent level and
** denotes a 1 percent level of significance

4.4. Sensitivity analysis

With other conditions remaining the same, Table 2 shows the percentage change in profits for both Topman and Topshop for the different markdown magnitudes *K*. As typically a discount was tagged to a particular type of promotional category, the change in profits was also simulated under promotion category "SP" (where the dummy variable "promos" equals 1) with the largest coefficient as an example.

Table 2: Percentage change in profits corresponding to percentage markdown under different assumptions for promotion categories if RP = 30 and C = 10.

	Change in Profits (%)	
Discount (%)	**Under no promotion category**	**Under promotion category "SP"**
5	−3	+164
10	−6	+155
15	−10	+145

5. DISCUSSION

The demand prediction model gave some understanding around the price-sensitivity of consumers as well as identifying variables that were statistically significant in influencing the demand for each franchised brand. The magnitude of the coefficients indicated the magnitude in which the demand could be impacted by a change in that particular variable.

It was noticed that the coefficients for percentage discount and average retail price per piece of item in the same department were negative, indicating an inverse relationship between the variables and the outcome variable quantity sold for the particular item. The finding for percentage discount was non-intuitive as one might assume that an increase in discount would lead to an increase in quantity sold. However, this was not the case. This could be due to the high percentage discounts that were given on items for clearance. Typically such items are limited in quantity so this could have been a supply issue instead. Alternatively, it was argued that it could be due to consumers being unwilling to buy the items on clearance, perhaps due to unsuitable size or items being out-of-fashion. On the other hand, the percentage change in the quantity sold for the item is a decrease of 0.42 per cent and 0.26 per cent for every dollar increase in average retail price per piece of item in the same department for Topman and Topshop respectively. This shows the extent to which price could affect demand. Consumers of Topshop were less price-sensitive than those of Topman.

It was interesting to notice that store locations were not significant in impacting demand. The Chinese New Year season had a more significant increase in demand compared to other seasons like Christmas and the Great Singapore Sale. Promotions were significantly useful in increasing demand, with promotional category "SP" consisting of bundle deals, category promotion, in-store promotions, sale events and PLP re-pricing having the greatest impact on demand.

Compared to the baseline, i.e. other departments not within the top eight contributing sales for Topman and top 12 contributing sales for Topshop, the demand for each of these departments was less than that of the baseline, with the exception of Dept 71: Short-sleeve leisure ("Deptrank1") and Dept 87: Suits ("Deptrank8") for Topman being demanded 1.14 and 1.33 times more than the baseline respectively.

Based on the findings above, price increases had little impact on demand and that the notion of promotions mattered more than the exact amount of discount offered. Furthermore, members tended to be more willing to spend than non-members, perhaps due to promotions offered exclusively to members. On the other hand, the demand across the various departments were statistically significantly different, as certain products were more popular.

6. CONCLUSIONS AND FURTHER WORK

With an understanding of the factors driving demand, it would be interesting to conduct a field experiment to address (i) whether price increases would affect demand and (ii) the impact of price increases on revenue. Further work could be done to find out more about the inverse relationship between discounts and demand; there could be other confounding factors that were not captured by the model. As the structure of a panel model relies heavily on capturing the behavior of individuals over time, increased membership amongst consumers can further improve the model as well as aid future analysis.

Appendix A: Sales for respective departments for Topman and Topshop

Topman			
Dept	**Total Sales $**	**% of total Sales**	**Rank**
33	991,661.66	6.9%	7
37	618,540.11	4.3%	
52	408,068.23	2.9%	
56	369,629.43	2.6%	
64	160,777.44	1.1%	
68	1,222,762.63	8.6%	5
69	1,090,433.35	7.6%	6
71	2,510,312.32	17.6%	1
76	74,444.70	0.5%	
77	540,098.07	3.8%	
78	4,603.67	0.0%	
79	71,090.12	0.5%	
80	88,819.47	0.6%	
81	140,378.55	1.0%	
83	1,785,919.70	12.5%	3
84	1,871,336.67	13.1%	2
87	967,103.96	6.8%	8
88	1,334,793.02	9.3%	4
90	9,251.67	0.1%	
NULL	39,443.53	0.3%	
Total	14,299,468.30	100%	
Topshop			
Dept	**Total Sales $**	**% of total Sales**	**Rank**
1	170,567.38	0.7%	
2	2,003,150.63	8.0%	5
3	371,496.09	1.5%	
4	4,061,781.41	16.2%	1
5	1,103,160.19	4.4%	8
7	92,938.52	0.4%	

(*continued*)

Appendix A: Sales for respective departments for Topman and Topshop. (*continued*)

Dept	**Total Sales $**	**% of total Sales**	**Rank**
8	154,889.77	0.6%	
10	2,056,127.94	8.2%	4
11	250,823.92	1.0%	
12	253,184.63	1.0%	
13	2,064,106.64	8.2%	3
14	548,370.18	2.2%	11
16	496,117.37	2.0%	12
17	379,742.25	1.5%	
19	211,641.92	0.8%	
20	395,243.21	1.6%	
21	15,038.14	0.1%	
22	74,525.44	0.3%	
23	734,682.05	2.9%	10
24	460,348.41	1.8%	
25	283,616.67	1.1%	
26	3,348,443.91	13.4%	2
27	1,174,501.53	4.7%	7
30	746.76	0.0%	
32	513,898.94	2.1%	
36	1,384,207.37	5.5%	6
42	1,046,454.15	4.2%	9
43	425,387.95	1.7%	
44	123,340.82	0.5%	
60	231,132.88	0.9%	
1D	450,440.28	1.8%	
1M	25,512.14	0.1%	
1O	71.00	0.0%	
PP	1,049.82	0.0%	
TA	118,073.70	0.5%	
Total	25,024,814.01	100%	

REFERENCES

1. Schrantz, M (2015). *The Best Retail Pricing Strategies by Sector IndustryView | 2015.* Retrieved from Software Advice on Research Web site: http://www.softwareadvice.com/retail/industryview/pricing-strategies-report-2015/

2. Liu, N, S Ren, T Choi, C Hui and S Ng (2013). Sales Forecasting for Fashion Retailing Service Industry: A Review. Mathematical Problems in *Engineering Volume 2013 (2013).* Retrieved from Hindawi Publishing Corporation. Retrieved from http://dx.doi.org/10.1155/2013/738675

3. Lee, S (2011). *Study of demand models and price optimization performance* (Doctoral dissertation). Georgia Institute of Technology. Retrieved May 3, 2015, from https://smartech.gatech.edu/bitstream/handle/1853/42914/lee_seonah_201112_phd.pdf

4. Wooldridge, J. M. (2010). *Econometric Analysis of Cross Section and Panel Data,* 2nd ed. The MIT Press, Cambridge, Massachusetts and London, England.

5. Philips, RL (2005). *Pricing and Revenue Optimization,* 1st ed. Stanford: Stanford Business Books.

CHAPTER 18

Skin Care Product Aggregator

Gong Yan

National University of Singapore

ABSTRACT

Before purchasing skin care products, online shoppers search the Internet for product details such as benefits, usage, ingredients, or similar products. This is time-consuming and the information is not organized in an intuitive way.

This study developed an application as a centralized information portal for various skin care brands. It crawls skin care official sites and generates indexes for users to search effectively. It also analyzes the ingredients of skin care products and provides an intuitive view for users to identify the potentially harmful ingredients. The application aims to help users make informed decisions during online purchases.

1. INTRODUCTION

Consumers are smarter these days, particularly in online shopping. Before making a purchase, customers also check other product details in addition to price. Taking skin care products as an example, customers also want to find out whether there are similar products from other trusted brands, what benefits and usage the product has, what skin concerns or problems this product will address, what type of skin this product is suited for, and what ingredients this product contains. Although people can make actual purchases from various online retailers whose websites usually provide limited information about product details, the most accurate and reliable source of product details is the official site of the skin care brands.

This study proposes an application framework that can retrieve and aggregate information from skin care product official sites. The application framework will provide a consolidated search and filtering functionality to users, and highlight the effective or potentially harmful ingredients in the products. It aims to help users to get more insights on the products before they make an actual purchase.

2. PROBLEM STATEMENT

In case of skin care products, the official sites only reveal product details for their own brands. This makes it difficult for online shoppers to compare products across brands to make purchase decisions.

Online shoppers usually search the internet for both retail and official websites, to get the lists of skin care products that probably meet their needs, and compare the descriptions, price, product reviews, and consumer opinions to find the most suitable one. This process is manual and time-consuming, and the information is scattered across multiple websites, and therefore not intuitive enough for customers to make purchase decisions efficiently. Usually, online shoppers tend to manage their frequently used websites in traditional ways such as bookmarking the websites or subscribe to their newsletters. To maintain the bookmarks and newsletter is tedious, and exposes the users to irrelevant promotions that they might not be interested in.

Besides, consumers are getting more conscious about the quality of skin care products. They are concerned about the potential damages to the skin caused by harmful ingredients of skincare products that they ingest or apply to their body, e.g., causing allergic reactions, irritating/dehydrating the skin, or clogging of skin pores. Some consumers would like to review the ingredient list to make sure they are compatible with their skin, avoid the ones which they are sensitive to, allergic, or otherwise individually reactive to. Based on a survey, 59 per cent U.S. adult women read beauty product ingredient labels prior to purchase, while nearly 40 per cent intend to increase their expenditure for all-natural beauty products.[1]

However, there is no ready-to-use online tool for customers to identify any potentially harmful ingredients they should be aware of. It is also difficult to come up with a complete and objective list on potential toxicity of skin care ingredients. Manufacturing companies usually assert that whatever ingredients they use are safe. It is largely up to manufacturer's conscience not only to ensure effectiveness but also safety of the consumers. On the other hand, it is up to consumers to buy wisely. Thus, consumers have to visit each official site, browse through the product information pages to read the ingredient list and identify the potentially harmful ones based on their own knowledge.

3. STATE OF THE ART

There are two types of websites where people can retrieve the skin care product information.

1) Retailer site, e.g., Sephora (http://www.sephora.sg/)

   These sites offer a number of skin care brands. The advantage of such websites is that it can auto-generate related products, and substitute products within or across brands. Users can easily manage their wish list to compare similar products from different brands. Some websites allow users to write reviews and comments, and also provide discount. However, they usually do not provide sufficient details of the products, but a short description, package size, and price. An example is shown in Figure 1 below.

2) Official sites, e.g., bareMinerals (http://www.bareescentuals.com/)

   These sites provide only products of a single brand. Some of them allow users to directly purchase online, while others provide only

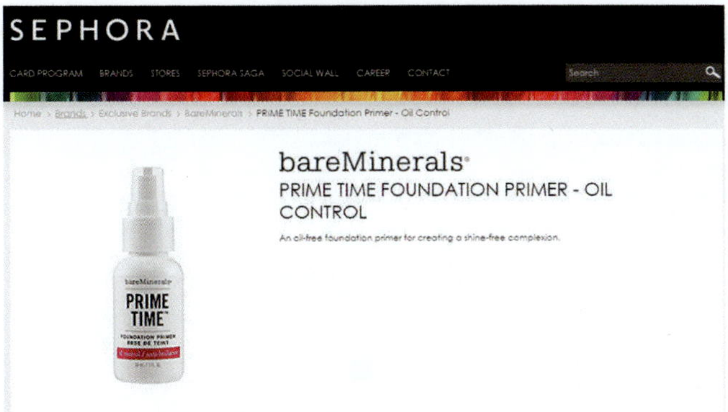

Figure 1: Product description from retailer site.
Source: http://www.sephora.sg/matte-spf-15-foundation/cid1340.html

product information and users need to make purchases in local stores. Official sites provide more details, such as usage instructions, ingredients, and the skin type it can be applied to. Its information is more accurate and reliable. An example of the same product from official site is shown in Figure 2 below.

However, the websites do not provide additional information, such as what are the active and inactive ingredients in the products. They will not highlight whether the ingredients used in the products can be potentially harmful, and whether some ingredients may cause allergy to sensitive skin. Without further details, the ingredient list is not much helpful to users. An example is shown in Figure 3 below. Without categorization and analyses, the long ingredient list does not provide any valuable information to users. However, there is no effective tool or websites that can help users analyze the ingredients lists.

4. SOLUTION: DESCRIPTION OF APPROACH

The project develops a solution using IBM Watson Explorer (10.0.0) content analytics component. It creates a content analytics collection that crawls the skin care brands official site information, parses and indexes the data, and provides search and analysis functionality to users, which include: search across multiple brands' products, and identify those effective and potentially harmful ingredients in the products.

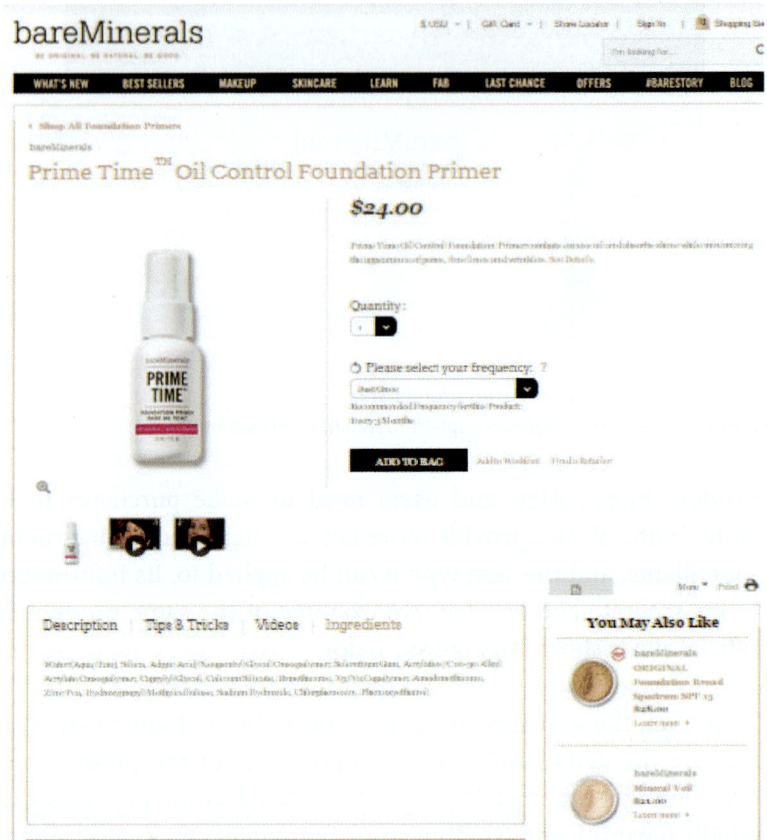

Figure 2: Product description from official s All manufacturers of skin care products have to list the ingredients on the label and official websites, as required by the law in most of the countries, such as The Fair Packaging and Labeling Act of U.S.[2]

Source: http://www.bareescentuals.com/PrimeTime-Oil-Control/US58927,en_US,pd.html

Description | Benefits | Tips & Tricks | Ingredients

Water/Aqua/Eau, Disodium Cocoyl Glutamate, Sodium Lauroamphoacetate, Glycerin, Carbomer, Cetearyl Alcohol, Coco-Glucoside, Sodium Lauryl Glucose Carboxylate, Benzyl Alcohol, Soil Minerals, Punica Granatum Extract, Persea Gratissima (Avocado) Oil, Actinidia Chinensis (Kiwi) Fruit Extract, Ananas Sativus (Pineapple) fruit Extract, Litchi Chinensis Fruit Extract, Garcinia Mangostana Fruit Extract, Zizyphus Jujuba Fruit Extract, Passiflora Incarnata Fruit Extract, Psidium Guajava Fruit Extract, Averrhoa Carambola Fruit Extract, Sodium Lauroyl Oat Amino Acids, Sodium Cocoyl Apple Amino Acids, Macadamia Integrifolia Seed Oil, Xylitylpolyglucosides, Anhydroxylitol, Xylitol, Sodium Hyaluronate, Cetyl Alcohol, Glycine Soja (Soybean) Oil, Lavandula Angustifolia (Lavender) Oil, Lavandula Hybridia (Lavandin) Oil, Anthemis Nobilis Flower Oil, Linalool, Lauryl Glucoside, Tetrasodium EDTA.

Figure 3: Product ingredients.

Source: bareMinerals <http://www.bareescentuals.com/Purifying-Facial-Cleanser/US53704, en_US,pd.html>

There are three major steps in this proposed method, as shown in the architecture overview in Figure 4:

1) Crawl or import data from skin care brand sites
2) Parse and index: generate the index fields, facets and categories required for users search; generate positive and negative ingredients
3) Analysis: search, filter, and view sentiment analysis results

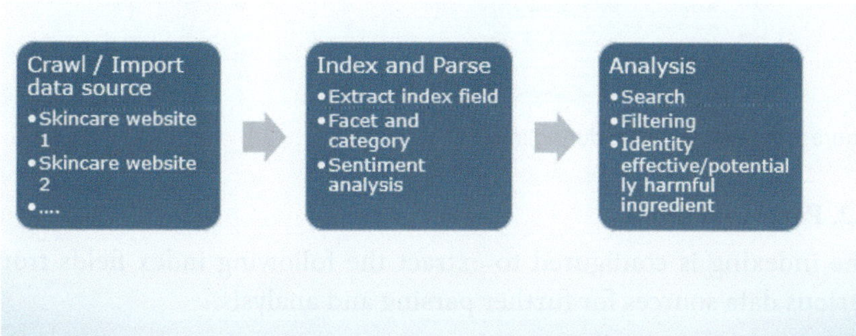

Figure 4: Architecture overview.

4.1. Crawling and importing data from different sources

This process discovers the original information from various sources, which can be files or websites, for further indexing and analysis.

As a proof of concept, CSV files were used to represent the data sources. To ensure the variety of the data, the data sources include multiple brands and product categories. The number of columns and column heads of the source files are not consistent, e.g., one source file uses "product-name_text" while another source file uses "title" to store the product name. Some records may have empty values in certain columns. The data source is imported into the content analytics collection for indexing and analyzing. Each source file can contain one or more brands or product categories.

Different data sources may use different column names whose content actually represent the same information e.g., some websites use "Description" while others may use "Benefit" to describe the usage and purpose of their products. To simplify users' search query into these inconsistent fields, the same index field was created for those columns in the source files that represent the same information when importing the source data. As shown in Figure 5, both "description" and "benefit" columns in the data files are mapped to "product_description" index field. If users do an advanced search by querying index field "product_description", the product items will be displayed in the result, if either "description" or "benefit" column contains the queried text.

Import	Column	Index field name		Returnable	Faceted search	Free text search	In summary	Fielded search
☑ All								
☑	Brand	brand	brand	✓	✓	✓	✓	✓
☑	productname_text	productname_text	productname_text	✓		✓	✓	✓
☑	description	product_description	product_description	✓		✓		✓
☑	productname_link	image	image	✓				
☑	category	productname_link	productname_link	✓		✓	✓	
☑	ingredient	category	category	✓	✓	✓	✓	✓
☑	concern	ingredient	ingredient	✓	✓	✓	✓	✓
☑	benefit	product_description	product_description	✓		✓		✓

Figure 5: Index field setup during import.

4.2. Parse and index

The indexing is configured to extract the following index fields from various data sources for further parsing and analysis.

- Brand: e.g., *Kiehls, L'occitane*
- Category: e.g., toner, moisturizer, cleanser
- Concern: e.g., anti-aging, hydration
- Product name: e.g., deep cleansing foam
- Ingredient: the ingredients list
- Description: the purpose and benefits of the products

For users to do further filtering and analysis, the above index fields were used to configure facets and pre-defined rule-based categories.

A facet is a way to organize or classify the search results so that users can refine and navigate along one or multiple fields, where each field presents a different view or perspective of the results. Facet can also help users to further explore the patterns or perform analysis based on certain index field(s). The facet tree as shown in Figure 6 is configured and mapped to these index fields: brand, category, concern, and ingredient. Users can select a facet to explore and analyze the values within the facet.

Categories enable users to group search results that share common characteristics based on pre-defined rules. Users can also explore search results within a category for further analysis. Some rule-based categories are defined in Figure 7. In the collection's user interface, they are displayed

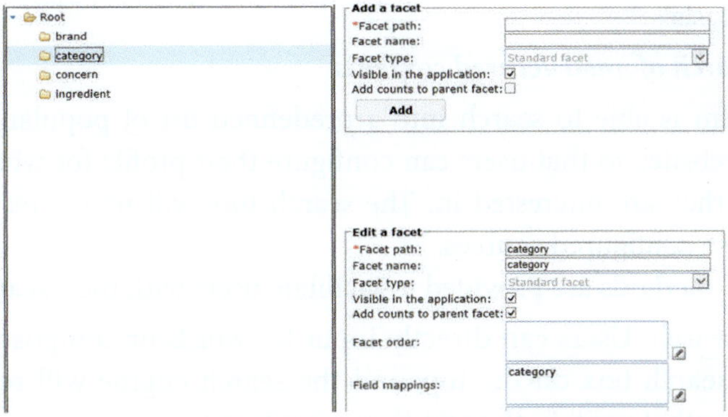

Figure 6: Facet tree.

as shortcuts under facet navigation of the left panel. Users can click on the pre-defined categories to zoom into a subset of the search results to further explore and analyze, without the need to compose their own search queries, as shown in Figure 8.

In addition to the pre-defined rules, users are also able to add their own rules (i.e., filtering criteria) into existing categories.

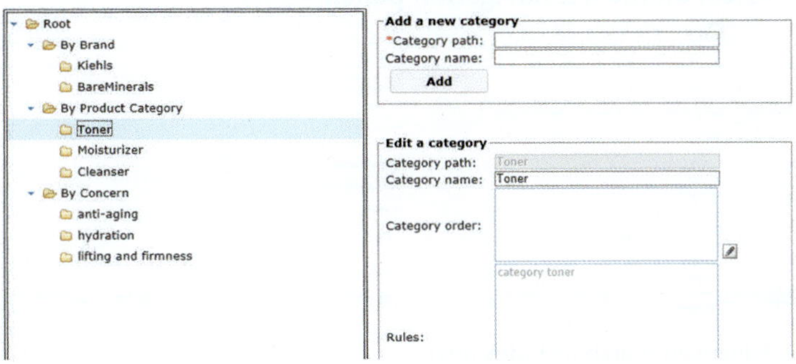

Figure 7: Category.

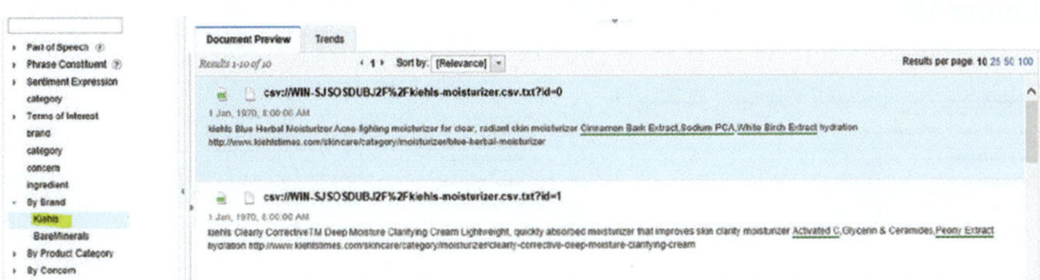

Figure 8: Search results based on category.

4.3. Analysis

4.3.1. Search of unstructured contents

The system is able to search into a predefined list of popular skincare brands websites so that users can configure their profile for what source websites they are interested in. The search tool will return results only from those configured sources.

Two methods are provided to facilitate users with their search:

- Open search: Users can directly input keywords or compose a query in the search box on the top, and the search engine will return the products that contain the text that users input.
- Search by property: The application has setup those frequently queried fields as index fields from the imported data. This provides users the ability to select or filter the results by index fields. Users can use the advanced search option to refine and narrow down the most lucrative search results. The search query can be based on any index fields, e.g., product category, brand, concern, description, or ingredient (refer to Figure 9). Users can also make use of the pre-defined search filtering (categories) on the left navigation panel.

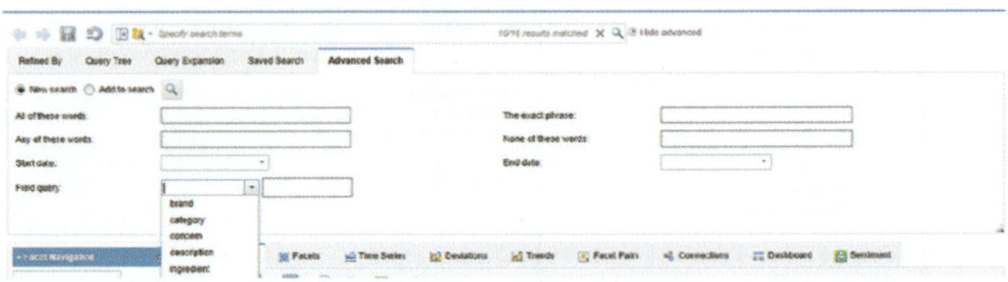

Figure 9: Advanced search by index field.

An example of user input on the search query page is shown in Figure 10:

Figure 10: Advanced search query page.

Figure 11 is an example of search result page which the application returns:

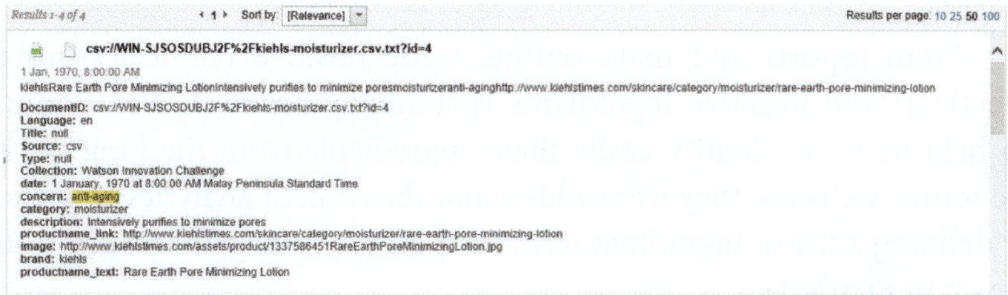

Figure 11: Advance search result page.

Users can also save their frequently used search queries as shortcuts, if they are only looking for a specific brand or a product category and can bookmark such search queries as shown in Figure 12. This allows users to execute the same queries by just clicking on the saved search.

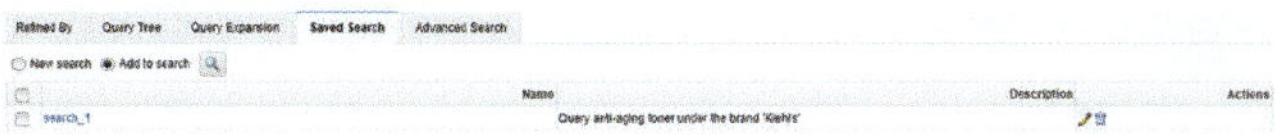

Figure 12: Saved search query.

An example of search result page using saved search is shown in Figure 13):

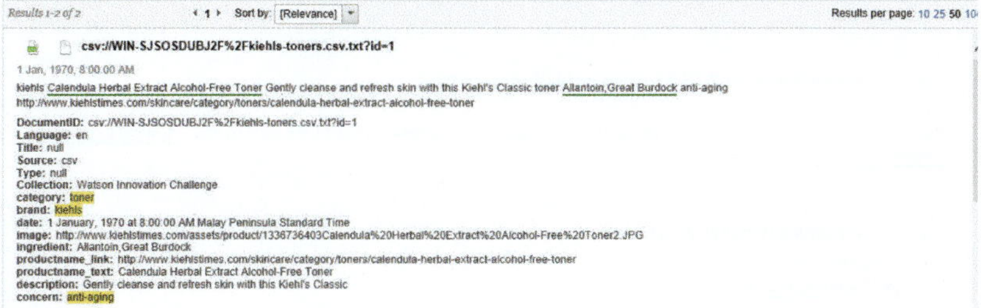

Figure 13: Saved search result page

4.3.2. Ingredient analysis

The application uses sentiment analysis feature in the content analytics collection to identify the positive and negative ingredients from the data sources.

From reports and news online, some positive (clinically proven effective)[3] and negative ingredients (potentially harmful) were found.[4] To help users to identify easily these ingredients from the long list on the source websites, they were added into the content analytics collection by defining a list of ingredient terms as positive or negative expressions, shown in Figure 14.

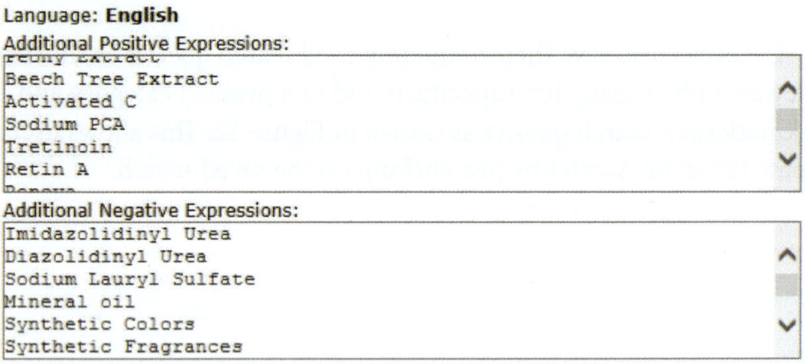

Figure 14: Sentiment analysis setup.

In the search result page, if a product item contains any of the configured ingredients, positive components will be highlighted in green while negative components will be highlighted in red. Thus, users are able to quickly differentiate the potentially harmful and effective ingredients.

Example of positive ingredient (in green, see Figure 15)

Figure 15: Positive expressions.

Example of negative ingredient (in red, Figure 16)

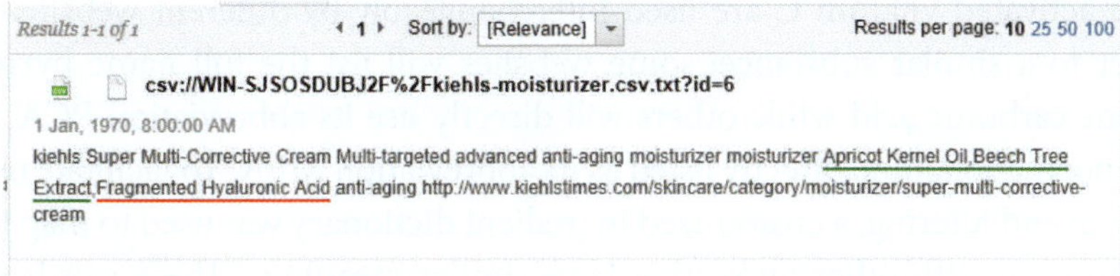

Figure 16: Negative expressions.

This feature can be used in combination with rule-based category. Users can select a pre-defined category, e.g., toners, and look into these products to further analyze their positive and negative ingredients (Figure 17).

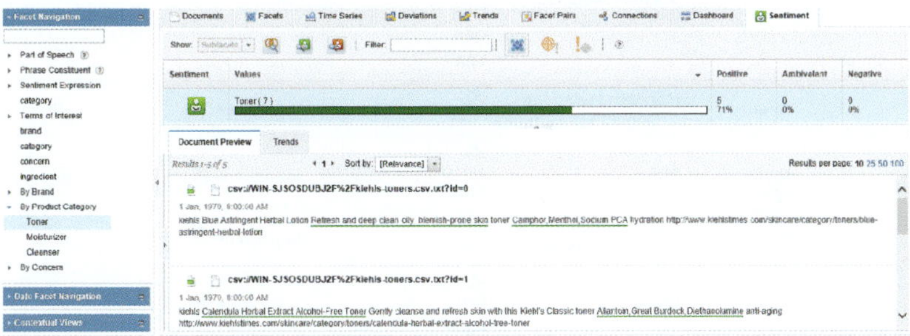

Figure 17: Sentiment analysis result by category.

Users can also click "ingredient" facet to explore more insights from the ingredient list (Figure 18). The application will list the set of unique values of "ingredient" field from all product items. For each value, you can zoom in the details, such as the number of occurrence, or positive and negative ingredients for these product items.

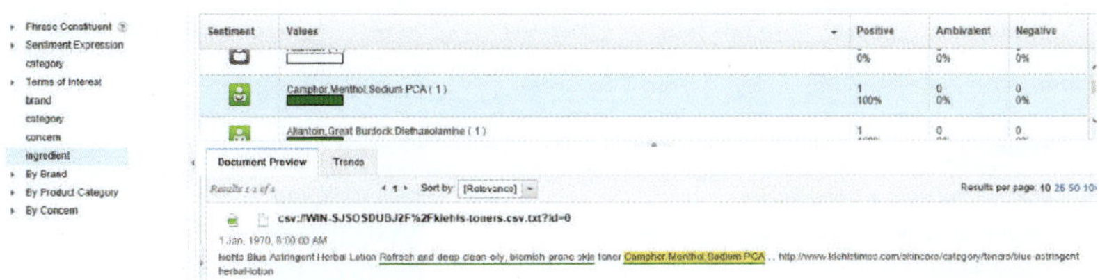

Figure 18: Ingredient facet.

As the data is from different sources (i.e., skin care product websites), the terms used to describe ingredients may vary, e.g., activated C, vitamin C, and activated vitamin C are used interchangeably by different websites to refer to a similar substance; some websites will list the full name pyrrolidone carbonic acid while others will directly use its abbreviation PCA, or monoethanolamine directly listed as its abbreviation MEA. To facilitate user search and filtering, a customized ingredient dictionary was used to map the main term with other terms that have similar meanings. These words are applied to "ingredient" facet, so that results with similar terms can also be shown when analyzing the main term using ingredient facet (see Figure 19).

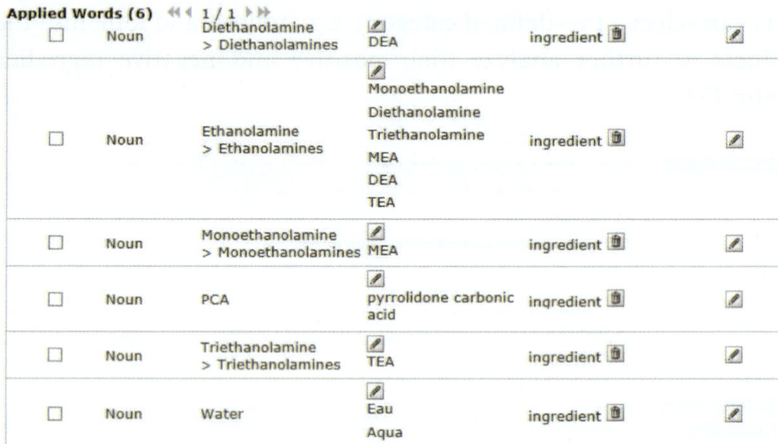

Figure 19: User dictionary setup.

When users execute a filter in the ingredient facet by inputting the main word, its equivalent terms will also be shown in the results. As in the example shown in Figure 20, diethanolamine and triethanolamine are defined as equivalent words of ethanolamine. When users do a filtering by ethanolamine, results containing its equivalent words are displayed as well.

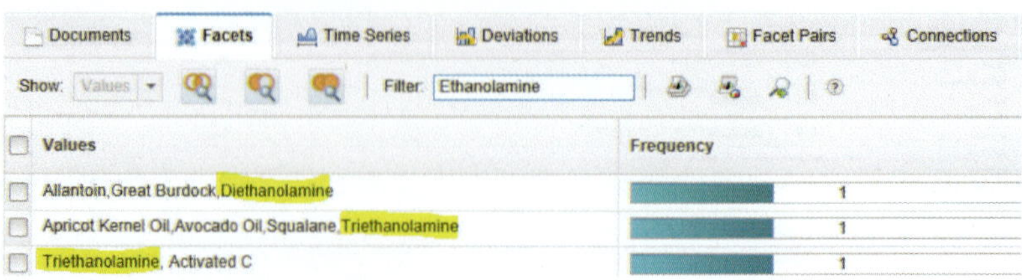

Figure 20: User dictionary example.

5. DISCUSSION

This application aims to act as one-stop platform to consolidate skin care product information. It can be used for information reference, and also help users to easily find the products they are interested in.

One of the advantages of this solution is that it utilizes information from the official sites as data sources. This ensures the completeness and reliability of the source information. Compared to the official sites which only provide product information of its own brand, the application is able to crawl multiple brands; thus users do not have to go to individual websites to view product information.

In addition, the ingredient analysis feature provided in this solution can be attractive to users. As there have been increasing concerns about the safety of skin care products, people are interested to know more about the ingredients used in the products before purchasing. No existing useful online tool was able to serve this need. The solution provides intuitive and easy-to-use ingredient analysis functions. Instead of manually scanning through the ingredient list, the application helps users to identify those potentially harmful ones from those effective ones. This can help users make quick judgments about the safety of the products.

6. CONCLUSION AND FURTHER WORK

Developed using Watson Explorer content analytics components, the application is able to provide features that help to resolve the problems as stated in Section 2. Watson Explorer provided administration features for content analytics collections, to achieve the required functionalities with setup and configuration, which makes it easy to maintain or extend this application in future.

The current ingredient analysis is still preliminary. Aside from identifying effective and potentially harmful ingredients, if more information is available, more in-depth analysis could be attempted. There are other factors that determine effective/potentially harmful ingredients that are not being evaluated in this solution, for example, the concentration of each ingredient is also an important factor to evaluate the effectiveness and safety of the product. If there is insufficient amount of an ingredient in the product, its effectiveness will degrade over the shelf-life of the product by reacting with air or other ingredients.

One such example is vitamin C (L-ascorbic acid) and alpha lipoid acid which have to be at least 10 per cent and 1 per cent, respectively.[5] If the application can get ingredient concentration information and date of manufacture, and analyze them against the standard concentration ratio, it will help users to have a better understanding of the effectiveness of the product's ingredients. However ingredient concentration data may not be available on the label or official websites, since this is not mandatory based on regulation. Although the ingredients are usually listed based on descending order of the concentration, it does not provide sufficient information for further analysis.

Moreover, whether an ingredient is considered as effective or potentially harmful also depends on the type of skin of the consumer, e.g., consumers with sensitive skin prone to acne would prefer to choose products with natural ingredients.[6] For dry skin, they will prefer ingredients such as Glycolic Acid, Aloe Vera, or Lactic Acid.[7] The application can be further customized and enhanced to allow users to select their profile, e.g., dry/oil/normal/sensitive, then the search results will analyze effective ingredients and potentially harmful ingredients based on the type of skin the users have. Such features will provide more relevant insights to the products for users to make purchase decisions.

REFERENCES

1. Kari Gran. Poll: Nearly 60 per cent of American women read beauty product labels, check for harmful ingredients, *Yahoo Finance*. 5 August 2015. http://finance.yahoo.com/news/poll-nearly-60-american-women-151500522.html;_ylt=AwrXgiPkfcRVTDIAjBLQtDMD;_ylu=X3oDMTByb2lvbXVuBGNvbG8DZ3ExBHBvcwMxBHZ0aWQDBHNlYwNzcg--

2. Fair packaging and labeling act, Federal Trade Commission. 31 July 2015. https://www.ftc.gov/enforcement/rules/rulemaking-regulatory-reform-proceedings/fair-packaging-labeling-act

3. Topical skin rejuvenation treatments, Smart Skincare. 31 July 2015. http://www.smartskincare.com/treatments/topical/

4. Potentially harmful ingredients, Smart Skincare. 31 July 2015. http://www.smartskincare.com/ingredients/harmfulingred.html

5. Alpha lipoid acid skin care: What is all the fuss about? Smart Skincare. 31 July 2015. http://www.smartskincare.com/treatments/topical/lipoic.html

6. 8 natural ingredients that soothe sensitive skin. 14 January 2014. http://www.annmariegianni.com/8-natural-ingredients-soothe-sensitive-skin/

7. Audrey Kunin. Top 5 skincare ingredients for dry skin. 7 October 2013. http://www.dermadoctor.com/blog/top-5-dry-skin-skincare-ingredients/

CHAPTER 19

Study on Factors Associated With Bounce Rates on Consumer Product Websites

SNG Yun Fei

ABSTRACT

This paper explores one of the often-ignored metrics with regards to web analytics: bounce rate. The bounce rate of a website refers to the percentage of visitors who navigate away from the website after viewing only one page. High bounce rates indicate that a website is not sustaining the attention of its visitors, or could reflect a technical issue that is preventing visitors from moving forward through the site. This paper seeks to identify ways in which the bounce rate of a website can be reduced, through both qualitative and quantitative research methods, including site analysis and regression methods applied on available demographic and technical information.

1. INTRODUCTION

The history of web analytics begin with the modest hit counter that quickly proliferated most websites in the 1990s. They provided webmasters with an indication of the number of visits their pages received. Slowly, these evolved into more advanced JavaScript tags that allowed webmasters to find out more about their visitors, where they arrived to the site from and even their physical geographic location. As the amount of information about each virtual visit became more detailed, the importance of such information was better understood and used to improve websites and build businesses. Indeed, entire companies are devoted to analyzing web data, helping big corporations to expand their empire.

2. PROBLEM STATEMENT

Product websites and campaign microsites are used extensively by fast-moving consumer goods (FMCG) companies to provide consumers with information on their products or events. Along with online advertising and social network websites, these sites form an integral part of their digital marketing strategy. However, some of these websites suffer from high bounce rates, meaning that a high proportion of visitors to the site navigate away from the site after viewing only one page.

The bounce rate of a website refers to the percentage of visitors to the website who navigate away from the websites after only viewing one page.

$$\text{Bounce Rate} = \frac{\text{Total Number of Visitors Viewing One Page Only}}{\text{Total Number of Entries to Page}}$$

A visitor may bounce under the following circumstances: clicking on a link to a different website, closing an open browser window, typing a new URL, clicking the "back" button and timeout of their current browsing session. High bounce rates indicate that a website is not sustaining the interest of its visitors, or could reflect a technical issue that is preventing visitors from moving forward through the site. Given the many advantages in keeping consumers on the website (generate purchase interest for the product, cross-selling of other products, build rapport with the brand), marketers are constantly looking for ways to increase customer engagement on product websites by reducing the bounce rate.

3. STATE OF THE ART

Much of the academic research available around digital marketing and website efficiency relates to advertising click-through rates (CTR) and conversion rates. CTR refers to the number of users that click on a specific link out of the total number of users that view a page, and is commonly linked to how successful an online campaign had been.

$$\text{CTR} = \frac{\text{Clicks}}{\text{Impressions}} \times 100\%$$

A similar metric is the conversion rate, which measures the rate at which a retail website (usually) 'converts' site visitors into paying customers. This definition could, however, be expanded to include any specific action that the webmaster wants the site visitors to take, for example submitting a product review, or tweeting about an article on social media.

$$\text{Conversion Rate} = \frac{\text{Number of Goal Achievements}}{\text{Visitors}}$$

In a particular study on identifying factors affecting CTR using neural networks, it was found that increased query reformulation, searching duration and query length correlate positively with future click-through (Zhang, Jansen and Spink, 2009). Other studies also looked at using clustering algorithms to identify features that would improve conversion rates (Ayanso and Yoogalingam, 2009), and identified expert and statistical evidence as important factors to improving performance of online advertising (Haans, Raassens and van Hout, 2013). One study also identified the importance of design in converting visitors using a scientific method, by quantifying the placement of elements and the type of elements on a web page (Gofman, Moskowitz and Mets, 2009).

There is limited academic research addressing website bounce rates specifically – discussions on this topic are often covered by professional marketers as part of agency blog posts as a means to build the agency's presence in the industry. This lack of academic coverage could largely be due to the relative novelty of the tools that allow companies to track the performance of their websites, constant renewal of web standards, content infrastructure and variables that are hard to quantify, which add to the complexity of researching the topic.

Bounce rates are indicative of overall user opinion of websites, and can be reasonably predicted using features extracted from sponsored advertising and their landing pages (Sculley, Malkin, Basu and Bayardo, 2009). Longer, and more engaged browsing sessions – and by definition, lower bounce rates – were found to be correlated with return visits by visitors (Plaza, 2009).

From a qualitative perspective, researchers and marketers have attributed content strategy and visual design as key to reducing bounce rates (Tan and Wei, 2007) (Marentis, 2014).

4. SOLUTION

4.1. Description of approach

4.1.1. Part I: Descriptive analytics

The first part of the research involved qualitative and quantitative analyses using Adobe Analytics data for a well-known FMCG company. Other external tools and resources, including literature reviews, were used to identify possible enhancements to reduce bounce rates and hence increase the 'stickyness of the visit'. The project focused on analysis of traffic entries and aimed at decreasing bounce rates, and did not go in-depth on e-retailer visit analysis, social media analytics, and other digital metrics.

The research focused on 10 websites across the company's most important personal care brands including baby, beauty, oral health and topical health categories, across a few key markets, including China, Japan, Korea and India. This part of the research utilized descriptive analytics to uncover digital insights and identify possible opportunities for the websites in reducing their bounce rates to a level below 55–60 per cent, which is considered to be the industry standard (Simpson, 2012).

The key metrics of each website, including visitor count, traffic flow, time spent on site, were examined. For each website, pages with the most traffic entering and highest bounce rates were identified, and a deeper look was taken at both quantitative metrics and qualitative qualities that could possibly be improved.

In the study, Japan and Korea were found to have a high 'mobile' focus, with 65–70 per cent of visitors arriving to the sites via mobile devices. Conversely, China visitors were mostly arriving on desktop devices, accounting for 80–90 per cent of the traffic, due to redirect of mobile traffic to microsites / social networking sites such as weibo and wechat. There is a growing need to make product websites more responsive and easier to read on mobile devices, thereby making visits more 'sticky', reducing the bounce rate. Due to the strong trend towards mobile, it was deemed important to retire Flash-powered pages as support for Flash on mobile devices no longer exists on many mobile operating systems.

From the data recorded on the Adobe Analytics server, it was discovered that the Chinese and Indian sites covered in the study experience significantly higher load times than the other websites. The hypothesis is that this is largely a reflection of the poor Internet Service Provider (ISP) infrastructure in these countries, rather than website size and composition. It is likely that the tags on the Adobe Analytics platform logs the time from the moment the page starts to load on the visitor's device until it finishes loading, thereby reflecting the speed of the visitor's connection. As a result, website speed testing was conducted across all the websites in this study with an independent online load time testing tool which attempts to access the same sites using servers located in various countries. It was found that, using this tool, all the websites in the study yielded similar load times. In fact, the Chinese websites had the highest performance grades (higher scores are better), and lower page sizes (lower scores are better). As a result of this finding, even though the websites in China and India are meeting global standards on usability, it is important to continue building even more lightweight websites for these markets to adapt to local needs.

From a technology perspective, certain websites with article content were not properly tagged using Adobe Analytics, resulting in data that records all article-related data as a single data point. If article pages can be identified uniquely by Adobe Analytics, greater insight can be gleaned on article quality and focus can be targeted on articles that promote 'sticky' visits

To summarize our findings, the following three-pronged recommendation was presented:

Action

- Ensure that the websites have a *clear call to action* that gives the visitor an understanding of how the websites can be useful to them, and where they can click to navigate through the site. This would convert potential bounces to stay on the site and keep them engaged.
- Ensure that there is *interactive content* to engage visitors. Visitors often leave a website because there is either no button where they can click on to progress through the website, or they cannot find it.

Content

- Ensure the *content strategy and execution* is well planned for. If website content is not kept up to date, visitors can easily switch to other platforms to look for content.
- Know who the visitors are, and understand why they are visiting the websites. This would allow the website to be tailored in such a way to ensure that the content presented is *relevant* to the audience. A disinterested visitor would only leave to find information elsewhere.
- Keep a clear, well-designed *information architecture* to help visitors navigate through the website. If visitors get frustrated with trying to find what they are looking for, they will leave.

Design

- Use strong *color contrast* to draw attention to important content and help users understand information.
- Maintain *visual appeal* using interesting graphics to keep visitor interest and focus.

4.1.2. Part II: Regression techniques

For the second part of the research, a deep dive was conducted into the visitor data for one particular website, to explore fundamental qualities connected with bounce rate. The goal of this section is to examine specific pre-determined factors, and how they relate to whether a chosen visitor would bounce from the site. A brand that specializes in personal care products (wash, powder, moisturizers, etc.) targeted at infants was chosen. This site was chosen due to the completeness of the data spanning across a period of all twelve months in the year.

Data was extracted for the period March 2014–Feb 2015 from Adobe Analytics. Data cleaning and the following data transformations were made:

- Converted date and time data in Adobe Analytics into standard date/time format recognizable by R
- Cleaned up naming convention of geographical variables
- Retained only records of visitor's initial entry into the website during each browsing session

- Created Bounce variable (Entry Page = Exit Page AND Path Length = 1 AND Time Spent on page < 1 min)
- Create dummy variables for Month
- Simplify OS Type by consolidating categories
- Simplify Device Type by consolidating categories
- Included internet penetration data for 2012 (Martin, 2012)

The final data set consisted of 364,801 observations with 15 variables: (Refer to Appendix 1)

The primary aim of this section is to predict the possibility of bounce before the visitor even enters the page. Any variables that occur after the visitor has accessed the page from this data set (for example, the number of web pages in the website the visitor has accessed in the current browsing session, the total time the visitor spent on the website) were removed.

Since the bounce variable has a binary range of [0,1], the data set was run through logistic regression models to identify the effect of variables on the bounce rate.

4.2. Logistic regression

A simple logistic regression of the dataset in R, trying out with various variable combinations.

$$\log\left(\frac{Y}{1-Y}\right)=b_0+b_1X_1+b_2X_2+b_3X_3+b_4X_4+b_5X_5+b_6X_6+b_7X_7+b_8X_8$$

where Y is the probability of a bounce

X_1 are the dummy variables relating to the 'State' variable

X_2 are the dummy variables relating to the 'Device Type' variable

X_3 are the dummy variables relating to the 'Referrer Type' variable

X_4 are the dummy variables relating to the 'OS' variable

X_5 are the dummy variables relating to the 'Month' variable

X_6 is percentage of Internet penetration

X_7 is the number of seconds taken to load the page

X_8 is the frequency of visits by the visitor in the last 30 days

Call:
glm(formula = Bounce ~ factor(State2) + factor(Device.Type) + factor(Referrer.Type) + factor(OS) + factor(Month) + Internet. Penetration + Seconds +
LastVisit + FrequencyMonth, family = "binomial", data = JBCN)

Deviance Residuals:
Min 1Q Median 3Q Max
−4.8745 −0.6647 0.4687 0.6406 1.9877

Coefficients: (1 not defined because of singularities)

Signif. codes: 0 '***' 0.001 '**' 0.01 '*' 0.05 '.' 0.1 ' ' 1
(Dispersion parameter for binomial family taken to be 1)
Null deviance: 12715 on 11183 degrees of freedom
Residual deviance: 10115 on 11127 degrees of freedom
(353617 observations deleted due to missingness)
AIC: 10229
Number of Fisher Scoring iterations: 9

		Model Likelihood Ratio Test		**Discrimination Indexes**		**Rank Discrim. Indexes**	
Obs	11184	LR chi2	2599.80	R2	0.305	C	0.803
0	2859	d.f.	56	g	1.424	Dxy	0.606
1	8325	Pr(>chi2)	<0.0001	gr	4.153	gamma	0.608
max |deriv|	0.005			gp	0.225	tau-a	0.231
				Brier	0.142		

The above combination of variables yielded the lowest AIC value, with an R^2 of 0.305.

4.2.1. Interpretation of results

By looking at the results from the State variable containing dummy variables of the provinces from which the website was accessed, compared to the omitted reference state Anhui, visitors from the less 'connected' provinces – including Inner Mongolia, Jilin, Shandong – were found to be more likely to bounce.

Visitors accessing the website on mobile devices were more likely to bounce. Possible reasons for this could be due to poor mobile design and increased likelihood of visitors to access the site unintentionally.

Visitors directed to the website from search engines are less likely to bounce (versus the baseline of an unknown entry method), possibly because they are specifically searching for content related to the brand. At the same time, visitors who directly enter the site by typing the URL or through an existing bookmark were more likely to bounce.

Visitors accessing the site in the summer months, relative to the month of January, were more likely to exit the site. This could be attributed to higher browsing activity during the winter months due to poor weather, or the fact that the brand's range consisted mainly of moisturizing products, which are in greater demand in colder and drier seasons.

Load time has a small, positive correlation with bounce rates. A higher load time increases the possibility of a bounce from any visitor. Intuitively, this is due to the visitor giving up on loading the page the longer the process takes.

The recency of the last visit is positively correlated with the visitor's decision to stay longer on the site. The more recent the last visit, the more likely the visitor is interested in finding information on the website, and thereby inducing them to revisit the website to find out more information about the product.

Finally, it was discovered that frequency also seems to play a part – the more times a visitor has visited the website in the last 30 days, the more likely he is to stay on the website as he continues to show interest in the product.

4.3. Panel (linear) regression

Panel regression was conducted on the data to analyze the impact of individual preferences and time variable choices. The 'State2' variable was dropped from the data as it is a time-invariant variable. Fixed effects and random models were run on the data, and a Hausman test was conducted to determine the significance of each method.

Hausman test: p-value < 2.2e−16

Because the p-value is significant (less than 0.05), the null hypothesis is rejected and the fixed effects model will be used.

Fixed effects

$$\log\left(\frac{Y}{1-Y}\right) = b_0 + b_1X_1 + b_2X_2 + b_3X_3 + b_4X_4 + b_5X_5 + b_6X_6 + b_7X_7$$

where Y is the probability of a bounce
X_1 are the dummy variables relating to the 'Device Type' variable
X_2 are the dummy variables relating to the 'Referrer Type' variable
X_3 are the dummy variables relating to the 'OS' variable
X_4 are the dummy variables relating to the 'Month' variable
X_5 is percentage of Internet penetration
X_6 is the number of seconds taken to load the page
X_7 is the frequency of visits by the visitor in the last 30 days

Call:
plm(formula = Bounce ~ factor(Device.Type) + factor(Referrer.Type) + factor(OS) + factor(Month) + Internet.Penetration + Seconds + LastVisit + FrequencyMonth, data = JBCN2, model = "within", index = c("Visitor_ID", "DateTime"))
Unbalanced Panel: n = 9146, T = 1–44, N = 11184
Residuals:
Min. 1st Qu. Median 3rd Qu. Max.
–0.919 0.000 0.000 0.000 0.952

Signif. codes: 0 '***' 0.001 '**' 0.01 '*' 0.05 '.' 0.1 ' ' 1
Total Sum of Squares: 303.51
Residual Sum of Squares: 291.5
R-Squared : 0.039588
Adj. R-Squared : 0.0071361
F-statistic: 3.77725 on 22 and 2016 DF, p-value: 8.0663e–09

Running a linear panel regression resulted in outputs which were quite different:

- Traffic from search engines still resulted in lower bounce rates.
- All months showed a reduced probability of bounce compared to January.
- The impact of the load time and visitor frequency on bounce rate is significantly reduced.

4.4. Panel logistic regression

Finally, a panel logistic regression was run due to the nature of the Bounce variable and the inability to explain the results of the panel linear model.

Maximum Likelihood estimation
BFGS maximisation, 147 iterations
Return code 0: successful convergence
Log-Likelihood: −5150.124
26 free parameters
Estimates:

Signif. codes: 0 '***' 0.001 '**' 0.01 '*' 0.05 '.' 0.1 ' ' 1
The results turned out to be very similar to the simple logistic model.

5. DISCUSSION

Identifying problematic pages on the website that contribute to high bounce rates helps in improving consumer engagement. For example, a particular webpage accounted for about 50 per cent of entry traffic for a certain website. However, it was an outdated promotion page which displayed a 'missing page' error and had a bounce rate of 80 per cent. By being able to identify this problem using website data, the digital team was able to correct the source of the problem and remove advertising material and sponsored links that referred visitors to that website. In addition to being able to reduce bounce rate for that website by five per cent one month after the promotional materials were removed, resources could be redirected to other parts of the business.

By being able to identify variables that can predict bounce rates, areas where the website can be further improved can be examined as well as whether there are specific customer segments (based on geography, mobile usage, etc.) the FMCG company should consider targeting to increase web engagement. Advertising spend on promoting the website, both on print and digital platforms, can be better allocated to make sure that finite resources are well utilized.

Looking at the results from this data set, the company could target high income individuals from more prosperous provinces who are more likely to purchase their products. Sponsored web advertising money could be poured into targeting desktop users, unless there are improvements to the user interface of the mobile website which would allow visitors to be able to better find the data they are looking for. Advertising spend could also be phased more heavily in the winter, to target customers who are more likely to purchase moisturizing products during the colder months.

6. CONCLUSION AND FURTHER WORK

Web analytics can be extremely useful for companies to identify problems with their digital face to consumers – their product website. By analyzing the bounce rate of their product websites, the company can get a better understanding of its customers browsing habits. This helps to improve the allocatation of advertising budgets by targeting potential consumers with a higher propensity to purchase the company's products. However, it important to note that the ultimate goal of a digital presence, like any other promotional campaign, is to increase conversion of consumers to utilize the brand's products and build consumer rapport with the brand, and it is towards this objective which analytics should focus.

Further studies could apply other analytics to this data set including keyword search analysis to identify keywords that the company could purchase for sponsored advertising. Funnel analysis could also be conducted to discover which pages visitors leave and why.

REFERENCES

1. Zhang, Y, BJ Jansen and A Spink (2009). Identification of factors predicting click-through in web searching using neural network analysis. *Journal of the American Society for Information Science and Technology*, 60(3), 557–570. doi:10.1002/asi.20993

2. Ayanso, A and R Yoogalingam (2009). Profiling retail web site functionalities and conversion rates: A cluster analysis. *International Journal of Electronic Commerce*, 14(1), 79–114. doi:10.2753/JEC1086-4415140103

3. Haans, H, VR Hout and N Raassens (2013). Search engine advertisements: The impact of advertising statements on click-through and conversion rates. *Marketing Letters*, 24(2), 151–163. doi:10.1007/s11002-013-9226-5

4. Gofman, A, HR Moskowitz and T Mets (2009). Integrating science into web design: Consumer-driven web site optimization. *Journal of Consumer Marketing*, 26(4), 286–298. doi:10.1108/07363760910965882

5. Sculley, D, R Malkin, S Basu and RJ Bayardo (2009). Predicting Bounce Rates in Sponsored Search Advertisements. In *Proc. of the 15th ACM SIGKDD Conference on Knowledge Discovery and Data Mining* (KDD-2009).

6. Plaza, B (2009). Monitoring web traffic source effectiveness with Google Analytics. An experiment with time series. *Aslib Proceedings*, 61(5), 474–482.

7. Marentis, C (2014). Search engine people blog: SEP 23: Decrease your website's bounce rate today. Chatham: Newstex. Retrieved from http://search.proquest.com/docview/1643207256?accountid=13876

8. Simpson, M (2012). Dissecting high homepage bounce rates. Multichannel Merchant, Retrieved from http://search.proquest.com/docview/1035205090?accountid=13876

9. Martin, R (2012). China Internet Penetration Map 2012. Retrieved July 29, 2015, from https://www.techinasia.com/china-internet-penetration-map/

Appendix 1

Variable Name	Variable Description
Visitor_ID	System-generated unique visitor ID
DateTime	Date and Time of the visit (e.g. 2014-03-25 02:00:00)
State	Provinces of China • anhui • beijing • china • chongqing • fujian • gansu • guangdong • guangxi • guizhou • hainan • hebei • heilongjiantg • henan

Variable Name	Variable Description
	• hubei • hunan • jiangsu • jiangxi • jilin • liaoning • nei mongol zizhiqu • ningxia • other • qinghai • shaanxi • shandong • shanghai • shanxi • sichuan • tianjin • xinjiang • xizang • yunnan • zhejiang
Device.Type	Type of Device used to access website • Mobile Phone • Other • PC
Referrer.Type	Where the visitor entered the website from • (blank) • other web sites • search engines • social networks • typed/bookmarked
Connection.Types	The type of internet connection the device is using • lan/wifi • mobile carrier • modem

(*continued*)

Appendix 1 (*continued*)

Variable Name	Variable Description
OS	Operating system on device used to access website • Android • Apple • Linux • Other • Windows
Month	Character of Month (e.g. 01, 02, 03, …, 12)
Internet Penetration	Internet penetration percentage of province in 2012
Seconds	Load time of site in seconds
Time.Spent.per.Visit	The amount of time the visitor spent during the visit, pre-grouped into the following intervals by Adobe Analytics • Group A: <1 min • Group B: 1–5 min • Group C: 5–10 min • Group D: 10–30 min • Group E: 30–60 min • Group F: 1–2 h • Group G: 2–5 h
Days.Since.Last.Visit	The number of days since the visitor's last visit, pre-grouped into the following intervals by Adobe Analytics • Group A: less than 1 day • Group B: 1–3 days • Group C: 3–7 days • Group D: 7–14 days • Group E: 14 days–1 month • Group F: longer than 1 month • Group G: first visit
LastVisit	Number of days since last visit
FrequencyMonth	Number of times visitor accessed the site in the last 30 days
Bounce	Binary bounce indicator (1 indicating bounce, 0 indicating no bounce)
	Definition of bounce: Entry Page = Exit Page AND Path Length = 1 AND Time Spent on page < 1 min

Appendix 2

	Est.	Std. Error	*z* value	Pr(>|z|)	
(Intercept)	0.0567	0.240	0.236	0.81339	
factor(State2) beijing	0.276	0.191	1.443	0.14895	
factor(State2) china	−0.0872	0.384	−0.227	0.82065	
factor(State2) chongqing	0.130	0.282	0.461	0.64488	
factor(State2) fujian	0.406	0.207	1.957	0.05037	.
factor(State2) gansu	0.0925	0.325	0.285	0.776	
factor(State2) guangdong	−0.0258	0.188	−0.138	0.89063	
factor(State2) guangxi	0.237	0.235	1.006	0.31451	
factor(State2) guizhou	0.586	0.295	1.988	0.04686	*
factor(State2) hainan	0.394	0.449	0.877	0.38047	
factor(State2) hebei	0.330	0.207	1.594	0.11093	
factor(State2) heilongjiang	1.08	0.272	3.97	7.18E−05	***
factor(State2) henan	0.541	0.209	2.584	0.00975	**
factor(State2) hubei	0.516	0.233	2.209	0.02718	*
factor(State2) hunan	0.560	0.260	2.159	0.03085	*
factor(State2) jiangsu	0.355	0.208	1.706	0.08796	.
factor(State2) jiangxi	0.403	0.266	1.513	0.1302	
factor(State2)jilin	0.864	0.260	3.326	0.00088	***

(*continued*)

Appendix 2 (*continued*)

	Est.	Std. Error	*z* value	Pr(>|z|)	
factor(State2) liaoning	0.598	0.236	2.537	0.01119	*
factor(State2) nei mongol zizhiqu	0.949	0.333	2.844	0.00445	**
factor(State2) ningxia	1.52	1.05	1.45	0.147	
factor(State2) other	−0.111	0.211	−0.525	0.59988	
factor(State2) qinghai	0.659	1.09	0.607	0.54417	
factor(State2) shaanxi	0.266	0.261	1.019	0.30809	
factor(State2) shandong	0.728	0.199	3.662	0.00025	***
factor(State2) shanghai	−0.0809	0.191	−0.425	0.67119	
factor(State2) shanxi	0.560	0.263	2.128	0.03331	*
factor(State2) sichuan	0.487	0.228	2.134	0.03287	*
factor(State2) tianjin	0.247	0.264	0.933	0.3506	
factor(State2) xinjiang	0.751	0.397	1.893	0.05833	.
factor(State2) xizang	8.97	119	0.075	0.94013	
factor(State2) yunnan	−0.00760	0.296	−0.026	0.97955	
factor(State2) zhejiang	0.406	0.210	1.938	0.05268	.
factor(Device. Type)Other	0.102	0.171	0.593	0.55294	
factor(Device. Type)PC	−1.13	0.200	−5.682	1.33E−08	***

	Est.	Std. Error	*z* value	Pr(>|z|)	
factor(Referrer.Type)other web sites	1.40	0.106	13.139	< 2e−16	***
factor(Referrer.Type)search engines	−0.208	0.0935	−2.228	0.0259	*
factor(Referrer.Type)social networks	0.565	0.933	0.605	0.545	
factor(Referrer.Type)typed/bookmarked	0.411	0.0942	4.363	1.28E−05	***
factor(OS)Apple	0.376	0.147	2.556	0.0106	*
factor(OS)Linux	0.930	0.226	4.113	3.90E−05	***
factor(OS)Other	1.02	0.666	1.53	0.12605	
factor(OS)Windows	0.351	0.200	1.75	0.08005	.
factor(Month)02	−0.176	0.139	−1.267	0.20528	
factor(Month)03	0.152	0.233	0.654	0.51286	
factor(Month)04	0.753	0.148	5.089	3.60E−07	***
factor(Month)05	0.900	0.148	6.062	1.34E−09	***
factor(Month)06	0.417	0.158	2.643	0.00821	**
factor(Month)07	0.407	0.157	2.6	0.00933	**
factor(Month)08	0.686	0.157	4.358	1.31E−05	***
factor(Month)09	0.0434	0.149	0.29	0.7715	
factor(Month)10	−0.333	0.162	−2.05	0.04033	*
factor(Month)11	−0.283	0.161	−1.758	0.07875	.
factor(Month)12	−0.396	0.156	−2.545	0.01092	*
Internet.Penetration	NA	NA	NA	NA	
Seconds	0.0718	0.00798	8.996	< 2e−16	***
LastVisit	0.0251	0.00247	10.167	< 2e−16	***
FrequencyMonth	−0.0280	0.0102	−2.741	0.00612	**

Appendix 3

	Estimate	Std. Error	*t*-value	Pr(>|t|)	
factor(Device.Type)PC	0.258	0.212	1.2197	0.222729	
factor(Referrer.Type)other web sites	−0.113	0.0634	−1.7842	0.074547	.
factor(Referrer.Type)search engines	−0.141	0.0328	−4.2904	1.87E−05	***
factor(Referrer.Type)typed/bookmarked	0.0279	0.0331	0.8428	0.399414	
factor(OS)Apple	−0.164	0.415	−0.3951	0.692821	
factor(OS)Linux	−0.0781	0.301	−0.2593	0.795453	
factor(OS)Windows	−0.649	0.296	−2.1902	0.028626	*
factor(Month)02	−0.0232	0.0870	−0.2668	0.789648	
factor(Month)03	−0.433	0.210	−2.0623	0.039311	*
factor(Month)04	−0.400	0.157	−2.551	0.010814	*
factor(Month)05	−0.299	0.149	−2.0116	0.044393	*
factor(Month)06	−0.203	0.145	−1.3953	0.163068	
factor(Month)07	−0.315	0.132	−2.3872	0.017068	*
factor(Month)08	−0.308	0.116	−2.6506	0.008098	**
factor(Month)09	−0.318	0.104	−3.064	0.002213	**
factor(Month)10	−0.225	0.0946	−2.372	0.017786	*
factor(Month)11	−0.168	0.0839	−2.0063	0.04496	*
factor(Month)12	−0.220	0.0778	−2.8216	0.004825	**
Internet.Penetration	0.211	0.188	1.1229	0.26163	
Seconds	0.00501	0.00112	4.4722	8.17E−06	***
LastVisit	−0.000307	0.000589	−0.521	0.602438	
Frequency Month	0.00671	0.00283	2.3734	0.017718	*

Appendix 4

	Estimate	Std. error	*t* value	Pr(> t)	
(Intercept)	0.530	0.108	4.914	8.90E−07	***
factor(Device.Type)Other	0.0629	0.0941	0.668	0.504003	
factor(Device.Type)PC	−0.653	0.113	−5.775	7.71E−09	***
factor(Referrer.Type)other web sites	0.958	0.0604	15.869	< 2e−16	***
factor(Referrer.Type)search engines	−0.0471	0.0557	−0.845	0.398203	
factor(Referrer.Type)social networks	0.248	0.577	0.43	0.667481	
factor(Referrer.Type)typed/bookmarked	0.319	0.0558	5.716	1.09E−08	***
factor(OS) Apple	0.138	0.0796	1.734	0.082861	.
factor(OS) Linux	0.542	0.128	4.238	2.26E−05	***
factor(OS) Other	0.394	0.341	1.155	0.247981	
factor(OS) Windows	0.148	0.113	1.312	0.189655	
factor(Month)02	−0.161	0.0812	−1.988	0.046818	*
factor(Month)03	0.0344	0.137	0.251	0.801676	
factor(Month)04	0.427	0.0862	4.953	7.32E−07	***
factor(Month)05	0.515	0.0858	5.998	2.00E−09	***
factor(Month)06	0.231	0.0917	2.516	0.01188	*
factor(Month)07	0.186	0.0925	2.006	0.04487	*
factor(Month)08	0.429	0.0910	4.712	2.45E−06	***

(*continued*)

Appendix 4 (*continued*)

	Estimate	Std. error	*t* value	Pr(> t)	
factor(Month)09	0.0421	0.0875	0.482	0.629908	
factor(Month)10	−0.256	0.0949	−2.695	0.00703	**
factor(Month)11	−0.265	0.0945	−2.807	0.005002	**
factor(Month)12	−0.263	0.0914	−2.875	0.00404	**
Internet. Penetration	−0.549	0.0960	−5.722	1.06E−08	***
Seconds	0.0260	0.00257	10.133	< 2e−16	***
LastVisit	0.0102	0.000902	11.321	< 2e−16	***
Frequency Month	−0.0198	0.005844	−3.388	0.000704	***

CHAPTER 20

Personalised Knowledge-Based Recommender System for Travel Planning

LI Yiwang Linus

ABSTRACT

Compared to many static tour packages or fixed itinerary suggestions in travel guidebooks, a personalized, knowledge-based recommender system for travel planning may provide a flexible schedule tailored to individual preferences and tastes. In this study, the feasibility and potential of implementing a personalized recommender system in the tourism industry was demonstrated through a case study of Singapore. The paper uses public data sources — TripAdvisor and HungryGoWhere — to form a knowledge database where queries are made to retrieve and suggest relevant places of interest and restaurants to the traveler.. The system is highly relevant to business travelers with scattered periods of leisure time in their schedule or budget travelers with free and easy travel plans.

1. INTRODUCTION

The latest United Nations World Tourism Organization (UNWTO) World Tourism Barometer estimated that international tourist arrivals grew by 4.7 per cent over the previous year and reached 1138 million in 2014.[1] Despite geopolitical and economic challenges, the number of international tourist arrivals has grown by 5 per cent a year on average since 2010.[3]

While online travel agencies (OTAs), such as Priceline, Expedia, and Orbitz are gaining popularity and often provide an option for users to book fixed local tours, the market lacks a travel service that can provide personalized recommendations of attractions based on individual preference and feedback. Such a feature can value-add to the manual search for the best flights, hotels and car rentals, for the best places of interest to visit, thereby providing a one-stop planning service to optimally piece together a travel plan that addresses individual needs.

The additional element of a personalized recommender system saves time and effort for tourists, and is highly relevant for business travelers. A fixed one-day itinerary suggestion extracted from the traditional travel guidebook might be a quick fix (see Figure 1), but it does not reflect the nuances of individual traveler preferences.

With the rise of low-cost carriers in the aviation industry, the proportion of budget airline travelers have also ballooned in the past decade.[2] The CAPA Centre for Aviation estimates that low-cost carriers accounted for at least 26 per cent of seats sold globally in 2013, a huge jump from 2001's 8 per cent.[4] With an increase in the number of budget travelers, the tourism industry has seen a greater demand for free and easy travel plans. A personalized recommender system that is able to provide quick and flexible tailored recommendations seems to be an appealing idea for this group of travelers.

Current state-of-the-art solutions include online trip planners such as Tripomatic, Travefy, and Triporama, but none of them suggests attractions and eating places intuitively based on user's preference and feedback.

Figure 1: One-day itinerary by lonely planet.[5]

2. PROBLEM STATEMENT

Personalized recommender system has the potential to complement the state-of-the-art technologies available in the tourism market. This study aims to identify and generalize the key components for building a personalized knowledge-based recommender system. To demonstrate the viability of such a feature, this study focuses on a localized case study in Singapore to build a working prototype with public data, Google APIs, and Python.

Information such as opening hours, entrance fees for the local attractions are generally not available readily and hence special efforts were taken to gather data by browsing and crawling many useful websites, Structured data was scrapped as much as possible and proxies had to be used as substitutes for missing data for approximation.

Methodology for calculating the journey duration for each mode of transport and the best routing schedule was built with Google Geocoding, Google Maps, and Google Directions API. The study only considered driving as the mode of transport.

3. STATE OF THE ART

3.1. Online travel planners in the market

Tripomatic is one of the most comprehensive online travel planners currently available in the market. It allows the user to add attractions of their choice from the available list. These attractions are then delineated on a map with photo icons, short descriptions, opening hours, and contact details. Once added to the itinerary, the user can choose their mode of commuting (i.e., driving or walking) between attractions, view the weather forecast, and add notes for the day.

Triporama is another online travel planner catering to group travelers. It simplifies group travel planning by allowing the user to create and manage a group trip home page, store and share trip research, assign and organize tasks, conduct polls, post announcements, and coordinate on travel deals. Snapshots of both the travel planners, Tripomatic and Triporama, are shown in Figure 2.

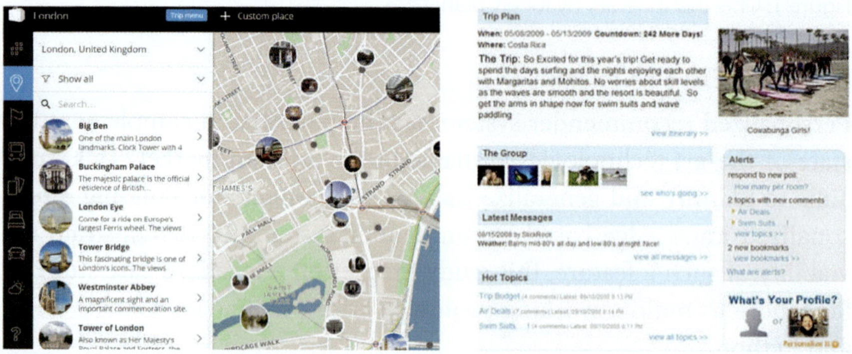

(a) Tripomatic[4] (b) Triporama[5]

Figure 2: Screenshots of online travel planners in the market.

3.2. Overview of recommender system

Many large-scale commercial and social websites, such as Amazon, Netflix, Facebook, and Instagram recommend options to their users, which include products or potential people that the customer might be interested in in. Recommendation engines sieve through copious amounts of data to identify potential user preferences. They revolutionized the manner inanimate websites communicate with their users. Instead of providing a static experience to users to search for and potentially buy products, recommender systems allow for interaction to build a richer experience.

Recommender systems can identify recommendations independently for each user based on his or her prior purchases and searches, and on other users' behaviors.[6]

Recommender system provides benefits for both customers and providers alike. It narrows down the set of choices and efficiently zeroes in on the most relevant options for the user. The provider has the potential to increase customer trust and loyalty, sales, click-through, and conversion rates with avenues for more effective advertising and persuasion.[7]

Recommender systems are necessarily dependent on the availability of reliable data corpus that can provide a basis for prediction of how a new individual is likely to rate items from a catalogue of possible recommendations. For a tourist arriving at a city that he or she never visited earlier, it would be difficult to identify which attraction to suggest as there can be variation in individual preferences.[8]

Many existing guidebooks and websites sought to recommend attractions that are generally popular. Highly personalized recommender systems, however, possess the advantage of providing recommendations that are aligned to individual preferences. For example, elderly travelers would likely not reckon attractions which are physically demanding, and introverts would probably relish places of interest with lesser human interaction as compared to extroverts.[8]

3.3. Types of recommender system

There are three main types of recommender systems — collaborative, content-based and knowledge-based. Collaborative filtering derives a recommendation based on a model of prior user behavior. The model can be built entirely from a single user's behavior or from a cluster of users with similar characteristics and patterns. In a nutshell, collaborative filtering uses group knowledge to construct recommendations based on an automatic collaboration of multiple users, filtered on those who exhibit similar preferences.[6]

Content-based filtering builds a recommendation based on the history of a user's behavior. This type of system might consider the user's historical browsing or purchasing information, such as items the user browses or purchases, and analyze the characteristics of such items.

It then leverages on the historical data to identify and recommend similar content.[6]

Knowledge-based recommender system consolidates the user's unique requirements on a particular product or service by posing questions to the users, and querying its knowledge repository to retrieve the items that best meet the user's expectations. Knowledge-based approach makes deterministic recommendation and does not require a starting database of users' preference, therefore facing no cold-start problem.[9] It can be applied more easily to meet the requirements of this study.

Figure 3a illustrates the input/output relationship used in the knowledge-based recommender system.

There is also a hybrid system, which combines two or more components of the recommender systems in varied ways to enhance recommendation performance. The combination of techniques might mitigate specific weaknesses of the individual approach, such as cold-start or data sparsity disadvantage, and result in a more versatile system.[10]

Figure 3b Summarizes the comparison of pros and cons of different recommender approaches.

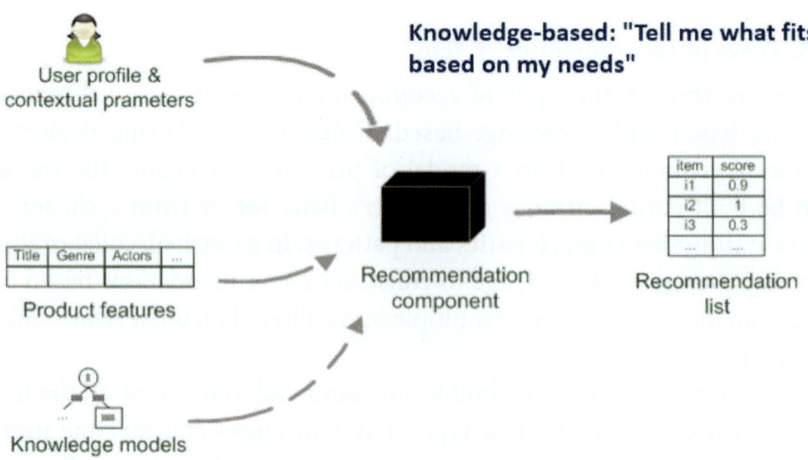

Figure 3a: Input/output relationship in the knowledge-based recommender system.[7]

	Pros	Cons
Collaborative	No knowledge-engineering effort, serendipity of results, learns market segments	Requires some form of rating feedback, cold start for new users and new items
Content-based	No community required, comparison between items possible	Content descriptions necessary, cold start for new users, no surprises
Knowledge-based	Deterministic recommendations, assured quality, no cold-start, can resemble sales dialogue	Knowledge engineering effort to bootstrap, basically static, does not react to short-term trends

Figure 3b: Comparison of recommender approaches.[7]

4. SOLUTION: DESCRIPTION OF APPROACH

4.1. Conceptual design model

General conceptual design model of the personalized knowledge-based recommender system is illustrated in Figure 4. Data sources are identified for crawling, cleaning, and formatting to build a knowledge repository. User inputs include the location of stay, period of travel, and other preferences. User parameters are processed and appropriate queries are made from the database to select the preferred items for recommendation. Travel plans are then optimized for the suggested items incorporating relevant constraints, such as weather considerations, opening hours of attractions, and choice of transportation. Recommendation outputs contain the travel schedule, with other information such as driving directions, cost of meals, etc.

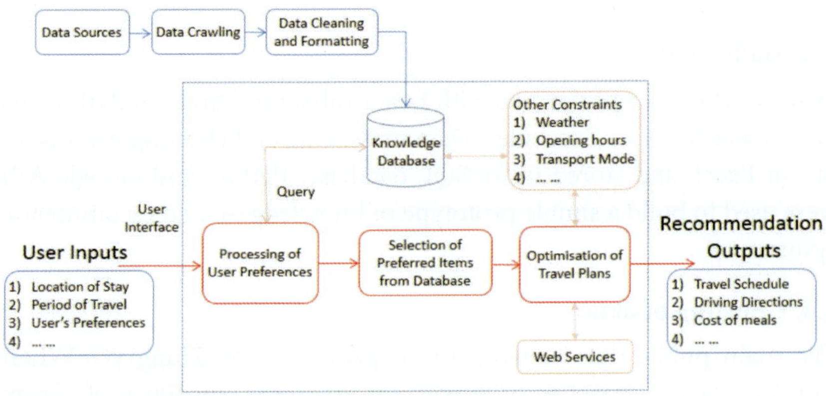

Figure 4: Conceptual design model of the recommender system.

4.2. Building the prototype

The skeletal architecture of recommender system is illustrated in Figure 5. Target audience for prototyping was assumed to be business travelers. User inputs include the hotel of stay, time period of travel, preferred type and nature of attractions and cuisine for meals. Based on the user inputs, system recommends the most popular places of interest and nearest restaurants with the preferred cuisine. It presents an output showing the optimized travel schedule, providing the driving directions, and informing the total cost of meals for the day.

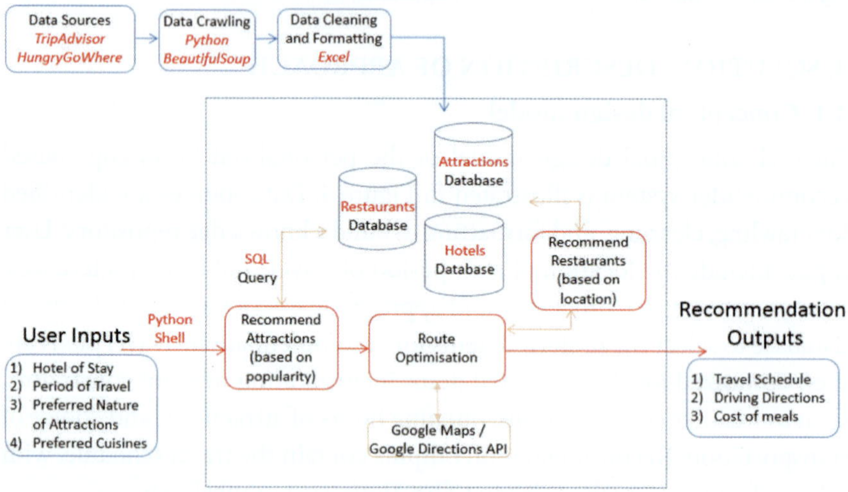

Figure 5: Skeletal architecture of the recommender system.

4.3. Tools used

Data crawling was performed with Beautiful Soup Library in Python and output was taken as Excel files. Data massaging and cleaning was carried out in Excel, and stored in MySQL database. Python and Google APIs were used to build a simple prototype of knowledge-based recommender system.

4.4. Crawling of data

The main public data sources are TripAdvisor and HungryGoWhere. TripAdvisor is a travel website with an extensive repository of accommodations, restaurants, and attractions. HungryGoWhere is a food and restaurant review website, containing a huge database of user-generated reviews of eating places in Singapore.

Data scrapped from TripAdvisor was used to set up the databases of hotels and attractions. Hotel features consist of the name and address of hotel and number of reviews, while attributes of attractions include name, address and contact details for the attraction, number of reviews, main category and subcategory of the attraction. As there was no public information on the amount of time to be spent at each attraction, such values were estimated arbitrarily and appended to the dataset.

Database of restaurants was set up with the name, address, contact details, and opening hours of restaurant, and its rating, number of votes, cuisine, and price. These databases form the basis for query depending on the user inputs. A summary of the attributes of hotels, attractions, and restaurants is tabulated in Figure 6.

Hotels	Attractions	Restaurants
Name of hotel	Name of attraction	Name of restaurant
Address of hotel	Address of attraction	Address of restaurant
Number of reviews	Phone number	Phone number
	Number of reviews	Rating
	Main category	Number of votes
	Subcategory	Cuisine
	Time to spend	Price
		Opening hours

Figure 6: Attributes of hotels, attractions, and restaurants.

4.5. Data cleaning and formatting

Data cleaning and formatting of the scrapped data was carried out using Excel. The total number of data points crawled from the data sources was over 10,000. Duplicates were removed, uniform formatting was applied, and relevant fields were created for subsequent easy identification and query. The field for the time spent at each attraction was also estimated for each type of attraction and inserted into the dataset.

4.6. Querying of knowledge database

Connection from Python to MySQL was set up and queries made to extract the list of relevant attractions and restaurants. Based on the user preferences, attractions and restaurants were sorted, and the most popular attraction and the nearest restaurant at mealtimes were inserted into the itinerary.

4.7. Route optimization and travel directions

Traveling salesman problem is one of the most famous computer science problems and it seeks to identify the shortest route that goes through a group of locations. In this study, deriving the driving directions from one location to another and route optimization were carried out using Google Geocoding, Maps and Directions API based on the shortest distance matrix, which is equivalent to selecting the route with the lowest cost.

Scenario Testing

To demonstrate the working of the system prototype, two scenarios were explored and the results displayed.

Scenario 1

In the first scenario, the following input parameters were used as shown in Figure 7.

Hotel of stay	Marina Bay Sands
Time of travel	07:00–22:00
1st preferred category of interest	Shopping
1st preferred subcategory	Shopping malls
2nd preferred category of interest	Nature and parks
2nd preferred subcategory	Gardens
3rd preferred category of interest	Museum
3rd preferred subcategory	Art museums
Preferred cuisine for lunch	Thai
Preferred cuisine for dinner	Korean

Figure 7: User parameters (Scenario 1).

The output travel schedule itinerary is illustrated in Figure 8. It recommends that the user first visits Clarke Quay and River Safari sequentially from Marina Bay Sands, before lunch at Nakhon Kitchen (Hougang), which is a Thai eatery located near the next attraction, Mustafa Centre. It recommends that the traveler shops at Mustafa Centre for the afternoon and Korean cuisine for dinner at Chicken up (Tanjong Pagar) before ending the day at Singapore Art Museum.

Time shown in the first column of Figure 8 is determined arbitrarily based on the estimated time spent at each recommendation, and provides a rough indication for the traveler. The approximate cost for the recommended meal is $40.

```
+-------+----------------------------+----------------------------+----------------------+
| Time  |            From            |        Destination         | Estimated Time Taken |
+-------+----------------------------+----------------------------+----------------------+
| 07:00 |      Marina Bay Sands      |        Clarke Quay         |         3.0          |
| 10:00 |        Clarke Quay         |        River Safari        |         4.0          |
| 14:00 |        River Safari        | Nakhon Kitchen (Hougang)   |         2.0          |
| 16:00 | Nakhon Kitchen (Hougang)   |       Mustafa Centre       |         3.0          |
| 19:00 |       Mustafa Centre       | Chicken Up (Tanjong Pagar) |         2.0          |
| 21:00 | Chicken Up (Tanjong Pagar) |   Singapore Art Museum     |         2.0          |
| 23:00 |    Singapore Art Museum    |      Marina Bay Sands      |         0.0          |
+-------+----------------------------+----------------------------+----------------------+
The cost for meals is approximately $ 40
```

Figure 8: Output travel schedule (Scenario 1).

An example of the output for distance, duration, and driving directions from Chicken Up (Tanjong Pagar), 48 Tanjong Pagar Road, to Singapore Art Museum, 71 Bras Basah Road, is shown in Figure 9. The short drive took 12 minutes and covered a distance of 4.1 km.

```
Distance:  4.1 km
Duration:  12 mins
Head  north  on  Tg Pagar Rd  toward  Duxton Hill  (DRIVING, 1 min, 0.1 km)
Turn  right  onto  Maxwell Rd  (DRIVING, 2 mins, 0.5 km)
Turn  left  onto  Robinson Rd  (DRIVING, 2 mins, 0.8 km)
Slight  right  onto  Collyer Quay  (DRIVING, 1 min, 0.3 km)
Continue onto  Fullerton Rd  Partial toll road  (DRIVING, 1 min, 0.2 km)
Continue onto  Esplanade Dr  (DRIVING, 1 min, 0.6 km)
Turn  left  onto  Stamford Rd  (DRIVING, 2 mins, 0.7 km)
Turn  right  to stay on  Stamford Rd  (DRIVING, 1 min, 0.1 km)
Turn  left  to stay on  Stamford Rd  (DRIVING, 1 min, 0.2 km)
Continue onto  Orchard Rd  (DRIVING, 1 min, 85 m)
Slight  right  onto  Prinsep St  (DRIVING, 1 min, 0.1 km)
Turn  right  at the 1st cross street onto  Bras Basah Rd  (DRIVING, 1 min, 0.3 km)
Turn  left  Destination will be on the left  (DRIVING, 1 min, 38 m)
```

Figure 9: Driving directions (Scenario 1).

Scenario 2

In the second scenario, following inputs were used as shown in Figure 10, with a different hotel of stay, time of travel and different travel interests.

Hotel of stay	Pan Pacific Singapore
Time of travel	09:00–17:00
1st preferred category of interest	Sights and landmarks
1st preferred subcategory	Farms
2nd preferred category of interest	Fun and games
2nd preferred subcategory	Escape games
3rd preferred category of interest	Spas and wellness
3rd preferred subcategory	Spas and wellness
Preferred cuisine for lunch	Hong Kong
Preferred cuisine for dinner	Indian

Figure 10: User parameters (Scenario 2).

The output travel schedule itinerary for the second scenario is illustrated in Figure 11. It recommends that the user first visits Bollywood Veggies from Pan Pacific Singapore, before lunch at Mayim Chinese Cuisine (West Mall), which is serves with Hong Kong cuisine. It recommends that the traveler plays games at The Escape Hunt Experience Singapore for the afternoon before ending the day at 5 p.m.

As mentioned earlier, the time shown in the first column of Figure 11 provide only a rough indication for the traveler, as information on the amount of time likely to be spent at each attraction was not available from data sources and therefore estimated. The approximate cost for the recommended meals is $17.

Time	From	Destination	Estimated Time Taken
09:00	Pan Pacific Singapore	Bollywood Veggies	3.0
12:00	Bollywood Veggies	Mayim Chinese Cuisine (West Mall)	2.0
14:00	Mayim Chinese Cuisine (West Mall)	The Escape Hunt Experience Singapore	2.0
16:00	The Escape Hunt Experience Singapore	Pan Pacific Singapore	0.0

The cost for meals is approximately $ 17

Figure 11: Output travel schedule (Scenario 2).

An example of the output for distance, duration, and driving directions from Pan Pacific Singapore, 7 Raffles Boulevard, Marina Square, to Bollywood Veggies, 100 Neo Tiew Road, is shown in Figure 12. The drive took 37 minutes and covered a distance of 34.5 km.

```
Distance:  34.5 km
Duration:  37 mins
Head  southeast  on  Raffles Blvd  (DRIVING, 1 min, 0.3 km)
Continue straight to stay on  Raffles Blvd  (DRIVING, 1 min, 0.2 km)
Slight  left  onto  Republic Blvd  (DRIVING, 1 min, 0.6 km)
Turn  left  to stay on  Republic Blvd  (signs for  E C P ) (DRIVING, 1 min, 0.2 km)
Keep  left  at the fork, follow signs for  ECP/Changi Airport  and merge onto  ECP  Partial toll road  (DRIVING, 1 min, 1.3 km)
Take exit  14  for  KPE  toward  TPE  Partial toll road  (DRIVING, 1 min, 1.0 km)
Continue onto  KPE  (DRIVING, 2 mins, 1.6 km)
Take exit  2B  to merge onto  PIE  toward  Tuas  Partial toll road  (DRIVING, 2 mins, 2.4 km)
Keep  right  to stay on  PIE  (DRIVING, 7 mins, 8.5 km)
Take exit  24  for  BKE  toward  Woodlands  (DRIVING, 1 min, 0.7 km)
Continue onto  BKE  (DRIVING, 7 mins, 8.3 km)
Take exit  8  for  Turf Club Ave  toward  Kranji Rd  (DRIVING, 1 min, 0.5 km)
Continue onto  Turf Club Ave  (DRIVING, 1 min, 0.4 km)
Continue onto  Turf Club Flyover  (DRIVING, 1 min, 0.4 km)
Continue onto  Turf Club Ave  (DRIVING, 1 min, 0.8 km)
Continue onto  Kranji Rd  (DRIVING, 3 mins, 1.5 km)
Turn  left  onto  Kranji Loop  (DRIVING, 1 min, 0.5 km)
Continue onto  Kranji Way  (DRIVING, 4 mins, 2.3 km)
Continue onto  Neo Tiew Rd  Destination will be on the left  (DRIVING, 4 mins, 3.1 km)
```

Figure 12: Driving directions (Scenario 2).

5. DISCUSSION

Value of a Personalized Recommender System in Tourism

The previous decade saw a tremendous increase in the amount of tourist information available online, and the use of web and mobile technology among tourists. There are numerous e-Tourism systems in the market that can offer recommendations based on the traveler's preferences and their current destination.[11]

General functionalities provided by tourism recommender systems can be broadly categorized into four groups — recommendation of a destination and forming a tourist pack, suggestion of relevant places of interest in a specific destination, construction of a detailed multi-day travel itinerary, and imbuing social capabilities into the system.[11] Figure 13 estimates the percentage of systems that offer the functionalities described above.

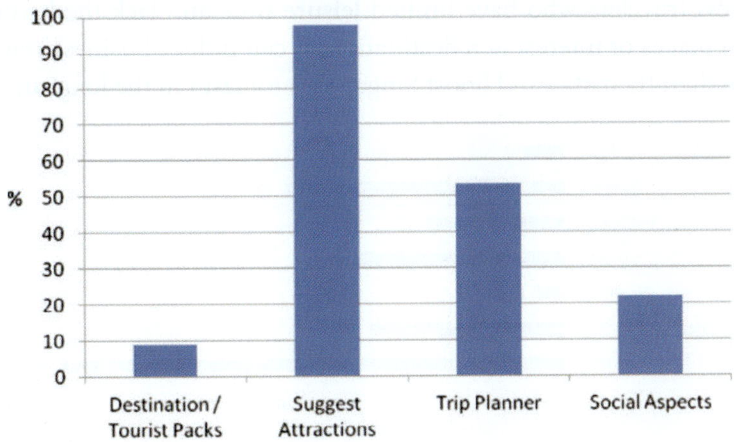

Figure 13: Distribution of functionalities available in the market.[11]

A large percentage of tourism systems in the market therefore focus on the ability to provide a ranked list of recommendations for attractions based on a specified destination. Several other systems provide an initial fixed set of recommended activities and a route through the list of attractions. Users can subsequently interact with the system to add or amend activities, change the order of visit, etc.[11] However, the viability of providing a highly personalized set of recommendations at the onset is rarely explored.

This study demonstrates the viability of a personalized recommender system applied to the tourism industry. It illustrated an example case of specific attractions and restaurants tailored to the travelers' preferences with route optimization and travel directions features. The study is confined to Singapore but could be easily replicated for other cities in the world, given that a rich database of hotels, attractions, restaurants, and users is readily available. It also lays the foundation for further expansion of capabilities of the system.

The monetary potential of the business value of a personalized recommender is evident. The number of international visitor arrivals to Singapore increased more than 1.5 times in the past decade and reached 15.6 million in 2013. From Figure 14, shows that apart from vacationing being the main reason for travel to Singapore, business and MICE together took up 23 per cent of the total international visitor arrivals in 2013, i.e., about 3.5 million visitors.[12] These segments are relatively substantial and represent the potential to provide an efficient personalized recommender system which can give quick relevant suggestions to business travelers who have limited leisure time and lack the luxury to search places of interest at a destination. It can induce business travelers to lengthen their stay and boost Singapore's tourism in the long run.

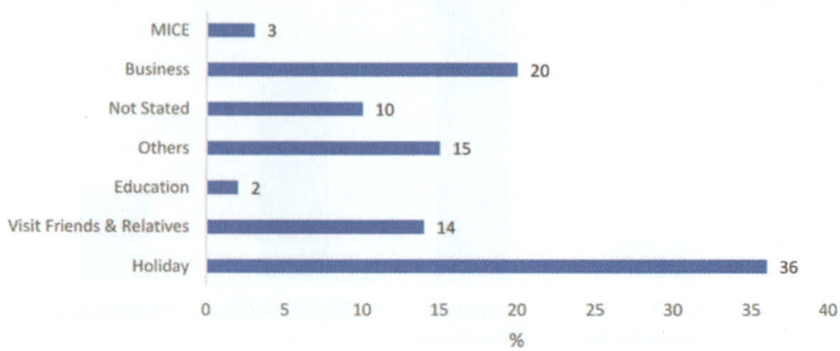

Figure 14: Main purpose of visit for tourists in Singapore, 2013.[12]

With the upsurge of budget traveling in the world, Singapore has also established itself as an attractive backpacking destination. This is evident from the increase in number of backpacker's accommodations in Singapore. Hotel Licensing Board (HLB) statistics indicates that there are currently 29 registered backpackers' hostels in Singapore and these are increasingly gaining popularity due to their affordable prices.[13] With the increase in budget travelers coming to Singapore, a personalized recommender system has the potential to effectively provide assistance to this group of travellers to piece together free and easy travel plans.

6. CONCLUSION AND FURTHER WORK

This study identifies the components of a personalized knowledge-based recommender system in a conceptual design model. A prototype was successfully constructed to provide personalized recommendations of tourist attractions and restaurants in Singapore using a knowledge-based approach. The system digests user inputs and outputs a travel schedule with driving directions, route optimization, and total cost of meals. The prototype was built using public data, Google APIs and Python, and tested with scenarios. The prototype demonstrated the viability, value, and business potential of a personalized recommender system in the tourism industry. There is room for expansion of the system capabilities of the simple prototype to provide greater interactivity and user-friendliness. The conceptual model can be replicated easily for other major cities in the world.

Search for useful data

One of the challenges encountered was the dearth of comprehensive public datasets containing essential information that could be used to build a robust and dependable recommender system. For example, there were no readily available public sources of information on the opening hours and entrance fee for each attraction. This missing piece of information is important for incorporating additional elements into the system to output a more reliable set of recommendations for the user. Going forward, more data might be required from a mixture of sources, with the need for data merger, standardization, and transformation.

Improving reliability of datasets

As the database was built using public data sources, the reliability of the datasets might be compromised in certain situations. The data on TripAdvisor and HungryGoWhere were provided by their users, and outdated information on places of interest and restaurants might be present. Some attractions and eating places might have already been closed, with little or no user review.

It is sensible to explore how such cases could be sieved out from the data and removed from the database. One possible solution might be to perform a classification on the datasets to categorize data points according to whether a review was written in the past 3, 6, or 12 months. Otherwise, it would be necessary to provide the contact details and inform the user that it would be prudent to check with the premises before visiting.

Improving flexibility of system

Flexibility is a key sought-after characteristic of any recommender system. Additional features such as the ability to plan for a longer period of travel, specify certain attractions or restaurants as must-go (for travelers who might have visited Singapore before), be able to swipe and replace unwanted recommendations with the next best alternatives would result in a more rewarding user experience. These can be embedded in a Graphical User Interface (GUI) for greater interactivity.

Many e-Tourism recommenders have used both web-based and mobile interface. For example, CT-Planner provides users with tour plans that could be refined as the system assimilates the user's preferences and requests, including tweaks made to duration, walking speed, reluctance to walk, etc. A snapshot of the CT-Planner2 user interface is illustrated in Figure 15.

Another service that builds its application on Android platform is EnoSigTur, with Figure 16 showing screenshots of the mobile version giving a list of recommended attractions, the recommended route of the trip, and more elaborate information of a place of interest.[11]

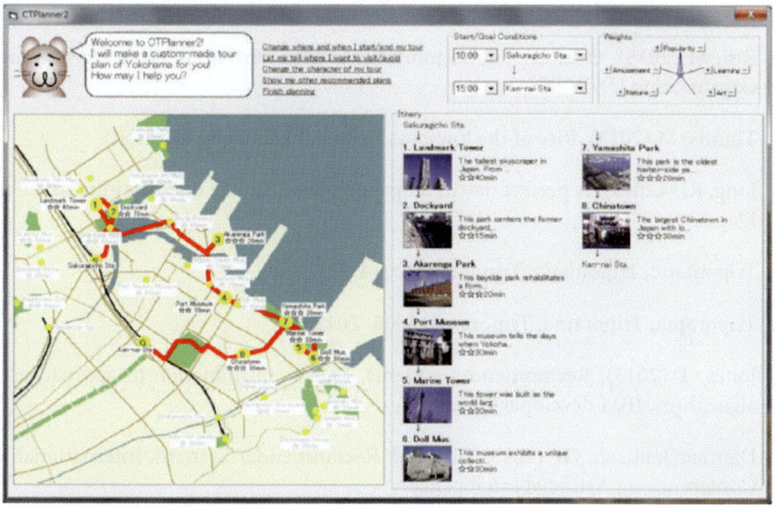

Figure 15: CT-Planner2 user interface.[11]

Figure 16: EnoSigTur mobile interface.[11]

Additional optimization constraints

There is high variability and subtle differences in travel preferences and tastes. There are also myriad of factors affecting the choice of visiting a specific sight or landmark. For simplicity, this paper did not consider some of these constraints, such as budget limitation, weather forecast, and the use of alternative modes of transport due to lack of available data for analysis. The versatility of the system could be enhanced with the consideration of these additional elements.

REFERENCES

1. Risi, M (2015). Over 1.1 billion tourists travelled abroad in 2014, World Tourism Organization UNWTO.

2. Timms, M (2013). Rise of the low-cost airline, Business Destinations.

3. Jong, RD (2015). A perfect day in Singapore: the ultimate one-day itinerary, Lonely Planet.

4. Tripomatic, Tripomatic, Tripomatic, 2014.

5. Triporama, Triporama, Triporama, 2005–2012.

6. Jones, T (2013). Recommender systems, Part 1: Introduction to approaches and algorithms, IBM developerWorks.

7. Dietmar Jannach, GF (2013). Tutorial: Recommender Systems, International Joint Conference on Artificial Intelligence.

8. Yoram Bachrach, SC, Kash, IA, Key, P, Radlinski, F, Porat, E, Armstrong, M and Sharma, V (2014). Building a personalized tourist attraction recommender system using crowdsourcing. In *Proc. of the 13th International Conference on Autonomous Agents and Multiagent SystemsParis*, PS Alessio Lomuscio, Ana Bazzan and Michael Huhns (eds.). France.

9. Hong, IS and Chun, IG (2001). The implementation of knowledge-based recommender system for electronic commerce using Java expert system library. In *Proc. of IEEE International Symposium on Industrial Electronics*, 3, pp. 1766–1770.

10. Amini, B and Othman, MS (2011). Discovering the impact of knowledge in recommender systems: a comparative study, *International Journal of Computer Science & Engineering Survey (IJCSES)*, 2.

11. Joan Borras, AM and Valls, A (2014). Intelligent tourism recommender systems: a survey, *Expert Systems with Applications*, 41, 7370–7389.

12. Board, ST (2014). Annual report on tourism statistics 2013. In *Singapore Tourism Board*, ST. Board (ed.). Singapore.

13. Chen, J (2012). *The Backpacking Tourism Boom in Singapore*, Ghetto Singapore: Heritage and Places.

CHAPTER 21

A Model for Sales Forecasting and Stock Management

Tom Stephens

ABSTRACT

This project worked with a bicycles and bicycle-related accessories retailer. The business is in its growing stage and is currently addressing a challenge around forecasting stock and inventory control. This study will attempt to address these challenges by developing an accurate model for sales forecasting and a template through which these forecasts can be tracked and backtested. Forecasting techniques trialed include Exponential Smoothing and ARIMA Models. Backtesting of forecasts of out-of-sample data for a selected number of product categories is positive, but some further improvements to the model may be possible before expanding to test across further products.

1. INTRODUCTION

99 Bikes (99bikes.com.au) is an Australian retailer for bicycles and bicycle-related accessories. It was founded in 2008 with one store in Brisbane, Australia. It has since grown to 22 physical stores and a web

store with annual revenues exceeding AUD 50 million and annual sales transactions exceeding 285,000. Around 140 people are employed in stores located on the East Coast of Australia in Brisbane, Sydney, Melbourne, and some major regional centers. The business is growing fast with plans to open between five and eight stores per year going forward.

A current focus for management is to develop a method to assess performance against forward-looking targets and budgets. Currently, performance is only assessed against past results which somewhat limits the ability to plan ahead. Therefore, they are looking to develop sales forecasts along with a template to easily display the forecasted information.

The most immediate requirement for forecasted sales data is to assist with purchasing of stock and inventory management. With more accurate information about likely future sales, management will be able to make better purchasing decisions, with the potential benefits being an improved return on capital through any of these outcomes:

- A reduction in the total investment in inventory for the same amount of sales.
- An enhanced quality of inventory leading to products selling at a faster pace and with a higher margin.
- Reduced levels of dead stock requiring clearance at a discounted margin.

2. PROBLEM STATEMENT

2.1. Business description

The business sells over 100 products, known as product categories, which are broken down into roughly 15 bicycle categories, 60 accessory categories and 25 parts categories. The bicycle categories include Road, Mountain, BMX, Kids boys, Kids girls and Hybrid; the Accessory category includes four helmets categories being Mountain Bike and Road, BMX, Kids, and Full Face. Product categories are further broken down into brand, model, and size. Given the aim of this study to forecast the purposes of inventory planning, management, it seems the best level of granularity to forecast will be at the product category level on an all-stores basis.

2.2. Current procedure

The current method for forecasting stock is manual and relies on the experience and judgment of management to determine how much they think needs to be purchased. There are currently two main parts to the purchasing process.

First is a range review of the product category to assess and make a determination as to whether a product should be in the category or not. Second is a determination of minimum stock level (MSL) that is required for each product category. Purchase orders are made based on the difference between MSL and stock on hand. MSL is reviewed at least quarterly to make sure stores have enough or not too much.

2.3. Anticipated change to procedure

It is anticipated that the major benefit of this study will be to improve the second area of the purchasing process around the determination of the MSL. The models and template developed in this study will have two advantages to the current process. First, a model provides for consistency in determining MSL and removes the risk of human error in calculating this number incorrectly. Management will still review these numbers for reasonableness but it will be done after a systematic and consistent forecast has been made. Second, it will save time as reviewing MSL on quarterly basis is a manual and timely process.

2.4. Problems to be solved

The business has requested that forecasts be within 10 per cent accuracy on the backtesting of out-of-sample data before they will be comfortable in relying on these models for use in the business. Therefore, this study will set out to address the best model for achieving this result. A simple and user-friendly template will also be developed where this forecasted information can be saved and used by management for decision making.

2.5. Scope

Due to 100-plus product categories that are sold by the business, the scope of the project will be limited to four product categories being:

- Helmets — Mountain Bike and Road
- Helmets — BMX
- Bicycles — Mountain Bike and Hard Tail
- Bicycles — Kids Boys

These were selected for analysis because they are the highest selling helmet and bicycle categories, respectively and contribute a high proportion of sales and gross profit. Section 4 will describe in detail the analysis performed to forecast Helmets – Mountain Bike and Road. Similar analysis was then also performed for the other three product categories and the forecasting results for all four product categories are discussed in Section 5.

3. LITERATURE REVIEW

3.1. Related work

This study will follow the procedures set out by Hyndman and Athanasopoulos in "Forecasting: principles and practice"[1] that describe exponential smoothing and ARIMA models as the two most widely used approaches to time series forecasting. Hence this study will look at both models.

This study will also follow work done by Ramos et al.,[2] who looked at the accuracy of both Exponential Smoothing and ARIMA models for forecasting sales of five categories of woman's footwear in a retail business concluding that both models are similarly accurate. However, they also found that multi-step forecasts were more accurate than one-step forecasts because they incorporate information that is more up to date.

3.2. Forecast error measures

Accuracy of forecasting will be assessed with three measures as described by Pena et al.,[3].

- Mean Absolute Percentage Error (MAPE) — given the challenge set by management to forecast sales to within 10 per cent accuracy, this will be the primary tool for assessing strength of models.

- Mean Absolute Error (MAE) — given that the capital invested in some product categories (i.e., bicycles) will be much higher than that invested in other product categories (i.e., helmets), this measure will be helpful as it will show the actual error in terms of quantity of units.
- Root Mean Square Error (RSME) — the business needs the forecasts to be accurate for every period in the forecast range. Therefore, this measure will be helpful as it penalizes large errors. This will be useful in the event that the forecast is accurate for most periods but very inaccurate in one period.

3.3. Exponential smoothing models

Exponential smoothing models are based on a description of trend and seasonality in the data. Forecasts produced using exponential smoothing methods are weighted averages of past observations, with the weights decaying exponentially as the observations get older.[1]

This study will follow the statistical framework to exponential smoothing developed by Hyndman et al.,[4] where models are described by error, trend and seasonality. This will be referred to as an ETS model going forward. The benefit of an ETS is that it is a stochastic model that will provide point forecasts, prediction intervals and a platform for choosing the best model.[1] Hyndman in the fpp package has developed an algorithm that will automatically provide the best estimate of ETS when provided with a time series and this algorithm will be used.[4]

An approach for selecting the best model is to use the Akaike Information Criteria (AIC), which penalizes the likelihood of the model to compensate for the potential overfitting of the data[2]. Therefore the model with the lowest AIC will be considered to be the best model.

3.4. ARIMA models

Autoregressive, Integrated, Moving Average (ARIMA) is a linear model for forecasting seasonal time series.[2] The procedure set out by Hyndman et al[1] for ARIMA modeling will be followed in this study:

1) Plot the data. Identify any unusual observations.
2) If necessary, transform the data to stabilize the variance.
3) If the data are nonstationary, take first differences of the data until the data are stationary.

4) Examine the Autocorrelation Function (ACF) and Partial Autocorrelation Function (PACF) to determine how many autoregressive and moving average periods are required.
5) Try your chosen models, and use the AIC to search for a better model.
6) Check the residuals from your chosen model by plotting the ACF of the residuals, and doing a Portmanteau test of the residuals. If they do not look like white noise, try a modified model.
7) Once the residuals look like white noise, calculate forecasts.

The output of an ARIMA model is described by (p,d,q) * (P,D,Q)m where:

- *p* and *P* are the number of autoregressive periods and the number of seasonal autoregressive periods required to remove autocorrelation in the data.
- *d* and *D* are the number of periods and seasonal periods that the data is differenced on in order to make the data stationary. This is assessed through reviewing ACF and PACF and also be performing a Dickey-Fuller Test.
- *q* and *Q* are the moving average and seasonal moving averages required to describe the data.
- *m* describes the seasonal structure of the data.

4. SOLUTION: DESCRIPTION OF APPROACH

4.1. Tools

A combination of Excel and R was used to perform analysis and forecasting. The business records its summary data in Excel so this was used to arrange the data in a usable format, run initial analysis and also to record the forecasts and track back testing. The R packages stats, [4] forecast[5] and fpp[6] were used to develop ETS and ARIMA models.

4.2. Review of the data

Since 2011, the business has recorded the key performance indicators for each store; quantity of units sold, gross sales, gross profit, and gross profit percentage for every product category in Microsoft Excel in four week period. Therefore, there are 13 readings of data per year, which management prefer over monthly periods as the number of days in the month can skew results. A new workbook is saved for each year and thus the business has provided five workbooks of data for analysis.

Initial cleaning of the data involved consolidating the sales and gross profit figures of each individual store for each period into a global/store wide figure, and then consolidating the four years of data into a single spreadsheet. Management advised that data for 2011 be ignored, partly because the data was not fully complete and also because they felt that performance in 2011 was not relevant to forecasting sales in the year 2015.

For model development, 36 periods of training data from Period 1, 2012 to Period 13, 2014 are used. Forecasts from the training data will be validated against one-step testing from Period 1, 2015 to Period 8, 2015. Multi-step forecasts will also be conducted from Period 1, 2015 onward, which will incorporate more up- to-date information.

4.3. Variables considered for modeling

After discussion with management, it was felt that the following variables would be significant in any model used for forecasting sales:

- Seasonality — from Figure 1, it is clear that seasonality is very strong and that Christmas/summer is the main peak of sales over the year.
- New store openings — the business is in growing phase and stores are opening at a fast pace. Any forecasts based on historical data will struggle to accurately predict future sales when there are more stores than in the historical periods. Three new stores have been opened to date in 2015 and therefore, forecasts will need to be assessed for accuracy after sales from new stores are stripped out. This will need to be taken into account for the final forecasting template and a column for new store sales will need to be added to estimate new store sales.

Other variables considered but not used for modeling:

- Sales campaigns — these are run year-wide across most product categories; hence it was considered too difficult to find a control period that could be used to measure any sales campaign.
- Pricing — the retail bicycle industry in Australia is highly competitive and management considers pricing to be the main driver of sales.

When pricing is competitive, sales will be strong, and vice versa. This project does not consider pricing in any model as obtaining pricing data of competitors is outside the scope of this study.

- Quality of store locations and quality of staff — these are both critically important factors for achieving excellent performance. However, this study is interested in consolidated/firm-wide sales data, these variables are not required. If forecasting on a store by store basis, these would be essential variables.

4.3.1. A detailed look at helmets — MTB and road

The rest of Section 4 will deal with a detailed analysis of the product category Helmets — Mountain Bike and Road, and a description of how ETS and ARIMA models were developed to forecast sales of this category. It will also include a review of the accuracy of both models.

4.3.2. Initial analysis and summary statistics of helmets — MTB and road

Table 1 shows that the business has sold 44,637 Mountain Bikes and Road helmets since 2012 and Table 2 shows an average of 744 sales per month with a maximum sales of 1562 at Christmas in 2014. A first glance of Figure 1 immediately shows a clear upward trend and seasonality in helmet sales. This is further confirmed with a decomposition plot of Helmets — MTB and Road in Figure 2. A very strong seasonal pattern is obvious, corresponding with Christmas sales as expected.

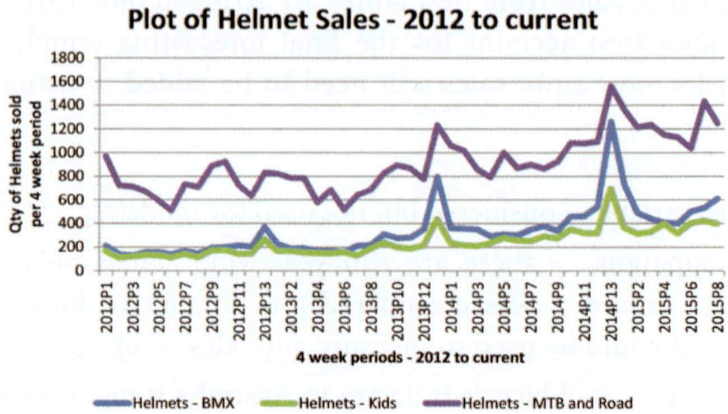

Figure 1: Plot of helmet categories — 2012 to current period.

Table 1: Historical results of helmets — MTB and Road, 2012 — current.

	Units Sales
2012	9,612
2013	10,075
2014	13,095
2015 - YTD (9 periods)	9,802
Total	44,637

Table 2: Summary statistics of unit sales of helmets — MTB and road, 2012 — current.

Average Sales	**744**
Median Sales	789
Standard Deviation	317
1st Quartile Sales	560
3rd Quartile Sales	1,005
Max Sales	1,562

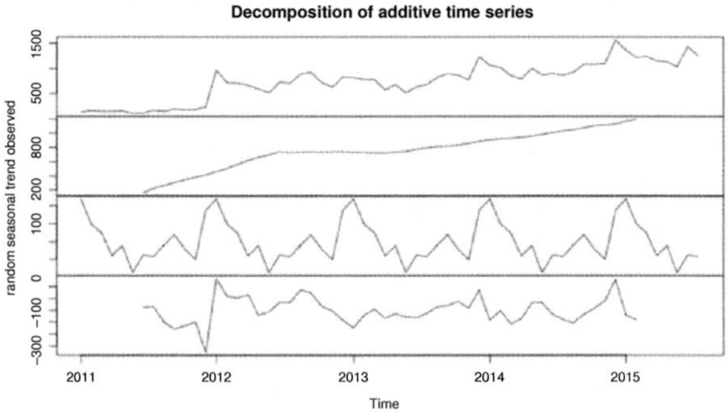

Figure 2: Decomposition of helmets — MTB and road.

4.5. Exponential smoothing model — helmets — MTB and road

The ETS function in the fpp package automatically selects the most appropriate combination of Error, Trend and Seasonality where the AIC is at its lowest. The package selects an M,N,M model, which means multiplicative error, no trend, and multiplicative seasonality. Attempts to improve this model and reduce the AIC by manually adjusting the parameters in the ETS model could not be made (see Figure 3).

Validating the model against the test period in Table 3 provides a MAPE of approx. 10 per cent and 124 helmets against the training set

```
ETS(M,N,M)

Call:
 ets(y = cleanets)

  Smoothing parameters:
    alpha = 0.6253
    gamma = 1e-04

  Initial states:
    l = 776.138
    s=1.3405 0.932 1.0089 1.1216 1.0347 0.8817
           0.9405 0.7473 0.9174 0.8541 0.9883 1.0409 1.1922

  sigma:  0.0937

     AIC     AICc      BIC
623.4230 638.9068 651.1752

Training set error measures:
                   ME     RMSE      MAE      MPE     MAPE      MASE      ACF1
Training set 21.02484 82.02875 69.44531 1.487204 7.897569 0.3454991 0.1291426
```

Figure 3: ETS model results from fpp package.

with a MAPE of 8 per cent and 66 helmets. Table 4 shows that while the MAPE is approx. 10 per cent on an overall basis, the variance in error on a month by month basis fluctuates from 2 per cent to 23 per cent, which is not ideal.

Table 3: ETS accuracy — training v test set on an overall basis.

	RMSE	MAE	MAPE
Training set	78	66	7.98%
Test set	158	124	9.97%

Table 4: ETS (M,N,M) forecast — accuracy over the test period on a month by month basis.

Period	Actual Sales	ETS Forecast	Absolute Error	Mean Absolute Percentage Error	Mean Square Error
2015P1	1,363	1,394	31	2%	932
2015P2	1,212	1,233	21	2%	460
2015P3	1,235	1,142	93	8%	8,640

Period	Actual Sales	ETS Forecast	Absolute Error	Mean Absolute Percentage Error	Mean Square Error
2015P4	1,149	978	171	15%	29,104
2015P5	1,129	1,095	34	3%	1,133
2015P6	1,036	889	147	14%	21,604
2015P7	1,432	1,098	334	23%	111,697
2015P8	1,246	1,085	161	13%	25,829
Mean			**124**	**9.97%**	

Given that sales from the three new stores have not been accounted for, accuracy is also assessed when sales for these new stores have been stripped out. Table 5 shows that the error is now smaller than in the training set by approximately 2 per cent. The month by month accuracy in Table 6 shows that error ranges between 1 per cent and 13 per cent, which is an improvement.

Table 5: ETS accuracy with new stores stripped out.

	RMSE	MAE	MAPE
Training set	78	66	7.98%
Test set	83	69	6.06%

Table 6: ETS (M,N,M) forecast against adjusted sales — accuracy over the test period on a monthly basis.

Period	Adjusted Sales	ETS Forecast	Absolute Error	Mean Absolute Percentage Error	Mean Square Error
2015P1	1,363	1,394	31	2%	932
2015P2	1,212	1,233	21	2%	460
2015P3	1,213	1,142	71	6%	5,034

(*continued*)

Table 6: ETS (M,N,M) forecast against adjusted sales — accuracy over the test period on a monthly basis. (*continued*)

Period	Adjusted Sales	ETS Forecast	Absolute Error	Mean Absolute Percentage Error	Mean Square Error
2015P4	1,088	978	110	10%	12,012
2015P5	1,034	1,095	61	6%	3,763
2015P6	974	889	85	9%	7,222
2015P7	1,259	1,098	161	13%	25,989
2015P8	1,098	1,085	13	1%	162
Mean			**69**	**6.06%**	

4.5.1. ARIMA models — Helmets — MTB and road

The procedures set out by Hyndman and Athanasopoulos are followed in Section 4.5.1 to 4.5.8.

4.5.1 Steps 1 and 2 — Plot the data. Identify any unusual observations. If necessary, transform the data to stabilize the variance

When there is a small increase in the seasonal variance, Hyndman recommends a transformation of the data to remove this. Per Figure 1, it appears that this may be the situation, so to be safe, the natural logarithm was used to ensure that the variance is stabilized. Figure 4 shows the natural log of sales quantity.

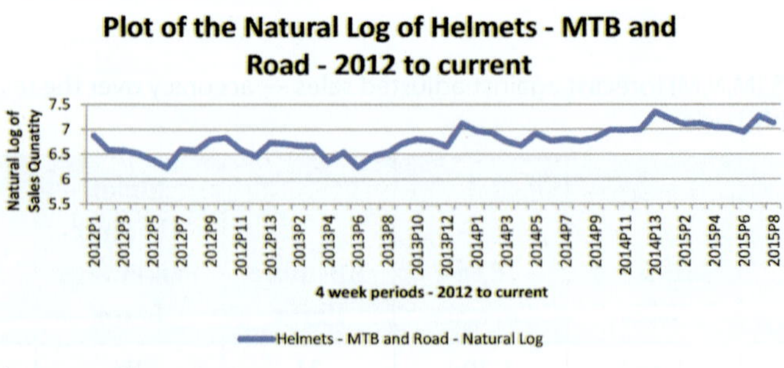

Figure 4: The natural log of sales.

4.5.2. Step 3: If the data are non-stationary: take first differences of the data until the data are stationary

The ACF and PACF functions in Figures 5 and 6 clearly show strong levels of autocorrelation.

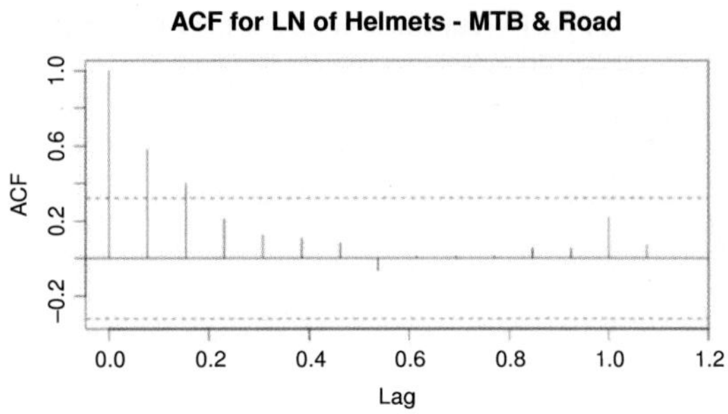

Figure 5: ACF of helmets — MTB and road.

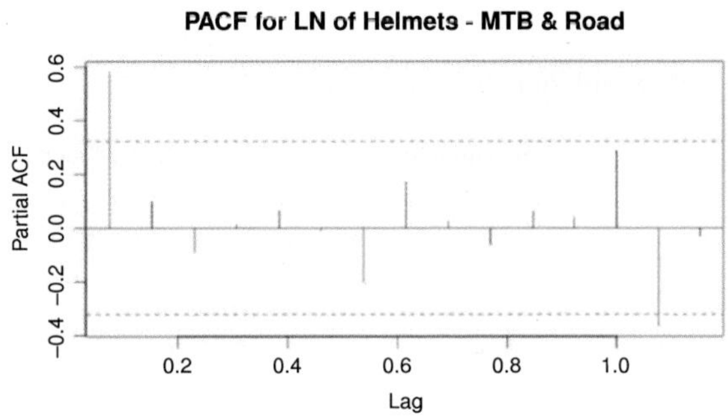

Figure 6: PACF of helmets — MTB and road.

A first difference is taken and the new correlation is showing in Figures 7 and 8. Most of the autocorrelation has been removed but there is still a spike at period 13. This is an indication that there is also seasonal autocorrelation. Therefore in Figure 9, first seasonal and first differences have been taken. The spikes have been removed and it can be taken that the remaining variance is white noise.

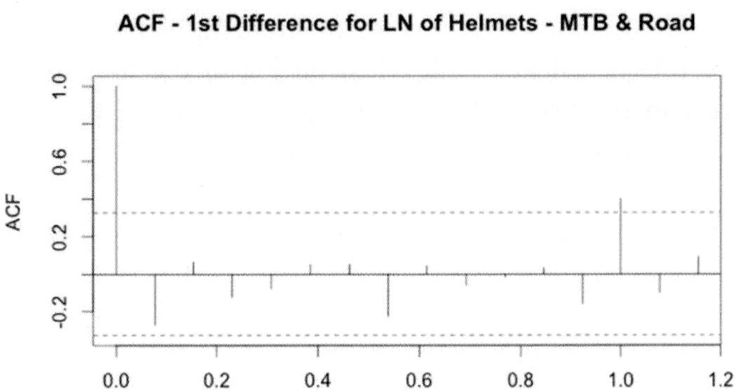

Figure 7: ACF with one differenced period.

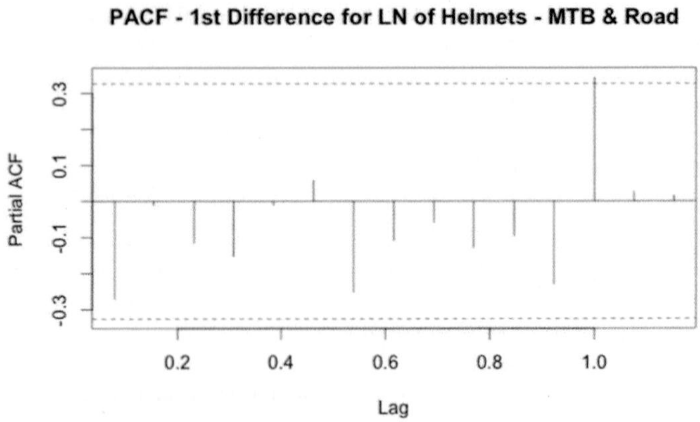

Figure 8: PACF with one differenced period.

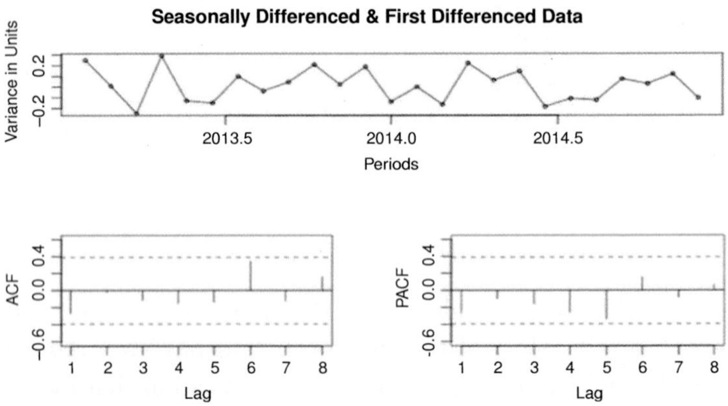

Figure 9: Seasonally differenced and first differenced data.

4.5.3. Dickey-Fuller test

Dickey-Fuller Test confirms the reading of the ACF and PACF. Log of sales (Figure 10) shows that further differencing is required given the *p*-value of 0.1846. Dickey-Fuller Test on log of the first seasonal first difference and the first difference in Figure 11 shows that no further differencing is required given the *p*-value of 0.02158.

```
        Augmented Dickey-Fuller Test

data:  clean
Dickey-Fuller = -3.3629, Lag order = 3, p-value = 0.07346
alternative hypothesis: stationary
        Augmented Dickey-Fuller Test

data:  Difference1
Dickey-Fuller = -3.9809, Lag order = 3, p-value = 0.02158
alternative hypothesis: stationary
```

Figure 10: Dickey-Fuller on first differenced sales and then first differenced and first seasonally differenced sales.

4.5.4. *Step 4 — Examine the ACF and PACF to determine how many autoregressive and moving average periods are required.*

Following the guidance of Ramos et al.,[2] a number of models were run where p and q took the values of zero to five and P and Q took the values of zero to two. The resulting model with the lowest in sample AIC will be used.

4.5.5. *Step 5 — Try your chosen models, and use the AIC to search for a better model.*

Based on the analysis in Section 4, it is clear that a seasonal difference will be required and also some first differencing. As with the ETS function, the fpp package has an algorithm that selects the best model called auto.arima. The Auto ARIMA function arrives at a (0,1,0)(1,1,0) model.

```
Series: train2
ARIMA(0,1,0)(1,1,0)[13]

Coefficients:
         sar1
       0.0551
s.e.   0.2989

sigma^2 estimated as 13905:  log likelihood=-154.74
AIC=313.49   AICc=314.03   BIC=315.92
```

Figure 11: Output of the auto ARIMA function in fpp package.

Manually adjusting the p and q parameters to levels between zero and five, and the P and Q parameters to levels between zero and two could not improve the model. Hence forecasts will be made with the ARIMA model (0,1,0) (1,1,0).

4.5.6. *Step 6 — Check the residuals from your chosen model by plotting the ACF of the residuals, and doing a portmanteau test of the residuals. If they do not look like white noise, try a modified model (See Figure 12 and 13).*

There is no pattern in the ACF or PACF of the residuals. The Ljung-Box test provides a p-value of 12.75 per cent, which also indicates that the

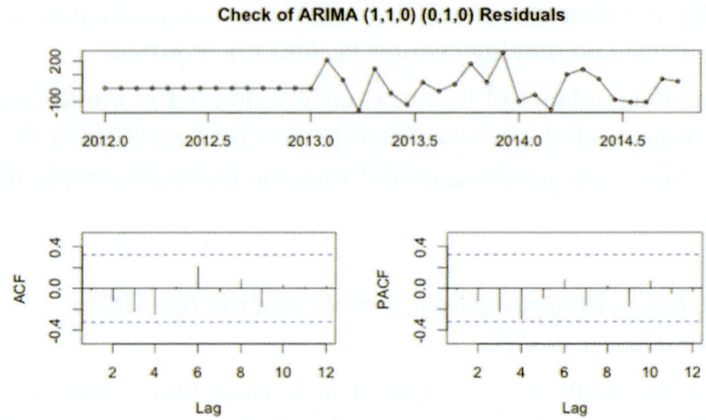

Figure 12: Residual check of ACF and PACF.

```
        Box-Ljung test

data:  residuals(Arima1_forecast)
X-squared = 2.3228, df = 1, p-value = 0.1275
```

Figure 13: Box-Ljung test of the residuals.

residuals are not significantly different from what would be expected from a white noise process.

4.5.7. Step 7 — Once the residuals look like white noise, calculate forecasts.

Forecasts based on ARIMA model (1,1,0) (0,1,0) are displayed in Table 7, which shows a training error of 7.45 per cent versus a test error of 9.12 per cent. On a month by month basis over the forecasting period, the error ranges between 1 per cent and 17 per cent, which is not ideal again (see Table 8).

Table 7: ARIMA accuracy on an overall basis.

	RMSE	MAE	MAPE
Training set	94	62	7.45%
Test set	130	**110**	**9.12%**

Table 8: ARIMA accuracy — training v test set on a month by month basis.

Period	Actual Sales	ARIMA Forecast	Absolute Error	Mean Absolute Percentage Error	Mean Square Error
2015P1	1363	1,381	18	1%	327
2015P2	1212	1,337	125	10%	15,519
2015P3	1235	1,171	64	5%	4,084
2015P4	1149	1,111	38	3%	1,463
2015P5	1129	1,326	197	17%	38,955
2015P6	1036	1,198	162	16%	26,106
2015P7	1432	1,221	211	15%	44,377
2015P8	1246	1,183	63	5%	3,978
Mean			**110**	**9.120%**	

When sales in new stores are stripped out of the out-of-sample data in Table 9, the accuracy is not improved as compared to the ETS model. Per Table 10, the error ranges from 1 per cent to 28 per cent on a month by month basis, which is a poor result.

Table 9: ARIMA accuracy on an overall basis with new stores stripped out.

	RMSE	MAE	MAPE
Training set	94	62	7.45%
Test set	142	105	9.89%

Table 10: ARIMA accuracy on adjusted data — training v test set on a month by month basis.

Period	Actual Sales	ARIMA Forecast	Absolute Error	Mean Absolute Percentage Error	Mean Square Error
2015P1	1,363	1,381	18	1%	327
2015P2	1,212	1,337	125	10%	15,519
2015P3	1,213	1,171	42	3%	1,756

(*continued*)

Table 10: ARIMA accuracy on adjusted data — training v test set on a month by month basis. (*continued*)

Period	Actual Sales	ARIMA Forecast	Absolute Error	Mean Absolute Percentage Error	Mean Square Error
2015P4	1,088	1,111	23	2%	518
2015P5	1,034	1,326	292	28%	85,481
2015P6	974	1,198	224	23%	49,986
2015P7	1,259	1,221	38	3%	1,418
2015P8	1,098	1,183	85	8%	7,213
Mean			**106**	**9.89%**	162,218

5. RESULTS AND DISCUSSION

5.1. Initial discussion

Section 4 describes the process as applied to Helmets — MTB and Road. This process was subsequently applied to the product categories; BMX Helmets, Mountain Bike and Boys Kids Bikes. Tables 11, 12, 13, and 14 describe the accuracy of the forecasts with MAPE, MAE, and RMSE analysis for both in-sample and out-of-sample data.

The results in general show that the ETS model provides better forecasts for both helmet categories and Kids boys bikes than ARIMA models. However, Bikes — MTB and Hardtail are forecasted more accurately with an ARIMA model. It is clear that the forecast accuracy from both models requires work as neither is able to forecast within 10 per cent on a consistent basis.

5.2. In Sample accuracy

Table 11: In sample accuracy.

	Model	MAE	MAPE	RMSE
Helmets - MTB and Road	ETS	66	7.98%	78
	ARIMA	62	7.45%	94
Helmets - BMX	ETS	33	10.37%	46
	ARIMA	24	6.65	49
Bikes - MTB Hardtail	ETS	19	10.05%	27
	ARIMA	21	7.83%	36
Bikes - Kids Boys	ETS	33	7.61%	41
	ARIMA	30	7.22%	46

Table 12: Out-of-sample MAPE — one step and multi-step.

	Model	One Step	Step-ahead of multi-step process - 2015				
			Period 2	Period 3	Period 4	Period 5	Period 6
Helmets - MTB & Road	ETS (M,N,M)	9.97%	2.75%	8.55%	5.22%	−7.49%	9.59%
	ETS with same store data	6.07%	2.75%	6.89%	−0.09%	−17.37%	3.84%
	ARIMA	9.12%	8.77%	15.57%	−0.76%	−9.96%	4.29%
	ARIMA with same store data	9.89%	8.77%	14.04%	−6.40%	−20.06%	−1.80%
Helmets - BMX	ETS (M,N,M)	12.70%	12.44%	17.82%	12.46%	−1.44%	24.64%
	ETS with same store data	10.63%	12.44%	19.73%	19.20%	−9.11%	19.14%
	ARIMA	18.21%	35.20%	30.76%	17.94%	20.82%	12.51%
	ARIMA with same store data	26.29%	35.20%	32.88%	25.01%	29.96%	6.12%
Bikes - MTB Hard tail	ETS (M,N,M)	14.55%	11.69%	26.50%	15.40%	24.68%	13.99%
	ETS with same store data	9.21%	11.69%	23.73%	8.73%	36.13%	3.97%
	ARIMA	10.21%	31.06%	22.23%	7.16%	12.78%	11.37%
	ARIMA with same store data	13.49%	31.06%	19.30%	−0.16%	23.13%	24.35%
Bikes - Kids Boys	ETS (M,N,M)	11.63%	3.58%	−9.40%	8.41%	35.46%	14.41%

(*continued*)

Table 12: Out-of-sample MAPE — one step and multi-step. (*continued*)

	Model	One Step	Step-ahead of multi-step process - 2015				
			Period 2	Period 3	Period 4	Period 5	Period 6
	ETS with same store data	18.09%	3.58%	11.65%	1.74%	50.68%	6.68%
	ARIMA	52.51%	2.45%	10.23%	−9.11%	34.67%	20.89%
	ARIMA with same store data	64.32%	2.45%	12.49%	17.06%	49.80%	13.75%

5.3. Out of sample MAPE — One step and multi-step

Table 13: Out of sample MAE accuracy.

	Model	One Step
Helmets - MTB & Road	ETS (M,N,M)	124
	ETS with same store data	69
	ARIMA	110
	ARIMA with same store data	106
Helmets - BMX	ETS (M,N,M)	72
	ETS with same store data	54
	ARIMA	87
	ARIMA with same store data	120
Bikes - MTB Hardtail	ETS (M,N,M)	49
	ETS with same store data	28
	ARIMA	31
	ARIMA with same store data	39
Bikes - Kids Boys	ETS (M,N,M)	64
	ETS with same store data	90
	ARIMA	296
	ARIMA with same store data	331

5.4. Out of sample RMSE

Table 14: RMSE accuracy — one month.

	Model	One Step
Helmets - MTB and Road	ETS (M,N,M)	158
	ETS with same store data	83
	ARIMA	130
	ARIMA with same store data	142
Helmets - BMX	ETS (M,N,M)	94
	ETS with same store data	69
	ARIMA	102
	ARIMA with same store data	125
Bikes - MTB Hardtail	ETS (M,N,M)	57
	ETS with same store data	37
	ARIMA	38
	ARIMA with same store data	47
Bikes - Kids Boys	ETS (M,N,M)	87
	ETS with same store data	122
	ARIMA	320
	ARIMA with same store data	362

5.5. Suggestions for model improvement

On an overall basis, the forecast error measures in out-of-sample data are reasonable. However, it is clear that the accuracy varies from month to month and some periods are not as accurate as anticipated. The main variable suspected of creating this variance is sales from new store openings. When these sales are stripped out from the out-of-sample data, the accuracy is improved for the ETS model. However, sales for new store openings have not been controlled for in the training data from 2012 to 2014, and further work is required to explore the impact that this is having.

Hyndman and Athanasopoulos describe a dynamic regression model that allows for the inclusion of additional predictor variables in addition to past observations in a time series.[7] It would be interesting to see if a variable for new store openings would improve results. Time constraints mean that this model is outside the scope of this study but will be trialed in ongoing work with the business.

5.6. A template to display forecasted data

Of equal importance to the accuracy of forecasting is the presentation of the forecasted data in a template that is easily understandable and usable for management to make business decisions. Given that the business has over 100 product categories, there will be many forecasts to make and significant amounts of data to analyze. Figure 14 is currently being worked on in consultation with management and is an example of how forecasted data will be set out for analysis. For confidentiality purposes, the dollar value of sales and gross profit are dummy figures.

FORECAST & VARIANCE TRACKER - HELMETS - ROAD & MOUNTAIN BIKE

		Actual				Prior Period				1 Month Forecast					
Period	Financial Year	Qu Sales Actual	$ Sales Actual	GP$ Actual	GP% Actual	Qu Sales Prior Perio	$ Sales Prior Perio	GP $ Prior Period	GP % Prior Period	Qu Sales Point Forecast	95% CI Low	95% CI High	Sales $ Forecast	GP $ Forecast	GP % Forecast
2015															
01	2015	1,363	100	10	10.0%	1,060	100	10	10.0%	1,431			100	10	10%
02	2015	1,212	100	10	10.0%	1,016	100	10	10.0%	1,360			100	10	10%
03	2015	1,235	100	10	10.0%	859	100	10	10.0%	1,157			100	10	10%
04	2015	1,149	100	10	10.0%	791	100	10	10.0%	1,181			100	10	10%
05	2015	1,129	100	10	10.0%	1,001	100	10	10.0%	1,266			100	10	10%
06	2015	1,036	100	10	10.0%	870	100	10	10.0%	1,091			100	10	10%
07	2015	1,432	100	10	10.0%	899	100	10	10.0%	1,055			100	10	10%
08	2015	1,246	100	10	10.0%	865	100	10	10.0%	1,337			100	10	10%
09	2015					922	57,882	22,641	39.1%	1,306			100	10	10%

Variance Analysis						Stock				
Qu Sales Prior Perio	Sales $ Prior Perio	GP $ Prior Perio	Qu Sales Forecast	Sales $ Forecast	GP $ Forecast	Stock on Hand	MSL	1 month forecast forecast - Units	Mgmt Adjust for New Strores	Under / Overstocked Units
22%	0%	0%	-5%	0%	0%	200				
16%	0%	0%	-12%	0%	0%	200				
30%	0%	0%	6%	0%	0%	200				
31%	0%	0%	-3%	0%	0%	200				
11%	0%	0%	-12%	0%	0%	200				
16%	0%	0%	-5%	0%	0%	200				
37%	0%	0%	26%	0%	0%					

Figure 14: Performance tracker — helmets — MTB and road.

The spreadsheet contains columns for:

- Actual Sales — units, dollar value, gross profit, and gross profit percentage
- Comparison to the same period in the previous year
- Comparison to forecasted sales
- The forecasts will include a point forecast and low/high forecasts at a confidence interval of 95 per cent
- Analysis of variance to both prior period and forecasted data
- An assessment of stock required based on current stock, MSL, forecast sales, and any adjustment required for new stores

5.7. Backtesting of rolling forecasts

The final spreadsheet being developed is one for backtesting of forecasts. As each period passes, new forecasts will be made with the updated information. It will therefore be important to track forecasts made in the past. Figure 15 demonstrates this table.

Back Testing Accuracy
Quantity - Helmets - Mountain Bike & Road

			Forecasts			Difference in Units			% Difference		
Year	Period	Actual Sales	1 Month	2 Month	3 Month	1 Month	2 Month	3 Month	1 Month	2 Month	3 Month
2014	13	1,562	1,255			307			19%		
2015	1	1,363	1,431	1,197		-68	166		-5%	12%	
2015	2	1,212	1,360	1,417	1,181	-148	-205	31	-12%	-17%	3%
2015	3	1,235	1,157	1,275	1,331	78	-40	-96	6%	-3%	-8%
2015	4	1,149	1,181	1,119	1,237	-32	30	-88	-3%	3%	-8%
2015	5	1,129	1,266	1,293	1,223	-137	-164	-94	-12%	-15%	-8%
2015	6	1,036	1,091	1,198	1,226	-55	-162	-190	-5%	-16%	10%
2015	7	1,432	1,055	1,101	1,214	377	331	218	14%	23%	15%
2015	8	1,246	1,337	1,039	1,086	-91	207	160	-7%	17%	13%
2015	9		1,306	1,383	1,064						
2015	10			1,381	1,465						
2015	11				1,381						

Figure 15: Example of backtesting template for rolling forecasts.

6. CONCLUSION AND FURTHER WORK

The development of accurate forecasts can be an effective way for management to make more accurate purchasing decisions and achieve greater profitability from the stock on hand.

The product category Helmets — Mountain bike and Road was used to develop ETS and ARIMA forecasting models. Based on the preferred measure of business (MAPE) an ETS model was able to more accurately predict sales for this product category. Accuracy was improved when sales from the three new stores opened so far in 2015 were stripped out of the out of sample data. However, the forecasts were still not in the required range of 10 per cent as requested by management. This was also the case when ETS and ARIMA models were used to forecast sales for a further three product categories being; BMX Helmets, Mountain Bike, and Boys Kids Bikes.

Further work will need to done to control for new store openings in the training data. A dynamic regression model as described by Hyndman and Athanasopoulos will be trialed in order to control this variable.

The development of the forecasting templates for analysis of results against past performances and forecast sales will be a helpful tool for the business. Further work will be done to build this out for more product categories.

REFERENCES

1. Hyndman, RJ and G Athanasopoulos, *Forecasting: Principles and Practice*. Online open text book. http://otexts.org/fpp/. Accessed on [13 November 2015.]

2. Ramos, P, N Santos and R Rubelo. (2014) '*Performance of state space and ARIMA models for consumer retail sales forecasting*'.

3. Penna, D, G.C Tiao, R.S. Tsay (2001). *A course in Time Series Analysis*. New York: John Wiley and Sons.

4. Hyndman, RJ, A.B. Koehler, J.K Ord and R.D Snyder (2008). *Forecasting with Exponential Smoothing: The State Space Approach*, Springer-Verlag.

5. R Core Team and contributors worldwide (2015). Stats: *R statistical Functions*. https://stat.ethz.ch/R-manual/R-devel/library/stats/html/stats-package.html.

6. Hyndman, R.J (2015). Forecast: "Forecasting Functions for Time Series and Linear Models." R package 6.2, https://cran.r-project.org/web/packages/forecast/forecast.pdf.

7. Hyndman, R.J (2013). *fpp: Forecasting: principles and practice*. R package 0.5, https://cran.r-project.org/web/packages/fpp/fpp.pdf.

CHAPTER 22

Business Analytics in Airport Operations for Improved Customer Experience

Himanshu Jaggi

ABSTRACT

This paper examines the projects Changi Airport Group Singapore (CAG) undertook to explore how it could improve its services to mobile phone users with location-based services, by mapping customer Wi-Fi data with certain locations in the airport. The results were used to better plan and allocate the key infrastructure and services across the premises. The investigations that were undertaken and results obtained from the exercise are discussed.

The paper also aims to present the findings and solutions developed to successfully integrate the data from two different source systems. This was done by creating mapping rules and logic to find the exact match and anomalies, a result that could be seen as a first step in implementing organizational level Business Intelligence (BI). An automated workflow was developed to find out the number of matching and non-matching records. Overall, 89 per cent of the records were matched with the logic developed, and non-matching records were assigned the best possible match, using Fuzzy logic transformation.

Best practices in the industry and architecture that are being employed by various organizations for developing a successful Enterprise level BI strategy are also discussed.

1. INTRODUCTION

Delivering an exceptional customer experience is not just about becoming more customer-centric. It also involves maximizing the opportunities of every interaction with the customer. BI, analytics and information technologies support key elements of a customer experience management solution. They provide an environment for delivering practical insights that guide or automate the decision-making process throughout the customer experience. Each insight in turn provides an opportunity to enhance and improve individual customer experience.

BI and Analytics help in two ways: firstly, conventional analytical stacks provide an environment for integrating and analyzing large volumes of historical customer information to support the planning and execution of the key customer experience decisions; secondly, operational analytics stacks enables analytic insights to deliver personalized and relevant actions at the point of action, which have to be integrated tightly with business process and actions. All these are aimed at achieving exceptional customer experience.

Different customer-oriented activities are of increasing interest in the transportation industry, particularly airport operations. Airports have shown considerable interest in becoming more customer-centric, looking beyond basic capabilities, to drive deeper insights into their businesses to create and sustain a competitive advantage.

Airports embarking on customer experience initiatives need to start by getting a complete view of their existing customer interactions and touch points, together with people and processes that support them. However, to get these deeper insights, airports need to rethink and optimize their existing legacy systems, as well as the processes that had been focused on the needs of the companies rather than the needs of customers. Customer experience strategy needs to work across multiple business functions: from sales and marketing, to customer service, finance and research and development. However, to effectively deliver these, a data integration layer that provides clean, consistent, timely and complete customer data is fast becoming a strategic imperative for organizations that want to pursue customer experience initiatives.

To effectively deliver the exceptional customer experience, the Changi Airport Group, Singapore (CAG) undertook three different initiatives:

i) Passenger Analytics: to understand the dwell time of passengers in the airport (for future infrastructure changes)
ii) The integration of two disjoint data sets: flight data (FLIRT) and sales data (POS) to achieve knowledge discovery in which the relationships between different data points are unknown or not understood and
iii) Enterprise BI level strategy to create an enterprise Business Intelligence Strategy to understand the different nuances and challenges that organizations typically face while implementing the enterprise-wide strategy.

This paper addressed these three projects with the objectives, challenges faced, results and lessons learnt from each project.

With smart phones being widely used, the digital and physical worlds are bridged. Public Wi-Fi networks and new indoor-location technologies are facilitating location-awareness indoors such as in office buildings, entertainment venues, retail stores, airports and other commercial environments. Harnessing both these technologies, it is now possible to accurately follow consumers in and around stores, stadiums, airports, hospitals, college campuses and other physical places, just as internet users are brought from one website to another. [1]

Many such applications to provide location-based services to users have received much attention, in research and commercially. Increasingly, companies are leveraging on technology to provide indoor location and place-based advertising and marketing ecosystem. [2] CAG used location analytics to understand its customers' behavior better so as to serve them better. With location service analytics in place, CAG hoped to deploy their (physical) real estate for maximum interaction with users.

The aim to understand passenger dwell time at certain locations and passengers' behavior for example the earliest and latest passenger arrival times, seeking to find any co-correlation between dwell time and a particular flight. The project was challenging as it required a thorough understanding of the framework used for location indoor analytics.

The other activity of the project required integrating data from various source systems and configuring the dashboards as per specific requirements. For the unmapped records, an exception report needed to be generated; this report had all the records that were not being mapped to any of the record in the other source system, and hence was called 'dangling records'. An automated workflow comprising various mapping rules to map both data sets together was designed. One such challenge for completing the project was to perform the data cleansing activities that are generic in nature and hence no information loss was accrued. To address this this problem, a type of clustering algorithm called Fuzzy logic [3], [4] was used to find the potential match for non-matching records.

Finally, research on implementation of enterprise BI level strategy to understand the challenges and the industry's best practices better was undertaken. [5]

2. PROBLEM STATEMENT

Recognizing the importance of identifying the unexpressed needs of passengers and using these insights to create an extraordinary customer experience, Changi airport focused on these three problem areas: passenger analytics, integration of sales data (POS) with flight data (FLIRT) to deliver sales insights and Enterprise Business Intelligence Strategy.

2.1. Passenger analytics

The primary users of airport terminals are airlines, air travelers, well-wishers and greeters, and a wide range of airport employees, government regulatory authorities, air carriers, concessionaires, and other airport tenants.[6] While facilities at airport terminals must first provide a good level of service (LOS) to the users, the planning and design of an overall terminal facility is greatly influenced by the more rigid requirements needed to accommodate maneuvering aircraft and ground access systems.

However, to provide exceptional customer experience and to distribute passengers uniformly across the terminals so that workforce could be better allocated, and point-of-sales could be uniform, CAG wanted to analyze the passenger footfall and the dwell time so that these findings could be incorporated into the designing of a new terminal. CAG would like to leverage the power of Wi-Fi data of passengers after they had connected to the airport Wi-Fi.

2.2. Integration of sales data with flirt data to deliver sales insights

The Pricing and Commercial strategy team had to perform sector sales analysis per passenger. However, the existing process was time-consuming and prone to error as it could not handle big data sets for example, performing yearly sales analysis. To avoid manual intervention and to reduce the time required to perform basic analysis, CAG wanted to create an automated solution that could effectively integrate flight data (source FLIRT) with sales data (source POS Data) to obtain sales by gate, countries and cities.

The project required creation of rules and logic to map the POS flight numbers to FLIRT flight numbers for both exact match and anomalies. The successful outcome of the project was an automated work-flow solution that performs business logic and effectively maps both the independent and disjointed data sets - an exercise that would reduce errors by being more systematic. This package loaded the data into tables, updated the requisite flags, monthly exception reports, and developed monthly tableau reports. The challenge was to detect and remove errors and inconsistencies to improve the quality of the data. Various data errors such as mis-spellings of data information, missing information and other invalid data presented in the POS data, which when integrated with FLIRT data lead to inconsistencies in business logic, leading to inaccurate sector sales analysis.

2.3. Enterprise business intelligence strategy

This area focuses on employing Business Intelligence Strategy at Enterprise level. CAG's approach was to use this strategy to align its goals, improve knowledge management, advance business (by making the best use of information), penetrating into business processes, and helping with strategic, tactical, and operational decision-making. Currently, CAG holds one subject area with supporting summarized data from the other division and the owner of the primary area owning the analysis. CAG looks to achieve Enterprise BI strategy where owner could be one but target audience can be many divisions i.e. cross analysis between various data sources available and how best to achieve this.

3. STATE OF THE ART

The aviation industry is processing huge amounts of data available that can be used to improve customer satisfaction. Different types of data: sensor data, Wi-Fi data, customer data, flight details and location data can be accessed to broaden customers' experience. As people turn on their mobile devices at various locations, a natural approach was to target potential customers in close proximity. Location data helps competitive locational targeting (the practice of promoting to consumers near a competitor's location) and characterizes the conditions under which it works. Mobile promotions were sent to customers at three similar locations in shopping areas.

The results showed that competitive locational targeting has the potential to take advantage of heightened demand that a focal retailer would not otherwise capture, generating incremental sales without cannibalizing profits. [3] Locational targeting has enormous potential as a competitive weapon to allow retailers to maintain a presence anywhere – including on a competitor's doorstep. The other application analyzes the movement patterns of passengers to optimise the work force deploying it in highly concentrated areas. Similarly, dwell time analysis was applied to the data. An example is Copenhagen airport [7] that used location data to discover:

- What routes passengers take through the airport.
- Real-time tracking.
- How passenger behavior changes by day, season, airline.
- What is the effect of new infrastructure.
- Indoor navigation.
- When departing passengers arrive at the airport.

- Behavior of frequent flyers.
- Facilitating mobility "You are at the wrong end of the airport for your departure gate. Turn left at Starbucks and proceed straight on."
- Opportunities for loyalty programs "We are aware that you are a fashion-conscious passenger. A three day sale is on now at the shop on your right."

Further studies have been conducted into customer behavior using mobile data. The findings suggest that although mobile trajectory-based advertising can lead to a significant increase in revenues of the focal advertising store, it can lead to a significant decrease in the overall revenues of the shopping mall during the weekend.[8] Research has been undertaken on localization technologies and their applications have received much attention, both in research and increasingly, commercially. Several commercial services can locate an end host with reasonable accuracy, using publicly available databases that map domain names and IP addresses to geographical locations and other proprietary mechanisms. [9, 10]

Several network-level techniques further enhance the accuracy of geo location. IP2Geo uses end-to-end latency and trace route information to pinpoint geographic location. [11] Octant enables accurate geo location by solving a system of geometric constraints. [12] More fine-grained geo location can be obtained by tracking the strength of the radio signals received by the phone from different cell towers, as shown by Varshavsky et al. for GSM cell phones.[13] Various new opportunities are available to provide value to users and business. In-Store browsing is such an example. [14]

Fundamentally, retailing is about connecting end consumers with the products and services in a way that serves the needs of both consumers (value for money) and businesses (increased sales). Therefore tracking and analyzing customer behavior in a physical store is valuable. Indeed, this has become an active space for startups looking to leverage existing technologies for indoor localization. All these activities are possible if the accuracy of the location data is high and can provide effective results in mapping the customer to the real location.

Identifying the location accuracy of the data and thus finding how well the passenger is being identified when mapped with Wi-Fi location signals was the most important activity that needed to be performed to accurately identify a passenger. Validating results on location accuracy was necessary to find out that the data has some signal in it; otherwise the possibility of noise in the data could affect the outcome.

Once the analytics project was identified, the first task was to gather data and make sure that that the data values were correct or, at the very least, conformed to some set of rules . For example, a variable called Gender would be expected to have only two values; a variable representing height in inches would be expected to be within reasonable limits. Sometimes, however, the source systems were badly designed or not validated thoroughly and thus impacted the data entries, making the data vulnerable to some invalid or illogical entries.

Handling data cleansing and data profiling task was time consuming and required best practices for example [21]:

- All data sources within the enterprise were standardized and documented at once, ensuring that each department was accounted for and determining what data elements were required to complete their required business tasks.
- A central data cleansing database was built and ensured that all locations using each item was referenced.
- The data-cleansing database included a balance of electronic scripting for data corrections and manual auditing.

However, after taking all these precautions, other sources of data errors remained for example, measurement errors and distillation errors. In addition, these errors were aggravated when multiple sources needed to be integrated. Each source had the potential to contain dirty data and the data in the sources could be represented differently, overlap or contradict. This was because the sources were typically developed, deployed and maintained independently to serve specific needs. This resulted in a large degree of heterogeneity with respect to data management systems, data models, schema designs and the actual data.

The data inconsistencies, data errors and unclean data presented difficulties in the integration of stand alone data sources and hence finding insights became difficult. To obtain a large number of sales records when matching identified data with the other sets of data using business logic was difficult. Hence it was necessary to clean the data.

Research on different aspects of data cleaning have been conducted in recent years for example, computational procedures to automatically or semi-automatically identify and, when possible, correct errors in large data sets [15]. This resulted in a large number of tools being developed in the market to support data transformation and data cleaning tasks, particularly for data warehousing. Some tools focus on a specific domain for example, cleaning name and address details or on a specific cleaning phase such as data analysis or duplicate elimination. Other tools such as ETL tools, provide comprehensive transformation and workflow capabilities to cover a large part of the data transformation and cleaning process.

This helped identify the most appropriate tool to use for performing data cleaning, data transformation and standardization, and thereby devising rules and logics for cleaning the data and then performing business logic to successfully integrate the data sets.

The introduction of a BI strategy aimed to align business processes with enterprise goals, improve knowledge management and advance business by making the best use of information. BI helps enterprise with strategic, tactical, and operational decision making [22]. The essential components of BI strategy empower all in the enterprise to work effectively on a daily basis, and hence driving better business performance. BI strategy explains the steps to bring together the forces that drive business operations - people, processes, and technology in a collaborative environment. It highlights the approach to enable successful adoption of BI to deliver true business value. The proven best practices for building a successful organizational BI strategy is as follows [5]:

- Create a business proposal and outline the expected benefits.
- Obtain buy-in from stakeholders, especially the senior executives.
- Have an enterprise-wide perspective.
- Establish criteria for success.
- Treat information as an asset.
- Adopt best practices and standards.
- Set up change management procedures.
- BI strategy should align with the overall IT strategy and enterprise goals.
- Do a current state, future state, and gap analysis.
- Think actionable and baby steps.

- Establish governance body.
- Use iterative implementation approach with parallel tracks.
- Work with frameworks and adopt proven methodologies.
- Assess BI readiness of the organization and identify related gaps and issues.
- Document and analyze the constraints and assumptions.
- Consider all BI components.

Figure 1 helped realize that transformation of insight into action was missing.

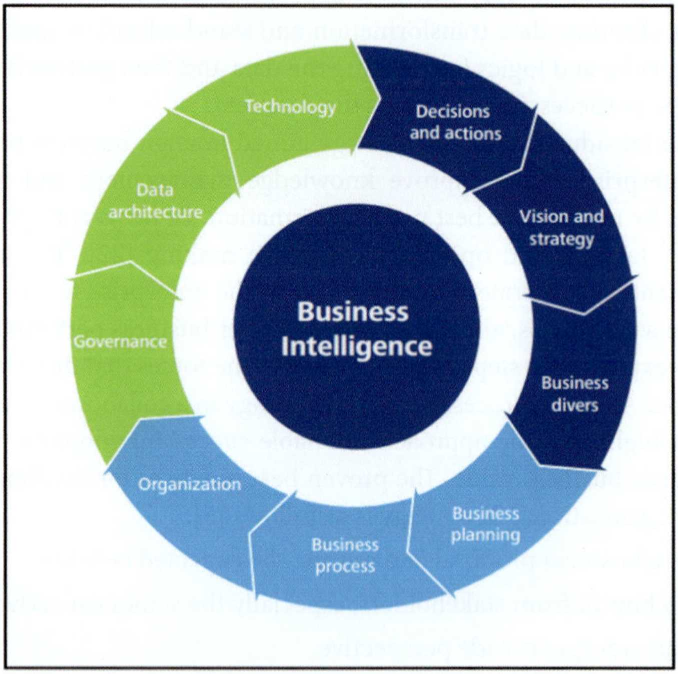

Figure 1: Business Intelligence components

4. SOLUTION

4.1. Description of approach

CAG hoped to understand its passenger and customers better with the help of data, so that more user-friendly services could be provided to them. The tasks were:

- to analyze the passenger footfall so that the data could be used to plan the new new terminal.

- to understand and perform the sector sales analysis and sales analysis by various gates, cities and countries so that those factors contributing to the most sales could be targeted and marketing campaigns designed.

Problem Statement 1:
Passenger Analytics

The first task was to accurately map the passenger to gate holding rooms and analyze passenger behavior and dwell time for individual flights. The data sets provided were Wi-Fi data along with Point of Information data and FLIRT data. The data required was an effective integration of both these data sets.

The functional requirements provided were as follows:

- To understand passenger dwell times within the airport premises at a given time.
- To identify the earliest time a passenger arrives at a gate holding room for a particular flight.
- To identify the latest time a passenger arrives at a gate holding room for a particular flight.
- to identify the average dwell time of a passenger for every flight.

The data set provided for analyzing customer behavior was Wi-Fi and Point of Information data with different conversion units

The Wi-Fi data had the following variables and attributes:

- Timestamp (continuous): Time Stamp for each snapshot.
- Mac Address (continuous) Passenger Mac Address.
- X Coordinate (continuous): X coordinate of passenger location(pixels).
- Y Coordinate (continuous): Y coordinate of passenger location(pixels).
- Terminal Id (ordinal): ID based on Terminal Zone.
- Terminal Level Id (ordinal): ID based on Terminal Level.
- STP X Coordinate (continuous): Snap to x coordinate.
- STP X Coordinate (continuous): Snap to y coordinate.
- Zone 1 id (ordinal): ID based on Zone Dimension.
- Dwell Time Zone 1 id (continuous): Zone 1 dwell time in seconds.
- Zone 2 id (ordinal): ID based on Zone Dimension.
- Dwell Time Zone 2 id (continuous): Zone 2 dwell time in seconds.

- Zone 3 id (ordinal): ID based on Zone Dimension.
- Dwell Time Zone 3 id (continuous): Zone 3 dwell time in seconds.
- Zone 4 id (ordinal): ID based on Zone Dimension.
- Dwell Time Zone 4 id (continuous): Zone 4 dwell time in seconds.

The Point of Information Data provided had the following variables and attributes:

- Type (continuous): POI Type.
- Shop Name (continuous): POI Description.
- Terminal (ordinal): TerminalDescription.
- Level (ordinal): Level Description.
- X (continuous): X coordinates(pixels).
- Y (continuous): Y coordinates (pixels).

Various activities including data preparation, data engineering and preliminary data analysis were conducted before analyzing passenger footfall behavior. The approach merged and cleaned all e-data together and then applied random sample of passengers to undertake a preliminary analysis to evaluate the signal and noise.

The following activities were performed for the preliminary analysis:

a) Data Preparation:

Tools Used: Microsoft SSIS package, Linux command line parameters, and relational database

Preparing the data set was the most challenging activity as the granularity of the data was at the 'second' level, and the data (in excel sheets) were stored at a common repository. Appending the data for all the passengers into one data file resulted in a file as big as 50Gb for one month. The initial files given were in compressed format and an ETL was created to uncompress the data and push it to the SQL server into the Staging tables. An automated work-flow took the files from a designated location and converted the data as required and pushed the data into the database. However, the power required for merging the data and pushing it into the database was underestimated, leading to performance issues.

The second approach of data ingestion was performed using Linux command tools by appending the data from the raw files into one large file. Indeed, the number of rows created for passenger data was 600 million rows for only one month of data.

The data preparation and validation phase required that the preliminary analysis made sense before starting on the full analysis. Using random sampling, all the corresponding records for 50,000 passengers was selected and pushed into the relational data base. The x and y coordinates were converted into geospatial data to effectively use the algorithm and to achieve results provided by some industry standard tools. Another advantage of converting into spatial coordinates was to effectively use joins and other geometries that are difficult to convert using the raw data.

For example, a passenger was mapped to a gate holding room if he was within a 10 meter radius of it; hence the need to use the 'circle' overlay of the sql geometry data types. Another effective use of the converted data type is that it was easier to find points patterns that could be identified as clustered, dispersed, or random. The ability to calculate distance easily and effectively was the basic use of converting raw x, y coordinates into the geospatial data types.

b) Data Analysis:

After the data preparation stage, preliminary analysis was undertaken to perform high level analysis to find the mapping of individual passengers to the gate holding room, an activity that set the basis for further work in this project. The validity of the data sets was achieved by using various methods such as using 'join' algorithm, mathematical evaluation and graphical analysis to evaluate whether both sets of x,y coordinates were recorded correctly and were on the same scale and having same units. Initial analysis of the variables showed that the coordinates should be on the same scale and have the same units. However, that was not what the results revealed.

The "join" algorithm performed on spatial coordinates failed to provide any mapping of the passenger with the Point of Interest (POI) location. To validate the algorithm, a more suitable mathematical approach was required to find out the minimum x and y coordinates that needed to be in the database to effectively map the passenger data with the poi location. Careful analysis and studying the mathematical results, revealed that the coordinates were out of bound and hence did not exist due to possible change in the units of both poi and passenger location data set.

The mathematical evaluation was as follows: a brief analysis to find a passenger within a 10-meter radius to certain gate holding room. The approach was to find Y minimum required to have in the data set that could help find the passenger at the gate holding location.

Gate C19/C26. The most conservative X and Y coordinate across all gates

Coordinates were: (5381,4571)

Using Euclidean distance formula,

Euclidean Distance: (x2–x1)^2+ (y2–y1)^2 = r^2

To find minimum of Y, we had to make X maximum.

The max found in database records for Wi-Fi data was 5686.37

Putting this value into the above formula, the Y minimum required was y >=3475. However, the maximum y coordinate that was in the database was 2314. Hence, the data could not be mapped.

The value of using graphs in guiding the analysis, and especially in detecting and diagnosing analysis problems, can be overstated. To view that data set and to confirm the results obtained earlier, the Cartesian set of variables was plotted. It revealed that it was not possible for both data sets be superimposed, a condition required for mapping the passenger to the gate holding room.

The graphical analysis confirmed the initial analysis that both data sets were mutually exclusive, or recorded in different units and hence required possible transformation to give a meaningful result.

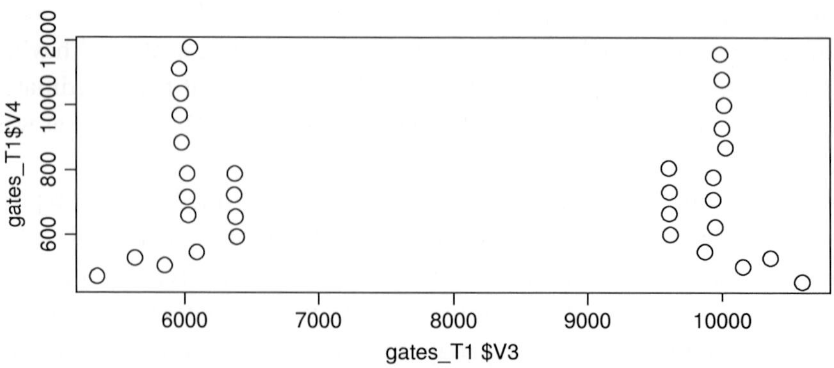

Figure 2: The graph shown above is the various Gate terminals having coordinates from 5000- 10,000.

Courtesy: Prof Tuan Phan, NUS

Figure 2 above shows the different Gate Holding location for Terminal 1. Each point is one gate location at terminal 1. The coordinates move from ~5000 to 12,000

Figure 3 above shows the randomly sampled passenger location. The co-ordinates range from 1800 to 2300.

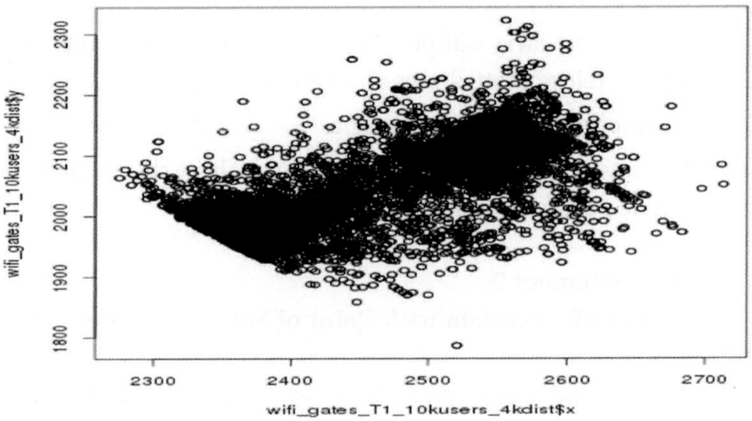

Figure 3: The graph shown above is passenger location data of random sample of 10,000 passengers.
Courtesy: Prof Tuan Phan, NUS

Superimposing both the data sets did not provide any useful analysis and confirmed that the passenger location data and the poi data had different units. Therefore, the data set could not be used for further analysis.

Although anticipating some insights might have helped CAG understand its customers behavior better, the data sets were unworkable due to the presence of noise.

It was proved mathematically that the data sets were disjointed and could not be integrated to establish any meaningful analysis. The data sets provided either contained different units or had other conversion factors that resulted in noise. The conclusion reached was that one or both of the data sets were noisy, making it impossible to effectively map the passenger with the point of information locations.

Recommendations:

It was strongly recommended that:

- both data sets have a standard conversion factor that could effectively and reliably convert one set of coordinates into another.

- the Wi-Fi data be validated thoroughly and effectively with the coordinates recorded in real time at some point of information location, and then confirm that the converted units pointed to the real location accurately.

Learning Points:

Although the project did not deliver any real insights that CAG was hoping for, the project provided the following learning points:

- It was important to carry out preliminary analysis on a smaller data set that has all the relevant attributes and behavior of the data.
- The importance of sampling technique.
- Not all data sets can bring insights, and data analysts should be aware of this fact while performing data analysis.

Problem statement 2:

Integration of sales data with Point of Sales (POS) data for sales insights

The Pricing and Commercial Strategy team faced a difficult time analyzing the net sales accounted to airlines, gates, cities etc. The data sets were mutually exclusive and required integration i.e. Flirt data and POS data had different data sources, to effectively analyze the data and provide some unseen insights. A solution was needed to perform business logic and rules were needed to map POS flight numbers to FLIRT flight numbers accurately. More sophisticated logic supported by the current database was required so a scalable approach was developed to reduce the amount of manual intervention.. In addition, management was not aware of the unmatched flight numbers, which resulted in less accurate net sales or insights. The process was time-consuming and so a need for an automated solution was necessary. The solution needed to deliver:

- Monthly tableau reports for sales match to gates, countries, and cities.
- Delivery of monthly exception reports to flag flights that don't match (percentage of accuracy).
- Creation of automated scripts for running monthly data reports.

The expected business objective was to create mapping rules and logic to map POS Flight code and Flight Numbers with the FLIRT flight code and flight numbers for both exact match and anomalies. The proposal was to find an automated solution that could perform data cleansing, data standardization and business logic to find the number of matching and non- matching records. As the solution needed time to be constructed and then the programmed to undertake monthly runs, Microsoft Business Intelligence Studio tool kit (specifically, SQL Server 2012, SSRS, SSAS and SSIS) was used to develop the entire solution.

The Microsoft Business Intelligence Studio Tool kit comprises:

Business Intelligence Development Studio - Microsoft Visual Studio 2012 with additional project types that are specific to SQL Server business intelligence. Business Intelligence Development Studio is the primary environment used to develop business solutions including Analysis Services, Integration Services, and Reporting Services projects.

The following are activities of proposed solution.

a) Data Preparation and Extraction:

The main goal of data preparation and loading is to off-load data from the source systems as fast as possible, making them less cumbersome and as less cumbersome for these source systems to handle as possible.

Since the PAX (FLIRT data) and POS (Point-of-sales) data sets used were different source systems, the raw data was provided in the form of excel spreadsheets. Data profiling was used to 'understand' the data better. Analytical techniques were applied to discover the true content, structure and quality of the data. This was completed by deciphering and validating data patterns and formats and by identifying and validating redundant data across the data source. Given the huge amount of data, it was imperative to use the correct data tools such as SSIS, without which it would have been impossible to move forward.

However, no data cleansing rules were applied onto the raw files.

The variables provided for the problem were:

FLIRT	Point of Sales
Date	Area
Time	Location
Terminal	Terminal
Country Name	Business Category
City Name	Product Category
Flight Code	TA

FLIRT	Point of Sales
Flight Number	TA Number
Airlines	Outlet Name
Gate No	Outlet Name 1
Gate	Flight Code
Arrival Departure indicator	Flight Number
PAX Movements	Nationality
Transit PAX	Day
TTL PAX	Net Sales

The first step was to export the data from monthly PAX and POS data file to the database (changi_pos). The PAX data was loaded into the table "PAXDATA" and the POS data was loaded into the table (POSDATA). The details are:

- File export names: PAX and POS Data(APR 14).
- Database name: changi_pos.
- Table name: dbo. POSDATA & dbo.PAXDATA.
- Utility Required: Import and Export Data (32 bit).

SQL server import and export wizard was used for importing the PAX and POS Data File.

After validating the number of records available in source and destination file systems, the solution was developed further and the files were no longer required.

b) Cleaning and Data Transformation:

Transforming and loading the data means to integrate then move the integrated data to the presentation area that can then be accessed via front-end tools by the end-users.. Here the emphasis should be on really using the offered functionality by the chosen ETL-tool (ETL - extracting, transforming and loading of the data) and using it in the most effective way.

The FLIRT and POS data sets required the mapping of certain common keys that would ensure that there was unique mapping between both PAX and POS. After carefully examining the data the important keys were found: Flight number, Flight Code and Date. However, the formatting of these fields was different and required transformation. Moreover, on careful analysis, it was found that in certain columns, the data was duplicated and needed to be rationalized before being used for providing insights. This was necessary because on slicing and dicing the data the insights would not have been exact and hence possible duplication of the results that needed to be roll up for further analysis. In addition, the data from one of the source data system required extensive cleaning, without which the analysis would have been impossible. For transforming and cleansing the data, ETL was used. For the data cleansing activities, the errors found can be fixed based on a pre-defined set of metadata rules. However, a distinction needed to be made between completely or partly rejecting the record by fixing the data through e.g. completing the record, correcting the inaccurate data fields, adjusting the data formatting and setting a flag to True, in case the record is dirty and is modified.

The results of the automated cleansing activities were as follows:

- Date time fields were adjusted and corrected.
- All the special characters from POS Flight Code and Flight Number were removed.
- The Nationality column was uniformed and rolled up.
- The terminal name was changed to ensure an effective join in the future.

The cleansed data was loaded into the new tables, so that staging could be served as base tables for future transfer of raw data. Also, it is best practice in BI to create staging tables and then move the data from staging to another table for performing any necessary activities.

Figure 4 illustrates the data analysis process

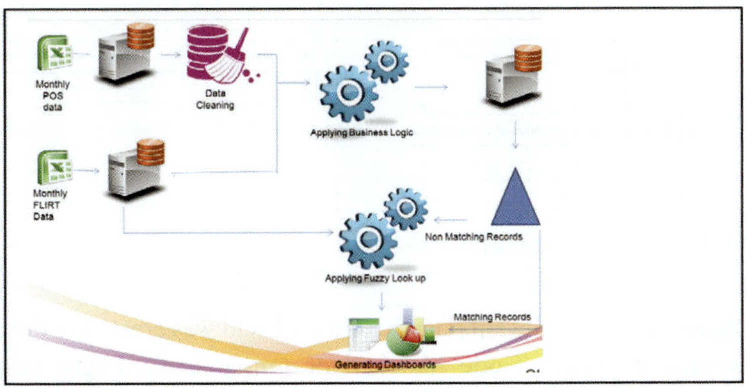

Figure 4: Data analysis process.

Three independent packages were created to produce a smoother work-flow. The function of the packages was as follows:

4.2. Package 1 "PackageCleaning.dtsx"

This package imported data from the POS data set and made the transformation for example, Date, Time, trimming of special characters in the Flight Number and Flight Code, cleaned the "Nationality" data and joined the PAX data set with the specified Business Key (Date, Flight Code and Flight Number). It also set the flag 'is_record_dirty' and 'is_record_modified' to 0 or 1 by performing a look up on FLIRT data set. The lookup transformation performed lookups by joining data in input columns with columns in a reference dataset for example, in the PAX dataset. This look up transformation data flow task looked for matching POS "Flight Code" records in the PAX dataset. Sequential looks up were created for example Date and Flight number to find out the number of records that were clean and able to be matched. The remaining data set that was dirty and could not be matched was been identified by the relevant flags (Figure 5).

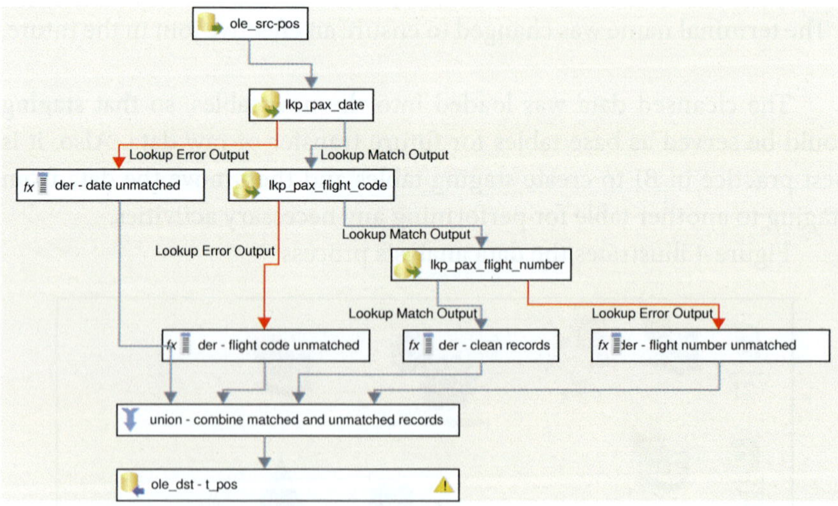

Figure 5: The package cleaning process.

Apart from the relevant flags, a Remarks field was created to describe errors such as 'Flight Code Matched or unmatched',, 'Flight number unmatched', or 'Date unmatched'. This was done to analyze effectively the number of unclean records with respect to the business key.

4.3. Package 2 "PackageFuzzyLookup.dtsx"

For the unmatched flight code and flight number records, this package looked for potential matches in the PAX data for the corresponding flight number and flight code. Microsoft Fuzzy was used to find the potential matches between the POS flight code and flight number, and PAX flight code and flight number. The Fuzzy Look Up contains 'built-in' operators and data cleaning operators. For wide usage, it was desirable to have generic, domain-neutral operators which were also used for the operators that allow domain specific customizations. Examples of such customizations included plugging in synonyms, domain specific tokenization and token weighting.

The operators identified and implemented in the Fuzzy logic included:

- Fuzzy Lookup (FL) that is used as one of the core operators to perform record matching. The matching was customized to configure the tokenization, token weighting and provide transformation rules. Efficiency was addressed by designing a similarity index.
- Fuzzy grouping that was used for reduplication. Fuzzy Grouping clustered the pair wise matches produced by Fuzzy Lookup.
- Column segmentation that segmented input strings based on specification of regular expressions that could also reference tables in a database.

Fuzzy Lookup uses the Error-Tolerant Index (ETI) to find matching rows in the reference table. Each record in the reference table is broken up into words (also known as tokens), and the ETI keeps track of all the places in the reference table where a particular token occurs. Take the name as an example, if the reference data contains John Sward, the ETI will contain entries for John and Sward. In addition, Fuzzy Lookup indexes substrings (known as q-grams) to better match records that contain errors. The more unique tokens and the more rows in the reference table, the more entries and longer the occurrence lists in the ETI. The ETI would be roughly as big as the reference table.

The Fuzzy Look up requires a few parameters to be set in, for finding the matching records. The similarity thresholds indicate how closely the input data resembles its proposed match. A similarity value of 1 indicates an identical match. The closer the value is to 1, the closer the match.

The similarity threshold was set to 0.25 per cent meaning the output only gave records that were 25 per cent matching when compared with Flight code and Flight number. The other non-matching records were transferred to a separately derived column.

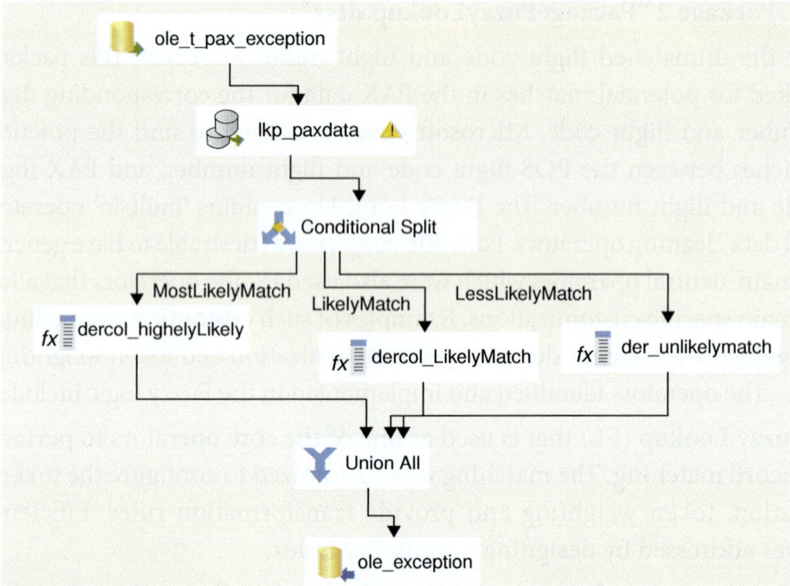

Figure 6: The control flow.

Another parameter was provided to set the maximum number of records to be five so that a maximum of five similar records were fetched. This provided more flexibility for managers to be able to better evaluate the results and to make informed decisions.

Once the Fuzzy Look up algorithm worked, the results were sent to the automated exception report in the form of an excel spreadsheet.

The exception report generated contained the ExceptionReport_ DateTime.xlsx format. The dynamic behavior of the excel sheet was also being automated and contained the following output columns:

- Date.
- Flight Code.
- Flight Number.
- Remarks.
- Referenced Flight Code.
- Referenced Flight Number.
- Overall Similarity.
- Similarity between Flight Code.
- Similarity between Flight Numbers.
- _isMatched or not.

4.4. Package 3: "Update_t_pos.dtsx"

The package updated the "t_pos" table for all the unmatched records with the potential PAX Flight Code and Flight number match. The pos table was updated for all the corresponding records that were dirty and the flag was_modified and set to 'True'. This helped in updating the POS record, specifically the flight code and flight number with the PAX flight code and flight number that had the maximum similarity between them. This was essential to roll up the net sales maximum likely flight required for analysis in the future. However, the approach had the flexibility to update the POS records with other criteria, a characteristic of dynamic and flexible ETL work flow that is best practice in the industry.

4.5. Package 4: "MasterPackage.dtsx"

As the name suggests, the Master package was created to monitor and drive the above mentioned slave packages. The package was created to run the abovementioned packages sequentially and did not have functionality from extracting, transforming and loading data per se. For each loop container is being used to run the packages sequentially and has been deployed in Integration Services Catalogue. This package was further used in the job agent of SQL Server Agent.

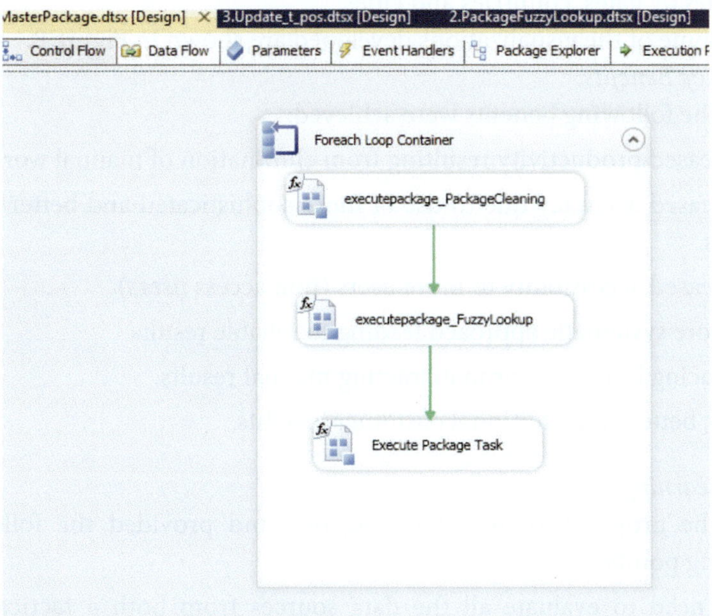

Figure 7: A view of the different packages.

All the packages were deployed in the SSIDB database and executing the Master package automatically executed all the functional packages mentioned earlier.

This package was required to automate the entire work-flow and was easily scheduled as per the frequency provided.

On executing the Master package, an exception report was created automatically with all the non-matching records. It updated the POS records with the maximum similar PAX flight codes and flight numbers. The developed solution was tested for logics and rules for accuracy.

Results: The statistics and the results achieved with this activity are:

Business Logic	Current approach	Earlier approach
Percentage of Matching Records	90%	78–80%
Fuzzy logic	2%	Not possible
Overall	92%	78–80%

Using this approach, a higher accuracy of results was achieved. For visualizations, a Tableau dashboard was built to effectively visualize the net sales by gates, countries and cities.

Some of the visualizations developed are shown in Figure 8.

Key Benefits:

The following benefits were achieved:

- Increased productivity resulting from elimination of manual work.
- Increased accuracy due to use of more sophisticated and better tested rules.
- Increased accessibility to more users (non access users).
- A more systematic approach leading to reliable results.
- Reducing human error in extracting manual results.
- Easy, better and additional customer insights.

Learning Points:

The project was an interesting one and provided the following learning points:

- The need to evaluate all the data sources from both a tactical and strategic perspective.

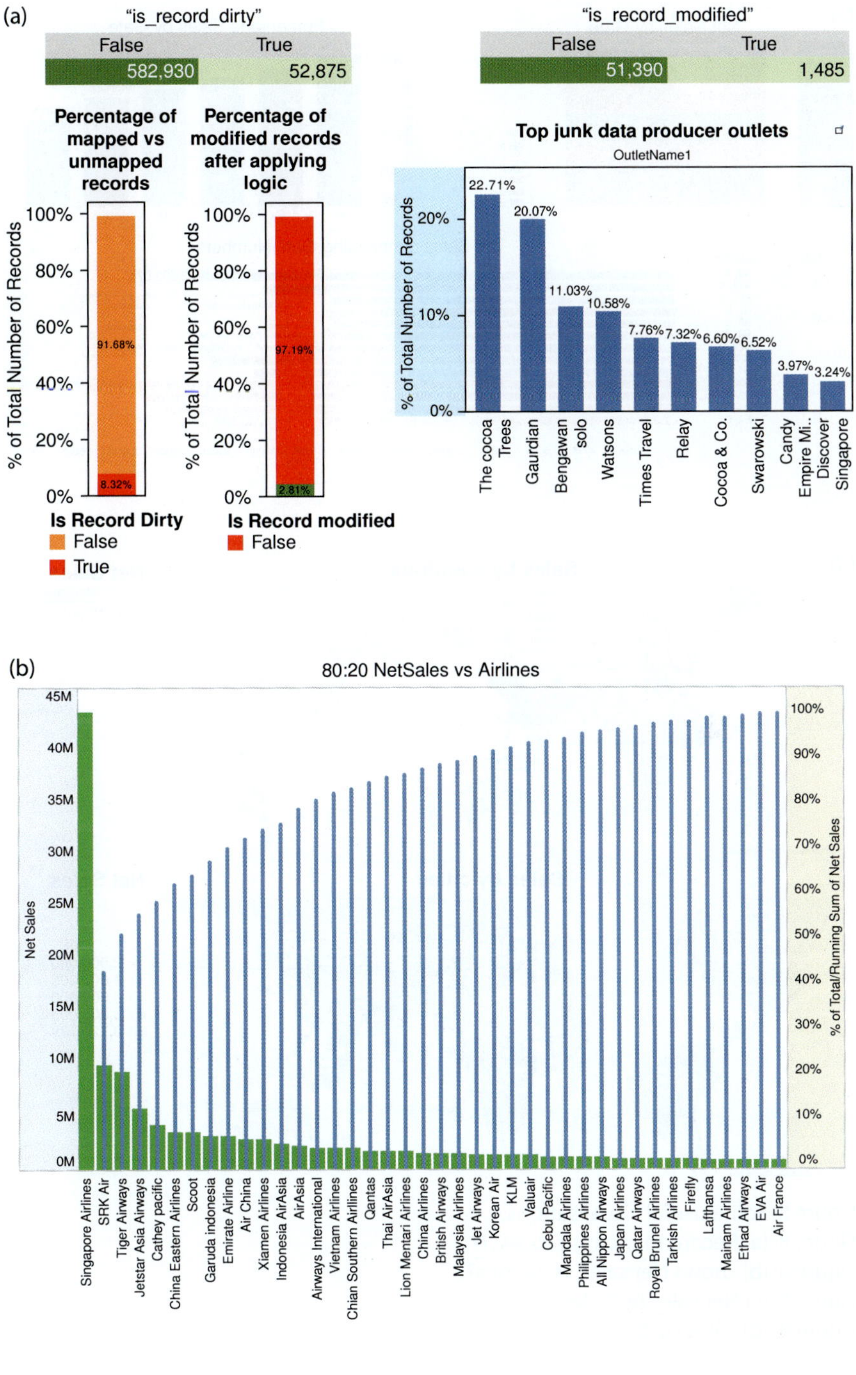
(a)
"is_record_dirty"
False
True
582,930
52,875
"is_record_modified"
False
True
51,390
1,485
Percentage of mapped vs unmapped records
Percentage of modified records after applying logic
% of Total Number of Records
100%
80%
60%
40%
20%
0%
91.68%
8.32%
97.19%
2.81%
Is Record Dirty
False
True
Is Record modified
False
Top junk data producer outlets
OutletName1
22.71%
20.07%
11.03%
10.58%
7.76%
7.32%
6.60%
6.52%
3.97%
3.24%
The cocoa Trees
Gaurdian
Bengawan solo
Watsons
Times Travel
Relay
Cocoa & Co.
Swarowski
Candy Empire Mi..
Discover Singapore
(b)
80:20 NetSales vs Airlines
Net Sales
45M
40M
35M
30M
25M
20M
15M
10M
5M
0M
% of Total/Running Sum of Net Sales
100%
90%
80%
70%
60%
50%
40%
30%
20%
10%
0%
Singapore Airlines
SRK Air
Tiger Airways
Jetstar Asia Airways
Cathey pacific
China Eastern Airlines
Scoot
Garuda indonesia
Emirate Airline
Air China
Xiamen Airlines
Indonesia AirAsia
AirAsia
Airways International
Vietnam Airlines
Chian Southern Airlines
Qantas
Thai AirAsia
Lion Mentari Airlines
China Airlines
British Airways
Malaysia Airlines
Jet Airways
Korean Air
KLM
Valuair
Cebu Pacific
Mandala Airlines
Philippines Airlines
All Nippon Airways
Japan Airlines
Qatar Airways
Royal Brunel Airlines
Tarkish Airlines
Firefly
Lafthansa
Mainam Airlines
Ethad Airways
EVA Air
Air France

(c)

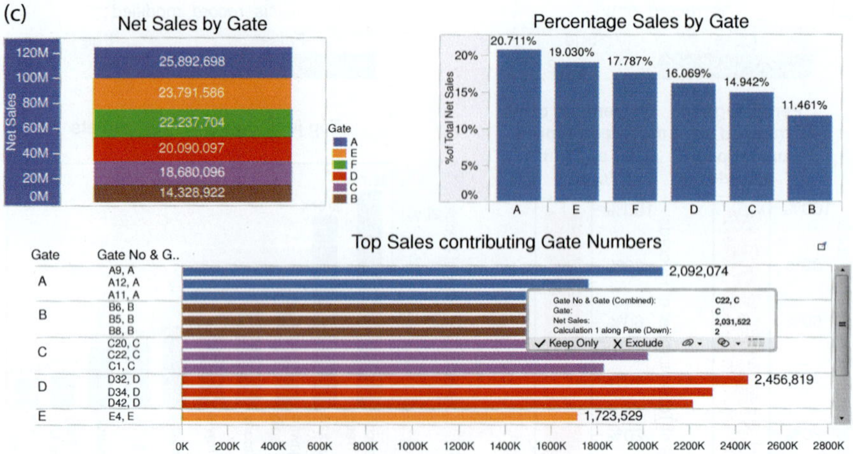

(d)

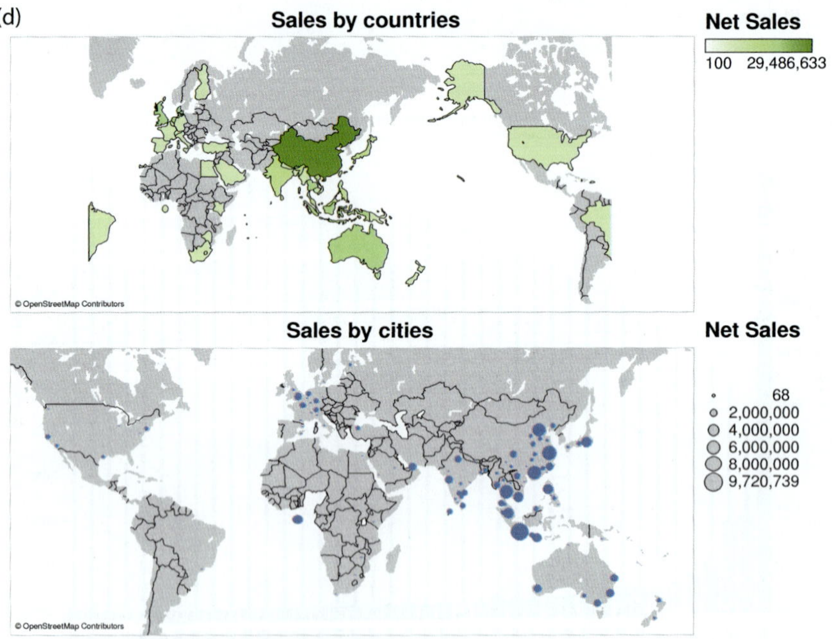

Figure 8: Some useful visualisations.
Figure 8: (a) Record mapping process??
Figure 8: (b) shows Net sales vs airlines??
Figure 8: (c) Net sales by Gate??
Figure 8: (d) Sales by country??

- The need to focus on the core information that is valuable to most business users.
- The importance of cleaning data as a first priority to avoid data quality issues.
- The importance of selecting the appropraite IT solution for the job is very important. Interactive dashboards and other analytics-based tools help business users conduct data analysis and mining to identify metrics, trends, interrelationships and anomalies.

Problem Statement 3:
Research work on Enterprise Business Intelligence Strategy

The objective of this work was to:

- understand and focus on building a BI strategy that aligned with the business goals.
- improve knowledge management and advance business by making the best use of information.
- incorporate BI into business processes to help in strategic, tactical and operational decision making.

The solution developed required an understanding of CAG standalone data sources and the current functional BI system. Complete assessment of processes, technology, and people in the current state were critical to the success of the changes made to the current environment. Moreover, various technologies and governance procedures were determined. In the current state analysis, pain-points and shortcoming were highlighted after an open dialogue with business partners.

After the current state analysis and understanding the BI environment, brainstorming on the future environment was done to achieve the BI vision. Multiple tools and technologies were used to come up with the desired method of delivery and the best fit.

In addition, assessment of immediate requirements and long-term business needs were considered to classify the project in phases.

The table below shows a comparison of the current state with the future state:

In the developed solution, a generic enterprise BI framework with an overview of different components of BI strategy fit together to serve the

As –is State (current state)	To – be state (future state)
Technology driven BI initiative	Business driven initiative
Multiple BI systems	One version of truth
No enterprise BI standards	Collaborative BI environment
Limited or no data governance	Effective data governance
Data in silos resulting in multiple unsynchronized reporting solutions	BI initiative align with overall enterprise goals
Lack of BI collaborative environment	Data quality issues addressed in holistic manner
Multiple BI standards	Uniform BI standards

BI vision. The framework connects BI, business processes, collaborative applications, and their underlying data store. A comprehensive approach incorporating technology, people, and other components in current and future behavior was developed in a 5-layered Enterprise framework

Although BI architecture varies from organization to organization, there are some common components of BI architecture in all BI solutions. What is included in BI architecture is driven by the objectives, goals and requirements of the enterprise. This was shared with end users.

The following are suggestions provided to CAG to better understand the activities and best practices helpful for them to achieve the end-to-end BI strategy

4.6. BI Architecture

A comprehensive representation of the typical BI architecture is shown in Figure 9 below. Multiple disparate Data sources, data integration services, data management services, reporting, analytical services, information delivery, and consumption services form the broad spectrum of the BI architecture.

An important outcome is a flow chart of the set of activities that are needed to achieve the enterprise BI see Figure 10. Each stage was discussed along with a set of activities, roles involved and deliverables that results from these activities. The deliverables were usually templates completed by various stakeholders involved during the entire project life cycle.

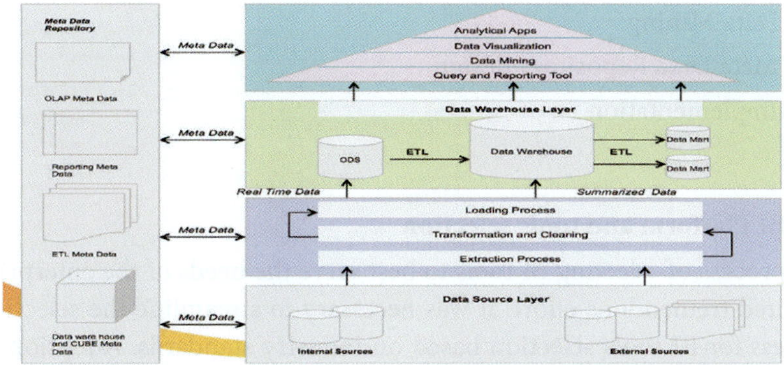

Figure 9: Flow Chart/Set of Activities involved in achieving Enterprise BI Architecture

The entire project life cycle was divided into 15 such sets of activities, with each set having its own set of deliverables. The recommendation provided was industry standard and usually considered the best practices by consulting companies such as Deloitte.

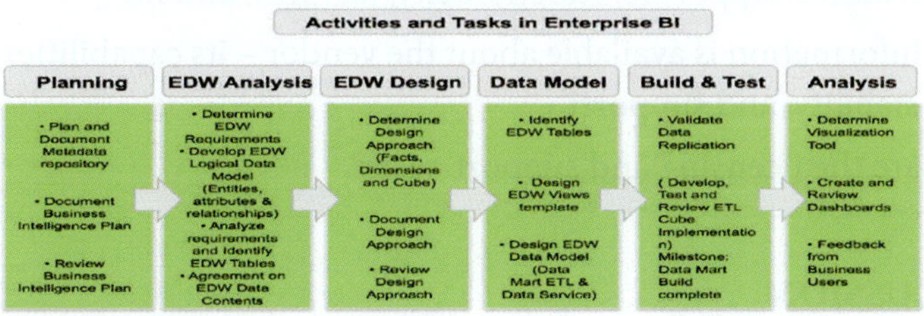

Figure 10: Main activities in Enterprise BI.

A summary of the outcomes follows

BI Project Plan

Project Requirements Definition

Data Analysis

Application prototyping

Meta Data Repository analysis

Database Design

ETL Load Design

Meta Data Repository Design

ETL Load Development

Application Development

Data Mining
Meta Data Repository design
Implementation

4.7. BI Platform and tools selection

The process of selecting BI tools to best serve the needs of the enterprise required tremendous effort. It was necessary to streamline the selection process for BI tools selection based on industry standards. Adoption of best practices helped to mitigate business risk and manage effort. The following factors were considered in the recommendation of tools:

- Is it capable of defining and classifying business, functional, and technical requirements?
- Can it categorize requirements as essential, important, and desired?
- What features support its functionality, features, and fit?
- What information is available about the vendor – its capabilities, framework, stability, and support?
- What are the licensing and support costs?

5. DISCUSSION

The passenger analytics project helped to better understand customer behavior at various locations. The results of accurate identification of customer location can help to develop heat maps and identify the concentration pattern of the passengers.

Another application could be detecting the queues and estimating service time of queues at various retail counters. The real time simulation of the project would help to understand common mobile trajectories taken by passengers and retail locations could be rented out accordingly. This would have helped CAG increase its bottom line. A slightly more advanced application is to combine physical movement and online usage to infer user preferences, interests and activities.

As the results of the exercise did not meet the expectations, a wide array of the abovementioned opportunities could be achieved if both the point of information data and the Wi-Fi data could be brought to the same unit or have a conversion that could help map the passengers with the intended location.

The solution provided has been a key deliverable to the Pricing and Commercial Strategy team. Automation of generating monthly reports not only reduced manual effort but increased accessibility to non-users as well. Since the whole process was automated, productivity has increased and human error reduced. The logic could be replicated to new POS BI. In addition, it helped business evaluate and analyze new insights that are more accessible and easy to interact with when making strategic and tactical decisions.

A key result that was achieved with this research work was that end-users are more aware of the industry best practices and standards that are used. Moreover, the research work has helped in understanding the factors and underlying architecture to design an effective BI strategy. Though CAG understands and has effective know-how of Business Intelligence and reporting, employing the Enterprise Business Intelligence Strategy helped the company become more aware of tools, technologies and challenges. As the BI environment matures, so will the formal documentation and depth of details identified in the BI strategy.

6. CONCLUSIONS AND FURTHER WORK

This project lends itself to further data analytics work. Mapping passengers and users of the airport can reveal deeper insights about their behavior. The integration of different data sets can help attribute sales behavior effectively. Lastly, understanding the challenges and best practices in adopting the Enterprise BI Strategy can help CAG develop deeper insights that are not possible otherwise.

REFERENCES

1. http://research.microsoft.com/pubs/204092/msr-tr-2013-107.pdf
2. http://opusresearch.net/wordpress/pdfreports/OpusIndoorReport_24_Jan2014.pdf
3. https://msdn.microsoft.com/en-us/library/ms137786.aspx
4. http://courses.cs.washington.edu/courses/cse590q/04au/papers/Chaudhuri03.pdf

5. http://www.loria.fr/~ssidhom/UE909R/1_BI_strategy.pdf

6. Airport passenger terminal planning and design Vol1: Guidebook

7. http://d2zmdbbm9feqrf.cloudfront.net/2013/eur/pdf/CCSEWN-1236.pdf

8. http://www.ip2location.com.

9. https://www.maxmind.com/en/home

10. http://www.quova.com.

11. Padmanabhan, VN and L Subramanian (2001). An investigation of geographic mapping techniques for Internet hosts. In *ACM SIGCOMM 2001*. San Diego, CA.

12. Wong, B, I Stoyanov and EG Sirer (2007). Octant: A comprehensive framework for the geo localization of Internet hosts. In *NSDI 2007: Fourth Usenix Symposium on Networked Systems Design and Implementation*. Camdbridge, MA.

13. Varshavsky, A E de Lara, A LaMarca, J Hightower and V Otsason (2007). Gsm indoor localization. *Pervasive and Mobile Computing Journal (PMC)*, 3(6), 698–720.

14. Zhang, B, J Teng, J Zhu, X Li, D Xuan and YF Zheng (2012). EV-Loc: integrating electronic and visual signals for accurate localization. In *ACM Mobihoc*, Jun 2012

15. Physical Analytics: A New Frontier for (Indoor) Location Research

16. Data Cleaning: Problems and Current Approaches

17. http://db.cs.berkeley.edu/jmh/papers/cleaning-unece.pdf

18. Mobile Trajectory-Based Advertising: Evidence from A Large-Scale Randomized Field Experiment Anindya Ghose, Beibei Li, Siyuan Liu

19. http://db.cs.berkeley.edu/jmh/papers/cleaning-unece.pdf

20. Book by: Business Intelligence Road Map by Larissa Terpeluk Moss, S Atre

21. https://jackiemroberts.wordpress.com/2015/05/29/why-to-enter-into-data-governance-and-data-cleansing-project/

22. Big Data Analytics Roadmap, Douglas Moore, Principal Consultant

CHAPTER 23

Profiling of Train Station Staff to Improve Customer Experience

ONG Pei Sin

ABSTRACT

Acknowledging the importance of using data to provide information and insights to their rail business, the Trains Business Unit wanted to build a dashboard that would provide information needed to inform critical decision-making.

As the station staff are the very first point-of-contact with SMRT Corporation Ltd's customers, the dashboard needed to offer insights supported by concrete figures on how station staff could improve the operations on the ground.

The objectives of this project were (1) to enable almost real-time monitoring of staff-performance, (2) to equip managers with performance information to reward staff or take pre-emptive actions, (3) to improve decision-making through analysis-driven insights, (4) to increase efficiency with work automation and (5) to pinpoint areas for improvement of work processes.

1. INTRODUCTION

SMRT Corporation Ltd (SMRT) is a leading multi-modal public transport operator in Singapore. The company's core business involves offering integrated island-wide transport services with a broad network of public transportation options such as trains, buses and taxis connecting commuters to their destinations seamlessly. Strategically, the company invests heavily in diversified portfolios relating to the transportation industry as well. Such efforts are fundamentally focused on the rental of commercial and retail amenities conveniently located within its premises and properties (Xchanges, MRT Stations, Bus Interchanges and Kallang Wave Mall), advertising related ventures, operations and maintenance services, project management, engineering consultancy and overseas rail expertise marketing.

Based on employee feedback gathered after the two major rail disruptions in December 2011, SMRT's President and Group Chief Executive Officer, Mr Desmond Kuek Bak Chye, set out five strategic thrusts to guide his company to be more efficient and streamlined (Tan, 2013). The five strategic thrusts are: Operational Performance, Customer Experience, Workforce Health, Organisational Excellence and Sustainable Growth.

In line with the second strategic thrust – Customer Experience and SMRT's dedication in delivering exemplary service to the commuters, SMRT partnered with Disney Institute and NTUC LearningHub to develop a Service Excellence Framework that bonds all 8,000 SMRT employees from across the ranks with a Common Purpose and four core Service Standards (SMRT Corporation Ltd, 2013). The collaboration aims to build a culture of service excellence to internal and external customers.

Since 2014, SMRT employees go through specially tailored Workforce Skills Qualification (WSQ) certified training to inspire them to "build trust and bring on smiles every day, and in everyone who journeys with us" (SMRT Corporation Ltd, 2015). They are also equipped with knowledge on the four core Service Standards ordered in terms of importance: Safety, Reliability, Care and Comfort.

According to SMRT's Annual Report published in 2015, approximately 80 per cent of SMRT employees have completed the WSQ course and embarked on their journey to Service Excellence. This includes frontline station staff who act as SMRT's ambassadors in engaging and providing customers with first-hand positive travel experience.

2. PROBLEM STATEMENT

Before the initiation of this project, the Trains Business Unit did not own a dashboard to guide them in making informed decisions. Understanding the importance of using data to make discoveries about their business, they wanted to design a dashboard to provide information needed to make critical decisions. As station staff are the very first point of contact with the organization's customers, the dashboard would supply insights backed by concrete figures on how station staff could impact the operations on the ground.

There were several objectives that the Business Unit wanted to meet with the creation of a new dashboard. These were:

1) to enable management to gain instant access to staff performance through a dashboard. As soon as data is entered into the system, the management or any relevant personnel would see the latest performance of any station staff, allowing almost real-time monitoring of staff performance.
2) to equip management with consolidated information about staff performance to inform decisions to reward or to take preemptive actions. Staff with exceptional performance can be recognized for their hard work and supervisors would have ample time to take preemptive actions such as sending under-performing ground staff for re-training or counselling.
3) to enable management, supervisors or recruiters to make informed decisions through data explorations, such as re-scheduling or re-grouping teams to boost ground staff morale or making informed decisions prior to hiring with the added knowledge-based on data.
4) to enable automation for preparation of data during appraisal and relief workload for other more critical functions.
5) to pinpoint areas for improvement to enhance work processes and increase efficiency.

The subjects of this research were working at the North-South and East-West Line (NSEWL) in 2014. Station staff follow a hierarchy of Service Operations Manager (SOM), followed by Station Manager (SM) and Assistant Station Manager (ASM). There are altogether 54 stations along the North-South East-West Line corridor and these stations are grouped into 16 zones or areas. Stations in a zone are consecutively next to each other along the train line. To illustrate, Admiralty, Sembawang, Yishun and Khatib are in Zone three (see Figure 1). Service Operations Managers oversee the zones and there are typically three to four stations under their supervision. Station Mangers and Assistant Station Managers are positioned at a particular station and may be rotated every three to four months when the need arises. Both Station Mangers and Assistant Station Managers are responsible for the daily operation of all facilities, equipment and services in a station in accordance with the rules, procedures and guidelines, as well as ensuring high standards of customer service extended to passengers utilizing SMRT's services for their journey. The difference between the two positions is the focus of their duty: Assistant Station Managers are expected to put more attention on providing exceptional service to passengers passing through the train lines, while Station Managers concentrate more on the operational aspect of their duty. In addition to that, Station Managers are required to supervise their subordinates and guide them to handle their tasks well and eventually progressing to the next grade (SMRT Corporation Ltd, n.d.).

3. STATE OF THE ART

Human Resource Analytics is not a new concept in the world of Business Analytics. In fact it has emerged and evolved over the past decade. Just at the end of the last decade, a Google search for the term produced over 1.5 million results (Levenson, 2010); Five years later, a Google search for the same term supplied 10 times as many results more than the last decade, over 15.2 million results. Though there has been an increase in the amount of literature, the proportion of companies not actively using Human Resource Analytics capabilities is more than half based on a survey by Deloitte (Bennett and Collins, 2015). However, it is noteworthy that another study by Harvard Business Review *Connecting Workforce Analytics to Better Business Results* (2013) concluded that "companies that are very effective at leveraging their workforce are more than three times as likely to say they're beating their competition on customer satisfaction, quality, and productivity.

Put simply, Human Resource Analytics enables organizations to make good use of the existing wealth of employee data to enhance workforce health and strive for operational excellence. As Mondore *et al.* (2011)

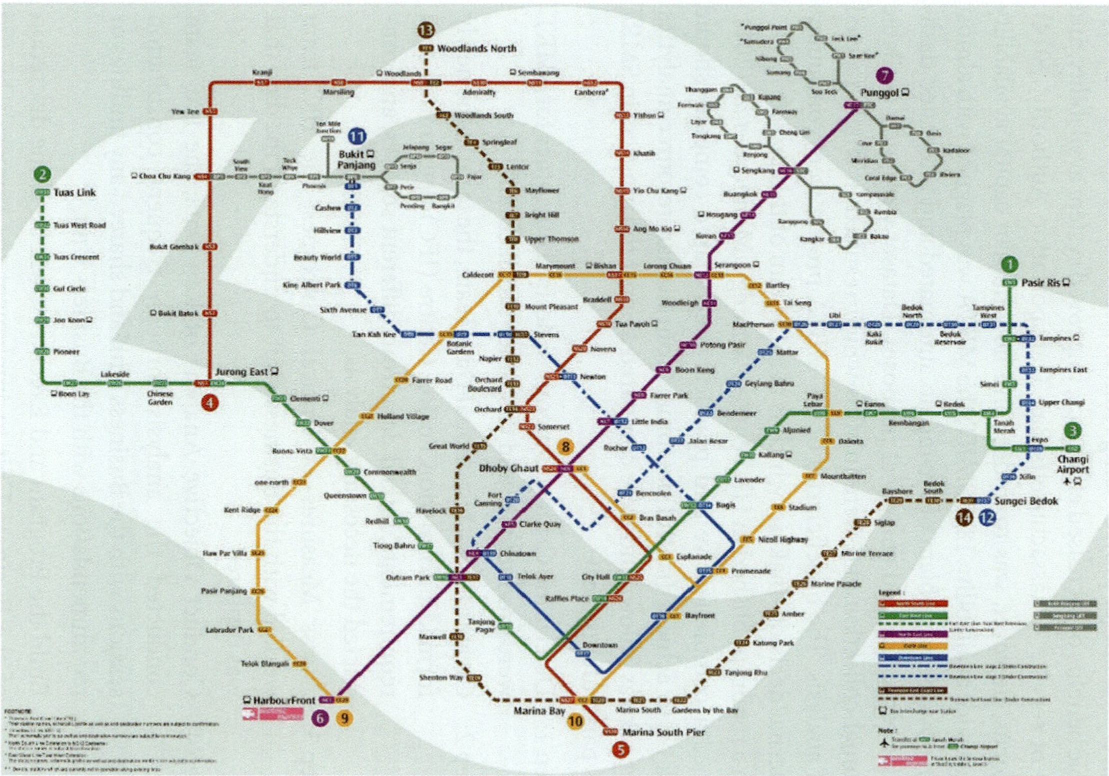

Figure 1: Singapore's Train System Map [Online image]. (n.d). Retrieved from http://www.lta.gov.sg/content/ltaweb/en/public-transport/mrt-and-lrt-trains/train-system-map.html

pointed out, "correlating people data and business data is definitely a step in the right direction" towards human resource analytics.

In 2014, the Massachusetts Bay Transportation Authority (MBTA) embarked on a similar project using Human Resource Analytics to deliver "tangible benefits of increased efficiency, improved system availability, and quality of service" (Massachusetts Bay Transportation Authority, 2014). Their focus, however, was to understand how human capital availability affects service availability. Like SMRT, the MBTA was plagued with almost the same business problem of having no automated and integrated dashboard for reporting and analytical purposes. Dataset were only available via manual collection and were in silos which resulted in single-faceted type of analysis. The beneficiaries of the MBTA project were commuters and internal decision-makers, which is also the aim of this project.

In a report published in HR People + Strategy, Mondore *et al.* (2011) described a comprehensive and practical road map a company should embark on to achieve fruitful outcomes from human resource analytics. The steps are as follows and were compared against the progress in SMRT for this particular project.

Step 1: Determine Critical Outcomes; desired outcomes for SMRT were productivity and customer satisfaction.

Step 2: Create a Cross-Functional Data Team; the team at the newly formed Information Fusion Centre (IFC) determined data requirements, linked data from different sources, and conducted the necessary analysis.

Step 3: Assess Measures of Critical Outcomes; the IFC team worked with the Business Unit to understand the data that was captured.

Step 4: Conduct Objective Analysis of Key Data; the IFC team conducted the analysis through frequent consultation sessions with the Business Unit and shareed any findings or recommendations with the Business Unit.

Step 5: Build the Program and Execute; it will be at the discretion of the Business Unit to implement the proposals by the IFC team.

Step 6: Measure and Adjust/Re-prioritize; should the suggestions by the IFC team be executed, the team would work with the Business Unit to assess the progress or results.

The Oracle White Paper (Martin, 2011) suggested several subject areas to explore and some of these ideas were expanded upon when developing the dashboard for SMRT. Workforce Profile "provides a starting place for analysis of headcount and headcount movement trends" and showcases other demographic trends, Human Resource Performance highlights strength and weakness of staff, while Recruiting and Retention optimizes candidate sourcing and bring to attention the group of employees to retain.

Visualizations used to present information on these subject areas must be appropriate to convey the right message. In the world of big data, one must be selective about what to include in the dashboard so that it fulfills a purpose and "is accessible to (its intended) audience and tells a holistic story" (Tableau Software, n.d.). Two other guides were used during the process of creating the dashboard - one on the best practice for selecting the right charts to transform data into effective visualizations (Hardin, Hom, Perez, and Williams, n.d.) and the other, a user guide (SAS Institute Inc, 2014) for the selected software.

4. SOLUTION: DESCRIPTION OF APPROACH

4.1. Proposed software

The proposed software utilized to solve the business problem presented by the Trains Business Unit was SAS® Visual Analytics. Before the introduction of a visualization tool such as SAS® Visual Analytics, Business Units in SMRT presented information either in Excel or PowerPoint formats. In some cases, the dashboards provided only simple charts with limited analytical capabilities. The IFC team in SMRT chose the SAS® Visual Analytics for its enhanced capabilities as a visualization tool over the Excel tool (see Table 1).

With the SAS® Visual Analytics installed in SMRT, Business Units were encouraged to utilize the tool for dashboarding purposes with added analytics function. The IFC team partners encouraged Business Units to develop a prototype through a series of discussions to understand their business requirements. Once the Business Units approved the base template, they took ownership of the dashboard to make further improvements and modifications to suit any future needs. Selected representatives from the Business Units undertook the entire process of building the dashboard to give them the necessary knowledge to make any further tweaks to the Business Unit specific dashboard.

Table 1: Comparison between Excel and SAS® Visual Analytics

	Excel	SAS® Visual Analytics
1. Security	No control over unauthorised access	Secured with user name and password log-in
2. Speed of Usage	Susceptible to lags with increased data points	Faster performance with in-memory technology
3. Data Transfer	Manual	Automated process for better efficiency and reduce risk of human errors
4. Access	Via email	Via web browsers (PC / Laptop) Via mobile app on tablets
5. Maintenance / Modification	Requires advanced knowledge in Excel	Drag & Drop Easy knowledge transfer
6. Analytical Capabilities	Limited	Decision Tree, Forecasting, Network Analysis, Text mining, Sentiment Analysis
7. No. of Users	Single user	Multiple users

To date, the Business Units that have participated in this project and actively use the tools are Trains, Buses, Taxis, Finance, Human Resource and Commercial.

4.2. Scorecard

The assessment of the performance of station staff is based on a scorecard devised by the Trains Business Unit. It accurately measures the performance of train station staff based on merit and focuses on six main areas of concern (labelled as main category): Service Excellence, Enforcement, Productivity, Discipline, Operation Excellence and Awards & Recognition. Each main category branches out to several subcategories (category elements) for example, Service Excellence contains three category elements – Compliments, Valid Complaints and Invalid Complaints. There are 31 category elements in total for Assistant Station Managers and 32 category elements for Station Managers.

The common category elements are Compliments, Valid Complaints, Invalid Complaints, NOO, EZCRAF, PFE, MC, Lateness, Report Sick No MC, Negative e-Logcard, Letter of Advice/Restriction of Panel Clinic, Verbal Warning, Written Warning, Final Written Warning, Suspension, AFC Non-Compliance, Audit Report, Non-Compliance, Incident Management, Positive e-logcard, Letter of Appreciation, Letter of Commendation, SMRTnI CEO Excellence Award, Service Achiever,

Best ASM/SM, EXSA Silver, EXSA Gold, Transport Gold, EXSA Star, LTA Excellence Award and National Champion, while the performance of Senior Managers will be assessed with one more added category element – Light Duty (see Table 2).

Table 2: Description of the Categories in the Scorecard

Main Category	Category Elements	Description
Service Excellence	Compliments	Feedback from external parties
	Valid Complaints	
	Invalid Complaints	
Enforcement	NOO	Notification of Offence issued to passengers for infringement of Rapid Transit Systems (RTS) regulations
	EZCRAF	
	PFE	
Productivity	MC	Sick leave certified by Panel Clinics
	Light Duty	Light duty assignments
	Lateness	Punctuality at work
	Report Sick No MC	Absence from duty without producing valid Medical Certificate
Discipline	Negative e-Logcard	Different levels of disciplinary actions taken for misconduct that impede smooth operations or compromise safety and security
	Letter of Advice/Restriction of Panel Clinic	
	Verbal Warning	
	Written Warning	
	Final Written Warning	
	Suspension	
Operation Excellence	AFC Non-Compliance	Non compliance of procedures during accounting of fare collection
	Audit Report	Audit findings for inappropriate procedures
	Non-Compliance	Non compliance not capture under Audit Report
	Incident Management	Assistance in restoration of normal service operations quickly following an incident to minimize impact
Awards and Recognition	Positive e-logcard	Extra duties for special circumstances
	Letter of Appreciation	Internal awards
	Letter of Commendation	
	SMRTnl CEO Excellence Award	
	Service Achiever	
	Best ASM/SM	
	EXSA Silver	External awards
	EXSA Gold	
	Transport Gold	
	EXSA Star	
	LTA Excellence Award	
	National Champion	

For every member of staff, a point is given based on the frequency or number of records for each category element. There may be a cap to the maximum number of points awarded for some main categories such as Awards & Recognition. The final score is computed by aggregating the points given for each category element.

Depending on the emphasis for the year, there may be changes to the weightage of each main category in the scorecard. In 2014, Operation Excellence was the emphasis with the highest percentage assigned among all the main categories.

4.3. Data

As the primary data provider, the Trains Business Unit supplied several datasets: a master file with nearly 7,000 entries of incidents pertaining to each Category element, a station score file and a bonus point file.

The master file contains information such as the employee number, designation, name, zone, station, incident date, category element, main category, count number and description/case number. These details were manually entered by the Service Operations Manager on a weekly or monthly basis and consolidated at the headquarters level.

The station score file contains a score calculated for each station based on several factors such as throughput passing the station (the average daily number of tap in and out), architecture of stations (interchange/interlocking stations are given extra to make up for the low throughput), additional workload at stations etc. The bonus point file contains bonus points awarded to selected staff based on the discretion of the Service Operations Manager.

After initial cleaning of the data, it was found that some of the personal particular fields such as name and station were inconsistent (as rotation may happen every three to four months), therefore Human Resource data was requested to solve this problem of inconsistency. Furthermore, more information from the Human Resource department was needed to enrich the existing database for a more comprehensive analysis. The Human Resource file contains almost 600 records of data necessary to replace the inconsistent information in the master file and includes additional columns such as age, gender, date of employment and postal code.

Also, to facilitate the Business Unit in conducting its half yearly assessment exercise, the inconsistent date formats were standardized. The Business Unit was also briefed on the importance of consistent formating during data collection to facilitate the automation of the work.

4.4. Problems encountered and solutions applied

As the master file only contains records of incidents that happened over the year, this naturally means that there is often no record pertaining to a particular category element for many employees. For example, if the raw data did not have any record for valid complaints for a particular individual, it is registered as a missing value. However, the dashboarding tool was unable to detect missing values as zero. Using the same example, an individual with a missing value for valid complaints will generate a missing score. Intuitively, the employee that did not receive any valid complaints should be rewarded with a positive high score for that component instead of a missing score.

Attempts were made to reflect missing values as zeros with formulas. However the dashboarding tool was unable to register that. To circumvent that, pseudo data points for each employee and the corresponding 32 measures were created as an interim solution. However, this may not be the best method longer term.

The problem was resolved by creating a new table with the Structure Query Language (SQL) tool provided by SAS® Visual Analytics. Using SQL, the multiple relational databases were joined using the employee number as the primary key and the Human Resource data assigned as the main dataset (see Figure 2). This was followed by grouping together records with the same category elements for each staff and the corresponding aggregation of count number of records for each category element for example, each employee may have multiple records on compliments, MC days or audit findings, these records were summed up and presented with employee number in the first column and column headings (compliments, MC or audit) and count numbers in subsequent columns. The result was a table with an entry created for every member of staff on the Human Resource record, including missing data recorded as zero.

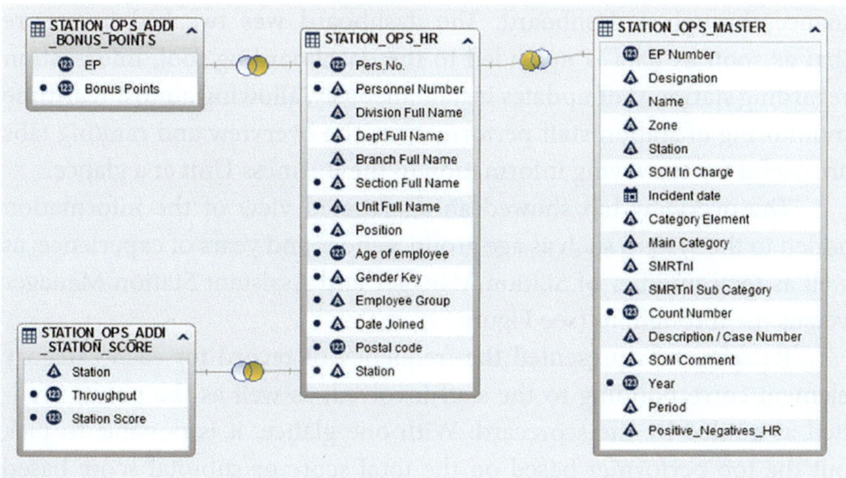

Figure 2: First query used to join the multiple relational databases.

The second challenge was having a subset of audit records in the master file not tagged to any employee. These records needed to be assigned to every member of station staff as everyone in the station is responsible for any audit findings deemed inappropriate from the proper procedures.

To solve the second problem, another SQL query was created by linking the first query output with the audit records without employee number by station. Similar to the first query, the audit records were summed up and assigned to every staff member in the particular station, resulting in an additional column documenting total number of unaccounted audit findings tagged to each employee in the final table output. The reason why this was not done in the first query itself was because the aggregation of audit records for each station would be augmented by the number of records each staff member has.

5. DISCUSSION

The creation of the dashboard addressed the Business Unit's immediate problem of not having an avenue to store and retrieve critical information of station staff. Several tabs or subject areas were made to achieve the objectives set out prior to the completion of the projected stated in Section 2 above (Note: Data has been masked.)

One, management was able to gain instant access to staff performance through a dashboard. The dashboard was tweaked to ensure that as soon as data is uploaded to the dashboarding tool, information regarding station staff updates instantaneously, allowing almost real-time monitoring of station staff performance. The overview and ranking tabs are useful for conveying information to the Business Unit at a glance.

The overview tab showed an aggregated view of the information added to the system such as age group, gender and years of experience, as well as total number of Station Manager and Assistant Station Manager versus the throughput (see Figure 3).

Ranking tabs presented the frequency of record for each category element corresponding to the staff involved, as well as the points credited as guided by the scorecard. With one glance, it is possible to pick out the top performer based on the total score or subtotal score based on each Main Category. During appraisal, these ranking tabs, with the ability to perform an employee name and number search, act as a tool

Figure 3: Overview tab in the dashboard.

to facilitate discussion among the supervisors. It also fulfils the second objective of giving management or supervisors enough information to reward performance or sufficient time to take necessary pre-emptive disciplinary actions. Staff with exceptional performance will be recognised or rewarded for their hard work, whereas under-performing ground staff can be encouraged through re-training or counselling.

Three, there are several tabs or components of the dashboard that enable management, supervisors or recruiters to make informed decisions through data explorations. Such information helps with re-scheduling or re-grouping teams to boost ground staff morale, reveal gaps in workforce requirements and propose alternatives or pick out traits of applicants most qualified for a specific position.

The Top 20 per cent Performer tab filters the top 20 per cent of Assistant Station Managers and Managers that performed well and their corresponding zones and stations. Since the majority of the top 20 per cent of Station Managers and Assistant Station Managers worked in the red zone, it was recommended that these top performing staff be posted to zones with higher number of poor performing staff to boost staff morale at these zones (see Figure 4). Through peer assessment, outstanding staff may be able to help encourage or guide poor performing staff to excel in their daily duties.

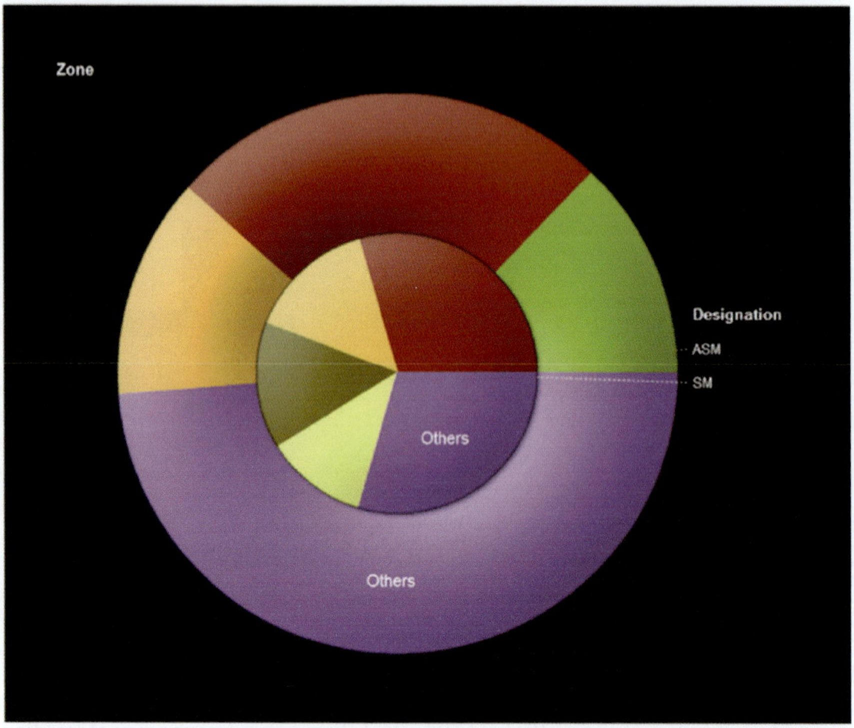

Figure 4: Top 20 per cent of staff came from the red zone.

In addition to the tabs above, there are other components of the dashboard which yield insights for the team.

A tree map was plotted with staff strength in each zone versus throughput (see Figure 5). Zones with higher throughput will be greater in size, while those with more manpower will be in blue. Intuitively, zones with higher throughput should be assigned more manpower to handle larger passenger flow, i.e bigger rectangles should be blue. It was recommended to the Business Unit that the map suggested Zone B may likely be understaffed and Zone C be overstaffed. Also it was highlighted that Zone D with the lowest number of staff has a higher throughput than Zone C but smaller staff strength to handle the workload or crowd.

The butterfly chart shows the proportion of the number of Assistant Station Managers and Station Managers with their corresponding years of experience in their posts (see Figure 6). Given the job scope, it was expected that most of the Assistant Station Managers would fall in the

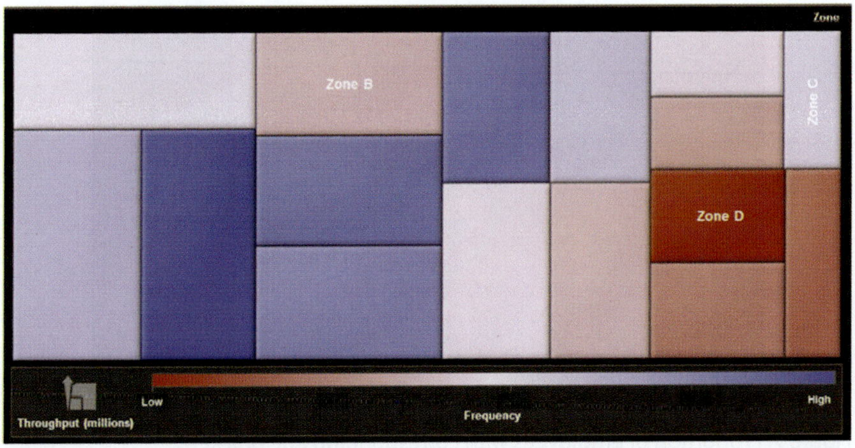

Figure 5: Tree map with staff strength versus throughput in each zone.

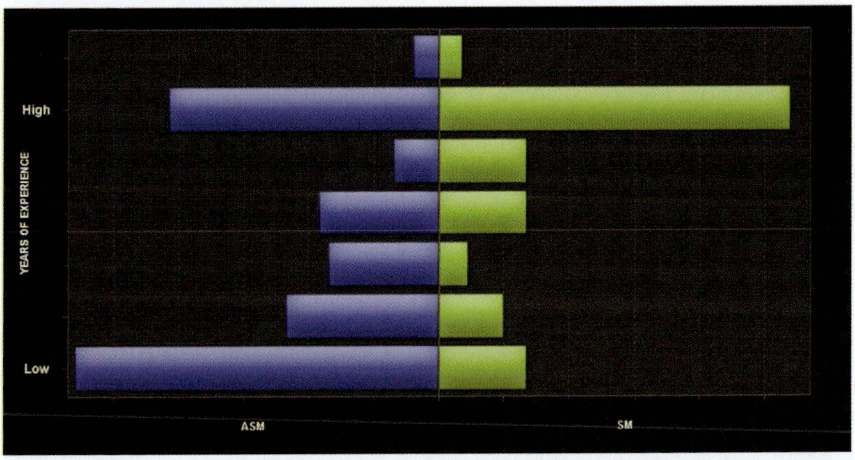

Figure 6: Proportion of employees with corresponding years of experience.

category with little experience and the Station Managers would fall in the range with many years of experience. Naturally, it was also observed that Assistant Station Managers are younger than Station Managers (see Figure 7). Station Managers have "a wealth of priceless intellectual capital" critical for the company, while Assistant Station Managers "offers innovative and creative ideas that are essential to navigate today's technologies and economic challenges" (Martin, 2011). What is interesting is that there is also high number of Assistant Station Managers that have accumulated

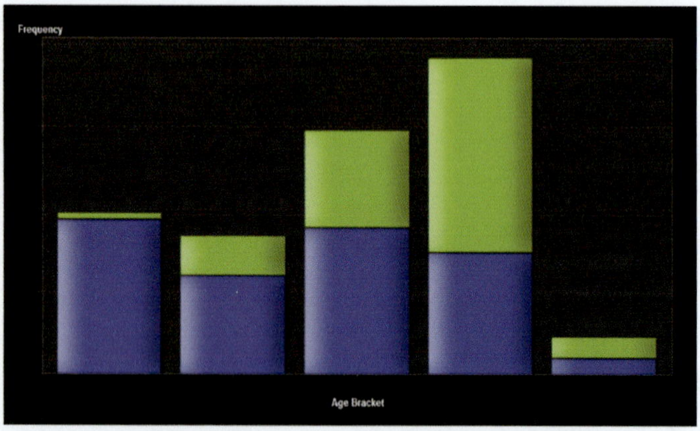

Figure 7: Proportion of employees with corresponding age bracket.

many years of experience. For the purpose of succession planning, it was suggested that the Business Unit look into grooming this group of people to take on a bigger role and responsibility.

Based on Figure 7, there is an impending need to plan ahead for replacement of older soon-to-retire employees which form a huge share of the entire population of station staff. In line with the suggestion above, there is potential in developing Assistant Station Managers with age bracket falling in Category one as these group of people would very likely be able to serve the company for a longer period of time (see Figure 8).

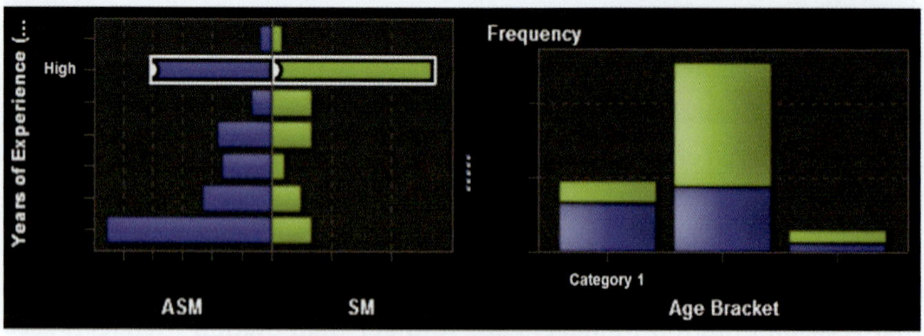

Figure 8: Filtering of staff with many years of experience by age bracket.

To determine the right employee to groom for the talent pool, it was suggested that the Business Unit refer to the improvised version of the Strategic Survey HeatMap introduced by Mondore *et al.* (2011). The scatter plot shows employees on a scatter plot based on their total score against the number of years of experience with the company, split into four quadrants by a horizontal axis showing the average performance score and vertical axis splitting those with lesser experience and the veterans (see Figure 9).

The top-left quadrant is labelled Maintain – these are the employees doing better than average with not much experience and should be maintained for future succession planning. The bottom-left quadrant is labelled Monitor – these are the employees that are not doing as well as their peers with the same experience, but should be given the opportunity to prove themselves with more time. The bottom-right quadrant is labelled Focus – these are the employees that are expected to perform with their knowledge but are under-performing. The focus should be on them as they are likely to be a valuable asset to the company with their expertise, but are not achieving their full potential. Lastly, the top-right quadrant is labelled Promote – these are the employees that are performing well according to expectations and should be considered for promotion to further build on their capabilities.

As Mondore *et al.* (2011) shared, the evidence-based advice that a company has decided to take will "result in tangible outcomes that benefit shareholders, customers and employees themselves".

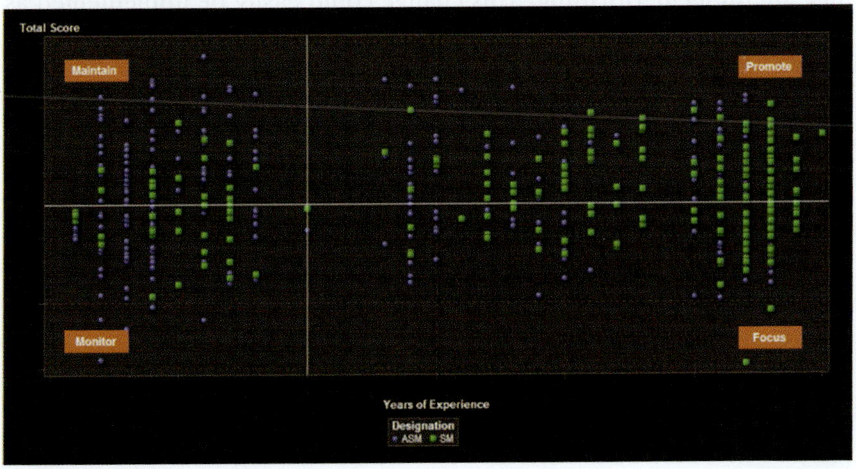

Figure 9: Scatter plot of total score against years of experience.

Through other charts used to improve the selection process, it was found that female staff generally did better in Service Excellence than their male counterparts. Also on deeper analysis, the Service Excellence scores improved with age. Younger male staff did better in terms of Service Excellence as compared to their older counterparts. Male staff only achieved marginally better scores than female staff in terms of Operation Excellence.

The fourth objective was to enable automation for the preparation of data during staff appraisals and this was achieved by taking into consideration the necessary formulae needed to formulate the scores while creating the dashboard. Raw data was requested to relieve the Business Unit of the need to manipulate the data. This reduced the number of steps required to monitor staff performance to simple data uploads, freeing-up several man-hours for other critical duties.

Five, two areas of improvement were identified to enhance work processes and increase efficiency – consistency during data collection and the frequency of performance review. Inconsistent inputs resulted in errors when the data was uploaded onto the dashboarding tool. To reduce the amount of work needed to clean the consolidated data, it was recommended that the data format be fixed during the collation process. Formal employee appraisals were performed once a year and it was proposed that this be increased to twice a year to allow staff ample time to improve if they are under-performing. This change could easily be implemented as the system was built to automatically reflect half-year scores.

6. CONCLUSIONS AND FURTHER WORK

The project kicked off an essential step in building a performance monitoring system for the Trains Business Unit to store and retrieve important information about its staff. It achieved all the objectives set out in the introduction for the first phase. With the core system in place, further work can easily be developed. Subsequently, historical data and new data points can be appended to the system "to understand the past and present to predict the future" (Mondore *et al.*, 2011).

To make the system more robust, there are plans to include more Human Resource data. Information such as training records, shift work records, remuneration, educational level, approved headcount and overtime hours that could help the Business Unit understand its workforce better. Future phases may also include assistance to improve data collection methods so that data format can be fixed during the collation process, or be extended to include Circle Line staff as well.

Finally, once the system has stabilized, it is also recommended that the data be applied to deeper analysis for other potential business problems. As aptly described by Bennett and Collins (2015), "do not let the perfect be the enemy of the good; it is better to do analytics based on less-than-perfect data than to do no analytics whatsoever."

REFERENCES

1. Tan, C (2013, February 17). SMRT chief exec: Man on a mission to change things. *AsiaOne*. Retrieved from http://transport.asiaone.com/news/transport/story/smrt-chief-exec-man-mission-change-things

2. SMRT Corporation Ltd. (2013, December 16). *A Review of 2013 and the Progress We Have Made - Customer Experience* [Press release]. Retrieved from http://www.mynewsdesk.com/sg/smrt/pressreleases/a-review-of-2013-and-the-progress-we-have-made-customer-experience-941473

3. SMRT Corporation Ltd. (2015). SMRT Corporation Ltd Annual Report 2015 – Keeping Singapore Moving. Retrieved from http://www.smrt.com.sg/Portals/0/Announcement/2015/Annual%20Report%202015.pdf

4. SMRT Corporation Ltd. (n.d.). *Electronic references*. Retrieved from http://www.smrt.com.sg

5. Singapore's Train System Map [Online image]. (n.d). Retrieved from http://www.lta.gov.sg/content/ltaweb/en/public-transport/mrt-and-lrt-trains/train-system-map.html

6. Levenson, A (2010, September 15). Using Targeted Analytics to Improve Talent Decisions. Retrieved from http://ceo.usc.edu/pdf/G11-03.pdf

7. Bennett, C and L Collins (2015). HR and people analytics: Stuck in neutral. Retrieved from http://dupress.com/articles/people-and-hr-analytics-human-capital-trends-2015/

8. Connecting Workforce Analytics to Better Business Results. (2013). *Harvard Business Review*. Retrieved from https://hbr.org/resources/pdfs/comm/sumtotal/hbr-sumtotal-report-aug.pdf

9. Mondore, S, S Douthitt and M Carson (2011). Maximizing the Impact and Effectiveness of HR Analytics to Drive Business Outcomes. Retrieved from http://c.ymcdn.com/sites/hrps.site-ym.com/resource/resmgr/p_s_article_preview/ps_34.2_hranalytics.pdf

10. Massachusetts Bay Transportation Authority (2014). Data-Driven Decision Making for Improving Public Transit: How A 360' Employee View Leads to a Better Commute for Bostonians. Retrieved from http://www.nascio.org/awards/nominations2015/2015/2015MA8-Massachusetts_Open%20Government%20and%20Data,%20Information%20and%20Knowledge%20Management%20_MBTA360_6.1.2015.pdf

11. Martin, L (2011, September). HR Analytics: Driving Return on Human Capital Investment [White paper]. Retrieved from http://www.oracle.com/us/solutions/ent-performance-bi/045039.pdf

12. Tableau Software. (n.d.) Visual Analysis Best Practices: A Guidebook. Retrieved from http://www.tableau.com/

13. Hardin, M, D Hom, R Perez and P Williams (n.d.). Which chart or graph is right for you? Retrieved from http://www.tableau.com/

14. SAS Institute Inc. (2014, October). SAS® Visual Analytics 7.1: User's Guide. Retrieved from http://support.sas.com/documentation/cdl/en/vaug/67500/PDF/default/vaug

CHAPTER 24

Data Mapping and Financial Dashboards

WONG Ai Wen

ABSTRACT

This project comprised two main activities. First, sales data under two different hierarchies had to be integrated from two different silos. Second, after successful integration of the data, a single financial dashboard was created and refined to showcase net trade sales data under these two hierarchies. The dashboard was shared with global managers at the end of every month. The aim was to produce useful, meaningful and practical dashboards for management decisions.

1. INTRODUCTION

Upon acquisition of another company, it is beneficial for the parent company to integrate data from the newly acquired one into the parent company's data system. However, this takes time if monthly financial reports are required to be published punctually.

An integrated financial dashboard was required to include data from the child company in order to showcase multiple views of product category hierarchy in use by both companies. To achieve a solution for the above, the work performed was two-fold:

- Integrating data from two silos after acquisition
- Refining existing financial dashboards

2. PROBLEM STATEMENT

The company grows both organically and through acquisitions - with a presence in different parts of the world. This results in a fragmentation that perpetrates inefficiency; for example, the decentralization of data poses a challenge to integrate and extract data from relevant fields of interest. This problem is further amplified when the parent company aims to integrate data from a newly acquired company.

For financial reporting, schedules and timelines of publication must be met. Hence extraction of sales data from two different systems followed by manual mapping of the multiple product hierarchies has to be done, until data integration is completed at the backend. In the interim, this manual mapping needs to be as comprehensive as possible.

In line with the company's mandate to standardize all financial reports, a dedicated team within a Centre of Excellence (COE) had to create, maintain, and refine financial dashboards for different business users. The main purpose of the dashboards was to provide a clear and meaningful overview of the monthly financial and sales situations in various countries, using the net trade sales data.

The task was to refine existing dashboards, particularly the financial dashboards for net trade sales across Asia Pacific countries which the company had a stake in. The challenge lay in transfering multiple views into a single integrated dashboard for different managers. Using different software tools such as Tableau provided purposeful and meaningful data delivery.

Upon acquisition of Company B, the data resided in two silos – one in the system of Company A, and the other in a totally different system of Company B. These two sources of data follow different reporting hierarchies causing problems in creating standardized financial reports for the company.

An example of double product hierarchies is shown in the diagram

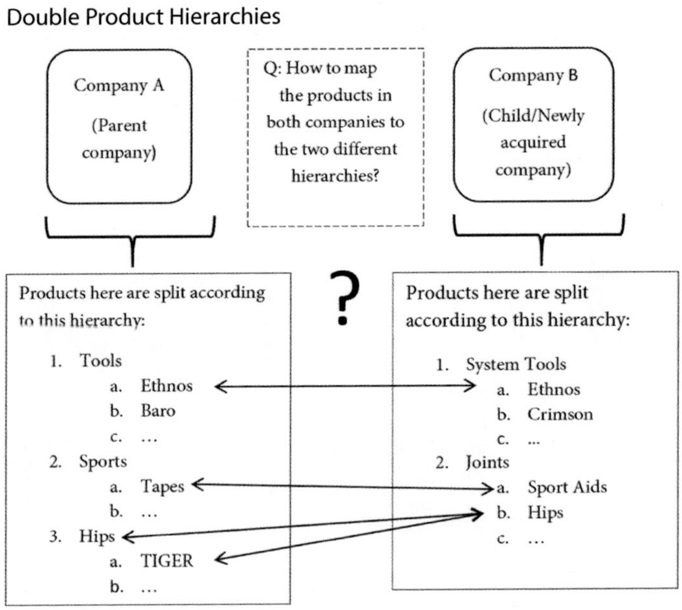

This problem was one of data integration, and much research has been done in this field of database systems management (DBMS), especially on acquired companies. Back-end resolution is dense but not difficult and Company A needed to build a globally integrated DBMS. However, regardless of when backend integration happened, the reporting team was required to produce financial reports at the end of each month.

Without the technological back-end in place, an automated process to quickly and accurately identify and map the product codes to both the hierarchies was needed, made more pressing by the fact that the monthly reports were distributed globally to all finance teams, including the Chief Financial Officer. This automated process was built from scratch and involved both text and numerical analytics.

The financial dashboards currently sent by the CoE team are plain figures in tables, without much in the way of supporting graphics. The task was to incorporate graphics (to provide a more holistic presentation) into the dashboards from the net trade sales data globally, to aid management decisions. This is illustrated in Figure 1 and Figure 2.

Business Units	Jan Sales (USD, 'MM)	Feb Sales (USD, 'MM)	...
Tools	10	12	
➢ *Ethnos*	*4*	*6*	
➢ ...	*6*	*6*	
Sports	21	22	
➢ *Tapes*	*15*	*15*	
➢ ...	*6*	*7*	
Hips	5	5	
➢ *TIGER*	*3*	*3*	
➢ ...	*2*	*2*	

Figure 1: Current dashboard.

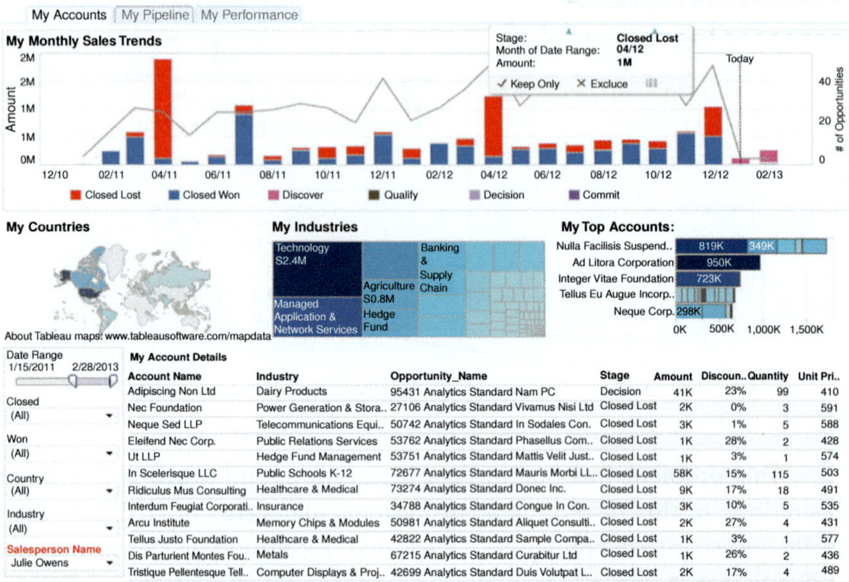

Figure 2: Improved / refined dashboard.

Extracted from Tableau – Examples

http://www.tableau.com/sites/default/files/blog/accounts-dashboard.png

3. STATE OF THE ART

According to Kimball, [1] data integration is a universal concern and most data warehouse projects strive to deliver integrated data that supports decision makers throughout the organization. However, this takes an extremely long time given the amounts of data produced by a giant in the industry. If data integration is rushed and if data-warehouse or business insights teams fail to focus on integration and consistency, their warehouse deliverables will merely result in easier, faster access to inconsistent data that, while addressing short-term needs, is not the long-term solution.

Back-end solutions were not possible immediately due to the size of the data from all the global subsidiaries of the parent company, and the hierarchy mapping process required manual intervention until the back-end solutions were settled.

In a business environment, data visualization can have two broad goals, which may be related: explanatory and exploratory. Visuals that are meant to direct the viewer along a defined path are explanatory in nature. The bulk of business dashboards in day-to-day scenarios fall in this category.[2]

Explanatory visualization starts with a question in mind e.g. “Which country has the highest value?” The answer is found in the visuals. This type of visualization is used in many scenarios for the following tasks:

- answer a question e.g. How much sales in the last quarter?
- support a decision e.g. the need to stock more football jerseys as these were sold out on most days the week before.
- communicate information e.g. Revenue is on track for this quarter.
- increase efficiency e.g. ‘Technical specifications’ should be given more profile as this is the most viewed section in the product page.

Exploratory visualization offers many dimensions to a data set, or compares multiple data sets with each other. The first step was to familiarize ourselves with the visualization, then identify an area of interest. Visuals were explored; questions asked, and solutions to those questions found for example ‘Which country’s population holds the best positive sentiments towards this product?’ The ‘Products’ section was then explored for the answer. The other areas of the visualization could be explored subsequently.

Many insights were found from a single visualization and further investigations to gain understanding rather than make a specific decision, were undertaken. It was important to balance explanatory and exploratory visualization when viewing the financial dashboard, moving away from simple numerical and table dashboards.

Research shoes that when designing the dashboards, pre-attentive attributes used by our working memory should be incorporated.[3] Colin Ware, Director of the Data Visualization Research Lab at the University of New Hampshire, terms the basic building blocks of the visualization process as ‘Pre-attentive attributes’ - attributes that immediately catch our eye when looking at visualization. They can be perceived in less than 10 milliseconds, even before making a conscious effort to notice them. Here's a list of the pre-attentive attributes:

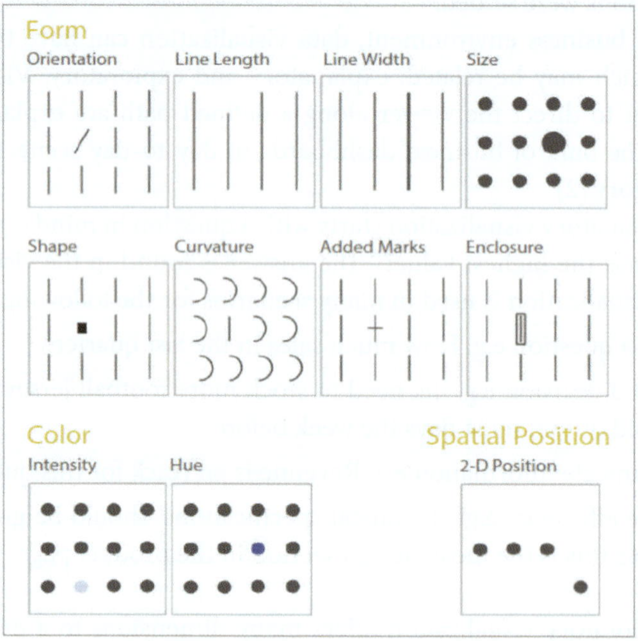

Of these, only position, and length can used to perceive quantitative data with precision. The other attributes are useful for perceiving other types of data such as categorical or relational data. For example, both the pie chart and the bar chart in Figure 4 below show the same data. But from the pie chart, one cannot easily tell with accuracy which is the biggest proportion. That is more clearly visible in the bar chart as it calls on the pre-attentive attribute of length.

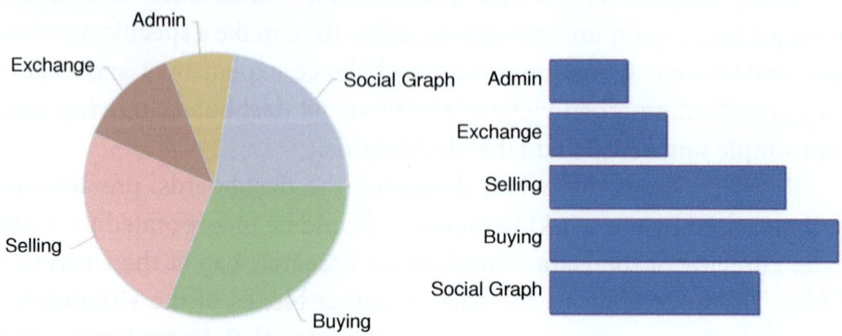

Figure 4: An example of pre-attentive attributes.

These pre-attentive attributes were incorporated into the dashboard, with the purpose of aiding management in asking the relevant questions and more importantly, finding the answers to those exact questions from the visualization dashboards that will be rolled out on a monthly basis to global managers.

4. SOLUTION

4.1. Description of approach

The tables below are visual examples of the sales data from two different sources that required integration. The sales numbers are immaterial in this example.

Data residing in system of Company A:

Majors	Jan	Feb	Mar	...
Sports	$1000	$1500	$80	...
Tools	$180	$200	$159	...
Hands	$250	$300	$400	...
Knees	$0	$80	$0	
Hips	$1000	$800	$1200	...
Neuro	$400	$300	$200	...
...	...	...	...	...

Data residing in system of Company B:

Majors	Jan	Feb	Mar	...
Sports	$1000	$1500	$80	...
System Tools	$180	$200	$159	...
Joints	$110	$980	$1300	...
Knees	$0	$80	$0	
Hips	$1000	$800	$1200	...
Others	$100	$100	$100	...
Spine	$400	$300	$200	...
...	...	...	...	...

The two tables above show an example analogous to the situation faced by Company A — the presence of two different product hierarchies, which are, by mandate of the acquisition, required to be integrated. The monthly report needed to show the sales of both companies A and B with a toggle between views of these two hierarchies. Essentially, this was a mapping problem involving analytics.

The first step to solving this problem was to obtain sales figures and the accompanying description for all products at the Stock Keeping Unit (SKU) level, which came up to approximately 37,000 distinct SKUs. Next, the SKUs that were present in both systems were filtered out as they had two product hierarchies mapped to them. Then the remaining SKUs that lacked either of the product hierarchies were mapped.

As with all analytics work, experimentation and exploratory data analysis were performed. Using the publicly available freeware R programming language, a quick check was performed to identify any patterns between the SKU descriptions and the categories these products fitted.under each of the hierarchies. It became evident that there seemed

SKU	Description	Hierarchy 1		Hierarchy 2	
		Major 1	Minor 1	Major 2	Minor 2
12345	CAVE Tape 1 m*50 mm	Sports	Tapes	Joints	Sport Aids
342.000.1	Ethno Drill – Handheld 200 g	Tools	Ethno	–	–
342.000.5	Ethno Bolt – Silver	–	–	System Tools	Ethno
678-CX	CAVE –2 m*50 mm	Sports	Tapes	–	–
789.013	Strips – CAVE Tape 10 mm*20 cm	–	–	Joints	Sport Aids
246-CN	TIGER Hip Implant	Hips	TIGER	Joints	Hips

to be a one-to-one relationship between the Majors/Minors and certain keywords in the descriptions.

In the above simplified example, there are three distinct inferences that can be made with high confidence:

a) CAVE is a keyword for Minor one to be Tapes and Major one to be Sports, Minor two to be Sport Aids and hence Major two to be Joints.
   - ▸ CAVE is likely a brand that deals with sport tapes exclusively.

b) Likewise, the word Ethno appears to be the keyword for both Minor one and Minor two, with the Majors being Tools and System Tools respectively.
   - ▸ Although there was no specific example showing (Tools, Ethno) in hierarchy one to coincide with (System Tools, Ethno) in hierarchy two, it was a highly likely match due to their Minors already being identical.

c) The Hips in Major one is the Minor two for product hierarchy two, with its Major two being Joints.
   - ▸ With more data points, it was highly likely that the product hierarchy one places brands as their Minor while product hierarchy two was more broadly defined with its Minors being less specific than those in product hierarchy 1.

The process of exploratory data analysis mentioned above was employed to secure quick wins, before the more time-consuming deeper analysis was undertaken. Further text analytics was employed to massage the data into more comparable text phrases; specifically, the descriptions of the SKUs had the following manipulations performed:

- Numbers and dots (.) were removed completely
- Dashes (-) were replaced with spaces
- All letters were transformed to upper case
- The widely-used symbol "Ø" in the description was changed to "O"
- And two additional columns containing the first three words and first two words from the SKU's corresponding description were added

The following is a table illustrating the above modifications to descriptions of a few fictitious product codes.

SKU	Original Description	Modified Description	First three words	First two words
000.130	Drill Bit Pie-ce 36	DRILL BIT PIECE	DRILL BIT PIECE	DRILL BIT
000.207	Bolt Little HPR Ø1.7 × 1.4	BOLT LITTLE HPR OX	BOLT LITTLE HPR	BOLT LITTLE
000.914.0	Ball-bearing 6.5 × 9.5 × 3.5	BALL BEARING XX	BALL BEARING XX	BALL BEARING
001.012.03	Heavy Type Pin Ø2.5 × 5	HEAVY TYPE PIN OX	HEAVY TYPE PIN	HEAVY TYPE
001.020.08	Compression Ø5 × 19 × 4	COMPRESSION OXX	COMPRESSION OXX	COMPRESSION OXX

These text manipulations enhanced the ease of comparison and aided the efficiency of lookup functions. After these changes, a lookup function was run to pick up matching descriptions for mapping of hierarchies. For the remaining unmapped SKUs, the first three words were used to pick up the matching descriptions; and for the products that remained unmapped, the first two words were used.

At this juncture, it was prudent to test the accuracy of the above methodology. The mapping achieved from the above steps was tested on past sales data at the SKU level – the resulting sales split under each of the two hierarchies from the mapping achieved an accuracy of above 90 per cent, an unexpected strong performance. This accuracy test did not include the unmapped SKUs.

To map the remaining unmapped product codes that did not respond to text comparison, numerical analysis of the product codes was employed. The following lists the observations and corresponding methodology to acquire the modified product codes, for further comparison and matching:

- Some product codes or SKUs had country specific codes tagged to the end, for example, a product in Australia had the code 123.456 while the same product in China had the code 123.456-CN.
- Modification: Dashes (-) and onwards were removed completely when found, and then looked up against existing mapped product codes.

- Product codes exhibited sequential behavior, whereby products of the same Minor and, more often, Major tended to cluster in running SKU numbers or similar numerical order.
- Modifications: The last digit was dropped, before mapping against the already mapped SKU database that similarly had the last digit dropped. For the product codes that did not respond to this, another trailing digit was dropped before mapping again to the database, which likewise had another digit dropped.

The result at this point culminated to a 99 per cent complete mapping of SKUs, with only 370 distinct product codes left unmapped. Barring these, the mapping was tested against past sales data for accuracy, which came up to a little more than 90 per cent, successfully extending the satisfactory performance from the previous check.

After text and numerical analytics, operational research skills were employed for the mapping of the remaining product codes (1 per cent) namely Open Solver, R, and Gurobi Solver.

The set-up of the variables, constraints, and objective is conceptually as follows:

- Variables: The sales figure of each product code is multiplied separately with n binary variables, where n is the number of Minor-Major pairs in database, and then summed up to form the calculated total sales. For example, for the Major "Sports",

$$\textit{Calculated total sales for Sports} = (BinKnees1 + BinTapes1 + \ldots) *SalesSKU1 + (BinKnees2 + BinTapes2 + \ldots)*SalesSKU2 + (BinKnees3 + BinTapes3 + \ldots)*SalesSKU3 + \ldots + (BinKneesn + BinTapesn + \ldots) *SalesSKUn, \textit{ where Knees and Tapes are Minors to Sports.}$$

- Objective: Maximize the calculated total sales for each Major to as close as possible to the actual total sales data for each Major.
- Constraints:
- Calculated total sales per Major ≤ Actual total sales per Major.
- The sum of the n binary variables for each product code must equal 1. In the above example for Sports,

$$(BinKneesn + BinTapesn + \ldots) = 1, \forall\, n \in [1, \text{number of Minors for Sports}]$$

Sales data at the Minor level are provided in the system, but not sales data at the SKU level. Hence, this optimization process aims to split the Sales data at the SKU level to achieve finer granularity for possible mapping to both product hierarchies.

The optimization was the final step, in this case, only on the remaining 1 per cent of data, because this solution process has an upper limit to the number of variables allowed. The sales figure for each SKU must, moreover, be distinct for the Solver method to attain higher precision and accuracy; hence the fewer SKUs involved, the higher the efficiency of the Solver.

The accuracy of the resulting full mapping hovered around 90 per cent, with a slight increase to 92 per cent.

This hierarchy mapping process was essential primarily because it linked crucially to the production of the financial dashboards in the upcoming sections of this report. Management office requested the integration of multiple views of the product hierarchies into a single dashboard for ease of making business decisions and drawing business insights quickly.

The next step was the construction and refinement of the financial dashboards. With the hierarchy mapping internally mapped to high accuracy, attention turned to the development and refinement of the financial dashboards to showcase net trade sales data under multiple hierarchy views, and also with both table and visualization enhancements.

Initially, the dashboards followed the template design shown below. This was the menu page with buttons to the eight financial reports (as boxed up in black dotted border) integrated into a single dashboard. Before refinements, there was only a single product hierarchy to view for net trade sales data.

The task for the CoE team is to integrate the commercial product hierarchy into this single dashboard Figure 5 for ease in management analysis of net trade sales under multiple product hierarchies.

Clicking on any of the buttons leads the user to the respective dashboards, with the design standardized as follows:

The two different product hierarchies, at the highest level, are shown in Figure 6, and the greyed out areas are filled with numbers in a table format. Note that the multiple views of sales data showcased under the two different hierarchies were made possible by the internal mapping performed,

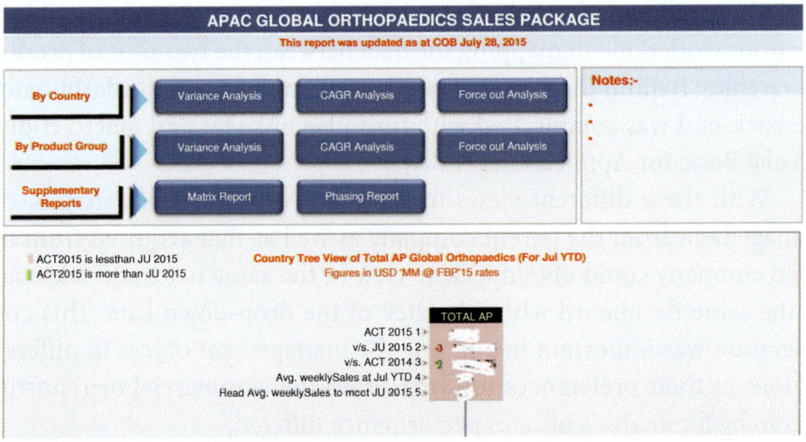

Figure 5: An example of integrated dashboard.

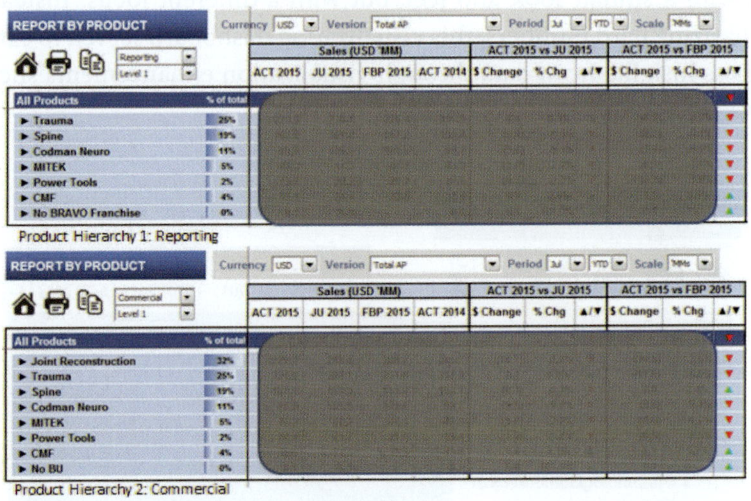

Figure 6: An example of two product hierarchies.

described earlier. Although complicated in the back-end formula linkages, the integration of the commercial hierarchy with the reporting hierarchy was a success, both in data integration and timely publication.

Under the separate views of the product hierarchies, net trade sales data was further displayed in more granular levels of product categories. For example, the data shown in the previous page is at Level one of the respective product hierarchies; the data shown in the following is at Level two of the respective hierarchies, with an option for Level three, the lowest / finest level of the hierarchies.

These refinements to the financial dashboards were made possible by the prior work done in mapping the data between the two silos of product hierarchies. Behind the simplicity of these refinements in the dashboards, the back-end was complicated with formulae linkages and macro coding (Visual Basic for Applications, VBA).

With these different views under the two product hierarchies, the management from the parent company as well as that acquired from the child company could obtain a clear view of the same net trade sales data in the same dashboard with one click of the drop-down lists. This consideration was important in aligning the management offices in different regions as their preferences towards either the commercial or reporting hierarchy for analysis of sales performance differed.

After refining the tabular dashboard, a visualization report was created, with a similar look and feel, but with a different focus. Instead of emphasizing hard numbers, this visualization dashboard served to extract business insights from data through visualization enhancements such as charts, lines, maps and geocoding.

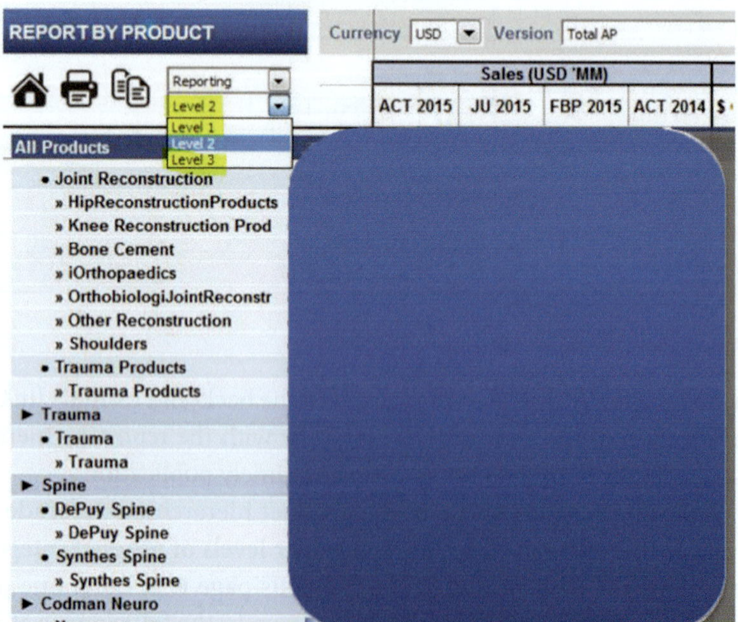

Figure 7: A view of the dashboard. Note that for confidentiality reasons part of the figures have been covered up.

Created on Tableau, the visualization dashboard had a menu as shown Figure 7. It was very similar to the menu of the tabular dashboard, except that the visualization had three more reports.

Line graphs were plotted to show the monthly phasing and variance of the net trade sales amongst region, period, and different product hierarchies. The aim was for the end-users to achieve is the ability to drill down to the specific region or product level or period, by accessing the drop-down filters (boxed up in dotted borders).

In line with the teachings of visualization best practices espoused by visualization techniques experts such as Stephen Few,[4] line graphs were used to appropriately display any trends in sales, while the bar charts were used to display the variances and how many more sales would be needed to meet targets. Although visually attractive, pie charts were avoided due to their lack of clarity and precision in displaying proportions especially when many sectors were involved, in this case countries. See for instance Figure 8.

Figure 8: An example of a dashboard.

Geo-mapping was another prominent feature of the visualization dashboard, where the data of products was tagged to their countries and displayed accordingly on the world map, for quick retrieval of sales of certain products in different regions. For example. in the following dashboard Figure 9, it can be seen that in the Country View (1), Indonesia is red-coded.

With a Mouse-over View (2), the sales performance and growth of the country were displayed, so that managers could easily identify the best and worst performers by the color codes.

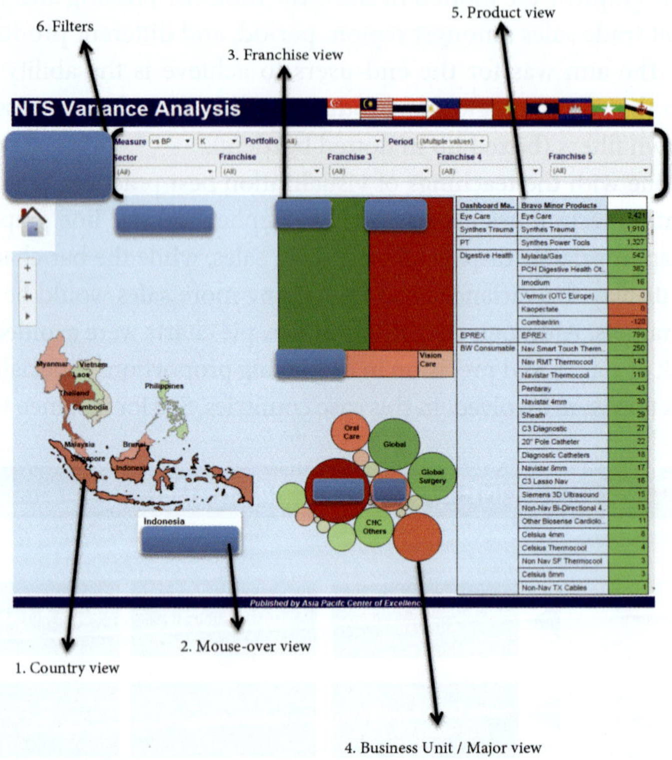

Figure 9: Dashboard with colour coding and other capabilities Figures shown are fictional.

Moreover, the dashboard showed the performance of the different franchises, for example, Consumer, Medical, Pharmaceutical, and Vision Care, also color-coded, alerting the end-user immediately to the franchise sector that needed the most help.

The Business Unit / Major View (4) that categorized the products are shown in bubbles or circles, with size proportionate to volume sold and color relative to the net trade sales, green being most profitable.

The Product View (5) showed the finest level of details of the products and their corresponding net trade sales.

Filters (6) were added to allow the visualization to showcase only data from a certain period, country or sector, franchise and business units, that allowed country leaders to focus on their respective countries of interest.

The end-user could also click on the specific country or countries of interest, for example Indonesia. This drilled down from the general bird's eye view of performances of the countries in Asia Pacific revealing a more detailed view of the franchises, business units and products relevant to only Indonesia. See Figure 10.

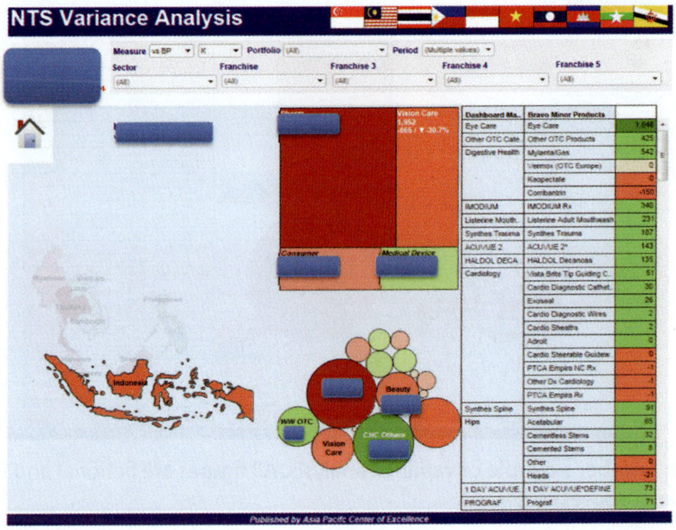

Figure 10: Dashboard showing variance analysis. All figures are fictional and for illustration purposes.

For example, the following image Figure 11 shows the view that pops up upon clicking on Indonesia. Choosing Indonesia in the Country View (1) cascades a filtering effect through to the views (2) to (6), showcasing only Indonesia's net trade sales data. As seen in the dashboard, the franchise view changes from having Medical Device as the franchise with the largest volume and healthiest net trade sales growth to having Pharmaceutical with the largest volume but the lowest net trade sales growth (largest and reddest box in the franchise view).

This was a concern to the management and simply looking at numbers may not provide comprehensive and swift answers. The visualization dashboard could easily and clearly trace the "problematic" segment to its roots. Clicking on the Pharmaceutical box in the Franchise View cascades the filtering effect to the other views, and obtains an Indonesia-Pharmaceutical-specific view as in Figure 11. The Mouse-Over View on the Pharmaceutical franchise also displays clearly the percentage of decrease in its net trade sales. The management end-users could access further information by clicking on Pharmaceutical in the Franchise View.

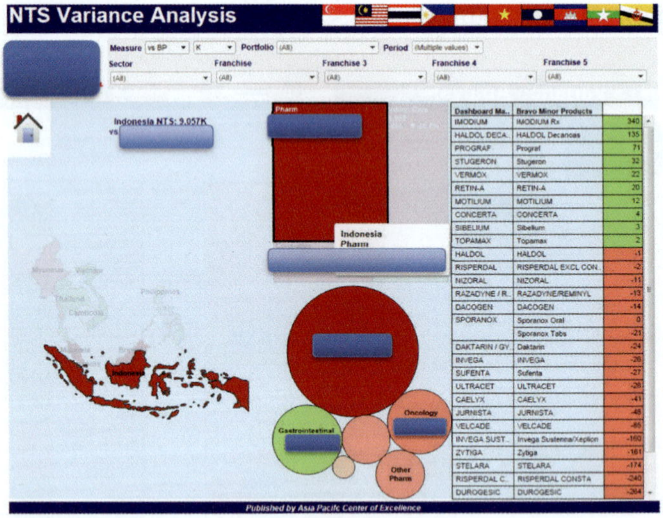

Figure 11: Another example of variance analysis. All figures are fictional and for illustrative purposes only.

After filtering to the Pharmaceutical in the Franchise View, the Business Unit View changed accordingly and showed that Neuroscience had the biggest volume but also sustained the most sluggish growth in net trade sales, while Gastrointestinal showed a healthy growth in net trade sales.

By clicking the Neuroscience bubble in the visualization financial dashboard, end-users could explore the problem of negative net trade sales growth in the Franchise View (3) -Neuroscience business unit of the Mouse-Over View (2) - Pharmaceutical franchise in the Country View (1) - Indonesia sector. This cascades a filter to the Product View (5), as shown in Figure 12

Notice that at this stage, the Indonesia map in the sector view, the Pharmaceutical box in the franchise view, and the Neuroscience bubble in the business unit view were the only highlighted pieces, with the rest faded in the background. This visual contrast allowed business end-users to access the point of interest quickly and accurately.[6]

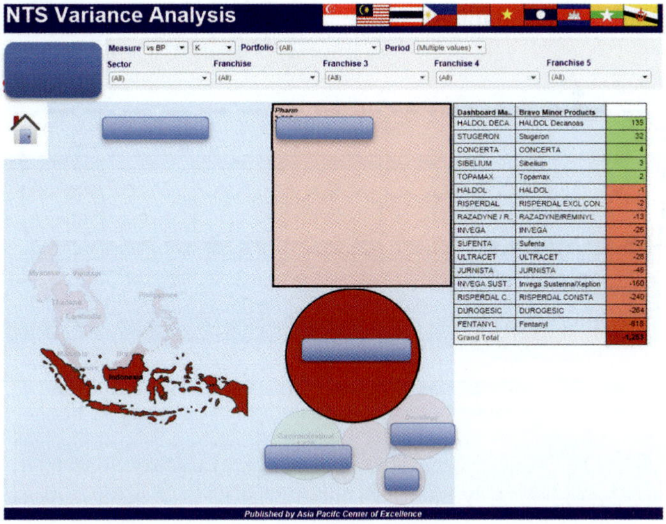

Figure 12: Another dashboard view for Neuroscience. All figures are fictional and for illustrative purposes only.

The product view on the far right shows only the products sold in the respective month in the country Indonesia, the Pharmaceutical franchise and the Neuroscience business unit. At this most granular level of detail, the products and their corresponding net trade sales performance are shown in colour code and sorted in decreasing order. This allowed the business users to identify instantly the top five selling products and also the worst performers in terms of net trade sales.

With this level of detail and filtering, the management could trace the problem of lowest net trade sales to the product, and accordingly draw up a business plan to assist the sales team associated with this product in Indonesia. What this brings to the business is the ease in reading the story that the net trade sales figures can tell. Visualization in this aspect drives growth for the business, as managers can now pick up the cues from the data that previously remained undiscovered or obscured for a long time.

Once the data integration with respect to the hierarchy was completed, and the visualization dashboard for front-end users constructed, the CoE team pushed a step further by providing the analytics to improve future net trade sales forecast, as shown in Figure 13.

Figure 13 Net trade sales forecast example. Blocked fields due to confidentiality of the data.

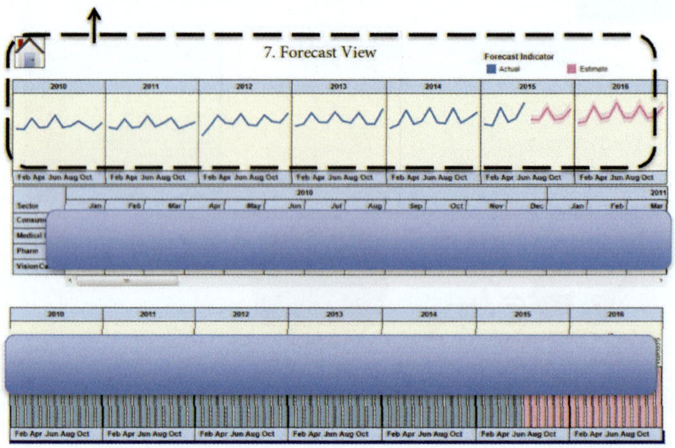

The Forecast View (7) shows the predicted cyclic pattern of net trade sales, calculated from the Holt-Winter's (HW) exponential smoothing model. Many companies use the Holt-Winters method to produce short-term demand forecasts when their sales data contain a trend and a seasonal pattern.[7,8] This 50 year old method is popular because it is simple, has low data-storage requirements, and is easily automated. It also has the advantage of being able to adapt to changes in trends and seasonal patterns in sales when they occur. This means that fluctuations in demand, or changing consumer behavior at key points in the year, can all be accommodated. It achieves this by updating its estimates of these patterns as soon as each new sales figure arrives.

While the Holt-Winters method remains a mainstay approach to business forecasting, it was extended to deal with three other problem areas.[9]:

- The presence of unusual values (outliers). Left unattended, outliers can distort HW forecasts.
- The prevalence of multiple seasonal cycles, such as a combination of day-of-week patterns and month-of-year patterns. Traditional HW could account for only a single seasonal pattern.

- The need for prediction intervals, which affect, for example, safety-stock calculations. Traditional HW intervals in use tend to be too narrow, resulting in inaccurate forecasts.[10]

The parameters of the model were derived from optimization: minimizing the mean absolute percentage error of the predictions. What made the optimization and modelling process easier is that the software Tableau has in-built functions and algorithms that can quickly and conveniently find the best output for parameters. This has proven to be of great technical help, but like all statistical software that automates the modelling processes, the statistical and technical knowledge and proficiency of the users should be well-honed before use.

5. DISCUSSION

The value of the mapping work had the following benefits:

1) it brought forward the distribution of the monthly sales report **by an entire day**, which subsequently gave the reporting team more time to focus on and publish the other financial reports, such as Profit and Loss
2) it developed a highly accurate and automated logic to minimize routine manual work, freeing up managers to focus on other areas of business development.

These improvements in timeline and staff efficiency paid dividends as they were replicated in other sectors in the company, as a solution to issues such as mapping of entities to a certain hierarchy. In the host company, the team delegated to sales reporting was reduced to half its initial size due to the automation of the hierarchy mapping process, thus the other half of the team were freed up to take on other projects and tasks.

The visualization financial dashboards were a step change to how management gained business insights through analytics, visualization techniques and enhancements. Previously, sales figures in tabular form were the primary source for telling the story of net trade sales performance throughout the Asia Pacific region. However, with the advent of the CoE set-up and the analytics that it brings coupled with managers' top-down support, sales data in its primitive tabular form was integrated into visualization dashboards that provided not only interactive usage for the business and management end-users, but invaluable business insights from the same sales data that would otherwise have gone undetected or unconsidered in business decisions.

The adoption of analytics in the company was a significant step towards maximizing informed business decisions, by gaining broader business insights through visualization, forecasting and predictive modeling.

6. CONCLUSION AND FURTHER WORK

Further work to speed up the automated mapping process of SKUs to the multiple hierarchies available should be considered. As different regional business management offices request for their local hierarchies to be integrated, it would be wise to slowly move away from Excel (spreadsheet) for dashboard purposes and adopt Tableau, where data is stored, connected and extracted more quickly than in the front-end Excel. The company and the CoE team are advocating and aiming for the total integration of multiple hierarchical mappings into the back-end to facilitate the creation of dashboards with more than two hierarchies in a single integrated view.

As backend integration is time consuming, the CoE team will need to continue to update the financial dashboards in both tabular and visualization forms. Further work in this line can be done to improve the accuracy of the mapping of the hierarchies. As for the visualization dashboards, further work can be done to explore the option of motion and animations to illustrate sales data.

Thereafter, analytics could be performed on the foundation of this back-end integration of data. Further work should be explored to perform predictive analytics and risk-modelling, especially when the plan to roll out visualization of Profit and Loss dashboard is in place. Risk-modelling could be beneficial to the supply chain department as the inventory could be optimized for distributorship should risk analytics be explored and incorporated into another financial dashboard for both tabular and visualization purposes.

REFERENCES

1. Kimball (2013). *Kimball Dimensional Modeling Techniques,* pp.14–20. Kimball Group. Stanford US.

2. FusionCharts (2012). *Principles of Data Visualization–What We See in a Visual,* White Paper, pp. 10–14.

3. Jacobs, J, and B Rudis (2014). *Data-Driven Security: Analysis, Visualization and Dashboards,* pp. 287–301. Singapore: Wiley.

4. Few, S (2007). *Data Visualization–Past, Present, and Future, Perceptual Edge, Cognos Innovation Center for Performance Management,* pp. 7–10.

5. Business Objects XI Release 2 MHF1 (2006). *Performance Management Visualization Analytics Information, Business Objects XI Release 2 MHF1,* pp. 9–15.

6. Juice (2009). *A Guide to Creating Dashboards People Love to Use,* Juice November 2009 Ed, pp. 25–40.

7. Bermúdez, JD, JV Segura and E Vercheri (2010). Bayesian forecasting with the Holt–Winters model. *Journal of the Operational Research Society,* 61, 164–171.

8. Gelper, S, R Fried and C Croux (2010). Robust forecasting with exponential and Holt-Winters smoothing. *Journal of Forecasting,* 29, 285–300. Holt, CC (1957). Forecasting trends and seasonals by exponentially weighted averages, Carnegie Institute of Technology, Pittsburgh ONR memorandum no. 52.

9. Hyndman, RJ, AB Koehler, JK Ord and RD Snyder (2005). Prediction intervals for exponential smoothing using two new classes of state space models. *Journal of Forecasting,* 24, 17–37.

10. Makridakis S and M Hibon (2000). The M3-competition: Results, conclusions and implications. *International Journal of Forecasting,* 16, 451–476.

CHAPTER 25

Procurement Demand Aggregation

CHEW Tze Hoong

ABSTRACT

A demand aggregation contract was established to combine purchases of common goods and services to yield better value for money through economies of scale. In an organization where common goods and services are not consolidated, the procurers are unaware of what the others are purchasing. There is a need for the central procurement department to sieve out the purchases to identify suitable items for demand aggregation, but can often be a manual and onerous process. To address this problem, a set of methods to analyze the textual description of the purchase order was developed to accelerate the process, producing a list of specific recommended goods commonly bought that would result in potential cost savings through demand aggregation.

1. INTRODUCTION

This project was conducted in a government statutory board. The data obtained for the project belongs to the statutory board and due to data sensitivity issues, the findings of the project are fictitious in order to illustrate the results of the algorithms and techniques used. The project examines the business domain of procurement and arose due to organization requirements to enhance the procurement capabilities of the different lines of operations, ranging from procuring and contracting to governance. This project aimed to assist the procuring operations, where analytics was applied to historical purchases to identify similar buys that could be aggregated to achieve potential cost savings. The envisaged outcome was a system that analyses textual descriptions of the buys, extracts identical or similar goods and services, and aggregates the amount to identify suitable items for demand aggregation.

2. BUSINESS UNDERSTANDING

2.1. Problem statement

In many organizations, disparate departments purchase goods and services that may be of the same nature or from the same supplier. Often, these purchases are not consolidated or communicated across the organization and procurers within the individual departments go ahead with their own plans. However, many purchases are suitable candidates for period contracts and framework agreements (PC/FA) that provide huge discounts when purchased in bulk. The main goal of this project was to develop an analytical model to identify similar goods and services purchases where PC/FA could be established.

The methodology that provides visibility into purchasing requests throughout the enterprise through the process of coordinating and consolidating requirements is otherwise known as demand aggregation. Demand aggregation facilitates the various departments of the organization to optimize their buying strength, resulting in potential savings on the cost of direct and indirect goods and services.

In addition, under the Ministry of Finance rules and guidelines for procurement, 'Value for Money' is one of the key principles and is described as the optimal balance of benefits and costs. The Auditor-General's Office (AGO) regularly carries out audits to ensure government agencies' compliance with the Government procurement framework to enhance public accountability by ensuring proper accounting of public monies. The key underlying concepts of demand aggregation could also be extended to a system safeguarding 'Value for Money' principles, by detecting extravagant purchases compared to other similar goods and services.

2.2. Business objective

The objective of this project was to build an analytics system that is able to extract specific information from the purchases description, identify identical or similar goods and services in the entire purchasing data set, and group them together. The groups that had the highest purchase amount were recommended for demand aggregation.

2.3. Scope

Due to the multitude of goods and services procured, the scope of the analysis was focused on IT (Information Technology) related purchases. IT goods and services contribute to a significant amount of the statutory board's purchases and would make an interesting case study. The number of procurement transactions over the years were numerous, and it was determined that the older data was not relevant due to the changing market. As such, only transactional data from 2012 to 2015 was considered.

2.5. Terminology

There are a few terminologies to note:

GeBiz: This is the Government-to-Business (G2B) Public eProcurement business center where suppliers can conduct electronic commerce with the Singapore Government. All of the public sector's invitations for quotations and tenders (except for security-sensitive contracts) are posted on GeBIZ.

Purchase Request: This is a document raised to initiate a purchase. It is a formal request that contains the requirements of the buyer and relevant information for the procurement agency to buy goods or services.

Purchase Order: This is a document issued by a buyer towards the seller, indicating the types, quantities and agreed prices for goods or services. The acceptance of a purchase order forms a contract between the buyer and the seller.

2.6. Business process

Figure 1 briefly describes the procurement process [1] in the government sector:

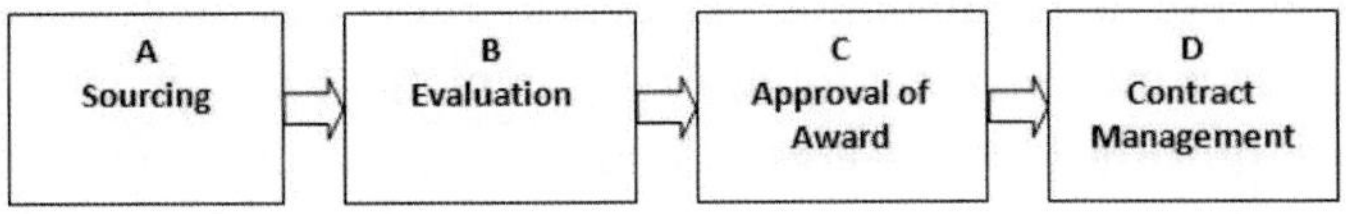

Figure 1: Procurement process.

a) Sourcing: This phase is where purchase requests are raised and approved. The category of the purchase is determined by the estimated procurement value, and falls into three main categories: Small Value Purchases, Quotations and Tenders.

b) Evaluation: This phase is where the different offers are being evaluated to determine the best option, according to the principle of value for money. Once the option has been decided, a purchase order will be raised to the awardee.

c) Approval of Award: This phase ensures checks and balances are included in the process by going through a number of approval processes.

d) Contract Management: A formal contract is set up between the buyer and seller to ensure that goods or services are supplied in accordance with the contractual agreements.

3. LITERATURE REVIEW

The idea of demand aggregation is closely related to the field of spend analytics. The literature revolves around knowledge extraction from the unstructured text through natural language processing, text classification and machine learning.

The idea of text classification by Mukherjee, Fradkin, & Roth (2008) [2] was explored where spend transactions were associated to a family of commodity codes, and each code represents a particular class of product or service. The commodity codes comprised a three level hierarchy that goes down to the details of the specific product or service, and the project was to develop automated techniques for spend classification by using the historical commodity codes to train multiple classification algorithms. The paper also demonstrated the use of a noisy channel technique for feature correction in the procurement description.

A similar implementation was conducted by IBM Global Process Services where a Compliance Analytics Tool was developed using advanced data mining techniques to segment/cluster large spend transactions to quickly identify areas of improvement [3]. Subsequently, a portfolio optimization tool was used to narrow the specific purchase categories to provide maximum benefits based on a desired budget. A two-step clustering approach was used, after which the importance of each feature in every cluster was calculated by measuring its homogeneity in that cluster. The application of the feature importance was found to be a necessary step in determining the significance of each feature.

Another applicable area of text analytics was the named entity recognition algorithm. Many out-of-the-box named Named Entity Recognition techniques (NER techniques) were constrained to a small number of predefined classes such as location, organization and people. A context aware named entity disambiguation implementation [4] was implemented by crawling linked data from DBpedia (see paragraph 4b below) and extracting out concrete instances of entities backed by a knowledge base. With the input of context relevant entities, the named entity recognition algorithm improved significantly.

4. SOLUTION

4.1. Architecture

The analytics tools used for this project were:

a) Rapidminer

Rapidminer is the main tool used for conducting text analytics and the aggregation of the procurement data. The community version is an open-source analytics tool that comprises a wide variety of text analytics and machine learning related algorithms. A number of extensions such as the linked open data extraction, text processing and information extraction were utilized.

b) DBpedia

The DBpedia project extracts structured content from the Wikipedia, and stores them inside a linked data structure. It allows users to semantically query relationships and properties existing in Wikipedia resources through the use of SPARQL queries, where multiple entities type could be queried and merged together in a single view.

c) KNIME

KNIME is another open-source analytics tool similar to Rapidminer. It was used for the Named Entity Recognition (NER) algorithm, where the OpenNLP NER tagger was available.

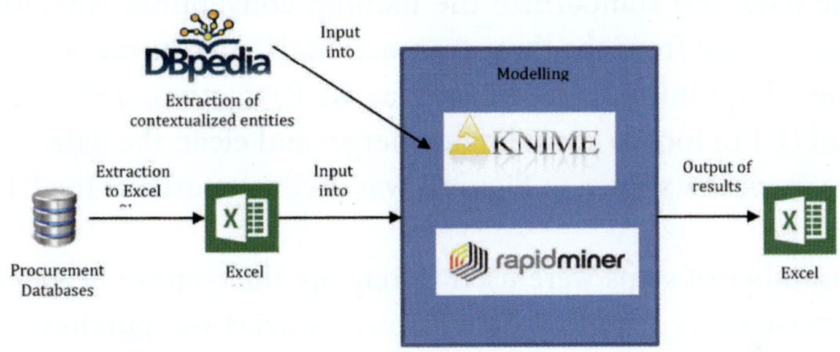

Figure 2: Architecture.

4.2. Data description

There were three different procurement databases and each served a specific purpose in the procuring operations. The representation of procurement data is standard across the three databases, mainly comprising purchase requisition, purchase orders and invoices. For this project, the main data analyzed were the purchase orders. The following data columns were selected:

a) Purchase Order No.: A unique key to represent a purchase order.

b) Purchase Order Line No: Within each purchase order, there are multiple line items. The order no. with the line no. formed a unique key of the procurement transaction.

c) Supplier Name: The name of the supplier whom the buyer is procuring from.

d) Order Date: The date which the purchase order was raised.

e) Buyer Name: The buyer or procuring officer who is purchasing the goods or services.

f) Price: The price of the purchase at the line item level.

g) Purchase Order Line Item Description: The detailed description of the type of goods and services purchased. This is the main column used for the analysis.

h) Source: Indicate which procurement database the transaction belongs to.

4.3. Data collection and transformation

The key task after collecting the disparate data sources was to consolidate the data and standardize the naming convention. After the data was extracted out from the three transactional data sources, and put into Excel files, Rapidminer was utilized as an Extraction, Transformation and Load (ETL) tool to consolidate, merge, and clean the data.

The workflow shown in Figure 3 was used to construct the ETL steps mentioned:

A number of steps were used to rename the column headers, parse the purchase order date to a date format, convert the purchase amount to numeric, and generate new attributes to identify the source. Since the focus was on purchase transactions which did not leverage on demand aggregation contracts, those transactions that did so had to be filtered out.

During the data exploration phase, it was also discovered that the purchase amount indicated was at the purchase order level, rather than the purchase order line item level. This meant that for each line item, the purchase amount reflected the total amount for the entire purchase order, which was incorrect. Due to time constraints, the data was not re-extracted with the correct logic, but rather, the average was calculated for each line item.

Example of the Data Cleansing

Order No.	Order Line No.	Purchase Amt
X123	1	15000
X123	2	15000
X123	3	15000

→

Order No.	Order Line No.	Purchase Amt
X123	1	5000
X123	2	5000
X123	3	5000

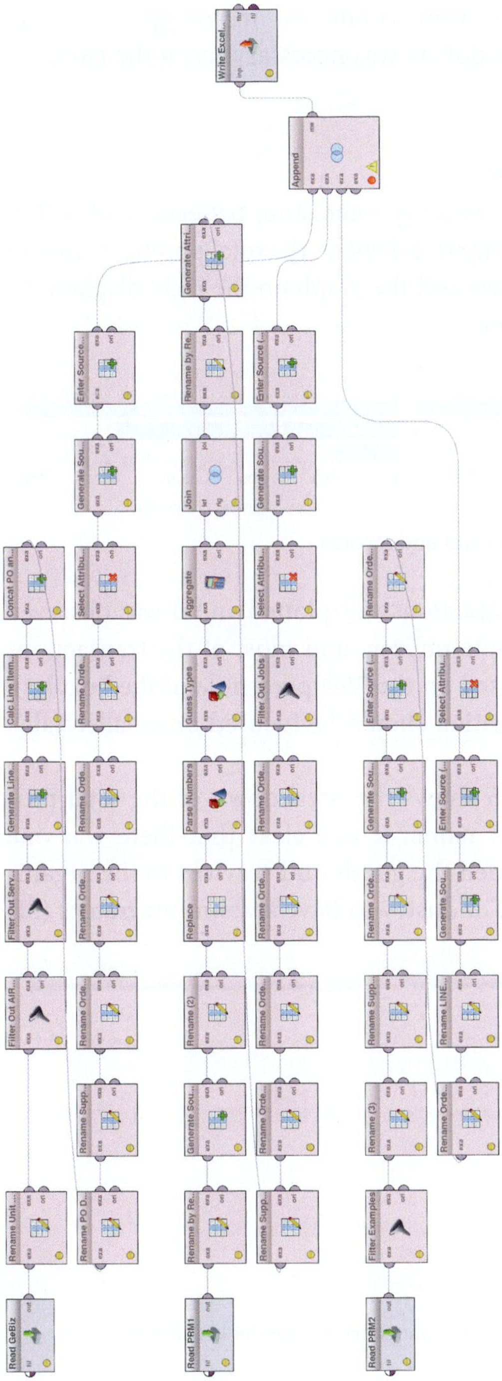

Figure 3: ETL workflow.

Some of the transactions were conducted in foreign currencies and a conversion to Singapore dollars was necessary using the currency exchange rate column.

4.4. Exploratory data analysis

The data was profiled to sieve out any interesting patterns or distributions. The graph on the left in Figure 4 displays the total purchase amount by the procurement data sources and the graph on the right displays the respective number of transactions.

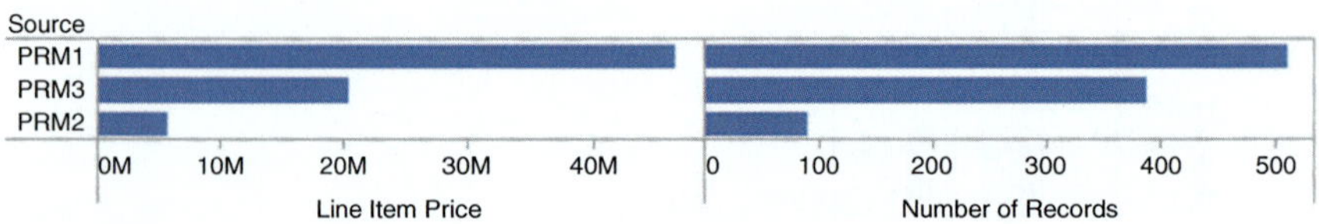

Figure 4: Breakdown of purchase amount and records.

Next a boxplot of the transactions was plotted and it was observed that the spread of data was quite uneven, and most of the transactions were less than SGD70,000 (based on the 75th percentile of the boxplot). It seemed that demand aggregation should be focused on smaller value purchases.

The bar chart in Figure 5 shows the breakdown of the total procurement amount by supplier name. It was clear that there was one dominant supplier who provided the goods and services to the organization. It is common in the IT industry to have system integrators (SI)

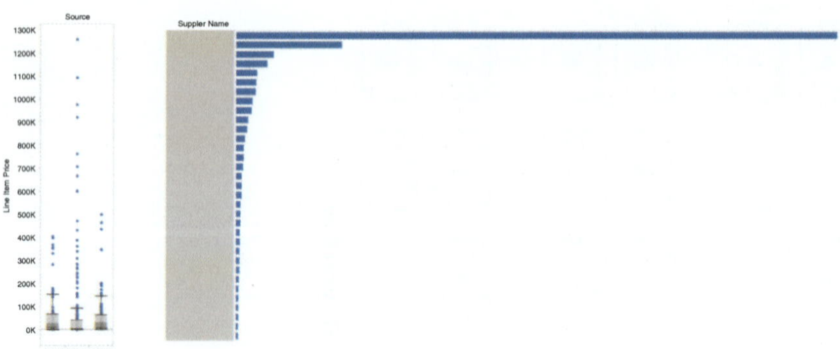

Figure 5: Boxplot of purchase amount and bar chart of supplier breakdown.

who are re-sellers of goods and the provider of services in a single project. For example, the reporting tool AA is sold by Company XX, but under the procurement transaction, the supplier name will be the IT systems integrator who is in charge of the IT project. Hence it is critical to conduct text analysis on the purchase description as data is not represented explicitly.

4.5. Text cleansing

A few steps were carried out to clean the text:

a) Lowering of Case

   In order to group properly the goods and services, all cases of text were lowered.

b) Tokenization

   Tokenization is the process of breaking a stream of text into words, referred to as tokens. During this phase, punctuation and whitespace were removed. After the tokenization, a word count was conducted.

c) Part of Speech (PoS) Tagging and Filtering

   This step tagged every word within the purchase order description to a verb/adjective/noun/adverb. As the project only focused on the goods and services name, naturally only the nouns were considered.

   The PoS tagging made use of the Penn Treebank set to annotate naturally-occurring text for linguistic structure. The Penn Treebank is one of the most comprehensive Treebank that was trained from many written text such as the Wall Street Journal and the Brown Corpus. The syntactic structure of the purchase order description exhibits similar characteristics to a normal sentence, thus part of speech tagging was used. During the initial phase, only the text that were tagged as nouns (NN: singular noun, NNS: plural noun, NNP: proper singular noun, NNPS: proper plural noun), were considered. However, after some sampling, it became evident that a number of important words or phrases that needed to be captured were left out, and these were tagged as adjectives by the Penn Treebank tagset. The decision was made to also include adjectives (JJ: adjective, JJR: comparative adjective, JJS: superlative adjective) as words to be analyzed.

d) Stemming and Lemmatization

Stemming is used for reducing inflected words to their word stem. For example, reports -> report, multiply -> multipli. This allows better grouping of words at their root form. There were a few algorithms available for stemming, mainly Snowball and Porter, and they depend on a crude process based on a set of rules to chop off the ends of words. After much experimentation with the stemming algorithms, the results were difficult to interpret as the root form was extracted rather than the base word.

Lemmatization is the process of using a vocabulary and morphological analysis of words to remove inflectional endings and to return the base or dictionary form of a word, also known as a lemma. For example, reporting -> report, management -> manage. In Rapidminer, there is a WordNet extension that executes the lemmatization based on a WordNet dictionary. WordNet is a lexical database for the English language and contains the lexical categories of nouns, verbs, adjectives and adverbs. This algorithm proved to be more acceptable than stemming as the lemma was more comprehensible compared to the stem.

e) Stop words Removal

There were many redundant words within the purchase order description and were not useful in the analysis of goods and services. A default stop word list was generated by the tool itself, and another list of stop word was downloaded from the Internet (http://www.ranks.nl/stopwords) to make the list more comprehensive. The common stop words were: a, the, is, are, then, we, they; the less common stop words downloaded from the internet were: sufficiently, maybe, whomever, together, themselves.

However, the stop word list from the Internet was insufficient as the context was different. To improve the stop word list, a word count was conducted to identify commonly occurring terms that were not useful in recognizing a good or service. Some of the stop words added through this step were: maintenance, renewal, license, support (Figure 6).

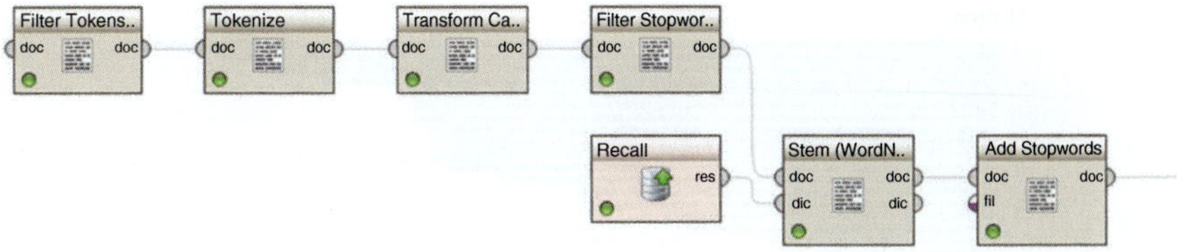

Figure 6: Workflow of text cleansing.

Using XX as a company name and AA as a product name, an example of the text cleansing process is:

'Five licenses of XX AA bought for ABC project'

Through the part of speech tagging:

'CD 5 **NNS** licenses **IN** of **NNP** XX **NNP** AA **VBD** bought **IN** for **NNP** ABC **NN** project'

After the POS Tag filtering, the only phrases left are the nouns and adjectives, which are 'licenses', 'XX', 'AA', 'ABC' and 'project'. The subsequent steps tokenize the sentence and lower the case of all words. Through lemmatization using WordNet, the word 'licenses' is reduced to the base form, 'license'. At the stop words removal step, 'project' and 'license' are deleted. The final end result of the text cleaning process is:

'xx aa abc'

4.6. Data exploration of text

A few data exploration steps were conducted on the purchase description, namely word count and creation of 2-grams and 3-grams.

The blue graph in Figure 7 represents the singular word count, the purple graph represents the 2-grams word count and the green represents the 3-grams word count. Note that the scale is nearly equal, where the blue graph's maximum value is 190, and the green and purple graph's maximum value is 130.

From the distributions, it was clearly observed that many of the purchase order descriptions contained the same phrases, up to 3-grams, and these are peculiar purchase order descriptions as the buyer has keyed in a similar description for more than 100 times. On further analysis of the text, it was understood that these purchases related to computer buys, and for each computer, a purchase order was raised with a near identical description.

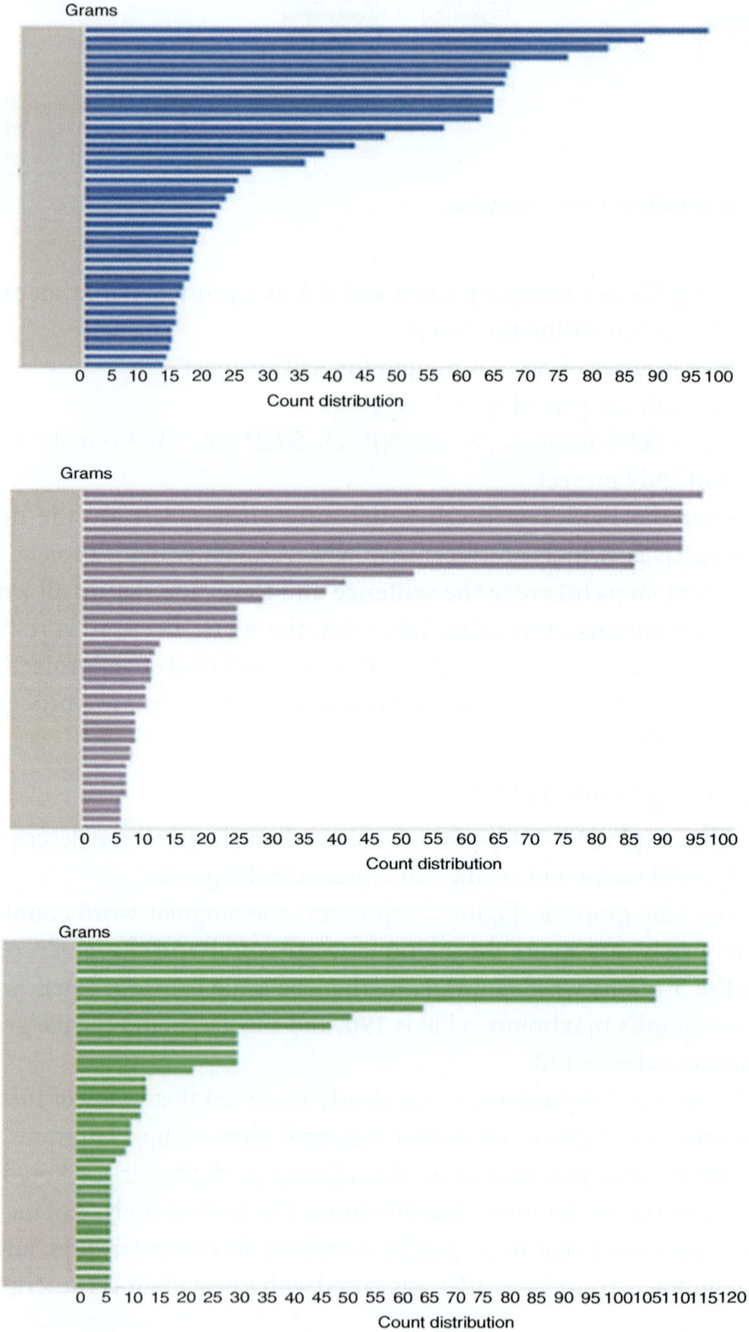

Figure 7: Word count, 2-grams and 3-grams count distribution.

4.7. Context relevant entities

Context aware named entity recognition is concerned with discovering entities that are relevant to the domain being analyzed. In DBpedia, there is a wealth of linked data that is built upon a comprehensive ontology based on Wikipedia. To obtain the entities data, SPARQL queries, which is an RDF query language, was written through the DBpedia ontology query platform, Virtuoso.

The following SPARQL queries were written:

1) Extract out a list of companies and their software that were developed:

```
SELECT *
  WHERE
   {
    ?company a <http://dbpedia.org/ontology/Organisation>;
         rdfs:label ?company_name.
    ?product <http://dbpedia.org/ontology/developer> ?company.
    ?product a <http://dbpedia.org/ontology/Software>;
         rdfs:label ?software_name.
FILTER (langMatches(lang(?company_name ),"en"))
FILTER (langMatches(lang(?software_name),"en"))
}
```

The list of companies and software were analyzed and found to be inadequate as they were missing a large number of software from the major vendors. The decision then was to focus on names of companies to determine the entity that the purchase order description referred to. Moreover, many of the software listed related to computer and video games which were not required.

2) Extract out a list of IT related companies from the hardware and software industries.

```
SELECT DISTINCT ?company_name
 WHERE
{
  {
    ?company a <http://dbpedia.org/ontology/Organisation>.
         ?company rdfs:label ?company_name.
?company <http://dbpedia.org/ontology/industry>
```

```
<http://dbpedia.org/resource/Computer_hardware>.
FILTER (langMatches(lang(?company_name ),"en"))
   }
.
.
.
UNION
   {
      ?company a <http://dbpedia.org/ontology/Organisation>.
           ?company rdfs:label ?company_name.
?company <http://dbpedia.org/ontology/product>
<http://dbpedia.org/resource/Software>.
FILTER (langMatches(lang(?company_name ),"en"))
   }
UNION
   {
      ?company a <http://dbpedia.org/ontology/Organisation>.
           ?company rdfs:label ?company_name.
?company <http://dbpedia.org/ontology/product>
<http://dbpedia.org/resource/Enterprise_software>.
FILTER (langMatches(lang(?company_name ),"en"))
   }
}
```

The query extracted companies whose industries are in the Computer Hardware, Software and Enterprise Software line of businesses. The list included every major IT company in the market, but it may have excluded some smaller companies. A total of 1,408 companies were extracted from DBpedia.

After the company entities were extracted, the next step was to clean the data extracted from DBpedia. Many of the company names had the words "software", "technologies", "pte ltd", "inc", "products" within it. The user entering the purchase order description often would not spell the product's company name in full, and this resulted in the company name not being recognized. Therefore, the company entity list needed to be cleaned and simplified: the company names were converted to lower case, lemmatization was applied and the common words were removed.

4.8. Named entity recognition

After the list of entities were extracted, the next task was to tag every purchase order to a company entity. Rapidminer did not have a named entity recognition algorithm for the text processing, and this step had to be done over at another tool, Knime.

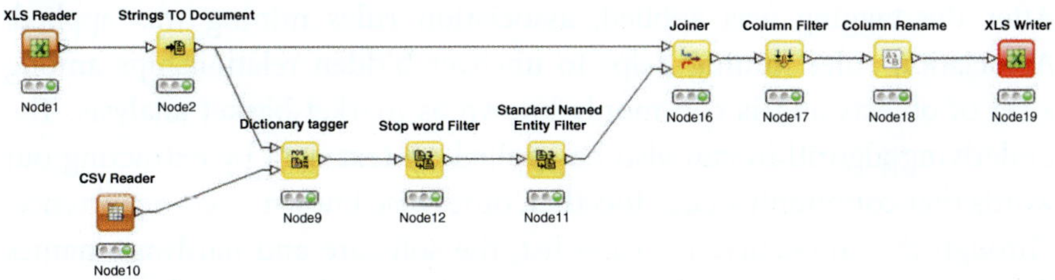

Figure 8: Knime named entity recognition workflow.

The purpose of the named entity recognition was to identify organizations within the text, using the dictionary extracted from DBpedia and the OpenNLP Named Entity Tagger. The OpenNLP package offers a number of name entity recognition models which are pre-trained on various available corpora. There is a training tool that allows custom corpora to be trained, but due to the time constraint, the out-of-the-box named entity recognition algorithm was used. Using OpenNLP, a few entities can be recognized: name, location, time, organization, and money. For this workflow, the organization entity recognizer was used, together with the company dictionary gathered from DBpedia.

After the named entity recognition algorithm was applied, the next step was to filter out all the words that were not tagged to the organization entity. The final data set included an additional column indicating the organization that the purchase order description is tagged to.

An example is listed below:

Purchase Order Description	Organization Tag
10 licenses of XX AA with two years maintenance.	XX

An iterative process was conducted to improve the accuracy of the tagging. The dictionary of companies from DBpedia had to be enhanced through sampling the data, and a number of words that belonged to the

DBpedia list were removed as they were found to be generic, e.g. some companies were called Check Point, Storage Technology Corporation, and purchase descriptions that contained the words 'Storage', 'Check' were wrongly tagged to these organizations.

4.9. Association rules

After the tagging was applied, association rules mining was applied. Association rules mining helps to uncover hidden relationships among a set of objects and is commonly known as market basket analysis. The underlying algorithm can also be applied on text data by extracting out words that commonly occur together, otherwise known as co-occurrence. Through the co-occurrence rules list, the software and hardware names that were associated with the companies were sieved out. The data was first converted into a binary term document matrix and subsequently placed into the table shown below:

Text	CC	XX	YY	ZZ	AA	BB
10 licenses of XX AA Modeler with two years maintenance.	false	true	false	false	true	false
Five licenses of XX BB Explorer	false	true	false	false	false	true
Two user license of YY	false	false	true	false	false	false
ZZ CC support maintenance for 10 years	true	false	false	true	false	false

Frequent pattern mining was then carried out to extract the frequent item sets. There were a few algorithms suited for frequent pattern mining, such as Apriori, Eclat and Frequent Pattern-Growth Trees. FP Growth trees were selected as they were much faster than Apriori and Eclat. There were a few parameters that needed to be adjusted for the algorithm to work properly. Since aggregating purchases were being examined, there needed to be more than one purchase, therefore the minimum support was set at a value where purchases were more than one. The maximum number of item sets was limited to two because the project was only interested in pairs of words.

Once the frequent item sets were obtained, the next step was the creation of association rules. In this step, the minimum confidence value had to be adjusted. The value set was lenient as there is a possibility that a company may produce different types of software. E.g. XX has AA, BB, DD, EE products. If the confidence value was set high, no association rules would be produced when the premise is the word XX. Assuming all the tools mentioned were bought, the result would be:

Premise	Conclusion
xx	aa
xx	bb
xx	dd
xx	ee
xx	warranty

Through the co-occurrence rules list, the software and hardware names that were associated with the companies could be sieved out. However, a number of irrelevant words that did not represent much were also part of the conclusion. Therefore, a comprehensive stop word list needed to be developed.

4.10. Aggregating

After the associated words were extracted, the next step was to aggregate the purchase orders that contained the premise and conclusion. The premise represented the company name, and the conclusion represented the product name. After tagging the purchase orders with the premise and conclusion, the purchases were grouped and aggregated to display the total amount purchased. For example:

Text	Total Amount	Premise	Conclusion
XX AA BI tool with deployment services and warranty of one year	$50,000	xx	aa
Five user license and 20 core license XX AA Business Intelligence	$160,000	xx	aa

The end result is:

Company name	Software name	Purchase Count	Total Amount
xx	aa	2	$210,000

From the final step, a list of goods and services identified as possible candidates for demand aggregation was produced.

4.11. Other methods trialed

This section mentions some of the other methods attempted, with minimal success.

4.11.1. Clustering

One of the initial ideas for the project was to conduct clustering on the text to group similar purchases. The text clustering converted the entire corpus to a term-frequency inverse document frequency matrix, and a few clustering algorithms, k-means, hierarchical and DBSCAN were utilized with cosine distance. The text clustering algorithm, despite many rounds of tuning, did not display accurate results. It grouped purchases that seemed similar, but in reality were fundamentally different. For example, '5 licenses of JJ Server database' and '4 licenses of KK database' were phrased similarly, and most of the time were clustered together, but they represent two different products. If the business objective was to cluster similar purchases (not identical), then the text clustering algorithm would suffice.

4.11.2. Chunking

Chunking is associated with parts-of-speech tagging where strings of words belonging to a pre-defined pattern is extracted. The idea was to extract chunks of nouns that represented an item purchased and group them to determine if they were suitable for demand aggregation. The result was that the parts-of-speech tagging and chunking did not perform accurately, and the chunks were not sufficiently representative of the purchase order, often missing out key organization names and entities.

5. DISCUSSION

Out of approximately 1,000 purchase orders, about 100 items could be aggregated. The resulting list of goods and services recommended provided strong justification for demand aggregation. The rest of the purchases were either too generic in nature, services based, or the required information could not be extracted. The techniques used, despite being able to meet the objective, had some flaws:

1) The techniques were very dependent on a comprehensive list of stop words to remove the irrelevant descriptions. It was an iterative process where words and phrases that did not represent anything needed to be identified and filtered out from the association rules.
2) Many organizations, especially the local ones, could not be found through DBpedia. Therefore, human intervention was required to scan through the untagged data, pick up those organization entities that were missed out, and add them to a controlled dictionary.
3) The assumption here was that the purchase order description was phrased in a manner equivalent to speech, where natural language processing can be applied. However, there were numerous occurrences of text that did not have a clear structure. For example, 'FF scanner, part no. P101X'.

There are other additional methods that could improve the results, but were not executed due to time constraints:

1) Train the parts-of-speech tagging algorithm: The algorithm used was based on a training data set of Wall Street Journal, and despite some encouraging initial level of accuracy, could be improved if a corpus taken from the procurement context is used for training.
2) Train the named entity recognition system: Similarly, training the NER tagger using procurement data would improve the accuracy of recognizing entities.
3) Use the Stanford named entity recognition algorithm: The Stanford NLP NER tagger uses a technique called CRF (Conditional Random Fields), and is widely recognized as one of the most accurate and robust methods. This could replace the OpenNLP NER tagger.

6. CONCLUSION AND FURTHER WORK

This project explored and demonstrated a number of natural language processing techniques to meet the business objectives. The most effective method was through named entity recognition coupled with a context relevant dictionary and word co-occurrence analysis.

However, there remains the opportunity to do much more as the procurement data consisted of many other types of products and services besides IT. Further work could be undertaken to identify demand aggregation opportunities in other areas, although this may require other types of techniques that are dissimilar from those used here. It would be desirable create an alert system or an event processing system that informs the procurement contract management team of suitable candidates for demand aggregation.

REFERENCES

1. Government Procurement Process (2015). [Online]. Available: http://www.mof.gov.sg/Policies/Government-Procurement/Procurement-Process [Accessed: 10-Jul-2015]

2. Mukherjee, S, D Fradkin and M Roth (2008) Classifying spend descriptions with off-the-shelf learning components, in *Proceedings of the IEEE 20th International Conference on Tools with Artificial Intelligence*, Dayton, OH, pp. 53–60. doi:10.1109/ICTAI.2008.95

3. Chowdhary, P, M Ettl, A Dhurandhar,S Ghosh,G Maniachari,B Graves, B Schaefer and T Yu (2011). Managing procurement spend using advanced compliance analytics, in *Proceedings of the IEEE 8th International Conference on e-Business Engineering*, Beijing, pp. 139–144, doi:10.1109/ICEBE.2011.57

4. Lasek, I and P Vojtas (2012). Context aware named entity disambiguation, in *Proceedings of the 2012 IEEE International Joint Conferences on Web Intelligence and Intelligence Agent Technology*, Washington DC, pp. 139–144.

CHAPTER 26

Understanding Buffett Indicators in Different Industries

WU Keyuan

ABSTRACT

Buffett Indicator (BI) is the ratio of Market Capitalization to Gross Domestic Product (GDP) in the United States of America. In 2015, the Buffett Indicator reached over 130 per cent, indicating a potentially bad time to invest. In this study, the concept of the Buffett Indicator is extended to individual industries and calculated based on published datasets for Industry Market Capitalization and industry GDP. The historical data shows the average Buffett Indicator from 1970 to 2014 was less than 50 per cent for industries such as Agriculture, Construction, Wholesale Trade, and Services. Mining, Utilities, Manufacturing and Information are popular industries for investors and got their Buffett Indicators greater than 150 per cent. Regression analysis shows that the Buffet Indicators for Mining, Utilities, Manufacturing, Information, Finance, and Services significantly affect the trend for the entire set of industries.

1. INTRODUCTION

As a long-term valuation indicator, “Buffett Indicator” has been popular since 2001 when Warren Buffet said “it is probably the best single measure of where valuations stand at any given moment” during a *Fortune* interview.

The raw data for “Buffett Indicator” can be traced back to middle of the 20th century. The US quarterly GDP can be found on Fed’s B.102 Balance sheet. Fed has quarterly updated GDP beginning in Q4 1951. The information of market capitalization is available on the Federal Reserve website. It is equal to “Market Value of Equities Outstanding” from the FRED designation for Line 39 in the B.102 balance sheet.[a] The graph for “Buffett Indicator” is plotted using market capitalization divided by US quarterly GDP. It has been widely spread on research paper and online blogs. The average ratio of “Buffett Indicator” during 1950–2015 is 69.5 per cent.

2. PROBLEM STATEMENT

The first objective of this study is to produce similar Buffett Indicator per industry. Based on the North American Industry Classification System (NAICS), the research was focused on the following eleven industries: Agriculture, Mining, Utilities, Construction, Manufacturing, Wholesale Trade, Retail Trade, Transportation, Information, Finance, and Services.

The second objective is to compare the patterns of Buffett Indicators across the eleven industries and identified one or more segments which contribute the most to the entire set of industries.

3. STATE OF THE ART

At of the end of the first quarter in 2015, the market capitalization to GDP of the companies listed on New York Stock Exchange and NASDAQ is about 150 per cent.[b] Hence the “Buffett Indicator” is now at its highest

a http://www.advisorperspectives.com/dshort/updates/Market-Cap-to-GDP.php

b http://www.checkthemarkets.com/index.php/market-analysis-a-insights/2286-are-stocks-in-danger-of-a-2011-style-crash level since the dot-com era, and higher than the historical average of 119 per cent over the past 20 years.

Benchmarking to Warren Buffett's rule of thumb: buying stocks has high chance to work well when the "Buffett Indicator" is in range of 70 per cent to 80 per cent; but when the market is overvalued and the indicator approaches 200 per cent (as it did in 1999), then this is not a good time to invest.

In the past 20 years, there were two significant stock market crashes. The first crisis occurred in 2000 as a product of over-investment in dot-com stocks. Since 1997, stock prices on Internet-based companies have risen dramatically. Investors blindly believed in technological advancements instead of analyzing traditional metrics, such as P/E ratio. Venture capitals were widely available at that time. The market collapse took place during 1999–2001 as people began to question how internet companies could turn future profits. The "Buffett Indicator" spiked at 130 per cent from 1999 to 2000 and then dropped to its historical average of 60 per cent in two-year time. The second crisis was a financial crisis in 2007–2008 with the failure of several large investment banks. The financial crisis was caused by excessive loans for subprime borrowers and overlook the risk of bundled subprime mortgages. When the housing bubble burst, stock market crashed as people questioned regarding bank solvency, credit was tightened and international trade declined. The "Buffett Indicator" rose above 110 per cent during 2005–2007 but dropped to 60 per cent when subprime crisis happened, which is the lowest point since 1994.

The "Buffett Indicator" has risen since the bull market began six years ago, causing a debate as to whether stocks can keep advancing. At Berkshire's annual meeting conducting in May 2015, Warren Buffett gave public his point of view on the importance of how interest rates would change going forward would ultimately affect the valuation of stock market. He has pointed out that if the cost of borrowing normalized, stocks would be on the high side on a valuation basis.[c]

However, there have been some arguments on the "Buffet Indicator". Most concern is about market capitalization to GDP assumes that the US economy is the driver of capitalization. In addition, it does not take into

c http://blogs.wsj.com/moneybeat/2015/06/15/buffett-indicator-flashes-warning-for-stocks/

account globalization. The percentage of income that S&P 500 derives from overseas activity significantly increases compared to 20 years ago.[d]

4. SOLUTION: DESCRIPTION OF APPROACH

The data for Market Capitalization is obtained from Compustat. The dataset contains stock price and stock quantity for each company in each quarter in US. Also, either SIC or NAICS or both are available in the dataset. The main data-preparation steps conducted for market capitalization are following:

1) All the companies have SIC codes, but some of them do not have NAICS codes. Each SIC code was mapped to NAICS code firstly to make sure each company has got its respective NAICS code. Each company was classified to one industry based on its NAICS code then
2) Using stock price multiplied by stock quantities to get capitalization for each company in each quarter. The quarterly market capitalization for each industry would be the sum of capitalizations of all companies in the respective industry

The quarterly GDP was obtained from FRED directly.

In order to be comparable to the "Buffett Indicator" published online, some adjustments were made to Compustat's data to have the equal total market capitalization as FRED. The process of the reconciliation is following:

1) The total market capitalization for each industry per quarter using data from Compustats was calculated
2) Dividing market capitalization for each industry by the total market capitalization to get the percentage of market share for each industry
3) Multiplying the percentage of market share calculated from previous step by the total market capitalization in FRED Balance Sheet to get the adjusted market capitalization for each industry

The graphs of adjusted market capitalization and GDP for each industry are shown in the Appendix 1.

---

d http://www.bloombergview.com/articles/2014-02-26/even-warren-buffett-can-be-wrong-ritholtz-chart

5. DISCUSSION

5.1. Descriptive analysis

5.1.1. Agriculture

The value of Buffett Indicator for Agriculture is relatively small compared to other industries such as Mining, Manufacturing, Finance, etc. The average ratio is 11 per cent over 45 years. The ratio has been stable from 1970 to 1998. There was a steep increase from 2003 going forward and reached its historical highest point in 2007 just before subprime crisis happened and dropped half in the following three years. The ratio has been showing an upward trend in recent four years.

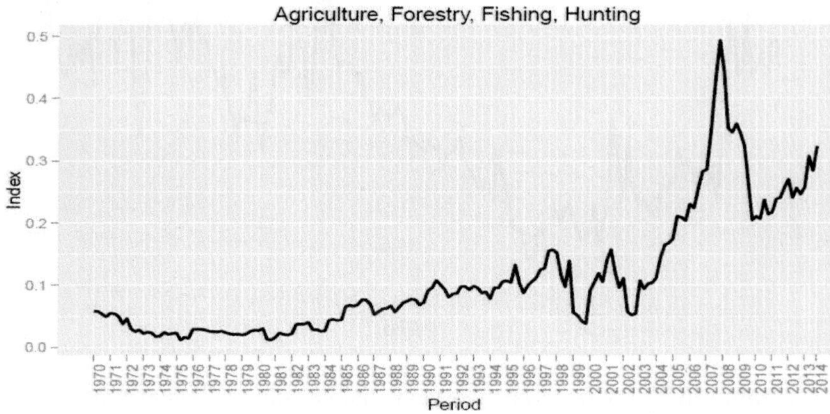

Over the past 150 years, the agriculture share of US GDP accounted for by farm value-added declined from 37.5 per cent of GDP in 1860s to 0.8 per cent in 2000s.[1] This significant decline in share of GDP in agriculture is not actually due to declining farm sector. Indeed, farm value-added has increased rapidly over this period, however, along with the industrial revolution and technology advancement, the US economy has expanded even faster.

Overall, farmers have found ways to adapt to the changes and improve efficiency over years. [2] Those who stay in agriculture are able to maintain profitability by expanding and specializing their operations to take advantage of economies of scale, or by identifying niche markets. Before 2008, the ratio rose to 50 per cent due to good economic and investment environment. Affected by the following financial crisis, the ratio dropped back to 20 per cent, but still much higher than it was in 19th century.

5.1.2. Mining

The ratio of market capitalization to GDP for Mining industry is very volatile. The ratio is above 100 per cent for most of the time since 1987. The average ratio is 161 per cent over 45 years. There are two peaks on the graph: one is appeared in 1997; the other is appeared in 2010. The ratio fell to bottom in 2000 and 2008. Not coincidentally, these are the two time period when economic crisis happened in US.

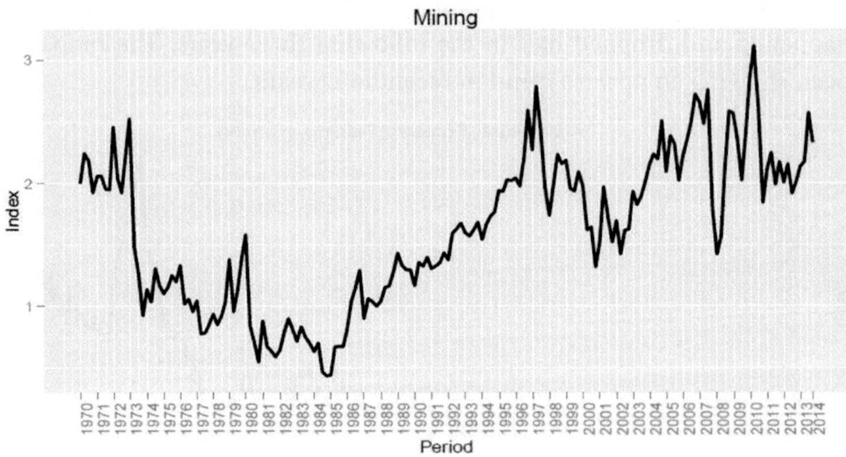

Mining industry has played a very visible role in the early industrialization of US. It has been a very profitable industry to the investors. The first two big drops in 1970s are due to the two oil crises first in 1973 and another in 1979. In October 1973, the OPEC members proclaimed an oil embargo, following by the dramatic rise of oil price from $3 per barrel to nearly $12. In 1978–1979, in conjunction with the revolution, Iranian oil output declined. Also due to the widespread panic, the oil price began to rise rapidly in mid-1979, more than doubling between April 1979 and April 1980. There are a few local minimum point appeared from mid-1970s to early 1980s on the graph. From 1985 onwards, the Buffett Indicator has kept increasing until financial crisis and dot-com bubble in late 1990s. However, some study has pointed out that the positive economic benefit of mining has been exaggerated seriously. [3] The decline in transportation costs since the middle of the 20th century has dramatically changed the likelihood that mining can be the basis for sustained economic development. That could be one of the reasons that ratios have become more volatile after mid-2000s.

5.1.3. Utilities

The ratios of market capitalization to GDP for Utilities industry are relatively large. The average ratio is 165 per cent during 1970–2014. It indicates that Utilities is a profitable industry that many investors prefer. Except the big jump in 1970–1972 due to lack of data, from 1973 onwards, the ratios move within the range of 100 per cent to 200 per cent till mid-2000s. In 2006, the ratio has reached historically highest value of 285 per cent, following by a big drop in 2008 due to subprime crisis

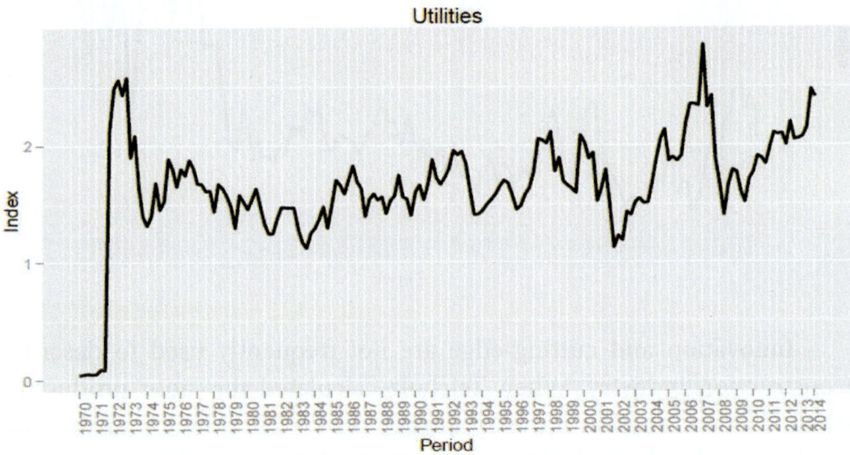

The first big drop in 1973 is because of the oil crisis. As mentioned earlier, one scene is that US people were waiting in long queue at gas stations to pay higher prices for petroleum. Besides fuels, the alternatives, such as coal, increased price as well. Higher energy prices caused higher cost of living. Data shows that inflation rate jumped to about 10 per cent by early 1975. [4] Investors in the stock market had little confidence in economy; consumers spent less on daily goods; business activities slowed down. Dow Jones Industrial average dropped 45 per cent from its 1973 high to tis 1974 low.[e]

5.1.4. Construction

Construction industry is always not as attractive as other industry to investors. The average Buffett Indicator is 7 per cent. It has reached to

e http://useconomy.about.com/od/stockmarketcomponents/a/Dow_History.htm

the peak recently in 2013–2014 at 15 per cent, doubled the average. The ratio has been stable before 2000 and become volatile after that. There is a big rise from 2001 to 2005 following by a big drop in 2007. It has been increasing recently from 2010 onwards.

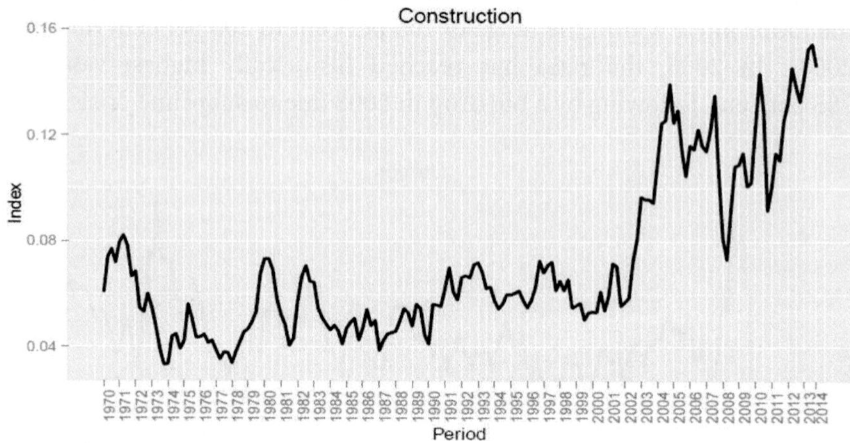

Innovation and cutting-edge are not frequently used to describe Construction industry. When Teicholz calculated the labor productivity in US Construction industry during 1964 – 2012, he found that the productivity has been declining at a rate of about 0.32 per cent per year. [5] Generally speaking, the negative changes, for example lack of consistent engagement by construction project stakeholders to each other, have outpaced the positive changes over the last three decades. Probably due to the good economic environment, there is a big jump of the ratio from 2002 – 2005. The ratio reached double-digit for the first time in 2004 and stayed above 10 per cent in recent years except 2008 financial crisis period.

5.1.5. Manufacturing

The ratio of market capitalization to GDP for the manufacturing industry is relatively large. The average ratio is 195 per cent and kept on increasing since 1980s. It reached its highest 390 per cent in 1999 followed by a big drop to 200 per cent in 2002. It reached another peak at about 400 per cent in 2014. The current ratio is nearly eight times compared to 50 per cent in 1970s.

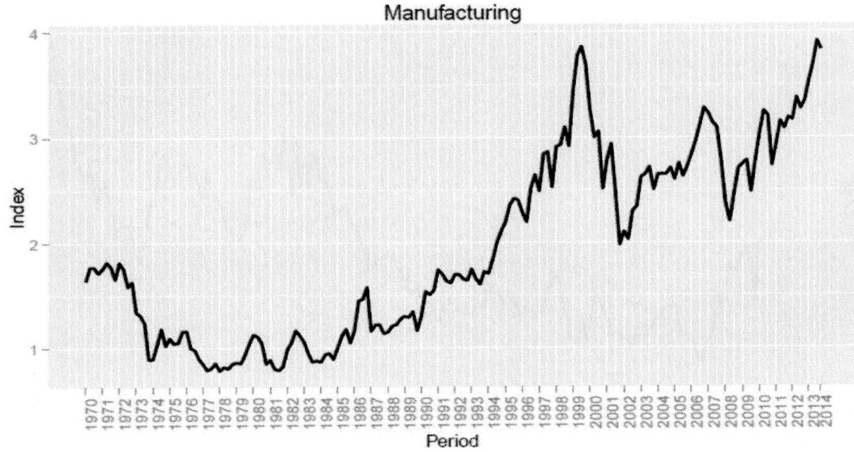

Manufacturing is a big and important industry to US economy and the most attractive industry to investors. The Buffett Indicator for the manufacturing industry is one of the closest to the BI graph. Despite an upward trend in absolute value of overall production and manufacturing, the portion of US production attributable to manufacturing has steadily declined since 1965. [6] In 21st century, along with technology advancement, machines have replaced labor force and unemployment rate in Manufacturing has increased. Obama Administration has undertaken various related initiatives to increase Manufacturing employment rate and congress members have also introduced hundreds of bills to support domestic manufacturing activities. [7] In 2010, US had the world's largest manufacturing sector, and has remained one of the biggest manufacturer in the world.[f]

5.1.6. Wholesale trade

Buffett Indicator for Wholesale Trade industry indicates that it is not a popular industry to investors. The average ratio over past 45 years is about 15 per cent. In 2013, it reached its highest value at 30 per cent. The ratios are quite volatile during 1996 – 2000.

f http://www.brookings.edu/research/papers/2014/02/us-manufacturing-past-and-potential-future-baily-bosworth

Wholesale inventories are the stock of unsold goods held by wholesalers. Generally speaking, a high inventory volume indicates economic downturn, while a low inventory volume signs economic revival. Data shows from 1992 – 2015, the average wholesale inventories rate is 0.4 per cent, highest rate of 2.38 per cent happened in October 2010 and lowest rate of -2.07 per cent was in March 2009. [8] However, the inventory changes did not reflect to Buffett Indicator. It has kept increasing after the end of 2008 financial crisis. All the fluctuations of the ratios on the graph are actually affected by large economic events, such as the oil crisis in 1970s, dot-com bubble in 2000 as well as the subprime crisis in 2008.

5.1.7. Retail trade

Buffett Indicator for Retail Trade industry is generally bigger than the Wholesale Trade industry. The average ratio from 1970 to 2014 is 63 per cent, very close to the average "Buffett Indicator" for the entire set of industries. There are some similar patterns between Wholesale and Retail Trade industries. For example, both ratios keeps going down at the beginning years and remains increasing before dot-com bubble. The difference is that the ratio for Retail Trade industry reached 100 per cent in 1998–1999, but the ratio for Wholesale was always below 25 per cent. After 2000, both graphs show an upward trend though some fluctuations happening.

The means in which consumers shop have changed due to globalization, technology advancement, and proliferation in a variety of shopping channels over decades.

Affected by oil crisis, Buffett Indicator went down in 1970s. However, at mid-1970s, Retail industry actually has been through massive changes including innovation in food processing, synthetic material fabrication and emergence of warehousing and discount stores. [9] A new era has started.

From 1980 onwards, along with a good investing environment and stable economic situation, Buffett Indicator has risen dramatically. Except the influence of macro-economy, the rise of Buffett Indicator could also due to the developments in direct marketing the technology which made it easier for retailers to experiment with different ways of reaching customers. Data shows catalogue shopping experienced resurgence in last 20 years of the 20th century, especially among boutique retailers such as Pottery Barn, Williams Sonoma, and Victoria's Secret. [10]

After 2000, though the ratio went down affecting by the dot-com bubble, the overall trend is upward. With the advent of internet, e-Commerce touches virtually every aspect of the retail value chain, from product development to operations. More recently, social-networking websites, online product reviews, and other forms of interactivity with customers have provided retailers two-edged sword, narrowing the distance with customers and amplifying the flaws at the same time.

5.1.8. Transportation

The Buffett Indicator for Transportation industry is a unique one. It keeps an exponential increase since 1970. The average ratio is 60 per cent. The highest value is the most recent one in the data in 2014. From 2008 to 2014, the ratio starts with 65 per cent and ends with 180 per cent, nearly three times higher in only six years.

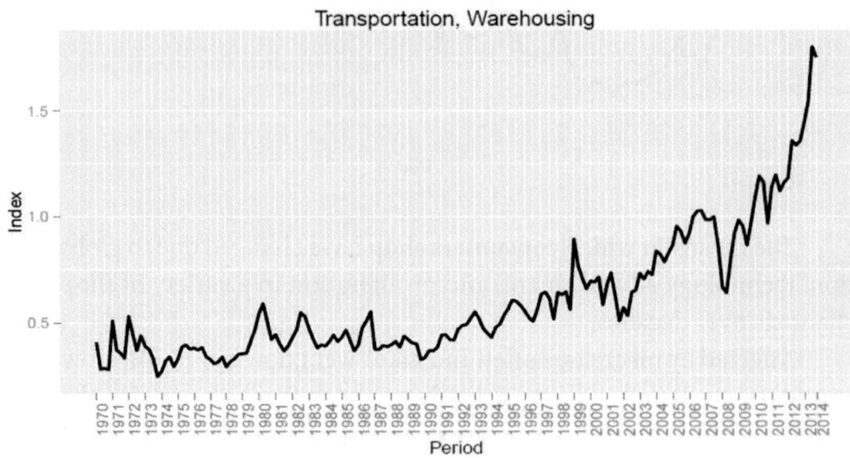

Because of its intensive use of infrastructures, the transport sector is an important component of the economy and a common tool used for development. At the macroeconomic level, transportation is related to output, employment and income in the country. At the microeconomic level, transportation is linked to producer, consumer and production costs. Generally, higher transportation expenses are associated with higher income levels. Along with globalization, the economic opportunities increasingly depend on the mobility of people, goods and information. When transport systems are efficient, people have better accessibility to markets, employment and additional investment. Efficient transport systems provide economic and social opportunities, and benefits that result in positive multipliers effects. Since US GDP increased every year, Buffett Indicator for Transportation industry also increased every year, showing investors consistently have confidence in Transportation industry in US.

5.1.9. Information

Buffett Indicator for Information industry is most exaggerated among all industries. The average ratio is 200 per cent. The highest ratio is 800 per cent in 1999 before the burst of internet bubble. The ratio started with 200 per cent in 1996 and rapidly increased to 800 per cent only in three years, but dropped back to 200 per cent within one year. It has kept increasing after 2001 and recently hit to 400 per cent. It has been a very popular industry for investors. From historical data, the trend in Information industry have significant impact on overall economy in US.

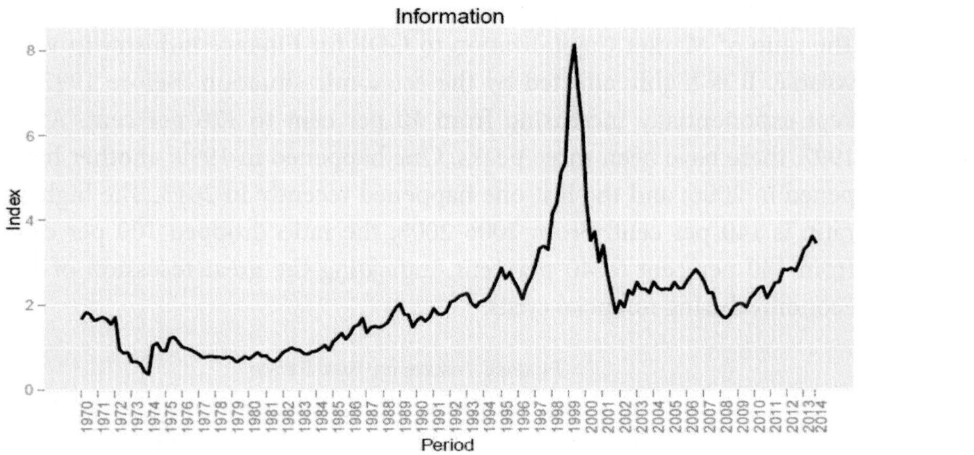

The period 1997–2000 was marked by the founding of several new internet-based companies commonly referred to as dot-coms. During that time, the practice of just adding an "e-"prefix to company's name or a ".com" to the end would easily increase company stock price. Market has enormous confidence in these new internet of things and strongly believed companies would realize profits in future.

In late 1990s, there is a dramatic jump of Buffett Indicator for Information industry. At the time, as access to the internet expanded, computers has become more and more important in people's daily lives. E-commerce is one of the biggest drivers of this growth. Due to the excitement of investors and good investment environment, data shows the value of NASDAQ grew from around 1000 points to more than 5000 points in 2000.[g]

However, in mid-2000, people started questioning the profitability that dot-com companies could eventually bring. Records show that from 10 March 2000 to 6 April 2000, in less than one month, nearly a trillion dollar of stock completely evaporated. One JP Morgan analyst told TIME magazine in April 2000 that a lot of companies were losing between 10 to 30 million for a quarter.[h] Buffett Indicator also dropped dramatically and touched the bottom in 2011, which was even lower than the beginning in 1996 when the internet bubble started to build-up.

5.1.10. Finance

The ratio of Market Capitalization to GDP for Finance industry in very volatile. It is highly affected by the economic situation. Before 1997, it kept exponentially increasing from 10 per cent to 120 per cent. After 1997, there have been three peaks. One happened in 1999; another happened in 2006; and the last one happened recently in 2013. The highest ratio is 140 per cent. From 2006-2008, the ratio dropped 100 per cent from 140 per cent to 40 per cent, indicating the great recession of US economy during financial crisis.

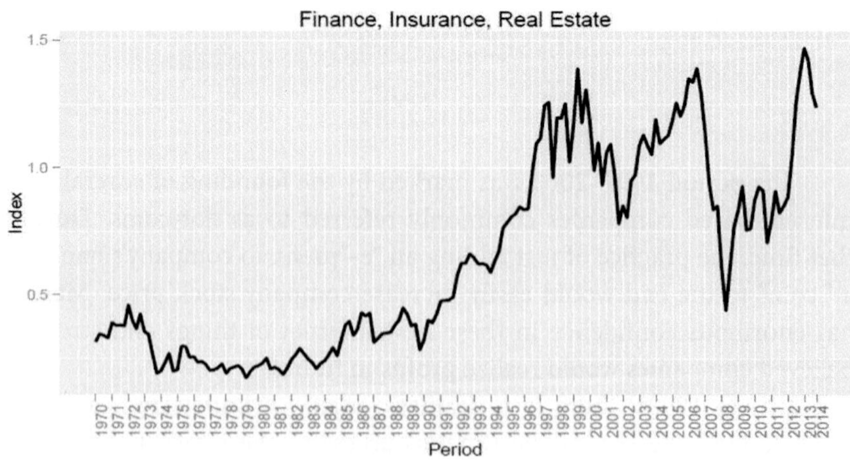

g http://marketrealist.com/2015/03/nasdaq-5000-dot-com-bubble/
h http://time.com/author/ben-geier/

Buffett Indicator for Finance industry is one of the graphs closest to the BI graph. Data shows that the US finance industry comprised only 10 per cent of total non-farm business profits in mid-1950s, but the percentage grew up to 50 per cent by 2010. Over the same period, finance industry income as a proportion of GDP rose from 2.5 per cent to 7.5 per cent, and the finance industry's proportion of all corporate income rose from 10 per cent to 20 per cent.[i]

The interactions between Finance and rest of the economy are actually complex. At the beginning of 1970s, the Buffett Indicator shows a downward trend due to the oil crisis. However, the ratio started to grow in late 1980s. Financial industry grew fast onwards, that is partially due to the "deregulation", where the federal government reduced the distinctions between banks and other financial institutions. [11]

The 2008 financial crisis is considered as the worst financial crisis since the Great Depression in 1930s. In late 2005–2006, home prices started to fall and many subprime borrowers could not afford the high interest rates and started defaulting on their loan. In early 2007, many subprime lenders filed for bankruptcy. It has brought all public attention when Lehman Brothers filed for bankruptcy, Bear Stearns was acquired by JP Morgan Chase and Fannie Mae and Freddie Mac were put under the control of the US federal government in 2008. The crisis played a significant role in leading to the 2008–2012 global recession and contributing to the European sovereign-debt crisis. In later 2008, US government came out the "Emergency Economic Stabilization Act of 2008" to spend up to $700 billion to purchase distressed assets, especially mortgage-backed securities. From 2011 onwards, the Buffett Indicator has gone up again and reached historical highest value in 2012, even higher than in 2006 when the house bubble just started to build-up.

5.1.11. Services

Buffett Indicator for Services industry is not popular to investors, just like Agriculture, Construction and Wholesale industries. The average ratio is 23 per cent over past 45 years. The graph has two peaks. The first one happened in 1971; the second one happened in 1999. After two-year's time since the two peaks took place, the ratio dropped to around 10 per cent.

---

i https://en.wikipedia.org/wiki/Banking_in_the_United_States

From 2008 onwards, the ratio has kept going up and reached 30 per cent in 2014.

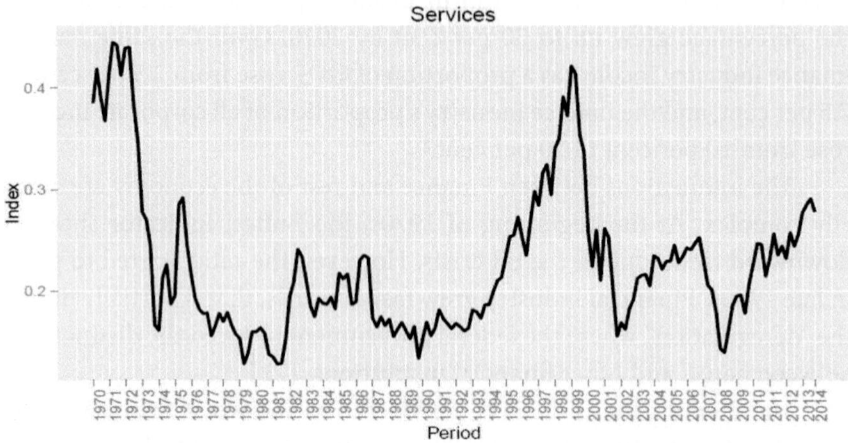

From mid-20th century, white-collar workers outnumbered blue-collar workers for the first time in US. The Service industry is actually where the most new companies are formed during 1979 – 2011. Records show that by 1999, the Service industry employed about twice as many employees as manufacturing or government and by the beginning of 21st century, Services accounted for approximately 70 per cent of the national income and 80 per cent of the jobs. [12] Although the US economy today is characterized as a "service economy" and this long-term shift from manufacturing to services is expected to continue, investors are not so attracted to this industry at all.

5.2. Correlation and regression analysis

5.2.1. Correlation analysis

The result of correlation matrix between industries is given in the Appendix 2.

The correlation matrix shows that Manufacturing, Wholesale Trade, Retail Trade and Finance have very strong positive correlations with each other. The correlation co-efficiency of Buffett Indicators are above 0.9. Manufacturing industry also has relatively strong positive correlation with Mining, Transportation and Information. Besides Manufacturing, Transportation has relatively strong positive correlations with Construction, Wholesale Trade and Retail Trade. The correlation coefficiency of Buffett Indicators for them are above 0.8.

5.2.2. Regression analysis

The result of linear regression is given in Appendix 2.

Except for Agriculture, the coefficients for other industries are all positive. However, the *t*-stat for Agriculture is −1.9, not significant with a 95 per cent significance level. The *t*-stat for Mining, Utilities, Manufacturing, Information, Finance and Services are over +2. These are the industries which significantly impact the "Buffett Indicator" of the entire set of industries.

6. CONCLUSIONS AND FURTHER WORK

From 1970 to 2014, the average Buffett Indicator for Agriculture is 11 per cent. But at the beginning of 2014, it has reached 33 per cent, exactly tripled the average value. The average Buffett indicators for Construction, Manufacturing, Retail Trade, and Transportation from 1970 to 2014 are 7 per cent, 195 per cent, 63 per cent, and 60 per cent, respectively. However, the most current indicators show that the ratios have reached 15 per cent, 390 per cent, 130 per cent, and 175 per cent, respectively, more than double the average. In fact, the current Buffett indicators for all the eleven industries are higher than the average value in the period of 1970 to 2014. According to Warren Buffett, all industries are overvalued based on their Buffett Indicators.

Among the industries, the graphs of Buffett Indicator for Manufacturing and Finance show most similar patterns to the graph for the entire set of industries. They are also the industries which have the strongest correlations with other industries such as Wholesale Trade and Retail Trade. Finally, the *t*-stat and *p*-value in the regression analysis show the significance that Manufacturing and Finance can affect the whole set of industries. It indicates the leading positions that Manufacturing and Finance industry are holding for US economy.

However, it is interesting to find out a common pattern in all graphs. Using Agriculture as an example. In 2002, the ratio grew from a local minimum point of 5 per cent, reached to nearly 50 per cent in 2007, and then it started crashing. It kept dropping but stopped at 20 per cent at the end of 2009. It did not drop back to the starting phase before it restarts to grow. All the graphs show this pattern: at one point of time, the ratio starts growing, but when it reaches maximum and starts dropping, it will not drop to original level; it ends at between the starting level and maximum point, and goes up again. Hence, some investors question about the capability of "Buffett Indicator". They think knowing if something has a higher or lower value compared to its historic mean does not provide much insight as to whether you should buy or sell it; indeed, stocks can become, and stay, oversold or overbought for long periods of time. In an easy way, the future will tell us whether Buffett Indicator is still "the best single measure of where valuations stand at any given moment".

REFERENCES

1. Springer (2010). *A Brief History of US Agriculture.* http://faculty.apec.umn.edu/ppardey/documents/9781441906571-c1.pdf

2. United States Department of Agriculture. *The 20th Century Transformation of US Agriculture and Farm Policy.* http://www.ers.usda.gov/media/259572/eib3_1_.pdf

3. Thomas Michael Power (2002). *Digging to Development? A Historical Look at Mining and Economic Development.* http://www.oxfamamerica.org/static/oa3/files/OA-Digging_to_Development.pdf

4. Richard Geddes, R (1992). *A Historical Perspective on Electric Utility Regulation.* http://object.cato.org/sites/cato.org/files/serials/files/regulation/1992/1/v15n1-8.pdf

5. National Society of Professional Engineers (2014). *Construction Productivity in Decline.* http://www.leanconstruction.org/media/docs/PEJune14_Construction.pdf

6. Martin Neil, B and B P Bosworth (2014). *US Manufacturing: Understanding Its Past and Its Potential Future.* http://www.brookings.edu/~/media/research/files/papers/2014/02/us-manufacturing-past-and-potential-future-baily-bosworth/us-manufacturing-past-and-potential-future-baily-bosworth.pdf

7. Levinson, M (2015). *US Manufacturing in International Perspective.* https://www.fas.org/sgp/crs/misc/R42135.pdf

8. Miller, J and W Abraitis (2007). *Monthly Wholesale Trade: Sales and Inventories.* http://www.census.gov/mwts/www/currentwhl.html

9. KPMG LLP. *The Evolution of Retailing: Reinventing the Customer Experience.* http://www.kpmg.com/CN/en/IssuesAndInsights/ArticlesPublications/Documents/Evolution-retailing-o-200912.pdf

10. Carden, A (2011). *Retail Innovations in American Economic History: The Rise of Mass-Market Merchandisers*. http://www.independent.org/pdf/working_papers/78_retailinnovations.pdf

11. Philippon, T (2008). *The Evolution of the US Financial Industry from 1860 to 2007: Theory and Evidence*. http://www.betterregulation.com/external/The%20Evolution%20of%20the%20US%20Financial%20Industry%20from%201860%20to%202007%20Theory%20and%20Evidence.pdf

12. Haksever, C and B Render (2013). *The Important Role Services Play in an Economy*. http://www.ftpress.com/articles/article.aspx?p=2095734&seqNum=3

APPENDIX 1: Graphs of Market Capitalization and GDP per Industry

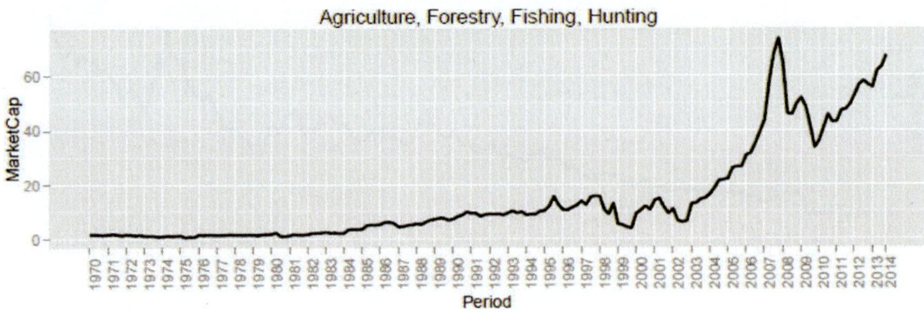

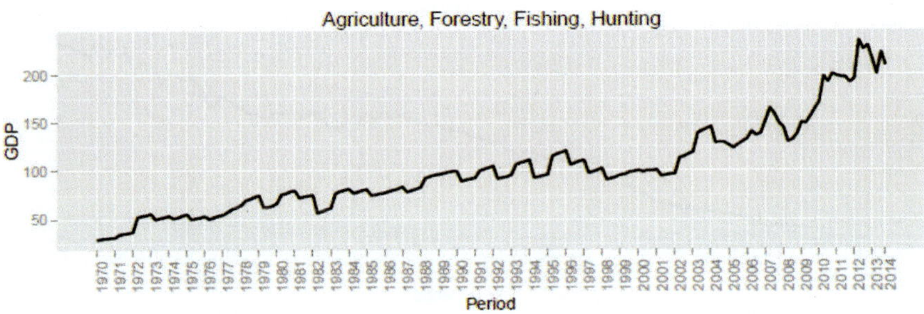

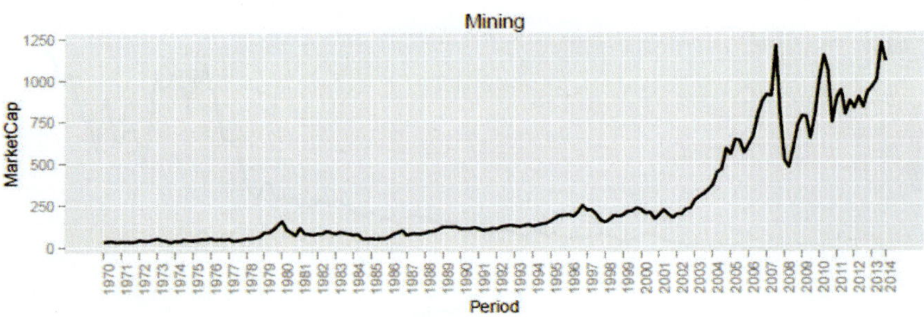

(*continued*)

APPENDIX 1: Graphs of Market Capitalization and GDP per Industry (*continued*)

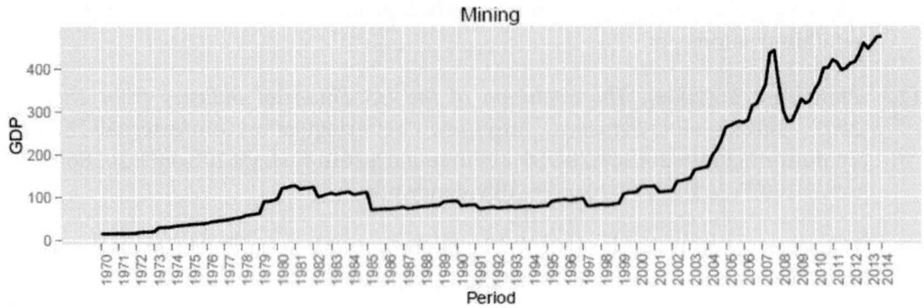

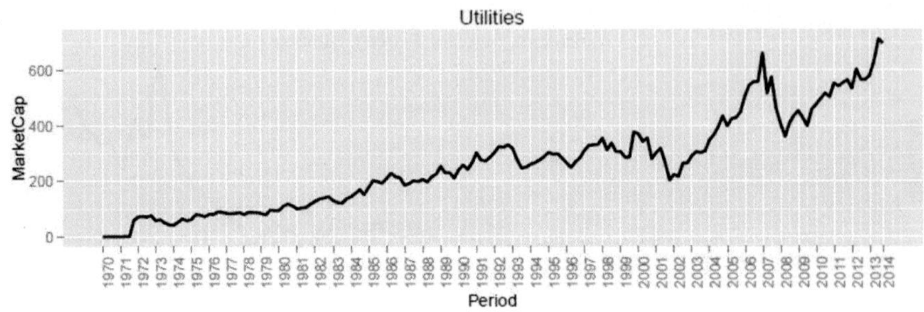

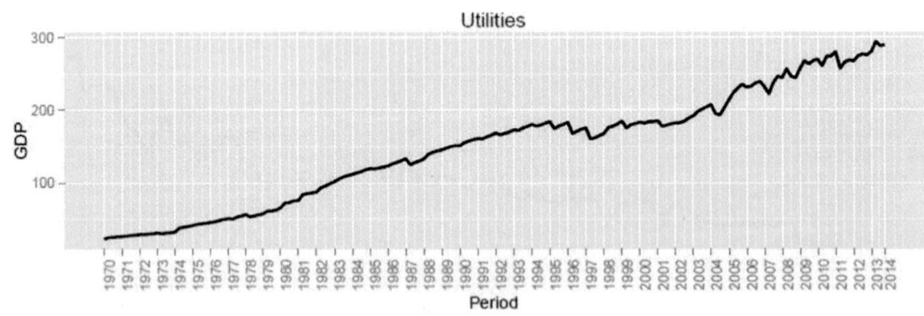

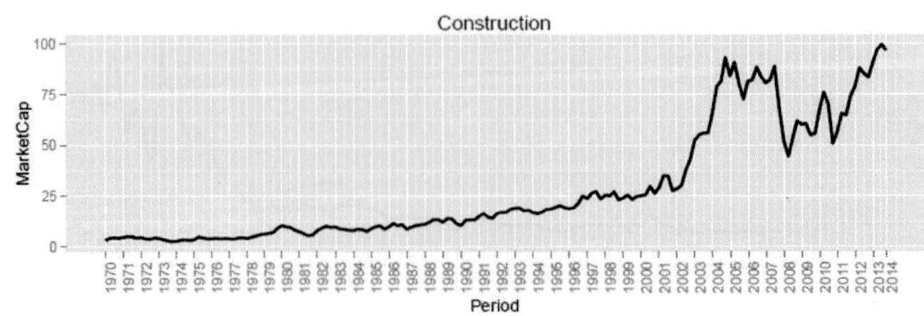

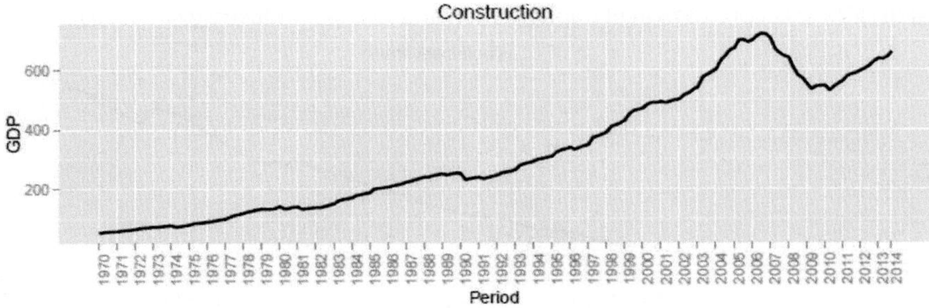
Construction
GDP
200
400
600
Period
1970 1971 1972 1973 1974 1975 1976 1977 1978 1979 1980 1981 1982 1983 1984 1985 1986 1987 1988 1989 1990 1991 1992 1993 1994 1995 1996 1997 1998 1999 2000 2001 2002 2003 2004 2005 2006 2007 2008 2009 2010 2011 2012 2013 2014

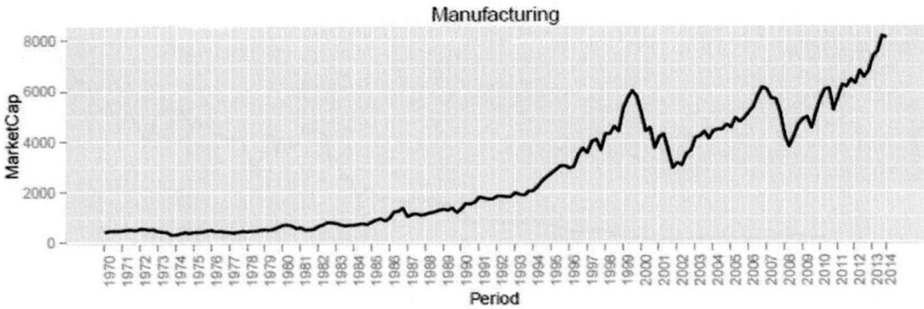
Manufacturing
MarketCap
0
2000
4000
6000
8000
Period
1970 1971 1972 1973 1974 1975 1976 1977 1978 1979 1980 1981 1982 1983 1984 1985 1986 1987 1988 1989 1990 1991 1992 1993 1994 1995 1996 1997 1998 1999 2000 2001 2002 2003 2004 2005 2006 2007 2008 2009 2010 2011 2012 2013 2014

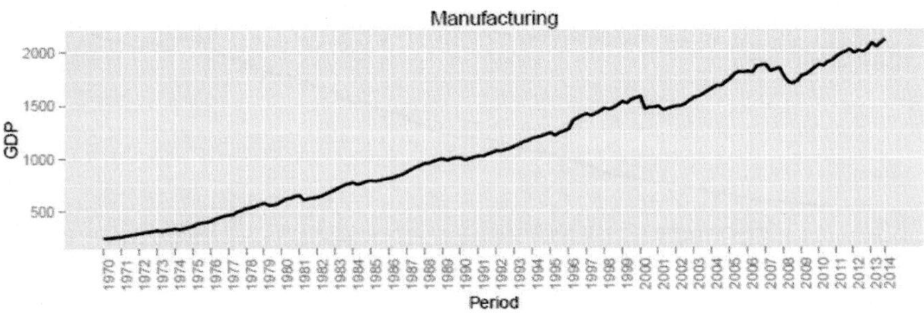
Manufacturing
GDP
500
1000
1500
2000
Period
1970 1971 1972 1973 1974 1975 1976 1977 1978 1979 1980 1981 1982 1983 1984 1985 1986 1987 1988 1989 1990 1991 1992 1993 1994 1995 1996 1997 1998 1999 2000 2001 2002 2003 2004 2005 2006 2007 2008 2009 2010 2011 2012 2013 2014

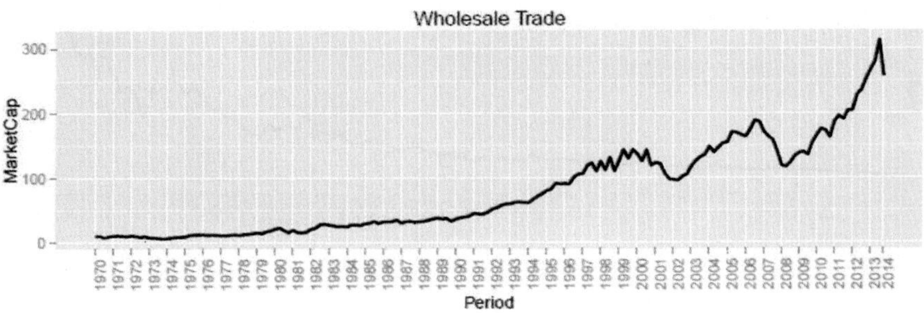
Wholesale Trade
MarketCap
0
100
200
300
Period
1970 1971 1972 1973 1974 1975 1976 1977 1978 1979 1980 1981 1982 1983 1984 1985 1986 1987 1988 1989 1990 1991 1992 1993 1994 1995 1996 1997 1998 1999 2000 2001 2002 2003 2004 2005 2006 2007 2008 2009 2010 2011 2012 2013 2014

(continued)

APPENDIX 1: Graphs of Market Capitalization and GDP per Industry (*continued*)

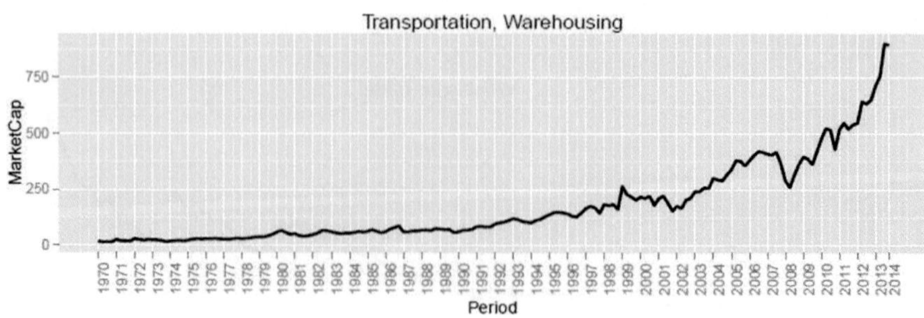

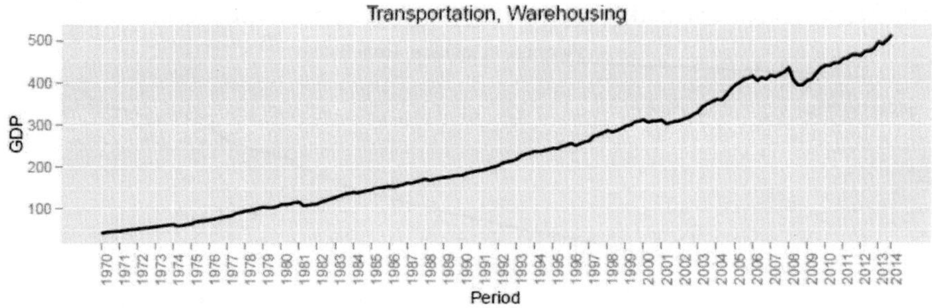
Transportation, Warehousing
GDP
500
400
300
200
100
1970 1971 1972 1973 1974 1975 1976 1977 1978 1979 1980 1981 1982 1983 1984 1985 1986 1987 1988 1989 1990 1991 1992 1993 1994 1995 1996 1997 1998 1999 2000 2001 2002 2003 2004 2005 2006 2007 2008 2009 2010 2011 2012 2013 2014
Period

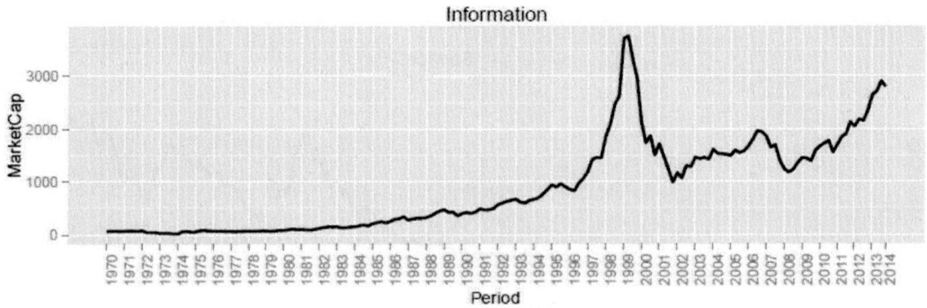
Information
MarketCap
3000
2000
1000
0
1970 1971 1972 1973 1974 1975 1976 1977 1978 1979 1980 1981 1982 1983 1984 1985 1986 1987 1988 1989 1990 1991 1992 1993 1994 1995 1996 1997 1998 1999 2000 2001 2002 2003 2004 2005 2006 2007 2008 2009 2010 2011 2012 2013 2014
Period

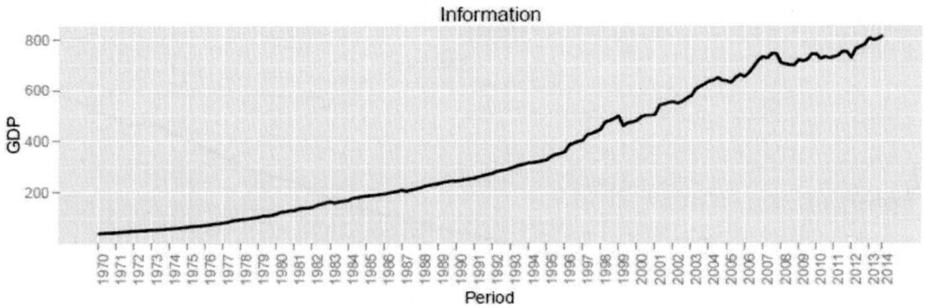
Information
GDP
800
600
400
200
1970 1971 1972 1973 1974 1975 1976 1977 1978 1979 1980 1981 1982 1983 1984 1985 1986 1987 1988 1989 1990 1991 1992 1993 1994 1995 1996 1997 1998 1999 2000 2001 2002 2003 2004 2005 2006 2007 2008 2009 2010 2011 2012 2013 2014
Period

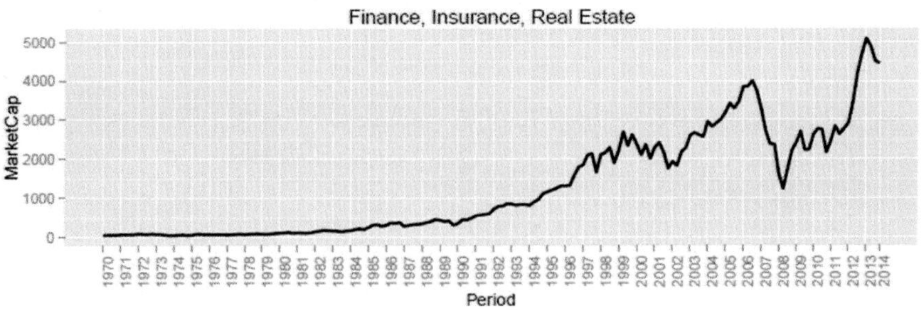
Finance, Insurance, Real Estate
MarketCap
5000
4000
3000
2000
1000
0
1970 1971 1972 1973 1974 1975 1976 1977 1978 1979 1980 1981 1982 1983 1984 1985 1986 1987 1988 1989 1990 1991 1992 1993 1994 1995 1996 1997 1998 1999 2000 2001 2002 2003 2004 2005 2006 2007 2008 2009 2010 2011 2012 2013 2014
Period

(continued)

APPENDIX 1: Graphs of Market Capitalization and GDP per Industry (*continued*)

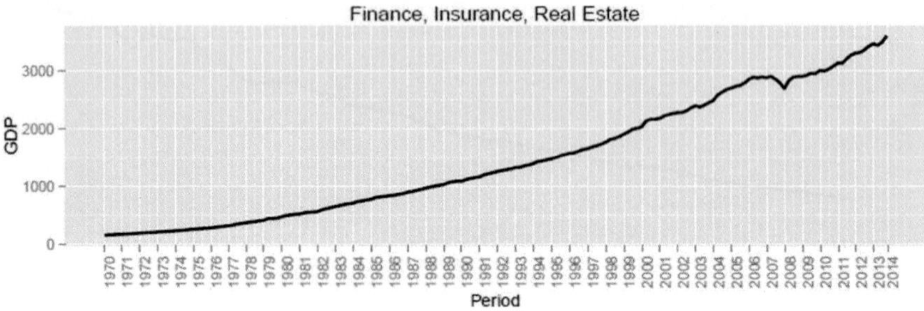

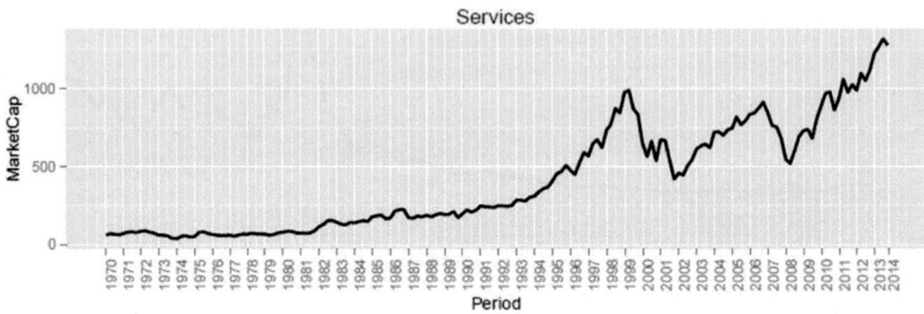

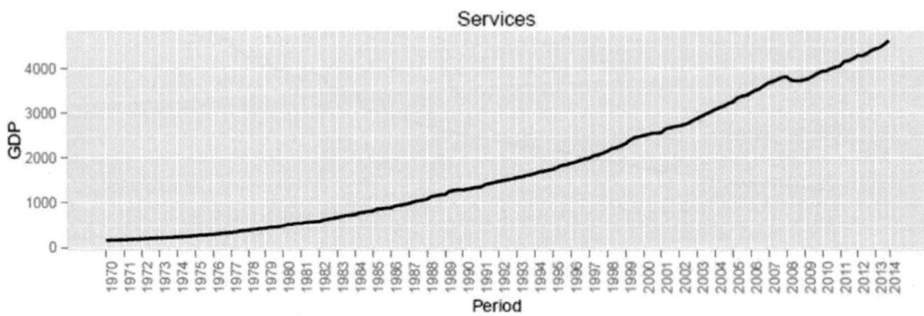

APPENDIX 2. Correlation Matrix and Regression Result

	Agriculture	Mining	Utilities	Construction	Manufacturing	Wholesale trade	Retail trade	Transportation	Information	Finance	Services
Agriculture	1										
Mining	0.62654709	1									
Utilities	0.412356314	0.325012212	1								
Construction	0.786481965	0.714931732	0.36820564	1							
Manu-facturing	0.720621915	0.831241917	0.417556843	0.74908368	1						
Wholesale trade	0.646560641	0.771009845	0.375576419	0.74777514	0.95662342	1					
Retail trade	0.759750737	0.786383205	0.40863604	0.779467041	0.968294859	0.933187238	1				
Trans-portation	0.786149986	0.655037521	0.497929868	0.89993855	0.840203291	0.836792225	0.848191243	1			
Information	0.342377005	0.566274219	0.257365746	0.331054341	0.811550343	0.785482295	0.760014707	0.507272129	1		
Finance	0.617819554	0.754466225	0.444906073	0.688163578	0.935470223	0.948441762	0.915091019	0.7644326	0.795779511	1	
Services	0.011396187	0.529417737	-0.0310705	0.186865538	0.43734036	0.447000071	0.385332036	0.179829171	0.495615379	0.352898406	1

Regression Statistics	
Multiple R	0.99936187
R Square	0.998724147
Adjusted R Square	0.998638571
Standard Error	0.010501832
Observations	176

	Coefficients	Standard Error	t Stat	P-value
Intercept	0.021242303	0.005986745	3.548222644	0.000506025
Agriculture	-0.034812742	0.018290412	-1.90333279	0.058748907
Mining	0.019048965	0.003336983	5.708438361	5.21972E-08
Utilities	0.025240329	0.002366301	10.66657452	1.65286E-20
Construction	0.075493986	0.088298991	0.854981291	0.39380879
Manufacturing	0.13327533	0.006679515	19.95284664	9.98057E-46
Wholesale trade	0.153539691	0.079462479	1.932228806	0.055054702
Retail trade	0.001000575	0.011278703	0.088713661	0.929417715
Transportation	-0.012332335	0.01069403	-1.153198103	0.250507052
Information	0.056928943	0.001827942	31.1437376	9.29792E-71
Finance	0.194226386	0.009080064	21.39042103	2.57984E-49
Services	0.464351531	0.017872693	25.98106108	5.111E-60

CHAPTER 27

On the Possibility of Arbitrage Around Announcements

Karthik Narayan Pasupathy

ABSTRACT

This paper aims to look at stock price movements around earnings announcements, to check if there are any patterns preceding the announcements that are dependent on the nature of earnings. A quick visual study appears to find some commonality but deeper analysis to check the dependency of nature of earnings announcements on stock variations yielded no correlation.

Further study was undertaken using industry verticals of stock and trend before announcement to come up with significant pattern using decision trees to predict nature of earnings announcements. This study suggests that while there is a significant improvement in accuracy when using industry vertical as an independent variable, there were no strong patterns. Thus the study concludes (1) there is no correlation between stock dip and nature of earnings announcements on aggregate level and (2) correlation between stock price movements, industry vertical and nature of results while do to exist, without strong patterns of emerging.

It could be beyond the observable parameters in the study and could be driven by other intangible factors while having some correlation with industry verticals.

1. INTRODUCTION

Stock prices always fluctuate abnormally during key events. One such key event tends to be quarterly earnings announcements. On a superficial analysis of the recent quarterly earnings announcements, there appeared to be a recent trend where the stock dips on the eve of announcements while picks up post announcements despite the nature of the results announced.

There has been lot of interest around the movement of stock prices around earnings announcements and resulting price drifts (see Figure 1). This abnormal shorting of stocks around announcements was studied by Christope *et al.* (2004) who measured the aggregate pattern of short selling around earnings announcements. It was revealed that in aggregate, shorting over entire sample does not rise over earnings surprises but for a specific set of stocks, indicating the possibility of insider trading. However, it showed that the short sellers are not always correct in the assessment of earnings. To add this line of study, Qureshi *et al.* (2012) studied the pre-announcement returns and found that there were abnormal stock returns around earnings announcement.

In fact, their studies showed similar "Nike tick" patterns, where the prices of stocks shot up before announcements but dipped just after the announcements. The study further went on to show that the price movements were similar across industries. This led to question if this pattern was a result of insider trading or an independent occurrence.

This study focuses on the movement of stock prices around the (−25, 25) day window of announcement. Checks to see if the occurrence of minimum of the stock price around the announcements is related to the nature of announcements. That is, if occurrence of minimum before announcements is indicative of bad results. It should be noted that the project classified announcements as positive, if results beat Earnings Per Share (EPS) estimate by Wall Street by more than 2.5 per cent and negative if it fell short more than 2.5 per cent or neutral. The study suggests that true to observations in Christope *et al.* (2004), short sellers are not always correct and there is not any correlation among occurrences of minimum.

Figure 1: Movement of stock prices on (–25, 25) days around announcements.

This study also tries to check useful patterns in the movement of stock prices before announcements, industry of the stock prices, and the nature of results. This has been attempted using C5.0 decision tree. While it was observed that no specific actionable patterns were available, some interesting insights were obtained.

2. PROBLEM STATEMENT

The key objective of this study is to investigate the phenomenon of "Nike tick" in detail and study the movement of stocks around earnings. This has been approached by breaking down into following sub objectives.

- To investigate further on the observed "Nike tick" to check if there exists a consistent pattern in the fall of stock prices before announcement.
- To check if the nature of announcements affect the pattern of occurrence of minimum around announcements.

- To identify possible arbitrage/insider trading if the relationship between occurrence of minimum of stock prices and nature of announcements is proved.
- To check for patterns between movement of stock prices, industry (or vertical) and nature of announcements.

3. STATE OF ART

As already stated, there has always been a lot of interest in earning announcements. Research work includes studying post earnings drift (Bernard and Thomas, 1989), analyzing insider trading before announcements, (Kea *et al.* 2003), and stock price prediction around announcements (Lobo and Tung, 1998), to name a few.

This study focuses on abnormal shorting of stocks around announcements, followed by a rise leading to what this study described as Nike tick pattern. Abnormal shorting of stocks around announcements was studied by Christope *et al.* (2004) who examined the short-selling behavior of investors prior to earnings announcements of 913 Nasdaq-listed stocks. A basic conclusion from this study was that the abnormal short selling is an indicator of future stock returns at earning announcements. It is not a perfect indicator, e.g., an unusual increase in short selling does not precede all negative earnings announcements. Nonetheless, in the majority of cases, announcement period stock return is negative following unusually high short-selling. Further interest in this line of study was sparked by Qureshi *et al.* (2012). The core objective of this study was to observe the movement of share prices around earnings announcement dates in Pakistani market. This was studied by examining the impact of the earnings releases on the stock prices, which was depicted in the abnormal or excess return as compared to any other random day selected. Results showed that there were significant abnormal returns in the whole event window, that is, the days surrounding the earning announcements and further went on to show similarities in behavior between companies belonging to same industry. On similar lines, moving from investigative analysis on financial trends to predicting financial trends, decision trees have been used for long finance. Tiwari *et al.*, (2010) predicted future trends in stock market based on historical stock market data using hybrid decision trees. This also contributed to decision to adopt similar techniques in the study.

This study adds to the similar line of research by investigating further on the "Nike tick" to check if occurrence of minimum of stock prices is correlated with the nature of results. It goes one step further by using a decision tree to predict the nature of announcements with the movement of stock prices around announcements, industry, and the trend before announcements as independent variables.

4. SOLUTION

Description of Approach

This section describes how the problem was approached and the steps taken to arrive at the solution. It is divided into four major sections:

- Section 4.1 deals with dataset and data collection.
- Section 4.2 describes the test for correlation between occurrence of minimum and nature of quarterly earnings announcements.
- Section 4.3 describes briefly checking for patterns using decision tree in the dataset.
- Section 4.4 describes the optimization and visualization of decision tree obtained in Section 4.3, and checking for accuracy in predicting the earnings results.

4.1. Dataset and visual observation

Data is the foremost requirement to perform a study. Four major attributes of stock data were required for this study.

1) Quarterly earnings announcement date
2) Wall Street estimate of earnings per share
3) Wall Street estimate of quarterly revenue
4) Actual earnings per share
5) Actual quarterly revenue
6) Stock prices around the window of announcements.

It was decided that the window of stock prices to be studied would be (−25,+25) days of earnings announcements. This was because, beyond this, the movement of stock prices need not necessarily be a result of effect of earnings announcements but other operational factors. The challenge with data collection was getting historical Wall Street estimates of EPS, quarterly revenue, and the announcement dates. Initially, Bloomberg terminal and financial websites were used to get the information manually. The problem with a manual approach was that getting each and every attribute manually after reading. There was no structured format available.

However tabulated source for the information was discovered online at http://www.estimize.com. This formed the basis of all the data that have been used for this study. Sanity checks for the accuracy of data was undertaken and found to be accurate for use in this analysis.

A sample of the information collected from this website is shown in Table 1 below.

Table 1: Sample of data set collected for the study using estimize.com.

Company	EPS Wall Street	EPS actual	Revenue Wall Street	Revenue actual	Reported date
Apple Inc	$1.22	$1.28	$38,002.00	$37,432.00	22/7/14
Abbvie Inc	$0.76	$0.82	$4671.00	$4930.00	25/7/14
Barrick Gold Corp	$0.14	$0.14	$2425.00	$2432.00	30/7/14
Auto Desk	$0.28	$0.35	$600.93	$637.00	14/8/14
Advent Software Inc	$0.34	$0.38	$97.70	$100.37	28/7/14

The dictionary for the above data table is as follows.

- **EPS Wall Street**: EPS estimate of Wall Street for the quarter (essentially consensus estimate of EPS for the given quarter)
- **EPS actual**: Actual EPS as shared by the company during quarterly earnings

- **Revenue Wall Street**: Quarterly revenue estimate of Wall Street for the quarter (essentially consensus estimate of quarterly revenue for the given quarter)
- **Revenue actual**: Actual quarterly revenue as shared by the company during quarterly earnings
- **Reported date**: Quarterly earnings announcement date

This information was collected for approximately 70 companies across eight quarters from Q4′12 till Q3′14. Once this information was collected, the stock prices around the earnings announcements were required, so as to study the price variation patterns for these companies. These stock prices around the earnings announcement dates were collected using Tseries and Zoo packages in R.

Visual analysis was undertaken to check for the "Nike tick" and to observe the movement of stock prices around earnings announcements. While it was observed in pronounced pattern in some cases, effect of "Nike tick" was not so pronounced in other cases. This analysis was undertaken in Excel using the graph plotting features. A sample of the observations is as shown in Figure 2.

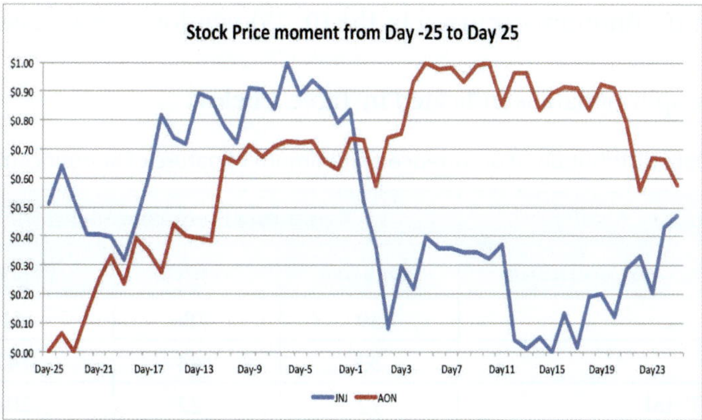

Figure 2: Sample visual analysis of movement of stock prices around the (−25, 25) day window.

In the above graph the prices are normalised between zero and one to ensure equal scale. As already stated, while the "Nike tick" pattern was observed in a lot of stocks, it was however not consistent across quarters/companies to significantly conclude on the occurrence of the pattern.

4.2. Test of independence

Moving a step further, it was decided to check if there was any relation between the nature of earnings announcement and occurrence of minimum as observed in a "Nike tick", i.e., to check if occurrence of minimum before or after the results was dependent on the nature of the results.

As a first step, the quarterly earnings results were classified as "Positive", "Negative," and "Neutral" based on EPS. If EPS of a company as disclosed in the quarterly earnings exceeded expectations of Wall Street for that quarter by 5 per cent, it was classified as positive quarterly earnings results. It was negative if there was a miss on actuals vs expectation by 5 per cent and neutral otherwise.

Excess EPS = (EPS Actual – EPS Wall Street)/EPS Wall Street.
If Excess EPS≥ .05 then positive
Else If EPS ≤ -.05 then negative
Else neutral

The occurrence of minimum of the stock price in the (–25, 25) day window was also classified as "Before" if it occurred in the (25,–1) day window. If minimum occurred in the (0, 25) window, it was classified as "After".

The split of data is indicated in Table 2 below.

Table 2: Data distribution of occurrence of minimum vs nature of announcements.

Minimum vs results	Announcement classification		
Occurrence of minimum	**Negative**	**Neutral**	**Positive**
After	39	78	61
Before	33	144	147
Grand Total	72	222	208

It can be observed that with 5 per cent variation of EPS between actual and Wall Street as the limit, data is more skewed towards neutral. The data now consists of 502 data points across eight quarters and 70 companies that could be checked for independence. To achieve this, checks for the following hypothesis were made.

Null Hypothesis: The occurrence of Minimum and Nature of earnings announcements are independent.

Alternate Hypothesis: The occurrence of Minimum and Nature of earnings announcements are dependent.

At a significance level of 0.05 in the Chi-Square test, reject a null hypothesis of independence. This test was conducted within the same quarter as well as across the quarters to check this hypothesis. The tabulated observation is as shown in Table 3 below.

Table 3: Chi-square results from the test of hypothesis for independence.

Quarter	Q4'12	Q1'13	Q2'13	Q3'13	Q4'13	Q1'14	Q2'14	Q3'14	All quarters
p value	0.236	0.095	0.012	0.029	0.524	0.119	0.805	0.631	0.001
Reject null hypothesis	No	No	Yes	Yes	No	No	No	No	Yes

It is to be noted that "All Quarters" column in Table 3 refers to test of hypothesis across all quarters, while otherwise, it refers to within the same quarter. The study found that for most quarters the test does not reject the null hypothesis that occurrence of minimum is independent of the nature of announcements.

It was then decided to check for the sensitivity of the test by reducing the cut for classifying the nature of earnings announcements to 2.5 per cent variation of EPS between actual and Wall Street estimate from 5 per cent. Thus, under the new classification,

If Excess EPS>=.025 then positive
Else If EPS <=-.025 then negative
Else neutral

The split of data was improved and more evenly distributed with slight skewness toward the positive classification as Table 4 shows.

A similar hypothesis test was carried out and the results are as shown in Table 5 below.

It can be observed that though the *p*-value has come down closer to 0.05, the no. of quarters rejecting the null hypothesis in the tests remain the same in both cases. Now that it was established that the nature of announcement does not necessarily influence the occurrence of minimum in the stock prices, the next step was to check if there was

Table 4: Data distribution of occurrence of minimum vs nature of announcements at 2.5 per cent EPS variation.

Minimum vs results	**Announcement Classification**		
Occurrence of minimum	**Negative**	**Neutral**	**Positive**
After	53	37	88
Before	47	66	211
Grand total	100	103	299

Table 5: Chi-square results from the test of hypothesis for independence at 2.5 per cent EPS variation.

Quarter	**Q4′12**	**Q1′13**	**Q2′13**	**Q3′13**	**Q4′13**	**Q1′14**	**Q2′14**	**Q3′14**	**All quarters**
p value	0.08076	0.3599	0.03198	0.04158	0.5186	0.2328	0.6049	0.178	0.00
Reject null hypothesis	No	No	Yes	Yes	No	No	No	No	Yes

a staggered reaction. That is if this quarter's announcement affects next quarter's stock price moments.

Null Hypothesis: *The occurrence of minimum in a given quarter and Nature of announcements in previous quarter are independent.*

Alternate Hypothesis: *The occurrence of minimum in a given quarter and Nature of announcements in previous quarter are dependent.*

In this test, the earnings result classifications were tested against the corresponding next quarter's occurrence of minimum. It is to be noted that the earnings announcements are classified at 2.5 per cent EPS variation. The tabulated results are as shown in Table 6 below.

Table 6: Chi-square results from the test of the hypothesis for independence between quarters.

Quarter	**Q1′13–Q2′13**	**Q2′13–Q3′13**	**Q3′13–Q4′13**	**Q4′13–Q1′14**	**Q1′14–Q2′14**	**Q2′14–Q3′14**
p value	0.525	0.3461	0.2624	0.1942	0.1348	0.8738
Reject null hypothesis	No	No	No	No	No	No

It was observed that this test did not reject the null hypothesis of independence between occurrence of minimum in a given quarter and nature of announcements in the previous quarter for any of the quarters. Thus, this concludes that there is no staggered effect either.

4.2.1. Visual observation of density of minimum days

As a last step before concluding the test of independence between occurrence of minimum and nature of earnings results, it was necessary to observe if there were any patterns in days of occurrence of minimum in the (−25, 25) day window. This was done in order to remove any data bias and to check visually if there were any indications of pattern requiring further work.

This was done by plotting a density graph of the day of occurrence of minimum. Here the density refers to the kernel density of the count of the number of times the minimum occurs on a given day. In the graphs below, three density plots are layered on each other. That is, the densities of occurrence of minimum for negative, neutral and positive cases are layered on top of each other for easy comparison.

Figure 3 shows All Quarters (density plot of occurrence of minimum across quarters).

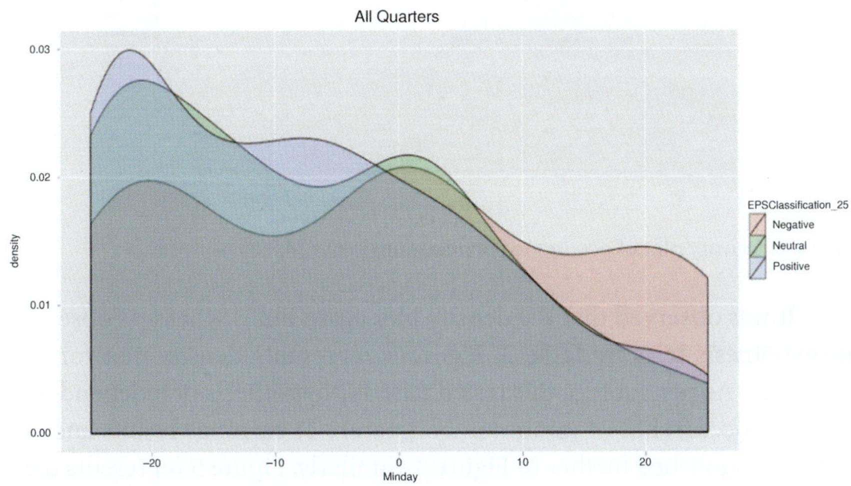

Figure 3: Density plot of occurrence of minimum across all quarter.

Figure 4 shows Q2′13 (density plot of occurrence of minimum in Q2′13).

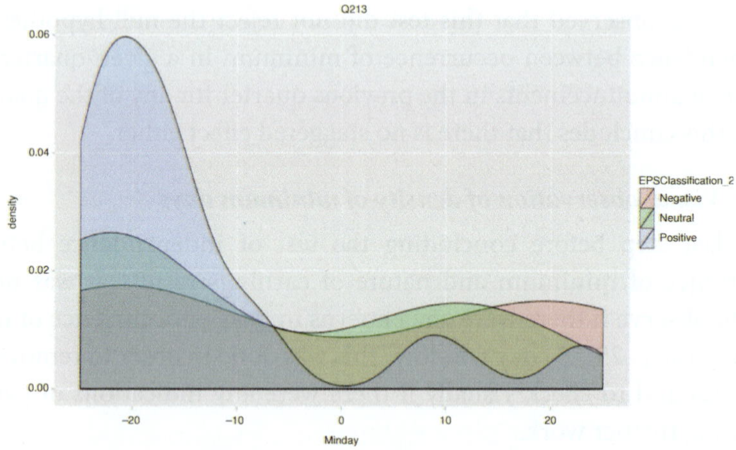

Figure 4: Density plot of occurrence of minimum in Q2′13.

Q2′14 (Density plot of occurrence of minimum in Q2′14)

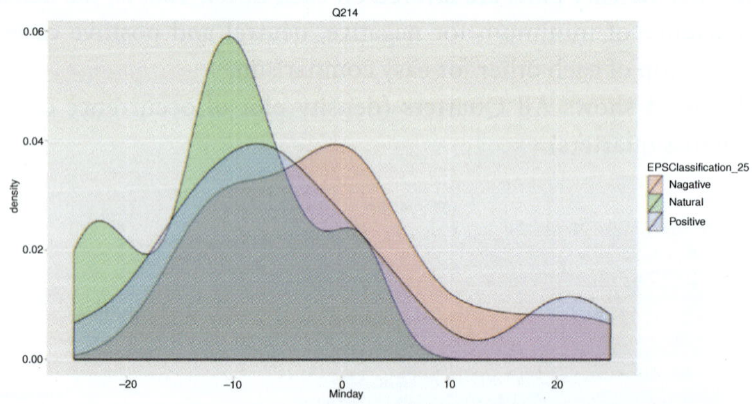

Figure 5: Density plot of occurrence of minimum in Q2′14.

It was observed that the density plot again holds what was observed in hypothesis tests in Table 3. Figure 3 represents density plot for "All Quarters" As per Table 3, this tested false for hypothesis of independence between occurrence of minimum and nature of earnings results and the same is established further in Figure 3. Similarly, Figure 5 represents density plot for Q2′14. As per Table 3, this did not test false for hypothesis of independence between occurrence of minimum and nature of earnings results. Figure 5 represents the same result visually. In Table 3, it can be observed that between Q4′12–Q3′14, it was only Q2′13 and Q3′13 that tested false for the hypothesis test. While in all the other remaining quarters, a hypothesis of independence was observed between occurrence of minimum and nature of results and were not proved false. Essentially, if these were plotted, a similar plot would be observed as in Figure 5 where there is no clear-cut distinction between occurrence of minimum and earnings results.

4.3. Check for patterns: decision tree

The next step was to identify if there was any relationship between the movement of stock price before announcements and nature of quarterly earnings announcements, i.e., to identify if there was any strong and conclusive patterns in the data.

For this as a first step, the data was modified with Day–25 to Day 0 as *X* variable and results as *Y* variable, and decision tree was run.

```
Decision tree:
Day −19 > 9.94671: Positive (470/183)
- Day 19 ≤ 9.94671:
:... Day −24 ≤ 5.473561: Neutral (7/3)
Day −24 > 5.473561:
:...- Day 7 ≤ 9.08: Positive (19/7)
Day −7 > 9.08: Negative (6)
Evaluation on training data (502 cases):
Decision Tree
----------------
Size Errors
4 193(38.4%) <<
(a) (b) (c) <-classified as
---- ---- ----
6  3   91  (a): class Negative
   4   99  (b): class Neutral
      299  (c): class Positive
```

DT showed that there was no pattern and the prediction of the nature of quarterly earnings announcements was inefficient. The decision tree was also not deep with just size of four. Even trying to detect the most important variable using Random Forest didn't yield any conclusive results.

Next steps were to check if there was some kind of pattern in the dataset, based on minimum and maximum price of the stock in the 50-day window (–25, 25). For this, the occurrence of minimum/maximum was classified as "After" if it occurred after quarterly earnings announcement and vice-versa. The tree was still shallow and continued to show weak correlation between nature of announcements and stock price movements.

Decision tree:
MinSide = Before: Positive (324/113)
MinSide = After:
:...MinPrice ≤ 14.60336: Negative (28/11)
MinPrice > 14.60336: Positive (150/72)
Evaluation on training data (502 cases):
Decision Tree
---------------- Size Errors
3 196(39.0%) <<
(a) (b) (c) <-classified as
---- ---- ----
17 0 83 (a): class Negative
1 0 102 (b): class Neutral
10 0 289 (c): class Positive

It can still be seen that most of the data is classified incorrectly with the positive quarterly announcements in general causing bias.

4.4. Optimization of decision tree

Based on the earlier research work, it was then decided to optimize the tree to ensure it takes more depth. To achieve this, following steps were undertaken:

4.4.1. Defining the trend (slope) of stock price movement before announcement

A 10 day window before announcement was taken and attempt to classify the movement of stock price as upward, downward or neutral was made. However, this again appeared to have lot of human judgment involved. To overcome this, the slope of the data points were obtained

(Stock price for 10 days before announcement) and used as an attribute in the dataset. This was worked in excel using the slope function. The syntax is as below:

SLOPE(known_y's, known_x's)

The slope function essentially runs linear regression to figure out the best-fit line. It then returns the slope of the line. The equation for the slope of the regression line is calculated using the below formula:

$$b=\frac{\sum(x-\bar{x})(y-\bar{y})}{\sum(x-\bar{x})^2}$$

This is a differential of the 10 points. This accurately defined the trend of stock movements from 10 days prior to quarterly earnings announcements.

4.4.2. Grouping companies into specific verticals

In order to classify companies into their respective verticals, the following verticals were used.

1) Banking
2) Healthcare
3) Manufacturing
4) Mining
5) Technology
6) Others

The following verticals were selected after a lot of trials to ensure at least 10 per cent of data was available in each category. Final split of the data is as shown in Table 7 below.

Table 7: Data summary across verticals.

Finance	Healthcare	Manufacturing	Mining	Technology	Others
64	63	95	48	120	112

4.4.3 Normalization of stock prices across rows (i.e., within the same quarter and company)

The normalization of stock prices between zero and one was done for a given quarter and company, i.e., across rows and not across columns. Table 8 and Table 9 shows the rows before and after normalization, respectively:

Before normalization

Table 8: Data sample before normalization across rows.

Ticker	Quarter	Day–25	Day–24	Day–23	Day–22
AAPL	**Q114**	$62.06	$61.89	$61.56	$61.65
JPM	**Q314**	$50.68	$51.41	$51.50	$50.67

After normalization

Table 9: Data sample after normalization across rows.

Ticker	Quarter	Day–25	Day–24	Day–23	Day–22
AAPL	**Q114**	$0.37	$0.25	$0.00	$0.07
JPM	**Q314**	$0.27	$0.92	$1.00	$0.26

Thus, the potential scaling issues in the decision tree were also eliminated.

4.4.4. Process of decision tree optimization

Once the data was modified as above, the C5.0 Decision Tree with 25 days of stock prices before announcements and two new attributes (slope, vertical) was run. The results are shown below:

```
Evaluation on training data (502 cases):
Decision Tree
----------------
Size    Errors
 72     63(12.5%)   <<
 (a)    (b)  (c)   <-classified as
----  ----  ----
85   1   14   (a): class Negative
```

3 66 34 (b): class Neutral

5 6 288 (c): class Positive

The results improved from 41% error last time to 12.5 per cent error. However it has to be remembered that this is not the accuracy against a test set. On checking the attribute usage, results were as shown below:

Attribute usage:

100.00% Day −15

84.46% Vertical

69.92% Day −1

66.93% Day −7

46.22% Day −24

2.99% Slope

1.99% Day −20

It was observed that categorization of companies into corresponding verticals has resolved most of the error in the classification and is an important attribute also shown by previous research by Christope *et al.* (2004). In order to extract meaningful rules and visualize the tree, pruning of the tree was done based on minimum cases per node at 10 per cent of the data. The resultant tree was as follows:

Evaluation on training data (502 cases):

Decision Tree

Size Errors

43 121(24.1%) <<

(a) (b) (c) <-classified as

---- ---- ----

60 8 32 (a): class Negative

8 55 40 (b): class Neutral

12 21 266 (c): class Positive

Attribute usage:

100.00% Day −14

84.46% Vertical

It was observed that the terminal nodes of the tree had come down to 72 from 37. It can also be seen that as shown in the importance of attribute, Day −14 and vertical form important attributes for prediction. Visualization of the C5.0 tree was undertaken using a tool called

Graphviz, as there is no package available yet for visualization of C5.0 decision tree. The process consisted of two steps where in the first step, the decision tree was pushed to text file in prescribed format of the tool. It was then visualized using Graphviz tool. The visual representation of the tree is seen in Figure 6 below:

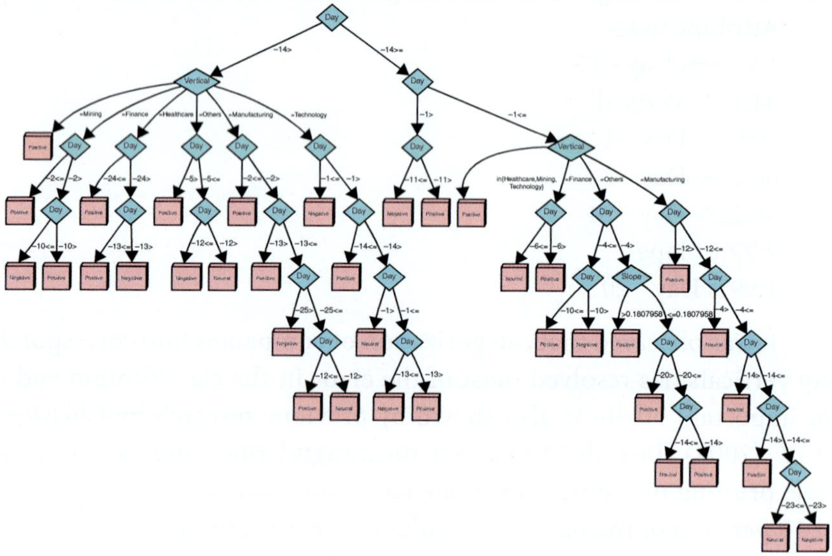

Figure 6: Visualization of pruned decision tree.

It can be seen from the above figure that Day–14 forms the root node and is the most important attribute in the dataset. That is, essentially, stock movements two weeks prior to announcement appear to be most decisive attribute to predict the nature of announcements. Descriptions of a few rules are as follows:

Day −14 > 0.4512491:
:...Vertical = Mining: Positive (15/7)
Day −14 ≤ 0.4512491:
:... Day −1 ≤ 0.8353141:
:...Vertical in {Healthcare,Mining,Technology}: Positive (106/32)

The rules above shows information like (15/7), (106/32), etc. Here, the pattern (x/y) refers to (total dataset applicable to rule/ no. of rows testing accurate to this rule). While this might be interesting, the accuracy of the rule is not high.

4.4.5. Over sampling, 10-fold cross-validation and testing

It was observed that while verticals formed important component of the tree, no strong and conclusive pattern was observed from the decision tree. However, it was important to check for accuracy of the prediction against a test set. As a first step, a test set of 10 per cent of the original data using stratified sampling was created.

Stratified sampling maintained the same ratio of dependent variable as original dataset.

Original Dataset

Negative	Neutral	Positive
100	103	299

Train Dataset

Negative	Neutral	Positive
90	93	269

Test Dataset

Negative	Neutral	Positive
10	10	30

It can be clearly seen that 10 per cent of the data as test set in the same ratio as original data. It was then important to do an oversampling of negative and neutral cases to make the data balanced while not losing any information. The negative:neutral:positive was in the ratio 1:1:3. Therefore, it was necessary to over-sample, or copy and insert the negative and neutral cases twice to achieve balanced data. Once the oversampling was done, the dataset was now balanced as shown below:

Oversampled Training Dataset

Negative	Neutral	Positive
270	279	269

With this dataset, a 10-fold cross validation was performed to get the accuracy after removing any bias or "Random luck" in the model. For this purpose, a function was written where the dataset was divided into 10 folds. The decision tree was run on folds 2–10 while testing the accuracy on 1st fold. Similarly in the second iteration, decision tree is run on fold 3–10 and one while testing the accuracy on 2nd fold. The process is explained diagrammatically in Figure 7 below.

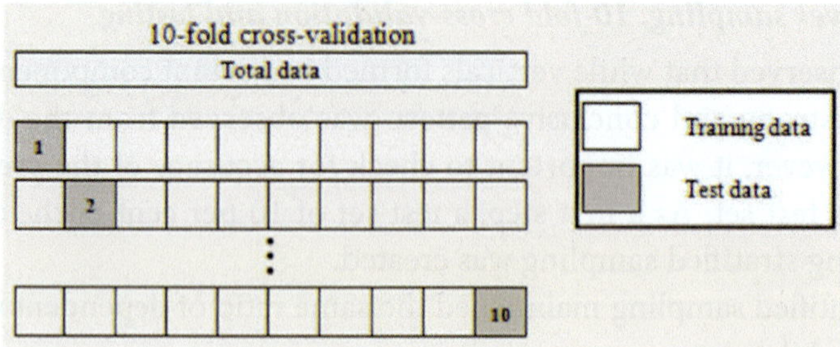

Figure 7: 10-Fold cross validation.

Accuracy was measured at every run, i.e., across each of the 10 trees. Overall accuracy of the 10-fold cross-validation model was the average of the 10 runs. The output is as shown below:

Accuracy of tree 1 is: 0.8641
Accuracy of tree 2 is: 0.8641
Accuracy of tree 3 is: 0.8888
Accuracy of tree 4 is: 0.7654
Accuracy of tree 5 is: 0.8641
Accuracy of tree 6 is: 0.8148
Accuracy of tree 7 is: 0.8148
Accuracy of tree 8 is: 0.7654
Accuracy of tree 9 is: 0.8888
Accuracy of tree 10 is: 0.8271
Accuracy of overall model (Average) is: 0.8358

Thus the overall accuracy of the model was 83 per cent. However this was not based on the test set and thus was not the actual accuracy. To get the accuracy on test set, the test data was predicted for accuracy using the trees in the cross-fold validation model. Thus the test set was predicted for accuracy across the 10 trees and the average was taken as accuracy of test set. Results are as shown below:

Accuracy on test data: 0.316

It could be seen that the accuracy of the test data was 31.6 per cent on average. This shows us that across test set, or unknown data, the model is not accurate and needs further work. However, the study has shown us that verticals play an important part in the nature of results. While this model can be used to obtain an overall guidance during quarterly earnings, it cannot be taken as accurate without further work.

5. DISCUSSION

This study started off with data collection and visual analysis of the stock price movement around announcement data. It was observed that while many stocks exhibited the occurrence of "Nike tick" pattern, it was not consistent across companies and quarters. In order to explore this occurrence further, checks for independence between occurrence of minimum and nature of earnings announcements were performed. The study clearly showed that the nature of earnings announcements was not dependent on the occurrence of minimum.

In the effort to study further, checks for patterns in stock price movement around earnings announcements were made. In addition to this, efforts to predict the nature of announcements based on the stock movements were also made. It was noticed that the industry vertical of the company played a significant role in the nature of earnings announcements. However, no clear-cut patterns emerged. The prediction accuracy of the model also requires further improvement.

This study leads to the question whether the movement of stocks is totally dependent on the nature of announcements. Intuitively, bad announcements leading to minimum in the stock price occurring after the announcement were expected. However what was observed in the dataset showed that this was not the case. It also led to a broader question of "If EPS is not a way to classify announcements, could there be other intangible factors that determine the nature of announcements?"

6. CONCLUSION AND FUTURE WORK

It was observed from the study that there is no conclusive proof to the hypothesis that the occurrence of minimum around the announcement window is actually dependent on the nature of announcements. However, it can be seen that there is a strong indication of macroeconomic factors within verticals affecting the results. Further work is required for model optimization using other market factors that could have been missed as well as testing of existing model against coming quarters. Also the "Nike tick" pattern could be a segregated occurrence that requires further study for any conclusion of patterns.

Future work could include a segregated study of the movement of stock prices around earnings announcement within a given industry vertical. This could throw further light on the factors that could be making companies within the vertical exhibit similar behaviors while leading to potentially more insights.

REFERENCES

1. Christope, S, M Ferri and J Angel (2004). Short-selling prior to earnings announcements. *The Journal of Finance*, 59(4), 1845–1875.

2. Qureshi, MA, A Abdulah and M Imadullah (2012). Stock price variability around earnings announcement dates at Karachi stock exchange. *Economics Research International*, Article ID 463627.

3. Bernard, VL and JK Thomas (1989). Post-earnings announcement drift: Delayed price response or risk premium? *Journal of Accounting Research*, 27(2), 1–36.

4. Kea, B, S Huddarta and K Petroni (2003). What insiders know about future earnings and how they use it: Evidence from insider trades. *Journal of Accounting and Economics*, 35(3), 315–346.

5. Lobo, G and S Tung (2000). Financial analysts' earnings forecast dispersion and intraday stock price variability around quarterly earnings announcements. *Review of Quantitative Finance and Accounting*, 15(2), 214–225.

6. Tiwari, S, R Pandit and V Richhariya (2010). Predicting future trends in stock market by decision tree rough-set based hybrid system with HHMM. *International Journal of Electronics and Computer Science Engineering*, 10, 1–10.

CHAPTER 28

Application of Predictive Analytics to Stock Price Directional Volatility and Direction

BOO See Yang

ABSTRACT

The current study employs an amended heuristic to stock price data to predict stock price direction and directional volatility. This heuristic was further extended to implied volatility data, as a proxy for the market consensus for volatility of the underlying stock price, and support vector machines (SVMs). The heuristic performed better than both implied volatility methods and SVM in prediction of stock price directional volatility. No significant result was obtained for the prediction of stock price direction using either the heuristic or SVM. A potential trading methodology was postulated to take advantage of this improvement over the market consensus on stock price directional volatility.

1. INTRODUCTION

In a previous study, a heuristic was developed to predict the propensity of a customer to respond to targeted marketing on a different brand. This heuristic performed well relative to linear regression. The objective of this part of the study is to determine if this heuristic can be generalized by applying it to another set of data.

Based on the experience of implementing it in the previous study and the specific requirements of prediction of stock price volatility and direction, the current study will analyze this proprietary heuristic to determine the areas of improvement.

The new set of data will include stock prices and corresponding financial ratios extracted from Compustat Monthly Updates: Fundamentals Annual Dataset. The magnitude of directional volatility[a] and direction of stock prices will be predicted specifically over a time period of five years and will be further determined by the magnitude of the linear regression slope of annual closing prices over same period. The direction of stock prices will be represented by the sign of the slope.

The results will be bench-marked against SVMs and implied volatility data as of the date of prediction, which will be used as a proxy to the market expectations of volatility of each stock. The implied volatility data will be extracted from the OptionMetrics: Option Prices dataset.

2. PROBLEM STATEMENT

The study aims to determine the required changes/improvements to heuristic developed in the previous work, so that it can be amended for prediction of stock price directional volatility and direction and to test the heuristic against established methodologies.

3. STATE OF THE ART

Stock price volatility prediction was investigated extensively in many studies. Harvey and Whaley (1991) showed that while high accuracy in stock volatility prediction was possible, it alone was not enough to generate returns, as the market was efficient enough to price in the volatility.

---

a Refer Sect. 4.1 for a detailed description of directional volatility.

Hence the need to investigate stock price direction prediction as well. Huang *et al.* (2005) showed that SVM performs better than linear and quadratic discriminant analysis and Elman backpropagation neural networks methods in prediction of Japanese stock price direction, using only macroeconomic indicators as inputs. Similarly, Kim (2003) showed that SVM worked well in predicting 1-day change in direction of stock prices compared with backpropagation neural networks and case-based reasoning methods. With Tay and Cao (2001) showing that SVM performs better than multi-layer, back-propagation neural network in predicting the prices of futures contracts, point prediction of stock prices has also been well investigated.

Apart from prediction methodologies, Black and Scholes (1973) established an approach for reaching a market consensus for option prices. The calculated metric of implied volatility represents the market consensus on the volatility of each option contract. Since option prices are closely related to the underlying prices of stock, this metric can be used as a proxy for the market consensus of volatility of the price of underlying stock.

4. SOLUTION: DESCRIPTION OF APPROACH

4.1. Dependent variables

This study aims to perform two separate predictions, namely stock price directional volatility and stock price direction. However, these dependent variables are not measured conventionally. Since the eventual objective of any stock prediction algorithm is to generate consistent positive returns, it is postulated that the prediction of volatility in a given direction would be more effective than the typical standard deviation. To achieve this end, the linear regression slope for the last five closing stock price points must be calculated. The directional volatility measure is the absolute magnitude of the slope, while the direction measure is the sign of the slope. Hence, large volatilities in a single direction are measured, while large volatilities around the mean are considered as "low volatility" samples.

If both predictions stand true, a trader would simply need to purchase a set of high directional volatility stocks identified in the direction predicted, to generate a consistent, positive return.

4.2. Datasets

4.2.1. Data description

The initially used dataset comprised approximately 6,000 daily stock tickers, prices and 65 financial ratios/categorical variables[b] for each stock for a period of 4 August 2014 to August 2015 The implied volatilities were scrapped from Yahoo Finance for the purpose of benchmarking the prediction results from the heuristic. However, after reviewing the implied volatility data, it was found that the numbers given on Yahoo Finance were not the ones calculated with standard Black and Scholes model. Hence, in the absence of a clear calculation methodology used by Yahoo Finance, it was decided to abandon this and the corresponding daily stock dataset.

Subsequently, it was decided to perform the prediction analysis on an annual time frame. TCompustat Monthly Updates: Fundamentals Annual dataset was used to provide independent variables[c] for the prediction models. Data was collected for the period of 1996–2014, which resulted in 23,000 data rows, comprising 1596 unique stock tickers.

Data for the implied volatilities of the stocks in the same period was extracted from the OptionMetrics: Option Prices dataset. The use of this as a benchmarking tool is discussed further in Sect. 4.5.

4.2.2. Data cleaning

The data for the daily stock dataset was received in a fairly clean state, with only missing values that were not available to the market. The data was merged into a large, single file before taking into R for further analysis, where the dependent variable was calculated.

For the annual fundamentals stock dataset, independent variables below 90 per cent completion were removed, leaving 186 independent variables. This added up to approximately 4.2 million data points for the final dataset used. Similarly, the annual data was combined before reading into R, and the dependent variable was calculated.

4.2.3. Data division

The data was divided into a training and test set. Thus, daily stock dataset had three month data for training and one month data for test sets.

b See Appendix 1 — Daily Stock Data Set Variables.

c See Appendix 2 — Annual Fundamentals Stock Data Set Variables.

Last five days of the training set were ignored, as there was not enough information for calculation of dependent variable when performing the prediction.

In case of annual fundamentals stock dataset, since the dependent variable measure required five data points, the training set was taken from 1996 to 2005, while the last five years of data (2010–2014) was separated out as the test set. Since the period 2006–2009 didn't form a five years span, only the closing price data was used to calculate the dependent variable, while the independent variable data was not considered.

4.3. Heuristic summary

A summary of the original heuristic is as follows. Variables were initially selected using a *t*-test, that is, only variables that significantly affected the dependent variable, direction of the effect and cut-off value for each data row were chosen. Next, each data row is tagged according to the *t*-test results, for example, while tagging for stock price direction for a particular variable with mean positive direction two and negative direction one, all data rows with a variable greater than two are assigned a one. All other data rows variable is assigned as zero. For a variable with mean positive direction lower than the negative direction, all data rows with a variable value lower than the mean of the positive direction is assigned as −1, and the remaining assigned a zero to account for variables that negatively correlate with the dependent variable.

Next, a coefficient, representing the magnitude of association each predictive variable has with the dependent variable, is assigned to each variable. Each data row's final score is determined by the sum of the multiplication of the tag with each variable's coefficient. To find a local optimal for each coefficient, an iterative optimization algorithm is used:

1) For one variable, the algorithm assigns the coefficient values as increments of 0.5 to each variable.
2) The score of each data row from all the variables is computed.
3) A comparison table is populated, with each row representing the cumulative count of positive and negative directions that has at least the corresponding score.
4) The percentage of data rows in each row is calculated for both the positive and negative direction.

5) The difference between the percentage of positive and negative direction is calculated for each row.
6) The maximum percentage difference, if is larger than the previous, is saved.
7) If the maximum percentage difference is changed, the coefficient for that particular variable is also saved.

The algorithm iterates through steps 1–7 for each variable until the maximum percentage difference remains unchanged for one full cycle of all the variables.

4.4. Heuristic improvement

Even though the heuristic performed very well in the first implementation on sales transactional data for fashion goods, improvements were necessary so that it can be adapted for implementation on stock price data.

4.4.1. Stock price data noise

Stock prices that display a small change could be due to this noise. Hence, to allow the algorithm to only use data rows that display a large change in the dependent variable, the heuristic was amended to filter out the data rows with a dependent variable close to the mean. For example, to predict the directional volatility, only top 20 per cent most volatile and bottom 20 per cent least volatile data rows are used as inputs into heuristic. The heuristic was run several times with the training dataset using various cut-off percentages and it was found that using the top and bottom 10 per cent of data rows worked the best.

4.4.2. Tagging of variables

The original heuristic tagged data rows with variable values did not meet zero cut-off criteria. Hence, only the data rows that had significant values in both positive and negative correlated variables had an interaction in the scoring mechanic between the two sets of variables (see Figure 12.1). To allow a more representative interaction, the new heuristic will have data rows that do not meet the cut-off criteria for variables to be tagged with −1 instead.

4.4.3. Local optimal

Each heuristic run generates a local optimal, so different runs for the same input dataset would produce different results. To reduce the variation of results, the heuristic was amended to complete multiple runs in a session. Five separate random number seeds were used for five different runs, which were repeated five times each, resulting in 25 total outputs. The final prediction for each data row of new heuristic was the average result of 25 runs. This entire computation took 4 h for the input dataset. The stability of the output will only increase if ample computation time is given to obtain more runs (see Figure 12.2).

4.4.4. Granularity of coefficients

The original heuristic assigned coefficients in multiples of 0.5, with a cap of three, i.e., six different calculations per variable were conducted. To discover more granular effects of the coefficients, this multiple was reduced to 0.1, with a similar cap of three, i.e., 30 different calculations per variable were conducted.

4.4.5. Runtime

The original heuristic ran for about 12 h with an input of about 6000 data rows. After investigating each part of the heuristic, several changes were made to optimize the memory usage and reduce the runtime, including consolidation of runtime-only tables, eliminating the need for a comparison table, by performing the comparison calculations using the original consolidated tables, etc. This effort resulted in the runtimes for the same dataset to be reduced from 12 h to about 15 min, which effectively allows for much larger datasets to be processed. The final runtime of the heuristic, with 23,000 data rows and 5 × 5 runs in total, on a computer with an Intel Quad Core i7-4770 CPU @3.40 GHz, came to approximately 4 h. This improvement takes into account the increased number of coefficient trial runs per variable, as stated in Sect. 4.4.4.

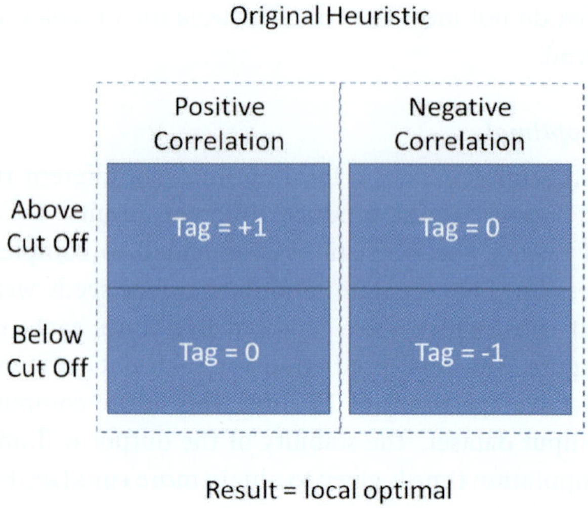

Figure 1: Original heuristic.

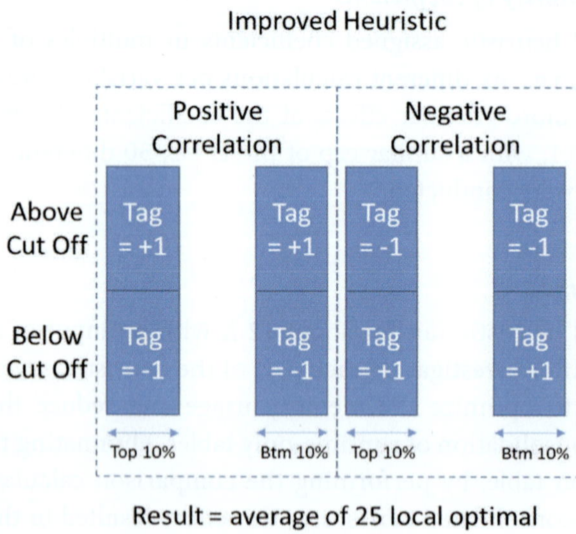

Figure 2: Improved heuristic

4.5. Benchmark metrics

4.5.1. Multi-variate stepwise linear regression

Initially, three forward, stepwise multi-variate linear regression models were completed on the initial daily stock dataset for the prediction of magnitude of forward 5-day directional volatility, for periods of 201501–201503, 201502–201504, 201503–201505. Linear regression was chosen as the initial benchmark, as it was methodology used in the previous study.

The multi-variate stepwise linear regression methodology used was as follows:

1) Transformation of the dependent variable to a normal distribution.

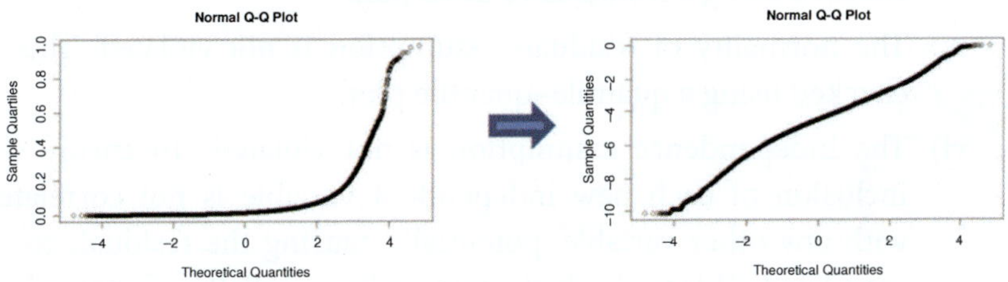

2) Removal of outliers from independent variables and transformation of each independent variable to linear relationship with dependent variable, e.g., earnings per share.

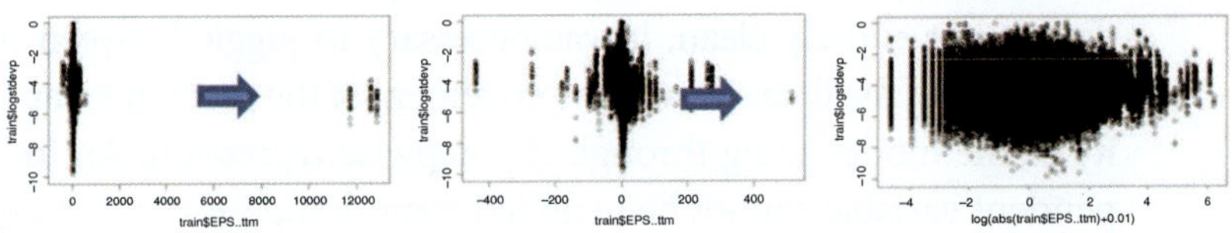

Base data *Outliers removed* *Log transformation applied*

3) Calculate the bivariate correlation between each independent and dependent variable.
4) Stepwise forward regression starts by including the independent variable with the highest correlation and continues to include independent variables until all the variables are covered. Following is a checklist for selection of each independent variable.
   i) The adjusted R-squared increases: This explains the predictive capacity of the model built. The adjusted R-squared instead of R-squared was used to take into account the degrees of freedom.
   ii) The significance of the independent variables: The p-value of the independent variables shall remain below 0.05 at each step. Those with the highest p-value are removed if the p-value assumption is violated.

iii) The linearity assumption is not violated: The independent variables continue to vary linearly with the dependent variable. This is checked using a component cum residual plot.

iv) The homoscedasticity assumption is not violated: To ensure the variance in the model is same throughout the dataset. This is checked using a residuals vs fitted plot.

v) The normality of residuals assumption is not violated: This is checked using a quantile–quantile plot.

vi) The independence assumption is not violated: To ensure the inclusion of each new independent variable is not correlated with any other variable, potentially causing the residuals to be correlated. This is checked using variance inflation factor calculation, with the cut-off point of 5.

vii) The number of data used does not decrease significantly due to missing data points: For regression to work, each data input needs to have complete data for each of the independent variables. As the data is not entirely clean, it was necessary to juggle between the reduction of the data size and improvement of the predictive capacity of the model going through the stepwise regression. An independent variable cannot be included even though it improves the *R*-squared, as it may reduce the representativeness of the model.

Final regression model for period 201501–201503:

Y = Industry + 0.02926*log(Volatility..Week) + 0.02248*log(abs(X52.Week.High)) + 0.01319*log(abs(X50.Day.High)) + 0.004319*log(abs(X200.Day.Simple.Moving.Average)) + 0.005111*log(abs(Performance..Week.)) + 0.003497*log(abs(X50.Day.Simple.Moving.Average)) + 0.006775*log(abs(X50.Day.Low)) + 0.02067*log(abs(X52.Week.Low)) − 0.0006941*log(Volume) + 0.005759*log(Average.True.Range) + 0.001369*log(Relative.Volume)

Residuals:

Min	1Q	Median	3Q	Max
−0.31842	−0.04335	0.00661	0.04895	0.33611

With an *R*-squared of 0.2612

Final regression model for period 201502–201504:

Y = Industry + 0.02755*log(Volatility..Week.) + 0.02385*log(abs(X52.Week.High)) + 0.01156*log(abs(X50.Day.High)) + 0.006652*log(abs(X200.Day.Simple.Moving.Average)) + 0.006724*log(abs(Performance..Week.)) + 0.003225*log(abs(X50.Day.Simple.Moving.Average)) + 0.006557*log(abs(X50.Day.Low)) + 0.02008*log(abs(X52.Week.Low)) – 0.001041*log(Average.Volume) + 0.004551*log(Average.True.Range)

Residuals:

Min	1Q	Median	3Q	Max
–0.31815	–0.04353	0.00549	0.04849	0.33963

With an *R*-squared of 0.2738

Final regression model for period 201503–201505:

Y = Industry + 0.03338*log(Volatility..Week.) + 0.02625*log(abs(X52.Week.High)) + 0.003756*log(abs(X20.Day.Simple.Moving.Average)) + 0.008968*log(abs(X200.Day.Simple.Moving.Average)) + 0.001699*log(abs(X50.Day.Simple.Moving.Average)) + 0.005399*log(abs(Change.from.Open)) + 0.008812*log(abs(X50.Day.Low)) + 0.01655*log(abs(X52.Week.Low)) – 0.0007962*log(Average.Volume) + 0.003908*log(Average.True.Range)

Residuals:

Min	1Q	Median	3Q	Max
–0.32227	–0.04317	0.00599	0.04780	0.36568

With an *R*-squared of 0.2821

As discussed earlier, it was decided to switch to benchmarking the heuristic based on guidance drawn from state of the art. Hence no linear regression model was produced for the stock price direction analysis. The analysis moved from the daily stock dataset to annual stock dataset for analysis with SVM and implied volatility.

4.5.2. Support vector machines

As determined from the state of the art investigation, SVM is known to be one of the most effective algorithms to perform various types of stock price prediction. Hence the study will benchmark outputs from the heuristic and SVM. The SVM prediction model will be implemented using the e1071 library in R. Since there is no variable selection or variable transformation being performed, the final SVM model for both the directional volatility and direction analysis is the same, with full set of variables included.

4.5.3. Implied volatility

Implied volatility is a calculated metric using Black and Scholes model based on various attributes of an option (strike price, underlying price, time to maturity, put/call, risk free rate, etc.). This metric is generally considered as the market consensus on the volatility of option and hence will be used as a proxy for the market consensus on the volatility of the underlying stock price.

4.6. Results comparison

4.6.1. Volatility prediction

As the heuristic does not output a point prediction, instead produces a sorting of the stock tickers based on the dependent variable, it would not be possible to use the standard mean-squared-error-based measures to determine the accuracy of the models. Likewise, it would be unfair to directly use the implied volatility values as predictions for direct calculation of mean-squared error, as it is only a proxy for the volatility of the underlying stock price.

Instead, two measures will be used:

1) Average directional volatility of top X stocks
2) Count of top X stocks sorted by predicted directional volatility similarly appearing in top X stocks sorted by actual realized directional volatility

The first measure will take into account the magnitude of realized directional volatility. This measure will be skewed easily by large outliers, which in the first place is not desirable. However, if the objective of generating disproportionate returns is considered, having a methodology that can identify stocks that turn out to be large outliers is actually desirable. The second measure will only take into account the positioning of the stocks in the sorted output to determine accuracy.

4.6.1.1. Daily stock data

Data from 201501 to 201504

1) Average directional volatility of the top X stocks

Top X	Heuristic	Linear regression
25	0.90%	4.25%
50	0.95%	3.37%
100	1.21%	2.82%
250	1.16%	2.41%
500	1.26%	2.11%
1000	1.23%	1.68%
6085	0.69%	0.69%

2) Count of top X stocks sorted by predicted directional volatility similarly appearing in the top X stocks sorted by actual realized directional volatility

Top X	Heuristic	Linear regression
25	0 (0%)	3 (12%)
50	0 (0%)	7 (14%)
100	3 (3%)	21 (21%)
250	22 (9%)	83 (33%)
500	105 (21%)	208 (42%)
6085	6085 (100%)	6085 (100%)

Data from 201502 to 201505

1) Average directional volatility of the top X stocks

Top X	Heuristic	Linear regression
25	0.78%	2.16%
50	0.76%	2.44%
100	1.07%	2.13%
250	1.11%	1.86%

(continued)

Top X	Heuristic	Linear regression
500	1.15%	1.65%
1000	1.09%	1.53%
6085	0.95%	1.32%

2) Count of top X stocks sorted by predicted directional volatility similarly appearing in top X stocks sorted by actual realized directional volatility

Top X	Heuristic	Linear regression
25	0 (0%)	1 (4%)
50	1 (2%)	5 (10%)
100	5 (5%)	17 (17%)
250	31 (12%)	62 (25%)
500	94 (19%)	165 (33%)
6143	6143 (100%)	6143 (100%)

Data from 201503 to 201506

1) Average directional volatility of the top X stocks

Top X	Heuristic	Linear regression
25	2.32%	3.29%
50	1.97%	2.82%
100	1.69%	2.69%
250	1.43%	2.29%
500	1.43%	2.00%
1000	1.25%	1.71%
6137	1.03%	1.40%

2) Count of top X stocks sorted by predicted directional volatility similarly appearing in the top X stocks sorted by actual realized directional volatility

From all three runs over different time periods, the linear regression algorithm put forth in Sect. 4.5.1 performs better than

Top X	Heuristic	Linear regression
25	1 (4%)	2 (8%)
50	4 (8%)	9 (18%)
100	6 (6%)	24 (24%)
250	44 (18%)	76 (30%)
500	125 (25%)	194 (39%)
6137	6137 (100%)	6137 (100%)

heuristic in both measures. Unfortunately, the linear regression was removed as a viable benchmark while transitioning to annual stock fundamentals data.

4.6.1.2. Annual stock fundamentals data

1) Average directional volatility of the top X stocks

Top X	Heuristic	Implied volatility	SVM
25	0.54	0.41	0.32
50	0.45	0.46	0.26
100	0.37	0.36	0.29
250	0.27	0.29	0.27
500	0.23	0.25	0.24
1055	0.21	0.21	0.21

There were only 1055 unique tickers that had previously implied volatility data, hence only these stock tickers were selected for comparison.

The top 25 stocks selected by heuristic had an average realized directional volatility of 0.54, which was significantly higher than that achieved by implied volatility or SVM. Further down the table, heuristic prediction results roughly match the market consensus, while the results produced by SVM are quite far off.

2) Count of top X stocks sorted by predicted directional volatility similarly appearing in the top X stocks sorted by actual realized directional volatility

Top X	Heuristic	Implied volatility	SVM
25	3 (12%)	3 (12%)	3 (12%)
50	11 (22%)	15 (30%)	4 (8%)
100	26 (26%)	27 (27%)	13 (13%)
250	87 (35%)	93 (37%)	82 (33%)
500	232 (47%)	253 (51%)	246 (49%)
1055	1055 (100%)	1055 (100%)	1055 (100%)

Using this metric, the implied volatility based prediction performed slightly better than heuristic, but SVM again did not perform well.

4.6.2. Direction prediction

Direction prediction was done only with the annual stock fundamentals data. Since the direction prediction has a binary output, standard confusion matrix can be used to measure accuracy of the outputs. Since implied volatility is only a proxy for the market consensus and not for the direction of stock price movement, only compare the results of runs between the heuristic and SVM are compared.

Confusion Matrix Comparison:

	Heuristic			SVM		
		Prediction up	**Prediction down**		**Prediction up**	**Prediction down**
	Actual up	493	530	Actual up	481	542
	Actual down	159	124	Actual down	113	170
Accuracy (correct predictions/ total count):	47.24%			49.85%		

There were a total of 1306 predictions as there was no need to restrict the dataset to that which had implied volatility data. Both heuristic and

SVM results have below 50 per cent accuracy and hence did not perform better than random chance.

5. DISCUSSION

Using the daily stock dataset, the study runs show the linear regression methodology consistently outperforming the heuristic.

Using the annual stock fundamentals data, the study run results show that the heuristic is able to identify a small selection of stocks that, considering the magnitude of the realized directional volatility, on average will beat the market consensus in terms of directional volatility. Without considering the magnitude, the results are slightly worse than the prediction generated by the implied volatility predictor. Hence, there is evidence to show that the stocks selected by the heuristic tends to identify significant outliers with a much higher directional volatility magnitude than those identified by using implied volatility as predictor.

Unfortunately, no significant results were obtained for the stock direction prediction using either the heuristic or implied volatility as the predictor; hence the original trading scheme will need to be adjusted.

As the option prices would be determined by the market consensus on volatility, a potential trading scheme would be to purchase both the put and call options of the identified stocks with time to maturity that matches the time duration of the predictions. This trading scheme would work if the difference in directional volatility of heuristic predicted stocks is large enough to cover the bid/ask spread of both the put and call options, and the underlying price of either, assuming the price corresponds to the implied volatility. As the previous prices of individual options are not available, the viability of this trading scheme will need to be tested in the present term.

6. CONCLUSIONS AND FURTHER WORK

The results obtained from this study again shows that the developed heuristic is able to beat both SVM and market consensus measured via implied volatility. However, using the daily stock data, linear regression performed far better than was expected. This result is surprising and a logical next step would be to perform the direction prediction using linear regression, to see if it can generate a statistically significant result, and to apply the linear regression algorithm to annual fundamentals stock data, to see if the improvement over heuristic (and consequently SVM and implied volatility) holds constant over different datasets.

Since this implementation for heuristic was semi-successful, the next steps would be to further implement heuristic on other publically available datasets.

Specifically for the results of the stock price directional volatility result, the next step would be to start collecting data on option prices and perform the same prediction, but on the daily time frame, hence reducing the time taken to test the proposed trading methodology. An additional confirmation on the viability of this heuristic would be obtaining a similar improvement over the market consensus while using a daily time period based dataset. Another source for the daily calculation of implied volatilities will need to be found to perform a proper benchmark. Otherwise this may be calculated manually from the available options data.

Another future direction may be to draw from the work of Huang *et al.* (2005) or Kim (2003), both of whom successfully predicted price direction/price direction change using SVM. The combination of the results of work from this study and the referenced papers should allow for the implementation of the original trading scheme.

Appendix 1 – Daily Stock Data Set Variables

Industry
Market.Cap
P.E
Forward.P.E
PEG
P.S
P.B
P.Cash
P.Free.Cash.Flow
Dividend.Yield
Payout.Ratio

EPS..ttm.
EPS.growth.this.year
EPS.growth.next.year
EPS.growth.past.5.years
EPS.growth.next.5.years
Sales.growth.past.5.years
EPS.growth.quarter.over.quarter
Sales.growth.quarter.over.quarter
Shares.Outstanding
Shares.Float
Insider.Ownership
Insider.Transactions
Institutional.Ownership
Institutional.Transactions
Float.Short
Short.Ratio
Return.on.Assets
Return.on.Equity
Return.on.Investment
Current.Ratio
Quick.Ratio
LT.Debt.Equity
Total.Debt.Equity
Gross.Margin
Operating.Margin
Profit.Margin
Performance..Week.
Performance..Month.
Performance..Quarter.
Performance..Half.Year.
Performance..Year.
Performance..YTD.

(*continued*)

Appendix 1 – Daily Stock Data Set Variables (*continued*)

Beta
X20.Day.Simple.Moving.Average
X50.Day.Simple.Moving.Average
X200.Day.Simple.Moving.Average
X50.Day.High
X50.Day.Low
X52.Week.High
X52.Week.Low
Relative.Strength.Index..14.
Change.from.Open
Gap
Analyst.Recom
Average.Volume
Relative.Volume
Price
Change
Volume
Days.to.Earnings.Date

Appendix 2 – Annual Fundamentals Stock Data Set Variables

Symbol	Description
acchg	Accounting Changes — Cumulative Effect
aco	Current Assets — Other — Total
acox	Current Assets — Other — Sundry
act	Current Assets — Total
ao	Assets — Other
aoloch	Assets and Liabilities — Other — Net Change
aox	Assets — Other — Sundry
ap	Accounts Payable — Trade
aqc	Acquisitions
at	Assets — Total

Symbol	Description
bkvlps	Book Value Per Share
caps	Capital Surplus/Share Premium Reserve
capx	Capital Expenditures
capxv	Capital Expend Property, Plant and Equipment Schd V
ceq	Common/Ordinary Equity — Total
ceql	Common Equity — Liquidation Value
ceqt	Common Equity — Tangible
ch	Cash
che	Cash and Short-Term Investments
chech	Cash and Cash Equivalents — Increase/(Decrease)
cogs	Cost of Goods Sold
cstk	Common/Ordinary Stock (Capital)
cstkcv	Common Stock-Carrying Value
cstke	Common Stock Equivalents — Dollar Savings
dclo	Debt — Capitalized Lease Obligations
dcpstk	Convertible Debt and Preferred Stock
dcvsr	Debt — Senior Convertible
dcvsub	Debt — Subordinated Convertible
dcvt	Debt — Convertible
dd	Debt — Debentures
dd1	Long-Term Debt Due in One Year
dd2	Debt — Due in 2nd Year
dd3	Debt — Due in 3rd Year
dd4	Debt — Due in 4th Year
diladj	Dilution Adjustment
dilavx	Dilution Available — Excluding Extraordinary Items
dlc	Debt in Current Liabilities — Total
dltis	Long-Term Debt — Issuance
dlto	Other Long-term Debt
dltr	Long-Term Debt — Reduction
dltt	Long-Term Debt — Total

(*continued*)

Appendix 2 – Annual Fundamentals Stock Data Set Variables (*continued*)

Symbol	Description
dm	Debt — Mortgages & Other Secured
dn	Debt — Notes
do	Discontinued Operations
dp	Depreciation and Amortization
dpact	Depreciation, Depletion and Amortization (Accumulated)
dpc	Depreciation and Amortization (Cash Flow)
dpvieb	Depreciation (Accumulated) — Ending Balance (Schedule VI)
ds	Debt-Subordinated
dudd	Debt — Unamortized Debt Discount and Other
dv	Cash Dividends (Cash Flow)
dvc	Dividends Common/Ordinary
dvp	Dividends — Preferred/Preference
dvpa	Preferred Dividends in Arrears
dvt	Dividends — Total
ebit	Earnings Before Interest and Taxes
ebitda	Earnings Before Interest
epsfi	Earnings Per Share (Diluted) — Including Extraordinary Items
epsfx	Earnings Per Share (Diluted) — Excluding Extraordinary Items
epspi	Earnings Per Share (Basic) — Including Extraordinary Items
epspx	Earnings Per Share (Basic) — Excluding Extraordinary Items
esopct	Common ESOP Obligation — Total
esopt	Preferred ESOP Obligation — Total
esub	Equity in Earnings — Unconsolidated Subsidiaries
exre	Exchange Rate Effect
fiao	Financing Activities — Other
fincf	Financing Activities — Net Cash Flow
fopo	Funds from Operations — Other
gdwl	Goodwill
gp	Gross Profit (Loss)
ib	Income Before Extraordinary Items
ibadj	Income Before Extraordinary Items — Adjusted for Common Stock Equivalents

Symbol	Description
ibc	Income Before Extraordinary Items (Cash Flow)
ibcom	Income Before Extraordinary Items — Available for Common
icapt	Invested Capital — Total
intan	Intangible Assets — Total
intc	Interest Capitalized
intpn	Interest Paid — Net
invch	Inventory — Decrease (Increase)
invt	Inventories — Total
itcb	Investment Tax Credit (Balance Sheet)
ivaco	Investing Activities — Other
ivaeq	Investment and Advances — Equity
ivao	Investment and Advances — Other
ivch	Increase in Investments
ivncf	Investing Activities — Net Cash Flow
ivst	Short-Term Investments — Total
lco	Current Liabilities — Other — Total
lcox	Current Liabilities — Other — Sundry
lct	Current Liabilities — Total
lifr	LIFO Reserve
lo	Liabilities — Other — Total
lse	Liabilities and Stockholders Equity — Total
lt	Liabilities — Total
mib	Noncontrolling Interest (Balance Sheet)
mii	Noncontrolling Interest (Income Account)
mrc1	Rental Commitments — Minimum — 1st Year
mrc2	Rental Commitments — Minimum — 2nd Year
msa	Marketable Securities Adjustment
ni	Net Income (Loss)
niadj	Net Income Adjusted for Common/Ordinary Stock (Capital) Equivalents
nopi	Nonoperating Income (Expense)
nopio	Nonoperating Income (Expense) — Other

(*continued*)

Appendix 2 – Annual Fundamentals Stock Data Set Variables (*continued*)

Symbol	Description
np	Notes Payable — Short-Term Borrowings
oancf	Operating Activities — Net Cash Flow
oiadp	Operating Income After Depreciation
oibdp	Operating Income Before Depreciation
opeps	Earnings Per Share from Operations
oprepsx	Earnings Per Share — Diluted — from Operations
pi	Pretax Income
pnca	Core Pension Adjustment
pncad	Core Pension Adjustment Diluted EPS Effect
pncaeps	Core Pension Adjustment Basic EPS Effect
ppegt	Property, Plant and Equipment — Total (Gross)
ppent	Property, Plant and Equipment — Total (Net)
ppeveb	Property, Plant, and Equipment — Ending Balance (Schedule V)
prca	Core Post Retirement Adjustment
prcad	Core Post Retirement Adjustment Diluted EPS Effect
prcaeps	Core Post Retirement Adjustment Basic EPS Effect
prstkc	Purchase of Common and Preferred Stock
pstk	Preferred/Preference Stock (Capital) — Total
pstkc	Preferred Stock — Convertible
pstkl	Preferred Stock — Liquidating Value
pstkn	Preferred/Preference Stock — Nonredeemable
pstkr	Preferred/Preference Stock — Redeemable
pstkrv	Preferred Stock — Redemption Value
re	Retained Earnings
reajo	Retained Earnings — Other Adjustments
recch	Accounts Receivable — Decrease (Increase)
recco	Receivables — Current — Other
rect	Receivables — Total
recta	Retained Earnings — Cumulative Translation Adjustment
rectr	Receivables — Trade
reuna	Retained Earnings — Unadjusted

Symbol	Description
revt	Revenue — Total
sale	Sales/Turnover (Net)
seq	Stockholders Equity — Parent
siv	Sale of Investments
spce	S&P Core Earnings
spced	S&P Core Earnings EPS Diluted
spceeps	S&P Core Earnings EPS Basic
spi	Special Items
sppiv	Sale of Property, Plant and Equipment and Investments — Gain (Loss)
sstk	Sale of Common and Preferred Stock
tstk	Treasury Stock — Total (All Capital)
tstkc	Treasury Stock — Common
tstkp	Treasury Stock — Preferrred
txc	Income Taxes — Current
txdb	Deferred Taxes (Balance Sheet)
txdc	Deferred Taxes (Cash Flow)
txdi	Income Taxes — Deferred
txditc	Deferred Taxes and Investment Tax Credit
txfed	Income Taxes — Federal
txfo	Income Taxes — Foreign
txo	Income Taxes — Other
txp	Income Taxes Payable
txpd	Income Taxes Paid
txr	Income Tax Refund
txs	Income Taxes — State
txt	Income Taxes — Total
txw	Excise Taxes
wcap	Working Capital (Balance Sheet)
xacc	Accrued Expenses
xi	Extraordinary Items
xido	Extraordinary Items and Discontinued Operations

(*continued*)

Appendix 2 – Annual Fundamentals Stock Data Set Variables (*continued*)

Symbol	Description
xidoc	Extraordinary Items and Discontinued Operations (Cash Flow)
xint	Interest and Related Expense — Total
xintopt	Implied Option Expense
xopr	Operating Expenses — Total
xoptd	Implied Option EPS Diluted
xopteps	Implied Option EPS Basic
xpr	Pension and Retirement Expense
xrent	Rental Expense
xsga	Selling, General and Administrative Expense
cshtr_c	Common Shares Traded — Annual — Calendar
dvpsp_c	Dividends per Share — Pay Date — Calendar
dvpsx_c	Dividends per Share — Ex-Date — Calendar
prcc_c	Price Close — Annual — Calendar
prch_c	Price High — Annual — Calendar
prcl_c	Price Low — Annual — Calendar
cshtr_f	Common Shares Traded — Annual — Fiscal
dvpsp_f	Dividends per Share — Pay Date — Fiscal
dvpsx_f	Dividends per Share — Ex-Date — Fiscal
prcc_f	Price Close — Annual — Fiscal
prch_f	Price High — Annual — Fiscal
prcl_f	Price Low — Annual — Fiscal

BIBLIOGRAPHY

1. Harvey, CR and RE Whaley (1991). Market volatility prediction and the efficiency of the S&P 100 index option market. *Journal of Financial Economics*, 31(1), 43–73.

2. Huang, W, Y Nakamoria and S-Y Wang (2005). Forecasting stock market movement direction with support vector machine. *Computers and Operations Research*, 32(10), 2513–2522.

3. Kim, K (2003). Financial time series forecasting using support vector machines. *Neurocomputing*, 55(1–2), 307–319.

4. Tay, FEH and L Cao (2001). Application of support vector machines in financial time series forecasting. *Omega*, 29(4), 309–317.

5. Black, F and M Scholes (1973). The pricing of options and corporate liabilities. *The Journal of Political Economy*, 81(3), 637–654.

CHAPTER 29

Profiling of Patient Waiting Times at Hospital Outpatient Pharmarcy

LIM You Seng Eric

ABSTRACT

The Main Outpatient Pharmacy of National University Hospital (NUH) Medical Center aims to achieve 95th percentile of patient waiting times at the pharmacy to within 15 minutes. It was 30 minutes at the commencement of this project.

This study sought to understand how the factors that can influence the time taken for completion of tasks - for example dispensing medicine in the pharmacy - can impact patient waiting times. These factors could then be shared with the pharmacy in order to fine-tune their processes to reduce patient waiting times. Factory physics principles, in particular Kingman's formula, were used to study the processes involved, and identified areas for improvement.

1. INTRODUCTION

The Main Outpatient Pharmacy of National University Hospital (NUH) Medical Center was conducting an operational efficiency study to reduce patient waiting times at the pharmacy – the target hoped to achieve 95th percentile of patient waiting times within 15 minutes. The eventual objective was to improve patient satisfaction, as longer waiting times are associated with lower patient satisfaction rates. (Anderson *et al.*, 2007).

The pharmacy was using a pharmacy IT workflow system, namely Outpatient Pharmacy Automation System (OPAS) that integrated and orchestrated the work processes between the pharmacists, automated dispensing machines (Rowa VMax & Parata Max) and Radio Frequency Identification (RFID) technology to facilitate the fulfilment, assembling and dispensing of medications. The aim of OPAS was to reduce patient waiting times at the pharmacy and enforce patient safety by maximizing the use of automation for picking medications (Fitzpatrick, 2004).

This project sought to assist this operational efficiency study to uncover the factors that influence the time taken for fulfilment and dispensing tasks in the pharmacy, and how these factors can affect patient waiting times.

The principles in Factory Physics (Hopp and Spearman, 2011) were used to study the processes in the pharmacy and identify areas for improvement. More specifically, the Kingman's formula (Kingman, 1961) was used in this project. The operational data in OPAS were used to aid the understanding and measurement of the processes in the pharmacy before and after changes were made in the processes.

2. PROBLEM STATEMENT

The following were objectives of this project to reduce patient waiting times at the outpatient pharmacy:

a) To identify factors that significantly impact patient waiting times for example the time wasted due to walking to different shelves to select medication; delays in the packing and dispensing processes.

b) To develop strategies and recommendations to the process that can potentially lead to significant improvement in patient waiting times (for example process re-engineering or workflow re-design; man-power redeployment; software enhancements). This was with the final aim of achieving 95th percentile of patient waiting times at the pharmacy within 15 minutes.

c) To design an approach to extract and analyze data that would demonstrate the effectiveness of the strategies and propose recommendations to the process.

At the commencement of the project, the 95th percentile of patient waiting times at the outpatient pharmacy was approximately 30 minutes, which was twice the target time of 15 minutes.

3. STATE OF THE ART

There were various projects that looked into the reduction of waiting times in healthcare, and simulation model analysis (Fetter and Thompson, 1966; Vemuri, 1984) and process re-design (Choi *et al.*, 2006; Yu & Yang, 2008) had being used in these various studies. In this project, the principles of Factory Physics (Hopp and Spearman, 2011) were used to investigate and study the pharmacy processes, and to identify process bottlenecks.

The award-winning book 'Factory Physics' details the approach created by Professors Wallace Hopp and Mark Spearman to analyze manufacturing operations from a scientific perspective. It includes a series of principles, such as Little's Law, the law of variability and the law of utilization. Despite Factory Physics originating from the manufacturing industry, the Factory Physics principles have being applied successfully in many industries, including healthcare.

An important principle in Factory Physics is Kingman's formula (Kingman, 1961) which can be used to compute the approximate mean waiting time in a queueing system, and is a product of three factors – V (variability), U (utilization), and T (process time). It is also known as the VUT equation in Factory Physics. Kingman's formula has shown a few behaviors in a queueing system.

a) Increasing variability always degrades the performance of a production system, and variability comes in two forms – Process and Arrival variability.
b) Utilization is the fraction of time that the system is not idle. When utilization is increased without making any other changes, it is noted that the lead time will increase in a non-linear trend.

This Kingman's formula is stipulated below:

$$CTq \approx V\ U\ T$$

$$= \left(\frac{p}{1-p}\right)\left(\frac{c_a^2 + c_s^2}{2}\right)(t_e)$$

$$p = \frac{r_a}{r_e}$$

CTq: Approximate Mean Cycle Time in queue

V: Variability (Process Variability c_s + Flow Variability c_a)

U: Utilization

T: Mean Effective Processing Time

p: Utilization Rate

r_a: Arrival Rate (the rate of arrivals in jobs per unit time)

r_e: Capacity (the rate of completion of jobs per unit time)

These three factors can also be used to assess the mean waiting time from a non-quantitative perspective.

Figure 1 illustrates the factors that can help to reduce waiting times based on Kingman's formula. In this project, Kingman's formula was used as a theoretical model to profile the factors influencing the fulfilment waiting time in the outpatient pharmacy.

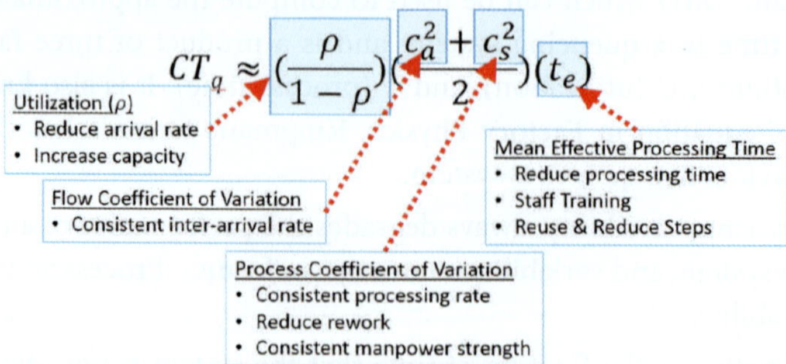

Figure 1: Factors influencing mean waiting time based on Kingman's formula.

4. SOLUTION

Description of Approach

In this section, the high-level pharmacy processes used in facilitating the data analysis of the work processes will be elaborated. This allows the reader to better understand the proposed solutions. Then, the various findings from the data analysis are explained. Finally, the proposed solutions that were implemented to reduce patient waiting times in the pharmacy will be discussed.

The key data sources for analysis carried out in this project were mainly from OPAS and iPharm systems. Their data was meshed so as to provide a more complete picture for data analysis:

a) The fulfilment and dispensing tasks performed by the pharmacists and automated dispensing machines were captured in OPAS.

b) The patient registration and first queue call time were captured in iPharm.

The range of data from OPAS and iPharm used in the analysis were based on prescriptions confirmed from April to June 2015.

4.1. High-level pharmacy workflow

The doctor prepares a prescription for a patient in the ePrescription (eRx) system. Once that has been confirmed, the prescription information is sent electronically to the pharmacy IT system iPharm via a HL7 message (a healthcare messaging standard). When the doctor completes the consultation with the patient, the patient proceeds to the pharmacy to collect his/her medications. A pharmacist (typist) will review the prescription with the patient prior to confirming the prescription at iPharm. Once the prescription is confirmed, the prescription information will then be sent to OPAS for further processing. The below diagram depicts the high-level interactions between the three IT systems (Figure 2).

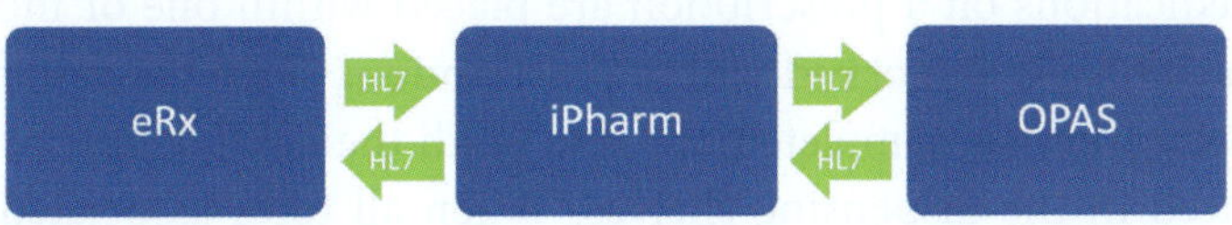

Figure 2: High-level Interactions between the 3 IT systems.

The process at the pharmacy from preparation to dispensing of the prescription goes through a chain of activities. The following diagram illustrates the high-level process flow at the NUH outpatient pharmacy (Figure 3).

Figure 3: High-level process flow at NUH outpatient pharmacy.

- Receiving: The patient arrives at the pharmacy and proceeds to the registration counter. A pharmacist (also known as a typist) will review the prescription with the patient. This is to review the prescription and to provide a queue number to the patient. Undertaking a more thorough assessment of the prescription with the patient at this stage has the potential to reduce delays at later stages of the workflow (for example, a patient requesting to collect a different quantity of a medication at the dispensing stage). At end of this stage, the typist will confirm the prescription at iPharm, and the prescription information will be sent to OPAS.
- System Pre-fulfilment Processing: Once OPAS receives the prescription information, the system will perform a series of tasks (prescription prioritization, translation from item to Stock Keeping Unit SKU level, and breakdown of user tasks) before the prescription fulfilment by the pharmacists and automated dispensing machines can commence. The total time taken for these tasks to be completed are in multiples of a second and therefore can be regarded as making a negligible contribution to the entire patient waiting time at the pharmacy.
- Fulfilment: The fulfilment tasks are to pick and assemble the list of medications on the prescription for the dispensing task. Each prescription can have a different combination of fulfilment tasks to be handled by the pharmacists and/or automated dispensing machines (Rowa & Parata). All medications on a prescription are placed within one or more tote, and each tote is associated with a prescription. Once the fulfilment of the medications is completed, the tote (with the medications) will then be placed in the dispensing shelves. When all totes associated with a prescription are placed in the dispensing shelves, this means that the prescription is set to the state of Ready for Dispense (or RFD for short).

- The pharmacists are accessing OPAS from a computer equipped with RFID scanner, barcode scanner and a label printer, and this setup is called a terminal. Broadly, there are two types of terminals in the pharmacy for fulfilment: Rowa terminals and non-Rowa terminals. Rowa terminals are terminals that are designed to receive medications from Rowa dispensing machines via conveyor belts, so this reduces the walking time by the pharmacists. There is a total of eight Rowa terminals in the pharmacy, and pharmacists who are using these Rowa terminals are able to perform fulfillment for a combination of all routes, which means Manual, Rowa and/or Parata. For the non-Rowa terminals, the pharmacists can only perform fulfilment on the Manual and Parata routes.
- Dispensing: The dispensing pharmacist will request a dispensing task from OPAS, which will then inform the pharmacist which patient's prescription should be dispensed. The pharmacist will pick up the tote(s) of the prescription to be dispensed from the dispensing shelves, and then call the patient (via queue system) to the dispensing counter to collect the prescribed medications. Counselling on the medications is provided to the patients, especially if the patients are not familiar with the medications or the medications are new to the patients.

The start time of the patient waiting time begins at the point when the prescription is confirmed by the typist, and the complete time of the patient waiting time is the first queue call of the patient to the dispensing counter.

Note that throughout the entire pharmacy process, rework (or more commonly known as amendment) can occur. The reason of rework can be due to many reasons, such as prescription changes by doctor, drug allergy, request by patient etc. Ideally, rework should be minimized as much as possible, as rework can extend the total time required to fulfil the prescription (Graban, 2011). For this reason, it is important for the typist to anticipate all possible causes of rework before the fulfilment work starts.

4.2. Priority of short prescriptions over long prescriptions

The following table shows the distribution of prescriptions by the number of item. An item is defined as a medication defined by their name, strength and form. The prescriptions are segregated into Short and Long prescription, where the short prescriptions are those with four or less items, and the long prescriptions are those with more than four items (see Table 1).

Table 1: Breakdown of Short & Long Prescriptions in February to April 2015

Month	Total	Feb 2015	Mar 2015	Apr 2015
Number of Prescriptions	28170	8274	11120	10914
Number of Short Prescriptions (<= 4 items)	24757 (87.9%)	7276 (87.9%)	9742 (87.7%)	9630 (88.2%)
Number of Long Prescriptions (> 4 items)	3401 (12.1%)	995 (12.1%)	1373 (12.3%)	1279 (11.8%)

Short prescriptions constituted approximately 88 per cent of all prescriptions. Generally, short prescriptions took less time to dispense than long prescriptions. Therefore, it was decided to focus on giving higher priority on fulfilling and dispensing short prescriptions over the long prescriptions. With this prioritization, more short prescriptions can be fulfilled faster, thus providing a higher likelihood of achieving the 95th percentile of patient waiting time at 15 minutes.

Although long prescriptions only constituted 12 per cent of the total prescriptions, the percentage of reworks was three times more than the short prescriptions (see Table 2). Such an observation was to be expected because when more items are ordered in a prescription, there will be a higher likelihood of rework for that prescription. Rework is understandably known to extend the total time required to fulfil the prescription. Due to this reason, this further justifies the decision to give higher priority in the fulfilment and dispensing of the short prescriptions.

Table 2: Breakdown of reworks between Short & Long Prescriptions in February to April 2015

Rework in	Total	Feb 2015	Mar 2015	Apr 2015
All prescriptions	9.40%	9.89%	9.08%	9.12%
Short prescriptions	7.53%	7.85%	7.22%	7.57%
Long prescriptions	23.08%	24.82%	22.36%	20.80%

4.3. Co-Starting of rowa and manual tasks

There is a mechanism in OPAS that allows a user to work on more than one fulfilment task of a prescription from different routes concurrently, and this is termed as co-starting of the tasks. For instance, the user can work on Rowa and Manual fulfilment tasks at the same time at a single terminal. For co-starting to be possible, the pharmacists must be seated at a Rowa terminal. Rowa terminals are specially designed terminals with conveyor belts connected to the Rowa machines, so that the medications picked by the Rowa machines for a prescription can be transported to the Rowa terminals through the conveyor belts. A key advantage of co-starting is that while the medications are picked by the Rowa machines and transported via the conveyor belt to the Rowa terminals, the pharmacist can pick the medications from the medication shelves manually at the same time.

If a prescription is worked out to have tasks for both Rowa and Manual routes and the pharmacist is seated at a non-Rowa terminal, he/she will only be able to work on fulfilling the Manual task as this terminal has no linkage to the Rowa machines. This is equivalent to the Rowa and Manual tasks are not co-started. In other words, this means that the opportunity of performing both Rowa and Manual tasks at a single terminal simultaneously is missed.

A study was conducted on the effect of co-starting versus no co-starting of Rowa and Manual tasks. As at April 2015, only 52 per cent of all prescriptions with multiple routes are co-started in the outpatient pharmacy. A hypothesis testing (Wilcoxon rank-sum test) was performed on 3,838 prescriptions with two samples:

- 2,001 co-started prescriptions with Rowa and Manual articles
- 1,837 not co-started prescriptions with Rowa and Manual articles

It was noted that there was statistical difference in the mean of fulfilment time if Rowa & Manual tasks were co-started (p-value = 1.688e^{-12}). Generally, co-starting Rowa and Manual tasks took less time to complete. Table 3 below compares the time taken for Rowa and Manual tasks that were co-started and not co-started. With this finding, NUH configured OPAS to adopt more co-starting of Rowa and Manual tasks.

Table 3: Time difference between No Co-start and Co-start of Rowa and Manual tasks

Time Taken	25th Percentile	50th Percentile	75th Percentile	95th Percentile
No Co-start (Sec)	504	838	1243	1984.2
Co-Start (Sec)	412	708	1117	1811
Difference (Sec)	92	130	126	173.2
Difference (Min)	1.53	2.17	2.10	2.89

4.4. Identification of frequent prescribed items in a prescription

Medication items that are to be picked manually are placed across several medication shelves in the pharmacy. When a prescription comprises multiple items to be picked manually, the pharmacist might need to walk to more than one shelf to gather the medication items. One way to reduce the walking time incurred by the pharmacist is to place the frequent prescribed items near to each other. For this purpose, Association Rules is performed on the manual items for 10,907 prescriptions that were ordered from January to March 2015.

With a minimum support and confidence of 1 per cent and 70 per cent respectively, a series of frequently prescribed item set was identified. It was also observed that different days of the week had different sets of frequently prescribed item sets. These lists of item sets were shared with the pharmacists who were already aware of these frequent item sets. Therefore, the placement of these items across the shelves were already optimized at the point of discovery.

4.5. Predictive classification modeling of patient waiting time

Two multivariate logistic regression models were developed to assist the pharmacist to make better assessment of the patient waiting times in the pharmacy. The 15 minute patient waiting time was used as the class label in these models, and two predictor variables were selected via stepwise regression from a pool of 30 variables. These classification models were trained with a total of 12,261 prescriptions dispensed within 27 working days (4 May – 12 Jun 2015), and 5,255 prescriptions were used as validation data.

Other classification models - Classification and Regression Tree (Breiman, 1984) and Random Forest (Breiman, 2001)) - were built and evaluated. Despite the fact that logistic regression is a simpler classification model, it provided the highest accuracy at approximately 78–79 per cent compared to the models built with other classification techniques in this project.

4.5.1. Logistics regression model 1: Predict if a prescription (upon confirmation) will exceed 15 minute patient waiting time

$$Y = 2.253 - 0.1845A - 0.3102B$$

- A: Number of other prescriptions waiting in Fulfilment Queue when the prescription (to be predicted) is confirmed
- B: Number of Items of the prescription (to be predicted)

The optimal cut-off is identified at 0.49. This means if the predicted value for a prescription upon confirmation is greater than 0.49, this implies that the prescription has high likelihood of not meeting the 15 minutes patient waiting time upon confirmation of the prescription. This model has an accuracy of 78.34 per cent based on the training data, together with sensitivity of 82.21 per cent and specificity of 75.18 per cent.

Table 4: Observations of Logistic Regression Model 1

Number of Pending Prescriptions in Fulfillment Queue upon Confirmation	Number of Items in Prescription upon Confirmation	Outcome (Meet/ Cannot Meet)
0	8	Cannot Meet
6	4	Meet
7	4	Cannot Meet

There were two interesting findings that were derived from this model (see Table 4).

a) A short prescription (four or less items) upon confirmation has a high likelihood of not meeting the 15 minutes patient waiting time when there are already more than six prescriptions in the fulfilment queue. This observation was presented to the pharmacists, and they concurred with this observation as there was likely to be only up to six Rowa terminals occupied during the peak operational hours.

If the pharmacy wished to increase this cutoff at six prescriptions in the fulfilment queue, they would need to increase the number of active Rowa terminals accordingly. However, increasing Rowa terminals is a costly option, as there was a need to construct additional conveyor belts linking the Rowa machines and the Rowa terminals. Therefore, this option was set aside at this point in the project.

b) If the prescription had more than seven items upon confirmation, there is a high likelihood of not meeting the 15 minutes patient waiting time.

The first finding of this logistic regression model can be corroborated by both Figure 4 and Figure 5. In both charts, each dot represents a prescription that is confirmed at a point in time (with reference to the horizontal axis). The vertical axis denotes the number of other prescriptions already waiting in the fulfilment queue when the prescription is confirmed. The yellow-shaded region marks the "safe" area (i.e. less than seven pending prescriptions in the fulfilment queue that is derived from the logistics regression model).

It is evident that there were many prescriptions that lie out of the 'safe' area in the chart for 2 Jun 2015, and only 22.88 per cent prescriptions met the 15 minutes patient waiting time. In the 19 Jun 2015 chart (Figure 5) most prescriptions fell within the 'safe' area, thus 97.15 per cent of prescriptions attained the 15 minutes patient waiting time.

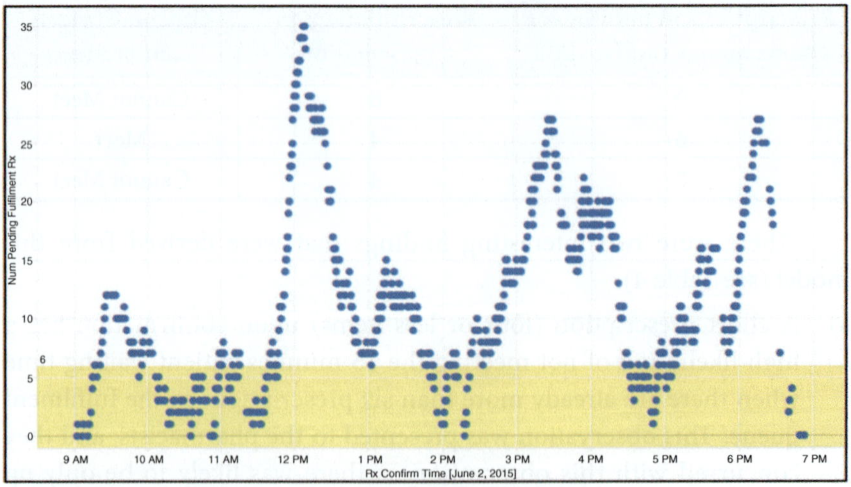

Figure 4: Number of pending prescriptions in fulfilment queue on 2 June 2015 (22.88 per cent of prescriptions met the 15 minutes patient waiting time).

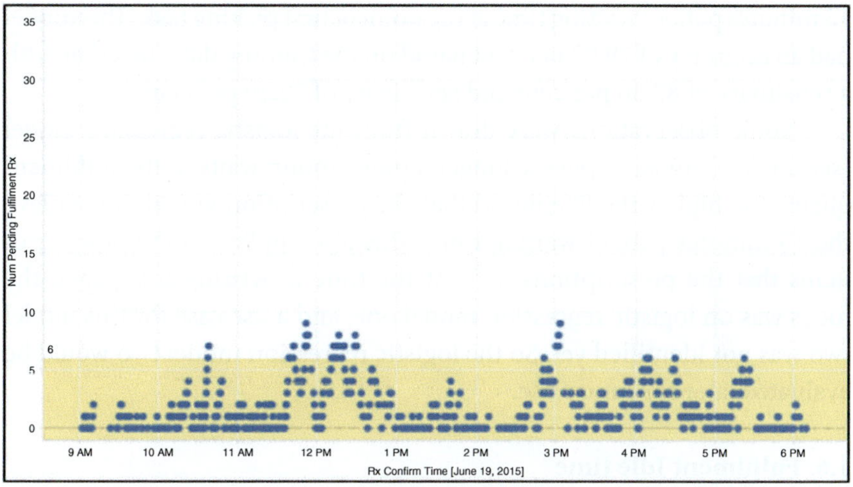

Figure 5: Number of pending prescriptions in fulfilment queue on 19 June 2015 (97.15 per cent of prescriptions met the 15 minutes patient waiting time).

4.5.2. Logistics regression model 2: Predict if a prescription (upon first picking task) will exceed 15 minutes patient waiting time

$$Y = 2.172 - 0.004487A - 0.3044B$$

- A: Number of seconds that the prescription (to be predicted) is waiting in Fulfilment Queue
- B: Number of Items on the prescription (to be predicted)

The optimal cut-off is identified at 0.46. This means if the predicted value for a prescription upon confirmation was greater than 0.46, this implied that the prescription had high likelihood of not meeting the

Table 5: Observations of Logistic Regression Model 2

Number of seconds that the Prescription was pending in fulfilment queue	Number of Items in Prescription upon Confirmation	Outcome (Meet/ Cannot Meet)
0	8	Cannot Meet
450	1	Meet
460	1	Cannot Meet
350	2	Cannot Meet

15 minutes patient waiting time at the point of first picking task. This model had an accuracy of 79.03 per cent based on the training data, together with a sensitivity of 87.36 per cent and specificity of 72.20 per cent.

Some observations were drawn from the logistic regression model (see Table 5) for example the longer a prescription waits in the fulfilment queue, the higher the likelihood that the prescription would not achieve the 15 minutes patient waiting time. This also applied to the number of items that the prescriptions had. At the time of writing this paper, the focus was on logistic regression model one, and a use case for this model two was not identified yet. So the logistic regression model two would be evaluated later for future use.

4.6. Fulfilment Idle time

The relationship between the fulfilment idle time and patient waiting time (see Figure 6) has a very strong correlation ($R^2 = 0.92$). The fulfilment idle time is the period from the time the prescription is confirmed until the start of the first fulfilment task. Therefore, it is evident that the fulfilment idle time is a stronger contributor to the patient waiting time than the

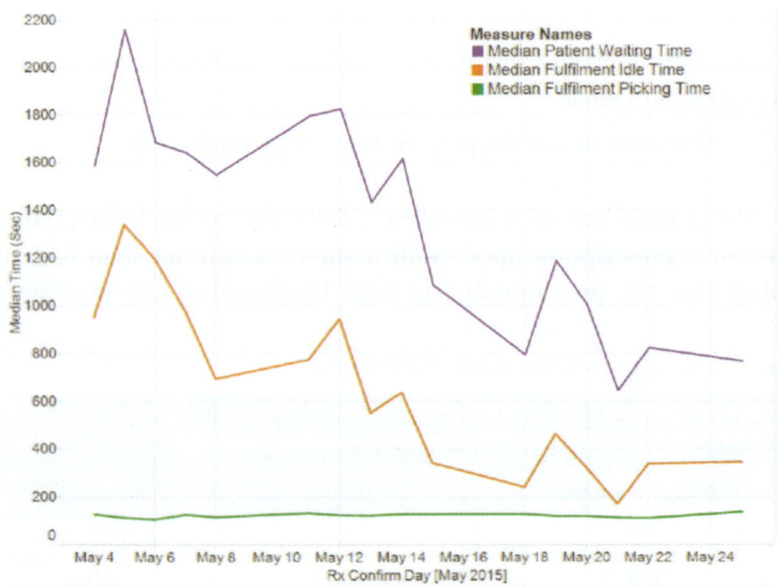

Figure 6: Correlation between patient waiting time, fulfilment idle time & fulfilment picking time.

fulfilment picking time, which is the productive time spent by the pharmacists in fulfilling the prescription.

It is also detected that the patient waiting time is exacerbated by faster rate of prescriptions confirmation by the typists. Figure 7 shows the histograms of time gap (in intervals of five minutes) between successive prescription confirmations, and the data based on prescriptions confirmed on 2 and 19 Jun 2015. Both histograms exhibit very similar Poisson-like distribution, but there were more prescriptions confirmed at shorter time gaps on 2 Jun 2015. It is also observed that there were a lower number of prescriptions attaining 15 minutes patient waiting time on 2 Jun 2015 (22.88 per cent) compared to 19 Jun 2015 (97.15 per cent). Similar observations on this relationship between the rate of prescription confirmation and patient waiting time were also noted on other days.

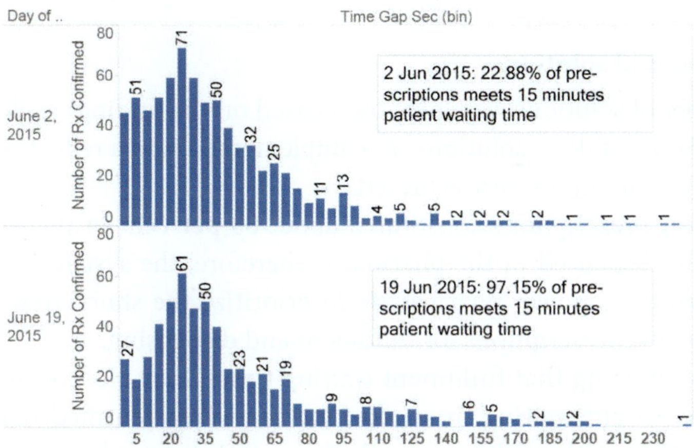

Figure 7: Histogram of prescription confirmation time gap between prescriptions on 2 and 19 June 2015.

Figure 8 illustrates the relationship between the number of active pharmacists who were working on fulfilling prescriptions against the number of prescriptions that were RFD across the day. This relationship shows that there was a close correlation ($R^2 = 0.75$) between these two variables. Another observation from this chart was that the manpower strength throughout the day working on fulfilling the prescription was not consistent. This was because the pharmacists had other duties to carry out in any given day, such as checking, ordering and replenishing stocks.

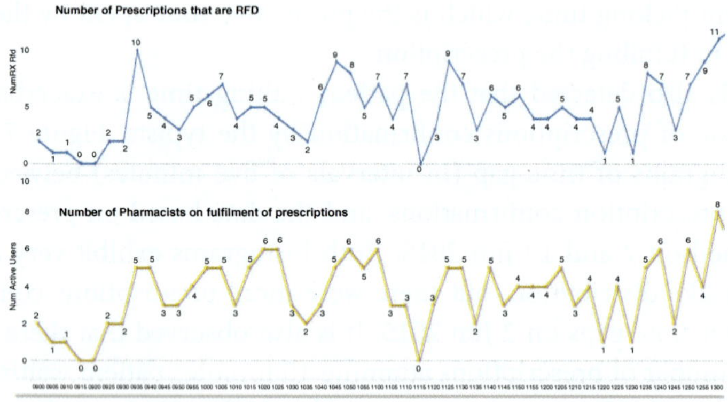

Figure 8: Relationship between the number of active pharmacists who were working on fulfilling prescriptions against the number of prescriptions that were RFD across the day.

4.7. Proposed solutions

A number of solutions were proposed based on the findings as discussed earlier. Some of these solutions were implemented, and a reduction in the patient waiting times were achieved.

Short prescriptions constituted about 88 per cent of the total prescriptions dispensed in the pharmacy. Therefore, the system OPAS was enhanced to empower pharmacists to prioritize the short prescriptions over the long prescriptions for fulfilment and dispensing.

Recognizing that fulfilment waiting times were closely correlated with the patient waiting times, two factors were identified that could help to reduce the fulfilment idle time (CT_q) based on Kingman's formula:

a) *To keep a constant rate of prescription confirmation throughout the day (to avoid sudden high bursts of prescription confirmation which can 'flood' the fulfilment queue)*

   By Factory Physics lingo, this is equivalent to maintaining a constant arrival rate r_a. By keeping a constant arrival rate, this could help to keep the utilization rate (ρ) constant as much as possible throughout the day, which in turn would reduce the fulfilment idle time.

b) *To ensure consistent manpower strength so that the prescriptions can be fulfilled at a constant rate*

This ensures a lower Process Coefficient of Variation (c_s^2), which will lead to a lower fulfilment idle time.

From a non-quantitative perspective of the Kingman's formula, Figure 9 summarizes the possible actions to reduce the mean waiting time in a queueing system.

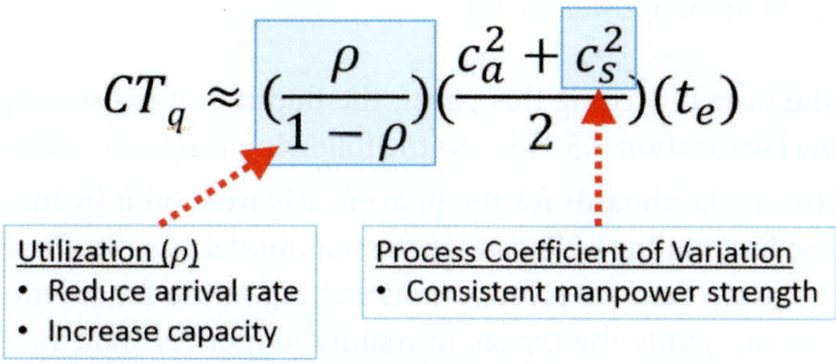

Figure 9: Using Kingman's equation to reduce fulfilment idle time.

A number of measures were implemented to reduce the fulfilment idle time based on these two factors.

a) An electronic dashboard was implemented to aid the pharmacists to monitor these two factors. One feature of this dashboard as a control chart was to assist the typist at the registration counter to throttle the prescription confirmation at a consistent rate. This is to prevent the pharmacists working on the downstream activities (fulfilment and dispensing) to be swamped with sudden high influx of prescriptions. The other benefit of this approach was the typist was able to spend equivalent time with each patient to review the medications, so rework on the prescription can be mitigated in advance. The other feature of the dashboard was to display the number of active pharmacists that were working on fulfilment and dispensing tasks, to assist the Pharmacy Floor Manager [refer to (c) below]

b) The pharmacy staff were instructed that if they needed to leave the fulfilment terminals to work on other duties, they were required to find replacement staff to take over the fulfilment work. This helped to ensure a consistent manpower strength required to fulfill the prescriptions.

c) A new role - Pharmacy Floor Manager - was created to coordinate the tasks and manpower in the outpatient pharmacy. The Pharmacy Floor Manager also reviewed the electronic dashboard regularly, so he/she could respond to situations promptly, especially during peak operational hours. For example, when there is a sharp drop in the number of pharmacists fulfilling the prescriptions, the floor manager is alerted by the dashboard and he/she will investigate and respond to the drop of manpower swiftly.

At the time of writing this paper, the findings of logistic regression model one (see section 4.5.1) led to the following proposed solutions:

a) Electronic dashboards for the pharmacists were built by incorporating the first finding of logistic regression model one (i.e. there should not be more than six prescriptions waiting in the fulfilment queue), so this can guide the typists in maintaining a constant rate of prescription confirmation. The dashboard will display an alert to the typists if the number of pending prescriptions in the fulfilment queue exceeds six. The typists will then need to throttle their prescription confirmation at a lower rate. With the 'extra' time afforded by a lower prescription confirmation rate, the typists can devote more time to review the prescription and interact with the patients, and such practices can help to reduce potential prescription reworks after the fulfilment has started.

b) With regards to the second finding of the logistics regression model one, the typists can offer home delivery service to the patient if there are more than seven items in the prescription. This allows the pharmacists to fulfill such prescriptions at a later time (after operational hours), and the patients need not wait for their prescriptions in the pharmacy. The patient waiting time for such prescriptions are recorded as zero, but will still contribute to the overall calculation of the 95th percentile of patient waiting times.

5. DISCUSSION

Since the implementation of the solutions, the patient waiting time has reduced significantly as shown in Table 6.

Table 6: Patient Waiting Time in June 2015

Date	% Patient Waiting Time < 15 min		
	All prescriptions	Short prescriptions	Long prescriptions
2 Jun 2015	22.99%	25.15%	5.88%
3 Jun 2015	59.94%	68.11%	13.33%
4 Jun 2015	49.45%	55.52%	6.33%
5 Jun 2015	57.95%	62.55%	20.69%
8 Jun 2015	82.59%	87.97%	45.45%
9 Jun 2015	86.50%	91.09%	56.38%
10 Jun 2015	94.64%	97.89%	66.67%
11 Jun 2015	90.66%	93.65%	67.14%
12 Jun 2015	91.62%	94.72%	70.27%

6. CONCLUSION AND FUTURE WORKS

From the outcome of this project, it was clear and apparent that the principles of Factory Physics can be used to study and improve the processes of a large outpatient pharmacy effectively. The objectives of this project were met by identifying the factors affecting patient waiting times, developing and implementing strategies to mitigate these factors and ultimately reduce the patient waiting time significantly. The proposed solutions discussed in this paper can potentially be used in other outpatient pharmacies to reduce patient waiting times. A potential area for future works is to build a discrete event simulation model to test and verify process changes prior to implementing them on the ground.

REFERENCES

1. Anderson, RT, FT Camacho and R Balkrishnan (2007). Willing to wait?: the influence of patient wait time on satisfaction with primary care. *BMC Health Services Research*.

2. Breiman, L (1984). Classification and regression trees. CRC press.

3. Breiman, L (2001). Random forests. *Machine learning*.

4. Choi, YF, TW Wong and CC Lau (2006). Triage rapid initial assessment by doctor (TRIAD) improves waiting time and processing time of the emergency department. *Emergency medicine journal.*

5. Fetter, RB. and JD Thompson (1966). Patients' waiting time and doctors' idle time in the outpatient setting. *Health Services Research.*

6. Fitzpatrick, R (2004). Automated dispensing—developing a business case to support investment. *Hospital Pharmacist*, 109–111.

7. Graban, M (2011). *Lean Hospitals: Improving Quality, Patient Safety, and Employee Engagement.*

8. Hopp, WJ. and ML Spearman (2011). *Factory physics.* Waveland Press.

9. Kingman, JF (1961). The single server queue in heavy traffic. *Mathematical Proceedings of the Cambridge Philosophical Society*, 57(4).

10. Vemuri, S (1984). Simulated analysis of patient waiting time in an outpatient pharmacy. *American Journal of Health-System Pharmacy.*

11. Yu, Q and K Yang (2008). Hospital registration waiting time reduction through process redesign. *International Journal of Six Sigma and Competitive Advantage.*

UNCITED REFERENCES

1. ASEAN Agreement on Transboundary Haze Pollution (2015). *Hotspots.* Retrieved from ASEAN Agreement on Transboundary Haze Pollution: http://haze.asean.org/?page_id=251

2. Asia Insurance Review (2015, April 15). *India: Less than 1/5 of farmers insure crops.* Retrieved from Asia Insurance Review: http://www.asiainsurancereview.com/News/View-NewsLetter-Article?id=32525&Type=eDaily

3. BAE, S (2015). *AML Transaction Monitoring.* Retrieved from http://www.baesystems.com/what-we-do-rai/financial-crime/financial-crime-solutions/aml-transaction-monitoring [16 August 2015].

4. Baker, J. and M Cameron (1996). The effects of the service environment on affect and consumer perception of waiting time: An integrative review and research propositions. *Journal of the Academy of Marketing Science.*

5. Bartlett, J (2014). *Area Under the ROC curve.* Retrieved from http://thestatsgeek.com/2014/05/05/area-under-the-roc-curve-assessing-discrimination-in-logistic-regression/ [16 August 2015].

6. Davenport, TH (2015). The Rise of Automated Analytics. *The Wall Street Journey.*

7. Delong, ER-P (1988). Comparing the areas under two or more correlated receiver operating characteristic curves: a nonparametric approach. *Biometrics*, 837–845.

8. Edelman, KD (2015, July). *What 'digital' really means*. Mckinsey Insights.

9. Feinerer, I (2015). *Introduction to the tm Package*. Retrieved from https://cran.r-project.org/web/packages/tm/vignettes/tm.pdf [16 August 2015].

10. FINCEN (2014). *SAR Stats*. Retrieved from http://www.fincen.gov/news_room/rp/sar_by_number.html [16 August 2015].

11. Gerdeman, D (2015, June 29). *Harvard Business School*. Retrieved from HBS Working Knowledge: http://hbswk.hbs.edu/item/consumer-centered-health-care-depends-on-accessible-medical-records

12. Hai, PT (2015, May 26). *Head of the Department of Information Systems at the School of Computing*, National University of Singapore. (F.-Y. Liang, Interviewer)

13. ICA, IC (2015). *What is Money Laundering*. Retrieved from http://www.int-comp.org/what-is-money-laundering [16 August 2015].

14. Karapiperis, D (2015). *Usage-Based Insurance and Vehicle Telematics: Insurance Market & Regulatory Implications*. Kansas City: NAIC Central Office.

15. Lam, SL (2012). *Rough Set Approach to Marine Cargo Risk Analysis*. Retrieved from International Centre for Maritime Studies: http://www.icms.polyu.edu.hk/ifspa2012/Papers/M26.pdf

16. Lee T (2006). *CARe 2006: Marine Reinsurane*. Retrieved from Casualty Actuarial Society: https://www.casact.org/education/reinsure/2006/handouts/tookey.ppt

17. Makino, T (2010, April). *What's Next: The Search for Disruptive Technologies*. Retrieved from CELENT: http://www.celent.com/system/files/disruptive_innovation_using_mobile_devices_tokio_marine.pdf

18. McKinsey & World Economic Forum (2014, May). *The rising strategic risks of cyber-attacks*. Retrieved from McKinsey&Company: http://www.mckinsey.com/insights/business_technology/the_rising_strategic_risks_of_cyberattacks

19. McKinsey Global Institute (2011). *Big data: The next frontier*. McKinsey & Company.

20. McKinsey&Company (2015). *The Internet of Things: Mapping the Value Beyond the Hype*. McKinsey&Company.

21. MetLife Asia (2015, July 16). *MetLife Launches LumenLab*. Retrieved from Business Wire: http://www.businesswire.com/news/home/20150716005707/en/MetLife-Launches-LumenLab---First-of-its-Kind-Innovation-Centre#.VcMHIf4cTL8

22. Park, K (2013). Expression of stress response HSP70 gene in Asian paddle crabs, Charybdis japonica, exposure to endocrine disrupting chemicals, bisphenol A (BPA) and 4-nonylphenol (NP). *Ocean Science Journal.*

23. Rohde, RA (2015). *Air Pollution in China: Mapping of Concentrations and Sources.* Berkeley: Berkeley Earth (of UC Berkeley) Press.

24. Sequeira, I (2015, June 20). *Fintech Leader* (Strategy and Analytics). (F.-Y. Liang, Interviewer)

25. SINTEF (2013, May 22). *Big Data, for better or worse.* Retrieved from ScienceDaily: www.sciencedaily.com/releases/2013/05/130522085217.htm

26. Strathclyde, UO (2015). *What is Logistic Regression.* Retrieved from https://www.strath.ac.uk/aer/materials/5furtherquantitativeresearchdesignandanalysis/unit6/whatislogisticregression/ [16 August 2015].

27. The Times of India (2015, August 13). *25% of Indians may die of lifestyle diseases before they are 70: Study.* Retrieved from The Time of India: http://timesofindia.indiatimes.com/india/25-of-Indians-may-die-of-lifestyle-diseases-before-they-are-70-Study/articleshow/48460601.cms

28. The World Bank (2012, March 6). *India Groundwater: a Valuable but Diminishing Resource.* Retrieved from The World Bank: https://www.worldbank.org/en/news/feature/2012/03/06/india-groundwater-critical-diminishing

29. UNODC (2015). *The Money-Laundering Cycle.* Retrieved from https://www.unodc.org/unodc/en/money-laundering/laundrycycle.html [16 August 2015].

30. Van, S (2015a). *APAC Big Data Market Watch.* Singapore: Swiss Reinsurance Company Ltd.

31. Van, S (2015b). *Closing the Protection Gap in APAC.* Singapore: Asia Insurance Review.

32. Weiss, U (2015). *Uwe Weiss On Predictive Analytics.* Interview by Lutz Finger.

33. Wikipedia (2015a). *Bank Secrecy Act.* Retrieved from https://en.wikipedia.org/wiki/Bank_Secrecy_Act [16 August 2015].

34. Wikipedia (2015b). *Text Mining.* Retrieved from https://en.wikipedia.org/wiki/Text_mining [16 August 2015].

35. Willis Energy Market Review (2014). *Cyber Attacks: Can the Market Respond?.* London: Willis Limited.

36. WinfWiki (2014). *Analyse Text Mining SAS Text Miner.* Retrieved from http://winfwiki.wi-fom.de/index.php/Analyse_Text_Mining_mit_SAS_Text_Miner [16 August 2015].

CHAPTER 30

Automated Analytics Process – The Next Stage of Competition on Analytics

LU John Jian An

ABSTRACT

This report explores the possibility of an automated process for carrying out retail banking analytics. While the practice of using data and quantitative techniques for decision-making has long been carried out by business analytics professionals, this report explores potential automation of some business analytics activities usually carried out by humans.

As business analytics matures, the role of senior analysts will shift from creating advanced models to creating advanced processes that are capable of automating the creation of decision-assisting analytical models. The 'automated analytical process' requires highly advanced business analytics skills to set up, maintain and improve the process – these are jobs that cannot be automated. If established correctly, this process can assist daily decision-making in either automated or semi-automated modes.

This report demonstrates the creation and testing of such an automated analytical process.

1. INTRODUCTION

Banks believe that digital innovation will have a big impact on the future of the business, and that analytics will be a critical success factor for a digital strategy. While this is well-accepted, there is a lack of clarity on how exactly analytics will achieve such an impact.

The appraoch can be summarized in three words – embed, integrate and productize. 'Embed' means that analytics are provided sufficiently quickly to business managers so that inputs are automatically fed into the sequence of their daily actions. 'Integrate' means that once the analytics output is produced, there is a straight throughput process to design and test an experiment using real campaign data. Successful ideas can be leveraged into standard practice, allow analysts to move on to the next idea. 'Productize' means the creation of products wherein analytics are consumed directly by end users, including consumers, business partners and employees such as call center agents that take immediate actions as a result of using these products.

The objective is to create value propositions beyond simple transaction processing yielding unique competitive advantages.

For example, instead of sending promotions to the customer, an application can be created which allows the customer to get a tailored promotion based on preferences (such as past purchase, frequent locations, etc) and current status (where he is now, what he wants to do, etc).

This type of product can also be used by business partners. For example, instead of sending out mass promotions on behalf of merchant partners, an application can be created that allows the manager of a restaurant to attract business by sending real time offers to nearby consumers by combining recommendation engines and location analytics.

Thus, digital communication channels together with analytics can create value in core businesses through decision making, customer interactions and business innovation (Dorner and Edelman, 2015).

To achieve this, the following capabilities need to be built:

1) Automated and highly effective analytical process that will lower the cost of creating and consuming analytics. This creates the ability to embed analytics into everyday decision making and interaction with each customer.

2) Integrated and extremely user friendly systems to assist automated testing of ideas using historical data and simulation. This makes it easy for an organization to adopt the new culture of analytics-assisted decision making.
3) IT architecture that can quickly design and deliver products that embed analytics for both internal and external consumption. This enables competition with industry leaders such as Apple Pay, Google Wallet and Bitcoin.

2. PROBLEM STATEMENT

How can business analytics be **measured**, **improved** and **embedded** to assist routine management decisions and customer interactions? One possible answer is the **automated analytic process**.

Analytics have been used to assist critical business activities, such as credit scoring, logistic and warehousing decisions, statistical quality control process, air ticket pricing and genome research. Many of these usages are based on purpose-built models that follow the traditional analytics process such as SEMA, CRISP-DM or other similar frameworks.

The traditional analytics process refers to an analytical process based on the principle where understanding the cause and the ability to explain the model are essential requirements for output generation. It emphasizes domain specific knowledge, understanding a specific problem and an interactive process that requires the analyst to interpret the outcome at each stage before moving into the next stage.

This process tends to be highly iterative and may lead the analyst back to previous stages to include new variables, re-select the appropriate variable or modify existing variables.

Full transparency and interpretation of the process (not the model) are ensured. Simultaneously, the analyst's skill helps to reduce the risk of false positive conclusions from high dimension data and repeated experiments.

The automated analytics process uses regularization and empirical tests to search for suitable models while avoiding the problem of over-fitting.

An automated analytics process must have the following characteristics:

1) The process must be fully preconfigured and able to produce a 'working' model with no human intervention during the modeling process, except for defining the problem.
2) The process must be able to produce comparable data containing parameters of the configuration, the problem, the input data, the model produced and the quality of the model.

What is the distinction between the 'automated analytics process' and the 'automated analytics tool?' 'Automated analytics tool' refers to a tool with a simplified user interface that can be used by those not trained in, for example, statistics to 'automatically' make predictions or inferences. Many solutions of this type have some underlying assumptions, such as having the input data with target and input variables correctly specified, knowing the correct algorithms, and having relevant training / testing samples.

The analytics process can be described as follows:

1) Set up the parameters for automated modeling tasks (which are to be re-used across problems).
2) Introduce new data that contains targets and variables.
3) Partition the data into training and testing.
4) Initial training on a large set of candidate models can be fine-tuned for optimal parameters. The training process can be arranged so that smaller training data can be used in the initial assessment. The risk of over-fitting is addressed by techniques such as repeated *n*-fold cross validation.
5) Identify the best subsets of candidate models and perform further model building and selections using larger training and testing data.
6) Evaluate final models by re-sampling the test data to produce an empirical distribution of the measurement such as Area Under the Curve (AUC) instead of using just one single test data set.

This process needs to be custom built by organization; it is unlikely to be based on a canned product capable of providing the full benefit of this multiple organizations. Nor is it possible for an organization to outsource the creation of this capability, for the following reasons:

Firstly, there is no theoretical answer to what kind of variable selection process, or which algorithm, will provide the best solution for different problems faced by the organization. So analysts have to test different criteria for selecting and evaluating the models and learning from the result.

Secondly, as results are reproducible and comparable across different problems, analysts will need to study past results and improve this process for different types of problem, data and solution objective.

Thirdly, as analysts are freed from the mechanical process of model fitting, they will spend more time on the activities of understanding the business problems and identifying potential use for this process.

A comparison of the traditional modeling process and automated modeling process is listed below:

	Traditional Modeling Process	**Automated Modeling Process**
Pros	Able to identify data abnormality in the early stages of modeling process Able to re-assess and validate business/data assumptions during the modeling process Results are easily explained and often provide hints for further improvements; thus an iterative process. Can lead to insights for the business to improve beyond the application of the model	The process is fast and automated; hence can be applied to solve more problems and as input for trigger events. The process can take in more recent data; improvements are made on models even after the models have been rolled out for production It is possible to learn from the past and adjust the process for different types of problem in the organization Able to generate a larger set of candidate models and recommend the best through validation and test process
Cons	Resource consuming; takes long time to build a model and the result depends on the skill of the modeler Start with limited set of candidate, and seldom do complete search for the optimal solution Difficult to continuously improve the models by learning from more recent data Success and lessons learned from each model exercise are domain-specific and not easy to institutionalize	Susceptible to garbage-in, garbage-out syndrome Does not incorporate subject matter expert's input during the automated process, so unable to capture early signs of a poorly defined use case Usually does not generate insights for the business problems beyond the direct output from the model Usually does not directly provide ideas on how to improve the result of the models

Traditional analytics process and automated analytics process should be used to complement rather than replace one another.

For example, when working on an explanatory model, the automated analytics process can be used to form a baseline of the predictive power, then the resultant models can be deployed to outline the main features of the problem, and finally the traditional analytics process can create the explanatory model and select the relevant factors for retention.

3. STATE OF THE ART

This problem was termed 'automated modeling process' at the outset of this project. During subsequent literature reviews, other discussions on this topic were identified, using terms such as "automated analytics" (Davenport, 2015) and "automated decision making" (Weiss, 2015). Hence, the term 'automated analytics process' is used throughout to avoid confusion with these other studies.

At the time of writing, it was not clear if there a mature commercial solution existed. But there are statistical learning methods and open source packages that can be utilized to solve such problems.

The following table highlights potential problems and proposed solutions in developing the 'automated analytics process'.

Problem	Solution
Differing t variables	With the lowered cost of storage, it is possible to create an analytics data layer on Apache Hadoop that contains pre-processed variables where new variables can be added as more models are built via this approach
Different population bases	The analytics data layer can contain all the potential observations and allow the problem to drive the applicable population base
Irrelevant variables	Regularization and cross validation during training can be used to avoid over-fitting
Different sampling strategies	A structured analytical process can help to discover the learning rate for different types of problem and thus enable conclusions to be drawn about rates of machine learning

Problem	Solution
Different trade-offs between complexity and degrees of freedom	Grid search with re-sampling allows the use of empirical evidence to decide optimal complexity
Suitability of algorithm	Re-sampling on test data and class invariant measurements such as AUC (Delong *et al.*,1998) can be used to select the best model

4. SOLUTION

Will the automated analytics process create inferior models because of a lack of interactive expert input?

An automated process should establish strong and repeatable models in a short timeframe. The discussion below compares models built via an automated process with those built by the traditional process.

4.1. Business problem

A business unit wants to increase the usage of a particular type of transaction; the modeling team is given the task of identifying those customers who are more likely to respond to the campaigns promoting the transaction. As there is no existing campaign to promote this transaction, a look-alike model is proposed as a potential solution.

Construction of modeling file The modeling terminologies used in the report is listed below:

- **Population** is the collection of all customers eligible to perform the transaction.
- An **observation** is each month when a customer is in the population. When the customer is in the population twice in two different months, he will be counted as two observations.
- An **event** is each observation than contains the transaction. If an observation performs 10 transactions in the same month, he is still considered

as one event. But if the observation performs two transactions in two different months, there are two events.

- A **non-event** is each observation that does not contain the transaction.
- **In-time** data refers to the observations over six months from Apr 2014 – September 2014.
- **Out-of-time** data refers to the observations over two months from October 2014 – November 2014
- **Training** data is created by performing simple random sampling from 70 per cent of in-time data.
- **Validation** data is the remaining 30 per cent of the in-time data.
- **Testing** data refers to the out-of-time data.
- **Shifting-window** approach is a technique to create variables for each observation. Each time a customer appears as an observation, the past x months' variables of the same customer are used to create attributes for this observation. As illustrated below, Customer one appears twice in observation one and observation *N*-1 over two different periods.

The variables of Customer one from February 2014 are used to form part of the attributes for both observations. For example, Customer 1's balance in February 2014 is used to create the past six months' average balance for observation one. The same customer's balance in February 2014 is used to create the past six month's average balance for observation *N*-1.

This process can be automated by storing the data to allow for the efficient generation of shifting window attributes.

Traditional Modeling Process In the traditional modeling process, in-time data was modeled into training, validation and testing; final models were evaluated using out-of-time data as the test data.

The entire modeling process, which takes approximately two months, comprises the following factors:

1) An initial evaluation of 1,662 variables from five different source systems, including:
    a) customer demographic (e.g. age and gender)
    b) account (e.g. number of accounts and balance)

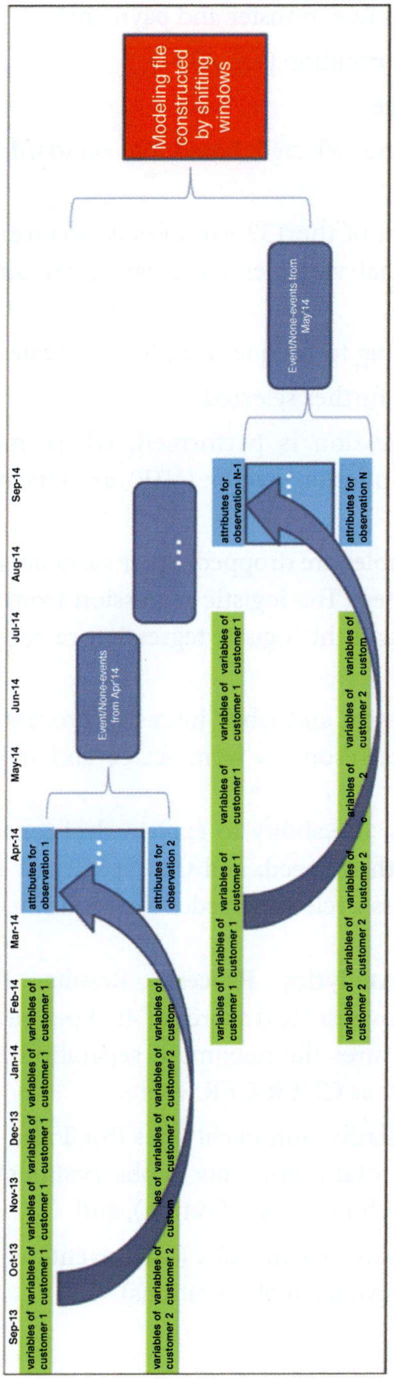
Sep-13
Oct-13
Nov-13
Dec-13
Jan-14
Feb-14
Mar-14
Apr-14
May-14
Jun-14
Jul-14
Aug-14
Sep-14
variables of customer 1
variables of customer 2
attributes for observation 1
attributes for observation 2
Event/None-events from Apr'14
attributes for observation N-1
attributes for observation N
Event/None-events from May'14
Modeling file constructed by shifting windows

   c) transactions (e.g. transfer and payment)
   d) channel information (e.g. ATM)
   e) branch usage
2) 139 variables are selected based on standard information value criteria.
3) Profiling of each of the 139 variables is performed by the modeler, and 35 additional variables are created, bringing the variable list to 174.
4) Variable clustering technique is applied to create 39 clusters.
5) 94 variables are further selected.
6) A logistic regression is performed, where metrics like *p*-value and Variance Inflation Factor (VIF) are checked to assess those variables.
7) Whenever variables are dropped, other variables from the same cluster are substituted. The logistic regression from the same cluster is substituted in, and the logistic regression re-run to include the new variables.

This is an iterative and labor intensive process originating from a time when analytics resources were scarce and models were used for many years.

In this process, the ability to explain decisions made in each step is more important than speed, and the capacity of analytics to smooth out over the business cycle supersedes the requirement to have optimal sample data.

Traditional Analytics Process: Results Two models with Kolmogrove-Smirnov test (KS) scores of 45.0 per cent and 49.4 per cent were built. KS measures the maximum separation between events and non-events, measure as CNER-CER where:

CNER is cumulative non-event rates (total non-events with prediction below *p* / total non-events in observations) with *p* going from zero to one (for binary classification), and

CER is cumulative event rates (total events with prediction score below *p* / total events in observations).

KS is commonly used in the industry, and a value above 0.4 is generally considered acceptable.

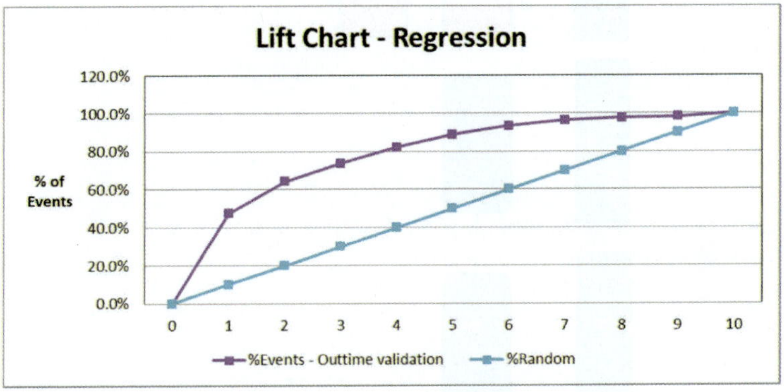

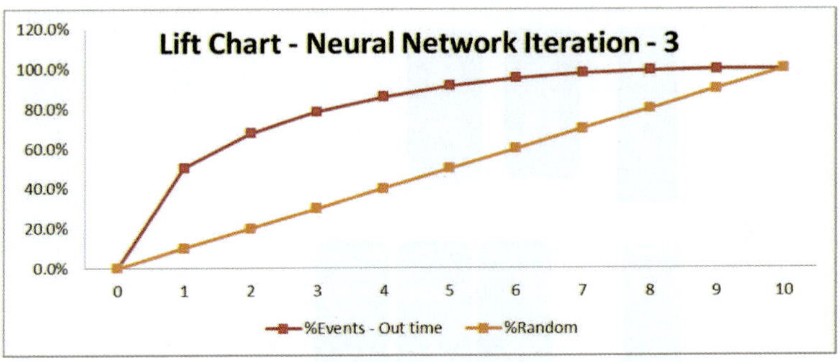

4.2. Automated modeling process: comparative study

The proposed automated process comprises the following six stages:

1) Pre-processing of data
2) Automated model building
3) Automated model selection
4) Ensemble
5) Re-train with full training data
6) Compare with traditional modeling process.

The above process is performed manually in both SAS and R, with details described below:

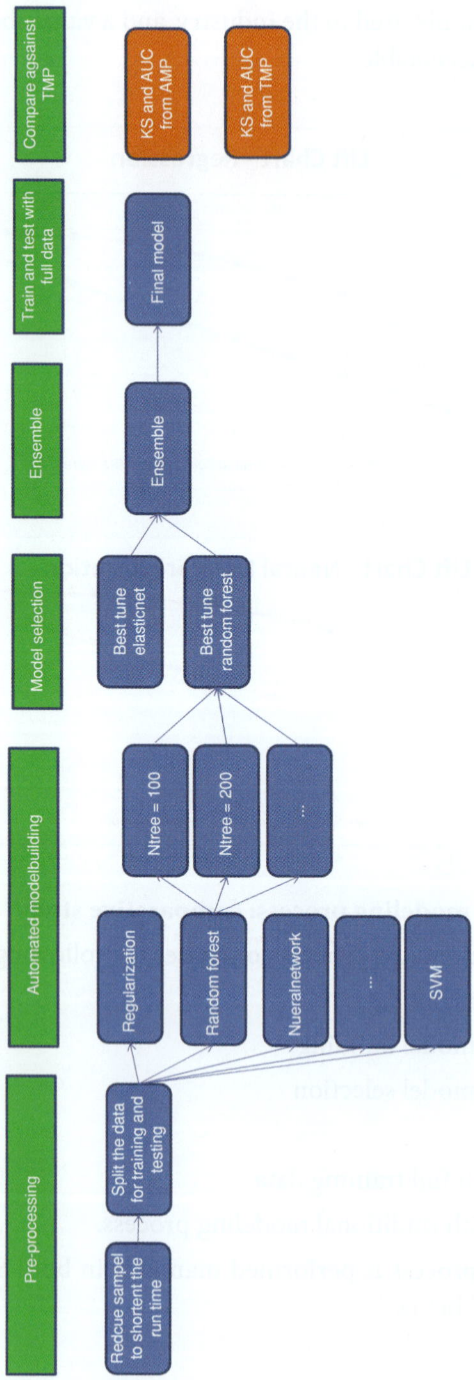
Pre-processing
Automated modelbuilding
Model selection
Ensemble
Train and test with full data
Compare agsainst TMP
Redcue sampel to shortent the run time
Split the data for training and testing
Regularization
Random forest
Nueralnetwork
...
SVM
Ntree = 100
Ntree = 200
...
Best tune elasticnet
Best tune random forest
Ensemble
Final model
KS and AUC from AMP
KS and AUC from TMP

4.3. Pre-processing of data

Data pre-processing consists mainly of automated variable pre-processing and creating samples that are much smaller than the traditional modeling approach. There are two reasons for this. Firstly, the end result is expected to apply to frequent decision making, where the data size could be small for many problems. Secondly, the success of this new approach depends on the ability to perform a large number of search and empirical tests using re-sampling. A smaller sample size will allow faster computation.

The following results use these definitions:

n – count of non-events in the original in-time sample

e – count of events in the original in-time sample

N – count of non-events in the original out-time sample

E – count of events in the original out-time sample

The sample rate used in SAS Enterprise Miner environment is reduced to 10 per cent of both events and non-events from the original sample.

	Traditional		Automated in SAS EM+HP		Automated in R	
In-time Sample	Counts	%	Counts	%	Counts	%
non-event	n	96.2%	n/10	71.9%	n/100	71.9%
event	e	3.8%	e	28.1%	e/10	28.1%
Total	p	100.0%		100%		100%

Out-time Sample	Counts	%	Counts	%	Counts	%
non-event	N	98.2%	N/10	84.3%	N/100	84.3%
event	E	1.8%	E	15.7%	E/10	15.7%
Total	P	100.0%		100%		100%
Out-time Sample	Counts	%	Counts	%	Counts	%
non-event	N	98.2%	N/10	84.3%	N/100	84.3%
event	E	1.8%	E	15.7%	E/10	15.7%
Total	*P*	100.0%		100%		100%

The sample rate used in R environment (32 bit, 2GB ram) is further reduced to 10 per cent of events and 1 per cent of non-events from the original sample.

Only automated transformation is applied to the data, namely:

- Remove variable with low variability
- Remove high correlation and multicollinearity
- Centering and scaling
- Missing value imputation using kNN (k – nearest neighbor)

The R code sample for the above task is:

```
# removes NZV
nzv <- nearZeroVar(x[train,], saveMetrics = TRUE)
x <- select(x,-one_of(vars.nzv))

# evaluate correlation
highCorr <- findCorrelation(correlations, cutoff = .9)
vars.highCorr <- colnames(x[,highCorr])
x <- select(x,-highCorr)

#find linear combos
multiCorr <- findLinearCombos(complete.cases(x[train,]))
x <- select(x,-multiCorr$remove)

#pre process with center and scale
preProc <- preProcess(x[train,], method = c("center", "scale"))
x<-predict(preProc,x)

# impute missing values
train.imputed <- impute.knn(data = train.preProc, k = 10,
rowmax = 0.5, colmax = 0.8, maxp = 1500, rng.seed = 362436069)
```

4.4. Automated model building

This process can be implemented either in SAS EM or R.

A SAS EM diagram with 1 LARS, 1 regression, 2 SVM, 4 neural networks and 5 random forests is shown below:

Simultaneously, a comparison is made between models built with engineered variables and those built via a fully automated process.

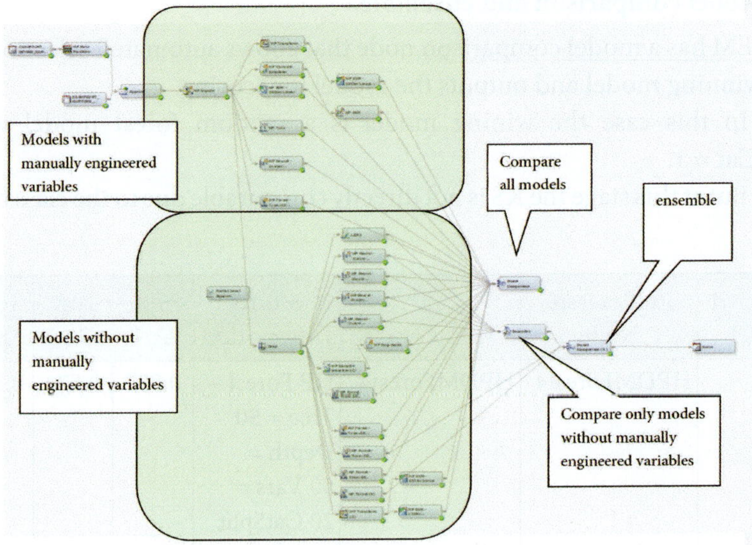

R has additional features that allow for grid search of optimal parameters. Below is the sample code using caret for automated tuning of parameters.

```
# parameter tuning for elastic net using caret
set.seed(123)
trControl <- trainControl(method = "cv", number = 5,
    classProbs = TRUE,summaryFunction = twoClassSummary)

glmnet.cv <- train(x = x[train,], y = y[train], method = 'glmnet',
  metric = "ROC", trControl = trControl)

# parameter tuning for gbm
ctrl <- trainControl(method = "repeatedcv", number = 5, repeats = 3,
    classProbs = TRUE, summaryFunction = twoClassSummary)

gbm.fit = train(x = x, y = y, method = "gbm", metric = "ROC",
  trControl = ctrl, verbose = FALSE)
# parameter tuning for svm
svm.poly <- ksvm(x = x[train.small,], y = y[train.small], scaled = TRUE,
kernel = "polydot", prob.model = TRUE)
svm.test <- predict(svm.poly, x[test,], type = "probabilities")
```

4.5 Model comparison and ensemble

SAS EM has a model comparison node that allows automated selection of the winning model and outputs the model for scoring.

In this case the wining model is a random forest model with MinCat = 1.

But at this stage the KS is not directly comparable due to the class bias.

Selected Model	Predecessor Node	Model Node	Model Description	Test: AUC	Test: Gini	Test: KS
Y	HPDMForest4	HPDMForest4	HP Forest – Tree = 50 Depth = 50 Vars = 20 CatSplit = 30 MinCat = 1	0.837	0.674	0.503
	HPDMForest2	HPDMForest2	HP Forest – Tree = 50 Depth = 50 Vars = 20 CatSplit = 30 MinCat = 5	0.834	0.669	0.497
	HPDMForest3	HPDMForest3	HP Forest – Tree = 50 Depth = 50 Vars =. CatSplit = 30 MinCat = 5	0.834	0.669	0.501
	HPDMForest5	HPDMForest5	HP Forest – Tree = 50 Depth = 50 Vars =. CatSplit = 30 MinCat = 1	0.834	0.668	0.499

Selected Model	Predecessor Node	Model Node	Model Description	Test: AUC	Test: Gini	Test: KS
	HPDMForest	HPDMForest	HP Forest – Tree = 50 Depth = 50 Vars = 20 CatSplit = 30 MinCat = 5	0.834	0.668	0.499
	HPNNA	HPNNA	HP Neural – 1 Layer 3 Hidden Identify Normal 2 Tries	0.826	0.652	0.496
	HPTree	HPTree	HP Tree	0.823	0.647	0.482
	HPSVM2	HPSVM2	HP SVM – 25 Iter Linear, External Transform	0.82	0.641	0.488
	HPSVM	HPVM	HP SVM – 25 Iter Linear	0.82	0.641	0.488
	HPNNA4	HPNNA4	HP Neural – 1 Layer 5 Hidden Tanh Normal 5 Tries	0.817	0.633	0.484
	HPNNA3	HPNNA3	HP Neural – 1 Layer 10 Hidden Identity Normal 5 Tries	0.817	0.635	0.483
	HPGLM	HPGLM	HP GLM	0.817	0.634	0.481

(*continued*)

Selected Model	Predecessor Node	Model Node	Model Description	Test: AUC	Test: Gini	Test: KS
	HPReg	HPReg	HP Regression	0.815	0.63	0.477
	HPNNA5	HPNNA5	HP Neural – 2 Layer 5 Hidden Tanh Normal 5 Tries	0.811	0.622	0.483
	HPSVM3	HPSVM3	HP SVM–25 Iter Linear	0.81	0.62	0.395
	HPNNA2	HPNNA2	HP Neural – 1 Layer 2 Hidden Identity Normal 2 Tries	0.807	0.614	0.478
	LARS	LARS	LARS	0.806	0.612	0.459
	HPSVM4	HPSVM4	HP SVM–25 Iter Polynomial2	0.56	0.119	0.128

The best model built under R is also from random forest models.

Note that the best model built in R has a slightly higher AUC than the SAS counterpart because ntree = 200 in R was used. This was possible because of the smaller sample size in R and the ability to perform multi-core processing using %dopar%.

```
# R code to perform multi-core processing
cores <- detectCores()
cl <- makeCluster(cores)
registerDoParallel(cl)

set.seed(123)
rf1 <- foreach(ntree = rep(50, 4), .combine = combine, .multicom-
bine = TRUE,
    .packages = 'randomForest') %dopar% {
    randomForest(x, y, na.action = na.omit, importance = TRUE,
ntree = ntree)}
```

Result from R

Model	package	Method	Test: AUC
Random Forest	randomForest	Ntree = 200	0.8399
Component wise gradient boosting with generalized additive model	mboost	gamboost mstop = 200, nu = 0.05	0.822
Lasso	glmnet	10-fold CV	0.8109
Elastic Net	glmnet	10-fold CV	0.8109
GBM	gbm	5-fold repeats = 3	0.8095
Ridge	glmnet	10-fold CV	0.8089
SVM	kernlab	Kernel = polydot	0.8078
SVM	kernlab	Kernel = vanilladot	0.8078
Component wise gradient boosting using generalized linear model	mboost	glmboost mstop = 200, nu = 0.05	0.8066
Decision tree	tree	Tree prune size = 5	0.7884
Decision tree	rpart	rpart, cp = 0.011	0.7463

4.6 Final model building

The final step was to train the full data on the Random Forest model. Due to running on a single test machine, it was not possible to train the random forest to ntree = 200 in SAS, which is the optimal according to a previous study on a smaller data sample.

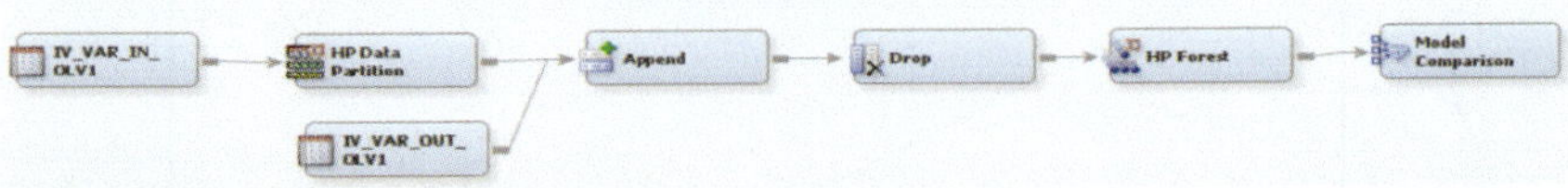

Model Description	Target Variable	Test: AUC	Test: Gini	Test: KS
HP Forest	target_bin	0.833	0.666	0.498

Note that the final model produced by an automated process using SAS software was superior to results produced by traditional modeling process logistic regression, and of a comparable standard to the tune neural network. An automated process using R produced the best model of the three.

5. DISCUSSION

It was encouraging to note that the output from rapidly-constructed automated methods was comparable to that produced by a model built over months using traditional analytics processes.

This fact can be explained by search cost; in the traditional process, search cost was absorbed by the modeler's time, which is very expensive and of limited supply. As a consequence, the modeler could only attempt a very small number of searches. For example, logistic regression in the traditional process is only a dot in the search space of elastic net method used in the automated process.

As shown in the chart below, the search space for elastic net is a two dimensional space represented by the different lines. Logistic regression is only a single point (with both parameters equal to 0).

In this case, the optimal solution depends on both parameters, and a modeler is unlikely to uncover the best solution with a few heuristic guesses.

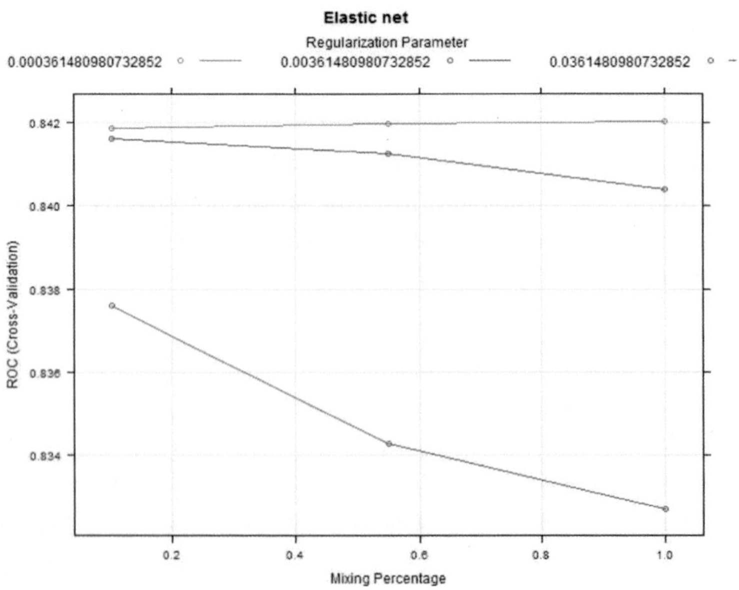

The solution with 10 per cent sampling on events and 1 per cent sampling on non-events produced a better result on test data than the other two solutions, which used full training data and 10 per cent training data respectively.

This provided another example of a trade-off between sampling adequacy and search cost. When the number of observations exceeds a certain threshold, the marginal benefit of having additional observations will decrease while the cost of computing resource and time will increase. This will eventually reflect in reduced search space.

In this particular example, the R software was able to run repeated cross validation on ntree = 200, while SAS hits the memory boundary at ntree = 100. This was despite R being run on a laptop with 3GB ram while SAS is run on an industry server.

This was due to the fact that, when implementing the solution in R, 1 per cent of non-events were sampled, with repeated sampling used to control over fitting. This aggressive sampling strategy paid off, as it facilitated the search for a more complex solution.

Another interesting discovery was that random forest provided the best solution when applied to applicable sampling strategies and executed over both software types. This was less surprising, however, as random forest is versatile method and requires the least variable transformation / engineering.

It can also be easily implemented for parallel processing and distributed computing, providing optimal cost effectiveness for this proposed approach.

Another noteworthy method was the elastic net, which produced strong results regardless of its simplicity when compared to SVM, Neural net and other boosting algorithms. Its role in regularizing allows it to handle noise effectively.

In the traditional process, there is no manual variable selection outside of the modeling stage, meaning that many weak features can potentially enter the model. Regularization plus cross validation is very effective in reducing the impact of these weak features and correlated variables.

This method is especially well suited for problems with $p >> N$, which is one of the practical challenges that requires consideration with the automated analytics process.

6. CONCLUSIONS AND FURTHER WORK

This project explored the next stage of competition on analytics as business embraces the digital revolution. It demonstrated the possibility of using a combination of techniques to speed up model building without compromising the quality of output.

It should prompt increased discussion on the automation of analytics from both practitioners and academics, and generate interest from open-source communities in developing solutions for 'unified modeling frameworks' such as caret and mlr.

Subsequent work to create an automated process and test how models produced by this process perform against the incumbent models could be undertaken.

REFERENCES

1. Davenport, TH and. JG Harris (2007). *Competing on Analytics*, Harvard Business School Press.

2. Dorner, K and D Edelman (2015). *What 'digital' really means*. Mckinsey Insights.

3. Davenport, TH (2015). The Rise of Automated Analytics. *The Wall Street Journey*.

4. Weiss, U (2015). *Uwe Weiss On Predictive Analytics*, interview by Lutz Finger.

5. Delong, ER, DM Delong and DL Clarke-Pearson (1998). Comparing the areas under two or more correlated receiver operating characteristic curves: a nonparametric approach. *Biometrics*, 44, 837–845.

6. Thomke, S and J Manzi (2014). *The Discipline of Business Experimentation*. Harvard Business Review.

CHAPTER 31

Discovering Actionable Insights from Online Reviews Using Unstructured Content Analytics

JI Jun Yao

ABSTRACT

This project aims to introduce an analytics framework to allow product manufacturers to consolidate product information and customer reviews from various social media sources. Based on the information gathered from social media, the project seeks to provide insights as to how to enhance the product quality and give a better understanding of the market trends of the new product development. Python and XPath were used to crawl the data from multiple data sources on the Internet, producing consolidated information of product details and user feedback. IBM Watson Content Analytics was used as the main platform to conduct text analytics on the unstructured data, and Tableau was used to enrich the analysis with data visualization. A case study of mobile device is presented in this report to show how to improve the product design based on the proposed framework.

1. INTRODUCTION

Interactions involving social media have become an integral part modern life and social media has changed the way people interact with each other. Sites like Facebook, Twitter, LinkedIn, Instagram and many others make it easy for people to stay connected with their friends, family or even people they may never meet face to face.

There are more than 1.4 billion active users on Facebook monthly who 'like' or comment on billions of posts shared by the users.[1] Twitter has more than 300 million active users generating more than 500 million tweets per day.[2] More importantly, social media has also changed consumer behaviors. Nearly nine out of 10 consumers have read online reviews to evaluate a product before they make the decision to make a purchase.[3] There are thousands of online review websites and discussion forums for people to share their thoughts and opinions. From a business point of view, the importance of social media is unquestionable. However, for many companies who invest in social media, the key focus is around online marketing or simply using it as channel for corporate communications. This paper aims to introduce a new framework that allows companies to derive insights from social media to enhance their product's quality and inform new product development.

The report is organized as follows:

- Section 2 elaborates the current problems and challenges faced by many companies.
- Section 3 highlights and summarizes the state of art research on text analytics of social media data for product quality management.
- Section 4 presents the proposed solution and key findings.
- Section 5 discusses the value and practical usage of the proposed solution.
- Section 6 concludes the key lessons learnt and potential future developments.

1 http://newsroom.fb.com/company-info/
2 https://about.twitter.com/company
3 https://www.brightlocal.com/2014/07/01/local-consumer-review-survey-2014/

2. PROBLEM STATEMENT

Shortly after Microsoft launched the Xbox 360, customers started complaining about widespread product failures. Although Microsoft stated that failure rates were within normal ranges, blogs, chat rooms and social media sites were bombarded with comments about these problems. The Internet quickly dubbed the onboard diagnostic code of three red lights the "Red Ring of Death."[4] Commenters were quick to propose potentially dangerous fix-it-yourself remedies and extol the virtues of competitive products. The Red Ring of Death quickly grew into a public relations nightmare and eventually caused Microsoft to extend customer warranties at a cost of more than $1 billion.[5]

Microsoft was not alone. Apple's issue with the iPhone 4 antenna[6] and Toyota's sudden acceleration[7] complaints are two more examples of how social media can shape perceptions of product quality. Understanding those perceptions is essential to identifying actual or potential quality issues and for being able to react effectively.

The importance of quality management is not new to companies, but social media today makes it more challenging to manage such incidents and mitigate the negative impact. In the past, a dissatisfied customer might tell 10 friends, but now he/she can share their experiences with more than 10,000 friends within seconds. People talk about their experiences with all kinds of products and make comparison of different brands. Some may be ambassadors and advocates, while others may be detractors and malcontents – and all of their voices can greatly influence customers' buying decisions. At a time when product recalls, government intervention and lawsuits are front-page news (and customers are questioning brands that seem to be above reproach), the ability to monitor, measure and manage these perceptions has a significant impact on the ability to detect field issues, differentiate the products and develop better products in the future.

It is important for a company to know its customers' buying behavior and their perception of the brand. These are influenced by what they

4 https://en.wikipedia.org/wiki/Xbox_360_technical_problems

5 http://www.computerworld.com/article/2542455/mobile-wireless/xbox-360–red-ring-of-death–costs-microsoft-more-than–1b.html

6 http://edition.cnn.com/2012/02/20/tech/mobile/iphone-4-antenna-settlement/

7 http://www.bbc.com/news/business-26650173

see on the Internet. The proposed solution below describes how text analytics and data visualization can be applied to derive insights from social media, to help the company to monitor the online reviews, improve their products based on the feedback from the users, and eventually gain a competitive edge over rival companies.

3. STATE OF THE ART

In this section, the state of the art research on text analytics of social media data for product quality management is explored.

Due to the massive amount of data exchanged every day and the increasing need for better data-based decisions, businesses are increasingly looking for ways to efficiently manage and optimize these huge datasets. Moreover, because of the emergence of social media, the huge online information flow in the form of collaboratively created content presents new opportunities and challenges to both information producers and consumers. With the large amount of data produced online, text analytics provides an effective way to meet users' diverse information needs. Particularly for product manufacturers, who have been used to traditional online marketing campaigns with knowledge based on common sense, this is a great opportunity to leverage text analytics on understanding social media feedbacks and better facilitate the process of product quality management.

Among the various formats of data exchanged in social media, text plays an important role. The information in most social media sites is stored in text format. Text analytics refers to the discovery of knowledge that can be found in text archives [1]. This field has received much attention due to its wide application as a multi-purpose tool, borrowing techniques from Natural Language Processing (NLP), Data Mining (DM), Machine Learning (ML), Information Retrieval (IR), etc.

The traditional text analytics framework consists of three consecutive phases: text preprocessing, text representation and knowledge discovery [2]. Text preprocessing aims to make the input documents more consistent to facilitate text representation, and preprocessing methods depend on specific application. Knowledge discovery is a process that successfully transforms the text corpus into numeric vectors, so the existing machine learning or data mining methods like classification or clustering can be applied.

But there exists some distinct features of text in social media that cause new challenges - including time sensitivity, short length, unstructured phrases, and abundant information [2]. Corresponding to these distinct aspects of text in social media, different techniques are required, but are not be discussed here.

Though text analytics on social media is a current trend in big data analytics, very few research studies or business applications tackle analytics of textual content from a product quality management perspective. However, product quality management is vital especially for manufacturers of electronic or topicality-possessed products.

Product quality encompasses both performance and conformance attributes of the product, and is an important aspect of product competitive advantage. Increased marketing - manufacturing integration is associated with greater product competitive advantage, and in turn, greater product success and higher return on investment [3]. Hence, product quality management plays an important role for manufactures.

One of the most popular research papers on this topic was conducted by Alan S. Abrahams, Weiguo Fan, G. Alan Wang and Zhongju (John) Zhang in 2014 [4]. In the study, they synthesized existing research studies on text mining and proposed an integrated text analytic framework for product defect discovery. By performing product defect discovery using user-generated content (UGC) in both the automotive and the consumer electronics domains, they showcased the usefulness of the framework. Subsequently, more business insights related with product defection were gained. However, the study is subject to the existence of possible biases in both defect information sharing and defect information utilization with a focus only on a single process of product quality management – defection.

Another study [5] provides a brief introduction on how to use unstructured text analytics to drive decision making in new product development and customer identification. In this study, they emphasized that critical product development decisions can be improved by using unstructured text analytics to convert text into data that can support well-informed decisions. The authors put many effort on introducing the basic logic and concept of natural language processing and critical thinking strategy to analyze unstructured data. The authors also illustrated a few examples on how to apply the text analytics in some real-world use cases for example, text analytics can be applied to find news or articles on the Internet that a competitor is creating new jobs or building a new facility, or assess the probability of a recall of defective parts by tracking complaints in blogs and other forms of social media. Just as Voice of the Customer (VOC) initiatives search for answers to what customers need in interviews, text analytics uncovers customer needs, competitor actions, emerging market trends, and other information necessary to inform critical product decisions.

4. SOLUTION: DESCRIPTION OF APPROACH

The proposed solution consisted of three major steps:

a) Crawling social media data using Python, and transforming the data into a more structured format using XPath.

b) Unstructured text analytics using IBM Watson Content Analytics which provides the analytics-driven solution that uses natural language processing (NLP) and text analytics to extract, normalize and derive additional information from the unstructured content.

c) Data Visualization and Exploration using Tableau. Figure 1 depicts the overview of all the main tools been used for this project and the overall solution architecture.

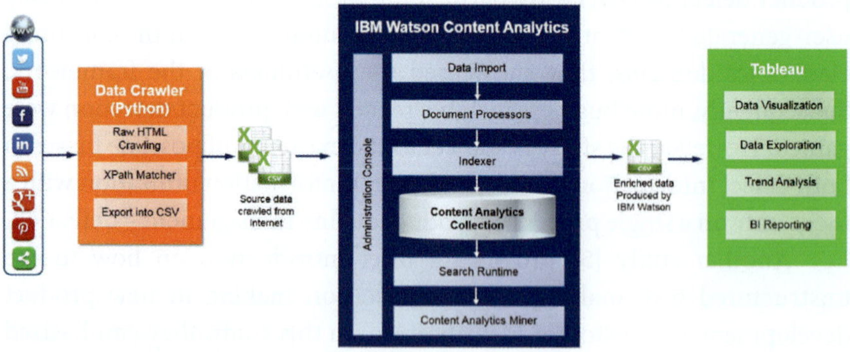

Figure 1: Solution architecture overview.

4.1. Data crawling

One of the main challenges for analytics projects using data from public source is data crawling. Web crawling can be a very complicated and technical subject. Different channels on social media require different techniques to access and download the information. For online social networking platform such as Twitter and Facebook, it is only possible to crawl the data via the Application Programme Interfaces. (API) But in most cases, those APIs will have certain constraints that can limit the volume and frequency needed to download the data. For blogs and discussion forums, the raw html files were downloaded and it was necessary to design an additional data cleansing layer to remove the markup language and to only keep the information that was relevant to the study.

GSMArena (http://www.gsmarena.com/) was the main data source for the project. GSMArena is one of the most popular websites that provides the latest information and updates on mobile devices including both cell phone and tablet for all kinds of brands and models. It also provides a central location for users to share and exchange their opinions. In this project, two types of information were crawled and extracted from GSMArena:

1) Device specifications – Detailed specifications for each device such as brand name, model name, release time, weight, thickness, operation system, storage, screen size and resolution, camera, battery, etc.
2) User comments – User comments for each model, together with the user name and posted time (Figure 2).

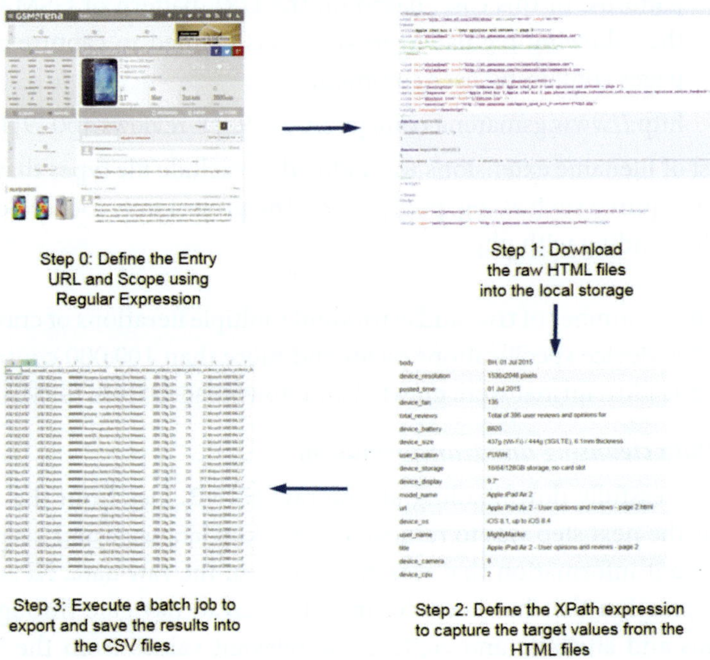

Figure 2: Data crawling process flow.

4.1.1. Define the scope for the crawler

Every website has its own structure and may contain hundreds of thousands of webpages so it was unrealistic to download every single page from the target website. Also, not all the information on the website was useful for the analytics project. To define the scope of the crawler written in Python, the following parameters needed to be defined:

1) The Entry URL - The crawler traverses web pages, following links from one to the next. It starts with the URLs specified as the Entry. For this project, http://www.gsmarena.com/makers.php3 was defined as the entry point. It was the main page that contained the list of brands and their URLs.
2) The URL Pattern – This is to control the sites that the crawler goes to by specifying what should be allowed and what should be excluded.
    a) A list of URL prefixes is defined to capture all the pages containing device specifications. For example http://www.gsmarena.com/samsung was defined as the URL prefix for all the models belonging to Samsung.
    b) Regular Expression is defined to capture URLs that have similar patterns. In this case, based on the URL pattern of GSMArena, the following regular expression was defined to capture all the pages containing user comments:

       http://www.gsmarena.com/[a-zA-Z0-9_]+-reviews-[p0–9]+\.php
3) List of filename extensions was defined to exclude file types that were not required such as jpg, png, gif, etc. The project only focused on the URLs ending with php.

After a number of trial and errors and multiple iterations of crawling, near 8,000 device specifications pages and more than 100,000 comments pages in HTML format were crawled and downloaded from GSMArena.

4.1.2 Data cleansing and transformation

After successfully downloading all the raw HTML files from the target website, the next step was to remove the markup language and keep only the relevant information that was embedded in the raw data. XPath is a path expression that has been commonly used to navigate through the elements and attribute and capture the relevant values from the XML/HTML documents.

In this case, two sets of expression was defined to capture the device specifications and user comments separately. A document level XPath expression was used to segment the HTML files based on the structure of the webpage. In this case, one comment page contains up to 20 comments posted by different users.

XPath expression to segment a single HTML file into multiple documents:

//div[@class="user-thread"]

Device specification variables and the corresponding XPath expression (Table 1 and 2):

Table 1: XPath Expression for Device Specification Variables

Variable Name	XPath Expression
Title	/html/head/title/text()
URL	/html/head/title/text()
model_name	//div[@id="body"]/div/div[3]/span/text()
device_release_time	//div[@id="body"]/div/div/div/div[2]/ul/li/span
device_size	//div[@id="body"]/div/div/div/div[2]/ul/li/span[2]
device_os	//div[@id="body"]/div/div/div/div[2]/ul/li/span[3]
device_storage	//div[@id="body"]/div/div/div/div[2]/ul/li/span[4]
device_display	//div[@id="body"]/div/div/div/div[2]/ul/li[4]/strong
device_resolution	//div[@id="body"]/div/div/div/div[2]/ul/li[4]/text()[3]
device_camera	//div[@id="body"]/div/div/div/div[2]/ul/li[5]
device_cpu	//div[@id="body"]/div/div/div/div[2]/ul/li[6]
device_battery	//div[@id="body"]/div/div/div/div[2]/ul/li[7]
device_popularity	//div[@id="body"]/div/div/div/div[2]/ul/li[2]
device_fan	//div[@id="body"]/div/div/div/div[2]/ul/li[3]/a/strong

User comment variables and the corresponding XPath expression:

Table 2: XPath Expression for User Comment Variables

Variable Name	XPath Expression
Title	/html/head/title/text()
URL	mm:metadata("id")
model_name	//div[@id="body"]/div/div[3]/span/text()

Variable Name	XPath Expression
user_name	ul/li
user_location	ul/li[2]/span/text()
posted_time	ul/li[3]/time/text()
body	P

After finalizing the variable name and XPath expression, a Pytho script was executed to ingest all the raw HTML files in batch and save the output into CSV files. After removing the duplicated records, 6943 device specifications and near 800,000 user comments are extracted and will be used as the main data source for text analytics and data exploration in the next step.

4.2. Apply text analytics to derive actionable insight

IBM Watson Content Analytics is used as the main solution to analyze the user comments extracted from GSMArena. IBM Watson Content Analytics provides the analytics-driven solution that uses natural language processing (NLP) and text analytics to extract, normalize and derive additional information from the unstructured content. Text analytics is a general term that refers to the automated techniques of converting textual data into structured data. After the information in the text is converted to a structured form, the data can then be processed by conventional business intelligence tools such as Tableau and Qlikview. For this project, the main input for the text analytics is the variable BODY from the comments CSV files.

4.2.1. Set up the watson content analytics project

IBM Watson Content Analytics consists of the following major components:

1) Data Import/Crawler: Extract content from enterprise data sources. For this project, crawling is done outside the IBM Watson Content Analytics. Data is imported directly from the CSV files.
2) Document processors: The document processor component is responsible for processing crawled documents and preparing them for indexing. In this component, the various text analytics are applied to the crawled documents. Each text analytic is referred to as an annotator because its job is to annotate a document with additional information that it extracts or deduces from the document content. IBM Annotators are built according to the Unstructured Information

Management Architecture (UIMA) standard. UIMA is an open source standard sponsored by the Apache organization. IBM Watson Content Analytics is UIMA-compliant and has a UIMA document processing pipeline built in. For this project, the following annotators is defined and enabled:

a) Language Identification annotator: Identifies the language of each document. This identifier is critical when analyzing data from open source. In most cases, the data may contain multiple languages and different NLP engines will be required. For this project, only documents identified as English are kept for the next step.

b) Linguistic Analysis annotator: Applies linguistic analysis for each document.

c) Dictionary Lookup annotator: Matches words and synonyms from a dictionary with words in the text.

d) Named Entity Recognition annotator: Extracts person names, locations, and organization names.

e) Sentiment Analysis annotator: Extracts sentiment expressions in documents.

f) Content Classification annotator: Classifies content into categories.

3) Indexer: Builds a document index for high-speed text mining and analysis.
4) Search run time: Services user search and analytic requests.
5) Content analytics miner: A web based UI for end users to perform text analysis.
6) Administration console: Used to configure and administer Content Analytics project.

All the configuration and settings can be defined in the Administration Console. Once the data collection is defined successfully in the Administration Console and all the data are imported and indexed, it is possible to start our exploration in Content Analytics Miner. Below is the screenshot of the Mobile Devices Online Reviews collection created in Administration Console. In total, near 800,000 documents/rows are imported and indexed (Figure 3).

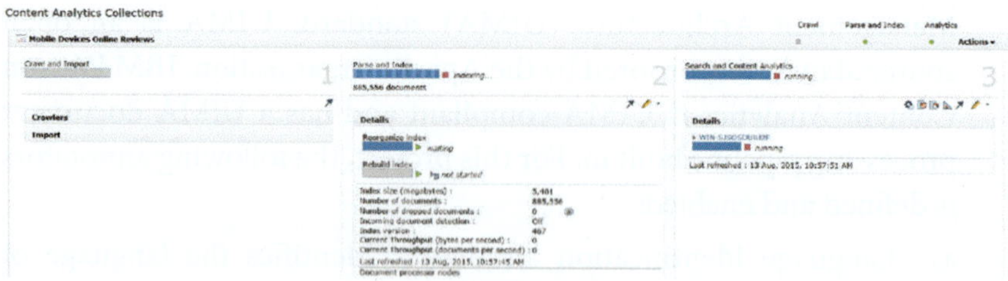

Figure 3: IBM watson content analytics administration console.

The out of box Market Analytics solution package is selected and used to speed up the project development process. This package is designed to analyze comments on products or services to understand the market which is very similar to the objective of our study.

4.2.2. Exploring text using content analytics miner

The comments dataset imported into Watson contains user comments posted on GSMArena for the past 15 years and year 2014 has the highest number of comments. By drilling down into some of the specific brands it is possible to see that the trends for some of the brands are quite distinct from each other. For Apple, the buzz only started after the announcement of the first generation iPhone on January 9, 2007 (Figures 4 and 5).

The number of comments related to Samsung started to increase significantly in 2013 which is one year later after its announcement of the Samsung Galaxy S3. Galaxy S3 is a historical smartphone for the Korean tech giant. When it was launched as a flagship smartphone by Samsung in May 2012, it became the turning point for the Korean tech company to become the biggest smartphone maker in the world, shipping an unprecedented number of over 50 million units of the handsets worldwide (Figure 6).

For brands like Nokia and Motorola, the number of comments have dropped tremendously over the past few years. Indeed, the volume of the comments is a very accurate reflection of the market share and how it changed over the time. Nokia and Motorola, once the mobile world's pioneer, are now struggling to survive and searching for the lost glory. In early 2014, Microsoft completed the acquisition of Nokia's devices and services business. For Motorola, it is first acquired by Google in 2012 and sold by Google to Chinese personal computer and mobile device maker Lenovo for $2.91 billion in 2014 (Figure 7 and 8).

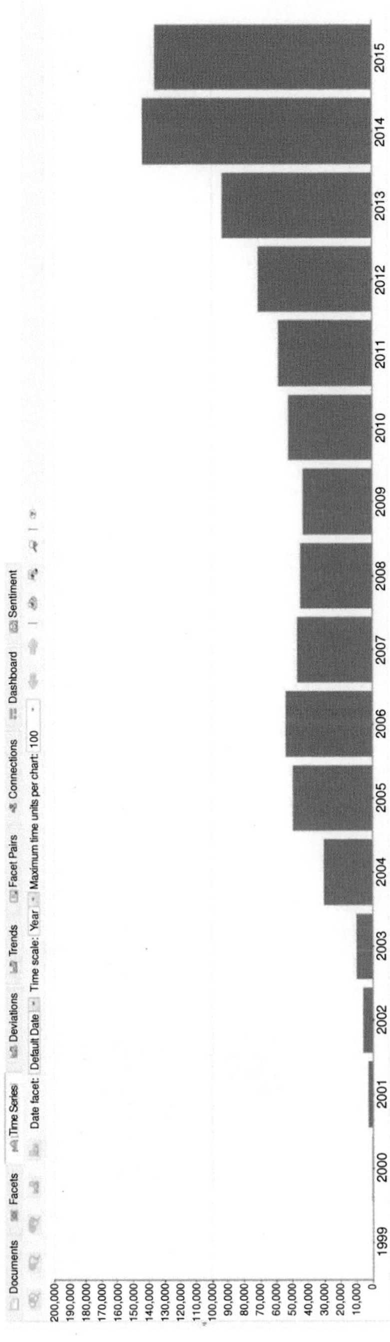

Figure 4: Total number of comments from 1999 to 2015.

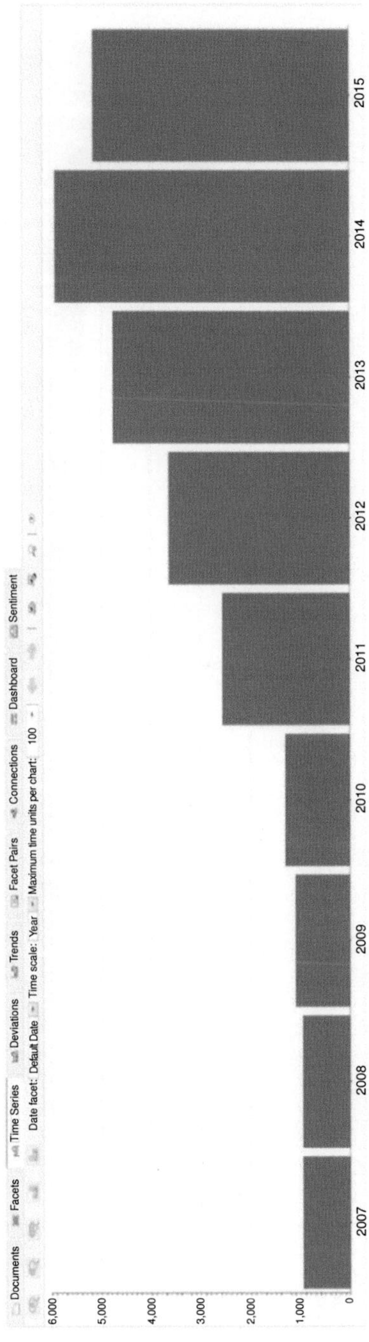

Figure 5: Total number of comments from 2007 to 2015 for Apple.

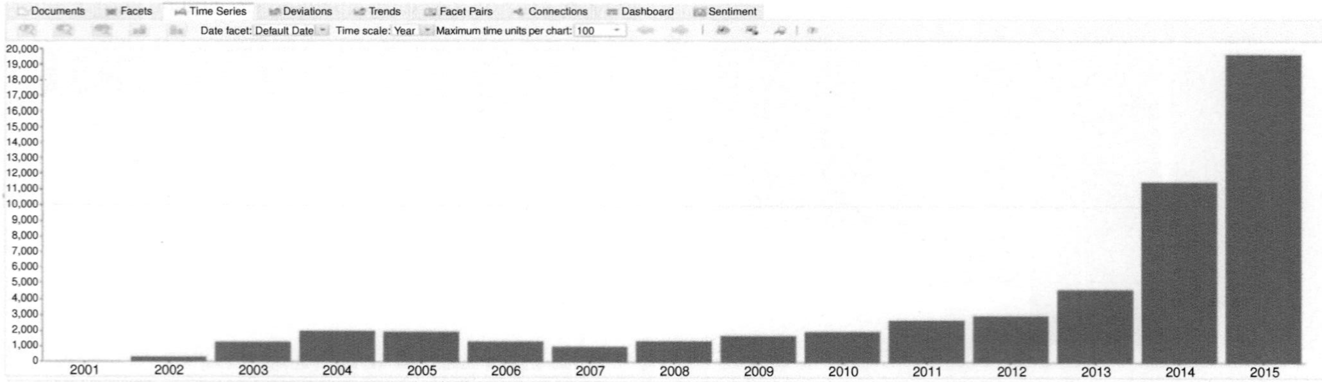

Figure 6: Total number of comments from 2001 to 2015 for Samsung.

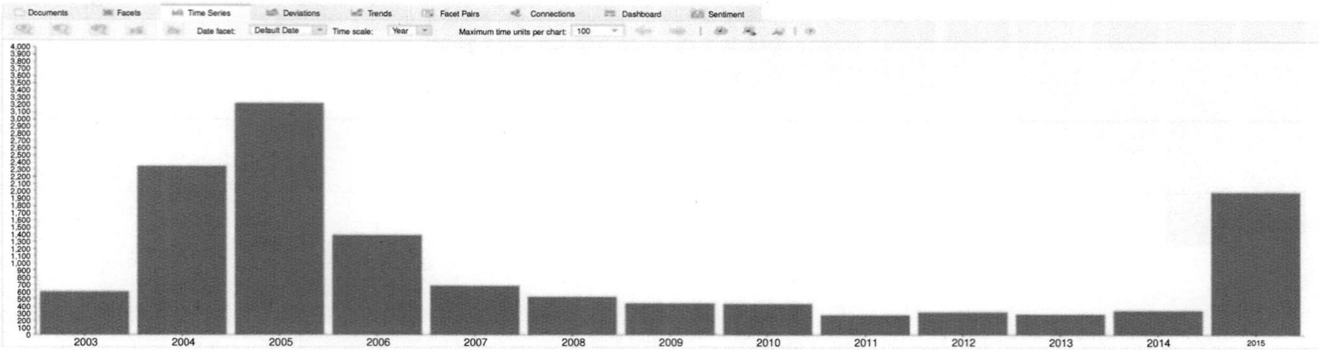

Figure 7: Total number of comments from 2003 to 2015 for Nokia.

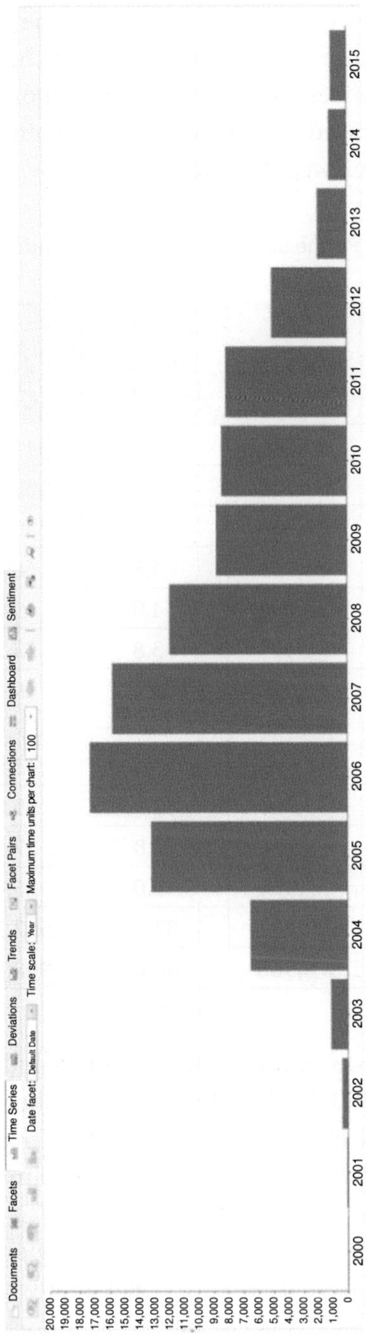

Figure 8: Total number of comments from 2000 to 2015 for Motorola.

Over the past five years, Samsung has become the world leader for mobile devices with more than 20 per cent of the market share in 2014. Table 3 below summarizes the top 11 mobile phone manufacturers in 2014.[8] This project focused on Samsung as the main company to understand how the users reviewed its products.

Table 3: Worldwide Mobile Phone Sales to End Users by Vendor in 2014 (Thousands of Units)

	Company	**2014 Units**	**2014 Market Share (%)**	**2013 Units**	**2013 Market Share (%)**
1	Samsung	392,546	20.9	444,472	24.6
2	Apple	191,426	10.2	150,786	8.3
3	Microsoft	185,660	9.9	250,835	13.9
4	Lenovo*	84,029	4.5	66,463	3.7
5	LG Electronics	76,096	4.0	69,094	3.8
6	Huawei	70,499	3.8	53,296	2.9
7	TCL Communication	64,026	3.4	49,538	2.7
8	Xiaomi	56,529	3.0	13,423	0.7
9	ZTE	53,910	2.9	59,903	3.3
10	Sony	37,791	2.0	37,596	2.1
11	Micromax	37,094	2.0	25,431	1.4
	Others	629,360	33.5	587,764	32.5
	Total	**1,878,968**	**100.0**	**1,808,600**	**100.0**

When drilling down into the list of models under Samsung, it was observed that Galaxy S6 Edge has the largest number of comments. One potential reason could be it is the latest model released by Samsung. In addition, all the top 10 models are under Samsung Galaxy series (Figure 9).

When drilling down into the product components, the top four components that users were most concerned with were Battery, Camera, Screen and Memory. "Tab" was considered as a noise because the word

8 http://www.gartner.com/newsroom/id/2996817

Values	Frequency	Correlation
Samsung Galaxy S6 edge	512	14.1
Samsung Galaxy J7	493	14.0
Samsung Galaxy J5	492	14.0
Samsung Galaxy E5	460	14.0
Samsung Galaxy E7	459	14.0
Samsung Galaxy Core Prime	442	14.0
Samsung Galaxy A5	442	14.0
Samsung Galaxy A7	432	14.0
Samsung Galaxy Grand Prime	431	14.0
Samsung Galaxy Grand Max	430	13.9
Samsung Galaxy Note 4	426	13.9

Figure 9: List of most frequently discussed models for Samsung.

"Tab" is part of model name for Samsung Galaxy Tab series (Figure 10 and 11).

Looking at the sentiment breakdown in Figure 12, Samsung in general has more positive sentiment than negative ones.

In Figure 13, drilling down into all the negative comments under Battery revealed that poor battery life was the main complaint. In the Negative Expression Window, some of the common expressions identified were "battery life is the worst", "battery life is very bad" and "battery is very poor".

In Figure 14, drills down into the list of specific models. Notice that Samsung Galaxy S Duos 2 S7582 has a much higher frequency as compared to other models for negative sentiment and a much higher correlation score (101.5) with "Battery".

After drilling down into this specific model in Figure 14, it was noticed that the negative expression users posted for this specific model is much more negative than other models - "Battery life is very very very bad"; "very good but battery problem" and "Phone Is Very Good But Battery Problem". This model obviously has a severe problem or defect related to its battery.

4.3. Data visualization and exploration using tableau

Device specifications extracted from GSMArena are imported into Tableau for data exploration and trend analysis to understand how the mobile industry evolves over the time. Insights and trends discovered can be used for new product development.

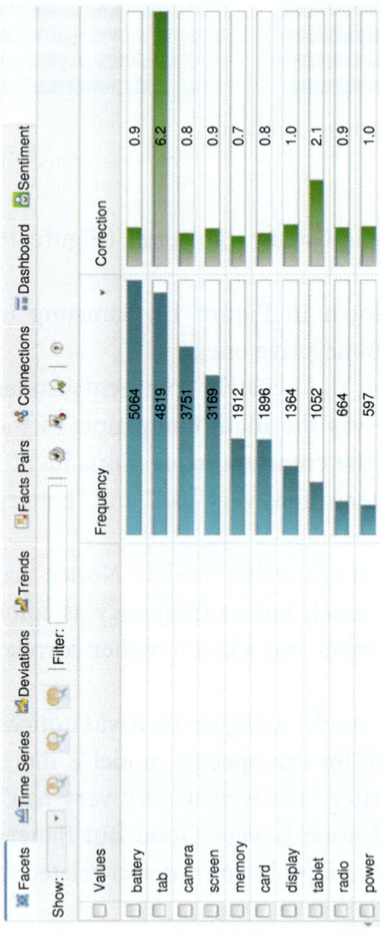

Figure 10: List of most frequently discussed components for Samsung.

Figure 11: Sentiment distribution of the product components for Samsung.

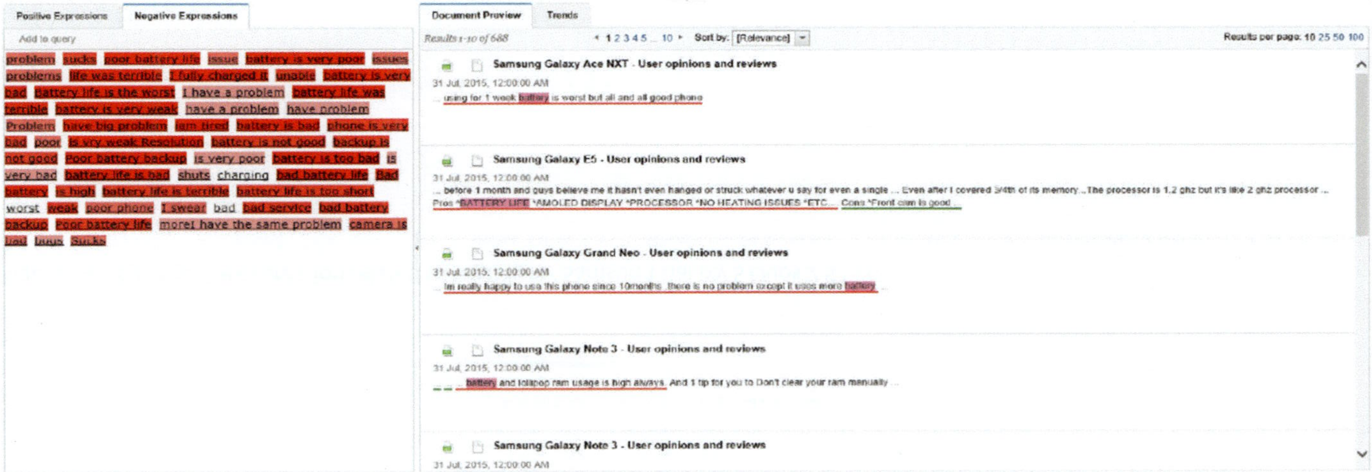

Figure 12: Key negative expression related to battery for Samsung.

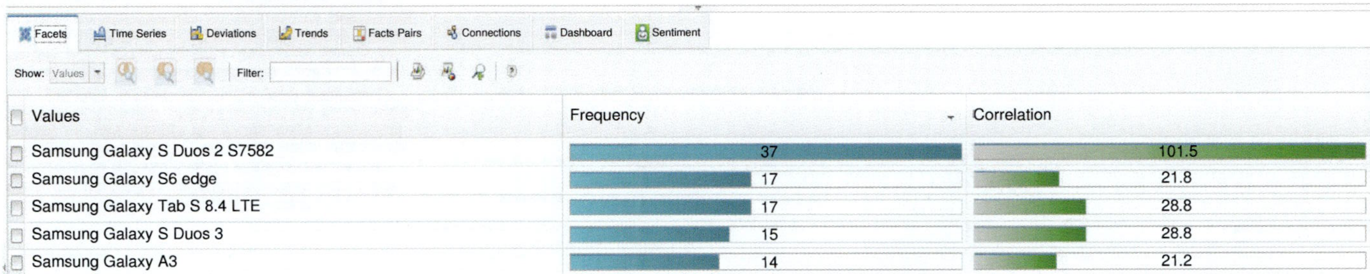

Figure 13: Top models with negative sentiment related to battery for Samsung.

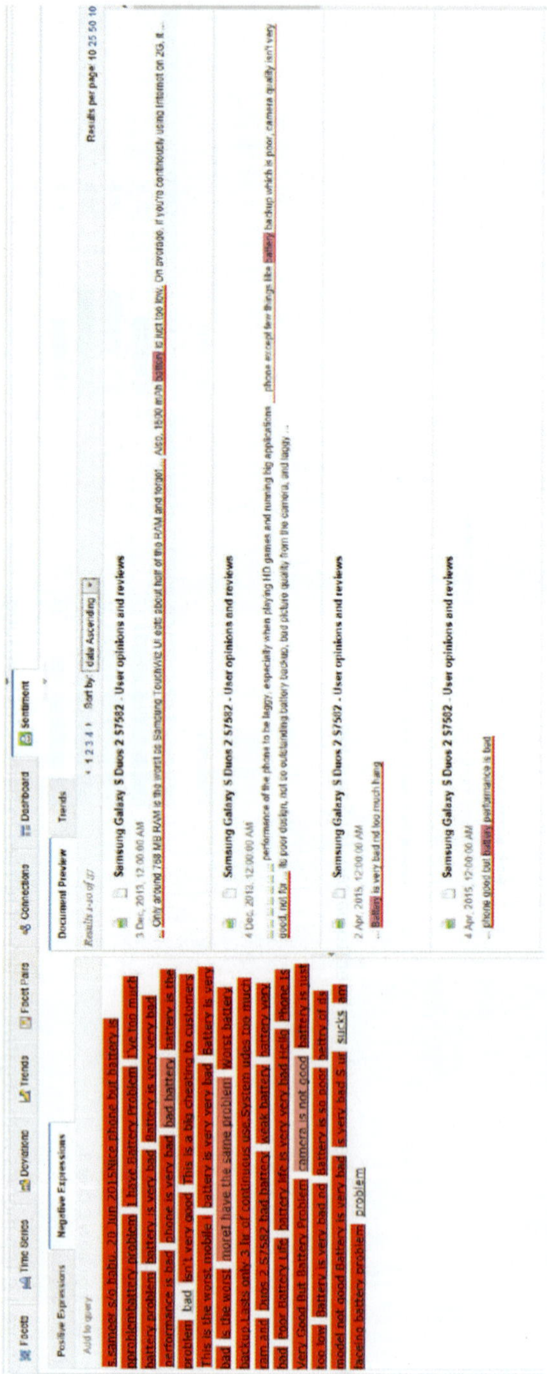

Figure 14: Key negative expression related to battery for Samsung Galaxy S Duos 2 S7582.

From 1994, the number of mobile devices released every year has increased tremendously over the past 20 years. Year 2014 has the highest number of release - about 844 models being released in a single year.

When the total number of models were broken down into different brands (see Figure 16), it was clear that Samsung has the highest number of models released over the past 20 years. In year 2009, Samsung released 129 models in different countries setting the record for the largest number of models released in a single year from one manufacturer.

One interesting pattern identified on the cell phone specifications is the change of the average battery capacity in mAh over the past 20 years. In Figure 17, the blue graph represents battery capacity in mAh. It was noticed that the capacity started to drop from 2000 reaching the lowest

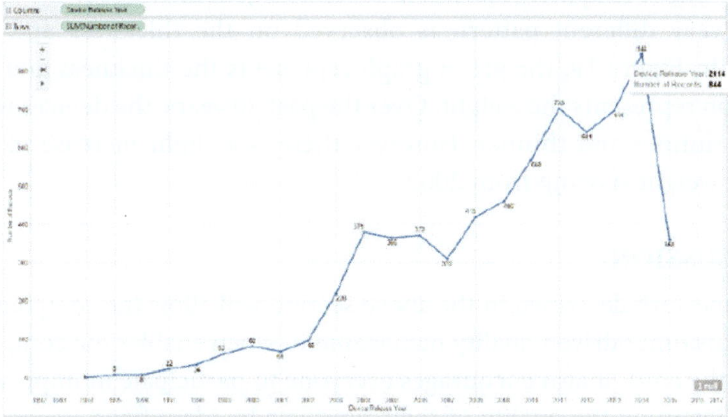

Figure 15: Total number of models released from 1994 to 2015.

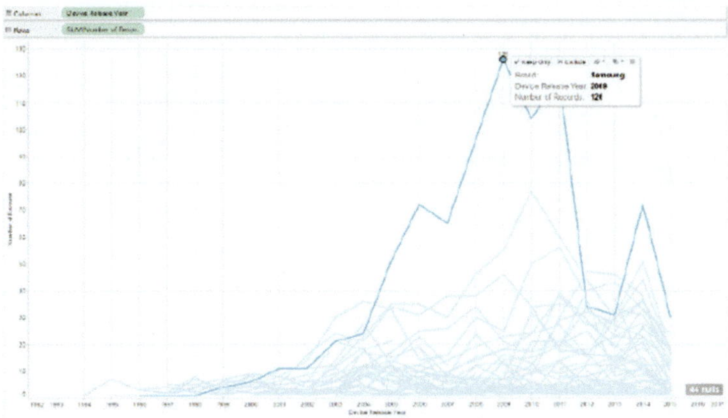

Figure 16: Total number of models Released by different brands from 1994 to 2015.

value in 2008. It started to increase again in 2009 and has been trending up since then.

Lithium ion (Li-Ion) batteries are a type of rechargeable battery commonly used in consumer electronics including cell phones until today, but it is not the driver behind the change in the battery capacity. Before 2008, cell phone manufacturers were able to design and release new models that were more energy efficient and that is why the battery capacity was dropping from 2000 to 2008. However, after Apple released the first generation iPhone in 2007 with a revolutionary multi-touch screen, touch screen soon become the most demanding feature in the market. The main drawback for touch screen is that it consumes more battery power than the traditional keypad. This is one of the main reasons the battery capacity started to increase again after 2008.

A very different pattern is observed on the thickness and the weight. In Figure 18, the green graph represents the thickness and the red graph represents the weight. Over the past 20 years, the devices were getting thinner and thinner. However there is a slight increase in the average weight starting from 2002.

5. DISCUSSION

The framework described in the above section will allow the company to have a customer driven quality management which enables the company to 'pull the cord'. It also encourages everyone to participate in improving and maintaining the quality of their products by identifying issues and

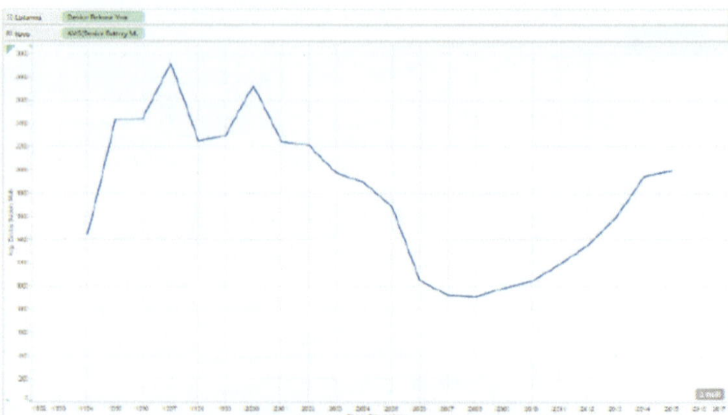

Figure 17: Average battery capacity in mAh from 1994 to 2015.

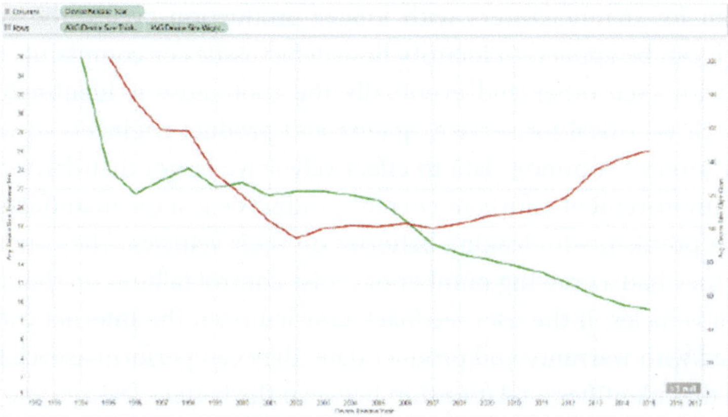

Figure 18: Average device thickness and weight from 1994 to 2015.

solving problems. Analyzing data from social media resulted in another dramatic improvement in return on quality, greatly improved customer satisfaction, and valuable brand equity.

This is achieved through collecting data from social media, both structured and unstructured, integrating data from different sources, and making them easily available to those responsible for maintaining quality. It involves leveraging analytics to exploit the data to find potential defects and allow people across different departments in the company to collaborate on fixing the issue quickly. The earlier an issue can be resolved, the less it will cost the company in terms of money, brand equity, and customer satisfaction.

In the case of a major mobile phone manufacturer, it has very short product lifecycles and are constantly developing new versions of products in order to keep pace with competitors. The new product development usually involves 80 per cent or more of the components from the previous version of the product. It is critical that engineers have access to the latest feedback describing the performance of those components in the field. If, for example, they fail to identify a reliability problem with battery in time to change the supplier or design in the new version, they may manufacture millions of new phones with the same issue. With a platform which allows them to ingest the data from different social media sources and automatically apply text analytics to derive insight that is beyond traditional BI reporting, quality engineers can raise the alarm early, and product engineers are able to address the issue prior to release of the new product.

Even for manufacturers with longer production cycles, the same approach can be applied to identify how defect issues or complaints correlated with each other and eventually the root cause is identified. In this case, it is critical for service, quality and product engineers to work together around common data to effectively solve issues that drive continuous improvement efforts in current products e.g. a car manufacturer noticed a problem with leaking batteries on their vehicles. They are also noticed they had a growing number of cruise control failures on the same model of vehicles. If the user feedback crawled from the Internet can be integrated with warranty and product data, they can perform association analysis that identifies a relationship between the battery leakage and the cruise control, and may eventually identifies that the cruise control failure occurred after the battery repair.

Competitive pressures are high, and competitive data is often difficult to acquire. The public nature of social media makes it ideal for competitive analysis. Competitive data can be analyzed using the same framework as mentioned above, allowing for direct comparisons of the customer sentiments and feedbacks. Understanding the position on specific issues relative to the competitors can give the company critical insights for issue detection and prioritization.

6. CONCLUSION AND FURTHER WORK

Quality is in the eyes of the beholder, and the customers' perceptions of the product quality are more public than ever. Understanding those perceptions is essential to identify quality issues and responding to them effectively.

In this paper, the end-to-end process on how to crawl the data from social media using Python and XPath was demonstrated, text analytics using IBM Watson Content Analytics to identify potential product issues was applied, and Tableau used to visualize and understand how the market trends have changed over the past 20 years.

The analytics framework introduced above allows us to make sense of these large volume of unstructured data crawled from social media. Insights derived using text analytics can guide the product designers and engineers to focus on the critical issues and resolve them before they grow out of control. Taking advantage of this information and integrating it into the quality process is an important step in avoiding costly quality issues and public relations nightmares.

Although social media is an effective channel for understanding and interpreting customer perceptions, it is not the only source of conversation. To evaluate sentiment, conversations, topics and what people care about or do not care about, it does not make sense to isolate social conversations in one silo and other customer communications in a different silo. It becomes interesting when social media data is blended with internal data sources.

Call centers, surveys, customer service records and customer emails generate volumes of comments that can be integrated with social media data. Each of these data sources brings its own pros and cons. Some are faster. Some are more detailed. Some are more reliable. Bringing all of this information together gives a 360 degree view of customer conversations and feedbacks. One area that is definitely interesting and worthwhile exploring is to merge some of the internal data with data crawled from social media and identify what additional insights can be discovered.

REFERENCES

1. Stavrianou, A, P Andritsos and N Nicoloyannis (2007). Overview and semantic issues of text mining. *ACM SIGMOD Record*, 36(3), 23–34.

2. Hu, X and H Liu (2012). *Text Analytics in Social Media[M]//Mining Text Data.* Springer US, pp. 385–414.

3. Swink, M and M Song (2007). Effects of marketing-manufacturing integration on new product development time and competitive advantage. *Journal of Operations Management*, 25(1), 203–217.

4. Abrahams, AS, W Fan, G Alan Wang, et al. (2014). An integrated text analytic framework for product defect discovery. *Production and Operations Management.*

5. Markham, SK, M Kowolenko, TL Michaelis (2015). Unstructured Text Analytics to Support New Product Development Decisions. *Research-Technology Management*, 58(2), 30–38.

CHAPTER 32

Knowledge Discovery on Unstructured Data

LIANG Nanxing, Ethan

ABSTRACT

A significant portion of organizational knowledge resides in the form of unstructured data such as emails, customer feedbacks and internal reports. Many Chief Information Officers (CIO) and Chief Technology Officers (CTO) consider this data to be crucial in business re-engineering.

A non-profit organization, faced with the problem of understanding large volumes of unstructured data, wanted a knowledge discovery solution that could improve their efficiency in extracting business intelligence. A long-term deliverable was co-developed with all stakeholders from which an intermediate goal suitable for the study timeline was carved out. IBM *Watson Content Analytics* was used to help business users understand two pre-processed textual sources in tandem. User tests with evaluation questionnaires were also performed to quantitatively and qualitatively evaluate the efficacy of the developed knowledge discovery solution. This study details the work done in constructing the knowledge discovery solution, and the value delivered to the non-profit organization.

1. INTRODUCTION

A Singapore-based non-profit organization (NPO) has produced and accumulated massive amounts of textual reports originating from different sources, which makes it difficult for managers and analysts to read through to form a coherent historical view of the issue. The NPO would like to explore analytical solutions to aid unstructured data exploration.

Managers of the NPO overseeing multiple projects need to monitor both qualitative and quantitative growth of textual data, and make strategic decisions based on how situations, as depicted in reports, evolve. An NPO analyst, newly-assigned to the domain, need to read through hundreds (sometimes up to thousands) of textual reports to gain an in-depth understanding of the historical background of the issue, before value-adding to the organization. For instance, an analyst may be tasked to provide qualitative evaluations on the same issue (e.g., reach of Islamic State of Iraq and Syria (ISIS) in Southeast Asia) from different NPO-internal and external information sources, and subsequently provide a coherent view on the issue.

2. PROBLEM STATEMENT

The workflows detailed in Section 1 have multiple areas for improvement: (i) it is overly time-consuming for NPO managers and analysts to analyze (potentially) massive amount of reports before value-adding, (ii) the diverse origins of textual report makes it difficult for NPO managers and analysts to adopt a fixed strategy (e.g., source-by-source or chronological) to analyze reports, and (iii) NPO managers and analysts have issues slicing and dicing the textual reports to zoom into specific focus across reports.

The rest of the study is organized as follows:

- Section 3 captures the literature research performed to understand text mining methodologies, as well as established tools which organizations use to tap on their unstructured data.
- Section 4 details the student's efforts in understanding the users of the knowledge discovery solution (KDS), managing their expectations. This section also captures the student's efforts in preparing data for ingestion into the KDS, and reviewing the features delivered.

- Section 5 qualitative and quantitatively assesses the benefits brought about by the KDS, providing explanations to why each feature was or was not well-received.
- Section 6 concludes this report and provides some directions in which the study could be developed further.

3. STATE OF THE ART

This study focuses on the extraction of business intelligence (BI) from unstructured data, specifically in the domain of text mining. From this perspective, scholarly views on management of unstructured data, text mining, and ontology building were explored. Knowing the fundamental text mining techniques alongside their strengths and weaknesses will help us understand how end-to-end data mining solutions function, and the extent to which these solutions inherit the drawbacks of the techniques they adopt. This section details the abovementioned findings deemed relevant by the student; selected end-to-end data mining solutions are further looked into in later section.

3.1. Mining of unstructured data

It is logical to assume that an organization's data grows (both in terms of storage space and content richness) organically along with the age and complexity of the organization. Traditional BI solutions focus on describing structured data of the organization, mainly comprising machine-generated transactional data. There is however, a paradigm shift of data source under the spotlight as organizations find unstructured data to be especially important — more than 60 per cent of CIOs and CTOs considered unstructured data to be critical for improving operations or for creating new business opportunities.[1] The unstructured data typically includes emails correspondence with organization and external parties, project reports in the form of word processing text, summaries and graphs in the form of spreadsheet files, and web pages.

The core difficulty in analyzing unstructured data is the extraction of metadata, so that the resultant semi-structured data may be analyzed using data mining techniques/systems which are already matured.[2] This widely adopted approach of unstructured data mining facilitates co-analysis of structured and semi-structured data, so that the joint-analysis may yield actionable insights. Another additional benefit is that these semi-structured data may be easily handled and stored in a knowledge mart alongside other relevant data.[3] Figure 1 illustrates the envisioned setup.

A type of unstructured data mining especially relevant to this study is text mining, as it aims to yield actionable BI from textual data containing reports and comments in natural language form. Subsequent readings focus on existing methodologies related to text mining.

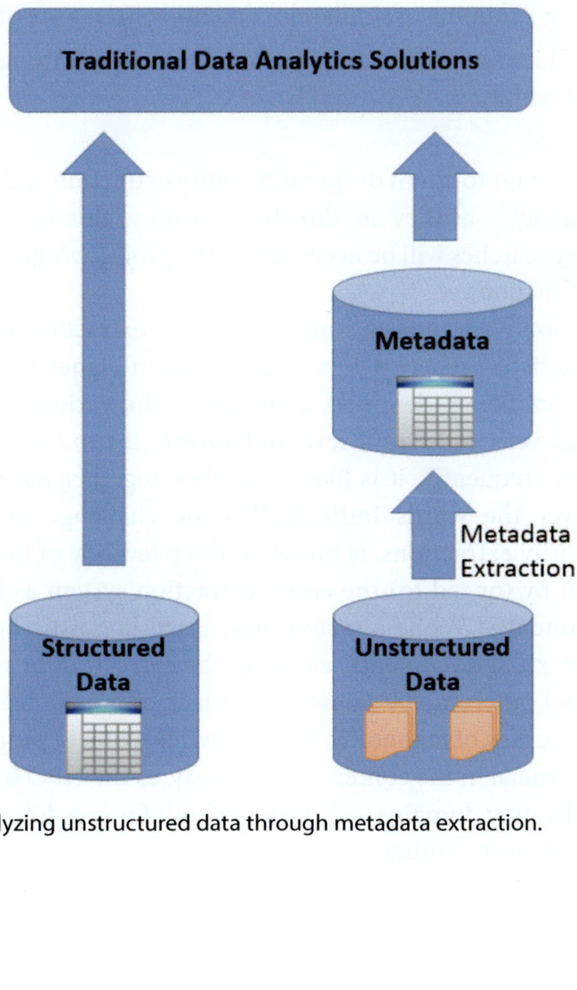

Figure 1: Analyzing unstructured data through metadata extraction.

3.2. Text mining

Text mining aims to derive information from textual, linguistic data, and does so through following few high-level approaches[4]:

1) Entity extraction: identification of key phrases within a corpus and assigning logical relations between key phrases;
2) Topic racking: identification of segments of document which can be of interest users, through keywords matching;
3) Summarization: provide overview on lengthy document to allow users make assessment on whether the entire dataset is worth going through;
4) Categorization: identification of the main theme of document;
5) Clustering: grouping of similar documents by relevance of topics; and
6) Concept Linkage: connecting related documents through common concepts within.

It is important to zoom deeper into entity extraction and categorization methodologies, as they are directly relevant to this study, at current stage. Broader searches will be necessary as the project progresses to more complex BI functions.

A commonly adopted technique in entity extraction is the use of collocation statistics, where words co-occurring at higher-than-expected probabilities are being identified, factoring in the various types of collocations, e.g., verb and noun, verb and adverb. If two (or more) words co-occur very frequently, it is likely that they together have additional meanings over the words individually. The challenge in using this method of entity extractions, is however, the relevancy of linguistic taxonomy learnt by (or fed to) the entity extraction system as it processes textual documents.[5] While a system may learn linguistic taxonomy as it processes textual documents, allowing the extraction of proper entities that would otherwise be missed out, a lack of human feedback does not ensure accuracy of taxonomy, thus allowing errors to propagate. This limitation is crucial in the context of this study, as the NPO has multiple, loosely-overlapping domains — taxonomy built for one domain may not be well-applied over another.

Automated text categorization assigns category labels to documents based on evaluated probabilities on association with a training corpus of already labeled documents. This classification task is often achieved through statistical learning methods, with these few popular techniques: (i) support vector machine, (ii) k nearest neighbor classification, (iii) linear least squares fit, (iv) neural networks, and (v) naive Bayes classification. Controlled tests evaluating the abovementioned techniques suggested support vector machine and k nearest neighbor approaches to be consistently more accurate than others in text classification.[6]

Support vector machines (SVM) work by arriving at a hyperplane that, as best as possible, splits observations into homogeneous groups. It was explained[7] that SVMs does away with the need for feature selection as it inherently generalizes well in high-dimensional spaces, and suitable for text categorization. Additionally, SVMs do not require parameter tuning, as satisfactory parameter settings may be found through the SVM classification process itself. Last but not the least, SVMs tend to be robust, and as such, can be applied to different corpus without catastrophic loss in accuracy — this feature is crucial in the context of this study, due to same reason of multiple domains which the NPO works on.

3.3. Ontology learning

An ontology defines the properties and inter-relationships between entities, and is often domain-specific — the same word can invoke different meanings in different domains, e.g., the word 'ball' in domain of sports can mean 'basketball', but is more likely to mean 'ball bearing' in the engineering. Again, as the NPO works on multiple domains, it is important that a suitable ontology is adopted, or a set of ontologies may be constructed so that appropriate ontology may be used for each domain.

Construction of domain ontology often involves a comprehensive analysis of the domain, examining the vocabulary that represents entities, relationships, and processes in the domain, followed by developing rigorous definitions about concepts in the vocabulary, and ending by defining the relationships between these concepts.[8] With an already built domain ontology, techniques to automatically enrich and expand the ontology are present,[9] and they leverage on developed natural language processing (NPL) technologies to identify linguistic patterns within documents, and to surface semantic relationships between entities extracted. *SysOntos* [9] is one such system that automatically expands ontologies.

WordNet is a lexical database of English words, grouping words of similar meanings together, made freely available online. This database often functions as a fundamental starting point on which text mining projects are based, and success has been gained in using *WordNet* to recognize phrases so as to facilitate the retrieval of relevant documents.[10] The proposed technique first extract entities (phrases) from the document, expands the collection with synonyms using *WordNet*, followed by finding similarities between documents. This approach is relevant to this study due to a large overlap in problem statements of retrieving relevant, important texts upon which business users base their decisions.

4. SOLUTION: DESCRIPTION OF APPROACH

This section aims to describe the problem and data sources in detail, examining the potential performance restrictions as a result of the data characteristics for each data source. A system architecture was then proposed, specifying the process flow from raw data to BI. This section captures the efforts taken in each phase of the process flow, leading to the customization of a selected knowledge discovery tool. Lastly, this section details the capabilities of KDS as a whole, providing illustrations on the KDS output.

4.1. Gathering of user requirements and solution usage scenarios

The problem statement was overly high-level for a solution to be constructed upon. Identified stakeholders to this project were brought together so as to achieve common understanding on (i) long-term deliverables from KDS and (ii) a suitable module of KDS to achieve through this project. The discussion sessions were held days apart so as to reaffirm users' needs through visual, computer-generated mock-ups to guide them through their analytics workflows. Special attention was paid to the formats and characteristics of each data source to be included to the KDS — this will be elaborated in later part of the section.

KDS users face the need to answer qualitative questions based on their views on multiple data sources, both generated internally (e.g., past reports in the domain of interest), and externally (e.g., Wikipedia entries for background knowledge). For example, the analyst may be tasked to assess the extent of *Islamic State of Iraq and Syria* (ISIS) reach in Southeast Asia, and he/she does so by assessing the global situation through relevant terrorism-related intelligence reports, and assess if the reasons that fuel ISIS's growth in Middle East are applicable to the Southeast Asian region. The analyst also keeps a lookout for indicators of ISIS presence, and applies it to the regional context. This requires a good depth of understanding on the domain of terrorism, as well as the current Southeast Asian regional outlook. The analyst typically needs to surface and read through twenty-relevant reports on the domain, before value-adding to the task. Additionally, if the domain is not well-documented, the analysts will still need to spend time scanning through irrelevant reports before discarding them.

4.2. Statement of work

The following statement of work (SOW) defined by the author was deemed to be sufficient by NPO management and stakeholders, in bridging the need for a KDS.

1) KDS shall minimally include a dashboard that monitors:
   i) Qualitative growth of unstructured data, through appropriate visualizations that highlights:
      a) newly-surfaced keywords of interest, and
      b) sudden spikes in flagged keywords
   ii) Quantitative growth of unstructured data:
      a) intuitive ways of presenting the growth to be proposed
2) KDS shall categorize surfaced keywords through a semantic dictionary (e.g., the word 'bank' is to be classified under 'finance' category).
   i) The dictionary should be user-customizable.
3) KDS shall allow the user to restrict the corpus of interest by defining:
   i) The period which the reports are dated; and
   ii) The data sources to be included.

4) KDS shall identify and highlight texts of relevance to up to five predefined topics/questions of interest.
5) KDS shall support slice and dice operations on logical hierarchies, allowing the user to zoom down into texts of interest.
6) The vendor shall propose any other features that intuitively support the conveyed problem statement.
7) Table 1 summarizes the data which the KDS is to ingest:

Table 1: Summary of data sources to be included to proposed KDS.

Source_ID	Origin	Characteristics	Format
INT_1	Externally originated, internally enriched	Colloquial; mixed languages	csv
INT_2	Internally generated	Formal language	eml
INT_3	Internally generated	Formal language	doc
INT_4	Externally originated, internally enriched	Colloquial; mixed languages	eml
EXT_1	Externally originated Wikipedia	Formal language	txt
EXT_2	Externally originated	Formal language	pdf
EXT_3	Externally originated (blogs)	Colloquial; mixed languages	html

It was jointly evaluated between NUS and NPO that this project shall focus on the inclusion of sources INT_1 an EXT_1 to the KDS.

4.3. Data characteristics

Table 1 summarizes data deemed to be crucial to decision making, for inclusion in the KDS. The fields describing the data are especially important to have an initial gauge on how well each data source may be explored through the KDS:

1) **Source_ID**: Unique identifier to each data source. The prefix indicates whether the data source is internal or external to the NPO.
2) **Origin**: Specifies if the data source is internal or external to the NPO. External data which is subsequently enriched by NPO is

considered to be internal data source. This information is needed for long-term planning to ensure KDS sustainability, as special attention may be given to external data sources (e.g., data quality checks).

3) **Characteristics**: Specifies whether the data source contains only English or contains multiple languages. As the project focuses on mining of English unstructured data, having non-English texts as data source may introduce noise to the KDS, especially when non-language agnostic text mining techniques are used. This information is thus necessary to evaluate if inclusion of the data source will bring about net benefits to the KDS. This field also specifies the style of text in the data source, whether it is colloquial or formal reporting — this will have direct impacts on the performance of KDS, especially if upstream analytics processes such as entity extraction could not be properly achieved.
4) **Format**: Specifies the file format of each data source. This determines if addition processing efforts (e.g., parsing) is required prior to ingesting to the KDS system.

Sources INT_1 and EXT_1 were examined deeper to assess if they were suitable for immediate ingestion into the KDS or if pre-processing was required.

INT_1 consisted of online articles/views on specific issues of interest, followed by appending of internal textual comments/reports on each article. It was understood that instead of updating each record (i.e., article/view) when internal comments were made, a new record was generated with the comments appended to the back of the previous record. This resulted in severe duplication of textual contents within the data, and there was no system-generated data field that allows easy identification of internally generated records to the root external record. This duplication of data can potentially limit entity extraction efficacy, especially if it functions on collocation statistics techniques as covered in the earlier section. Table 2 illustrates the manner in which duplication takes place.

EXT_1 consisted of Wikipedia content on pages deemed to be relevant to the domain of interest. As the content could be downloaded from the internet, either through web scraping or via APIs provided,

Table 2: Desensitized records showing the extent of duplication in INT_1. Only the first three columns are extracted data fields from INT_1.

[data field] Record_ID	*[data field]* Date/time	*[data field]* Content	*comments*
134567938	4 Jun 2014:15:21:30	There is a low probability of precipitation in the next five days.	External
140838389	7 Jun 2014:17:24:19	There is a low probability of precipitation in the next five days. *Officer1: This corroborates with meteorological forecasts.*	External, *Internal*
140838511	7 Jun 2014:17:29:40	There is a low probability of precipitation in the next five days. *Officer1: This corroborates with meteorological forecasts.* Officer2: Forecast is reliable given previous track records.	External, *Internal,* [Note: This record is the richest in content and should be retained.]

it was evaluated that manipulation to provide semi-structured output could be achieved with some programming efforts. Furthermore, (English) Wikipedia contents are mostly in proper English language, making this data source ideal for text mining.

4.4. System architecture

From an overarching view, a structured process flow was required to bring multiple sources of data to the KDS system so that analysts may discover knowledge with the texts. The system processes could be grouped in accordance to their logical phases. Figure 2 shows the system architecture of KDS, using processes on INT_1 and EXT_2 to illustrate the actual works on the data.

Data Universe: Data in the phase is allowed to grow without intervention of the KDS. Special attention will have to be made to look out for changes in data structures, as this will have impacts on the downstream processes.

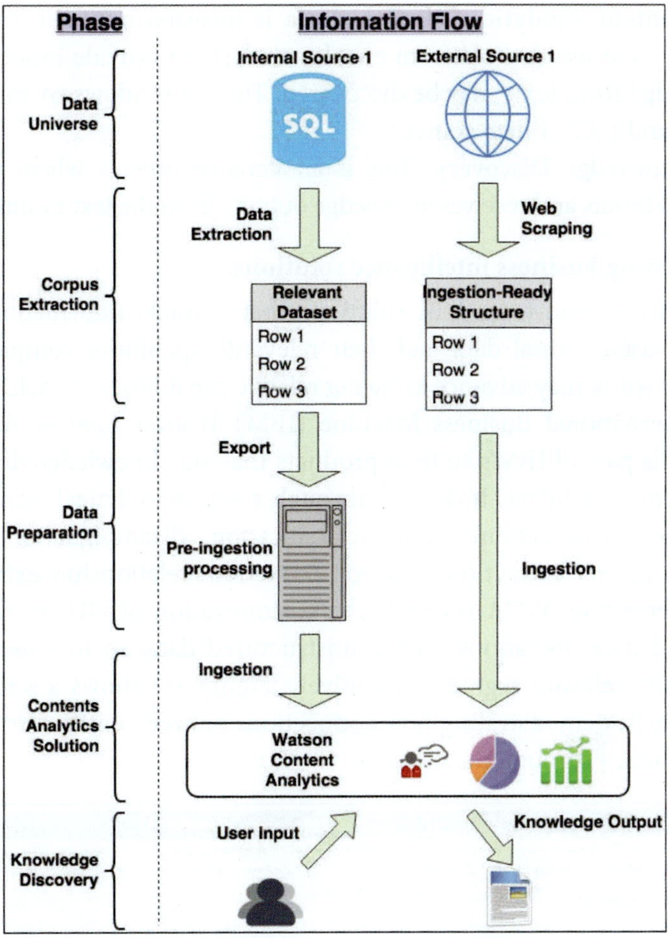

Figure 2: System architecture of KDS.

Corpus Extraction: Due to system sizing limitations, as well as potential introduction of noises (irrelevant data) to the KDS, only relevant data for ingestion to the KDS was extracted. This is done through SQL queries on INT_1, and web scrapping for the case of EXT_1.

Data Preparation: Not all data is immediately suitable for ingestion into the KDS, some will require format changes, while others may require data enrichment to make the information more meaningful. De-duplication was carried out on INT_1, along with enrichment of fields with internal identifiers. EXT_1 required no data preparation efforts since it was possible to control the output structure at upstream processes.

Content Analytics Solution: Data is ingested into a text mining tool for analysis. This platform enables analysts to provide input so that knowledge from texts may be discovered. This stage allows co-mining of INT_1 and EXT_1 data sources.

Knowledge Discovery: This is an iterative process where analysts provides inputs and receives knowledge outputs from the text mining tool.

4.5. Existing business intelligence solutions

Two existing end-to-end BI solutions that extracts information from unstructured textual data had their relevant capabilities compared, so that this study may advance knowing relative capabilities of each.

International Business Machine (IBM) *Watson Content Analytics* (WCA) is part of IBM's suite of products that aids knowledge discovery on unstructured data. It does so through a set of analytical techniques: language identification, textual classification, disambiguation, entity extraction, fact extraction, concept extraction, relationship extraction, and inferencing. WCA supports the customization of GUI to facilitate slice and dice operations on the unstructured data, so that users may zoom into relevant segments intuitively. Figure 3[11] shows a screenshot from WCA, demonstrating how connections between entities extraction are visualized through the product.

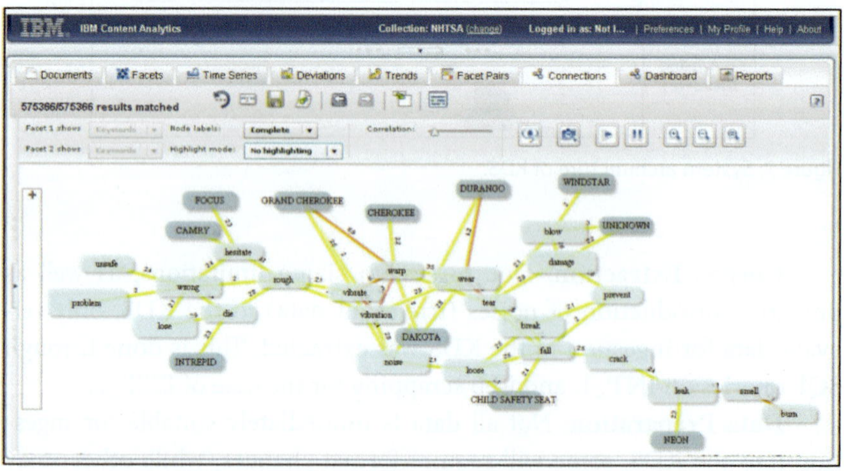

Figure 3: WCA visualizing connections between extracted entities.

Statistical analysis system (SAS) *Text Miner* is a solution aimed to allow discovery of themes and concepts with documents. The strong integration with SAS's suite of products makes it easy for already structured, quantitative data residing on SAS servers to be co-mined with textual data. *Text Miner* output can also be easily exported to other SAS products to conduct quantitative analysis. *Text Miner* in itself, however, is lacking in visualization, and analysts less *au fait* in programming may find its learning curve steep.

Figure 4 shows a typical topic mining output from *Text Miner*, showing collocation statistics on extracted entities.[12] Another product from SAS, *Visual Analytics*, addresses the need to visually and graphically navigate through textual data, but this product is not available to the NPO for evaluation at the time of this study.

Understandably, either text mining solutions from SAS or IBM would have to be considered together with its full suite of analytical tools for proper technical comparison of features. For this study however, it was not possible to access all tools from both solution providers; so technical comparisons will have to be based on existing SAS data mining infrastructure, and IBM WCA software made available for the study. The core strength of SAS *Text Miner* was identified to be its tight integration with *Enterprise Guide*, which allowed data to be pre-processed before ingestion into *Text Miner*, and with *Enterprise Miner* which allowed machine learning models to be built upon output of the *Text Miner*. The lack of SAS Visual Analytics limited the ease of solution deployment to analysts who required a GUI to explore textual data through visualization means. The core strength of IBM WCA was identified to be its integration of textual analytics and visual navigation into the same tool; data pre-processing could not be fully performed on WCA direct, and had to be executed on a separate tool before exporting the data for ingestion into WCA. Pertaining only to text analytics, both *Text Miner* and WCA had similar claims on features: entity extraction, topic identification, keyword trend analysis, and relationship extraction.

An end-to-end solution that ingests textual data, to discover knowledge visually was preferred by the NPO. WCA was thus selected to be uses as the analytics solution in KDS. Furthermore, WCA was made available to the NPO only through hosting collaboration for this study which will cease with the end of the study — the NPO would like to tap on this opportunity to experience the Watson suite of products.

Topics

Category	Topic ID	Document Cutoff	Term Cutoff	Topic	Number of Terms	# Docs
User	1	0.001	0.001	company and president	1	72
Single	2	0.001	0.001	+macro	1	193
Single	3	0.001	0.001	+report	1	156
Single	4	0.001	0.001	+data set	1	173
Single	5	0.001	0.001	+server	1	130
Single	6	0.001	0.001	+variable	1	179
Single	7	0.001	0.001	web	1	163
Single	8	0.001	0.001	+program	1	176
Single	9	0.001	0.001	+technique	1	186
Single	10	0.001	0.001	information	1	290
Single	11	0.001	0.001	access	1	153
Multiple	12	0.111	0.035	+statement,+select stat...	54	64
Multiple	13	0.079	0.038	+program,+time,+date,+...	104	109
Multiple	14	0.101	0.037	+method,+sample,+test...	116	108
Multiple	15	0.102	0.036	+graph,graph software,...	68	103
Multiple	16	0.119	0.035	+macro,+macro variable...	48	107
Multiple	17	0.099	0.037	+application,+developm...	109	138
Multiple	18	0.104	0.037	web,+page,+browser,+s...	83	144
Multiple	19	0.105	0.037	+output,+system,+templ...	86	117
Multiple	20	0.117	0.037	+value,+data set,+variab...	77	152
Multiple	21	0.101	0.037	+performance,+server,+...	103	115
Multiple	22	0.104	0.037	+programmer,+techniqu...	95	155
Multiple	23	0.116	0.036	+data warehouse,+ware...	66	112
Multiple	24	0.106	0.036	+report,print,+tool,+solut...	78	121
Multiple	25	0.108	0.037	java,+technology,+apple...	80	110
Multiple	26	0.096	0.038	+analysis,+developmen...	107	134

Figure 4: Topic mining output from SAS Text Miner.

4.6. Web scraping from Wikipedia

The general structure of Wikipedia articles was observed to follow a general schema, comprising of the article title, one article summary, one or multiple sub-headers, and content falling under each sub-header. Embedded within the Wikipedia summary and sub-header contents are also linked to other Wikipedia articles, which took up the same observed Wikipedia article structure. Identified Wikipedia articles were scrapped parsed from *en.wikipedia.org* using *Python* and package *Beautiful Soup*. Python code responsible for scraping and parsing Wikipedia articles is explained below:

```
#imports libraries/packages to be used by Python
from bs4 import BeautifulSoup
import urllib2, re

# defines constants, result lists and URLs to start crawling from
i = 0
sections = []
links = []
urls = ["https://en.wikipedia.org/wiki/Terrorism"]
```

```
# loops through remaining URLs
while i < len(urls):
  page = urllib2.urlopen(urls[i])
  soup = BeautifulSoup(page.read())
  i + = 1

  # obtains title of current page
  title = soup.findAll("h1")[0].string

  # searches for subtitles on page
  subtitles = soup.findAll("span", {"class":"mw-headline"})
  for subtitle in subtitles:
    # stop scraping the rest of the page if footer sections hit
    if subtitle.string == "See also" or subtitle.string == "References" or
subtitle.string == "External links":
      break
    else:
      # follow the parse tree to obtain the section's content
      content = u""
      for p in subtitle.parent.find_next_siblings():
        # if element is a header, the next section has been reached
        if p.name == "h2" or p.name == "h3":
          break
      # if element contains links to internal Wikipedia URLs, store and
add to list of URLs to crawl
        for l in p.findAll("a", {"href":re.compile("^\/wiki")}):
          links.append({"title":title, "link":l["href"]})
          urls.append("https://en.wikipedia.org" + l["href"])
  # handles newline characters by converting to unicode
        content += unicode(p).replace("\n", u' ')

    # add title, subtitle and content to result list
      sections.append({"title":title, "subtitle":subtitle.string,
"content":content})
```

There were two main considerations for the need of Wikipedia textual content as a source for KDS:

1) While the KDS will benefit from a large volume of textual data, relevancy of the Wikipedia articles to the domain of interest must be maintained; and
2) The scraped textual data must be in a semi-structured format which facilitates ingestion by the KDS.

To tackle the first abovementioned consideration, Wikipedia articles were scraped from a strategically chosen article which was assessed to be central to the domain of interest. Internal links embedded within contents were extracted and presented to analysts as Wikipedia article titles, so that they may make the judgment call on relevancy of those articles to the domain of interest. Only shortlisted articles were subsequently crawled for inclusion to the KDS. This process could be iterated so that volume of Wikipedia articles ingested by the KDS may expand. The process is illustrated in Figure 5. Two scraping loops were achieved through the cycle illustrated in Figure 5, collecting 850 relevant Wikipedia articles with the article on 'Terrorism' as a starting point.

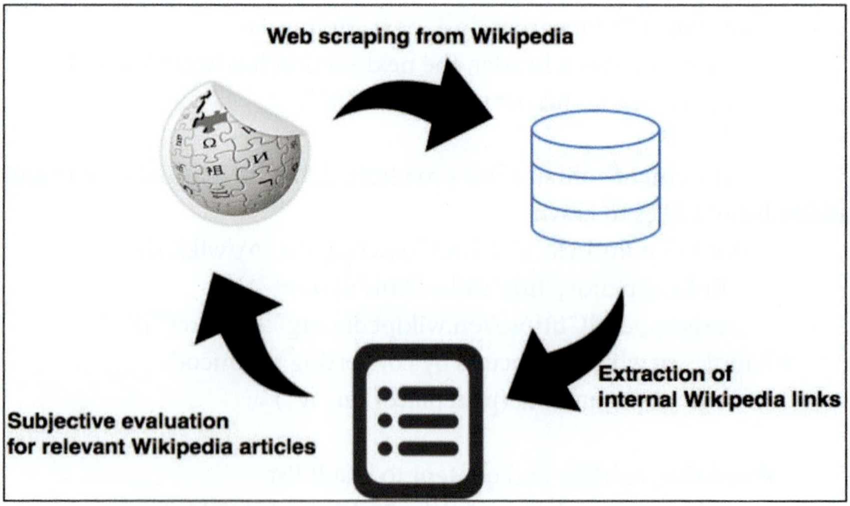

Figure 5: Visual illustration on scraping for relevant Wikipedia articles.

To tackle the second consideration mentioned above, textual data was structured in a manner which the KDS should ingest with good results. Table 3 is a sample extraction of the output from the web scraper.

Table 3: Extracted sample from Wikipedia scraper output.

Title	Sub-header	Content	URL	Extraction date
Terrorism	Summary	Terrorism is commonly defined as violent acts (or the threat of violent acts) intended to create fear (terror), perpetrated for an economic.	https://en.wikipedia.org/wiki/Terrorism	2015-06-20
Terrorism	Types	Depending on the country, the political system, and the time in history, the types of terrorism is varying.	https://en.wikipedia.org/wiki/Terrorism	2015-06-20
Religious terrorism	Summary	Religious terrorism is terrorism carried out based on motivations and goals that have a predominantly religious character or influence.	https://en.wikipedia.org/wiki/Religious_terrorism	2015-06-20
Religious terrorism	Definition	According to Juergensmeyer, religion and violence have had a symbiotic relationship since before The Crusades and even since before the Bible.	https://en.wikipedia.org/wiki/Religious_terrorism	2015-06-20

Title	Sub-header	Content	URL	Extraction date
Terrorism financing	Summary	Terrorism financing came into limelight in the United States after the terrorist attacks in the United States on 11 September 2001.	https://en.wikipedia.org/wiki/Terrorism_financing	2015-06-20
Terrorism financing	Money laundering	Often linked in legislation and regulation, terrorism financing and money laundering are conceptual opposites.	https://en.wikipedia.org/wiki/Terrorism_financing	2015-06-20

4.7. Data de-duplication and enrichment

It was described in earlier sections that data source INT_1 had data duplicity issues, and literature research suggested that data duplicity will adversely impact efficacies of entity extraction algorithms. Duplicate data will artificially increase counts of occurrences of words, causing collocation statistics to deviate from that of natural speech, thus negatively impacting text mining. To overcome the issue of data duplicity, a simple but effective approach was adopted for data cleansing. The data was first stored as an Oracle SQL database, and for each record, the "LIKE" operator was used to filter out records which were subset of subsequent records (up to 30 days later than the record of interest). Figure 6 shows the logic flow of the SQL de-duplication operation. The flow was looped for every record within the dataset.

#Partial code for decision node 2 in Figure 6, to arrive at duplicate records. These duplicate records were subsequently removed from INT_1 through a correlated query with NOT IN operator.

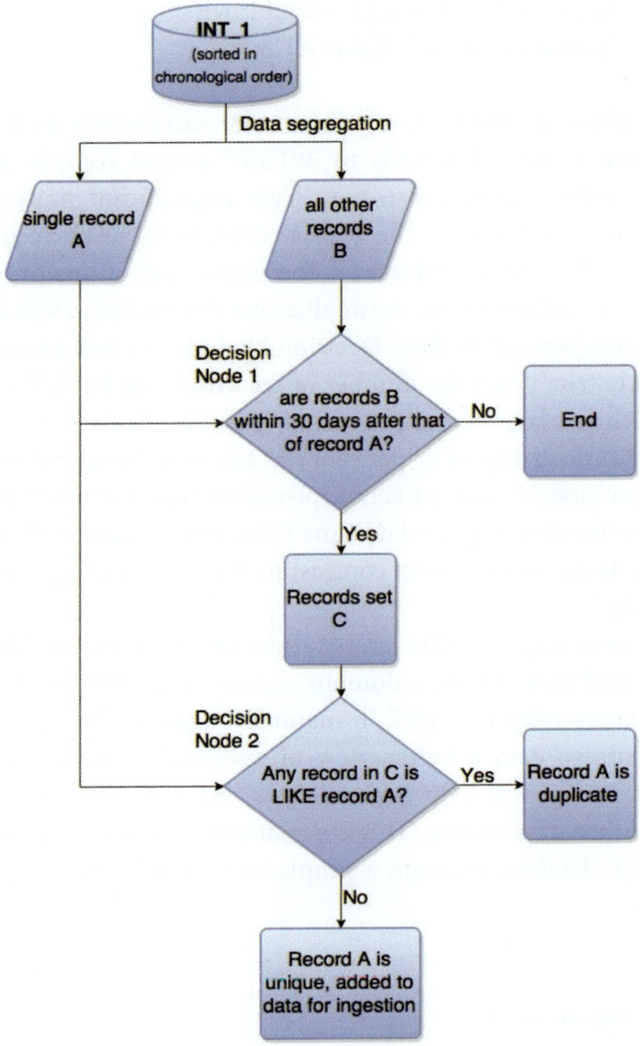

Figure 6: Logic flow of how unique records were identified for KDS ingestion.

#Actual code deployed was different as the SQL logic had to be executed through a SAS Proc SQL macro in the organizational setup, so as to achieve iterations to query through entire of INT_1.

SELECT DISTINCT [relevant fields].[Table A]
From [Table A], [Table C]

```
WHERE[textual contents].[Table C] LIKE
    """[textual contents].[Table A]"&"%""";
```

The above de-duplication efforts were satisfactory as it reduced INT_1 from 1,182,352 records to 391,187 unique records. Arguably, Decision Node 1 in Figure 6 may have insignificant impact on the de-duplication end result. The textual content for each record chain was sufficiently unique (at least for the magnitude of this project) that no records would match the de-duplication criteria (i.e., Decision Node 2) for records beyond 30 days. Decision Node 1 was instead included to significantly trim down the number of records, from 1,182,351 to about 2000, which was required to be fed into Decision Node 2 for each loop. Significant time savings of 23 per cent was achieved through the inclusion of Decision Node 1, and a likely explanation was that while additional SQL operations to compare date-time fields were incurred, these operations were faster to execute in contrast to the SQL LIKE operations that were avoided.

The next stage of data preparation involved the enrichment of de-duplicated INT_1 with a domain-specific data. NPO analysts often need to cross-reference INT_1 manually against the said domain-specific data to gain a better view of assigned scenario; correlating this information will help save analysts' manual efforts in referencing to another data source. This correlation effort was executed on an Oracle SQL database through a simple LEFT JOIN operation on both databases.

4.8. Data ingestion

Both INT_1 and EXT_1 were exported in comma separated value (CSV) format, one file for each data source, for ingestion into WCA to perform text analytics. Notably, the data must be ingested as a '*Content Analytics Collection*' through WCA's *Administration Console*', so that data exploration could be carried out using WCA. The *Administration Console* was intuitive to use, with proper status notification that notified user of the progress of ingestion, and the general phase on ingestion which the process was in. Figure 7 shows a screenshot of actual process of ingestion, with INT_1 successfully ingested in WCA.

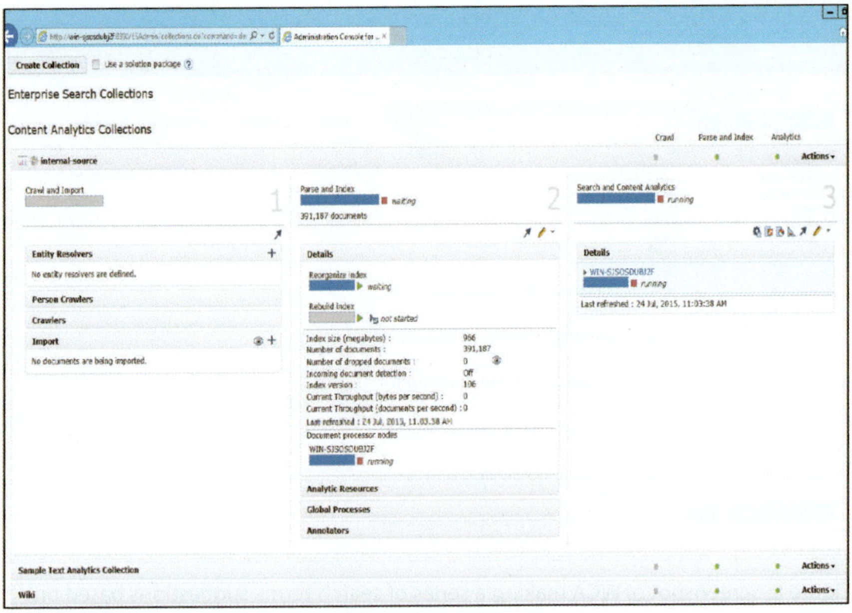

Figure 7: Ingestion of data on *Watson Content Analytics*.

4.9. Text analytics — fundamental search enhancement

As the domain of interest to the NPO could not be documented in this report, a sample of 91 Wikipedia articles on the domain of terrorism was ingested to WCA for illustration of text analytics capabilities achieved. While the key points surfaced through the KDS in this demonstration may seem to be common knowledge, the same success may be replicated on other less-known domains through the same analytical workflows.

The foremost benefit of the KDS achieved through WCA was textual search suggestions it provided as the analyst typed search terms into the textual search bar. Figure 8 shows the analyst typing in "terro", and the WCA made a series of word/phrase suggestions (e.g., 'terrorist', 'terrorism financing') containing the same character string, along with the count of articles containing the each search term. This feature encouraged the analyst to make explorations on keywords contained in the data source, and allowed them to search for words beyond their personal vocabulary. Clicking on any suggestion filters for all articles containing the word/phrase of interest allows the analyst to further drill down to view the article for in-depth analysis.

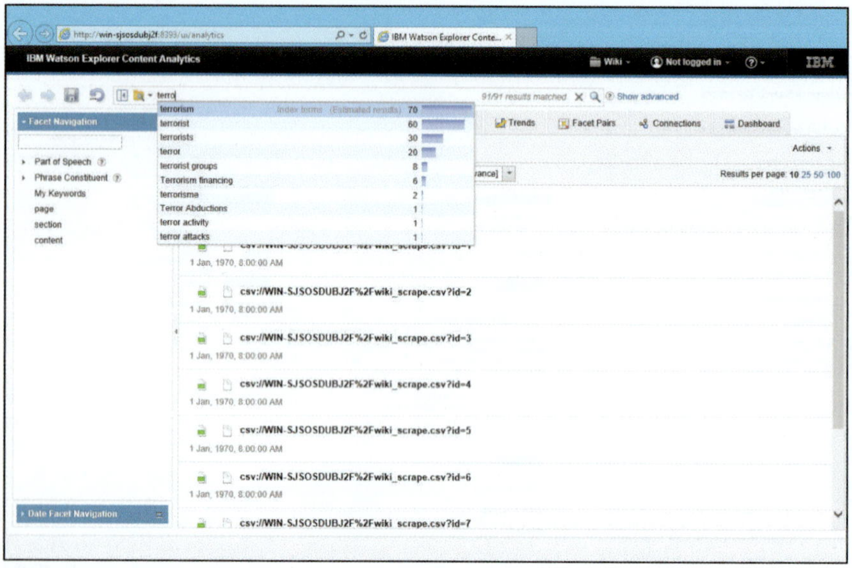

Figure 8: Screenshot of WCA making a series of search terms suggestions based on partial search term input.

4.10. Text analytics — knowledge discovery via single entity type

The developed KDS performed entity extraction, with WCA identifying parts of speech (i.e., noun, verb, adjective, adverb, conjunction, interjection, and numerals) and phrase constituent (i.e., noun phrase, predicate phrase, and conjunction phrase) using out-of-the-box text analytics engine configurations. Notably, the configurations could be adapted to better suit the project needs, but this required significant development efforts working on the WCA's language engine, and was thus excluded from this study. On selection of any parts of speech or phrase constituent, extracted entities are displayed along with their count of occurrences in articles. Figure 9 shows the adjectives extracted through the KDS, sorted in descending order of count of occurrences in articles. For illustration, the adjective 'political' appeared in 29 Wikipedia articles ingested for this demonstration.

The next natural step of the analytical flow was to repeat the extracted entities statistics generation based on previous selections, thus enabling the analyst to drill down to more specific articles. This iterative process should eventually lead the analyst to the article(s) which are of core relevance to the assigned task. KDS allowed such slice and dice operations through the use of Boolean operators: checking the checkbox beside words/phrases of interest and selecting relevant Boolean operations regenerates statistics based only on relevant articles.

Figure 10 shows a drilled-down view from selecting adjectives 'Militant' OR 'American'. An additional feature KDS provided on drilled-down view was correlation statistics, expressing whether the presence of each entity in the filtered articles was significant, in contrast to the overall dataset — the higher the correlation statistics, the more unique the entity was to the filtered articles. This additional feature again helped analysts to identify keywords so that they may first evaluate their relevance and repeat the iterative process of slice and dice, thus improving productivity.

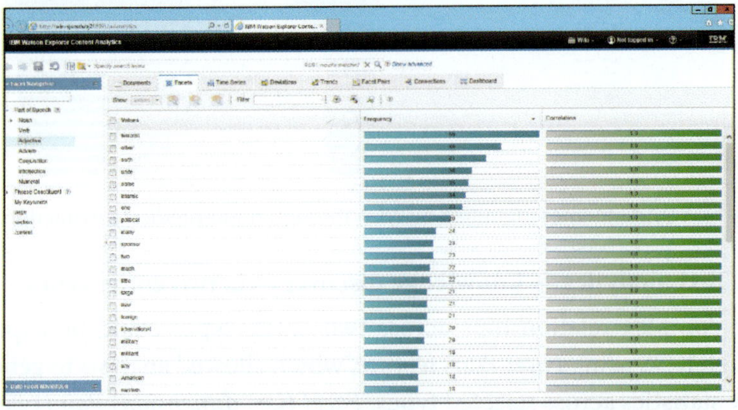

Figure 9: List of adjectives extracted through WCA, sorted by frequency count.

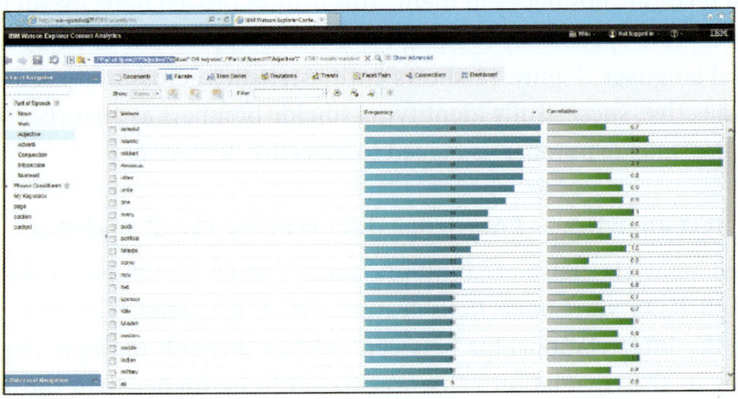

Figure 10: Slice and dice operations on WCA using Boolean operators.

Notably, KDS supported the extraction of noun-predicate pairs, which aimed to capture the central idea of sentences. This feature was found to be very useful for analysts to quickly understand the central themes which were repeated across multiple articles. Figure 11 shows noun-predicate pairs identifying themes such as 'money launder' and 'suicide attack'.

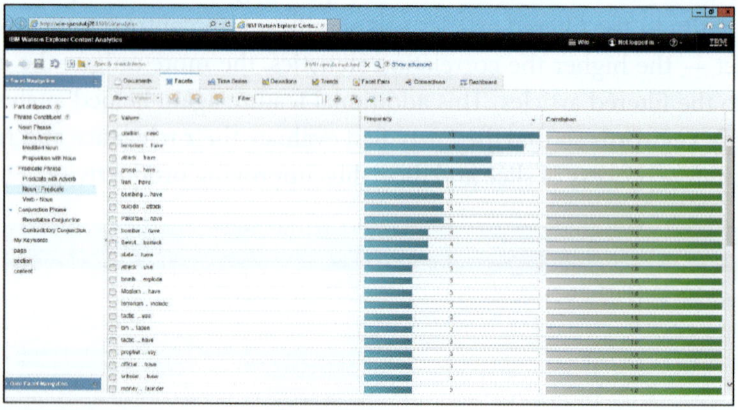

Figure 11: Central themes identified by WCA through noun-predicate extraction.

4.11. Text analytics — knowledge discovery via two entity types

More complex relationships across two entity types could be explored through KDS using *Facet Pairs* feature, which allowed analysts to generate entity statistics across selected types. *Facet (i.e., dimension) Pairs* refers to the co-analysis of textual entities across two different dimensions, so as to reveal relationships between them. This feature proved to be useful when analysts were specifically looking for a richer expression of ideas in the natural language, Figure 12 shows entity statistics across noun sequence and adjective, successfully identifying suicide bombers as terrorists: *noun sequence* 'suicide bomber' is tagged to *adjective* 'terrorist'.

4.12. Text analytics — knowledge discovery via visual analytics

Linked analysis between multiple entity types could be performed through KDS via *Connections* feature WCA provided. The link chart maps the interrelationships between entities through multiple degrees, as long as the correlation value was found to be higher than the specified threshold. This enabled analysts to visualize distance relationships

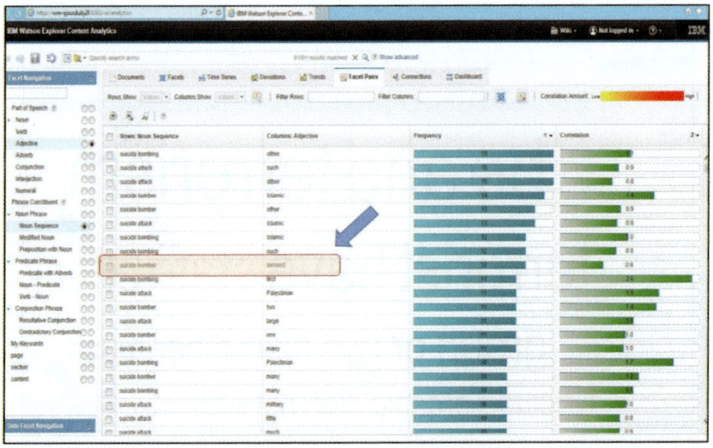

Figure 12: WCA generating entity statistics across different entity types.

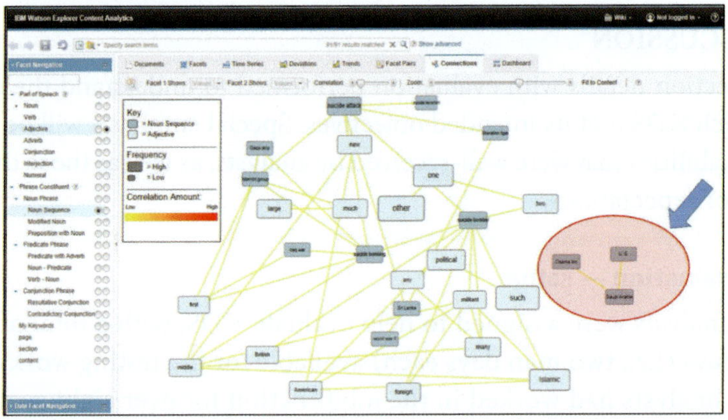

Figure 13: WCA performing link analysis between entities to aid understanding of complex relationships.

to gain a holistic view across articles of interest. Figure 13 shows link analysis achieved through KDS, highlighted portion of screenshot identified USA's interest in Saudi Arabia and Osama bin Laden's significance to Arabia.

Tag cloud was generated through KDS, expressing relative prominence of entities through the size of the font. This gave a quick overview of frequently occurring words in the articles. Figure 14 shows a tag cloud based on the sample articles ingested, identifying 'organized terrorism' and 'targeted attacks on states' as the central theme of the texts.

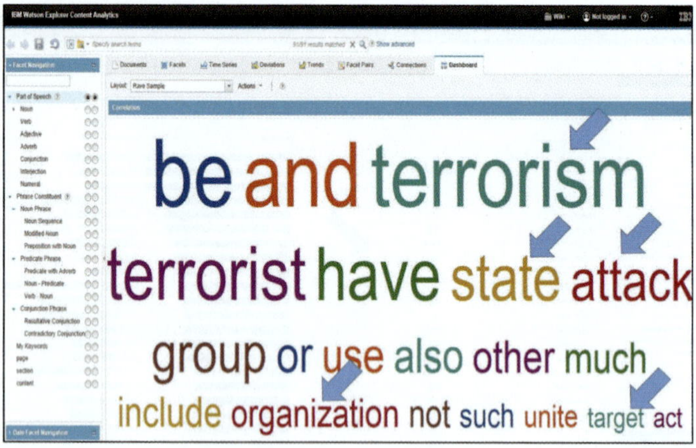

Figure 14: WCA-generated tag cloud, identifying 'terrorism' as central theme.

5. DISCUSSION

This section details with evaluation performed to understand the extent to which KDS met its intended objectives. Special emphasis will be made on capabilities that were well-received by analysts, as well as those that fell short of expectations.

5.1. Evaluation — setup

Four analysts were assigned to help evaluate KDS, with a total of eight man days (i.e., two man days each) available for the testing works. Two of the analysts had worked in the job function for over eight years and could be considered as *experts*, and the remaining two were in the job for less than one year and considered as *trainees*. While qualitative evaluations were directly achieved through interviews and questionnaires, quantitative evaluations aimed to understand time savings that KDS delivered were designed factoring individual proficiency and experienced differences in.

On the first day, all analysts were introduced to KDS through a 3-h training session. The remaining of the day was given to all analysts to perform self-exploratory of KDS using a partitioned dataset which is distinct from the actual dataset which the tests would be based on.

On the second day, all four analysts had to perform two analytics projects each, with both projects to be of similar complexity and which typically take an experienced analyst 2 h to complete. For each analyst, one analytics project was performed with traditional resources (internet, company-proprietary query systems, and internally-generated reports), while the other project was completed using KDS on top of traditional resources.

It was determined that for each experience group (i.e., experts vs trainees), the first project would be completed by one analyst using KDS, and the other analyst would not use it. The analyst who used KDS for the first project will complete the second project without the KDS, and the converse is true for the other analyst. Time taken to complete the projects was averaged for direct comparisons to understand if KDS indeed brought about time savings. Figure 15 illustrates the process of quantitative testing to negate impacts of individual proficiency within the experienced groups.

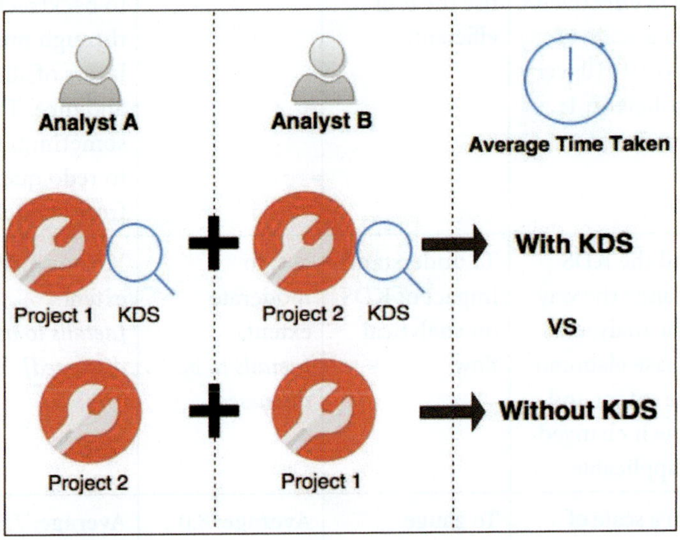

Figure 15: Quantitative testing procedures to even out individual proficiency differences, within an experienced group (i.e., trainees and experts).

5.2. Evaluation — qualitative

A questionnaire was given to analysts at the end of the evaluation, and the following table summarizes the questionnaire results. NPO-proprietary sections were excluded from the summary (see Table 4).

Table 4: Summary of KDS evaluation questionnaire results.

No	Question	Objective	Summarized response	
			Trainee	**Expert**
1	Did you have issues understanding objectives of the project?	For isolation of cause, if analysis done by analysts do not result in the same general direction.	No issue.	No issue.
2	Do you find yourself navigating through the KDS effectively? On a scale of 1 to 10 (10: very proficient, 1: very inept)	For isolation of cause, to understand if analysts can use the tool efficiently.	**Average:** 7.0	**Average:** 6.5 **Comment:** Lack of "back" or "undo" button to backtrack through multiple layers of slice and dice. Thus sometimes need to redo query from scratch.
3	Did the KDS change the way you analyze? Please elaborate the extent and how it changed, if applicable.	To understand impact of KDS on analytical flow.	Yes, to moderate extent. *[details to be discussed]*	Yes, to small extent. *[details to be discussed]*
4	On a scale of 1 to 10*, indicate the usefulness of Search Suggestions on KDS. Elaborate if possible.	To gauge usefulness of Search Suggestions.	**Average:** 8.0 **Comment:** Search suggestions	**Average:** 7.5

(*continued*)

Table 4: Summary of KDS evaluation questionnaire results. (*continued*)

No	**Question**	**Objective**	**Summarized response**	
			Trainee	**Expert**
5	On a scale of 1 to 10*, indicate the usefulness of Facets on KDS. Elaborate if possible.	To gauge usefulness of statistics on single entity type.	**Average:** 8.0 **Comment**: Predicate identification was especially useful	**Average:** 6.5
6	On a scale of 1 to 10*, indicate the usefulness of Facet Pairs on KDS. Elaborate if possible.	To gauge usefulness of statistics on multiple entity types.	**Average:** 8.5	**Average:** 6.0 **Comment:** Accuracy doubtful, do not support non-English languages.
7	On a scale of 1 to 10*, indicate the usefulness of Connections on KDS. Elaborate if possible.	To gauge usefulness of entity link analysis.	**Average:** 5.5	**Average:** 5.0 **Comment:** Charts overly messy and were hard to understand.
9	On a scale of 1 to 10*, indicate the usefulness of Dashboard on KDS. Elaborate if possible.	To gauge usefulness of tags cloud.	**Average:** 2.0 **Comment:** Little use for this feature	**Average:** 3.0

*10: useful; 1: useless.

The macroscopic scale shows KDS impacting different experience levels of analysts to two extents — little impact on the experts' analytical workflow, while the trainees' ways of analyzing were altered to a greater extent. On further inquiry, it was then discovered that trainees started their analysis with KDS, making searches on data source INT_1 using traditional search tool when needed. The experts did the reverse — started with traditional search tool, using KDS only when the traditional tool yielded no result.

A likely explanation to this behavior was that the experts were already proficient in making use of current tools, and thus had behavior inertias to move on to the new tool; the trainees were open to beginning analysis with KDS. A possible way to gain acceptance (thus increasing usage) amongst expert analysts is to assign them more complicated projects to convince them of KDS's strengths — the structured slice and dice method the KDS adopts can handle large amount of data better than categorically going through all reports to gain an understanding of the scenario.

Search suggestions were equally well-received by analysts across all experience levels. A possible explanation was that analysts find the suggestions a straightforward way of exploring beyond the root words they type in, for example, typing "terror" in the search bar invokes KDS to suggest related words such as "terrorism", "terrorist", and "terrorism financing", bringing them to terms which they might have missed out.

Both facets and facet pairs proved to be useful to the trainees for analysis use, but less so for the experts. An insightful comment by an expert was that the facet and facet pairs seemed to have entities wrongly classified, and that entities occurrence counts and correlation statistics did not consistently point out words/phrases/concepts central to the theme of the data. One reason may be the relevance of KDS's entity extraction engine to the ingested textual data. This accuracy issue could not be easily handled, yet a possible route is to improve entity extraction engine through updating rules that better fit the writing style of the text. Overfitting the engine to specific writing styles should also be avoided as this limits the engine robustness. On a workflow level, this revealed that the experts were sufficiently detailed in their analytics to point out discrepancies between KDS's output and their evaluation of data through traditional analysis methods.

Another feedback on the facet and facet pairs was the lack of non-English entities extracted. This issue may be tackled through the use of foreign-language entity extraction engines, but the same problem of relevance of entity extraction engine to the text corpus applies to each newly added non-English engine, and thus may eventually call for the need for improvements on engines for other languages. The observation that only the experts pointed out the lack of English entities suggested that the trainees may not have actively analyzed text in non-English medium — the inclusion of non-English engines would have further enabled the trainees to perform even better.

Connection charting, that brought entity link analysis, was not well-received by all analysts. A feedback provided is that the connection chart was rather messy and lacked auto-layout function that arranges the entities in an intuitive manner for analysis — this caused the analyst to spend time rearranging the entities before even attempting to understand the connections.

Dashboard that provided tag clouds had the worst evaluated utility, and was rarely used. A good explanation was that tag clouds delivered high level views of the texts, but this was not required by the analysts as (1) the analysts already know the background of the project and did not enter the analysis blind, as such the high level view is not new to them, and (2) the high level view was less actionable than other features delivered by KDS.

5.3. Evaluation — quantitative

Quantitative evaluation focused to arrive at the time savings brought about by KDS. Limited resources was dedicated to the evaluation of KDS, with the direct result being the lack of number of projects completed for statistically significant sampling points to arrive at conclusions. Nonetheless, quantitative evaluation was still carried out to yield ballpark figures on time savings. Additionally, the same evaluation framework may be adopted in future to re-evaluate with better sampling sizes.

Table 5: Summary of time taken for each analyst to complete assigned projects.

	Analyst ID	Time take to complete project (minutes)			
		Project_1 with KDS	Project_1 without KDS	Project_2 with KDS	Project_2 without KDS
Analyst	**Expert_1**	Not assigned	127	104	Not assigned
	Expert_2	117	Not assigned	Not assigned	97
	Trainee_1	Not assigned	135	130	Not assigned
	Trainee_2	112	Not assigned	Not assigned	138

It was assessed that for each analytical project tasked, analysts' submissions had similar outcomes across the board, though the level of detail of work may vary slightly. This gave foundation for better isolation of the cause of time taken to complete projects, to effectiveness of the KDS. Table 5 details the time taken by analysts to complete the projects. For illustration, expert analyst number one took a total of 127 min to complete project one without the use of KDS, and trainee analyst one took 130 min to complete project two with the use of KDS.

Table 6: Aggregated statistics on time taken for projects to be completed, comparing across experience levels and with/without KDS.

Average timings	Expert	Trainee	% Difference (expert vs trainee) – (b)
Project with KDS	110.5	121.0	8.7%
Project without KDS	112.0	136.5	17.9%
% Difference (with vs without KDS) – (a)	1.3%	11.4%	

Table 6 averages the time taken for projects to be completed, across two dimensions: (1) experience level and (2) with/without KDS. It was immediately clear that on an aggregate scale across all experience levels, KDS brought about 6.84 per cent time savings. A great disparity in time savings due to KDS across different experience levels can be seen: with reference to values (a) in Table 6, KDS brought about 1.3 per cent time savings for experts, but 11.4 per cent for trainees. The reason for this could be explained with earlier discussions on qualitative evaluations — experts were already proficient with existing tools and used KDS less, while trainees were more open to new tools and used KDS more. This implied that KDS could bring time savings of up to 11.4 per cent, if the analysts do indeed make use of it.

Another dimension to explore is the extent to which KDS closes up the proficiency gap between experts and trainees. The values (b) in Table 6 explains the percentage time difference taken by experts to complete analytic projects, against that taken by trainees. Without KDS, experts take 17.9 per cent less time than trainees to complete projects. With KDS, experts take only 8.7 per cent less time than trainees to complete projects. From this perspective, the KDS enabled trainees to achieve proficiency closer to that of the experts, closing up the percentage time advantage experts had by 9.2 per cent.

6. CONCLUSION AND FURTHER WORK

This project achieved its intended objectives in business process research, literature research, and strategic capabilities planning. Technical prototyping brought together two data sources, cleansed and enriched for ingestion into IBM Watson Content Analytics. The outcome was a knowledge discovery solution (KDS) that brought text mining features, enveloping around results of entities extractions. It is important to understand that KDS was intended to complement current, traditional analytical tools available to analysts, not to replace all of them.

Qualitative evaluation revealed that search suggestions and extracted entities statistics indeed helped analysts to an appreciable extent, but its accuracy could be improved to reduce entities that were missed out. While this can be achieved by training and adapting the entity extraction engine to better suit the domain and language style of the text corpus, over-fitting may negatively affect the robustness of the engine. A balance must be struck between accuracy and robustness. Logical deduction of analysts' feedback led us to believe that non-English engines may be included to the KDS to enable less experienced analysts to perform close to the level to that of experienced analysts. Interestingly, not all features were found to be useful — entity link analysis and tags cloud proved to be of little use to analysts who already knew the context of the extracted data. Entity link analysis and tags cloud could be reserved for analytic scenarios where there is greater ambiguity in the context of the extracted data.

Quantitative evaluation revealed that KDS was successful in achieving time savings for the analysts, shortening the time taken for the less experienced to complete projects by 11.4 per cent. To add on to the benefits, KDS improved the proficiency of less experienced analysts, so that they may perform closer to what the experienced analyst could achieve (in terms of analysis timings).

It is recommended to improve the robustness of quantitative evaluation through the inclusion of more analytical projects done, as well as involvement of more analysts, to yield analysts diversity and more sample points. It was believed that with increasing complexity of projects, KDS will prove to be more useful as it allows slice and dice operations to arrive at data of relevance — traditional tools could not allow analysts to manage large datasets well. A good way to prove this is to include project complexity as a dimension for evaluation, i.e., to provide a mix of simple (typically 2 h) and complex (typically 8 h) projects, so as to study the difference and extent of impacts brought about by the KDS in contexts of varying project complexities.

By listing down concrete steps to improve KDS, the entity extraction engine could be improved by training the model to better suit the data sources, and including non-English entity extraction engines. Additionally, evaluation could be improved to more accurately gauge the time savings the KDS brought about, and to bring diversity in feedback on qualitative feedbacks on the KDS — this can be achieved through involving more analysts at different experience levels for the evaluation, and performing more analytical tasks with and without the KDS, so as to achieve statistical significance in the quantitative evaluations.

REFERENCES

1. Blumberg, R and A Shaku (2003). The problem with unstructured data. *DM Review,* 42–46.

2. Rao, R (2003). From unstructured data to actionable intelligence. *IT Pro,* 29–35.

3. Baars, H and H-G Kemper (2008). Management support with structured and unstructured data — an integrated business intelligence framework. *Information Systems Management,* 132-148.

4. Fan, W, L Wallace, S Rich and Z. Zhang (2006). Tapping the power of text mining. *Communications of the ACM,* 76–82.

5. Lin, D (1998). Using collocation statistics in information extraction. *Proceedings of the Seventh Message Understanding Conference.*

6. Yang, Y and X Liu (1999). A re-examination of text categorization methods. *Proceedings of the 22nd annual international ACM SIGIR conference on Research and development in information retrieval.* 42–49.

7. Joachims, T (1998). Text categorization with support vector machines: learning with many relevant features. *Machine Learning: ECML-98*. 137–142.

8. I. Knowledge Based Systems (1994). IDEF5 Method Report, Information Integration for Concurrent Engineering (IICE).

9. Missikoff, M, P Velardi and P. Fabriani (2003). Text mining techniques to automatically enrich a domain ontology. *Applied Intelligence*, 18, 323–340.

10. Liu, S, F Liu, C Yu and W Meng (2004). An effective approach to document retrieval via utilizing wordNet and recognizing phrases. *SIGIR '04: Proceedings of the 27th annual international ACM SIGIR conference on Research and development in information retrieval*, pp. 266–272.

11. IBM Knowledge Centre (2015). *Take Tours of the Content Analytics Miner*. Available: http://www-01.ibm.com/support/knowledgecenter/SS8NLW_10.0.0/com.ibm.discovery.es.tm.doc/iiyscviewlet.htm retrieved 13 June 2015.

12. SAS Institude (2015). *SAS Text Miner*. Available: http://support.sas.com/software/products/txtminer retrieved 20 June 2015.

